Teaching Reading in the 21st Century

Motivating All Learners

Peter Dewitz
Educational consultant and researcher

Michael F. Graves
University of Minnesota

Bonnie B. Graves
Children's Author

Connie Juel
Stanford University

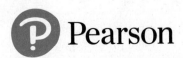

Director and Publisher: Kevin Davis
Portfolio Manager: Drew Bennett
Managing Content Producer: Megan Moffo
Content Producer: Yagnesh Jani
Portfolio Management Assistant: Maria Feliberty
Managing Digital Producer: Autumn Benson
Digital Studio Producer: Lauren Carlson
Digital Development Editor: Carolyn Schweitzer
Executive Product Marketing Manager: Krista Clark
Procurement Specialist: Deidra Headlee
Cover Design: Pearson CSC, Jerilyn Bockorick
Cover Art: Chinnapong/Shutterstock
Full Service Vendor: Pearson CSC
Full Service Project Management: Pearson CSC, Anitha VijayaKumar
Editorial Project Manager: Pearson CSC, Noribeth Santos
Printer-Binder: LSC Communications, Inc.
Cover Printer: LSC Communications, Inc.
Text Font: PalatinoLTPro-Roman

Library of Congress Cataloging-in-Publication Data
Names: Dewitz, Peter, 1948- editor. | Graves, Michael F. Teaching reading in
  the 21st century.
Title: Teaching reading in the 21st century: motivating all learners / Peter
  Dewitz, Educational consultant and researcher, Michael F. Graves,
  University of Minnesota, Bonnie B. Graves, Children's author, Connie Juel,
  Stanford University.
Other titles: Teaching reading in the twenty-first century
Description: Sixth edition. | Hoboken, New Jersey: Pearson Education, Inc.,
  [2019] | Previous edition: 2011. | Rev. ed. of: Teaching reading in the
  21st century / Michael F. Graves, Connie Juel, Bonnie B. Graves. 4th ed.
Identifiers: LCCN 2018059899| ISBN 9780135196755 | ISBN 0135196752
Subjects: LCSH: Reading (Elementary)
Classification: LCC LB1573 .G656 2019 | DDC 372.4--dc23 LC record available at https://lccn.loc.gov/2018059899

1 18

ISBN 13: 978-0-13-519675-5
ISBN 10:   0-13-519675-2

Dedication

This text is dedicated to my wife, Pam Dewitz, who provided continual support and encouragement and dealt with undeserved neglect as this new edition was being written. We continue to dedicate this text to Michael Graves' sister, Susan Jones, who in her 35 years of teaching led well over a thousand second-graders toward the high level of literacy they needed to succeed in the 21st century.

About the Authors

In writing and revising this book, each of us brought to the task his or her experiences and expertise, and we would like to briefly introduce ourselves.

Peter Dewitz

is an educational consultant and researcher who spends most of his time working with teachers and children in public schools. Peter has taught at the University of Toledo, the University of Virginia, and Mary Baldwin University and worked as a visiting researcher at the Harvard Graduate School of Education. He taught in the upper elementary grades and his major research interests are educational materials—specifically the efficacy of reading programs—the development and instruction of reading comprehension and the uses and abuses of assessments in our schools.

Michael F. Graves

is a professor emeritus of literacy education at the University of Minnesota and a member of the Reading Hall of Fame. Mike taught in the upper grades, and his research and writing focus on vocabulary learning and instruction and comprehension instruction. His current major research effort is an IES-funded research and development project on teaching word-learning strategies.

Bonnie B. Graves

is a full-time education writer and the author of 15 books for children. Bonnie taught in third and fourth grades, and her major interest is making literature enticing and accessible to beginning- and middle-grade learners. In addition to writing, Bonnie currently spends time working with children, teachers, and other educators on children's writing.

Connie Juel

is a professor of education at Stanford University. Her research centers on literacy acquisition, especially as it is affected by school instruction. She is noted for both her longitudinal research on reading development (often following children across multiple school years) and her work on interventions to help struggling readers. She was awarded the National Reading Conference's 2002 Oscar Causey Award for outstanding contributions to reading research and was elected to the Reading Hall of Fame by the International Reading Association in 2001.

Brief Contents

Contents

Features

In the Classroom

The Reading Corner

Preface

Welcome to the sixth edition of *Teaching Reading in the 21st Century*. In this edition we reaffirm the values that set our text apart. We believe that motivation underlies everything we do in school. Technology and efficiency can take us only so far down the road to fostering a new generation of students who read avidly for enjoyment and enlightenment. Motivation leads to children who read widely and deeply and with that their fluency, vocabulary and comprehension grows. Every chapter of this book is focused on developing students who *will* read and therefore *can* read. We believe this is especially vital in the digital age that dominates our lives.

When the fifth edition of this book was published in 2011 we were just digesting the impact of the No Child Left Behind Act and we paid little attention to the Common Core State Standards that were in their final draft. Since then the impact of NCLB has stayed strong, reinterpreted through the Every Student Succeeds Act and that of the CCSS has risen and begun to decline. The focus of all these national initiatives has been to make teaching and learning more precise and efficient. Assessment has taken a center stage in schools. In this text we put assessment in its proper perspective and give teachers the tools to determine what their students need, reaffirming the prerogative of the teachers in the classroom and questioning whether computer-based assessment should drive instruction.

The digital world plays an increasingly more prominent role in our classroom as a site for reading and writing. Students read for information online, write and revise online, and take tests online. In this edition of the book, we want to help new teachers and their students use these new technologies effectively and carefully. The Internet makes new demands on our students. They must know how to search for information, evaluate its truthfulness, and synthesize what they read. Not an easy task for an adult let alone a student.

New to This Edition

This new edition of *Teaching Reading in the 21st Century* is a significant rewrite of the previous editions of the book. We listened to the reviewers of the fifth edition, considered how the research was evolving, and rewrote the book in a number of ways. Rather than update each of the past chapters, we decided that new chapters were needed, especially in the areas of assessment, comprehension, and a careful consideration of the texts, both print and digital, we use for teaching students to read.

- **Rethinking assessment (Chapter 5).** Since the last edition, assessment has become a more powerful force in our schools, not just measuring the results of instruction but influencing the type of instruction. It is not just the high-stakes tests that have a critical effect on how we teach reading, but the increasing number of progress monitoring and interim computer-based assessments that are directing what we teach and how we teach. We wrote a new chapter on assessment to help teachers use intelligently the many assessments that pervade our schools. We believe that teachers are better suited to make instructional decisions than test developers within publishing companies who create new assessment products. We also added assessment advice to many chapters so that teachers can create their own tools to assess students' growth in word identification, fluency, vocabulary, and comprehension.

- **New chapter on texts for reading instruction (Chapter 6).** The Common Core State Standards made the reading of complex texts one of its ten anchor standards, and the Rand report on comprehension made text one of the four pillars when teaching comprehension. We wrote a new chapter to discuss how to select the right texts for beginning reading instruction and for developing comprehension. We also updated all of the children's literature suggestions and included more contemporary literature that reflects the diversity in our schools.

- **A focus on digital text.** Reading informational text continued its movement from the pages of trade and reference books to digital texts on the Internet. Throughout the book we have provided information and research on how to help elementary and middle school students learn to use Internet resources effectively and critically. We have provided strategies on how to find trustworthy, useful, and readable websites. We have included in several chapters strategies to help students comprehend and learn from digital text. In Chapter 6, we present strategies for helping students locate and assess the trustworthiness of Internet information. In Chapter 12, we help students comprehend and synthesize digital information.

- **Reading comprehension reinterpreted (Chapters 11 and 12).** The research on teaching children to comprehend has not changed, but our view of that research has evolved. Because much of what children read for information comes from the Internet, we devoted a full chapter to comprehending informational text and another to narrative text. Within each chapter we placed a stronger focus on developing students' knowledge and leading effective discussions. We also provided guidelines for developing curriculum that are more inviting and motivating than the skill-a-week pacing guides.

- **Understanding the history of literacy.** The teaching of reading has a long history and we believe it is important for all educators to understand it. When we can, we give you a look into the past and help you understand why new ideas were adopted, why some ideas persist, and why some old ideas should be rethought. In Chapters 1 and 2, we focus on the tortured history of reading instruction. Understanding that history will help you become a better consumer of new instructional ideas.

Key Content Updates by Chapter

- **Chapter 1, Reading and Learning to Read.** Because schools were not created yesterday, we begin with a look at the crises, trends, and fads of the past 20 years and sketch the current state of reading education in America. We remain focused on the belief that if teachers have a strong model of how children learn to read they will make the best choices for their students.

- **Chapter 2, Reading Instruction.** As we examine the basics of reading instruction, we take note of the slowly declining influence of the Common Core State Standards, the still rising influence of high-stakes assessments, and the enduring research-based principles of effective instruction. We believe that reading is a constructive act and through careful guidance when needed, all students can learn to read.

- **Chapter 3, Motivation and Engagement.** The increasing impact of digital devices on American children makes a focus on motivation vital. We have added to this chapter ideas on how to create or foster interest in children, not just discover it. We describe more motivating activities and provide our readers with a tool to determine what motivates individual students.

- **Chapter** 4, **Organizing Instruction So All Will Succeed.** The chapter helps teachers organize instruction so that all students can succeed because there are multiple reasons why children struggle to learn to read and enjoy reading. We believe and the evidence suggests that many learning problems can be handled in the general education classroom before the students need to go down the hall for extra help. We added information on interventions for English learners and students with learning problems.

- **Chapter** 5, **Classroom Assessment.** We completely rewrote this chapter to reflect the rising and negative impact of assessment on reading instruction and learning. We doubt that high stakes tests and the many tests that followed have improved teaching and learning. We have also provided teachers with many new tools to assess their own students and these tools are spread throughout Chapters 7 through 14, where we focus on specific components of reading.

- **Chapter** 6, **Choosing Texts for Reading Instruction.** This is a brand-new chapter. The Common Core State Standards pushed for students to read complex text. Other reports placed the text right next to the reader, the activity, and the context as the focus of reading instruction. In this new chapter, we help you evaluate texts, select them, organize them, and help children make the best use of the Internet.

- **Chapter** 7, **Emergent Literacy.** Emergent readers have not changed much in ten years, but our understanding of the factors that propel the development of literacy have. We have placed more emphasis on vocabulary as a driving force and on how it influences other components of the process. We have also added emergent literacy assessment tools.

- **Chapter** 8, **Word Recognition.** Learning to recognize words was central to the previous editions of the book. We continue to believe in the vital role of phonics, but every student needs a different dose. We have updated this chapter by adding more information on linkage between word identification and vocabulary and provided some resources for assessing students' development of word recognition skills.

- **Chapter** 9, **Fluency and Independent Reading.** We switched our focus from fluency as an activity to fluency as the outgrowth of motivating students to become independent, avid readers in school and out. Reading volume is critical. While isolated fluency activities are useful, our overall goal is to help you develop students who will read. We added some suggestions for developing fluency in small group and individual activities plus suggestions for assessing it.

- **Chapter** 10, **Vocabulary Development.** We continued our focus on a four-pronged approach to developing students' vocabulary and provided new material on selecting words for instruction and activities for teaching word learning strategies. Building knowledge of the world and of words is a major factor in becoming a strong reader.

- **Chapter** 11, **Teaching Reading Comprehension: Focusing on Narrative Text**. This is a new chapter pulling together what the research says about assisting children with literary texts. We compare and contrast different approaches to comprehension including basals, guided reading, scaffolded instruction, and a novel approach and merges read-alouds and book clubs. We have a strong focus on the importance of discussion and techniques for assessing students' comprehension.

- **Chapter** 12, **Comprehending Informational Text.** This, too, is a new chapter. Here we describe the knowledge, strategies, and motivation students need to read for information. Much of this reading now takes place on the Internet. We included new information on how to help students read for information on the Internet, a confusing, often untrustworthy place. We have added new information on teaching about text structure and fostering discussions that cause students to think deeply.

- **Chapter 13, Writing and Reading.**   In this chapter we have added some new ideas on the integration of reading and writing. We have also described how teaching writing can improve students' reading comprehension.

- **Chapter 14, Reading Instruction for English Learners.**   The number of English learners in schools is rising, and it is increasingly important for teachers to understand strategies for differentiating instruction. The revisions in this chapter have focused on new ideas about developing oral language skills and vocabulary.

Special Features

This text has a number of features designed to make understanding our sometimes-complex ideas easier. We have included different features for the print and the digital versions of the text.

In the print and digital versions:

- We start each chapter with a set of **Learning Outcomes** that list our purpose in writing each chapter. Each major section of the chapter addresses one of the learning outcomes.

- Within each chapter we have provided **In the Classroom** examples that offer specific lesson plans or teaching and assessment tools for measuring students' competence in each area we address.

- The **Reading Corner** in each chapter offers an updated list of children's books that can be used for specific curriculum goals. Some lists are focused on a genre, some on topics, and some reflect a range of text complexity.

- Within each chapter we provide **Reflect and Apply** questions and activities that we hope will help you think through the ideas and issues within each section of the chapter.

- We also provide references to the appendix for this book, where you can download lesson plans and other documents for your classroom instruction.

MyLab Education

One of the most visible changes in the sixth edition, also one of the most significant, is the expansion of the digital learning and assessment resources embedded in the eText and the inclusion of MyLab Education in the text. MyLab Education is an online homework, tutorial, and assessment program designed to work with the text to engage learners and to improve learning. Within its structured environment, learners see key concepts demonstrated through real classroom video footage, practice what they learn, test their understanding, and receive feedback to guide their learning and to ensure their mastery of key learning outcomes. Designed to bring learners more directly into the world of K–12 classrooms and to help them see the real and powerful impact of literacy concepts covered in this book, the online resources in MyLab Education with the Enhanced eText include:

- **Self-Checks.**   We have created short quizzes, *Self-Checks*, with which you can monitor your own learning. The self-checks are made up of self-grading, multiple-choice items that not only provide feedback on whether questions are answered correctly or incorrectly, but also provide rationales for both correct and incorrect answers.

- **Application Exercises.**   We also provide application exercises for each section of the chapter. These exercises help you apply what you have read, engage you in some critical thinking, and bring some of our abstract ideas into a real-world context. After learners provide their own answers to the questions, they receive feedback in the form of model answers written by experts.

- **Video Examples.** Throughout each chapter you will find videos of classroom instruction, opinions of other experts (yes, there are others), and at least one humorous take on our field by John Oliver.

Acknowledgments

Clearly, *Teaching Reading in the 21st Century* continues to change and evolve. With each new edition we have built on the combined expertise of many colleagues throughout the country who are dedicated to literacy education. To you, we extend a special thank-you for your valuable feedback and assistance.

- Our editors, Drew Bennett and Carolyn Schweitzer, who assisted us throughout the revision process; our production editor, Yagnesh Jani.

- The many people who granted us permission to cite their work and reproduce their materials in this text.

- The reviewers: Carol L. Butterfield, Central Washington University; Deborah A. Farrer, California University of Pennsylvania; Marie A. Fero, Eastern Illinois University; Kitty Y. Hazler, Morehead State University; Susan Hendricks, University of Nevada, Las Vegas; Kimberlee Sharp, Morehead State University; Maureen Siera, St. Martin's University; Linda Skroback-Heisler, University of Nevada, Las Vegas; and Christina D. Walton, Morehead State University.

- The reviewers of previous editions, who have been so helpful in shaping this text.

- The teachers, researchers, and students whose names you will see mentioned on nearly every page of this text, especially Sarah Collinge, Bethany Robinson, Jonni Wolskee, Babs Mowry, Alison Montano, Cheri Cooke, Lauren Liang, and Cheryl Peterson, who wrote outstanding lesson plans; Presley Williams and Cole Williams who lent us the thoughtful school work; Lili Claman who developed some book lists; Raymond Philippot, who assisted us with many of the other chapters; as well as Mark Aulls, Ann Beecher, Barbara Brunetti, Jerry Brunetti, David Carberry, Jim Hoffman, Susan Jones, Stephen Koziol, Anita Meinbach, Judy Peacock, Lynn Richards, Randall Ryder, Wayne Slater, Margo Sorenson, Kelly Spies, and Diann Stone. All lent their time and very special talents to this project.

- Our colleagues at the University of Minnesota and Stanford University, with special thanks to Lee Galda, Jay Samuels, Barbara Taylor, and Susan Watts, whose scholarship and dedication to the profession are without equal.

- Our students and teachers from kindergarten through graduate school, who over the years have inspired our thinking and contributed significantly to the ideas you will read about in this text.

- Our friends and family—especially my wife Pamela Dewitz, who listened, encouraged, and sustained me throughout this lengthy revision, and especially our accomplished, supportive children, Julie, Erin (Michael & Bonnie Graves), Rachel, David, and Erica, Presley and Cole (Peter and Pamela Dewitz).

Chapter 1
Reading and Learning to Read

 Learning Outcomes

After reading and studying this chapter you should be able to:

1.1 Discuss and debate the reading proficiency of students in the United States and identify where our major problems exist.

1.2 Explain how the cognitive view of the reading process influences instructional decisions and why it is important to understand this model of reading.

1.3 Describe the essential components of a reading curriculum and the knowledge teachers need to teach this curriculum well.

Classroom Vignette

It was the first day of summer vacation, and 10-year-old Carmella couldn't wait to meet up with her best friend Amber at the community pool. Just as she was considering which bathing suit to wear, she heard the patter of rain on the roof and looked out the window. "Daaang," she muttered. "No pool today." She flopped back on her bed and reached for Kate DiCamillo's *Because of Winn-Dixie* on her nightstand. Within minutes, she was deep into India Opal Buloni's new life in Florida, thoughts of the pool temporarily forgotten.

On the other side of town, when Carmella's friend Amber woke up and saw that rain had spoiled their plans for the community pool, she never thought of picking up a book. Unlike Carmella, she had not mastered the complex process of reading. Reading wasn't much fun for her, and she didn't do it often. Amber will probably spend most of the rainy day with her iPad, watching movies and playing video games.

For some children, like Carmella, mastering the complex process of reading comes easily, and by fourth grade they are quite accomplished readers. For others, like Amber, this is not the case. As Carmella and Amber progress in school, they both will face increasingly challenging reading tasks, and both will need help in meeting those challenges. Amber—and other students who struggle in reading—will, of course, need more assistance than Carmella and other accomplished readers, but all your students will need the very best instruction and encouragement you can provide if they are to become the sort of readers the 21st century demands.

The Reading Proficiency of U.S. Students

Critics of the U.S. educational system have frequently lashed out at what they perceive as the inability of U.S. schools to educate students as well as they once did, the poor performance of U.S. students compared to students in other countries, and the general failure of U.S. schools to teach all students to read. Crisis is a continual theme in American education, and many presidents including Eisenhower, Johnson, Reagan, Bush I, Clinton, Bush II, and Obama have staked part of their political reputation on solving the crisis in our schools. Almost always, the crisis centered on reading and mathematics.

The first contemporary educational crisis was an outgrowth of the Civil Rights movement, because the 1964 Civil Rights Act required that the government report on the equality of educational opportunity. James Coleman (1966) conducted a massive survey of our educational system, and his 737-page report concluded, in part, that there was a significant achievement gap between African American and White children. He also found that peers mattered more than materials. "If you integrate children of different backgrounds and socioeconomics, kids perform better" (Coleman, 1966, p. 537). Others in the U.S. Department of Education saw things differently and urged increased federal funding for reading and math. Congress them passed the Elementary and Secondary Education Act, Title I, that became No Child Left Behind (NCLB), then Race to the Top (RTT), and now Every Student Succeeds Act (ESSA).

The next educational crisis was identified in a report written in 1983 titled *A Nation at Risk*. This report stated, "Our Nation is at risk. Our once unchallenged preeminence in commerce, industry, science, and technological innovation is being overtaken by competitors throughout the world . . ." The reading community responded with its own report, *Becoming a Nation of Readers* (Anderson, Hiebert, Scott, & Wilkinson, 1985). The report had wide-ranging recommendations about teaching reading based on the best research at the time and concluded, "America will become a nation of readers when verified practices of the best teachers in the best schools can be introduced throughout the country" (p. 116). Some people, such as David Berliner and Bruce Biddle, saw this as *The Manufactured Crisis* (1995), that many of these claims were "myths, half-truths, and . . . outright lies."

Soon we were on to the next crisis under President George W. Bush. The *Report of the National Reading Panel* (NICHD, 2000) identified the five crucial components of reading instruction—phonemic awareness, phonics, fluency, vocabulary, and comprehension—but its detractors lamented the lack of emphasis on the child's oral language, the overemphasis on systematic phonics instruction and the total neglect of motivation. The National Reading Panel influenced No Child Left Behind and the $6 billion appropriated for Reading First, a program that leaned heavily on teaching phonological awareness, phonics, and fluency. NCLB put teeth into the nascent standards movement by creating mandatory testing in reading for all third- through eighth-graders and some high school students.

Under the President Barack Obama administration, the response to the crisis in education in general and reading in particular continued as states were urged to employ more carrots and sticks. End-of-the-year testing in reading was not sufficient, as Race to the Top pushed schools to regularly monitor the performance of their students. As of this writing, the backlash to testing has begun, but if past is prologue, a new educational crisis is just over the horizon.

Our task now is to carefully examine the reading proficiency of students in the United States looking at how students' proficiency has changed over time and how it compares to the reading achievement of students in other nations. Finally, and most importantly, we consider the sorts of reading proficiency required in today's and tomorrow's world. This, of course, is the proficiency you want to help all students to achieve.

The Current Reading Proficiency of Our Students

Frankly, achieving a clear picture of the reading ability of U.S. students is difficult. We will walk you the through the data, present our conclusions, and encourage you to draw your own interpretations. There is no right answer in this exercise.

We base our response primarily on three sources that provide the most reliable large-scale assessment data available—the National Assessment of Educational Progress (NAEP); the International Association for the Evaluation of Educational Achievement, also known as PIRLS; and some new data that directly compare the reading proficiency of U.S. students in 1960 to the present.

NAEP was established by the federal government 45 years ago to provide a periodic report card on U.S. students' achievement in reading and other academic areas. In other words, it was established to do exactly the job we are trying to do here—communicate about how U.S. students are doing in school. The NAEP reading achievement tests for long-term trends about every four years and reports data for ages 9, 13, and 17. Figure 1.1 shows NAEP results since 1971 (U.S. Department of Education, NCES Long Terms Trends, 2013). The trend line for 17-year-olds is basically flat, indicating little or no change in reading performance at the high school level since 1971. The trend line for ages 9 and 13 goes up very slightly from 1971 to 1999 and then just a bit more steeply from 1999 to 2012, indicating a small improvement in reading for this age level. Thus, over the past 45 years, the reading performance of 9- and 13-year-old U.S. students has gone up just a bit, and those of 17-year-olds has remained very much the same.

The picture becomes more complicated when we examine the data by racial or ethnic groups. While the gap in Black and White achievement has narrowed considerably since 1971, and since 1999, there is still a large gap between the performance of the two groups (see Figure 1.2). Similar results exist for 13-year-olds, eighth-graders, and between White and Hispanic students. Although overall reading achievement is improving, we have more work to do to bring all children to the same level of proficiency.

The International Association for the Evaluation of Educational Achievement (IEA) was established in the late 1950s to conduct international studies. Its most recent study of reading, Progress in International Reading Literacy Study (PIRLS), was conducted during the 2015–16 school year in 65 countries (Mullis, Martin, Foy, & Hooper 2017a). Figure 1.3 shows the results of this study, which gathered data from more than

Figure 1.1 U.S. Students' Reading Proficiency 1971–2012

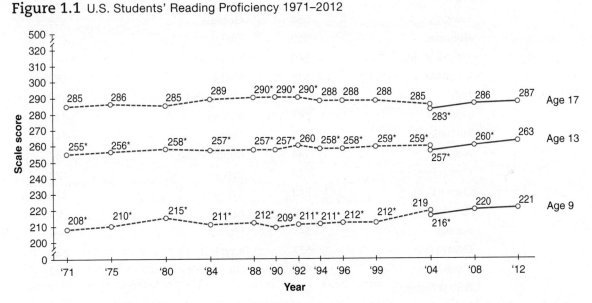

SOURCE: U.S. Department of Education, Institute of Education Science. National Center for Educational Statistics, National Assessment of Educational Progress (NAEP) Trends in Academic Progress, Reading 1971–2012.

Figure 1.2 Trend in NAEP Reading Average Scores and Score Gap for White and Black 9-Year-Old Students

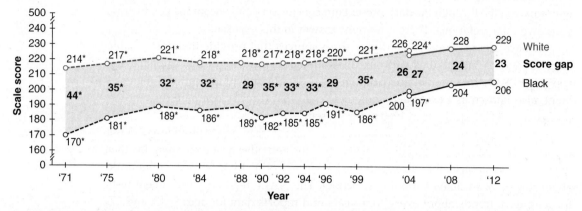

SOURCE: U.S. Department of Education, Institute of Education Science. National Center for Educational Statistics, National Assessment of Educational Progress (NAEP) Trends in Academic Progress, Reading 1971–2012.

Figure 1.3 PIRLS Overall Reading Average Scores of Fourth-Grade Students, by Education System 2016

Educational System	Overall Scaled Score	Educational System	Overall Scaled Score
Russian Federation	581	Slovak Republic	535
Singapore	576	Israel	530
Ireland	567	Portugal	528
Finland	566	Spain	528
Poland	565	Belgium (Flemish)	525
Norway	559	New Zealand	523
Chinese – Taipei	559	France	511
England	559	PIRLS scale centerpoint	500
Latvia	568	Belgium (French)	497
Sweden	555	Chile	494
Hungary	554	Georgia	488
Bulgaria	552	Trinidad & Tobago	479
United States	549	Azerbaijan	472
Lithuania	548	Malta	452
Italy	548	United Arab Emirates	450
Denmark	547	Bahrain	446
Netherlands	545	Qatar	442
Australia	544	Saudi Arabia	430
Czech Republic	543	Iran	428
Canada	543	Oman	418
Slovenia	542	Kuwait	393
Austria	541	Morocco	358
Germany	537	Egypt	330
Kazakhstan	536	South Africa	320
Slovak Republic	535		
Israel	530		

SOURCE: International Association for the Evaluation of Educational Achievement (IEA). Progress in International Reading Study (PIRLS) 2016.

150,000 fourth-graders. As you can see, the United States ranked thirteenth among the 65 countries. The United State scored below Russia, Ireland, Finland, and England, but above 26 other European, Asian, and Middle Eastern nations. Our students scored 49 points above the international average of 500. This is a very respectable showing indeed.

A second piece of the PIRLS study, ePIRLS, examined fourth-grade students' ability to read online for information (Mullis, Martin, Foy, & Hooper, 2017b). The study took reading into the digital age and examined how students can select, interpret, and integrate information while reading for information on the Internet. The students were given science and social studies tasks, each requiring students to read three websites with five to ten web pages per site. Students had to read text, study visual data, and work with pop-up and animated tasks. They had to use hyperlinks and navigate from one site to another, integrating visual and print information. All of the tasks required the students to answer multiple-choice and constructed response questions.

Fourteen countries participated in the ePIRLS study, all of which also participated in the regular PIRLS study. The students from the United States were ranked sixth out of the 14 nations. Students from Singapore, Norway, and Ireland performed better than our students, who scored the same as students from Sweden and Denmark. Students from China (Taipei), Canada, Israel, Italy, Slovenia, Portugal, Georgia, and the United Arab Emirates scored significantly lower than our students. Two other findings are worth noting. Our students performed better on the ePIRLS than on the regular PIRLS, and girls performed better than boys.

The final piece of data is a study that compares the reading efficiency of U.S. students now to students in 1960 (Spichtig, Hiebert, Vorstius, Pascoe et al., 2016). In the study, the students in both decades read the exact same texts under the exact same conditions. Two thousand students from grades 2 through 12 participated in the study. The students read graded passages silently, their eye movements and reading rate were recorded, and their reading comprehension was assessed. The study shows that the silent reading efficiency of U.S. students has declined and the severity of the decline is most apparent at the secondary level, as Figure 1.4 indicates.

The study demonstrates that comprehension-based silent reading rates are slower now than in 1960 (See the top left chart in Figure 1.4.). The gap first appears with fourth-grade students and widens over the next eight years. Students in middle school have hit a plateau, demonstrating no growth over three years. Eleventh- and twelfth-graders today read about as well as sixth-graders in 1960. These data provide a partial explanation why NAEP scores have changed little in middle school and high school. The other charts in Figure 1.4 demonstrate that students today make more eye movement fixation per word, dwell longer on each word and engage in more regressive eye movements. All this indicates that student today are less efficient readers.

The best data available presents an ambiguous picture of U.S. students' reading proficiency. Our students perform as well or better than students in other industrialized nations. However, the comprehension-based silent reading efficiency of our students has declined most strikingly in the upper grades. Our students perform better with digital tasks than with more traditional reading. Our interpretation of the NAEP data over the past 45 years suggests a troubling pattern of performance among U.S. students. By fourth grade, the vast majority of students can read easy material and answer simple questions. However, once the texts become slightly more difficult—the sorts of reading middle-grade students are expected to deal with—a large percentage of middle school students cannot read and understand the material, and neither can a sizable percentage of high school seniors. Once both texts and questions become demanding—the type of material one would need to read to understand political and social issues or enjoy relatively sophisticated literature—very few students, even those about to graduate from high school, can deal with them.

However, at the school level, NAEP is not an issue. Most schools are focused on their state high-stakes test, which will determine whether the school is accredited or punished at the end of the year. Compare state test results to NAEP and you will

Figure 1.4 Silent Read

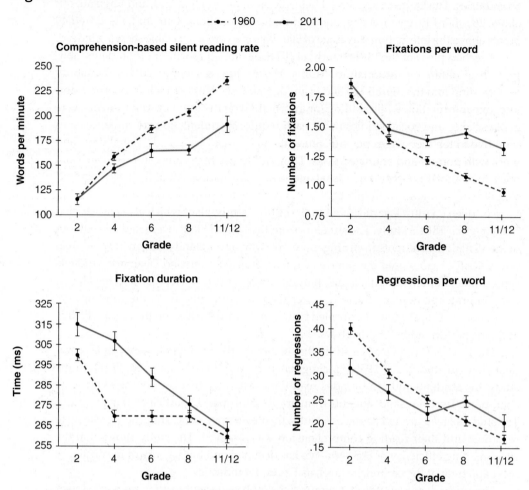

SOURCE: Spichtig, A. N., Hiebert, E. H., Vorstius, C., Pascoe, J. P., David Pearson, P., & Radach, R. (2016). The Decline of Comprehension-Based Silent Reading Efficiency in the United States: A Comparison of Current Data with Performance in 1960. *Reading Research Quarterly*, *51*(2), 239–259.

discover that, 40 percent of the students considered proficient on their state tests are not proficient on NAEP, and 75 percent of the states have a passing score that is below a basic level of reading on the NAEP (Koretz, 2017; U.S. Department of Education, 2007). The individual states are setting their standards low and may be institutionalizing a set of low expectations. Anthony Applegate and his colleagues compared state tests to NAEP and found startling differences (Applegate, Applegate, McGeehan, Pinto, & Kong, 2009). On the state tests, only 22 percent of the questions demand higher-order thinking, whereas 68 percent of NAEP questions do. Forty-six percent of NAEP questions ask readers to make interpretations and inferences about characterization and plot, but only 24 percent of the questions on state tests assess these skills. If state high-stakes tests continue as the norm and teachers teach students to pass these tests, we may undermine the literacy standards we have embraced, sacrificing higher-order thinking.

An increasing number of experts believe that high-stakes testing corrupts education (Koretz, 2017; Nichols & Berliner, 2007). Teaching to these high-stakes tests inflates test scores without improving basic reading ability. High-stakes tests narrow the reading/ language arts curriculum, undermine the attention to science and social studies, and distort how reading is taught—too many short passages and not enough books. At its worst, the focus on test scores has led to cheating scandals in several major school districts, with a few teachers and administrators serving jail time (Koretz, 2017).

The other continuing literacy concern is the persistent achievement gap in the United States. Many children raised in poverty score lower than their middle-class counterparts.

The same is true of many Black, Hispanic, and American Indian students when compared to White students. On the last NAEP assessment, the achievement gap between Black and White students had narrowed slightly but was still significantly wide. The United States still has a long way to go to ensure that all students become proficient readers.

Literacy for Today's and Tomorrow's World

It is important to understand how well U.S. students read, it is even more important to understand present-day literacy requirements and how those requirements are changing. At one time, literacy was defined as the ability to sign your name. At another time, it was defined as the ability to read aloud a simple text with which you were already familiar—typically a passage from the Bible (Kirsch & Jungeblut, 1986). Today, although there is no single definition of literacy, there is universal agreement that everyone needs a far higher level of literacy than at any time in our past, and that this requirement will continue to grow. Irwin Kirsch and Ann Jungeblut (1986) define present-day literacy as "using printed and written information to function in society, to achieve one's goals, and to develop one's knowledge." Lauren Resnick (1987) views present-day literacy as a "higher-order skill" and notes that it requires thinking that is complex, that yields multiple solutions, that involves multiple criteria, and that demands nuanced judgments. David Perkins (1992) notes that contemporary education must go beyond simply presenting students with information and must ensure that students retain important concepts, understand topics deeply, and actively use the knowledge they gain. Finally, the RAND Reading Study Group (2002) notes that the United States today "demands a universally higher level of literacy achievement than at any time in history" and goes on to say that "it is reasonable to believe that the demand for a literate populace will increase in the future."

Present-day literacy requires much more than passively absorbing what is on the printed page. It requires attaining a deep understanding of what is read, remembering important information, linking newly learned information to existing prior knowledge, knowing when and where to use that information, using it appropriately in varied contexts in and out of school, and communicating effectively with others. Literacy for today's world requires that readers be able to *do* something as a result of reading, not merely know something. Moreover, literacy for today's world requires that readers be able to do something with a variety of different texts—not just short stories, novels, poetry, and history texts, but also tax forms, computer manuals, complex directions for operating ever more complex machines, and increasingly the text that informs us about the critical issues of our democracy—immigration, health care, national defense, and the economy. These issues cannot be understood by listening to one-minute sound bites from CNN or MSNBC or by reading the latest tweet on your iPhone or Galaxy 8.

More and more, literacy means knowing how to use the Internet, reading digital text, and making complex decisions about the veracity of information on various websites, blogs, and tweets. These are New Literacies (Lew, Zawilinski, Forzani, & Timbrell, 2015). The Internet is the textbook of today, for most it will be the textbook of the future. The strategies that have been developed for printed textbooks and informational trade books must give way to new strategies. Readers today must search for information using key words, verify the trustworthiness of website, and synthesize information across a number of websites. These search tools will replace lessons on the Table of Contents and the Index.

Some suspect that the process of reading digital text is different from reading print on paper and presents new challenges for all readers. With digital text, we often resort to skimming, sacrificing deep reading understanding. With these new literacies "instead of hiking the trail yourself, the trees, rock and moss move past you in flashes with no trace of what came before and no way to see what lies ahead" (Jabr, 2013, p. 6). Kaufman and Flanagan (2016) demonstrated that young adults reach higher levels of abstractions when reading on conventional paper than they do when reading on screens. "The ever-increasing demand of multitasking, divided attention, and information overload that individuals encounter in their use of digital technologies may cause them to 'retreat' to the less cognitively demanding lower end of the concrete-abstract continuum" (Kaufman & Flanagan, 2016).

Literacy is the ability to read critically from a variety of sources, but literacy is also the desire to read for both pleasure and information. Without the inclination to read, without the habit of reading, higher-level reading skills are useless. In today's world, teaching children to read is only half the battle; we must motivate them to want to read. When the iPad and the Xbox One S are more engaging than a novel and cable news sound bites are easier than the *New York Times*, reading is hard to sell. Teaching the love of reading and inspiring children to use print for information may be the most difficult task, one for which we have not yet developed an effective curriculum. The child who can read but does not has no advantage over the child who cannot read.

To be sure, elementary and middle school students do not read all of these complex texts, but their early reading experiences should provide a foundation for dealing with complex material in the future. Moreover, given the lower level of reading proficiency demonstrated by many children raised in poverty and many Black, Hispanic, and American Indian students, we need to work especially hard to dramatically improve the reading instruction and the opportunity for these students to read. We particularly need to improve all children's higher-order skills and the desire to seek answers in complex materials. We must nurture and encourage students to become competent readers, who seek to read, in today's increasingly complex and demanding world.

Reflect and Apply

The arguments about the quality of education in the United States are old and increasingly political. To help you understand this debate, we include Reflect and Apply sections periodically throughout the text. Ideally, with many facts at your disposal you will discuss your responses with others—a study group, your class, or your course instructor.

1. Suppose you are sitting with a small group of parents at a school open house when one woman abruptly demands to know why today's students read so poorly compared to those in her day. A man picks up her prompt and with similar abruptness wants to know why American kids can't read as well as those in other countries. Compose a response in which you cite data to reassure these parents that U.S. students are certainly holding their own.

2. The concept of present-day literacy is complex. At this point, describe your understanding of the concept in a paragraph or two. Keep your description and add to it as you gain a broader knowledge of present-day literacy in later chapters.

MyLab Education **Self-Check 1.1**

MyLab Education **Application Exercise 1.1:** How Proficient Are Fourth Grade Readers in the United States?

The Reading Process

Why should you care about the reading process? Why is it vital to develop a deep understanding of it? The answer is straightforward. Regardless of what you learn about the specifics of teaching reading from this text, your university courses, in-service sessions, Pinterest, and discussions with other teachers, much of what you do in the classroom will result from your personal understanding of the reading process. The number of teaching options you have is so great, the needs of different students so diverse, and the specifics of a particular teaching situation so unique that it is impossible to anticipate all of the decisions about literacy instruction that you will make each day. But understanding the mental processes of a reader can prepare you to make wise choices.

Reading instruction is regularly buffeted by fads, and publishers create hundreds of reading programs, all claiming to be "research-based." Each new reading program is "new and improved" like a box of Tide, and is "guaranteed" to fix your students' reading problems and inspire them to reach the heights of literacy. Beyond the published programs, you have access to 2.4 million resources on Teachers Pay Teachers (www.teacherspayteachers.com) and an overwhelming number of suggestions on Pinterest. Much of what is available on the Internet is poorly conceived and not very useful. The only way to use these sites intelligently is to have solid grounding in the reading process.

Although different authorities view the reading process somewhat differently, over the past 40 years a widely accepted, balanced, and strongly supported view of the process has emerged. Here, we call this the *cognitive-constructivist view of reading*. This construct forms the foundation of the approach to reading presented in this book. In the next section, we explain several theories that elaborate, complement, and supplement this concept.

The Cognitive-Constructivist View of Reading

The cognitive-constructivist view of reading emphasizes that reading is a process in which the reader actively searches for meaning in what he reads. In fact, the reader makes connections between ideas in the text and then integrates these understandings with prior knowledge. This search for meaning depends very heavily on the reader's having an existing store of knowledge. The active contribution of the reader is significant enough to justify the assertion that she actually constructs much of the meaning she arrives at while reading.

For example, as Carmella reads *Because of Winn-Dixie*, she learns that India Opal is sad because her mother recently walked out on her and her father. Later in the book, when Carmella learns that Amanda Wilkinson, a girl India Opal does not at first get along with, is sad because her younger brother recently died, Carmella can construct the inference that Opal and Amanda share a similar experience and may become friends. Nothing in the text tells Carmella this; the inference comes from her knowledge that people who have things in common often become friends and from her active processing of the text. Notice in the accompanying classroom example how teacher Martin Cummings highlights this use of background knowledge and encourages active processing with his sixth-graders (In the Classroom 1.1). Mr. Cummings is helping his students realize that readers actively search for meaning in what they read and that the meaning they construct from a text depends on their own knowledge about the world and its conventions.

THE COGNITIVE ORIENTATION

The earliest influence on this view of reading came from cognitive psychology, the orientation that became the main perspective of American psychology beginning in the 1960s (Gardner, 1985). Cognitive psychologists view the learner and her background knowledge as central to learning and the study of learners' thought processes as a fundamental focus of their work. They also view learners as active participants, who act on, rather than simply respond to, their external environment as they learn. In the cognitive view, reading is very much an active process in which the meaning the reader gleans from a text is heavily influenced by the cognitive work that she puts into the reading process. Both the beginning reader—whom we might observe carefully sounding out words as she reads orally—and the accomplished reader such as Carmella—who appears to be effortlessly absorbing *Because of Winn-Dixie*—are in fact actively engaged in making meaning from the text.

In the Classroom 1.1

Using Background Knowledge

Martin Cummings wrote the first paragraph from Sharon Flake's novel *The Skin I'm In* on the board:

> The first time I seen her, I got a bad feeling inside. Not like I was in danger or nothing. Just like she was somebody I should stay clear of. To tell the truth, she was a freak like me. The kind of person folks can't help but tease. That's bad if you're a kid like me. It's worse for a new teacher like her.

He read the paragraph aloud to his sixth-graders and then said, "What does this paragraph tell us? What meaning do you get from it?"

Chris: The narrator's someone young, maybe our age.

Mr. Cummings: What makes you think so?

Chris: 'Cause it says "a kid like me" and sounds like the way kids talk.

Lateisha: Yeah, Black kids, not White kids. I think the person talking is Black.

Mr. Cummings: So you think the narrator's Black. What else do we know about the narrator from this paragraph?

Kyle: She has a low opinion of herself.

Mr. Cummings: How do you know that?

Kyle: 'Cause she calls herself a freak.

CONSTRUCTIVISM

The view of the reading process described here derives from a theory called *constructivism*, a political (Searle, 1993), philosophical (von Glaserfeld, 1984), social (Gergen, 1985), and psychological construct. We are using the term in its psychological sense. Constructivism emphasizes the idea that comprehending a text is very much an active process. Constructivism holds that the meaning one constructs from a text is subjective—the result of one particular person's processing of the text. Each reader is influenced by the sum total of her experience as well as by her unique intellectual makeup. Because of this, each reader constructs a somewhat different interpretation of the text, the text as she conceptualizes it (von Glaserfeld, 1984). The three student journal entries listed in Figure 1.5 illustrate this concept. All three students were responding to a prompt for the picture book *Mama Bear* by Chyng Feng Sun. The story tells of a girl who bakes and sells almond cookies in order to earn enough money to buy a large, expensive stuffed bear for Christmas because she thinks it will help keep her and her mother warm. The students were asked to respond to this question: "What did Mei-Mei want most for Christmas?" Each answer in Figure 1.5, is, of course, correct, yet points to a different perspective on the story.

Having noted that constructivism emphasizes the subjectivity of meaning, we should also note that different texts vary dramatically in how much they constrain it (Stanovich, 1994). An abstract poem may prompt many appropriate interpretations, but a manual on how to install new software should prompt only one. In between these two extremes lies a range of texts that invite various degrees of individual interpretation. However, when reading straightforward stories and a good deal of informational material, most readers will construct quite similar meanings for what they read.

As noted, constructivism is a social construct as well as a psychological one. Most constructivists emphasize that the social world

Figure 1.5 Three Students' Responses to the Same Question About a Story They Read

Kaiya: Mei-Mei wanted a bear for Christmas.

Lawrence: Mei-Mei wanted her mother to be happy.

Ali: Mei-Mei wanted to be warm most of all.

in which we live heavily influences the meaning that we derive from our experiences, including our experiences with text. Thus, constructivism strongly supports the inclusion of a variety of discussion arrangements and group work as part of reading and learning (Calfee & Patrick, 1995).

Reading and Understanding Words

WORD RECOGNITION

Before the reader can make connections, before he can bring his knowledge and experience to bear on the text, he has to read the words. Reading is an ongoing, recursive process. Many operations happen at once, but we have decided word recognizing is a good place to start in describing the reading process. For the mature reader, word recognition is an effortless process beyond our awareness. Most words we read are recognized automatically, with the reader processing all the letter-sound associations simultaneously or recognizing the word as a whole unit. Only when a new word is encountered, such as *Bangladesh,* is the reader aware that some process must be invoked to identify the word. He may know that he has to break the word into chunks or syllables and then use patterns he knows—*ang, la, esh*—to pronounce the new word. These abilities come to most readers easily but not before moving through several developmental stages. We will outline these developmental stages when we discuss word recognition in Chapter 8.

AUTOMATICITY

Achieving automatic word recognition is vitally important because automaticity underlies reading ability. Charles Perfetti (2007) has developed a comprehensive theory called word reading efficiency, which links fluent word recognition and the automatic retrieval of word meanings from memory. When you see the word *cantankerous*, you should read it effortlessly and quickly know its meaning. If not, you resort to decoding the pronunciation and using context clues to infer its meaning.

The concept of automaticity is both crucial and straightforward. An automatic activity is one that we can perform effortlessly and with very little attention. As David LaBerge and S. Jay Samuels (1974) pointed out in their pioneering work on automaticity in reading, the mind's attentional capacity is severely limited; in fact, we can attend to only about one thing at a time. Recent research suggests that multitasking, despite what you may believe, is nearly impossible unless one of the tasks is automatic and requires no attention, like listening to music on your iPhone (Ophir, Nass, & Wagner 2009). If we are faced with a situation in which we are forced to attend to too many things at once, we will fail. For example, a number of people have reached a level of automaticity in driving a stick shift car. They can automatically push in the clutch, let up on the accelerator, shift gears, let out the clutch, and press on the accelerator—and they can do all this while driving in rush hour traffic. Beginning drivers cannot do all of this at once; they have not yet automated the various subprocesses, and it would be foolish and dangerous for them to attempt to drive a stick shift car in an attention-demanding situation such as rush hour traffic.

Reading includes a number of subprocesses that need to take place at the same time—such as recognizing words, assigning meanings to words, constructing the meanings of sentences and larger units, and relating the information gleaned from the text to information we already have. Unless some of these processes are automated, readers simply cannot do all of this at once. Specifically, readers need to perform two processes automatically: They need to recognize words automatically, and they need to assign meanings to words automatically. For example, if a student is reading and comes across the word *imperative*, she needs to automatically recognize the word and automatically—immediately and without conscious attention—know that it means "absolutely necessary." If the student needs to pause often and struggles to recognize and assign meanings to words, reading will be difficult and laborious, and the student will not understand much of what she is reading.

Fluency is the ability to "read a text orally with speed, accuracy, expression and comprehension" (Samuels, 2002b). The component of fluency should also include endurance, because good readers can sustain fluent reading page after page. Reading well for one minute, a common test of fluency, might not be the best way to assess it (Deeney, 2010). Fluency is not just an oral phenomenon—it applies to silent reading as well. Because fluent readers can decode a text automatically, they are able to decode and comprehend at the same time, resulting in oral reading that is accurate, smooth, and fairly rapid, with proper expression.

To become fluent readers, students need to do a lot of silent reading in material they find interesting, enjoyable, and relatively easy. To become fluent oral readers, students can engage in a variety of different reading activities such as paired reading, echo reading, and repeated readings (Rasinski, 2003). These and many other techniques for creating fluent readers, as well as the many prerequisite skills that underlie fluent reading (Pikulski & Chard, 2005), are discussed in Chapter 9. The bibliography on page 28 of this chapter provides examples and information about books beginning readers can use to build automaticity and fluency.

Achieving fluency is often a particular challenge for students learning English as a second language. In addition to going through the processes that native speakers do, nonnative speakers may need to translate English words into their own language in the process of arriving at meaning. Thus, becoming automatic in processing words and fluent in reading texts is extremely important for English language learners.

English learners need a strong emphasis on vocabulary if they are to achieve reading fluency. It is difficult and artificial to read quickly, with expression, a passage you do not understand. To build fluency with English learners, teachers need to actively build vocabulary. As words are encountered, teachers need to discuss meanings and relate them to prior knowledge. Pictures provide support for new words and new concepts, especially for young students. Cognates should be stressed to create links between the students' first and second languages. *Artistico* is *artist* and *conflicto* is *conflict*.

VOCABULARY KNOWLEDGE

Vocabulary knowledge is crucial to learning to read and understanding what you read. Children who enter school with a rich store of words will make relatively rapid progress learning to read. Disadvantaged students who enter school with smaller vocabularies will have more difficulty developing word identification and comprehension (Language and Reading Research Consortium, 2015; August, Carlo, Dressler & Snow, 2005). Vocabulary or word knowledge is essential for comprehension, and the relationship of vocabulary and comprehension is reciprocal. Reading engaging and challenging text with comprehension builds a student's vocabulary. If the reader does not know the meaning of the essential words in a text comprehension suffers. Teaching vocabulary build comprehension. This is true for native English speakers and English learners.

Building vocabulary knowledge requires an instructional program with many parts (Graves, 2016). Students need rich language experiences in the classroom, including interactive read alouds, engaging discussions, and ample time during which they can read independently. Teachers need to directly teach individual words, especially those essential to comprehending the texts. Teachers need to develop students' word learning strategies so that they can use word parts, context clues, and the dictionary to infer word meanings. Reading is a self-teaching process if students have the right tools and the opportunity to use them (Share, 1995). Finally, teachers need to foster word consciousness so that students find words interesting and a delight to learn. In Chapter 10 of this book we will focus directly on vocabulary instruction.

The Process of Comprehension: The Construction-Integration Process

CONSTRUCTION-INTEGRATION

While our reader is fluently recognizing the words, she also comprehends the message. We can break the comprehension process into at least three recursive parts—construction, integration, and metacognition. To grasp the process of comprehension, we turn to the theory with the greatest clarity—the construction-integration model, a detailed example of constructivism. Developed by Walter Kintsch (1998, 2004) and others, the process begins with construction, in which the reader comprehends sentences and then links ideas from one sentence to another. Integration is the process of using prior knowledge to expand and interpret the meaning the author has put on the pages. Consider these three sentences: *John got a cup of coffee. It was very hot. Now there is a big mess on the rug.* Construction is necessary to link the first sentence to the second. The pronoun *it* links the coffee and its temperature. The first two sentences are integrated with the third when the reader, using her prior knowledge, makes the inference that hot coffee was dropped, perhaps over an expensive rug. In the third phase, metacognition, the reader confirms that this makes sense.

We illustrate the construction-integration process in Figure 1.6. To construct ideas, the reader first applies his knowledge of vocabulary and syntax, grammar, to understand each sentence, a process used in oral language comprehension. Then the reader links one sentence or one idea to another using what he knows about the cohesive ties of language. A reader knows that the words *but* and *however* mean that the next idea somehow qualifies the first, that *because* and *since* signal that one idea caused another, and that *some* and *few* refer to a portion of the ideas already mentioned. As the reader integrates ideas using these cohesive ties, he is building a textbase—a relatively literal understanding of the text. A textbase is fleeting and it might be what a reader could immediately recall if you stopped his reading in mid-passage and asked him to retell it.

To preserve this textbase, the reader integrates text information and prior knowledge, creating his own mental model. This is the essence of the constructivist process. Reading the text—*Mary looked at the menu carefully trying to find the cheapest entrée, while John gazed lovingly in her eyes*—we know immediately that she is in a restaurant, concerned about money or at least wanting to make a good impression, and John is smitten. We have used our prior knowledge to interpret the text.

When psychologists first developed this constructivist view of cognition and reading, they wanted to explain how readers use knowledge and they developed the concept of schema theory, a theory that preceded the construction-integration model. Schema theory is concerned with knowledge, particularly with the way knowledge is represented in our minds, how we use that knowledge, and how it expands. According to the theory, knowledge is packaged in organized structures termed *schemata*. David Rumelhart (1980) states that schemata constitute our knowledge about "objects, situations, events, sequences of events, actions, and sequences of actions." We have schemata for

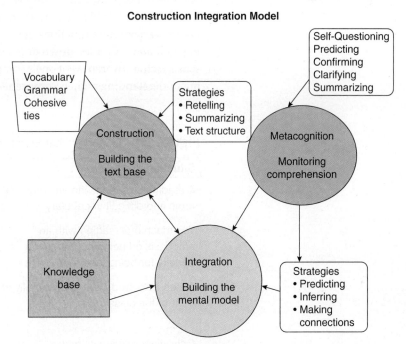

Figure 1.6 The Construction Integration Model of Comprehension

Based on: Kintsch. (1998) *Comprehension: A Paradigm for Cognition*. New York, NY: Cambridge University Press.

objects such as a house; for situations such as being in a class; for events such as going to a football game; and for sequences of events such as getting up, eating, showering, and going to work.

When we read the small scene with John and Mary, we use our dating schema to interpret the text. When a couple is having dinner together, it is likely a date. The word *menu* invokes the setting—a restaurant. *Gazed lovingly* signals affection or love, and reinforces the concept of a date. The words *cheapest entree* signals Mary's lack of money or her sensitivity to John's financial situation. We interpret our experiences—whether direct encounters with the world or vicarious experiences gained through reading—by comparing and, in most cases, matching those experiences to existing schemata, which constitute a vast and elaborate network of interrelationships. These networks of *organized* knowledge are virtually endless and constitute much of the intellectual capital that human beings have to work with.

One very important consequence of readers having these rich, internalized networks of schemata is that, once a particular schema is evoked, a huge store of knowledge becomes instantly available. Even when watching a motion picture, the director counts on us to have a rich background of information or schema to fill in what was left out. The more we know about the subject, the easier it will be to deal with that topic and learn more about it. Schemata assist the reader in initially making sense of what she reads, relating newly acquired information to prior knowledge, determining the relative importance of information in a text, making inferences, and remembering (Anderson & Pearson, 1984).

Good readers simultaneously rely on the text and on their background knowledge as they construct meaning. We as teachers need to provide students with the sorts of texts and tasks that promote this interplay of text and background knowledge. Sometimes we provide too little knowledge and comprehension suffers or too much knowedge and the students have little to. Figure 1.7 depicts situations that encourage too much or too little attention to the text, and that should be avoided.

METACOGNITION

The third component of the construction-integration process is metacognition. Someone has to keep an idea on the whole meaning construction process and ensure that it makes sense. Hence, think of your mind's eye, a part of your brain that observes your own cognitive functions, giving frequent thumbs-up when things are progressing well and a thumbs-down and stopping the whole process when it does not make sense. Active awareness of one's comprehension while reading and the ability to repair misunderstandings when comprehension breaks down are absolutely essential tools

Figure 1.7 Situations That Encourage Too Much and Too Little Attention to the Text

Situation	Result
A reading selection with an unfamiliar topic and difficult vocabulary	The reader will give too much attention to individual words and will bog down in the reading.
Too much oral reading with an emphasis on being correct and a penalty for being incorrect	The reader will focus on individual words, rather than on sentences, paragraphs, and ideas.
A less-able student's reading orally in front of the class	The reader will focus attention on correctly pronouncing individual words and give little attention to meaning.
Only silent reading with no postreading follow-up discussion	The reader will pay too little attention to the ideas in the text and guess at the meaning with little use of the text to confirm meaning.

for becoming an effective reader, and lack of such metacognitive skills is a particularly debilitating characteristic of poor readers.

Metacognitive readers have the ability to mentally step outside of themselves and view their own reading. By stepping outside of themselves, they can become self-regulated learners—learners who generate thoughts, feelings, strategies, and behaviors that help them attain their learning goals (Schunk & Zimmerman, 1998). Accomplished readers have several types of metacognitive knowledge, which we illustrate in Figure 1.8.

Metacognition begins with setting a purpose—why am I reading this text? For example, at the beginning of this section, you might have realized that you have no prior knowledge about metacognition (self-knowledge), noticed that the section is brief (task knowledge), and decided that the strategy of reading the section through several times would be fruitful (strategy knowledge). Thus, you exhibited metacognitive knowledge prior to beginning reading.

STRATEGIES

To keep the meaning construction process on track and to solve comprehension problems, the mature reader has at his disposal a set of cognitive tools or strategies. For example, if a reader comes across an unknown word as he is reading, one very reasonable response would be to read ahead a little to see if the context suggests a meaning; this is a strategy, something done automatically or deliberately to assist meaning construction. The list of comprehension strategies varies from one expert to another, but most agree that readers need to: set a purpose for reading, preview a text, predict, activate prior knowledge, monitor and clarify, create visual representation of text, draw inferences, self-question, and summarize or retell. Some strategies help drive the construction of the textbase, others assist the development of the mental model, and still others assist metacognition. A strategy like self-questioning might do all three. Asking questions before reading helps to set a purpose and build the mental model. Asking questions while reading, especially inferential questions, can drive the integration of text information and prior knowledge. When a reader asks himself a question after reading a portion of the text, he is checking his understanding. Figure 1.9 categorizes these research-based comprehension strategies by their functions. Some strategies do double duty.

In the teaching of reading, we use the terms comprehension skills and strategies loosely and interchangeably. In some reading curricula, finding the main idea is a skill while determining importance is a strategy (Dewitz, Jones, & Leahy, 2009). In fact, these skills/strategies are one and the same and share a type of thinking that is also critical to summarizing. Most of the mental processes of comprehension start out as strategies, something that requires deliberate thought and effort. At some stage of development,

Figure 1.8 Types of Metacognitive Knowledge

Types of Metacognitive Knowledge	What We Say to Ourselves
Self-Knowledge	"I love figuring out clues in detective stories." "If the book is too long, I know I won't finish it."
Task Knowledge	"It is best to skim the chapter first to learn what it is about, before reading it to take notes." "I wonder, what is the author's point? Why did he write this book?"
Strategy Knowledge	"When I get stuck on a word, I never use a dictionary and I should." "I am going to summarize this section of the chapter to see if I understand it."

SOURCE: Based on Schunk, D. H., & Zimmerman, B. J. (Eds.). (1998). Self-regulated learning: From teaching to self-reflective practice. New York: Guilford Press.

Figure 1.9 How Comprehension Strategies Affect the Process
of Meaning Construction

Textbase (Strategies that help readers relate ideas to each other)	Mental Model (Strategies that help readers relate text ideas to prior knowledge)	Metacognition (Strategies that help readers monitor and repair comprehension)
Anaphoric relationships	Predicting	Self-questioning
Retelling	Making inferences	Predicting-confirming
Summarizing	Making connections	Clarifying
Narrative structure	Self-questioning	Rereading
Expository text structure		Summarizing

comprehension strategies become automatic and readers can generate an inference or self-question without conscious effort. At this stage, we call strategies *comprehension skills* (Afflerbach, Pearson, & Paris, 2008). We want readers who are skillful and strategic.

Reading online within and across websites requires some additional strategies not typically used when reading print. Afflerbach and Cho (2009) argue that Internet reading requires a completely different style of reading because the reader is faced with multiple texts and multiple decisions about how and when to navigate from one text, image, or video to another. Some of us, especially children, are unschooled in this new media (Le Bigot & Rouet, 2007). Internet reading, compared to single text reading, requires more decisions about what to read and when (Afflerbach & Cho, 2009). The purpose for reading must remain fixed, or the disciplined reader becomes a random shopper. Leu, and his colleagues (2008) argue that there are distinct categories of strategies necessary for Internet reading. They include defining the problem, locating information sources by using key word search terms, critically evaluating information and determining its trustworthiness, deciding on the usefulness of information and integrating information from multiple websites.

MOTIVATION

Comprehension is more than skill; it is very much a matter of *will*. Students need to care whether they comprehend and be motivated to think and use strategies, especially when the going is difficult. Knowledge and strategies will only take the reader so far; the reader must want to comprehend the text (Alexander, 2003). That means reading that is enjoyable and interesting; reading that is personally valuable. The reader must have an important purpose for reading the text, and the reader should have some choice in what to read. The goal of reading instruction is much more than creating better readers. Reading is just a tool to enjoy text and understand ourselves, others, and the world. Adeptness with comprehension strategies can enhance motivation because the reader knows she has the tools to tackle a difficult text. The following factors help build motivation.

1. Read interesting texts. Texts written for the purpose of teaching comprehension (instructional websites, workbooks, leveled books) lack the interest of authentic novels, magazines, and informational trade books (Dewitz, Leahy, Jones, & Sullivan, 2010).

2. Allow students some choice in what they read. Choice gives students a sense of control. Choice allows them to seek out the genres they love—mysteries, adventures, fantasy—and engage their own curiosity.

3. Create tasks that students value. Reading to become a better reader is not as motivating as reading to learn or reading to enjoy.

4. Focus on student efficacy. When students believe that they have the tools to succeed, the strategies and the knowledge, and they attribute their success to these tools, their motivation grows. Students develop a sense of control and confidence.
5. Challenge your students. Many students like challenging projects. It is satisfying to read something difficult and create a complex report.
6. Stress competition at times. Some students thrive on competition. They like doing better than their peers or better than they did before.
7. Stress the social relatedness of learning. For many students, working in groups, being part of a larger effort is an important catalyst for effort.
8. Minimize the use of points, pizza, and other extraneous rewards.

The Meaning We Construct

As we pointed out earlier in this chapter, we do not all construct the same meaning from a text. The meaning we construct is influenced by our purpose for reading, the background and beliefs we bring to the text, and the social context in which we read. Take the often controversial Second Amendment to the Constitution.

> *A well regulated Militia, being necessary to the security of a free State, the right of the people to keep and bear Arms, shall not be infringed.*

A political liberal who is in favor of stricter gun controls emphasizes the *"well regulated militia"* part of the sentence and infers that guns exist for the militias but individuals do not have unrestricted rights to guns. Conservatives focus on the *"right of the people to keep and bear Arms, shall not be infringed"* and want as little gun control as possible. Each constructs a different meaning from the same sentence.

Before constructivism and the construction-integration model, two other theories competed to explain how we read and how we should read. These theories were New Criticism (see Ransom, 1941, 1979; Brooks & Warren, 1938), and Reader Response Theory (Rosenblatt, 1938/1995, 1978). Each of these theories can find a home within the construction integration model, and each emphasizes how the mental or situation model is built. Each of these theories has relevance for how to teach reading in today's classrooms.

New Criticism emphasizes that the meaning is in the text and the readers' task is to find and interpret the text. The contemporary example of New Criticism is close reading (Boyles, 2012), a style of reading in which the reader pays close attention to the ideas in the text and minimizes the role prior knowledge plays—if this is possible—in the construction of meaning. One consortium of educators, which developed assessments for the CCSS, offered this definition of close reading.

> Close, analytic reading stresses engaging with a text of sufficient complexity directly and examining meaning thoroughly and methodically, encouraging students to read and reread deliberately. Directing student attention on the text itself empowers students to understand the central ideas and key supporting details. It also enables students to reflect on the meanings of individual words and sentences; the order in which sentences unfold; and the development of ideas over the course of the text, which ultimately leads students to arrive at an understanding of the text as a whole. (PARCC, 2011, p. 7)

Reader-response theory puts greater emphasis on the reader; the meaning one gains from text is the result of a transaction between the reader and the text. Readers will have a range of responses to a literary work. Over the past 30 years, reader-response theory has had a very prominent influence on literature instruction (Beach, 1993; Galda & Graves, 2007; Marshall, 2000). When reading complex literary texts, students will derive a variety of interpretations. Many literary texts simply do not have a single correct interpretation, and readers should be allowed and encouraged to construct a variety of interpretations—if they can support them.

One important fact to keep in mind when considering reader-response theory is that it applies primarily to literary texts and certain purposes for reading. As part of explaining when and where reader-response theory applies, Rosenblatt (1978) points out that there are two primary types of reading: efferent, or informational, reading and aesthetic reading. In efferent reading, the reader's attention is focused primarily on what she will take from the reading—what information will be learned. Much of the reading of both students and adults is done for the sake of learning new information, answering questions, discovering how to complete a procedure, or gleaning knowledge that can be used in solving a particular problem. Most reading done in such subjects as health, science, math, and geography is informational reading. These texts, unlike many literary texts, often constrain meaning substantially, do not invite a variety of interpretations, and should yield quite similar interpretations for various readers (Stanovich, 1994).

The other sort of reading Rosenblatt considers, aesthetic reading, is quite different. In aesthetic reading, the primary concern is not with what students remember about a text after they have read it but with what happens to them as they are reading. The primary purpose when reading aesthetically is not to gain information but to experience the text. Although the aesthetic reader, like the reader whose goal is gaining information, must understand the text, he must "also pay attention to associations, feelings, attitudes, and ideas" that the text arouses (Rosenblatt, 1978). For the most part, literature is written to provide an aesthetic experience. Most adults read literature for enjoyment; they do not read literature to learn it, but often we do learn from it. And students need to be given opportunities to do the same. Before we leave the topic of meaning construction, we should consider sociocultural theory.

Sociocultural Theory

Sociocultural theory extends the influence on the cognitive-constructivist view out from the reader and the text into the larger social realm. Learning is viewed as primarily a social rather than an individual matter. This theory is still very similar to constructivism, in that learning is viewed as an active and constructive task and what is learned is viewed as subjective. As described by its originator, Vygotsky (1978), or by Vygotskian scholars such as James Wertsch (1998), sociocultural theory is complex. However, its implications for the view of reading and learning described here can be succinctly listed.

First, the social and cultural backgrounds of students have a huge and undeniable effect on their learning. Unless we as teachers take students' social backgrounds and modes of learning and thinking into account, little learning is likely to occur. Second, because learning is quintessentially social, much learning—particularly the best and most lasting learning—will take place as groups of learners work together. Dialogue— give-and-take, face-to-face discussion in which students strive to make themselves understood and to understand others—is a mainstay of learning. Third, the classroom, the school, and the various communities of students in a classroom are social contexts that have strong influences on what is or is not learned in the classroom, and each of them must be carefully considered in planning and carrying out instruction.

We take you into a fourth-grade classroom (see In the Classroom 1.2) where the students are reading *Shiloh* (Naylor, 1991) to illustrate how these various theories of meaning construction operate within the same book and occasionally in the same day.

In concluding this section on the reading process, it is worth pointing out that although constructivism as a theory was developed nearly 30 years ago, it is fully consistent with the model of reading comprehension developed by the RAND Reading Study Group (2002), a group commissioned by the U.S. Department of Education to review the research on reading comprehension: "We define reading comprehension as

In the Classroom 1.2

How Students Construct Meaning

In Ms. Gladwell's fourth-grade classroom, the students in one of her groups are reading *Shiloh* (Naylor, 1991), a novel about Marty, a ten-year old, who rescues an abused dog and faces several moral dilemmas. This is the first novel they will read during the school year and for several students, it is the first novel they have ever read. As the students read and discuss the book, Ms. Gladwell is aware that she must address their comprehension from an efferent, or close reading, perspective, and allow an aesthetic response to the text. She hope they become captivated by Marty's problem. Several theories of comprehension underlie her instruction.

At the beginning of the novel, Ms. Gladwell has the students focus on the facts and the structure of the text. They construct a character list and draw a map of the setting. In the character list, they identify each of the major characters and their relationships to the other characters. The characters are entered onto the chart as they are encountered in the text. Ms. Gladwell writes the list on a large piece of chart paper, and students copy the list into their reader's notebook. They are encouraged to update their list as new information is encountered (Collinge & Robinson, 2015).

From this largely efferent stance, collecting information and attending to text structure, the teacher gradually shifts the students' thinking into an interpretive stance. As the students read into the second quadrant of the novel, they discover the moral dilemmas that plague Marty. Marty wants to save Shiloh from his abusive owner, Judd, but Marty must do so secretly, lying to his parents. At this point, Ms. Gladwell and her students construct a new character list, one that grapples with the beliefs of each main character. They soon discover what Marty is learning about the complexity of moral life.

Character List
• Marty – 11 years old, likes animals.
• Dara Lynn – Marty's sister
• Becky – Marty's sister
• Ma – Mother
• Dad – a hunter, kind toward dogs
• Shiloh – dog, beagle, skinny
• Judd Travers – Shiloh's owner, hunter, cruel to his dogs

As the students read deeper into the novel, they are living through Marty's problem, what is the right thing to do. How can Marty save Shiloh, defying Judd, without incurring the wrath of his parents, punishment, and the loss of the dog?

At this point, the students are engaged in close reading, studying the book to extract the nuances of the plot, but they are also engaged in an aesthetic experience as they live through Marty's fears, indecision, and anxiety. Ultimately, they must be critical readers, taking a moral stance toward the book and in their own lives. As readers, they have to decide how to make decisions about right and wrong. This is why we read fiction to learn about the values, ethics, and morality of human life and to revel in the excitement of the story. The strategies and text structure knowledge that often are at the center of our curriculum are the tools that foster our pleasure and enable us to grapple with these deep human questions.

What the characters believe about right and wrong

Character	Belief
Marty	Shiloh's safety is more important than the law.
	You can lie by not saying anything.
	The Bible isn't always clear about what is right and what is wrong.
	It is wrong to steal from your family.
Dad	Right and wrong are defined by the law.
Judd	Right and wrong are defined by you. You should have the freedom to do what you want.

the process of simultaneously extracting and constructing meaning through interaction and involvement with written language." The RAND group goes on to note that comprehension entails three elements:

- The *reader* who is doing the comprehending,
- The *text* that is to be comprehended, and
- The *activity* in which comprehension is a part.

Figure 1.10 RAND Study Heuristic for Thinking About Reading Comprehension

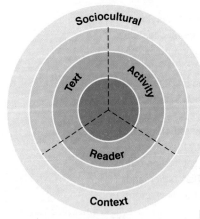

SOURCE: RAND Reading Study Group. (2002). *Reading for Understanding: Toward an R&D Program in Reading Comprehension*, MR-1465-OERI. Santa Monica, CA: RAND Education. Copyright 2002. Reprinted with permission.

Furthermore, the RAND group notes, these three elements operate within and are heavily influenced by a *sociocultural context*, as illustrated in Figure 1.10. The RAND group's orientation, in addition to being consistent with the interactive model, is consistent with the view of the reading process just discussed and with the program of instruction we recommend throughout this book.

Constructivism and the construction-integration model is also consistent with the Common Core State Standards (CCSS) that currently drive the reading curriculum in many states. The CCSS states four major goals. We present these goals in Figure 1.11 and indicate how they align with the construction-integration model. The CCSS set the goals for our reading curriculum, but with one glaring exception: the CCSS do not speak to the vital issue of motivation, and we will in Chapter 3.

Figure 1.11 How the Construction-Integration Model Aligns with the Common Core State Standards

Anchor Standards in the Common Core State Standards	Elements of the Construction-Integration Model
Key Idea and Details Read closely to determine what the text says explicitly and to make logical inferences from it.	This standard aligns with the **construction** phase of the comprehension model.
Determine central ideas or themes of a text and analyze their development; summarize the key supporting details and ideas.	This standard aligns with both the **construction** and **integration** phase of the comprehension model.
Craft and Structure Interpret words and phrases as they are used in a text, including determining technical, connotative, and figurative meanings, and analyze how specific word choices shape meaning or tone.	These standards align with both the **construction** and **integration** phase of the comprehension model.
Analyze the structure of texts, including how specific sentences, paragraphs, and larger portions of the text (e.g., a section, chapter, scene, or stanza) relate to each other and the whole.	
Integration of Knowledge and Ideas Integrate and evaluate content presented in diverse media and formats, including visually and quantitatively, as well as in words.	These standards align with the **integration** phase of the comprehension model.
Delineate and evaluate the argument and specific claims in a text, including the validity of the reasoning as well as the relevance and sufficiency of the evidence.	
Range of Reading and Level of Text Complexity Read and comprehend complex literary and informational texts independently and proficiently.	The construction integration model operates with any level of text complexity.

SOURCE: Common Core State Standards Initiative, 2010a. Common Core State Standards for English Language Arts & Literacy in History/Social Studies, Science, and Technical Subjects. Washington, DC: Council of Chief State School Officers & National Governors Association.

Reflect and Apply

Comprehension is an active, constructive process that we will reinforce throughout this book. This means if you are to understand and remember the ideas we present, as well as use them in your teaching, you must mentally manipulate them in some way. Ideally, as constructivist and sociocultural principles suggest, you will discuss your responses with others—a study group, your class, or your course instructor.

3. Suppose that one teacher taught the word *relax* by simply saying, "*Relax* means to loosen up," while another taught it by having students view several pictures of people relaxing, having them assume relaxing positions themselves, and then having them talk about situations in which they have felt comfortable and relaxed. Explain how the second teacher is demonstrating a cognitive-constructivist perspective.

4. Identify a schema that both inner-city students and suburban students are likely to have, one that inner-city students are likely to have but suburban students might lack, and one that suburban students are likely to have but inner-city students might lack. Why do certain groups of students share some schemata but not others? What does sociocultural theory say about the importance of students having different schemata?

5. As noted, a reader can be metacognitive before reading, during reading, or after reading. Now that you have read this section of the chapter, exercise your metacognitive skills by characterizing your understanding of it and noting some of the steps you could take to better understand the concepts presented.

The Reading Corner

Books to Help Build Automaticity and Fluency in Young Readers

As we have stated, to become automatic in reading, students need a lot of practice with easy, understandable, and enjoyable texts. For children who are just beginning to read—typically first-graders—books that include frequently repeated common words (for example, *run* and *book*) and common word parts (for example, phonograms such as *-ick* and *-ake*) are ideal. Consider series books like Junie B. Jones, Nate the Great, or the Magic Treehouse series. Like their predecessors, The Hardy Boys, Nancy Drew, and The Baby-sitters Club, the repetitive nature of these books builds fluency. The following list shows specifically designed, easy-to-read books from series that help build beginning readers' automaticity and fluency. Also provided are several sources of information on easy-to-read books.

Easy-to-Read Series Books

Norman Bidwell. *Clifford Goes to Dog School*. Scholastic, 2002. Clifford proves to be quite a challenge for dog school. Just one of dozens of books in the Clifford series. 32 pages.

Denys Cazet. *Minnie and Moo: The Attack of the Easter Bunnies* (I Can Read Book 3). HarperCollins, 2005. In this Minnie and Moo adventure, these unconventional cows try to find an Easter bunny for Mr. and Mrs. Farmer's traditional Easter egg hunt. 48 pages.

Lillian Hoban. *Arthur's Birthday Party*. Harper-Trophy, 1999. At his gymnastics birthday party, Arthur the chimp is determined to be the best. 48 pages.

Arnold Lobel. *Frog and Toad Are Friends*. Harper & Row, 1970. The earliest adventures of these two friends. 64 pages.

Cynthia Rylant. *Henry and Mudge and the Tall Tree House*. Simon and Schuster Books for Young Readers, 2002. Henry gets a new tree house but worries that his dog Mudge won't be able to share it with him. 40 pages.

Jean Van Leeuwen. *Oliver and Amanda's Halloween*. Dial Press, 1992. Oliver and Amanda scramble to get just the right costume for Halloween. 48 pages.

Information on Easy-to-Read Books

R. L. Allington. *What Really Matters for Struggling Readers: Designing Research-Based Programs*. Longman, 2001. Chapter 3, "Kids Need Books They Can Read," provides a number of suggestions for choosing books young readers can read.

I. C. Fountas & G. S. Pinnell. *Leveled Books (K–8): Matching Texts to Readers for Effective Teaching*. Heinemann, 2005. Lists thousands of books leveled for grades K to 8.

M. F. Graves & B. B. Graves. *Scaffolding Reading Experiences: Designs for Student Success* (2nd ed.). Christopher Gordon, 2003. Chapter 10, "Assessing Text Difficulty and Accessibility," discusses features that make books easy or difficult.

MyLab Education **Self-Check 1.2**

MyLab Education **Application Exercise 1.2:** Finding Examples of the Construction-Integration Process While Reading a Text

A Literacy Curriculum for Today's and Tomorrow's World

We are now going to describe the components of a reading program that lead students to the high level of literacy required in the 21st century. Before continuing, we should point out that the focus in this book is reading; therefore, some aspects of a comprehensive literacy curriculum are not discussed, including spelling and handwriting. Also, although we consider writing as it relates to reading, we do not present a comprehensive writing program. Finally, we do not present curricula for specific subjects such as history, science, and the like. However, the reading curriculum we describe in this book is both broad and deep.

In recent years, the federal government has taken an increasingly active role in influencing reading instruction. The federally sponsored report of the National Reading Panel (2000) and the Reading First provisions of the No Child Left Behind Act of 2001 identified five curricular components as having strong support from research and being key to effective reading instruction—phonemic awareness, phonics, fluency, vocabulary, and comprehension. Reading First—the massive federal program designed to ensure that the curriculum endorsed by the National Reading Panel (NRP) is implemented in kindergarten through third-grade classrooms—will likely continue to have an effect on reading instruction in the primary grades because the Common Core State Standards (NGA & CCSSO, 2010) has incorporated most of its recommendations.

Like most literacy educators (for example, Allington, 2002; Krashen, 2004; Pressley, 2002; Routman, 2002; Taylor, Pearson, Peterson, & Rodriguez, 2003), we believe a comprehensive and balanced literacy curriculum that addresses the needs of primary-grade students, upper-elementary students, and middle-grade students includes more than the five components endorsed by the NRP and Reading First. We specifically believe that motivation is vital and was ignored by these national reading initiatives, and it will be the central focus of our book.

Not long after the influence of NCLB and Reading First began to wane, the Common Core State Standards sought to redefine the goals of reading instruction in the nation. The Standards were reinforced by the federal Race to the Top (2009) initiative that provided funds to develop tests that assessed the Common Core. The standards, originally published in 2010 and adopted by 45 of the states and the District of Columbia, attempted to shift reading instruction in three key ways (Coleman & Pimental, 2012).

1. Regular practice with complex texts and their academic language. At each grade, students should be guided to read increasingly complex text and learn the vocabulary within so they are reading texts they will encounter on the job and in college.
2. Reading, writing, and speaking grounded in evidence from texts, both literary and informational. The Standards pushed the students to read closely and write informative and persuasive texts that were grounded in their reading.
3. Building knowledge through content-rich information. The reading curriculum in the elementary grades should include a 50/50 balance of literary and informational

MyLab Education
Video Example 1.1
Compare the approach the teachers take toward comprehension instruction to what you have experienced in your schooling. Later, return to this video when reading about comprehension in Chapters 11 and 12.
https://www.youtube.com/watch?v=JKvErP0Dx5o

texts, and the texts should be selected so that they build students' knowledge from one text to another and from one grade to another.

As of this writing, the influence of the Common Core is beginning to diminish under pressure from conservation politicians in the states and at the federal level. The assessments that were created to measure the impact of the CCSS, Smarter Balanced Assessment Consortium (SBAC), and the Partnership for Assessment of Readiness for College and Careers (PARCC), have been dropped by more than half of the states that originally adopted them. Recent history suggests the Common Core will not be the last literacy reform we will experience. Something new is just over the horizon. In the meantime, in this text we will discuss what we believe are the essentials for developing students who can and will read. In this section, we describe eight components that we believe are vital to help all students achieve the sort of literacy required for full participation and success in today's world (see Figure 1.12).

Figure 1.12 Components of the Present-Day Literacy Curriculum

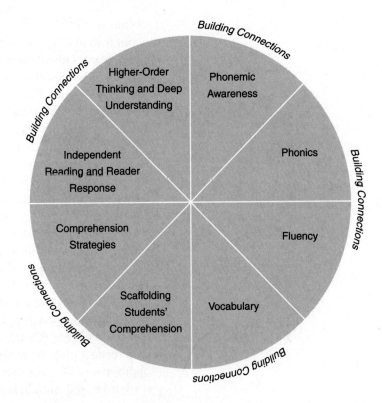

1. **Motivation**

    Our primary concern is motivating students to become literate and sustains their interest in reading for years to come. It is easy to view reading as just a skill, but all skills are learned because we have goals beyond the effortless performance of that skill. We learn to read because it is a rite of passage into the adult world. Most kids just want to learn to read. After the pleasure of performance must come the satisfaction from the book. Reading is a source of entertainment and escape. Reading is a tool that enables us to learn and understand the complex scientific, economic, and political world in which we live. Reading is essential for success in higher education and on the job. As our children are increasingly captivated by big screens and little screens, iPhones and flatscreen TVs, a world where Amazon's Alexa can report the weather tomorrow or identify the leading actress in *The Wizard of Oz*, we must find a way to make reading tantalizing again. Motivation is our focus in Chapter 3.

2. **Selecting the Right Text**

    All teachers must select texts for reading instruction and help their students select texts. Whether texts are packaged within a reading program or selected individually, there are important criteria for selecting texts for beginning reading instruction and other criteria for texts designed to build vocabulary and comprehension. For decades, the primary criteria for selecting texts has been reading level or readability. However, a teacher should also consider the ideas in a text, the interest of the text, the text's structure, the language the author employed, and how the themes of the text will resonate with the wide diversity of students in our classrooms. We will tackle the topic of choosing texts in Chapter 6.

3. **Phonemic Awareness and Other Aspects of Emergent Literacy**

    As part of learning to read, students need to internalize a substantial body of knowledge about print and the relationship between print and speech. One very important component of such knowledge is phonemic awareness—the insight that spoken words are composed of somewhat separable sounds. But there are many other aspects of emergent literacy. For example, students must recognize that the written language they are just beginning to learn about is in many ways similar to the oral language with which they are already quite proficient. Additionally, as part of emergent literacy, children need to develop positive attitudes about reading and about their ability to learn to read. We deal with emergent literacy in Chapter 7.

4. **Phonics and Other Word Recognition Skills**

   Phonics is the area of reading instruction that deals with the relationships between letters and sounds. Children use their knowledge of phonics to sound out written words they do not immediately recognize. If an adept reader comes to the word *bike* and doesn't immediately recognize it, she can follow a series of steps to arrive at its pronunciation. Phonics skills help children become independent readers. Other word recognition skills—for example, identifying syllables, blending sounds to form syllables and words, and dealing with word parts such as prefixes and suffixes—also assist children in becoming independent readers. We deal with phonics and other word recognition skills in Chapter 8.

5. **Fluency and Independent Reading**

   Fluency, as we have already noted, is the ability to "read a text orally with speed, accuracy, expression, and comprehension" (Samuels, 2002b). Additionally, it is important that students become fluent in their silent reading (Pikulski & Chard, 2005). When reading silently, students need to read smoothly, at an appropriate pace, and with good comprehension. There are a number of effective practices for building students' fluency, but none are more important than a powerful independent reading program in every classroom. Students need to do a lot of reading in appropriate texts, texts that are not too difficult and that they readily comprehend, learn from, and enjoy. It is not enough for students to read and comprehend texts they are assigned. Students must become independent readers who voluntarily choose to read for the pleasure, knowledge, and satisfaction that only reading can provide. We will discuss independent reading and fluency in Chapter 9.

6. **Vocabulary Learning and Instruction**

   A huge amount of research has been conducted on students' vocabulary knowledge, and reliable estimates indicate that many students have acquired reading vocabularies of something like 5,000 words by the end of the first grade and approximately 50,000 words by the time they graduate from high school (Graves, 2006). Obviously, vocabulary learning represents a significant task throughout children's years in school, and effectively fostering students' vocabularies requires a multifaceted and long-term program that includes rich and varied language experiences, teaching individual words, teaching word-learning strategies, and fostering word consciousness. Chapter 10 is devoted to vocabulary instruction.

7. **Teaching Reading Comprehension**

   Comprehension is both a complex process and the ultimate goal of reading, and, as a consequence, comprehension instruction needs to be powerful, long-term, and multifaceted. As one facet of comprehension instruction, we need to do everything possible to ensure that students comprehend and learn from each and every text they read—to scaffold their efforts with both narrative texts such as short stories, plays, and novels, and expository texts such as the chapters in their science and social studies texts and articles on the Internet. We want students to move beyond comprehension to higher-order thinking. Students should master such complex tasks as analyzing, synthesizing, and evaluating. As students read text, we want to promote deep and lasting understanding—teaching in such a way that students grasp topics deeply, retain important information, and actively use the knowledge they gain in a variety of tasks in and out of school.

   Comprehension is the product of knowledge, strategies, and motivation. Our comprehension curriculum must be organized so that knowledge builds from one text to another. Comprehension strategies are mental acts that facilitate our understanding of text (Lysynchuk, Pressley, d'Ailly, Smith, & Cake, 1989). Although many strategies have been identified, a handful of them have been repeatedly singled out as particularly useful, including establishing a purpose for reading, using prior knowledge, asking and answering questions, making inferences, determining what is important, summarizing, dealing with graphic information, imagining and creating graphic representations, and monitoring comprehension (Duke, Pearson, Billman, & Strahan, 2011). The active use of knowledge and strategies is dependent on motivation. Students must care; they must want to learn and revel with the text. In Chapter 11, we will lay out our approach to reading comprehension and then focus on narrative texts, fiction, biography and autobiography. In Chapter 12, we will discuss informational text and reading on the Internet.

8. **Building Connections and Fostering Critical Thinking**

   The final component of the critical literacy curriculum cuts across all of the others. Students need to build connections in several directions. First, we want students to realize that what they bring to school—the wealth of out-of-school experiences that they bring when they enter first grade and that are constantly enriched each year—is relevant to what they are learning in school. For example, the pride they felt when they were first allowed to go to the grocery store alone can provide insight into a story character's feelings when she successfully meets a challenge. Second, we want students to realize that the various subjects they study in school are interrelated in many ways. The understanding of the American Revolutionary gained in social studies can help them understand the motives of Johnny in Esther Forbes's *Johnny Tremain*. Third, we want students to realize that ideas and concepts learned in school are relevant to their lives outside of school. For example, a character's discovery that persistence paid off in meeting her goal may suggest to a student that similar persistence may lead to success as she tries to help a younger brother develop the habit of putting his toys away neatly.

Reading has always required critical thinking but in the Internet age it becomes a survival skill. Information floods our lives and it is vital for students to evaluate the trustworthiness of information. Students need to consider who wrote the information, what are their credentials, and their political point of view. An article on the weather will take a different slant coming from the National Oceanic and Atmospheric Administration versus a political website. Rather than devote a chapter to critical thinking and the Internet you will find it throughout the book in the chapters on selecting text, comprehension strategies, and reading informational text.

Making Instructional Decisions

To develop and implement a literacy curriculum, teachers must make instructional decisions, and they need the tools to do so. Over the last several decades, the populations in our schools have become more diverse. We have many English learners, large numbers of students living in or close to poverty, and increasingly large numbers of students who carry a special education label. The special education population increased from 8.3 percent in 1976 to 13.8 percent in 2015. English learners currently constitute 9.5 percent of the public-school population, whereas they totaled 7.3 percent in 1980 (U.S. Department of Education, 2012). Each of these groups demands some well-thought-through instruction that might be carried out by the classroom teacher, a specialist, or both. We need to consider what instructional approaches work best for these students and how general education teachers coordinate their efforts with the specialists. In Chapter 14, we will discuss English learners, and in Chapter 4 we will discuss students who struggle to learn to read.

To meet the eight curriculum goals and the increasingly diverse needs of the students in your classrooms, you will need some tools.

- The first tool is an understanding of the reading process. Teachers need to understand how children read and how they learn to read. A theory of the reading process underlies all instructional decisions. If you believe that reading is a series of neatly separated individual components, you will employ a discrete skills approach, teaching them one at a time. If you view reading development as the product of knowledge, strategies, and motivation, you favor a more constructivist approach. We explored these theories in this chapter.

- Next, teachers need to understand the basic principles of reading instruction. What are the dominant approaches to teaching reading, and where did they come from? In Chapter 2, we will give you a brief history of reading instruction, so you can avoid making the same mistakes as did your forefathers and foremothers.

- You will need to know how to organize the space and time in your classroom. The physical layout in your room helps you teach to the whole class, work with groups of students, and meet with individuals. Time is also critical. You will soon discover that you do not have enough time to do all that you desire. We will help you create schedules for your classroom and guide your principal to provide the time that you need. We will explore these topics in Chapter 4.

- We work in an era that is dominated by assessment. There are state assessments designed to evaluate programs and the quality of schools and teachers. There are district assessments designed to prep students for the state assessments and evaluate your students' progress from month to month. There are assessments designed to measure what students have learned. There are diagnostic tests for placing students in the right text and for determining their strengths and weaknesses. Preparing, giving, and interpreting tests can easily consume a third of your instructional time. In Chapter 5, we will explain these assessments and help you manage them. Good teachers make observations, and they employ both informal and formal assessments to understand their students and to gauge their progress. Often teachers do not need to give a test, they can just look and listen. Finally, we will guide you through the process of developing a differentiated curriculum—one that addresses the skills, interests, and motivations of your students.

MyLab Education
Video Example 1.2
From this video, you can learn more about the five components of reading outlined in the National Reading Panel Report.

MyLab Education **Self-Check 1.3**

An Overview of this Book

We have designed each chapter to facilitate your reading and learning as effectively and efficiently as possible, and most chapters have the same components and the same organization.

Each chapter begins with a set of learning objectives and a brief scenario in which we capture a problem you are likely to face and that anticipates one or more of the major themes of the chapter. Following the scenario is the body of the chapter, usually consisting of two to four main sections and a number of subsections. Within each chapter we have placed some recurring features. We will regularly consider how to differentiate instruction for English language learners. Whenever needed, we will discuss the impact of digital technology on reading and how to teach students to use it. We will also consider how to motivate and assist struggling readers. Finally, we provide concluding remarks, a summary, and commentary on the chapter.

Each chapter includes a number of additional features. Samples of children's work illustrate their growth toward present-day literacy. Reading Corner boxes provide annotated lists of children's literature useful in teaching particular literacy skills and topics. In the Classroom features offer a variety of examples of classroom interaction—student–teacher dialogues, vignettes, and the like—designed to nurture students toward literacy. We will also include features on motivation and differentiation throughout the chapters. To encourage reader involvement, Reflect and Apply sections are embedded at the ends of major sections to give you an opportunity to review and try out some of the central ideas presented.

Chapters end with two standard features. A section titled Extending Learning invites you to apply and elaborate on some of the major ideas presented by observing classrooms, talking with parents and teachers, or investigating a particular topic further. Following this, a section titled Children's Literature provides citations and brief annotations of the selections mentioned in the chapter and occasional citations of other sources of children's literature.

Concluding Remarks

In this chapter, we have emphasized four points. First, we described the concept of the reading process underlying this book—the cognitive-constructivist view. We also described several concepts that elaborate and complement this view—the construction-integration model of comprehension, automaticity, fluency, and metacognition. Second, we briefly characterized U.S. students' proficiency in reading, contrasted their proficiency today to what it was in the past and to the proficiency of students in other industrialized countries, and described the sort of literacy necessary in today's and tomorrow's world. Third, we listed the components of the present-day literacy curriculum that serve as the foundation for the book. Fourth, we gave an overview and explained the common organization that all chapters share.

The topics in this chapter are particularly important to internalize because they underlie the remainder of the book. As we have said several times, reading is enhanced by rich background knowledge. In the case of this book, the more you know about the view of the reading process that informs it, the level of present-day literacy it is designed to help you achieve for your students, the components of the curriculum, and the organization of the book and each chapter, the easier it will be for you to learn, remember, and use the information and procedures presented. We, therefore, strongly encourage you to review the chapter, take some notes, respond again to some of the prompts in the Reflect and Apply sections, make use of some of our suggestions in the Extending Learning section, and perhaps search out and read some works listed in the references.

Extending Learning

Here we suggest several activities that take you beyond this book—to schools, students, teachers, parents, libraries, and others sources of information—to help you more fully understand and appreciate your role in nurturing children toward present-day literacy.

1. One way to increase your understanding of new and complex concepts is to examine several perspectives on them. The concepts about the reading process that we have discussed have all been described in a variety of other texts, and all of them are complex enough to warrant further study. Pick two or three concepts that you would like to further explore, and read more about them either in the references that we have supplied or in a general text on psychology or educational psychology.
2. Go to the NAEP website (http://nces.ed.gov/nations reportcard/reading) and print out a copy of the sample test items. Then go to your state website and compare the passages and questions from the national and state tests. Which test is the more rigorous assessment of reading? Which test demands higher order thinking?
3. List the components of the present-day literacy curriculum we have outlined and interview some elementary school teachers to find out which components they deal with, which they don't, and the literacy activities they engage in that are not part of the curriculum presented in this chapter. Try to include teachers from primary, middle-elementary, and upper-elementary grades. Once you have completed your interviews, sum up what you have discovered and comment on (1) the extent to which the teachers you interviewed employ the curriculum we have outlined and (2) any components of the literacy curriculum that are not among the components we consider but that you probably want to include in your classroom.

Children's Literature

DiCamillo, K. (2000). *Because of Winn-Dixie*. Cambridge, MA: Candlewick Press. A poignant and well-told story of a young girl's building a new life after her mother left and she and her father moved to Florida—with, of course, a little help from her dog, Winn-Dixie. 182 pages.

Dolphin, L. (1997). *Our Journey from Tibet*. New York: Dutton. A true story based on interviews with a 9-year-old Tibetan girl, Sonam. Includes dramatic and stunning photos. 40 pages.

Flake, S. G. (1998). *The Skin I'm In*. New York: Jump at the Sun/Hyperion. Uncomfortable because her skin is extremely dark, 13-year-old Maleeka meets a new teacher with a facial birthmark and makes some discoveries about how to love who she is and what she looks like. 171 pages.

Forbes, E. (1998). *Johnny Tremain*. New York: Houghton Mifflin. Johnny Tremain, apprentice silversmith, takes on the cause of freedom as a message carrier for the Sons of Liberty in pre-Revolution Boston. CD available. 293 pages.

Giff, P. R. (2004). *A House of Tailors*. New York: Wendy Lamb Books. Set in the late 19th century, this novel for intermediate readers tells the story of how 13-year-old Dina adjusts to her new life in the United States after being sent from Germany to live in Brooklyn with her tailor uncle. 149 pages.

Lord, B. B. (1984). *In the Year of the Boar & Jackie Robinson*. New York: Harper and Row. In 1947, a Chinese girl comes to Brooklyn, where she becomes Americanized at school, in her apartment building, and by her love for baseball. Illustrated. 169 pages.

Snicket, L. (2002). *The Carnivorous Carnival: Book the Ninth*. New York: HarperCollins. The continued adventures and misadventures of the Baudelaire orphans in the Series of Unfortunate Events series. 286 pages.

Sun, C. F. (1994). *Mama Bear*. Boston: Houghton Mifflin. Young Mei-Mei bakes and sells cookies in order to earn enough money to buy a large and expensive stuffed bear for Christmas. Illustrated. 28 pages.

Chapter 2
Reading Instruction

 ## Learning Outcomes

After reading and studying this chapter you should be able to:

2.1 Describe the history of reading instruction in America from the mid-19th century to the present and use that history to understand how the current approaches to reading reflect the tensions of the past.

2.2 Understand the cognitive constructivist-principles of instruction and apply them to the design of effective reading instruction.

2.3 Compare and contrast the three major approaches to reading instruction—basal programs, guided reading, and reader's workshop.

Classroom Vignette

It is the beginning of the school year and the principal of Fargo North Elementary School is meeting with the teachers from each grade level to review the results from last year and discuss possible changes in instruction for the new academic year. During the 2016–2017 school year, the school did not meet its Adequate Yearly Progress (AYP) goal, as proscribed by their state department of education and the Every Student Succeeds Act (ESSA, 2015), the successor to No Child Left Behind. According to the law, 85 percent of all students had to pass the state reading test, and that includes 85 percent of African American students, Hispanic students, low-income students, and special education students, with only a few exceptions. The fourth-grade teachers assembled at this meeting are not happy. Last year only 74 percent of their students passed the test, not the required 85 percent. The teachers were given a set of reflection questions before the meeting to frame the discussion about improving instruction and learning.

1. If your grade level performed well last year, what aspects of the curriculum and instruction accounted for that success? How will you sustain those practices?
2. If your grade level performed poorly last year, what aspects of the curriculum and instruction caused the problem? What changes will you make this year?

The teachers did their homework and came with written answers; they had clearly thought through the questions. In response to the first question, they produced a list of factors that accounted for their success. In the second column, they listed the changes they would like to make (See Figure 2.1).

Figure 2.1 Fourth Grade Curriculum Reflections and Plans

What Made Your Instruction Successful?	What Would You Like to Add Next Year?
• Fluency program • Silent reading time • Timed readings • Graphic organizers • Accelerated reader • Small-group instruction • Reading coach • Practice books • Work stations • Websites • Reading consultants model lessons • Computer programs • Read-alouds • Highlighting • Data-drive instruction	• Weekly Reader • Workbooks • Novels • Parent involvement • Passages from ReadWorks • Vocabulary notebooks

The explanation for success was a scattershot of materials, instructional routines, and personal assistance from experts. Their suggested changes were additional materials and more parent involvement. Neither of the responses suggested that the teachers understood instruction. Their view of instruction consisted of materials (workbooks), outside assistance (the reading coach), classroom organizational practices (small-group instruction, workstations), and commercial programs (Accelerated Reader) where students take tests on the books they have read and earn points. They did not define instruction as a series of explicit teaching moves or student tasks.

Instruction is the procedures and practices teachers use to help students acquire new knowledge, skills, and attitudes. To help students with these acquisitions, teachers explain concepts and skills, show students how to use them, provide assistance as students try out new tasks, and provide ample opportunity to practice. Teachers organize the instruction so that students will use their new knowledge and skills long after they have moved on to another topic or another grade. Good teachers try to make all of this as lively and interesting as possible, because motivated students are deeply engaged in reading and writing. Good teachers provide the slower students as much help as possible while guiding and encouraging those who are surging ahead.

All teachers have a theory of instruction that guides their decisions even if they cannot articulate that theory. In our opening vignette the teachers' theories of instruction were primitive. Some teachers believe that teaching is modeling. If you show children how to do everything including silent reading, they will imitate those models. During sustained silent reading time, the teacher kicks back with her latest novel hoping to inspire her students. Other teachers believe that practice makes perfect, and their classroom is a blizzard of workbooks and worksheets with which students practice their reading skills. Instruction is more than modeling and practice; it has many components. The purpose of this chapter is to help you understand the principles of instruction and by the end of the chapter we hope you will have developed your own theory of instruction, based on what researchers have discovered about effective teaching. We will then apply these principles of instruction to the rest of the chapters as we discuss word recognition, fluency, vocabulary, and comprehension.

Reflect and Apply

1. Think about the best teacher or teachers you ever had—elementary, secondary, or higher education. What made the instruction of these teachers particularly strong? Try to ignore for now the personality traits of these teachers.

A Brief History of Reading Instruction in the United States

We begin this chapter with a brief look at the history of reading instruction, because how to teach reading has always been controversial and continues to be so. The history of the United States and its schools reveals cyclical changes in which alternating political and educational ideas at first receive widespread support, only to later draw heavy criticism and disapproval (Cremin, 1990; Graves & Dykstra, 1997; Schlesinger, 1986). Understanding this history will help you understand the present and perhaps avoid the pitfalls of the past. As Pearson and Cervetti (2017) write: "Ideas and practices come with ancestors and precedents, even when they appear to emerge suddenly, and they persist long after their theoretical and research foundation appear to have been overturned (p.13)."

Since the early 19th century, there have been many debates about the best methods for teaching young children to read, but fewer arguments about promoting the reading ability of older children. To understand the development of contemporary approaches to teaching reading, the history of reading instruction in the United States is best studied against the backdrop of tensions between a direct, or didactic, approach to teaching the skills of reading and a more holistic or child-centered approach that puts meaning making first. In the brief history that follows—parts of which rely heavily on information taken from Nila Banton Smith's *American Reading Instruction* (2002), David Pearson's "Reading in the Twentieth Century" (2000), and Pearson and Cervetti's (2017) work on reading comprehension—we focus on these tensions.

The Colonial Period and the 19th Century

The period extending roughly from 1600 to 1840 was relatively free of tensions over instructional approaches. The emphasis was on content. The purpose of reading instruction early in the period was clearly religious, as revealed by this excerpt from the Old Deluder Act passed by the General Court of Massachusetts in 1647:

> It being one chief point of that old deluder, Satan, to keep men from the knowledge of the Scriptures.... It is therefore ordered that every township in this jurisdiction, after the Lord hath increased them to the number of fifty households, shall then forthwith appoint one within their town to teach all such children as shall resort to him to write and read. (Quoted in Smith, 2002)

Beginning about the time of the American Revolution and continuing until about 1840, the purpose shifted, and reading instruction and textbooks reflected what Smith has termed a "nationalistic-moralistic emphasis," as exemplified in these lines from the preface to Lyman Cobb's *The North American Reader* (1835):

> The pieces in this work are chiefly American. The English Reader so largely used in our country does not contain a single piece or paragraph written by an American citizen. Is this good policy? Is it patriotism? (Cobb, 1835).

However, regardless of whether the reading material focused on religious or patriotic content, the method of instruction throughout the period was much the same—the alphabetic-spelling method, a plodding, step-by-step approach in which students first learned the alphabet, next learned to spell a large number of syllables, and then spelled words before they read them. At this point they memorized sections of text (usually religious, moral, or patriotic in content) and read orally (Smith, 2002).

Comprehension was largely an afterthought. In the early 19th century, the goal of reading was to read aloud familiar texts, the Bible or a hymnal, with expression and intonation. Oral performance was the measure of good reading. There was a small minority, educated white men who did read with strong comprehension, but this was not the goal for all people. Developing comprehension was not an explicit goal of instruction but a byproduct of memorizing text.

Not surprisingly, this approach eventually came under fire, most notably by educational reformer Horace Mann, who advocated instead a focus on whole words and letter sounds. In an 1842 report to the Board of Education in Massachusetts, Mann displays his disdain for the alphabetic-spelling approach and pushed for a meaning focused approach that foreshadows the controversy that, though modified, continues today:

> Compare the above method [the more meaningful approach Mann favored] with that of calling up a class of abecedarians—or, what is more common, a single child—and while the teacher holds a book or card before him, with a pointer in his hand, says, a, and he echoes a; then b, and he echoes b; and so on until the vertical row of lifeless and ill-favored characters is completed, and then of remanding him to his seat, to sit still and look at vacancy. (Mann, 1884/1965).

The Evolution of Reading Programs in America

From the American Revolution through the early 1800s, children spent little time in school so only one or two books were necessary to teach reading. At the beginning of the 19th century the most popular text was Noah Webster's *The American Spelling Book*; it was first published in 1783 but it stayed in print for over 35 years. As students stayed in school longer Webster added a second and a third book, *The Little Reader's Assistant* (1790) and *An American Selection of Lessons in Reading and Speaking* (1787). All of these texts emphasized pronunciation and oral expression with reading selections on history, morality, religion, and popular speeches of the time. See Figure 2.2 for the list of rules for reading well by Joshua Leavitt (1832) in his Easy Lesson in Reading.

By the mid 1800s, reading programs and reading instruction began to evolve as society and schools changed. As the population of the country grew and children stayed in school longer, they were divided into grades, and eventually publishers offered one book for each grade. The most popular was the *McGuffey's Eclectic Readers* published

---

Figure 2.2 Rules for Reading Joshua Levitt, 1832

If you wish to know how to read well, you must learn these rules by heart.

1. Be careful to *call* your words right.
2. Learn to *pronounce* them properly.
3. Speak with a *clear* and *distinct* voice.
4. Do not read too *fast*. Read *slow* and *carefully*, so as not to make any *mistakes*.
5. Be very particular to observe all the *Stops*.
6. Learn to use the proper *Emphasis* and *Inflections* of the voice. Ask your teacher to show you what that means, and how to do it.
7. Endeavor to *understand* every word you read as you go along. *Study* your reading lessons very carefully as you read.
8. Try to read as if you were telling a story to your mother or talking with some of your playmates. *Reading is talking from a book*.
9. Take pains to *read* the poetry and not to *sing* it.
10. The emphatic words are printed in *Italic* letters.

SOURCE: Based on Joshua Leavitt. 1829. Easy Lessons in Reading: For the Use of the Younger Classes in Common Schools. J. & J.W. Prentiss.

from 1835 until 1920 and selling over 120 million copies. McGuffey included a lesson plan with each selection, an idea he "borrowed" from Samuel Worcester (1830) (Worcester sued McGuffey for plagiarism and won an out-of-court settlement for $2,000.) Before reading the selection, there were rules for reading, the teacher provided a bit of background information, and after the selection was read there were lists of words and definitions to study, comprehension questions, and guides to common pronunciation errors.

By the end of the 19th and into the 20th century, basal reading programs began to look a bit more like the approaches your parents might have experienced. More robust teacher's manuals were developed just as teachers received more education in the process of teaching reading. Consider the irony. In 1900, *The New Education Readers* (Demarest & Van Sickle, 1900) contained a 13-page teacher's guide for the first-grade program. Today, the teachers' guide for *Journeys* (Houghton Mifflin Harcourt, 2016) numbers over 2,000 pages. Additional changes included carefully controlled vocabulary for introducing words based on word frequency, sequences for teaching reading skills, workbooks for practicing skills, tests for placing students and assessing their mastery, and grouping student by ability to differentiate instruction.

Basal Readers at the Beginning of the 20th Century

Basal readers at the beginning of the 20th century contained a collection of reading selections with accompanying worksheets, teacher's manuals, tests, supplementary material, and lots of workbooks. The books for the earliest grades employed strictly controlled vocabularies and generally contained very brief narratives, relying on pictures to convey much of their meaning. The books in the remainder of the primary grades continued to employ controlled vocabularies and contained largely fiction focusing on typical middle-class life, fantasy, safe adventures, and moderately preachy stories.

In the fourth-grade, selections became longer, vocabulary control eased, more genres of fiction were included, along with a few expository selections. Much of the instruction students received in these programs was organized around the directed reading lesson—which included preparation for reading, silent reading, and follow-up questions and discussion—on individual selections. These lessons were often punctuated by skills work in decoding, vocabulary, and comprehension, and students spent a good deal of time completing worksheets. Figure 2.3 shows pages from a first-grade reader in a 1950 basal series, typical of the readers of this period.

Figure 2.3 Pages from a Typical First-Grade Basal Reader of the 1950s

Oh, Jane.
Look and see.
See Baby go.
See Tim go.
See Spot and Puff go.

Sally said, "Come, Mother.
Come and see Father.
See Father jump and play.
Oh, oh.
Father is funny."

51   75

As basal reading programs grew, they began to incorporate more skill work—comprehension, vocabulary, and study skills. Prior to the 20th century, work on reading skills was largely absent from reading instruction. Some argue that comprehension skills —finding the main idea, distinguishing fact from opinion, or grasping an author's organizational pattern—had their origin in survey work conducted by William S. Grey who was also the author of the Curriculum Foundation Series, better known as Dick and Jane (Dewitz, Jones, Leahy, & Sullivan, 2010). Others suggest that the new comprehension assessments and reading skills grew up together with each influencing the other (Pearson & Cervetti, 2017). The developers of comprehension tests had to test something, *skills*, and the authors of basal programs tended to teach what was tested, *skills*.

The increasing number of skills raised two important questions for the publishers. In what order should the skills be taught? How much time or emphasis should be given to each skill? To answer these questions, the publishers created scope and sequence charts, curriculum maps that guided instruction over the academic year. As the scope and sequence charts became more complex and the number of skills grew, there was a greater need to give teachers more explicit guidance in the teacher's manual. The complexity of reading instruction was only one of the issues that sparked a backlash.

Although many controversies about reading materials and reading instruction arose during the 1950s and 1960s, the most persistent and frequent involved the tensions between more holistic and more segmented instruction, centering on letters, sounds, and words. The alphabetic-spelling method had disappeared, but the whole-word method and various approaches emphasizing phonics continued to be in conflict. In the whole-word method children were introduced to high frequency, common words, and these were repeated frequently insuring that students remembered them. The conflict between the whole word method and phonics reached a crescendo in 1955 when Rudolf Flesch published his best-selling *Why Johnny Can't Read*. Flesch charged that American children were not learning to read because they were not taught phonics. A decade later, in 1967, Harvard University professor Jeanne Chall published a very influential review of research, *Learning to Read: The Great Debate (1967)*, in which she concluded that phonics produced at least somewhat better results than the whole-word method. In that same year, the largest study of beginning reading ever conducted, the First Grade Reading Studies (Bond & Dykstra, 1967/1997), produced findings that tended to support Chall's conclusions.

Although these three publications did eventually change the content of basals (It took more than 20 years.), they did not seriously change the influence and prominence of basals in the schools (Pearson, 2000). Contrary to Flesch's charge, most basals had always included some phonics instruction, and basal publishers responded to criticisms by providing somewhat more phonics. As late as 1990, the vast majority of American children continued to be taught with basal readers, and most teachers, if asked, would have said that they used a basal reading approach.

Along with the basal reader, many school districts adopted a skills management approach to the teaching skills. A skills management system identified and sequenced the reading skills, provided worksheet for practicing the skills and provided tests to monitor students' mastery. The Wisconsin Design for Reading Skill Development (Otto & Askov, 1971) is an example of a management system for teaching word attack, vocabulary, comprehension, study skills, interpretative reading, and creative reading. Each of these broad areas was divided into a number of subskills numbering over 100. Each week, students, based on their need, would be working on different skills and taking tests to determine their level of mastery.

The skills management approach proved to be so popular that it was adopted by basal reading programs of the 1970s and early 1980s. The sequence of skills instruction became more precise and robust, more skills were taught, the number of worksheets increased, and students took more mastery tests. This approach was so consuming that reading for pleasure and meaning became rare in many classrooms. Reading instruction was now driven by an accountability system that assessed a proliferating number of reading skills (Johnson & Pearson, 1975). The joy out of reading was sucked out for many educators.

The Challenge to Basal Readers: Whole-Language and Literature-Based Approaches

Advocates of more holistic approaches—whole-language and literature-based instruction—began to challenge basal reading programs in the late 1970s. Whole language was widely popularized in the writings of Kenneth Goodman (1970) and Frank Smith (1971). The basic charge was that basal approaches break up language and learning to read in a way that is unnatural and artificial and actually makes learning to read more difficult. More specific charges were that basals included too much skills instruction, that instruction in phonics and other subskills of reading was not integrated with actual reading, that vocabulary was much too controlled, that stories were banal and not well constructed, that separating students into ability groups had dire results for less skilled readers, and that teachers were over-programmed and over-scripted.

Critics also noted that the selections in basals dealt almost exclusively with White, middle-class characters, themes, and settings and that many of the reading selections were mundane from a literary standpoint. Advocates of literature-based programs had similar criticisms, though they tended not to be as adamantly against basal anthologies and structured programs as their whole-language colleagues. Both groups had a marked effect on basal readers and a huge effect on the reading instruction taking place in U.S. classrooms. In fact, literature-based basals became the most common type of basal in the 1990s.

Advocates of whole-language and literature-based instruction had a specific agenda, but they believed that the reading curriculum and the methods of instruction should evolve as teacher considered the needs and interests of the students. Three general characteristics of whole-language stand out: the use of authentic children's literature, a child-centered approach, and a focus on learning to read by reading. Advocates argued that authentic children's literature—books written by professional authors to engage and entertain children—should be the mainstay of reading instruction. Moreover, whole texts should be used; excerpts should be avoided. Students and their needs, desires, and interests should be the focus of attention, the primary concern. A preset curriculum is suspect. Student-initiated learning is favored over teacher-initiated instruction. Instruction comes when and as needed, while students are actually engaged in reading, and in quite brief mini-lessons.

The influence of whole-language and literature-based instruction produced a significant change in basal reading programs, especially in first grade. Publishers of basals now picked reading selections by their literary value and not the control and repetition of the vocabulary. Hoffman and his colleagues carefully documented these changes, examining basal programs from 1987 and 1993 (Hoffman, McCarthey, Abbott, Christian, Corman, & Curry, 1994). In the newer programs, students had to learn more than twice as many individual words than in the older programs. Each word appeared with far fewer repetitions, and the overall reading level for first grade text was significantly more difficult. On the positive side, the material was judged to be more engaging. Educators and publishers were betting that interest and engagement would trump vocabulary and phonics control.

Instruction in skills and strategies still played a prominent part in these new basal reading programs. Phonics instruction was not as robust, but teachers were still directed to explain and model comprehension instruction even if these lessons were not always as explicit as they could be. These basal programs also included a process approach to writing, integration of reading with the other language arts, and the use of book clubs for literature study.

Comprehension instruction also changed during the 1980s and through the mid 1990s. Propelled by radical changes in psychological theory and by a large-scale research effort launched at the Center for the Study of Reading at the University of Illinois, researchers explored how knowledge influenced reading comprehension and how skilled readers used thinking strategies to make sense of text (Pearson & Cervetti, 2017). Because of these efforts, the creators of reading programs put a stronger emphasis on developing students' knowledge before they read passages and teaching comprehension strategies before and during reading. This made core reading programs even more complex as strategies took their place beside skills in the programs' scope and sequence.

Massive Federal Intervention in Reading and Core Reading Programs

In 1997, Congress directed the Director of the National Institute of Child Health and Human Development (NICHD), to convene a panel of experts to "assess the status of research-based knowledge, including the effectiveness of various approaches to teaching children to read." This resulted in two reports. The National Research Council, a prestigious scientific organization, published *Preventing Reading Difficulties in Young Children* (Snow, Burns, & Griffin, 1998), a book that reviewed and brought to prominence much of the research sponsored by the NICHD, on early reading. The report focused on young children and emphasized the importance of phonemic awareness and phonics especially for children who have difficulty learning to read.

In 2000, the National Institute of Child Health and Human Development Panel published the *Report of the National Reading Panel: Teaching Children to Read (NRP)* (NICHD, 2000). In this report, the NRP identified five elements of reading instruction that it saw as strongly supported by research: phonemic awareness, phonics, fluency, vocabulary, and comprehension. This report became the basis for many curriculum decisions in the years that followed. The National Reading Panel report was a back-to-basics movement that sought to fix the so-called poor reading skills of American students by strengthening early reading instruction. The message most educators took from the report was to put more focus on letter recognition, phonemic awareness, phonics, and fluency than on the development of language skills. In part, this was influenced by the test most districts used to measure students' growth.

The NRP report had both very strong supporters and very strong opponents, but both supporters and opponents agree that it has had a huge effect on reading instruction. Most notably, a massive federal funding program titled Reading First was specifically designed to promote kindergarten through third grade instruction in each of the five areas endorsed by the report—that is, in phonemic awareness, phonics, fluency, vocabulary, and comprehension. Reading First had a substantial influence on instruction despite the fact that the program had only marginal results. (Gamse, Jacobs, Horst, Bouley, & Unla, 2008). Only first graders improved in decoding ability, while second and third grade students did not improve in reading comprehension.

Basal reading programs responded to the Federal initiatives by updating their programs to reflect the new research priorities. They also changed their identity to become "core reading programs." The change in terminology was significant (Dewitz et al., 2010). Whereas *basal* means the base from which students begin reading instruction and then move into ever-wider ranges of literature, *core* conveys the idea that these published programs are *the* reading curriculum, encompassing the entirety of reading instruction. Core reading programs were marketed as being scientifically-based research programs after a number of states and one research lab certified the research base of their instruction. However, subsequent research, especially studies of comprehension instruction, have challenged the research base of these programs (Dewitz et al., 2009; McGill-Franzen, Zmach, Solic, & Zeig, 2006).

The core reading programs published after 2005, have provided a stronger focus on phonemic awareness, phonics, and fluency. They include more decodable books and leveled books. Vocabulary instruction has become more robust, conforming to the suggestions of Beck and her colleagues (Beck, McKeown, & Kucan, 2003). Yet, comprehension instruction still lacks direct explanation and has failed to follow the gradual release of responsibility model (Dewitz et al., 2009). These programs moved away from exclusive whole-group instruction that had been the hallmark of core programs in previous decades to provide guidelines for teaching small groups of students who have differing skill needs and reading levels. Just as publishers responded to literature-based instruction by building the programs around children's literature, now publishers have embraced the suggestions of the large federal initiative.

The Common Core State Standards Provide a New Disruption to Reading Instruction

The most recent national initiative to rock reading instruction in our country has been the adoption by 45 states of the Common Core State Standards (CCSS) (NGA & CCSSO, 2010). Figure 2.4 presents a shortened version of the standards. The standards urged educators to think about reading instruction at three levels. Students should grasp key ideas and details, understand how the craft and structure of the text influenced the meaning, and integrate knowledge and idea to produce new understanding. These standards, plus the requirement that students read increasingly complex text, were

---

Figure 2.4 An Abbreviated Version of the Common Core State Standards

Key Ideas and Details:
1. Read closely to determine what the text says explicitly and to make logical inferences from it; cite specific textual evidence when writing or speaking to support conclusions drawn from the text.
2. Determine central ideas or themes of a text and analyze their development; summarize the key supporting details and ideas.
3. Analyze how and why individuals, events, or ideas develop and interact over the course of a text.

Craft and Structure:
4. Interpret words and phrases as they are used in a text, including determining technical, connotative, and figurative meanings, and analyze how specific word choices shape meaning or tone.
5. Analyze the structure of texts, including how specific sentences, paragraphs, and larger portions of the text (e.g., a section, chapter, scene, or stanza) relate to each other and the whole.
6. Assess how point of view or purpose shapes the content and style of a text.

Integration of Knowledge and Ideas:
7. Integrate and evaluate content presented in diverse media and formats, including visually and quantitatively, as well as in words.
8. Delineate and evaluate the argument and specific claims in a text, including the validity of the reasoning as well as the relevance and sufficiency of the evidence.
9. Analyze how two or more texts address similar themes or topics in order to build knowledge or to compare the approaches the authors take.

Range of Reading and Level of Text Complexity:
10. Read and comprehend complex literary and informational texts independently and proficiently.

MyLab Education
Video Example 2.1
As you listen to this video think about the two-fold problem of teaching within the Common Core State Standards and developing your own curriculum.

applauded by many educators. They were consistent with model of reading employed by National Assessment of Educational Progress, our nations report card (Pearson & Cervetti, 2017). The writers of the CCSS quickly betrayed their own initiative by writing a second document, the Publisher's Criteria (Coleman & Pimental, 2012), intent on influencing the development of instructional materials consistent with the CCSS.

The betrayal took several forms. The Publisher's Criteria (Coleman & Pimentel, 2012) advocated an instructional method called close reading with little to no research support. Students were to reread a text several times, digging deeper into its meaning (Snow & O'Connor, 2013). The reader's prior knowledge was minimized, if that was possible, so personal interpretation took a back seat to the ideas of the author. The writers of the Publisher's Criteria advocated reading complex text not knowing if those were the texts that would produce the greatest growth in reading. In the state of New York, students began the year reading the Universal Declaration of Human Rights, studying it closely for two weeks or more. After several tortured rereadings of the text one students exclaimed, "I hate human rights."

The Obama administration urged states to adopt the CCSS and provided $350 million for the development of tests. Two interstate groups developed the Smarter Balanced Assessment Consortium (SBAC) and the Partnership for Assessment of Readiness for College and Careers (PARCC). Both were long complex tests requiring more than a day for students to complete. Thirty-two states participated in SBAC and twenty-six in PARCC (A state could participate in more than one). As of this writing, only 16 states still use SBAC and six use PARCC (Koretz, 2017). When the CCSS made contact with the robust state testing practices initiated by the Race to the Top, an Obama administration program, most of the joy was sucked out of reading instruction for elementary and middle school students. Testing dominated the lives of teachers and students with little change in achievement according the National Assessment of Educational Progress (NAEP, 2018).

It has now been 50 years since the Supreme Court's landmark *Brown vs. the Board of Education* decision requiring school desegregation. Yet, despite a number of strong efforts and the many gains that students of color have made over those 50 years, a large achievement gap continues to exist. By the twelfth grade, average African American and Hispanic students can read only about as well as White eighth-graders. In a recent policy statement on closing this gap (Gordon, 2004), the American Educational Research Association made two recommendations. First, we must "support programs that engage all students in a rigorous, standards-based curriculum. Provide additional time and instruction as needed, but do not lower expectations." Second, we must "create an environment that provides the necessary social support for learning. It is important for students to be surrounded by peers and family members who value and support academic effort." We very strongly support both recommendations, and we add one of our own: Do everything possible to ensure that students are motivated to succeed in school. Motivation is vital for all students, but it is particularly vital for many students of color. We take up the topic of motivation in depth in Chapter 3.

Reflect and Apply

2. How have our expectations for reading changed since the colonial period? Given the high expectations of the current era, can basal programs help us achieve these goals?

3. How has the increasing demands of high stakes assessments changed instruction in the classroom? What have been the unforeseen outcomes of this public policy?

MyLab Education **Self-Check 2.1**

MyLab Education **Application Exercise 2.1:** How Has the Past Influenced the Present in Reading Instruction?

Principles of Effective Reading Instruction

Although providing effective instruction has always been a concern of teachers, researchers, and policy makers, a huge proportion of the most productive research and theorizing on the topic has occurred in the past four decades. Researchers have used two methods to unlock the principles of effective instruction. Many researchers have designed instructional studies and compared one method of instruction to another to determine which is more effective. Through these controlled studies, researchers have learned about the importance of clear explanations, modeling, pacing, practice, and feedback (Duffy et al., 1986). Other researchers have taken a second approach and studied effective teachers. They have observed in classrooms, recorded the practices of successful teachers as well as less successful teachers for comparison, and related instructional practices to students' growth in reading. We will first describe the research on effective teachers and take you into successful first- and fourth-grade classrooms. Next, we will dissect these classrooms and highlight the instructional principles that underlie their success. We will conclude by taking a closer look at the three dominant models for teaching reading—basal reading programs, guided reading, and reader's/writer's workshop.

Highly Effective Teachers and Schools

Fortunately, research has identified a group of schools and classrooms in which students show particularly strong achievement in reading, achievement well beyond that in average schools and classrooms and well beyond what would be predicted from the economic background of students in those classrooms. Six studies stand out, four of which deal with instruction generally (Allington & Johnston, 2002; Pressley, Allington, Wharton-McDonald, Block, & Morrow, 2001; Taylor et al., 2003; Wharton-McDonald, Pressley, & Hampston, 1998) and two of which deal specifically with motivation (Bogner, Raphael, & Pressley, 2002; Dolezal, Welsh, Pressley, & Vincent, 2003). Each of these reports is well worth detailed study, and we encourage you to read them.

Studies of highly effective teachers start with the assumption that by studying experts we can understand the tools of their trade. Thus, psychologists have studied expert airplane pilots, radiologists, and teachers and tried to discern the thinking that underlies their expertise. In these studies the researchers, with the assistance of school personnel, identify teachers who achieve superior results as measured by both standardized tests and the professional opinions of their supervisors. These expert teachers, along with some more average teachers, are observed during the course of a school year, and their teaching practices are recorded, described, categorized, and then linked to outcomes such as students' test performance, reading levels, and the quality of their written work. From these studies, we can describe the instructional practices of these highly effective teachers.

In the classrooms of highly effective teachers, several important practices stand out. First, these teachers create a stimulating environment for their students. The classrooms are filled with print, including books of all kinds for students to read, print created by the students—reports, books, charts, and projects—print created by the teacher—instructional charts, word walls and topics being studied, and graphic organizers. Second, children are constantly busy, with multiple activities and tasks going on at the same time. Teachers instruct the whole class but also work with small groups and confer with individual students. A wide range of texts is employed to teach reading, including basal readers, children's literature, nonfiction books, magazines, and the children's own writing. Because children read many different texts, reading instruction is often integrated with the other content areas, so at times it is hard to tell if the topic is reading, science, or both.

These exemplary teachers demonstrate a rich combination of direct explicit skill instruction (phonemic awareness, phonics, comprehension, and the like) and more holistic activities like reading quality literature, book discussions led by the teacher, and in the upper grades book discussion led by the students. Process writing occurs at all levels; even the youngest students plan, compose, revise, and share what they have written. Exemplary teachers ignore the age-old fight between teaching phonics skills and whole language—they do both. They also ignore the fight between basal readers and literature-based instruction—they employ both. They select a basal story when it is useful to introduce a new concept and skill, and then students read literature to apply what they have learned. As students work with these more difficult texts they meet regularly in small groups and conference with their teacher for additional help so the teacher can gauge their progress. To orchestrate all of this, the expert teachers are masterful classroom managers who use many opportunities to motivate their students. Figure 2.5 summarizes the characteristics of these excellent teachers.

In addition to these findings about effective teachers, some of these same studies as well as others have revealed school-level factors that produce superior achievement in high-poverty schools. A summary of these findings reported by Taylor, Pressley, and Pearson (2002) is shown in Figure 2.6. Although these factors are not as directly under your control as are teacher characteristics, they are certainly factors you can look for in schools and work toward as a faculty member.

How High-Stakes Testing Is Changing Reading Instruction

The studies of effective teaching and effective reading instruction were conducted prior to the passage of No Child Left Behind and the federal mandate to assess annually the reading ability of all third through eighth graders. Not only did the states mandate testing, the results came with rewards for schools who did well and punishment for schools

---

Figure 2.5 Characteristics of Teachers Who Produce Outstanding Achievement in Reading

- The best teachers employ a rich combination of skills instruction (phonemic awareness, phonics, comprehension) and more holistic activities (reading quality literature and nonfiction texts, discussing and writing about what they read), focusing on important academic tasks.
- The best teachers teach a lot. They work hard, and their students work hard in turn. They employ a combination of well-planned small-group activities and whole-class instruction.
- The best teachers scaffold students' efforts so that if students put significant effort into learning, they will be successful.
- The best teachers employ higher-order thinking.
- The best teachers integrate reading instruction with language arts and the other content areas.
- The best teachers manage classrooms skillfully.
- The best teachers motivate continually and prominently and repeatedly recognize students' work.

Figure 2.6 Characteristics of Schools That Produce High Achievement
in High-Poverty Settings

- Strong focus on student learning
- Strong school instructional leadership
- Strong collaboration among teachers
- Consistent use of data on student performance to guide instruction
- Emphasis on professional development for teachers in the school
- Strong links to parents

that performed poorly. Against this backdrop of mandated testing, districts changed, schools changed, and classsroom instruction changed (Valli, Croninger, & Buese, 2012).

District administrators and school principals responded to federally mandated high-stakes assessments with heightened anxiety. They wanted to make sure that students would pass the tests in the spring, so they required interim or benchmark tests to determine which students might pass and with whom to concentrate their efforts. The schools focused on the "bubble students," those who, with extra help, just might pass the test, neglecting the strongest (these students were going to pass anyway) and weakest students (they had no chance) in the class (Diamond, 2012). They designed pacing guides so that instruction was aligned with the interim assessment and with the state high-stakes tests. The curriculum was narrowed to those concepts and skills most likely to be on the test. Teachers spent more time pouring over data, consulting pacing guides, and teaching to the test (Shepard, 2010). The amount of time preparing for, taking, and analyzing tests increased and the amount of time for instruction decreased.

In the classroom, high-stakes assessments narrowed what was taught and how it was taught. Without the pressure of high-stakes tests, teachers selected reading texts based on their literary value and student interest. When teachers worked with students in their small intervention groups to prepare for the test, passages were selected based on length and their ability to provide testing practice (Valli & Chambliss, 2007). All states have curriculum standards, many based on the CCSS, but not all standards receive equal emphasis. Because of the assessment demands, a standard such as employing metacognitives strategies, difficult to assess in a multiple-choice format, was ignored, while finding the main idea or drawing inferences became a focus because these skills were easily assessed. When assessment drives instruction, teachers talk more, student responses are more limited, and the rich discussions are sacrificed for getting to the right answer.

In this high-stakes environment, teachers feel compelled to conform to the policy dictates of the state and the district, teaching in ways they believe are in opposition to best practices (Valli, Croninger, & Buses, 2012). Despite what we believe to be the negative impact of high-stakes tests, we will still explore the best practices in reading instruction, keeping in mind that there are many pressures within and outside a school that shape reading instruction. We will start in the fourth-grade classroom of Mrs. Babs Mowry (see In the Classroom 2.1).

Traditional Perspectives on Instruction

Mrs. Mowry's class exemplifies many instructional principles that are essential for learning. These principles were developed from about 1960 to about 1980 as educators and researchers produced a rich body of basic information about effective instruction (see Good & Brophy, 2003). These traditional principles included:

- focusing on academically relevant tasks,
- employ active teaching,
- fostering active learning,
- providing sufficient and timely feedback so that students can learn from their mistakes, and
- distinguish between instruction and practice.

> ### Motivating Struggling Readers
>
> #### The Importance of Choice
>
> Life in Mrs. Mowry's classroom illustrates several important principles of motivation, but none more important than choice. Students are given choices about what to read and how to respond to their reading. There is a common text, the basal reader, that the teacher uses to introduce concepts and strategies, but beyond that students choose their own reading materials. When they are working in literature circles, the teacher allows them to select their own book to study from a small set approved by the teacher. The small-group processes of a literature circle promote motivation and engagement because all students are responsible to the group. When students are reading independently, they select their own book with some consult with Mrs. Mowry. If they can't pick, the teacher will offer suggestions. The classroom itself promotes choice and motivation by having a large, well laid out classroom library.

We will relate these principles to Mrs. Mowry's classroom and then develop them when we consider new instructional principles that derive from the cognitive–constructive perspective. For more information on these principles, Tom Good and Jere Brophy's *Looking into Classrooms* (2003) is an excellent source.

In the Classroom 2.1

A Portrait of Exemplary Fourth-Grade Instruction

Mrs. Mowry begins the period by reading aloud and discussing the survival book *Earthquake Terror* (Kehret, 1996), the story of Jonathan, an eleven-year-old boy and his family on a camping trip in Northern California when an earthquake strikes. Mrs. Mowry wants the students to describe the main character Jonathan who must care for his younger, handicapped sister while his parents go for help. The discussion today focuses on character traits and Mrs. Mowry first models and describes the concept of a trait. She and the students then list character traits on the board, including such traits as *responsible, caring, problem-solver, resentful*.

The students are also working in book clubs reading one of three related novels on the theme of survival—*I Survived* (Tarshis, 2011), *Kensuke's Kingdom* (Morpurgo, 1999) and *Hatchet* (Paulsen, 1987). Today, when the students meet with their book club partners, they will create a list of the main characters in their novel and note the traits of that character. The students are paired up so they can assist one another and apply what they learned in the read-aloud. Alongside each trait, they provide evidence, actions and thoughts of the character that they gleaned from the text. During the book club time the students are actively engaged in reading and taking notes. The room is quiet. Occasionally, a student will confer with his or her partner. Mrs. Mowry provides extra help to the struggling readers in the room conducting a guided reading lesson with their text, *I Survived*.

During book club time, five of Mrs. Mowry's students leave the room to work with the school's reading teacher. These students are reading well below a fourth-grade level, and continue to have difficulty with decoding and oral reading fluency. Mrs. Mowry has scant time to confer with the reading teacher, but regrets that their book club work is interrupted. She acknowledges that these students need extra help and the school district has mandated an intervention program. Thirty minutes later the five return.

Later in the period, Mrs. Mowry uses the concept of character traits in a writing task. She tells the students their task is to take what they have learned about character traits and write a poem about. Jonathan or a character from their book club selection. A handout helps the students structure their poem, somewhat like a cinquain. When they have finished writing their poem, the students are to return to their independent reading assignment while the teacher confers with individual students.

Mrs. Mowry conducts short reading conferences with five students a day while the rest of the class does their book club work or independent reading. During the conferences, she discusses what the students are reading, assess oral reading fluency as needed, assesses their comprehension and then probes students' critical thinking. The conferences afford her the opportunity to praise and support the students' efforts as readers and guide their reading choices. As the year progresses the conferences continue but the teacher also assesses comprehension by observing the students as they interact in book clubs. In Mrs. Mowery's class there is a free flow of activities moving from whole class instruction, to small group instruction to individual attention.

The Reading Corner

Informational Books That Give Students Opportunities to Make Critical Responses

One extremely relevant academic task is making critical responses to informational texts. The books listed here—science and social studies trade books about the world we live in—are interesting and involving and provide extended opportunities for students to make critical responses.

Deborah Chandra & Madeleine Comora. Illustrated by Brock Cole. *George Washington's Teeth*. Farrar, Straus and Giroux, 2003. This light-hearted account of the tooth problems that plagued Washington all his adult life provides a unique focus for a detailed timeline of Washington's life and accomplishments. 40 pages.

Rick Chrustowski. *Bright Beetle*. Holt, 2000. This colorful book, illustrated from a bug's eye view, describes the life cycle of a ladybug. The bright colors and accessible text make it a fun read-aloud, share-aloud book. Unnumbered.

Bonnie Graves. *The Whooping Crane*. Perfection Learning, 1997. This informational book begins with a narrative relating a true, potentially fatal incident in 1967 involving a whooping crane chick, then one of 55 remaining of a seriously endangered species; it ends with factual information about the whoopers and efforts to save the species. 54 pages.

Linda Lowery. *Cinco de Mayo*. Carolrhoda Books, 2005. This addition to the On My Own Holidays series, which encourages understanding of diverse cultures, features full-page illustrations by Barbara Knutson and describes the colorful holiday that honors Mexico's victory over the French army at the Battle of Pueblo in 1862. 48 pages.

Sandra Markle. *Outside and Inside Killer Bees*. Walker, 2004. One of the many books in Markle's Outside and Inside series, this edition, with striking photos and accessible text, focuses not only on factual information about bees, such as their anatomy, social behavior, and honey production, but also on the ecological impact of invasive species. 40 pages.

Wendy Pfeffer. *Dolphin Talk: Whistles, Clicks, and Clapping Jaws*. HarperCollins, 2003. From the Let's-Read-and-Find-Out series, this book focuses on dolphin communication while also revealing the basics of dolphin anatomy, behavior, and life cycle. 40 pages.

Laurence Pringle. *Snakes! Strange and Wonderful*. Boyds Mills, 2004. This book, by well-known nonfiction author Laurence Pringle and illustrated in watercolor paintings by Meryl Henderson, presents a wide variety of snakes and explains the unusual behaviors that characterize the various types. 32 pages.

Ken Robbins. *Seeds*. Atheneum, 2005. Through text and photos by the author, this book reveals the basic facts about seeds—their different shapes and sizes and the connections between a seed's structure and function in terms of its transport. 32 pages.

Pamela Turner. *Gorilla Doctors: Saving Endangered Great Apes*. Houghton Mifflin, 2005. This book in the Scientists in the Field series takes a look at mountain gorillas, one of the most endangered species in the world, and reveals through text and photos how veterinarians in Rwanda and Uganda are working to save them.

Carole Boston Weatherford. *Freedom on the Menu: The Greensboro Sit-Ins*. Dial, 2004. As seen through the eyes of a young southern Black girl, this book offers a unique perspective on the 1960 civil rights sit-ins at the Woolworth's lunch counter in Greensboro, North Carolina. Unnumbered.

FOCUSING ON ACADEMICALLY RELEVANT TASKS

If you are going to get really good at something, you need to do a lot of it. You need to have a lot of what educational researchers have termed "opportunities to learn," chances to learn about and practice whatever it is you are trying to get good at (Berliner, 1979). If students are going to become proficient readers, they need to do a lot of reading. Certainly, plentiful reading is the central academically relevant task in learning to read, but by no means is it the only one.

How much should students read every day is an open question. Brenner and Hiebert's (2010) data suggest that if students read everything in their basal program they could do so in 15 minutes a day or less. Clearly that is not enough reading to become fluent and competent. Allington (2001) and Fisher & Ivey 2006 argue that students in the middle grades should spend 45 minutes a day reading. Even more is needed for struggling readers. These students, who often receive multiple interventions from the reading teacher and a tutor, often read less than five minutes a day (Dewitz & Dewitz, 2003). Remember, the quality of reading matters. Randomly glancing at the pictures in a non-fiction text is not the same experience as deep engagement in an exciting novel or reading carefully to learn a new concept like the water cycle from a science book.

In addition to reading itself, several subtasks are important. If students are going to become proficient decoders—readers who can use their knowledge of letter-sound correspondences and spelling patterns to decode unfamiliar words—they need to be actively engaged in tasks like reading decodable books. If students are to become proficient at responding to literature orally and in writing, they need many opportunities to discuss and write about what they have read. And if students are to become critical readers and writers of informational prose, they need abundant opportunities to read, evaluate, and to make critical responses to informational text on the Internet. These are only some of the reading-related areas in which students must become proficient, but we think we have made our point: Curriculum—what students study—matters! In Mrs. Mowry's classroom, students read and write all the time in during whole class time and during small literature groups.

EMPLOY ACTIVE TEACHING

The term *active teaching* refers to a set of principles and teaching behaviors that research has shown to be particularly effective, especially in teaching basic skills. As noted by Brophy (1986), teachers who engage in active teaching are the instructional leaders of their classrooms; they are fully knowledgeable about the content and purposes of the instruction they present and about the instructional goals they wish to accomplish. Active teachers do a lot of teaching. Although they use discovery learning for some purposes, they do not generally rely on students to discover what it is they are supposed to learn, particularly when the learning deals with basic skills. The concept of active teaching became even more precise when cognitive-constructivists principles defined it in terms of direct explanation and modeling. The active teacher explains concepts and strategies, models strategies and thinking, and guides students as they attempt to use the new ideas. Mrs. Mowry employed active teaching when she explains the concept of character traits and has the students generate the traits that describe Jonathan the main character in the novel.

FOSTER ACTIVE LEARNING

Just as it is vital that the teacher be actively involved in teaching, it is also crucial that the learner be actively involved in learning (Good & Brophy, 2003). As we explained in our discussion of the cognitive-constructivist orientation in Chapter 1, the learner must do something with the material he is studying if he is to learn much from it. The students in Mrs. Mowry class room engage in active learning when they meet with their book club partner and together create a list of characters and traits for the novel they are reading. Fourth-grade teacher John Fitzhugh puts it well in the accompanying feature (In the Classroom 2.2).

In the Classroom 2.2

Actively Engaging Students in Reading and Responding to a Text

Students *must* be actively involved in order for any sort of learning to take place. That's simply a fact. But there are a number of ways this can happen. Say, for instance, a student is reading a trade book on sharks, perhaps Seymour Simon's *Sharks*. As he reads, the student can:

- think about the new things he is learning about sharks,
- discuss new insights with others,
- make outlines or sketches that depict his new knowledge,
- write a brief story about how he might respond if he were in the water and saw a shark fin nearby,
- draw relationships between the new knowledge and his existing knowledge of sharks, or
- attempt to implement the new knowledge (for example, simulate an underwater environment by making a diorama of sharks and their habitat, as one of my students did).

Or the student can undertake many other activities that cause him to grapple with the new knowledge and integrate it into his existing schema. As we all know, precious little new knowledge will be absorbed passively.

PROVIDING SUFFICIENT AND TIMELY FEEDBACK

Feedback is a long-standing precept of teaching and learning (see, for example, Bransford, Brown, & Cocking, 2000) and it has been more recently expanded as part of the formative assessment process. From the dialogues of Socrates to the answers included in programmed instruction, feedback has long been a central component of instruction. In the years before school, young children get a great deal of immediate, positive feedback—fussing brings a bottle; a smile, a lot of attention; saying "ball," a round object to play with. During these same years, young children also receive a good deal of immediate, negative feedback—too much fussing may bring only a closed door, a smile at the television set produces no response, and begging once too often to take the iPad to the restaurant may land you in time out.

Once in school, students continue to get feedback, although with one teacher serving perhaps 30 students, individual feedback is not as readily available as it was at home. But such feedback is every bit as necessary. There is no way for a learner to know whether he is on the right track unless he receives some sort of response. And this rule applies whether the newly learned material is the sound represented by the letter *m*, the pronunciation of the word *rabbit*, or the identification of the central theme in a story. Sometimes feedback can be embedded in the learning situation and does not require a response from another person. For example, when the child reads, "The rabbit really liked the carrots," his understanding of the sentence as a whole is established by his correct pronunciation of *rabbit*; the pronunciation brings the meaning to mind. At other times, peers can provide the feedback; for example, a group of fifth-graders read a novel and agree that the theme is the importance of friendship. But much of the time, such as in learning letter-sound correspondences, the feedback must come from the teacher. Figuring out how to provide timely, telling, and kind feedback for 30 or so students is a major task for a classroom teacher.

The concept of formative assessment (we will expand on this idea in Chapter 5) has given a structure to the feedback process. According to Black and Wiliam (2009) the teacher and the students discuss and clarify the learning task and criteria for success. Then the students engage in the tasks that elicit evidence of the students' proficiency. The teacher then provides feedback on their efforts and the students are encouraged to give each other feedback. As students understand this feedback, they embrace the criteria, moving to monitor their own learning. In Mrs. Mowry classroom the formative assessment process is employed as the students move from the initial explanation of character traits, to practice with a partner and to individual work. At each step the teacher and the students can provide feedback on the students' thinking about this new concept – character traits. By simply agreeing and disagreeing about a character's traits the students are provided feedback to each other.

DISTINGUISH BETWEEN INSTRUCTION AND PRACTICE

Effective teaching requires both instruction and practice, but the two need to be clearly distinguished. Practice involves asking students to do something they already know how to do or are beginning to do. Instruction involves showing or telling students how to do something that they do not yet know how to do. Simply asking students to do something does not constitute teaching them how to do it. Practice is appropriate *after* students have learned whatever it is they are to practice.

Emphasizing this distinction, Gerry Duffy and Laura Roehler (1982) coined the terms *proactive teaching* and *reactive teaching*. Proactive teaching consists of deliberately showing students how to do something before expecting them to do it themselves. Reactive teaching consists of first asking students to do something and then showing them how only when they struggle. Proactive teaching sets students up for success, whereas reactive teaching sets them up for failure. Reactive teaching is inefficient because it often leaves the teacher trying to clarify matters after the fact for students who became confused while working at something they did not know how to do; the confusion could have been avoided by providing instructions at the outset. Reactive teaching is especially demoralizing for students who repeatedly fail. Mrs. Mowry show active teaching when she she defines and elaborates on the concept of character traits.

Reflect and Apply

4. Think back as far as you can in your schooling—to elementary school, if possible, or to secondary school—and jot down a list of tasks you completed that you think were academically relevant and a list of tasks you completed that you think were not academically relevant. Then write about what does and does not constitute an academically relevant task.

5. Think of a teacher you have had or you have observed who has been particularly effective in gearing instruction to the students' zone of proximal development. Describe what he or she did that was so effective.

A Constructivist Perspectives on Instruction

The cognitive–constructive orientation underlying this book requires us to use different terms and concepts to describe instruction because these will take us deeper into a cognitive approach. In a nutshell, the cognitive-constructive orientation makes the process of instruction more explicit and outlines a process of learning that begins with direct instruction and ends with students using what has been taught in an effective independent manner. In the sections that follow we will describe these principles based on our cognitive orientations. These principles include:

- The Zone of Proximal Development
- The Gradual Release of Responsibility Model which includes: Direct Explanation, Cognitive Modeling, Scaffolding, Contextualizing, Reviewing, and Practicing
- Teaching for Transfer
- Cooperative Learning, and
- Teach for Understanding.

THE ZONE OF PROXIMAL DEVELOPMENT

To select learning tasks and activities it is important to consider the students' Zone of Proximal Development. Lev Vygotsky (1978), a Russian psychologist, put forth the concept of the zone of proximal development, which emphasizes the fact that learning is very much a social phenomenon; in fact, we acquire much of what we learn in our social interchanges with others. According to Vygotsky, at any particular point in time, children have a circumscribed zone of development, a range within which they can learn. At one end of this range are learning tasks that they can complete independently; at the other end are learning tasks that they cannot complete, even with assistance. In between these two extremes is the zone most productive for learning, the range of tasks in which children can achieve *if* they are assisted by a more knowledgeable or more competent other.

If left on their own, for example, many third-graders might learn very little from a *National Geographic World* article on the formation of thunderstorms. Conversely, with your help—getting them interested in the topic, focusing their attention, pre-teaching some of the critical concepts such as the effects of rising heat, arranging small groups to discuss and answer questions on certain parts of the article—these same students may be able to learn a good deal from the article. However, with other topics and other texts—for example, a chapter on gravity from a high school physics text—no amount of outside help, at least no reasonable amount of outside help, will foster much learning for these third-graders. The topic of gravity and its presentation in the high school text are simply outside their zone of proximal development. The zone of proximal development is a useful concept because it helps you think about the difficulty of the text and the task and find ways to adjust them to the abilities of your students.

THE GRADUAL RELEASE OF RESPONSIBILITY MODEL

The gradual release of responsibility model depicts an entire instructional cycle during which students learn new skills and knowledge and gradually assume increased responsibility for this learning. Within this model are several interrelated concepts—direct explanation, cognitive modeling, scaffolding, and contextualized review and practice. A particularly informative visual representation of the model developed by David Pearson and Margaret Gallagher (1983) is shown in Figure 2.7.

Figure 2.7 The Gradual Release of Responsibility Model

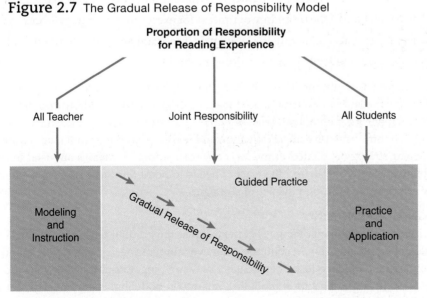

SOURCE: Reprinted from Pearson, P. D., & Gallagher, M. C., "The Instruction of Reading Comprehension," *Contemporary Educational Psychology, 8*, 317–344, Copyright 1983, with permission from Elsevier.

The model depicts a temporal sequence in which students gradually progress from situations in which the teacher takes responsibility for their successful completion of a reading task (in other words, does most of the work for them), to situations in which students assume increasing responsibility for reading tasks, and finally to situations in which students take total or nearly total responsibility for reading tasks—ideally, transfer of learning. This model can play out over a week, a month, or over a full school year. For some skills like decoding in the fourth grade, the students should be fully independent, needing little or no assistance from the teacher. At the same time, they might just be starting to learn how to determine the author purposes, and the teacher will assume full responsibility for explaining and modeling this thinking.

As is typical in education the gradual release of responsibility model has been adopted by other educators but with a new name: "I do it, we do it, you do it. (Fisher & Frey, 2007." This simplified language helps to explain the learning process to students but it looses the explicitness of the orginial terminology. We prefer that you keep the orginial model firmly in mind as a guide to instruction but use the simple language when talking to your students. They don't need the terms direct explanation or cognitive modeling.

As an example of this model, suppose a teacher decides that students need to learn to summarize. She begins by explaining what a summary is and how to construct one, trying to be as explicit as possible. Next the teacher models the process and lets students observe her thinking as she develops her summary. Then the teacher and students work on one together in a phase called *guided practice*. During guided practice the teacher asks students questions ("Does your summary contain just important ideas?"); provides hints ("Look for topic sentences."), and models the process again if students need it. After considerable guided practice students are ready to try it out on their own. This instructional cycle may play out over weeks, and the students may be at different stages of the cycle with different skills and strategies. The gradual release of responsibility model always begins with direct explanation, another term for proactive teaching.

DIRECT EXPLANATION

We use *direct explanation* to mean the first stage of the gradual release of responsibility model. Others see the term direct explanation as almost a synonym for the gradual release model (Duffy, 2002; Duke & Pearson, 2002).

When a strategy or concept is first introduced, the teacher has to provide:

- an explicit description of the strategy—what the students are going to learn to do,
- an explanation of the procedure or process for executing the strategy—how to do it,
- clear statements about why the strategy is important and when to use it, and
- modeling of the strategy with multiple pieces of text.

Your goal is to illuminate the thinking that underlies the strategy. Being clear and explicit is not easy because experienced readers are rarely aware of how they determine a word's meaning, find a main idea, or make an inference. Telling students when and why to do something provides motivation and helps the students understand how one particular strategy is related to the larger act of reading. Strategies are used to solve problems when we read, and the teacher needs to point out these problems and how they can be solved through the use of strategies.

COGNITIVE MODELING

After an explanation, modeling is the next step in the gradual release of responsibility model, but modeling should continue whenever students need greater understanding. When teachers model a task, they actually *do* something, rather than just tell students how to do it. A specific sort of modeling, cognitive modeling, is particularly useful in teaching students difficult concepts and strategies. In cognitive modeling, teachers use explicit instructional talk to reveal their thought processes as they perform the tasks

In the Classroom 2.3

Instructional Routines

Cognitive Modeling

Teacher: Suppose I'm reading along and I come to this sentence: "It was raining heavily and water was standing in the street, so before he left for work Mr. Nelson put on his raincoat, buckled on his galoshes over his shoes, and picked up his umbrella." Let me see—g-a-l-o-s-h-e-s. I don't think I know that word. Let's see. It's raining, and he picks up his raincoat and umbrella and buckles something over his shoes. Galoshes must be some sort of waterproof boots that go over shoes. I can't be certain of that, but it makes sense in the sentence; and I don't think I want to look it up right now.

that students will be asked to perform. For example, a teacher might model the mental process of determining the meaning of an unknown word in context, as shown in the accompanying feature (In the Classroom 2.3).

Cognitive modeling provides a window into the teacher's mind and constitutes one of the most powerful tools for showing children how to reason as they seek to understand a text. As we have stated, cognitive modeling is not easy. Duffy's (2009) *Explaining Reading* provides some strong examples for how to model many reading strategies. After the teacher models the strategy, the students should try it, and the teacher provides help as the students require it.

SCAFFOLDING

As students try out new tasks and new strategies, the teacher provides support by scaffolding the students' efforts. We believe that the term *scaffolding* was first used in its educational sense by David Wood, Jerome Bruner, and Gail Ross (1976), who used it to characterize mothers' verbal interactions when reading to their young children. In these interactions, mothers gently yet supportively guide their children toward successful literacy experiences. Thus, for example, in sharing a picture book and attempting to assist the child in reading the words that label the pictures, a mother might at first simply page through the book, familiarizing the child with the pictures and the general content of the book. Then she might focus on a single picture and ask the child what it is. After this, she might point to the word below the picture, tell the child that the word names the picture, ask the child what the word is, and provide feedback on the correctness of the answer. The important point to note here is that the mother has neither simply told the child the word nor simply asked him to say it. Instead, she has built an instructional structure, a scaffold that assists the child in learning. Scaffolding, as Wood and his colleagues have aptly put it, is "a process that enables a child or novice to solve a problem, carry out a task, or achieve a goal which would be beyond his unassisted efforts."

Teachers scaffold student learning in many different ways. Most frequently the language of the teacher guides the student through the process. If the student is stuck trying to determine the main idea of a passage, the teacher might remind her to reread the heading and look at the bold print, what we call "moment-to-moment verbal support." In another setting, the teacher might use a graphic organizer to support or scaffold the student. A story map reminds the reader to look for the critical elements of a narrative— setting, character, problem, and so forth. Even a stack of Post-it notes can remind students to jot down questions while they read—scaffolding a self-questioning strategy. Finally, a teacher might have two students work together on a task, with each student supporting the other. In the Classroom 2.4 expands on the idea of small group scaffolding for English learners. In each of these cases, the teacher is assisting students in doing

MyLab Education
Video Example 2.2
Watch this video of Ms. Sanchez modeling a reading strategy for her fourth grade students. How does thinking aloud help them?

In the Classroom 2.4

Scaffolding Small-Group Instruction for English Learners

Scaffolding student learning is accomplished most easily during small-group instruction. This is especially true for English language learners. We suggest that you bring together fluent speakers of English with students who are just learning English. The students who are stronger in English act as a model for the ELL students and help to support them. Pair up these students; after you ask a question, have them engage in pair-and-share activities. The two students take a moment to discuss the question and formulate an answer. Then one of the students shares the answer with the group. Through this process of pair and share, the ELL student learns how to formulate a response before taking a risk in front of the group.

The key to successful small-group instruction is thinking through how you will assist the students. Much of this assistance comes from moment-to-moment verbal support. Be prepared to ask some of the following questions that scaffold students' use of a main idea strategy. Be sure to have pair-and-share time before students begin responding.

- Can someone retell what we have learned? (Retelling)
- What was difficult to understand in this section? (Clarifying)
- What is the main idea of that section? (Main idea)
- How did you find the main idea?
- How did what you already know help you determine the main idea?
- Which text features helped you determine the main idea?

MyLab Education
Video Example 2.3
Watch Tim Shanahan discuss the components of reading as they relate to learning to decode. How many of the elements in this chapter does he mention?

something that they might not otherwise be able to do. Much of Chapter 11 describes ways to build supportive scaffolds for the many different types of reading students do.

CONTEXTUALIZING, REVIEWING, AND PRACTICING WHAT IS LEARNED

The release of responsibility model produces deep and lasting learning if students use their newly learned strategies in authentic contexts. Students need many opportunities to practice the strategies and make them their own, with periodic review from the teacher. Although review and practice are traditional instructional activities, the importance of contextualizing students' learning is something we have only recently recognized as absolutely vital to real and lasting learning, and thus we have decided to place all three practices in this section. The concepts are simple, but they must be heeded. If, for example, students learn the strategy of summarizing as part of reading instruction, they must be given opportunities and encouragement to use summarizing when they are working with social studies or science material or when they are gathering information in the library or studying at home. Moreover, students need many opportunities to use the strategy in these authentic contexts.

A literature circle is an excellent example (see Daniels, 2002). As students meet and discuss a novel, they summarize what they have read, clarify difficult vocabulary words, make inferences, and predict what will happen next. The structure of a literature circle reminds and prompts the students to use comprehension strategies, and if the teacher detects problems, she can review the strategies and, if necessary, provide more modeling and scaffolding. As students work in literature circles throughout the year, they are regularly reviewing and practicing strategies in a natural context.

Teaching for Transfer

Transfer is the use of knowledge or skills learned in one context and applied to another context. The well-known Chinese proverb "Give a man a fish, and you feed him for a day. Teach a man to fish, and you feed him for a lifetime." emphasizes the tremendous value of transfer. Knowledge and skills that transfer become tools that students can use throughout their lives. In a very real sense, transfer is the central purpose of schooling; schools are future oriented. Students attend school today so that they can use what they learn tomorrow. We want students to apply what they learn in the early grades to their learning in later grades; even more important, we want them to apply what they learn in school to the world outside of school.

Given the obvious centrality of transfer to schooling, it may shock you to learn that schools have often been unsuccessful in promoting it. Transfer is one of the oldest topics of educational research, and the repeated finding has been that students very frequently fail to use their school learning outside of school. The student who adds and subtracts quite competently during math class fails when she tries to calculate how much allowance she has left. The student who writes a competent letter of complaint as a class exercise never thinks of writing the distributor when his magazine fails to arrive two months in a row. As British philosopher Alfred North Whitehead (1929) aptly put it over 70 years ago, the knowledge students have gained in school has all too frequently been "inert"—fragile, tip-of-the-iceberg knowledge that might enable them to choose a correct answer on a multiple-choice test but does not last or serve much purpose in the real world.

Teaching for transfer requires thoughtful and well-planned instruction. The teacher must create learning tasks that facilitate transfer and remind students to use their new skills. Transfer can be achieved by following the gradual release of responsibility model. In fact the model leads the students to apply and transfer what the teacher has explained and modeled. In the guided practice stage of the model the students are beginning to transfer what has been taught but the teacher continues to provide some support. In the independent phase of the model the students are transferring what has been taught. Helping a student transfer the decoding or comprehension strategies modeled by the teacher requires that the teacher use texts where the strategies can be applied and then support, or scaffold, the student in the use of the strategies when he struggles.

COOPERATIVE LEARNING

David and Roger Johnson define *cooperative learning* as "the instructional use of small groups so that students work together to maximize their own and each other's learning" (Johnson, Johnson, & Holubec, 1994). Robert Slavin defines it as "instructional methods in which students of all performance levels work together toward a group goal" (1987). Cooperative learning is a set of procedures that scaffold student learning. It is a set of techniques that can be used during the guided and independent phase of the gradual release of responsibility model. As the Johnsons have repeatedly said, "None of us is as smart as all of us." Groups of students working together have the potential to achieve well beyond what a student working alone can do. Moreover, working in cooperative groups can produce multiple benefits, such as improving students' achievement, effort to succeed, critical thinking, attitudes toward the subjects studied, psychological adjustment, and self-esteem. Cooperative learning can also foster students' interpersonal relationships, improving their ability to work with others and build relationships among diverse racial, ethnic, and social groups. Additionally, as John Seely Brown and his colleagues note (Brown, Collins, & Duguid, 1989), group learning offers learners opportunities for displaying and recognizing the multiple roles that are often required to solve real-world problems and to recognize and confront their own and others' ineffective strategies and misconceptions.

Cooperative learning is consistent with many constructivist and sociocultural principles that we have mentioned. It relies on the belief that the best learning is often social, giving students an opportunity to scaffold one another's work and putting them in a position to respond to, and elaborate on, one another's thinking. Because of its great potential, throughout this book we frequently suggest group activities for elementary students, and many of the Reflect and Apply sections suggest group work.

TEACHING FOR UNDERSTANDING

As we have noted, over 80 years ago, British philosopher Alfred North Whitehead (1929) railed against schools' fostering what he called "inert knowledge"—fragile, shallow knowledge that is usually soon forgotten and too superficial to be of much use even if remembered. Today, educators are increasingly realizing the value of teaching for understanding—dealing with fewer topics but teaching them in such a way that students not only learn the content itself thoroughly but also appreciate the reasons for learning it and retain it in a form that makes it usable. As Harvard psychologist David Perkins (1992) puts it, teaching for understanding promotes three basic goals of education: understanding of knowledge, retention of knowledge, and active use of knowledge. Perkins anticipated the CCSS by twenty-five years.

We believe that teaching for understanding is terribly important; we address this topic especially in the comprehension chapters. Relying heavily on the work of Perkins and his colleagues (Blythe, 1998; Perkins, 1992; Wiske, 1998), we examine teaching for understanding in detail. Here we will note only that the key to teaching for understanding is teaching fewer topics but teaching them well and that teaching for understanding demands the sort of constructive teaching and learning advocated throughout this section of the chapter.

Reflect and Apply

6. In this section we presented two broad concepts: the gradual release of responsibility model and teaching for transfer. Consider how these two ideas are similar. In what ways does the gradual release of responsibility model promote transfer of learning?

MyLab Education **Self-Check 2.2**

MyLab Education **Application Exercise 2.2:** Applying the Gradual Release of Responsibility Model

---

Major Approaches to Reading Instruction

In the early 21st century, the revised core reading programs competed with two other trends in reading instruction; guided reading (Fountas & Pinnell, 1996, 2001) and the reader's/writer's workshop (Calkins, 1983) all hoping to be soldiers under the flag of balanced literacy (Pressley, 2006). Balanced literacy was supposed to put an end to the "reading wars" and create a balance between skill instruction and meaning centered approaches like whole language. Basal programs fly the flag of balanced literacy by including authentic fiction and non-fiction texts, presenting skill and strategy lessons, and the resources for independent student work. Guided reading does this by having the teacher share authentic literature, guide students through leveled texts by working with small groups of students, and provide skill instruction as needed: there is no scope and sequence. The reader's/writer's workshop offers even less instructional guidance. Students choose what they read with guidance from the teacher. They read independently with skill instruction delivered through mini-lessons when the teacher detects a need. In the workshop setting the students read independently, they confer with the teacher and ocassionally the teacher pulls a group together for a guided lesson. Both the guided reading approach and the reader's/writer's workshop trace their origins back to the whole-language movement and, if you want to push it back further, to Horace Mann.

When you visit schools or talk to teachers, you are apt to see a variety of approaches to reading instruction, some of them more effective than others. In many schools, you are apt to find a hybrid approach to reading instruction with teachers using elements of a basal program, guided reading, and the reader's workshop approach. We want to describe the most common instructional elements. While some educators advocate teaching programs, especially basal or core reading programs with fidelity, most recognize that reading instruction requires that the teacher make many decisions (Dewitz & Jones, 2013).

Whole Class Instruction

In almost all classrooms you will find a time where the teacher works with the whole class. In a basal program, the teacher uses this time to read aloud to the students to develop knowledge of genres and teach vocabulary. Basal instruction revolves around a primary anthology selection with a shorter piece of follow-up text. Frequently, these are introduced, read, and discussed with the whole class participating. Next, the teacher introduces and models phonics, vocabulary, and comprehension skills. Follow-up skills work, and instruction in spelling, grammar, and writing are also directed to the whole class. Compared to guided reading or the reader's workshop, whole class instruction dominates in many basal programs.

Guided reading typically includes a whole class time called shared reading. During shared reading, students and teachers read a common texts that may be beyond what students can read independently. Teachers use the shared reading time to introduce a new concept, strategy, or vocabulary words. Shared reading, according to Fountas and Pinnell (2001) is best suited for short pieces of text, dramatic stories, or poems. However, in some reading programs like the Collect-Interpret-Apply (Collinge, 2015) and Wit and Wisdom (Great Minds, 2012) the whole class time is used to read a complete picture book or novel and develop students' knowledge and strategies.

In the reader's workshop model, time for whole class instruction is used sparingly because much of what students do revolves around reading independently and conferring with the teacher. When the whole class is pulled together, typically for 10–15 minutes, the teacher delivers a mini-lesson called talking points. The term "mini-lesson" is deceptive. The length of a lesson is determined by the complexity of the content, the attention span of the students, and the motivational skills of the teacher. During this time, the teacher might model a strategy or introduce a concept of genre or text structure. Students are given an opportunity to try out the strategy with a partner. The whole class time is also used to survey the reading progress of the class—the status of the class. Here the teachers ask students to give a brief report on what they are reading, where they are in the book and explain something about their book.

Small Group Instruction

Small group instruction is central to the guided reading approach and more peripheral to basal instruction and the reader's workshop. Guided reading takes its name from the guided reading period during which students are organized into leveled reading groups and read a text as the teacher guides them through it. The guided reading period might consume 30 to 90 minutes of the reading time. A teacher might have three to five guided reading groups and meets with them from three to five times a week. The teacher works with the students to use decoding, vocabulary, and comprehension strategies that will improve their reading. When not meeting with the teacher the students read independently, write, or complete learning station activities.

Basal reading programs have brought small group guided reading within their programs. Most basal programs come with leveled texts, small books written for above, on, and below level readers. There is typically a fourth book written for English learners. All of these texts share the same topic or theme as the anthology selection. The key vocabulary words, introduced in the main selection, are reviewed in the leveled books. In most core reading programs, the guided reading portion of the program takes place two days a week with whole group instruction dominating during the rest of the week. Each leveled book comes with its own lesson plan in an attempt to differentiate instruction.

Within the reader's workshop approach small group instruction is an option. Teachers might bring together a group of students who are reading a similar genre to discuss the characteristics of the genre. The teacher can also create guided reading groups with students reading at the same level. This practice blurs the lines between guided reading and reader's workshop. These small group lessons are opportunistic with the teacher pulling together students who need help.

INDEPENDENT READING AND INDEPENDENT WORK

Independent reading defines the reader's workshop approach. Students read individually every day, often for 30 minutes or more, selecting a comfortable place to read within the room. Students read texts at their independent reading level. During the reading time, the students should be reading, not selecting books or wandering in the classroom. A well-stocked classroom library is essential to the success of the workshop. The teacher confers with her students weekly to assess their comprehension, note difficulties they might be having with reading strategies, plan their next book, and hold them accountable. While reading, students are encouraged to "talk back" to the book by using post-it notes or a reading journal to record their thoughts.

Independent reading is one of the activities within the guided reading design. When the students are not part of a small group guided reading experience, they are expected to read and write independently, sometimes with a partner. In a typical guided reading classroom, you will find a number of centers, places where students can read, write, work on an art project, make a scientific observation and record results, or play a language game. The centers are set up to encourage open-ended inquiry. Obviously, the classroom library with comfortable places to sit is a vital center in a guided reading classroom.

Within the basal reading system, independent reading, but not independent work, takes a backseat to the whole group work and the small group guided work. The teacher might meet with her guided reading groups two or three days a week, but that leaves considerable time for independent work. Often, students practice skills using their workbook or work in a learning center suggested by the program. Independent reading is not stressed in the basal programs and rarely mentioned in the lesson plans. There is a financial explanation for this lack of emphasis on independent reading. Basal publishers do not sell trade books the tools of independent reading.

As we noted in Chapter 1, we believe that phonemic awareness, phonics, fluency, vocabulary, and comprehension are vital parts of a reading program. But as we also noted, we and most other reading educators believe firmly that these five elements constitute only part of a comprehensive and balanced reading program that can lead all students to the sophisticated level of literacy necessary in the 21st century. A comprehensive reading program also requires a strong focus on motivation and building knowledge. It is important that children read frequently and widely. It is vital that children learn to read and want to read, since all of us are teaching into the headwinds of social media, iPhones and tablet and other seductive technologies.

Reflect and Apply

7. Basal reading programs, guided reading, and the reader's workshop each have their champions. Consider how the three approaches differ in terms of the teacher's role and the students' activities in the classroom.

8. Locate the teacher's manual from a basal reading program and analyze how comprehension skills are taught. Does the lesson provide for direct explanation, gradual release of responsibility, scaffolding, and contextualized practice?

MyLab Education **Self-Check 2.3**

MyLab Education **Application Exercise 2.3:** Debating Approaches to Reading Instruction

Concluding Remarks

In this chapter, we discussed three topics: First, we took you inside successful classrooms and looked at effective teachers. Next, we discussed traditional principles of instruction and newer constructivist and sociocultural perspectives on instruction. Third, we gave a brief history of reading instruction in the United States, including the most recent federal initiatives.

It is worth summarizing several main points. Both traditional instructional principles, such as fostering active learning and providing sufficient and timely feedback, and constructivist and sociocultural principles, such as cognitive modeling and scaffolding, are important. Instruction is not good simply because it represents an idea that has been around a long time or because it represents a new and different idea. Instruction is good because it is motivated by solid theory, backed by research, and able to be used by real teachers in real classrooms.

The history of reading instruction in the United States indicates that various approaches to reading have come and gone, that we have learned a lot and come to much agreement in recent years, but that tensions continue to exist. The most effective approach to instruction, the one most likely to lead the most children to a high level of literacy, is an eclectic, comprehensive, and balanced approach.

It is also important to realize that effective instruction emphasizes different parts of the curriculum, as students become increasingly competent readers. For example, most children will have mastered most of what they need to know about print and most decoding strategies by the end of second grade, and thus these elements constitute a small part of the literacy curriculum after that time. Conversely, all children should receive instruction in vocabulary and various facets of comprehension beginning in kindergarten and continuing throughout their years of school.

Extending Learning

As we noted in Chapter 1, in this section we suggest activities that take you beyond this book to observe and work with schools, teachers, and parents and to access various sources of information that can help you more fully understand and appreciate your role in fostering students' literacy.

1. Identify a simple skill that you have mastered but that many of your classmates probably have not. Choose

something specific that can be learned relatively easily, such as tying a square knot. Review the traditional and constructivist/sociocultural principles of instruction—active teaching, active learning, scaffolding, gradual release, feedback, and the like—and decide which can be incorporated into your instruction. Next, write out a specific plan for teaching your skill—a lesson plan—noting just what you are going to do and indicating which principles you are following at each point. Rehearse your instruction, with a partner if possible; then teach a small group of your classmates the skill. If possible, have a classmate who is not part of the group observe you. Finally, sit down with your classmates—both the learners and the observer—and critique your instruction, being sure to attend to how well people learned the skill, what did and did not go well, how you might improve the lesson, what instructional principles you followed, and what additional instructional principles you might incorporate to improve learning.

2. Identify two really excellent elementary teachers. These could be teachers who have been formally recognized as outstanding, teachers you know of from friends or colleagues, teachers you actually had, or teachers recommended by a principal or one of your professors. Make up some observation sheets listing the characteristics of teachers who produce outstanding achievement in reading. Go back to the section Highly Effective Teachers and Schools to develop your characteristics. Then, observe the two teachers, and make notes on the extent to which they demonstrate each of the characteristics on the list. Plan on at least three observations, but do more if you can. For each characteristic that the teachers demonstrate, jot down a specific example or two of how they do so. Once you are finished with your observation, write a summary statement on the extent to which the teachers did and did not demonstrate the characteristics and a statement about the extent to which you expect to incorporate the characteristics into your teaching. Finally, discuss your observations and conclusions with a classmate.

Children's Literature

Byars, B. C. (2002). *Keeper of the Doves*. New York: Viking. In this story set in the late 19th century in Kentucky, the precocious Amie McBee searches for her place in the family and discovers a talent of her own, writing poetry. 112 pages.

Inns, C. (2004). *Help!* London: Frances Lincoln. Doctor Hopper (a rabbit) and Nurse Rex Barker (a dog) zoom around to cure sick toys in this witty picture book. 32 pages.

Juster, N. (2005). *The Hello, Goodbye Window*. New York: Hyperion. A little girl visits her grandparents' house and finds a magic gateway in the kitchen window that leads her on a voyage of discovery. 32 pages.

Kehret, P. (1996). *Earthquake Terror*. New York: Puffin. A family is camping when a earthquake hits leaving the old boy to help his disabled sister while his parents go for help.

McDonald, A. (2001). *No More Nasty*. New York: Farrar, Straus and Giroux. Fifth grade becomes more than a bit embarrassing and challenging for Simon when his favorite, but eccentric, 74-year-old aunt becomes the substitute teacher in his unruly class. 172 pages.

National Geographic World. Washington, DC: National Geographic Society. This richly illustrated monthly periodical is designed for intermediate-grade students.

Morpurgo, M. (1999). *Kensuke's Kingdom*. New York: Scholastic. Washed up on an island in the Pacific with his dog, Michael a young teenager, struggles to survive on his own.

Paulsen, G. (1987). Hatchet. New York: Simon and Schuster. Brian, a fourteen year old boy is trapped in the Canadian wilderness after the plane he is riding in crashes. Weeks of difficult challenges lie ahead.

Simon, S. (1995). *Sharks*. New York: HarperCollins. With full-color photos and engaging text that describes fascinating details about 350 different kinds of sharks, Simon demystifies this greatly feared predatory fish. Unnumbered.

Tarshis, L. (2011). *I Survived Hurricane Katrina*. New York: Scholastic. A family must cope with the terror of a hurricane and the city flooding around them.

Chapter 3
Motivation and Engagement

 Learning Outcomes

After reading and studying this chapter you should be able to:

3.1 Understand why motivation and the creation of a literate environment is a top priority in any classroom.

3.2 Describe the components of intrinsic motivation and make decisions about how to implement these factors in the classroom.

3.3 Understand the limits of extrinsic motivation but indicate how and when they might be deployed in the classroom.

3.4 Assess students' motivation to read and use the results to craft a motivation program in your classroom.

Classroom Vignette

Last year, Cynthia Sanchez, who had spent five years working predominantly with inner-city Hispanic students, switched from teaching first grade to fifth grade, and her first year as a fifth-grade teacher was not an easy one. "What a difference four years make," she sometimes sighed to herself. Of course, she had to learn to teach very different aspects of reading than she had taught in first grade. None of her students needed to work on phonemic awareness, only a few needed help with phonics, and many read fluently. She also had to learn to teach fairly sophisticated lessons in social studies, science, math, and other subjects. What turned out to be much more of a challenge than learning how to teach new material, however, was motivating students. Cynthia's first-graders had come to school enthusiastic about their opportunities, excited about learning, confident that they could learn, and ready to put their best efforts into whatever subject they were studying. Some of her fifth-graders displayed very different attitudes. They were not enthusiastic about school or excited about learning. Nor were they confident about learning or prepared to put in their best efforts.

Cynthia soon decided that motivating and engaging students was her number one priority. As the year progressed, she talked regularly with her grade-level colleagues, who had many more years of experience in fifth grade. One colleague stressed that the key to motivation was selecting and reading the right books. She felt that her daily read-alouds from authors like Sandra Cisneros and Gary Soto would capture her students' imaginations. Another colleague urged her to incorporate Accelerated Reader software into her literacy program. Students like the computer-based assessments, and competing for points keeps them motivated. Her final colleague felt that the secret to motivating these students were the projects she developed for her class. Each year they studied the tide pools along the Pacific shore, the Spanish heritage in California, and space science, including a trip to Mt. Wilson observatory. These lengthy reading and writing tasks gave her students concrete goals and a reason to dive into books, articles, and the Internet.

Making Motivation a Top Priority

As you will see in this chapter, Cynthia is not alone in realizing that motivation should be a top priority and also not alone in being bombarded with theories of motivation. Other teachers, reading authorities, researchers, and policy makers are increasingly realizing that motivation is essential to learning (Wigfield, Gladstone, Turci, 2016; National Research Council, 2004; Pressley, 2006). Patricia Alexander properly focused on the role of motivation when she wrote

> . . .reading is an emotional domain, not a coldly cognitive enterprise. Reader motivation and affect are powerful forces in this journey toward competence. We may be able to move individuals into low levels of competence by attending only to their knowledge or strategic needs, but they will not have the personal interest to continue this journey especially as the demands of text-based learning become greater and the text more complex, less predictable (Alexander, 2003.p. 45).

Just as we developed a theory of instruction that should guide your instructional decision making, we will now develop a theory of motivation that should help you shape your students' experience in school. Motivation is complex and not all students are entranced and enticed by the same activities. In order for substantive learning to occur, students must have positive attitudes about themselves as learners, about their ability to succeed in school, and about the instructional goals they, their teachers, and their schools set. Students' reading abilities will grow in direct proportion to the extent to which they see reading as enjoyable, worthwhile, and valuable as a tool for learning.

Motivation is complex because there are many branches to this tree. Figure 3.1 presents a graphic view of motivation in the classroom. The two main branches are intrinsic and extrinsic motivation. Children who have an intrinsic motivation to read do so "because the activity is satisfying and rewarding in its own right" (Schiefele & Schaffner, 2016, p. 429). Extrinsically motivated readers read to get a positive outcome—points, praise, and better grades. To foster intrinsic motivation, teachers must create a literate environment, a physical and emotional space where literacy is valued, encouraged, and practiced. From this branch, each teacher has two major but interconnected goals: creating exciting and stimulating academic tasks that promote learning and motivating children to read as a lifelong pursuit. Academic motivation is fostered by interesting tasks, personal goals,

Figure 3.1 Modeling the Components of Motivation

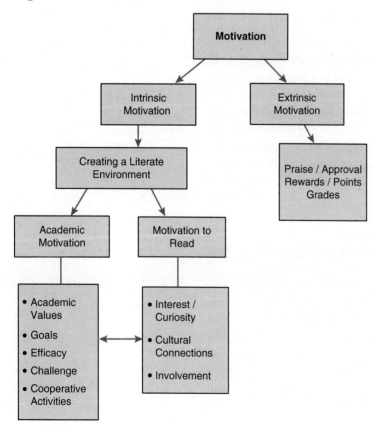

a sense of efficacy, choice, challenge, and cooperative activities. These factors, plus personal interest, cultural connections, and involvement with stories or informational text, also promote the motivation to read. Hanging off the side of the tree is extrinsic motivation, the praise, approval, grades, and points we award to keep some children moving forward but are not substitutes for longer term intrinsic motivation.

Much of the work in your classroom should revolve around interesting, gripping projects like studying a beloved author, a currently popular genre like fantasy, or a topic in science, global warming or social studies, immigration. An extended project like this must capture the interests your students. The student must value this project and see it as an attainable goal. These projects then give you the doorway to introduce the reading strategies students need for success with the project. This is the logic of Concept Oriented Reading Instruction (CORI, see Guthrie and Wigfield, 2000) that produces significant growth in reading achievement. If this logic is correct, then worksheets and workbooks have little value in the classroom.

Beyond academic projects, your students should become readers, individuals who value reading for enjoyment, escape, information, and enlightenment. The students' goal and your goal is not to reach the next reading level, be it a 40 on the Developmental Reading Assessment, or Q on the Fountas and Pinnell scales. Your goals are to foster literate students who read for information and pleasure. In the sections that follow, we will discuss the motivational principles necessary for students to become lifelong readers and to succeed with academic projects.

A dominant thought underlying not just this section of the chapter, but the whole of this book is the overwhelming importance of success. Research has repeatedly verified that if students are going to be motivated and engaged in school and learn from their schoolwork, they need to succeed at the vast majority of tasks they undertake (Brophy, 1986; Pressley, 2006). Students realize success when they gain a sense of efficacy after completing a challenging activity. This, of course, applies to reading just as it does to other schoolwork. Moreover, if students are to become not only proficient readers but also avid readers—children and adults who voluntarily seek out reading as a path to information, enjoyment, and personal fulfillment—then successful reading experiences are even more important.

A successful reading experience has at least three features. First, and most important, a successful reading experience is one in which the reader understands what she has read. Understanding may take more than one reading, it may require your assistance or that of other students, and it will often require the reader to actively manipulate the ideas in the text. Second, a successful reading experience is one that the reader finds enjoyable, entertaining, informative, or thought-provoking. Finally, a successful reading experience is often a means to a larger goal—to learn about galaxies or live in the fantastic world of the Hobbit.

Creating a Literate Environment

The term *literate environment* describes the sort of classroom, school, and home in which literacy is fostered, nurtured, and necessary (Gambrell & Mazzoni, 1999; Goodman, 1986). In a literate environment people read to themselves and to others. They write to others and to themselves. They read and write on paper and on screens. They read and write to manage their daily lives. In a literate environment print surrounds us. There is print on our bookshelves, on our tables, hanging on our refrigerators and bulletin boards. Our laptops and tablets have ads, information, novels, and news stories. Imagine managing your life without literacy. You could not send an email, a text, or a tweet. You could not locate a used car, a good restaurant, or create a shopping list. For students who do not come from a literate environment, we want to create one in their classroom.

Modeling

Probably the most important component of a literate environment is the modeling done by people children respect and love. In the best possible literate environment, children's teachers, principals, parents, brothers and sisters, and friends read a lot and openly display the pleasure reading gives them. These adults regularly demonstrate the fact that reading opens up a world of information and imagination from which they gain knowledge, insight, and joy. Unfortunately, many children come from homes where little or no reading takes place, and schools must be their literate environment (Heath, 1985). According to the Pew Research Center, in 2017, 26 percent of adults did not read a book last year. Among adults with a high school education or less, 40 percent did not read a book last year.

To be most effective, modeling should occur not just once but repeatedly—all the time, really. Modeling should include both repeated demonstrations—your reading along with students during a sustained silent reading period, your work during shared and guided reading, your looking up on the internet an answer to a question children have,—and direct testimonials—"Wow! What a story." "I never knew what fun river rafting could be till I read this article; I sure wish I'd read it sooner." "Sometimes I think the library is just about my favorite place."

Third-grade teacher Mary Lou Flicker has her own testimonial to the power of modeling.

> I never realized the importance of modeling the kinds of behaviors I would like my students to emulate until one rainy day in March. Normally the kids eat outdoors on picnic tables, but during this unusual California downpour we were forced inside for lunch recess. After the kids finished eating, I told them they could play games together quietly, draw on the chalkboard, read, whatever.
>
> Instead of doing paperwork or watching the kids, I decided to read a book that a young friend had recommended, one of Barbara Park's Junie B. Jones books, *Junie B., First Grader: Shipwrecked*. It turned out to be an extremely funny book that I enjoyed immensely. After I finished, I looked around the room. To my amazement, there in the library corner sat Ramon, one of my least-motivated readers, a kid who hardly ever read by choice, fully absorbed in a Junie B. Jones book. Later in the day, when I told Ramon I was so pleased to see him reading, he said, "Well, you looked like you were having such a great time reading that Junie B. Jones book, I just had to find out why!"
>
> —Mary Lou Flicker, third-grade teacher

Several aspects of this experience were motivating to students. First, Ms. Flicker modeled engaged reading. Second, she showed students how much she valued reading by spending class time on reading. Third, she shared her enjoyment. Fourth, she praised her student's good behavior.

Reading aloud to students is another way to demonstrate how much you value reading, and it also becomes an opportunity to teach students about the rewards that reading brings. What you choose to read aloud can serve to entice students to broaden the scope of their reading interests. It allows you to introduce new authors, new genres, and new ideas. All readers need to experience the power of a well-written story, poem, or piece of nonfiction so that they can remember the reward that reading can bring. Reading aloud offers you the opportunity to talk about writing in a way that is concrete and engaging; students enjoy learning about how writing works when they are engaged with a text.

Modeling literate behavior is not limited to reading aloud. We model literate behavior when we write a language experience story in first grade, when we record the number of students selecting pizza versus peanut butter and jelly for lunch, when we record what we have learned about snakes on a science chart, and when we write the new words we are learning on the word wall. In many classrooms the first literate activity after the read-aloud is the use of an agenda to record the work and homework for the day. When children observe adults using written language they begin to understand that written language is a powerful tool for recording, remembering, and planning life.

A Print-Rich Classroom

Three kinds of print should fill your classroom—books, print created by the teacher, and print created by the students. James Hoffman and his colleagues studied literary environments and found that they could link the amount and quality of print in the room to growth in students' reading comprehension (Hoffman, Sailors, Duffy, & Beretvas, 2004). In the best possible literate environment, the classroom is filled with books, books that are readily accessible for students to read in school or take home. Remember, in most schools, children to to the library only once a week. Certainly, some books will be in your classroom because they fit within your curriculum. Other materials should be selected so that students have a wide variety of topics, reading levels, and genres to choose from. Still other books should be chosen to reflect the diversity of your classroom—the range of abilities, interests, and cultural, linguistic, and social backgrounds of your students—as well as the diversity of the larger society outside your classroom. Reading well-written texts should become a tool students use to learn more about topics and ideas they are interested in, as well as supplementing their understanding of the required curriculum. This kind of reading gives students a purpose for practicing the craft of reading.

Digital texts have an important role in the classroom. A teacher should keep a computer nearby to lookup new words, find information on the Internet or project videos, pictures, and diagrams to bring clarity to topics in science and social studies. How much digital text and ebooks promote motivation is an open question, but the use of digital text is growing with 68 percent of children aged 8 to 16 indicating that they are more likely to read on screens outside of school than in school (Picton, 2014). Fifty-two percent of children said they preferred reading on screen rather than paper, while 32 percent preferred paper. Picton's study further reports that the avid readers, those who identify as readers, are those who read on paper and screens or read just on paper. One kind of reading promotes other types of reading. Clearly teachers need to incorporate digital resources as they build a literate environment.

In order to provide all students with appropriate texts and to match individual students with texts, it's important that you assess your students' attitudes toward reading and their reading interests. In the Classroom 3.1 presents an idea for building interest in books.

Finding out about your students as readers is vital to being an effective, motivating teacher. You can find books that will appeal to your students by looking at the following annotated lists:

- The Children's Choices and Teacher's Choice lists, which can be found on the International Literacy Association website https://www.literacyworldwide.org/get-resources/reading-lists
- The Notable Children's Trade Books in the Field of Social Studies list, which appears in the May/June issue of *Social Education*
- To find out what books are popular now look at Renaissance Learning annual report. They gather this data when children take an online test to get credit for a book read. https://www.renaissance.com/learning-analytics/wkar/
- The Outstanding Science Trade Books for Children list, which appears in the November issue of *Children and Science*

In the Classroom 3.1

Creating a Book Review File

Only a few students might read a book because you, the teacher, told them it was good, but most students will read a book that a peer has recommended. Kathy, a third-grade teacher who has a way of maximizing her efforts, developed a quick and effective book review system. When a student finished reading a book, she went to the file (a small box of 5-by-8-inch index cards) and looked it up by the author's name. If someone else had read it, there was a card on file; if not, the student created a card with the author's last name, the author's first name, and the book title. Then, either on a new card or below the comments of others on an existing card, the student wrote a one- or two-sentence opinion of the book. This file became a favorite aid when students were looking for new books for independent reading and often sparked impromptu conversations between students who had read the same book. It was also an opportunity for students to learn the difference between writing an opinion with a supporting reason and writing a brief summary. Summaries weren't allowed in the file.

Another effective strategy for identifying books that your students might enjoy is to talk with your school media specialist or the librarians at a local library. Librarians track the books that children read and check out. They have access to the American Library Association's resources and can give you lists of books that librarians have identified as being of interest to readers of various ages and levels of proficiency. A third way to identify exciting books is to watch the kids. Just like adults, children have their own "bestsellers." Right now, second-graders like *Click, Clack Moo: Cows that Type* (Cronin, 2000), third-grade boys are hiding Captain Underpants books (Pilkey, 2001) in their desks, and many fourth-graders are reading the *Diary of a Wimpy Kid* (Kinney, 2007) or Rick Riordan's Percy Jackson series. Although the literary quality of some books may be questionable, teachers must first help students develop the reading habit; then they can refine taste.

The social, linguistic, and cultural backgrounds of your students and of the greater society constitute yet another important factor in selecting books. Readers shape their views of themselves and of the world partly through what they read. Recognizing yourself in a book is a powerful affirmation that you are part of the human endeavor—and the world of books. Recognizing the humanity of others who might seem different from ourselves is an important part of becoming a citizen of the world. Good books can act as both a mirror and a window for readers (Galda & Cullinan, 2016), reflecting their own lives and offering them a chance to understand the lives of others. Perhaps the best books offer an experience that is similar to looking through a window at twilight. At first you can see through the window into another place, but, as the light gradually fades, you end up seeing yourself (Galda, 1998; Galda & Cullinan, 2016). Thinking and talking about experiences like this can help students develop an understanding of themselves and others. And reading books from many cultures exposes students to many wonderful authors. The Reading Corner provides some books that reflect a variety of cultural experiences.

Beyond books, teachers can and should create print for their classrooms that informs, guides, and reflects learning. The posters, anchor charts, and graphic organizers a teacher creates are far more powerful than the ones bought at the teacher supply store. Those are just wallpaper. If students are studying how to determine the main ideas, teachers should create a chart that reflects the rules and procedures that underlie this strategy. Figure 3.2 is an example of such an anchor chart created by the teacher and students in a fourth-grade classroom. This chart is powerful because the students' thoughts and ideas, guided by the teacher, make up the essence of the strategy.

The Reading Corner

Books about Food and Families in Many Cultures

Alma Flor Ada. *Gathering the Sun: An Alphabet in Spanish and English*. HarperCollins, 2001. Dedicated to Cesar Chavez, this alphabet book recounts stories of family farmworkers during the 1960s. For example, "A is for *arboles*" (trees) shows the fruit trees—plum, pear, peach, and orange—that are so much a part of these families' lives. 40 pages.

Debby Atwell. *The Thanksgiving Door*. Houghton Mifflin, 2003. After burning their Thanksgiving dinner, an elderly couple find themselves the guests of honor at the New World Café, a restaurant owned by welcoming Russian immigrants. 32 pages.

Carmen T. Bernier-Grand. *In the Shade of the Nispero Tree*. Orchard, 1999. Because her mother wants her to be part of the world of high society in their native Puerto Rico, 9-year-old Teresa goes to a private school but loses her best friend. 186 pages.

Nora Dooley. *Everybody Cooks Rice*. Carolrhoda, 1991. Young Carrie gets to sample rice recipes from Barbados, Puerto Rico, Vietnam, India, and more when sent out to fetch her little brother at dinnertime. 32 pages.

Ziporah Hildebrandt. *This Is Our Seder*. Holiday House, 1999. This book provides a simple description of the food and activities at a seder, the ritual meal of Passover, including an explanation of its historical and symbolic significance. 32 pages.

Aylette Jenness. *Families: A Celebration of Diversity, Commitment, and Love*. Houghton Mifflin, 1990. Black-and-white photo essays celebrate the lives of 17 children of many cultures, races, and lifestyles. 48 pages.

Angela Johnson. *The Wedding*. Orchard, 1999. An African American wedding is viewed through the eyes of the bride's younger sister. 32 pages.

Dayal Kaur Khalsa. *How Pizza Came to Queens*. Clarkson N. Potter, 1989. When Mrs. Pellegrino comes to visit May's family, she laments that there is no pizza. So May and her friends, with the help of the librarian who defines the word, buy the ingredients and get Mrs. Pellegrino to make pizza. 24 pages.

Susan Kuklin. *How My Family Lives in America*. Bradbury, 1992. Three young children, an African American, Chinese American, and Hispanic American, describe their families, customs, and favorite recipes. Includes nine recipes for rice. 32 pages.

Patricia McMahon. *Chi-hoom: A Korean Girl*. Boyds Mills, 1993. This photo essay depicting a week in the life of an 8-year-old girl in Seoul gives a sense of an individual's place within a Korean family and culture. 48 pages.

Shulamith Levey Oppenheim. *Ali and the Magic Stew*. Boyds Mills Press, 2002. A beggar helps a young Muslim boy save his seriously ill father by telling him how to get the ingredients for a stew with special healing powers. 32 pages.

Lynn Reiser. *Tortillas and Lullabies/Tortillas y concioncitas*. Greenwillow, 1998. A young girl tells about tortilla making, flower gathering, dress laundering, and lullaby singing—activities her great-grandmother, grandmother, and mother all did and that she does with her doll. The text is in English and Spanish and includes a musical score. 40 pages.

Lisa Shulman. *The Matzo Ball Boy*. Dutton, 2005. In this Jewish version of the "Gingerbread Man," a lonely old *bubbe* makes a matzo ball boy in her chicken soup so he can join her for the Passover seder. 32 pages.

Janet S. Wong. *Apple Pie 4th of July*. Harcourt, 2002. After a young Chinese American girl frets that no one will come to her parents' market to buy Chinese food on the 4th of July, she is happily proven wrong. 32 pages.

Paul Yee. *Roses Sing on New Snow: A Delicious Tale*. Macmillan, 1991. When the governor of South China visits Maylin's home, she creates a new dish in his honor, and her lazy brothers try to take all the credit. However, their attempts to duplicate the recipe only infuriate the emperor, while Maylin triumphs, demonstrating that cooking, like painting, is an art. 32 pages.

Figure 3.2 Main Idea Anchor Chart Developed by Fourth-Graders

How to Find the Main Idea

1. Think about the author's purpose. What did he or she want to write about? Why did he or she write it?
2. Look at the title, headings, and bold print words. What is the topic of the passage?
3. Look for a topic sentence—at the beginning, end, or middle of a paragraph.
4. If you can't find a topic sentence, invent your own main idea.
5. Check: Do the other sentences or ideas support the main idea?

The students' thinking is then preserved as a reminder of how to find the main idea and the students can refer to the chart when they are stumped in the midst of a reading task. You and your students should create all sorts of instructional charts—charts that capture the essence of a strategy or charts that reflect what has been learned—such as a time line of the American Revolution—or charts that serve as a model for good writing—the tall tale created by the class. The very act of creating a chart and hanging it on the wall stresses the importance of the strategy or the concept being taught.

Children's writing should be displayed in the classroom. It is important for teachers to display the stories, reports, and books that students write. You can put their work on a bulletin board; you can bind their stories and add them to the classroom library. These simple acts validate the importance of their writing and encourage others to write. We write well when we have a real audience and the first audience is the other children in the classroom. At least one major bulletin board in your classroom or in the hall should be devoted to students' work and it should change regularly to celebrate achievements.

Organizing Physical Space

The layout of your room influences students' literate behaviors. You need a table at which to meet with small groups. You need desks, arranged in groups for students to work together, and places to hold the computers and print resources that are essential for writing and inquiry. Probably the most important area is the classroom library. It should be large enough, with comfortable seating, so that several children can relax and get lost in books. The classroom library should have at least six to eight books for every child in the room organized by reading level, by genre, and by topic. Some of the books should be displayed with the cover forward to attract the attention of the students. Posters, puppets, beanbag chairs, and an old pole lamp help to set a mood. Rotate the books regularly so that there are always new books to discover. When you introduce new books or a new author, make sure that you call students' attention to these books. Several teachers we know let the students organize the classroom library. This is an excellent way for them to take ownership and as they categorize the books they will learn genre and authors. If you want more ideas about how to merchandise books visit a local bookstore and see how they display books to capture the interest of customers.

Choice

Students need to have choices about what they read and how they respond to their reading. This does not mean that you never assign selections for students to read or prescribe tasks for students to complete after they have read. It does mean that you structure regular opportunities for students to choose their own reading materials and to also choose their own response mode. Allowing students some choice often helps motivate them to spend time reading. In one classroom we observed, the teacher started a literature circle by giving each group a choice of two or three books. The students considered the three selections and then decided which book they wanted to read. This is minimal choice, but enough for the students to exert control and to have their say in the curriculum. Too much choice, as in the expanded types of Oreo cookies or cranberry juices in your local supermarket, is overwhelming. Figure 3.3 will help you find culturally diverse books for your students.

Independent reading provides one opportunity for students to choose. Although students, especially those who are struggling readers as well as many English language learners, need support and guidance in selecting books that they can and will want to read, students should choose their own books for independent reading. Some teachers insist that students choose only from the classroom or school library. We suggest that, if reading is the goal, students ought to be able to read all kinds of texts, print and digital, including newspapers, comic books, and magazines. If we want students to spend

Figure 3.3 Resources for Finding and Evaluating Culturally Diverse Books

Some basic questions to ask yourself as you are selecting culturally diverse literature:

- Does the book qualify as good literature?
- Is the culture accurately portrayed, demonstrating diversity within as well as across cultures if appropriate and avoiding stereotypes?
- Is the book a positive contribution to an understanding of the culture portrayed? (Galda & Cullinan, 2009)

As you are learning to evaluate literature in terms of literary excellence and cultural authenticity, you may want to rely on published lists of books that have been carefully evaluated by experts in the field. Here are some of the better ones:

- Harris, V. (1997). *Using Multiethnic Literature in the K–8 Classroom*. Norwood, MA: Christopher-Gordon.
- Helbig, A. K. & Perkins, A. R. (2000). *Many Peoples, One Land: A Guide to New Multicultural Literature for Children and Young Adults*. Westport, CT: Greenwood.
- International Board on Books for Young People. (Quarterly). *Bookbird: A Journal of International Children's Literature*. Basil, Switzerland: Author.
- Miller-Lachmann, L. (1992). *Our Family, Our Friends, Our World*. New Providence, NJ: Bowker.
- National Council of Teachers of English. (Multiple editions). *Kaleidoscope: A Multicultural Booklist for Grades K–8*. Urbana, IL: Author.
- Stan, S. (2002). *The World Through Children's Books*. Lanham, MD: Scarecrow.
- Tomlinson, C. M. (1998). *Children's Books from Other Countries*. Lanham, MD: Scarecrow.

You might also consult publication lists from publishers such as Lee and Low, Jump at the Sun/Hyperion, Kane/Miller Book Press, Open Hand, Children's Book Press, Arte Publico, and North-South Books, all of which focus on culturally diverse literature.

And here are some of the major awards given for multicultural books:

- Notable Books for a Global Society (February issue of *The Reading Teacher*, International Reading Association /www.reading.org)
- Coretta Scott King Awards (American Library Association /www.ala.org)
- Pura Belpré Award (ALA)
- Mildred Batchelder Award (ALA)

time reading, we must allow them to choose what they read as often as possible. In the Classroom 3.2 offers a suggestion for helping students develop an interest in poetry by making use of these motivating elements—including time for browsing through books, something that often looks unproductive but has been found to be important.

Classroom Climate

In a literate environment, everything that happens in the classroom sends the message that reading—including learning from what you read, having personal responses to what you read, talking about what you read, and writing about what you read—is fantastic! In such a classroom, students are given plenty of time to read, they are given ample opportunities to share the information they learn and their responses to what they have read with each other, they are taught to listen to and respect the ideas of others, and they learn that others will listen to and respect their ideas. A literate atmosphere is a thoughtful atmosphere in which values and ideas are respected especially the values and ideas of others.

This kind of climate is developed when teachers, in a positive and supportive manner, help students learn how to engage in discussions and other forms of sharing what

In the Classroom 3.2

Poetry Browsing to Create Interest

Teacher lore has it that it is often difficult to get upper-elementary students engaged in poetry. Whatever the reasons, upper-elementary readers tend to avoid poetry, unless it is humorous verse by authors such as Shel Silverstein and Jack Prelutsky. But this doesn't always have to be the case. Amy McClure and her colleagues (McClure, Harrison, & Reed, 1990) found that, given time and choice, their upper-elementary students came to really enjoy poetry, even selecting books of poetry for independent reading. After assembling a collection of poetry that might interest their students, McClure and her colleagues added it to the classroom library, displaying it so that students were tempted to look at the books. Then they gave students time to browse—to dip in and out of books, finding poems they enjoyed and wanted to read to their buddies and then moving on. Over time, this freedom to simply enjoy and sample a lot of poetry without any task being assigned broke down the negative attitudes that students began with.

they have read. One way students learn to do this is through watching you modeling how to be positive and supportive as you scaffold students' reading experiences. Even when students are wrong find a tiny kernel of truth to build upon. Modeling and directly teaching students ways to conduct themselves in the classroom, coming up with an agreed-on set of rules for discourse in the classroom, and prominently displaying the rules will also help set the right tone. Trust, respect, and responsibility are important ideas in a safe and supportive classroom, and talking about these concepts and how the successful operation of the class rests on them is crucial, especially at the beginning of the year.

Grouping Students for Instruction

One of the most important decisions you make in your classroom, and one that will have a huge effect on motivation and engagement, is how to group students. Students can be grouped in a variety of ways for a variety of purposes, yet in all too many cases grouping has not been used effectively and has had a negative effect on many students, specifically those students placed in the low-ability groups.

A typical class of 25 to 30 students brings with it 25 to 30 different sets of interests, abilities, attention spans, and reading skills, and it is very difficult to attend to each of these when working with the class as a whole. When teaching the entire class as a single group, teachers tend to teach to an imaginary mean; that is, they gear their instruction to what they perceive to be the middle range of interest, attention span, and ability. Such instruction does not meet the needs of those who are not in this range. Furthermore, in large-group situations, the teacher must work hard to ensure that all students participate.

Dividing students into smaller groups is often helpful for a number of reasons. First, keeping smaller groups of students on task is generally easier than keeping larger groups on task. It is easier to manage the engagement of students in small groups than the whole class and for longer periods of time. Second, smaller groups allow you to provide instruction designed to meet the needs of specific students, differentiating your reading instruction. Especially in the primary grades, the amount of time students spend in small groups has been linked to growth in reading achievement (Taylor, Pearson, Clark, & Walpole, 2000). The more time spent in small group instruction the more students grew in achievement. Finally, smaller groups allow more students to be actively involved in discussions. In a group of six, for example, it is possible for each student to respond to a question and for you to deliver individual feedback.

Given these advantages, it is not surprising that students have often been grouped for reading instruction. But grouping has its downside that requires diligence. Grouping—the high, average, and low group—has typically been based on reading ability (Anderson et al., 1985), leading to a number of disadvantages, particularly for students in low-ability groups. As compared to students in other groups, students in low-ability groups are often given less time to read, spend more time on worksheets and less time being actively instructed, and are asked fewer higher-order questions (Allington, 1983, 1984). None of this is ordained. Effective teachers will have weaker readers read more; they will ask higher-order questions and avoid worksheets. The negative impact of being in the low group—lower self-esteem and lower motivation—can be mitigated by teaching the skills students need and working hard to bring children from the low group to the middle or high group.

Recently, we have become slaves to putting students in the just-right reading level, ignoring students' interests and the knowledge they bring to the book (Hoffman, 2017). Many children can read books above their level, especially if they are interested in the topic. Groups should not be permanent; students in the low-ability group in kindergarten and first grade should not stay in that group throughout the elementary school years (Juel, 1990). At the end of every grade period teachers should ask, how many students from my low group have moved to the middle groups and how many from the middle group have moved to the high group? In the Classroom 3.3 illustrates one way for small groups of students of different reading levels to learn about genre.

In the Classroom 3.3

Heterogeneous Small Groups Learn about Genre

Early each year Ms. Weiss sets the goal of helping her second-graders learn to work in groups and, at the same time, discover the books and genres in the classroom library. She begins with a short whole-class lesson and reads to the students a fantasy (*Ralph's Secret Weapon*, Kellogg, 1986), a biography (*Jackie Robinson*, Prince, 2007), a realistic fiction story (*One Morning in Maine*, McCloskey, 1950), and a folk tale (*Ming Lo Moves the Mountain*, Lobel, 1982). She also discusses the characteristics and purpose of each genre and lists them on the board. The results are recorded on a genre chart that the class will maintain for the next few months. The chart will be kept up in the room and new titles added to the chart over the coming weeks and months as new books are read aloud. The accompanying genre chart is in its early stages. More genres and titles will be added as the students read and discuss more books.

Keeping Track of Our Reading

Genre	Purpose	Characteristics	Examples
Realistic fiction	To entertain, to learn about the big ideas in life	Fiction with real characters, real setting, likely problems and solutions	*One Morning in Maine* *The Voyage of the Frog*
Fantasy	To entertain, to amaze through magic	Fiction with strange or otherworldly settings or characters; fiction that invites suspension of reality	*Ralph's Secret Weapon* *Jumanji*
Biography	To entertain, to inform, to inspire	Narrative of a person's life, a true story about a real person	*Jackie Robinson* *Lincoln: A Photobiography*

Students are then assigned heterogeneously to separate tables and each group is handed a stack of 40 to 50 library books and four large cards labeled Fantasy, Information, Realistic Fiction, and Folk Tale. The students must sort the books into genres by reading a bit of each book and noting the kinds of illustrations or photographs. Because the teacher has organized each stack of books to have at least a few of each genre at a variety of reading levels, all of the students in the group will be able to read some of the books. As the students begin the work, the teacher circulates around the room and provides help as needed. Sometimes it is difficult to distinguish a folk tale from a fantasy. When the students have finished their sorting, each group must pick one book from each pile and share it with the class. Students learn about some interesting books, they begin to understand genre, and the classroom library gets a necessary clean-up.

MyLab Education
Video Example 3.1
Think about the factors that develop motivation from Figure 3.1. How does the teacher develop motivation? What might she add?

Reflect and Apply

1. Describe a successful reading experience you have had in school and an unsuccessful one you have had. What could your teacher have done to make the unsuccessful one more successful?

2. Think about how you choose the books you read as an adult. Do you have favorite authors, topics, genres? Do you follow the recommendations of friends? Do you read book reviews or best-seller lists? How could you incorporate these ideas into your classroom?

MyLab Education **Self-Check 3.1**

MyLab Education **Application Exercise 3.1:** How to Create a Literate Environment

Reading and Learning in the Classroom—Intrinsic Motivation

Students who are intrinsically motivated to read and learn do so because they expect positive and successful experiences. They do not expect praise or points (Schiefele & Loweke, 2018). Intrinsic motivation has been linked to the amount of reading, students' successful use of comprehension strategies, and their growing sense of competence (Schiefele & Schaffner, 2016). Several factors promote students' intrinsic motivation in the classroom: first and foremost is interest. However, interest alone is not enough. The day the bunny escaped from Mrs. Greenwich's classroom was downright enthralling, but it promoted little learning. To promote learning students must value the tasks they are assigned, they need personal goals, they must have confidence in their ability to meet those goals, and, for many, working with others makes the tasks easier and engaging.

Interest

Interest is the liking of a topic, genre, and author and the willingness to engage with that topic or read a book about it. Interest has been shown to influence a student's attention (Hidi, 1995), goals (Pintrich & Zusho, 2002) and levels of learning (Schraw & Dennison, 1994). Interest is not easily distinguished from background knowledge. When a child has a deep interest in skateboards, video games, or Marvel comics, she is also knowledgeable about the topics. At some initial point, knowledge was meager, and curiosity lead the child to the topic or author. As knowledge grew so did interest. As the student explores a topic and builds knowledge the payoff is psychological satisfaction.

Psychologists distinguish between personal interests and situational interests. Personal interests are intrinsic and endure over time, while situational interests can be content specific and activated by the teacher or other student. The escaped bunny prompted situational interest. Teachers tend to think that students either have or do not have an interest in a topic or genre, because we view interests as either on or off. I like basketball, broccoli, and jazz and dislike soccer, carrots, and chamber music.

Our goal as educators is to consider how to create a situational interest and turn that into a personal or enduring interest. Hidi and Renninger (2006) suggest a four-phase model for doing so. We will explore the steps in that model.

1. *Triggered Situational Interest.* A situational interest can be triggered by personal identification with a character in a story or a topic. For example, the teacher decides to read aloud, *Chains* (2008) by Laurie Halse Anderson. In some students this sparks an interest in the American Revolution, in others slavery, and still others want to try another book in Anderson's trilogy—*Forge* or *Ashes*.

2. *Maintained Situational Interest.* The situational interest develops and is nurtured by persistent work with a book, or books, or a topic. The reader is gently hooked. Many instructional conditions can deepen this situational interest, including cooperative group work, project-based learning, or literature circles. The more meaningful the task the more students' interest develop.

3. *Emerging Individual Interest.* After working with a book, a genre, or a topic for some time, the student begins to embrace the author or topic. If given a choice, she is likely to read more books by the same author or on the same topic. She becomes curious and seeks answers when new issues arise. This emerging individual interest is supported by the teacher or other students who might suggest new books or articles on a topic.

4. *Well-Developed Individual Interest.* Having a well-developed personal interest means that the student has very positive feelings for the topic, genre, or author and considerable knowledge about it. Think of the people you know who became passionate about Harry Potter. At this point, interest, knowledge, and value are all linked. A well develop individual interest is rarely self-generated. Often a librarian, a classroom teacher, or another student supports that interest through modeling, providing resources, and discussions.

Making Connections to Students' Cultures and Lives Outside of School

It is not at all surprising that students are more engaged and motivated to learn if they feel that what they are learning is related to their out-of-school lives. Although not every topic in the curriculum is going to be connected to students' home lives and cultures, many of them certainly should be. One of the easiest ways to do this is to carefully select the reading material for your classroom so that it reflects the issues, concerns, and cultures of your students. At the same time, however, we must admit that assuring cultural matches is easier said than done.

For example, Mr. Augustus, a sixth grade teacher, had developed a differentiated literature unit around the theme of survival. One group of boys was reading *The Upstairs Room* (Reiss, 1972), two other groups were reading *The Voyage of the Frog* (Paulsen, 1989), and a few were reading *Baseball Saved Us* (Mochizuki, 1993). Five African American boys were giving up on *The Upstairs Room*, a story about three young Jewish girls hiding in a closet in Holland to escape the Nazis. The boys complained that they just didn't get the book. "Who cares about some girls living 75 years ago." "What does that have to do with me?" Mr. Augustus began to discuss the boys' lives and wondered if they had ever experienced any persecution or discrimination. The boys acknowledged that they and their parents had. The teacher led them from their own experience to that of their parents and grandparents under Jim Crow, the Civil Rights movement, and finally back to life under slavery. With these facts in mind, Mr. Augustus helped the boys make connections between discrimination and persecution in different times and places. The boys made a connection, and the plight of Annie, Sinni, and Rachel hiding in that closet in Holland became important.

Helping students connect to literature requires selecting the right books and making deliberate efforts to link those books to students' lives. Your students all come from families and communities that have as Moll (1992) describes it "funds of knowledge." It is up to you to tap into that knowledge. Well-crafted book talks can move that process along. Teachers should regularly give book talks, at least twice a week, that discuss the genre, theme, and characters of new books. The book talk should make an obvious attempt to relate the book to the students' lives and interests. Although a culturally diverse classroom and school libraries are important no matter whom you teach, it's also important to think about the universals that engage all students. Reading fiction that explores topics such as family, friends, and issues of growing up (such as Lindsay Lee Johnson's middle-grade novel *Worlds Apart*), nonfiction about the wonders of the natural world (such as *Penguin Chick* by Betty Tatham), and inspirational biographies (such as *The Sky's the Limit: Discovery by Women and Girls* by Catherine Thimmesh), can draw your students into the world of reading and help them realize that reading, even the reading they do in school, often relates to their lives outside of school.

Class projects can also help students connect home and school. Rather than researching and writing about a topic that has little connection to their community, students can choose to pursue a topic that has relevance to their lives. For example, a group of sixth-grade students in the Pacific Northwest spent a year doing research and writing about how pollution had destroyed the salmon stream that ran by their school. They read, discussed, and wrote while they also cleaned up the stream. The result was a cleaner stream, heightened community awareness of issues of pollution, and a book, *Come Back, Salmon!*, that chronicled their project. Eventually, the salmon even came back.

English language learners experience more success when they can make connections between what they already know and what they are learning to do (Bear, Helman, Templeton, Invernizzi, & Johnston, 2007). One way to do this is to have children create an identity text. An identity text is one that is grounded in and reflective of children's lives. When completed, these texts "hold a mirror up to students in which their identities are reflected back in a positive light" (Cummins, Brown, & Sayers, 2007, p. 219). One way to do this is to have children create memoirs. Memoirs are, by their nature, grounded in and reflective of children's lives. Every child in the classroom can create a memoir. The children who are English language learners can create memoirs that are dual-language texts. On each page, sentences are first written in the child's home language. Then they are written in English, one language on top of the other. When completed, these texts "hold a mirror up to students in which their identities are reflected back in a positive light" (Cummins, Brown, & Sayer, 2007, p. 219).

Promoting Academic Values and Goals

Ultimately, motivation and engagement are intrapersonal values, and it is the student herself who must become motivated and engaged—with school and schooling. The fact is that a good deal of schoolwork is just that—work—and we need to find ways to help students truly value that work. All students approach an assignment by asking themselves a complex question. "How hard do I want to work given the interest of the task and the likely payoff?" Worksheets are boring and there are many, so students place little value on completing them. In contrast, reading about aerodynamics to construct paper airplanes that will be launched from the roof of the school to win a trophy has intrinsic interest and a powerful goal.

Every school day should start with a very short discussion about what we are going to do and why it is important. Students need to think about school not as a set of activities that they dutifully complete, but as important tasks chosen by the teacher and the students to build their skill and knowledge. In this short introduction to the day, plant a sense of anticipation, give students something to look forward to—a video from the Internet, a new read-aloud, an experiment in science. Much as the news teases us with an upcoming segment, we can keep the students engaged with less than brilliant activities—we are not always that creative—while they look forward to some exciting event in the afternoon. End every day with a short statement about what the class accomplished and what they learned. At home that night students will have something interesting to talk about school.

Keep in mind that students have different goals when they enter your classroom. Some are looking forward to the book you are reading aloud or the topic they are studying. The intrinsic interest drives them. Others work hard because they want a good grade and all A's on their report card will make them and their parents proud. Still others are willing to work if they can work with others. Keep these different goal orientations in mind as you interact with different students. Some can be prompted to work hard for the grade, for others the grade is less important than the topic or the task.

Our final suggestion for promoting academic values and goals is to make learning experiences enjoyable. As Nel Noddings eloquently argues in *Happiness and Education* (2003), happiness should be a major goal of education, but frequently is not. We have already said that a good deal of schoolwork is indeed work, and there is no getting around that. But nothing says that work cannot be made as enjoyable as possible. If, for example, students are learning how to make inferences, teachers can choose texts that students find enjoyable to make the point. For example, "getting" jokes often require inferences, and reading them is wonderful practice. Stories also often require inferences about, for example, a character's motives. Speculating about why a compelling character is behaving in a particular way is much more interesting than filling out a worksheet so students can practice making inferences by circling the correct answer from four choices.

Efficacy and Positive Attributions

Students' self-perceptions influence their motivation, their performance, and especially their sense of efficacy or confidence. Educators and psychologists who study motivation know that the way people view their successes and failures, what has come to be called their *attributions*, has a powerful effect on motivation. Students should enter a new task or open a new book with the sense that they will succeed. If they do succeed, their sense of efficacy grows as does their motivation. If they fail and do so repeatedly, they acquire a sense of learned helplessness. Students need appropriate challenge, and they need to learn how to interpret their success and failures.

Attribution theory helps to explain and underscore the importance of success to student motivation and engagement. Attribution theory deals with students' perceptions of the causes of their successes and failures in learning. As Merlin Wittrock (1986) explains, in deciding why they succeed or fail in reading tasks, students can attribute their performance to ability, effort, luck, the difficulty of the reading task, or the kindness of teachers. All too often, children who have repeatedly failed in reading attribute their failure to factors that are unchangeable and beyond their control—such as their perceived innate inability. One student in our experience simply stated, "I can't read; I have dyslexia." Whether we like it or not, placements in special programs contribute to these negative self-perceptions. Once this happens, children are likely to lose their motivation to read and to doubt their ability to learn. From the children's perspective, there is no reason to try because there is nothing they can do about it. Moreover, as long as they do not try, they cannot fail; you cannot lose a race if you do not enter it.

LEARNED HELPLESSNESS
As Peter Johnston and Peter Winograd (1985) have pointed out, one long-term outcome of children's repeatedly attributing failure in reading to forces beyond their control is the learned helplessness syndrome. Children who exhibit learned helplessness in reading are apt to be nervous, withdrawn, and discouraged when they are faced with reading tasks. They are unlikely to be actively engaged in reading, to have goals and plans when they read, to monitor themselves when they are reading to see if the reading makes sense, or to check themselves after reading to see if they have accomplished their reading goal.

Obviously, we need to avoid this debilitating cycle of negative attributions and learned helplessness. Second-grade teacher Jerry Costello suggests four approaches:

> The first, and almost certainly the most powerful, way I have found to help students understand that they are in control of their learning is something I hear stressed over and over again by my colleagues and read in the literature: Make students' reading experiences successful ones; make them so frequently successful for students that they will be compelled to realize that it is they themselves and not some outside force that is responsible for their success.
>
> Second, I tell students that their efforts *make a difference*, and when they are successful in a reading task, I talk to them about the activities they engaged in to make them successful. Teaching specific strategies is critical. If a student learns to predict and reread and their performance on a test or project improves I can help them attribute their success to these very specific actions. If they understand that their success stemmed from specific strategies they can control then they can alter their attributions. I usually confer with individual students and help them understand how their efforts and their strategies made a difference. This gives them a sense of control.
>
> Third, I avoid competitive situations in which students compare how well they read a selection to how well others read it and instead focus students' attention on what they personally gained from the selection.
>
> Finally, I try to provide a number of reading activities in which the goal is simply to *enjoy reading*, have fun, and experience something interesting and exciting rather than only offering reading activities that are followed by answering questions or some other sort of external accountability.
>
> —Jerry Costello, second-grade teacher

The Importance of Appropriate Challenges

All readers need to undertake some challenging tasks; unless they are willing to take some risks and make some uncertain attempts they are not certain of, there is little room or reason for learning to take place (Pressley, 2006; Taylor et al., 2002). As Mihaly Csikszentmihalyi (1990) has learned from three decades of research on what makes people's lives happier and more meaningful, that facing and meeting significant challenges is one of the most self-fulfilling and rewarding experiences we can have. However, when we present students with challenges, we need to be certain that they clearly understand the goals toward which they are working, to give them challenges appropriate for their skills, and to provide them with whatever support they need to meet these challenges. This is, of course, true for all students, but it is particularly true for those students who have often found school difficult. In the Classroom 3.4, which is based on an actual lesson one of the authors observed, shows how one teacher managed this balancing act. About half-way through the lesson the teacher and I looked at each other and nodded, acknowledging the fact that the students were so engrossed that there was little for any adult to do.

Can you see how this activity appropriately challenged the students? The anticipation guide provided a task that all of the students could complete. It also created a sense of intrigue or mystery. The students wanted to see if they were right or wrong. They wanted to solve the puzzle. The original book, *All About Snakes*, was at the students' reading level and the initial instruction on text features helped the students navigate the text. The library books provided additional information, and because these books came from a variety of reading levels, all students could find additional books they could read. Even difficult texts could be used because the students knew how to locate

In the Classroom 3.4

Providing Both Challenges and Supports

Mrs. Montano's goal is to teach her second-graders how to read informational text. For one of her groups she has selected the book *All About Snakes*—an intriguing topic. She starts the lesson by discussing the features of informational texts and their purpose. She points out the title and asks the students why a book has a title. "To tell what it is about." "So you can decide if you want to read it." These ideas are recorded on the chart. Next, the students consider the purpose of the table of contents, index, headings, bold print words, charts, graphs, pictures, and captions. Each feature is noted on the chart and its purpose is described. Mrs. Montano explains how we will use these features to help us understand what we are reading and to locate information. She models this briefly with a book about spiders.

Conventions and Purposes Chart for Exploring the Structure of Informational Text

Text Conventions	Purposes
Title	Identifies topic or subject, creates interest
Table of contents	Helps to locate specific topics
Headings	Identify the topic or purpose of a section
Subheadings	Identify the topic or purpose of a paragraph or more
Bold print	Highlights important concepts that demand attention and understanding
Picture	Helps us understand more about the text
Caption	Explains a picture or a chart
Index	Helps to locate specific information

The class then moves to their reading groups and one group of nine students begins to work with the teacher. In addition to *All About Snakes*, the teacher has brought from the library 25 additional books about snakes at various reading levels. Mrs. Montano presents the anticipation guide shown here. The students' task before they read the book is to guess, based on their knowledge, the truth of each statement about snakes. Working independently, the students ponder and complete the guide. Then the teacher explains that they are to work with a partner and read *All About Snakes* to determine whether their guess is correct. If they can't find the information in the book, they are free to read in any of the other books from the library.

The students begin to work. They read, they search, they argue. Some answers are found and others are not. They grab other books and turn to the index or the table of contents to locate information about statements they have not yet verified. Note how the Conventions and Purposes chart used at the beginning of the lesson helped the students locate the information they needed. There is a very high level of engagement in the group. Some students begin to argue with each other and point to books to substantiate their claims. The students talk almost exclusively to each other and the teacher is largely ignored. Occasionally, Mrs. Montano has to quiet the group, but otherwise they continue to work. The anticipation guide task is completed quickly, but the students continue to read the library books.

Anticipation Guide

Before Reading	Statement	After Reading
1. True False	Farmers do not like to have snakes on their farms.	1. True False
2. True False		2. True False
3. True False		3. True False
4. True False		4. True False
5. True False		5. True False
6. True False		6. True False
7. True False		7. True False

information. Finally, the students worked with a partner. This provided additional support; if one could not locate the necessary information the other could.

Using Cooperative Activities to Insure Active Participation

Students are a lot more motivated when actively engaged in learning. This is true for elementary students and for college students; if you are using this book as part of a college class, we hope you are engaged in active learning as part of your class. Such activities include constructing models, role-playing teaching situations, doing experiments, creating examples, and observing in classrooms and reporting back to your peers. Students in one study (Boaler, 2002), for example, noted that "you learn more by doing something on your own," "you feel more proud of the projects when you've done them yourself," and "because you had to work out for yourself what was going on, you had to use your own ideas."

Cooperative learning is another form of active learning that has become very widely used, and it offers different benefits and motivation. Importantly, the advantages of cooperative learning have been found to occur in a variety of domains(Johnson & Johnson, 1989). Students in cooperative groups showed superior performance in academic achievement, displayed more self-esteem, accommodated better to mainstreamed students, showed more positive attitudes toward school, and generally displayed better overall psychological health. Students in cooperative groups displayed better interpersonal relationships; and these improved interpersonal relationships held regardless of differences in ability, sex, ethnicity, or social class. Moreover, cooperative learning has been shown to be successful in teaching students how to resolve conflicts (Johnson & Johnson, 2002). Finally, cooperative learning can create a classroom in which students share the responsibility for each other's learning rather than compete with each other—a very positive situation. The reduces the alienation for students who often do not do well in school and often on their own performing more poorly than their classmates (Cohen, 1994). For some students, the social nature of school—that's where their friends are—is more important than the academic tasks. Working in groups satisfies their social needs while they learn new content and skills.

A number of authors (Aronson & Patnoe, 1997; Cohen, 1994; Johnson et al., 1994; Slavin, 1987) have described approaches to cooperative learning, and using more than one approach can provide variety and accomplish somewhat different purposes. Moreover, as the title of this section suggests, variety itself tends to be motivating and engaging for students. No one likes to do the same thing in the same way all the time, and sometimes adding variety just to add variety makes good sense. Cooperative groups can work as literature circles, book clubs, inquiry groups developing a report, or teams experimenting with a new science concept (see Chapter 11).

To close this section, we want to reiterate that you have two goals: engaging students in motivating academic tasks and motivating students to read. Similar factors underlie each goal. Choice, challenge, and efficacy are essential for deep involvement in academic tasks and for turning reluctant readers into avid readers. Interest and tasks that students value motivate them to work on a project or read a book.

MyLab Education
Video Example 3.2
Think about how a growing sense of competence and choice builds motivation.

MyLab Education **Self-Check 3.2**

MyLab Education **Application Exercise 3.2:** Designing a Lesson to Maximize Motivation

Motivating Students Extrinsically

Extrinsic motivation is frequently employed by teachers and parents. They are using it when a child earns points for reading a book, praise for completing an assignment, or when a class receives a pizza party at the end of the year for reading 500 books. Even earning an A in reading can be considered an extrinsic reward. Extrinsically motivated readers strive to attain some goal that is outside the book or the task (Wigfield & Guthrie, 1997). Extrinsic motivators such as grades, competition, and social recognition seem unrelated to how much students choose to read or to their development of reading fluency and comprehension (Schiefele & Schaffner, 2016). But extrinsic motivators are not all bad, especially when used in combination with the strong intrinsic tools we have already discussed (Gambrell & Marinak, 1997).

Praise and Points

Praise can be an effective motivator, and it is certainly a widely used tool. Nevertheless, praise is not without its potential drawbacks. Most importantly, it must be honest, and students must perceive it as honest. According to Guthrie and Wigfield (2000), effective praise is given only in response to students' efforts and achievements, specifies just what students have accomplished to earn the praise, and helps students better appreciate their work. Guthrie and Wigfield also note that effective praise makes it clear to students that they should attribute their success to effort and to the strategies that they used to accomplish the task for which they are being praised.

Before we can praise we have to help students set goals. Students who set goals to learn certain content or strategy are more motivated to learn than students who do not. Teachers who work with their students to set appropriate learning goals are helping to foster students' long-term engagement and learning (Ames, 1992; Maehr & Midgley, 1996). Once the goals are set, we should help students understand how they are progressing in meeting those goals. Praise has an effect once students recognize their own achievements.

Grades

Grades are an essential extrinsic motivation tool. It is hard to imagine a school without some system for reporting achievement and progress to students and parents. Like most extrinsic tools, grades have little effect on the students' motivation to read, but they can be useful to motivate some learning activities. For students who set their goals on earning good grades, the inducement of a higher grade can spur them on to work harder on a project. Other students are motivated by the interest in the project and the possibility of public recognition at the school-wide science fair. As you get to know your students, you can tailor your motivational messages to each individual. Grades seem to have more effect on the motivation to read and on reading achievement for some students while others are more motivated by the project or the activity (Schiefele, Schaffner, Möller, & Wigfield, 2012)

Rewards other than praise—points, stars, books, pizzas—can sometimes be effective in the short run. However, one of the most consistent and strongest cautions in the literature on motivation is that extrinsic rewards can undermine motivation in the long run (Guthrie & Wigfield, 2000; National Research Council, 2004; Stipek, 2002). When students become accustomed to getting extrinsic rewards for reading, they may begin reading solely or largely to get the extrinsic reward and actually discontinue reading when the extrinsic rewards are no longer available. Our goal should always be to demonstrate to students that reading is worthwhile for its own sake—for the learning, enjoyment, and satisfaction that it brings. Our greatest tools in accomplishing this goal are giving students good books and other materials to read and scaffolding their efforts so that they can successfully comprehend.

Technology

Two computer-based programs, Accelerated Reader (Renaissance Learning) and Reading Counts (Scholastic), are widely used to promote reading and provide motivation. These very similar programs are designed to motivate reading, promote increased time for reading, assess comprehension with computer-based tests, and reward students with points when they have successfully read a book and passed a test. Many teachers and schools believe that these two programs are at the core of their efforts to motivate students. However, the programs have their pitfalls—some students don't like to read for points, and many books are not yet on the system. Yet the largest problem is that points or other extrinsic rewards do not build a long-term love of reading (Krashen, 2003). Students who actively use these programs in school have no increased motivation to read on their own.

Factors That Undermine Motivation

In order to understand just what something is, it is often useful to understand what it is not. Although we certainly do not want to dwell on the negative, we do want to list some factors that undermine motivation. Pressley and his colleagues (Bogner, Raphael, & Pressley, 2002; Dolezal, Welch, Pressley, & Vincent 2003; Pressley et al., 2003) have identified a number of these factors. A few of them are listed in Figure 3.4. Pressley et al. (2003) provide a much longer list. Most unfortunately, when Pressley and his colleagues (2003) observed primary-grade classrooms, they found many of these factors present.

Figure 3.4 Some Factors That Undermine Motivation

Physical Environment

- Few examples of students' work and accomplishments are shown on the walls.
- The room is sparsely decorated, with few posters, pictures, or other elements to make it more attractive and inviting.

Psychological Environment

- The teacher does not have or communicate to students that she has high expectations for their learning.
- The atmosphere fostered by the teacher is not cooperative, and no sense of community and students helping and respecting each other is developed.
- The teacher communicates to students that getting the right answers and high grades are the most important part of school.
- The teacher gives students very little praise.

Classroom Instruction

- The teacher does not check for understanding before moving on.
- The teacher does not use opportunities to connect lessons to other concepts in the curriculum, to previous learning experiences, or to the world outside of school.
- The teacher does not give students time to process questions and think about answers before calling on them.
- The teacher is not fully prepared for the day's lessons.

Classroom Management

- The teacher does not check students' progress as they work and fails to notice students' confusion or off-task behavior.
- The teacher uses negative, punishing techniques to maintain order in the classroom.

SOURCE: Based on Pressley, M., Dolezal, S. E., Raphael, L., Mohan, L., Bogner, K., & Roehrig, A. (2003). Motivating primary grade students. New York: Guilford Press.

Reflect and Apply

3. Explain two or three things you might do to help a shy second-grader who tends to lack confidence in her ability develop a more positive attitude toward herself as a learner.

4. Now explain two or three things you would not do so that you do not further undermine her attitude toward herself as a learner.

5. Suppose you want to convince your fourth-graders that although schoolwork can be challenging, it is worth doing well and doing their schoolwork well will give them a sense of accomplishment and pride. Jot down what you might say to them.

MyLab Education **Self-Check 3.3**

Nancy Masters, a Superstar at Motivating Students

Nancy Masters is a truly outstanding teacher who was observed by Pressley and his colleagues as part of their in-depth studies of motivation in primary-grade classes (Bogner et al., 2002; Pressley et al., 2003). Here is a description of her efforts.[1]

On a typical day, Nancy Masters used more than 40 different positive motivational mechanisms to inspire and engage her students. Her classroom was filled to over-flowing with motivating activities and a positive tone. Cooperation was emphasized consistently during both whole-group and small-group instruction. Thus, when students read books with partners, Ms. Masters reminded them that, "The point is, you're supposed to help your partner." She provided reassurance and interesting scaffolding when students took on challenging activities. Thus, before a test requiring application of phonics skills, Ms. Masters reminded her students of the phonics they had been learning and emphasized that they should apply what they knew about phonics on the upcoming test.

Ms. Masters emphasized depth in her teaching, covering mature and interesting ideas. For example, during Black History Month, students not only completed detailed group book reports about five prominent African Americans, she led a discussion about the Jim Crow laws, one in which the students participated enthusiastically, demonstrating they had learned a great deal about discrimination during the month. During this conversation, Ms. Masters talked about different ways that people can affect social change, covering civil disobedience, disobeying unjust laws, and working within the system to change such laws. She and the first-grade students discussed equality and inequality, with student comments reflecting their grasp of some very difficult concepts.

Nancy Masters' teaching connected across the curriculum and community, between school and home. During the first month of the school year, she took her class to visit the kindergarten room. In doing so, she began to become acquainted with her future students while forging connections across grade levels for the kindergarten and grade-1 students. Her students wrote in their journals about this visit. When they wrote stories a few weeks later, Ms. Masters held out as a carrot another visit to the kindergarten room. She told her grade-1 students, "Maybe we'll show the kindergarten [your stories]." Nancy also pointed out times when students' home experience connected with school. Thus, when a student read the word "little" very quickly, Ms. Masters commented, "Have you been working at home with your Mom? I'm so proud of you!" In doing so, she simultaneously emphasized the importance of effort and homework while connecting to the student's home life. Ms. Masters also hosted a career day during which parents talked about and demonstrated their professional skills. After the visits, the students wrote in journals and did an at-home art project about their favorite profession. This special home assignment complemented the regular homework, which consisted of reading 15 minutes a night, doing a short math worksheet, and practicing spelling words.

Nancy Masters gave many opportunistic mini-lessons. In-class assignments seemed appropriately challenging and engaging (i.e., students could not finish them quickly, and they seemed interested in them). Her emphasis on good literature, the writing process, and comprehension were apparent during every class visit. Also, the class constructed many products, which were tangible evidence of accomplishment, including big books that were displayed prominently in the classroom and discussed often. Ms. Masters promised the class that each one of them would be able to take home one class-constructed book at the end of the year. She made many across-curriculum connections for her students (e.g., having students use the internet and the library to find material about Black History Month, material then used in writing an essay).

Ms. Masters expressively communicated with students. As she read to students, she modeled her interest and enthusiasm and reflected her curiosity about what would happen next in a story, often creating a sense of suspense about the events in a reading. When the class received a new basal reader, she opened it and said, "A brand new book!! It's like a present. I know you want to open it and look inside. Go ahead and look inside. See anything interesting? Anything you've read?"

Ms. Masters provided clear learning objectives and goals. Thus, at the beginning of the school year, she had the students copy stories she had written on the board, explaining they were copying stories so that "You can see what good writing looks like." Similarly, when she taught strategies during writing workshop, Ms. Masters emphasized that the use of the strategies would help students write as they needed to write by the end of grade 1.

Nancy Masters emphasized effort attributions. Thus, on the day report cards were distributed to students, she told the students twice that their most important grade was their grade for effort. She and her students often used the term "personal best" to describe how they were doing.

Nancy Masters monitored the students well. She often said, "When I come around, I want to hear you reading or helping your partner or discussing the story." During her walk-arounds, she provided help to students who were struggling.

Of course, Ms. Masters' efforts to motivate her students paid off. There was consistently high engagement in her class. The pace was always quick. The assignments were always interesting. She excited her students about their work. Her students were always engaged in productive work!

Reflect and Apply

6. Reread the description of Nancy Masters's motivational activities in her first-grade class and pick out five activities that would work just as well with fourth- or fifth-graders. Now look back at the description and see if you can find any activities that would be inappropriate for fourth- or fifth-graders. How many did you find? What does this suggest about the extent to which motivational principles are applicable across grade levels?

7. Because grouping can have such a strong effect on students' learning, it is important that you fully understand its possible effects. Toward this end, get together with a small group of your classmates, generate a list of positive and negative effects of grouping, and brainstorm a list of ways in which you can maximize the positive effects of grouping and minimize the negative ones.

Assessing Students' Motivation

Spend a few minutes in an elementary classroom and it becomes relatively obvious who are the readers and who are not. The readers have books on their desks, often more than one. The non-readers do not, or often the book they hold is beyond their reading level or mostly pictures with captions. During free time readers read and non-readers wander the room looking for a book that is quickly abandoned. During the weekly visit to the library readers easily find the next book, non-readers need considerable guidance. Your observations in the classroom and the library yield many insights about students' reading motivation. Simply asking students about the book on their desk will tell you more than the Accelerated Reader report that your printer spits out. In the Classroom 3.5 gives you another way to assess your students' motivation.

Beyond classroom observations there are a number of tools, or surveys, that a teacher can use to gain a deeper understanding of students' reading motivation. McKenna and his colleagues (1995, 2012) developed a survey tool that helps to quantify

In the Classroom 3.5

Assessing Students' Reading Attitudes and Interests

It's important that you get to know your students as readers early in the academic year. You can find out about their reading habits and preferences by having a one-on-one book conference with each of them, and with primary-grade children that's what you need to do. But with older students, a faster and more efficient way to get the information you need is to have them fill out a brief written survey. You can easily create a set of questions that will give you the information you need, such as the following:

- Do you like to read? Why or why not?
- Are you reading anything for fun at this time? What is it? Why do you like it?
- Do you have any favorite authors or titles? Why are these your favorites?
- Is there a certain kind of text that you prefer—books, magazines, fiction, nonfiction, or some other format?
- How do you choose what to read when you go to a library or book store?
- What do you do if what you are reading is too hard or too easy for you?
- What makes a good reader?

Figure 3.5 Assessing Home and School Preferences for Reading Print and Digital Text

	Academic Reading	**Recreational Reading**
Digital	• How do you feel about reading news online for class? • How do you feel about reading a book online for class?	• How do you feel about texting your friends in your free time? • How do you feel about being on a social website like Facebook?
Print	• How do you feel about reading a textbook? • How do you feel about reading a novel for class?	• How do you feel about reading a book in your free time? • How do you feel about getting a book or magazine as a present?

SOURCE: Based on McKenna, M. C., Conradi, K., Lawrence, C., Jang, B. G., & Meyer, J. P. (2012). Reading attitudes of middle school students: Results of a U.S. survey. Reading Research Quarterly, 47(3), 283–306.

a students' motivation for reading at home, recreational reading, and their motivation to read in school with either print or digital sources. The students respond to questions like, "How do you feel about reading news online?" (Academic and digital), or "How do you feel about reading anything printed?" (Recreational, print) on a six-point scale—Very Good (6) to Very Bad (1). Figure 3.5 presents some examples of the survey. The results of this survey could help teachers understand students' attitudes toward reading in school versus reading at home with different types of text.

If you want to deepen your exploration of students' motivation, you could use the Motivation for Reading Questionnaire (MQR) developed by Wigfield and Guthrie (1997). This tool examines eleven dimensions of motivation—curiosity, involvement, competition, recognition, grades, challenge, work avoidance, social, compliance, efficacy, and importance. The MRQ provides considerable information but so far no one has demonstrated that the information provided would help a teacher create a successful motivational program.

We recommend the somewhat simpler tool, the Reading Motivation Questionnaire (RMQ) that looks at six factors of reading motivation (Schiefle & Schaffner, 2016). Curiosity, involvement, and emotional regulation are aspects of intrinsic motivation. Grades, competition and social recognition are part of extrinsic motivation. In Figure 3.6 we present a sample of items from each category. In the Appendix you will find the complete survey.

MyLab Education
Click here to download a printable version of Figure 3.6

Figure 3.6 Assessing Reading Motivation from the Reading Motivation Questionnaire*

Intrinsic Factors	**Extrinsic Factors**
I read...	*I read...*
Curiosity *because I can learn more about things of interest to me.*	**Grades** *Because it helps me get better in school.*
Involvement *because some stories stimulate my imagination.*	**Competition** *because it helps me perform better in school than my classmates.*
Emotional regulation *because it helps me when I am sad.*	**Social recognition** *because it is important for me to be among the best students.*

SOURCE: Based on Schiefele & Schaffner, 2016. Factorial and Construct Validity of a New Instrument for the Assessment of Reading Motivation. Reading Research Quarterly, 51(2), 221–237.

The information from the RMQ could possibly help the teacher design her classroom motivational program. If the new class is highly motivated to read for intrinsic reasons, the teacher might spend less time on developing interest herself, and let the students inform one another. Sharing books would be an excellent idea. A troubled student who is high on emotional regulation might find solace in a book that addresses personal issues similar to her own. Knowing that a student reads for mainly extrinsic reasons might guide a teacher to stimulate a student curiosity or heighten his involvement through the selection of very compelling books. The RMQ could also be used in the classroom, to evaluate a teacher's success in building reading motivation over the year.

MyLab Education **Self-Check 3.4**

MyLab Education **Application Exercise 3.3:** Assessing Reading Motivation and Applying the Results

---

Concluding Remarks

Creating a motivating and engaging classroom means creating a literate environment—a place, a space, a collection of texts, and an atmosphere—where reading and learning thrive. In motivating and engaging classrooms, students learn to attribute their successes and failures to factors under their control and to avoid learned helplessness. And in motivating and engaging classrooms, teachers employ myriad approaches to motivating students—including but not limited to ensuring student success, fostering higher-order thinking, employing meaningful tasks, and making connections to students' cultures and lives outside of school.

We close the chapter with two sets of recommendations, found in Figure 3.7, for motivating students. The first is a set that Pressley and his colleagues (2003) gleaned from the work of Brophy (1986, 1987), recommendations made nearly 20 years ago. The second is a set that one of us (Graves, 2004b) gleaned from the work of Pressley and his colleagues (Bogner et al., 2002; Dolezal et al., 2003; Pressley, 2006; Pressley et al., 2003). As you read them, we hope that you will notice two points. First, the two sets of recommendations overlap a good deal with each other. Second, both sets overlap a good deal with the recommendations we make in this chapter. Our point is this: We know how to motivate and engage students; our task is to put this knowledge into action. In the remainder of this book and in our day-to-day teaching in our own classrooms, we keep these recommendations at the center of our thinking. We encourage you to do the same.

Figure 3.7 Research-Based Motivational Strategies

Motivational Strategies Gleaned from Brophy

- Model interest in learning…. Communicate to students that there is good reason to be enthusiastic about what goes on in school. The message should be that what is presented in school deserves intense attention, with the teacher doing all that is possible to focus students' attention on important academic matters.
- What is being taught, in fact, should be worth learning!
- Keep anxiety down in the classroom. Learning should be emphasized rather than testing.
- Induce curiosity and suspense, for example, by having students make predictions about what they are about to learn.
- Make abstract material more concrete and understandable.
- Let students know the learning objectives so that it is very clear what is to be learned.

- Provide informative feedback, especially praise when students deserve it.
- Give assignments that provide feedback (to your students and to yourself).
- Adapt academic tasks to students' interests and provide novel content as much as possible. (Do not cover material students already know just because it is the mandated curriculum.)
- Give students choices between alternative tasks (for example, selecting one of several books to read).
- Allow students as much autonomy as is possible in doing tasks. Thus, to the extent students can do it on their own, let them do it.
- Design tasks to contain an engaging activity (for example, role playing), product (for example, a class-composed book), or game (for example, riddles).

SOURCE: Pressley, M., Dolezal, S. E., Raphael, L., Mohan, L., Bogner, K., & Roehrig, A. (2003). Motivating primary grade students. New York: Guilford Press.

(*Continued*)

Figure 3.7 (Continued)

Motivational Strategies Gleaned from Pressley and His Colleagues

- Demonstrate your deep concern for students.
- Do everything possible to ensure students' success.
- Scaffold students' learning.
- Present appropriate challenges.
- Support risk taking and help students realize that failures will sometimes occur.
- Encourage students to attribute their successes to their efforts and realize that additional effort can help avoid failures.

- Encourage cooperative learning and discourage competition.
- Favor depth of coverage over breadth of coverage.
- Communicate to students that many academic tasks require and deserve intense attention and effort.
- Make tasks moderately challenging.

SOURCE: Graves, M. F. (2004b). Theories and constructs that have made a significant difference in adolescent literacy—but that have the potential to produce still more positive benefits. In T. Jetton & J. A. Dole (Eds.), Adolescent literacy research and practice (pp. 433–452). New York: Guilford Press.

Extending Learning

1. Spend some time observing a classroom at a grade level you find particularly interesting. Take notes on what you see. What opportunities for engaging in literacy activities are present? How welcoming is the physical setting? What materials are available? Then watch how the teacher and students interact in the classroom. Is the atmosphere safe and supportive? Are students enthusiastic and engaged? Finally, create a list of things to do and a list of things to avoid doing in order to best motivate students.

2. The lists that you created in the activity in item 1 represent your judgment based on your observation.

There are other sources of information that deserve to be considered. One is the teacher you observed. Talk to the teacher and get his or her perceptions on what motivates students and which specific things he or she does to motivate them. The other source is, of course, students. Talk to a half dozen or so students and get their perceptions of what is and is not motivating in their classrooms. Once you have the teacher's and some students' perspectives, compare them to your lists and revise or fine-tune your lists as seems appropriate.

Children's Literature

Anderson, L. H. (2008). *Chains.* New York: Atheneum. The author explores the themes of slavery and power during the American Revolution. This is the first in a trilogy followed by *Forge* and *Ashes.*

Cronin, D. (2016). *Click, Clack, Moo Cows that Type.* New York: Simon Spotlight.

Gibbons, G. (2002). *Giant Pandas.* New York: Holiday House. A well illustrated information book about the life and habitat of the giant panda. 32 pages.

Johnson, L. L. (2005). *Worlds Apart.* Ashville, NC: Front Street. Winnie is devastated when her family moves from Chicago to the grounds of a mental institution in small-town Minnesota where her physician father goes to work. 126 pages.

Kellogg, S. (1986). *Ralph's Secret Weapon.* New York: Puffin. Ralph, his aunt, and his bassoon conquer another strange monster. 32 pages.

Kinney, J. (2007). *Diary of a Wimpy Kid.* New York: Amulet Books. The hilarious story of an undersized tween trying to get through life and middle school while surrounded by morons and bullies. 215 pages.

Lobel, B. (1982). *Ming Lo Moves the Mountain.* New York: Scholastic. A Chinese fable about a naïve husband and wife, fools who eventually learn from experience. 32 pages.

McCloskey, R. (1950, 1987). *One Morning in May.* New York: Puffin. A young girl loses her tooth while clamming and learns to accept disappointment. 32 pages.

Park, B. (2004). *Junie B., First Grader: Shipwrecked.* New York: Random House. In another exciting adventure, Junie B. wins a starring role as the *Pinta*, the "fastest" of Columbus's ships, in a play to be presented on parents' night. 96 pages.

Parker, S. (2005). *Pond & River* (DK Eyewitness Books). London: Dorling Kindersley. A wonderfully illustrated introduction for the upper elementary student to the plants and animals that live in or near ponds and rivers. 72 pages.

Paulsen, G. (1989). *The Voyage of the Frog*. New York: Doubleday Dell. A boy, grieving for his uncle, inherits his sailboat and learns to survive when caught in a dangerous storm. 160 pages.

Pilkey, D. (2001). *The Adventures of Captain Underpants*. New York: Blue Sky Press. The hilarious and subversive adventures of George and Harold, who are usually responsible for the misdeeds that occur around them. 132 pages.

Reiss, J. (1972). *The Upstairs Room*. New York: HarperCollins. Two sisters must hide in a small room when the Nazis invade Holland during the second world war. 196 pages.

Riordan, R. (2014). *Percy Jackson and the Olympians*. New York: Disney-Hyperion. Percy's thrilling adventures with Greek gods, monsters and anything the author can dream up. This is a five part series.

Skurzynski, G. (2004). *Are We Alone? Scientists Search for Life in Space*. Hanover, PA: National Geographic. 92 pages.

Spinelli, J. (2002). *Loser*. New York: Joanna Colter Books. Spinelli explores the cruelty of the student body who pick on a very inept kid who really is a quite lovely boy. 224 pages.

Tatham, B. (2002). *Penguin Chick*. New York: HarperCollins. This information book focuses on one emperor penguin family's survival. 40 pages.

Thimmesh, C. (2002). *The Sky's the Limit: Stories of Discovery by Women and Girls*. Boston: Houghton Mifflin. In this compelling, cleverly illustrated tribute, the author recounts the contributions of many curious and brilliant women who have changed the world with their findings. 73 pages.

Chapter 4
Organizing Instruction So All Will Succeed

 Learning Outcomes

After reading and studying this chapter you should be able to:

4.1 Compare and contrast the reasons why some children have difficulty learning to read and others do not.

4.2 Understand how to organize a classroom and create a strong core program that enables all students to read and love reading.

4.3 Differentiate instruction within a strong core reading program.

4.4 Implement a variety of intervention activities that assist children who struggle with reading to overcome their difficulties.

Classroom Vignette

Mrs. Wright is concerned. It is the beginning of her second year as the principal of Pearson Elementary, a small 325-student elementary school in Virginia. Her school is in a rural area where the population is diverse—40 percent are Caucasian, 35 percent are African American, and 24 percent are Hispanic. Twelve percent of the students are in a special education program. Her concerns are triggered by test scores, not the high-stakes scores that schools live and die by in this era of accountability, but informal assessments of beginning reading skills that were conducted at the end of first grade and again at the beginning of second grade. This test, the Phonological Awareness Literacy Screening (PALS, Invernizzi, Juel, Swank, & Meier, 2015) is used throughout the state to assess skills like letter-name knowledge, letter-sound knowledge, phonemic awareness, spelling, and word and passage reading ability. She has just reviewed the assessments on her entering second-grade students and many of them appear to have word and passage reading skills at or below a first-grade level. That means 25 of her 72 entering second grade students are struggling with reading. Eight students are already in special education and another seven students are reading as poorly as the special education students. Mrs. Wright has decided that she, the three second-grade teachers, the school's reading teacher, and the special education teacher need to talk about the problem and devise a plan for accelerating the reading growth of their second-grade students.

Three days later at the second-grade team meeting, the teachers and Mrs. Wright begin to offer ideas and suggestions. It is the district policy to group students heterogeneously into classrooms; so one option—homogeneous classrooms—is off the table. That means each teacher is likely to have students reading from a beginning first grade reading level to a fourth-grade level in her room. The teachers offer various suggestions; one suggests purchasing a new phonics program that would help the students catch up. Another suggests a focus on reading fluency, and others think they need more leveled texts. Some want to enlist parent volunteers to work in the classrooms and read with the students. Another suggests that the high school students who must complete community service projects can work a few hours a week with the struggling students. All agree that their current core program offers few ideas for teaching such a wide range of students in a classroom.

Individual Differences in Learning to Read

The problem we have outlined is a real problem, one that is repeated across the country in many, if not most, classrooms. How do you deal with the diversity of abilities and accomplishments in the typical classroom? In any class you will find a range of abilities and interests that make the task of teaching all children to read a challenge. It is especially so given the demands of accountability of the Every Student Succeeds Act (ESSA, 2015), the successor to No Child Left Behind. According to this federal legislation, each state sets standards for the percentage of students who must be proficient in reading with the percentage rising each year. To compound the current problem, a school cannot achieve these goals by averaging the results across ability or ethnic groups; the same percent of African American students, Hispanic students, special education students, and students from poor economic backgrounds in the school must pass the test. This egalitarian stance on reading achievement puts even greater pressure on Mrs. Wright and her staff.

A Variety of Cultural Experiences

Students struggle to learn to read for a variety of reasons. Some find learning to read difficult because their homes and communities did not prepare them for the literacy demands that await. Our goal is not to cast aspersions on cultural or ethnic groups, but to simply document the differences in literacy experiences among children. Some children come from home backgrounds with little focus on literacy. There were no bedtime stories and there were few books in the home (Delpit, 2006; Heath, 1985). Conversely, many grew up in a home that was literacy rich. Parents read to their children on a daily basis, and through this experience they learned how books worked. By the time they entered school they knew how to hold a book, turn the pages, which part told the story, and they developed a love of books. Other experiences in the home, such as the notes and print on the refrigerator and the shopping lists father made, deepened their understanding of print and its uses. When children learn to spell their own name they discover some of the principles that underlie our alphabetic language. Heath estimates that children growing up in middle-class families will experience 1,500 hours of reading instruction before they start school. Those from economically disadvantaged homes might experience only 50 hours of reading "instruction" before entering kindergarten. For the fortunate children, this is a tremendous foundation on which to start classroom instruction. Delpit (2006) reaffirmed this point and called for schools to explicitly teach what many children learn by having a bed time story every night.

The language skills a child acquires growing up create a foundation for the acquisition of reading. If you grew up in a middle-class professional home, researchers tell us that you entered school having an oral vocabulary at least twice the size of a classmate being raised by parents at or near the poverty line (Hart & Risley, 1995). How much and how your parents talk to you affects the growth of your vocabulary. Vocabulary then affects reading in several ways. First, having a larger store of words seems to facilitate the acquisition of phonemic awareness (Snow, Burns, & Griffin, 1998). Some researchers suggest that the number of multisyllabic words in a child's vocabulary attunes the child to the rhythm of sounds within a word—a precursor to phonemic awareness. Second, the Language and Reading Consortium (2015) found that vocabulary affects word identification. If a child decodes a word for which he has no meaning (*chat* versus *hat*), that word is not easily retained. Third, knowing many words makes it easier to learn even more words as children build connections between words. Some children enter school speaking a language other than English, and they must traverse two languages while learning to read in one.

Learning Disabilities

Some students enter school lacking the talent, the cognitive wiring, that is necessary to easily unlock the printed code of English (Shaywitz, 2003). A variety of labels have been used to designate these children. They have been called learning disabled and dyslexic. Some suffer from a reading disability or a reading disorder. Others have an attention deficit disorder that prevents them from attending to or processing the print. Whatever the label, a small percentage of students have a basic reading disability that stems from some inner neurological or cognitive problem. For the moment we will avoid the problem of finding the right label, because in each generation the label changes as old labels take on pejorative connotations (mentally retarded became intellectually disabled) or as theories of learning evolve.

Frank Vellutino and his colleagues decided to determine just how many children actually have a learning disability that affects reading (Vellutino et al., 1996). They answered the question by identifying a large number of kindergarten students who appeared to be at risk for learning to read and an equal number of kindergarten students who were not at risk. A child was deemed to be at risk because of poor scores on a number of reading measures, such as phonological awareness, letter and word identification, and print awareness. Nine percent of the students were judged to be at risk, even though they had average intelligence. The at-risk group was randomly split in half and half of those students received extensive one-on-one tutoring 30 minutes a day for the entire year. The other half received no tutoring but continued in the regular kindergarten curriculum. By the end of kindergarten only 3 percent of the at-risk students who were tutored were experiencing difficulties learning to read. So that 3 percent is close to the number of students with a true cognitive or neurological impairment. But what of the other children who initially struggled?

The Matthew Effect

The last cause of individual differences in learning to read is the school itself. Not all teachers are equally adept at teaching children to read. If we return to Pearson Elementary School, we might want to examine the data on these entering second-graders. Over 95 percent of the students came from the five first grades in the school. Because these students were heterogeneously assigned to first-grade classrooms, some of the differences in achievement can be attributed to differences in instruction. Some teachers spent more time in small-group instruction and that factor has been linked to higher achievement (Taylor, Pearson, Clark, & Walpole, 2000). Within those small-groups, some teachers spent more time on teacher-directed phonics instruction, and that factor has been linked to higher achievement (Connor, Morrison, & Underwood, 2007). Finally, within the small-group instruction, the least experienced of the teachers was not very skillful in coaching students to apply their new word identification skills. Not knowing how to coach or scaffold learning has been linked to lower student achievement (Piasta, Connor, Fishman, & Morrison, 2009).

Difficulty with reading promotes disinterest, dislike, and avoidance. What happens to these children is called the "Matthew Effect" (Stanovich, 1986), or the rich get richer and the poor get poorer. Children who read well tend to read more. Conversely, children who struggle in reading read less and their skill level does not advance. The students who read less may do so because teachers assign less reading to such students. They read less because core reading programs make fewer demands on the below-level students than on the above-level students (Dewitz, et al., 2010). Finally, they read less because the process of reading is not rewarding, like playing golf without any talent.

The final cause of reading problems is poor instruction. If a primary teacher does not attend to phonics and phonemic awareness, some of her students will not make adequate progress. If an upper grade teacher neglects comprehension strategy instruction or fails to follow the gradual release of responsibility model, some of his students will struggle with comprehending texts. All teachers must have a powerful vocabulary program. If any teacher fails to organize and manage the classroom well, little work will be completed. Every child will occasionally have a poor teacher, but those from weak literacy homes suffer more from poor instruction than those from homes that can compensate for the inadequacies of a given teacher (Snow, Barnes, Chandler, Gooodman, & Hemphill, 1991). Two weak teachers in a row can be devastating for some students.

For a variety of reasons, classrooms are not homogeneous assemblies of students. Students vary in ability, in interests, in attention, and in temperament. Yet when the year is done, the teacher's goal is to have them reading well and ready for the next challenge. To create children who are alike—children who all read well—demands that we treat them differently. The goal of this chapter is to help you differentiate instruction for all students in your classroom and specifically meet the needs of those who struggle with learning to read, as well as those who excel and the rest in the middle. We will explore differentiation practices in the general education classroom and then examine how classroom teachers, special education teachers, and reading specialists can assist the students experiencing the greatest difficulty learning to read. This last topic will lead us to discuss Response to Intervention (RtI), a model for assisting all students and a process that can be used to identify students for special education.

MyLab Education
Video Example 4.1
This video addresses the causes of reading problems that we have outlined in this chapter.

Reflect and Apply

We have discussed at least three causes of reading problems, with the obvious possibility that any child's difficulty learning to read can be the result of two or more interacting problems.

1. Considering the different roots of reading problems, which ones do you feel are most easily solved by the general education teacher and which might take the intervention of a specialist?

2. Think about the expectations in your classroom. How much do you think second-graders, fourth-graders, and sixth-graders should read in a school year? How much of this reading should be guided by the classroom teacher and how much should the student be reading independently?

MyLab Education **Self-Check 4.1**

MyLab Education **Application Exercise 4.1:** Exploring the Causes of Reading Difficulties

Creating a Strong Core Program

In the opening vignette you learned that one-third of Mrs. Wright's second graders were entering second grade reading below grade level, some significantly below level. This is not the time to sound the alarm and call in the special education and reading teacher cavalry, but to critically examine the core reading program, to study what classroom teachers do on a daily basis to build reading skills and positive attitudes. While it is tempting to solve this problem with special assistance, interventions for struggling readers achieve the strongest results (Mathes, Denton, Fletcher, Anthony, Francis, & Schatschneider, 2005) when the core reading program is sound. In this section of the chapter, we will describe how to create a strong core reading program. We touched on some of these issues in Chapter 3 when we described the motivational climate that propels students to excel. In this section we will focus on the physical arrangement of your classroom, the management of time, and working with the whole class, small-groups, and individuals. With some skill and a bit of luck you will have a smooth-running classroom that only devolves into chaos on rare occasions.

The Physical Arrangement of the Classroom

MyLab Education
Video Example 4.2
Consider how a focal area is beneficial to the teacher, the students, and how it promotes interaction.

How you organize your classroom should be dictated by your instructional goals and your concern for motivation. Children learn to read by reading and they learn to write by writing. So, the classroom should be organized so that these two goals can be met. Students need comfy places to read—do you like reading sitting in a straight back chair?—and they need space to write because writing is messy and requires several tools. With that in mind, a classroom should have at least three focal areas plus space to explore science and social studies ideas.

First, you need a place to meet with the whole class. It should be comfortable, with a rug, and easy sight lines to the white-board, the Smartboard, and charts for you, the teacher, to write on. The teacher needs a high stool or director's chair (Figure 4.1 depicts the focal area in two different classrooms.) This is the place where you will give the class the directions for the day and if you are a primary teacher you can present the interactive morning message. In this whole-class area you can read to your students,

Figure 4.1 These are two photographs, one with high stool and the other with director's chair

introduce vocabulary words, and explain and model reading strategies. Putting all the students on the rug holds their attention on you and the content. Most students will enjoy coming to the class meeting area, but a few, especially older students, will rebel. If you are a fifth or sixth grade teacher don't push everyone to sit on the rug. A few will sit at their desks or on them, but keep them close to you.

Second, you need a place to meet with small-groups of students. A place for guided practice, a place for discussions, a place to attend to individual needs. Many schools have kidney shaped tables that seat the teacher and five to seven students. At this table the culinary concept of *mise en place* rules, meaning all your ingredients in their place. You need books, paper, extra pencils, dry erase pens, chart paper, everything at hand to teach the lesson. Planning and organization prevent management problems. If the students have to wait for you, then their behavior is likely to deteriorate.

Third, every student needs a desk, and we suggest that the desks be organized into groups of 3 to 5 depending on the size of the class and the size of the classroom. You will want your students to work in groups and you save time and reduce commotion if they don't have to get up to join their group. Organizing the classroom into groups helps with activities like pair-and-share in which students discuss a question, develop a question, or elaborate on a concept before continuing with the whole-class discussion. The desk is also vital for writing, research, and studying in other content areas. We belabor the desk because in some classroom systems of organization students keep their work in a cubby and land at different centers for specific activities—a writing center, a science center, an art center and so forth. Academic life requires work and students need a place to do it.

Fourth, all students need a classroom library. We focused on the classroom library in Chapter 3 but we will restate its most important characteristics. We want students to read often, widely, and deeply and, therefore, they need access to books. A weekly visit to the school library is not enough. The classroom library should be a space that invites reading. A rug, pillows, posters and an arrangement of books by genre and level causes students to want to read. It is a place where students can go to read independently and find the next book when they have finished the current one. Every elementary classroom should have a classroom library and the same holds true for the middle school English classroom.

Managing Time

Time is a precious resource; manage it well. In a typical elementary classroom, the principal allocates time to each subject area and reading/language arts receives anywhere from 90 to 150 minutes a day, a longer amount of time in the primary grades and shorter in the upper grades. As a classroom teacher, you will have little influence over the allocation of time, but if you do consider the following issues:

- You want a large uninterrupted blocks of time are preferable to having your reading/language arts block bisected by lunch, recess, and assemblies.

- It does not matter if reading is in the morning or afternoon, but some teachers seem to believe the primary aged children do better in the morning.

- Hope that you work in a school where the principal and the secretary stay off the public address system. Continual announcements are not conducive to attention and concentration.

- You want flexibility in how you mange time within your literacy block.

- The students who need intervention, additional help in reading, need to experience as much of the reading/language arts block as possible. It does not make sense to take these students from reading in the classroom to reading with a specialists. It is important to supplement instruction not supplant it.

Within your reading/language arts block you need to allocate time so you can work with the whole class, with groups of students, and with individuals. We recommend a whole-group time every day. Whole-group time can last from 20 to 40 minutes, but you can vary that time depending on what you need to accomplish. During whole-group time you will set the agenda for the day, conduct interactive read-alouds, share exciting new books, conduct the morning message lesson in the kindergarten and first grade, and introduce skills, strategies, and vocabulary words to the whole class.

You will need a large block of time to meet with the small-groups, typically 60 minutes a day. During this time, you can conduct guided reading lessons and work with book clubs and literature circles (more about these in Chapter 11). Because you can only meet with one group at a time, it is important to first plan what the students do when they are not meeting with you. Richard Allington (2001) divides classroom activities into three categories—reading, writing, and stuff. Reading and writing are obvious and stuff is everything else—worksheets, workbooks, games, word sorts, computer games, and skill practice programs on the computer. Students should spend most of their time reading and writing and very little time doing stuff. Allington raises this challenge for all teachers; prove that what you are asking students to do is more important than reading a book or writing a composition. As you plan your small-group time, plan what the students will be doing during their independent time.

Some educators advocate a center approach to the management of the classroom; we have some reservations. In a center approach, each guided reading group meets with the teacher for 15 to 30 minutes and then spends the rest of the time rotating through centers. A class might have some of these centers:

• computer center	• art center
• ABC center	• buddy reading center
• writing center	• poetry center
• listening center	• math center
• word center	• science center
• book club center	• social studies center

In the center approach, the focus is on the activity in the center and not on the learning objective or the project (Fountas & Pinnell, 1996). For example, a student might go to the word center and sort words and then to the poetry center one day; the next day to the listening center and the buddy reading center. The center approach emphasizes isolated activities, what Allington calls stuff. We prefer to put the focus on the project, the ideas, the content. Some students might be writing a report on the underground railroad while others are studying parasitic plants. Their independent time is devoted to reading and writing a report that will be shared with the class. They might also be preparing for guided reading by developing questions or researching vocabulary words for tomorrow's discussion. In the Classroom 4.1 describes how one second grade teacher structures his independent reading time.

There are many ways to provide productive and beneficial independent work for all students. Solve the independent work problem first, and the small-group instruction will almost take care of itself. These are our guidelines for independent work:

- Make reading the priority, reading books and articles in print and from the Internet. Students need regular reading assignments and plenty of self-selected reading.

- Reading is not something students do when the rest of their work is completed. Reading comes first.

In the Classroom 4.1

Managing Small-Group and Independent Work

Each week Mr. Kovarsky plans his second grade reading work around a topic or a theme. One week in October the students studied bats. During whole-group instruction he reads the story *Stellaluna* (Cannon, 1993) and a nonfiction book, *Bats* (Gibbons, 1999). The students were studying bats and learning how the reading of fiction and nonfiction differ. When reading *Stellaluna*, the students complete a story map listing the characters, setting, problems, events, and resolution (see story map in Chapter 11). When reading *Bats* they complete a main idea details chart (see Figure 4.2).

MyLab Education
Click here to download a printable version of Figure 4.2.

Figure 4.2 Main Idea Detail Chart

Book Title _____		Author _____
The Topic _____		
Main Idea 1 _____ _____ _____	**Main Idea 2** _____ _____ _____	**Main Idea 3** _____ _____ _____
Supporting Details	**Supporting Details**	**Supporting Details**

Mr. Kovarsky has planned the students' independent work to focus on reading and writing about bats. He first went to the library and checked out 25 books on bats. During a whole-group lesson the students generate questions about bats. Then each student is required to read three books during the week about bats and complete a graphic organizer for each book. They may choose either fiction or nonfiction books. When they choose a fiction book they complete a story map. If the students are reading nonfiction books about bats they record main ideas and important facts. By Wednesday most of the students are becoming "experts" on bats. They have answered many of their questions and raised new ones. Next, Mr. Kovarsky uses his whole-class time to introduce two new websites about bats: Kidzone (http://www.kidzone.ws/animals/bats/index.htm) and Kids Biology (kidsbiology.com/animal-types/bats/). Now the students can extend their research and answer additional questions about bats. They also gain experience reading and taking notes from the Internet.

- Vary the purpose for reading. There is reading for information to write a report, or reading for pleasure to share enjoyment. There is reading for enlightenment developing new insights about self and others.

- Make writing your second priority and we will elaborate on this in Chapter 13. Have the students write to the teacher in a response journal, write to a friend in a dialogue journal, and write to themselves to think about new insights from a book.

Small-group time is when a teacher has the best opportunity to differentiate instruction. The teacher can differentiate the amount of time he spends with each group. He can vary the texts that they read, choosing books that match their reading levels and interests. He can vary the tasks that the students preform and the explicitness of his teaching. In the next section we will focus on differentiating small-group instruction.

Differentiating Instruction

In Chapter 2 we introduced the Zone of the Proximal Development (Vygotsky, 1978). At one end of the zone a student can read books and complete tasks with great ease. At the other end of the zone it is nigh impossible for the student make sense of a book or complete the task. Learning takes place when the students are in the middle of the zone; they must work, think, and practice. The teacher's goal is to keep the child in the middle of that Zone of Proximal Development and differentiation of instruction provides the tools to do so.

A teacher can differentiate time, tasks, texts, and teaching techniques. Teachers should devote more direct instructional time to struggling readers and less time to more advanced students (Connor et al., 2007). Students in the primary grades should read text at their instructional level and texts that match their interests (O'Connor, Bell, Harty, Larkin, Sackor, & Zigmond, 2002). In third grade and up, precisely matching students to just the right text is often not necessary (Hoffman, 2017). Interest and background knowledge play a larger role. Finally, teachers should differentiate tasks. Strong readers, who decode well, are better served by focusing on vocabulary and comprehension development, whereas struggling readers need to spend more time on decoding tasks. Some students require more explicit instruction while others do not.

Differentiating Time

When Connor and her colleagues studied first-, second-, and third-grade classrooms, they found that small differences in the amount and type of instruction produced large differences in student learning. Students who had weak word recognition skills in first grade benefited from more time in teacher-managed instruction, with more work on phonics and word identification. It was important that students worked directly with the teacher and less important that they independently played word games, sorted words, or copied spelling words. It was particularly important that second-grade teachers continued to work hard on decoding activities, because second grade gave these students a second chance to succeed. If teachers added just 5 minutes a day to their decoding instruction, the second-grade students made significant gains in achievement, and almost all were reading at a third-grade level or higher by the end of the school year. Five minutes of instructional time each day is the equivalent of 13 extra hours of instruction over the course of a school year (25 minutes per week × 32 weeks of instruction). Although Connor and her colleagues do not say so explicitly, this additional instructional time can be added to the small-group work, reducing the amount of time teachers work with the stronger readers.

We can reach several conclusions about the use of time within the classroom.

- Maximize the amount of instructional time. This requires an organized and efficient classroom. Well-practiced instructional routines reduce the amount of down time and makes the best use of the available time.

- Students who struggle to learning to read need more of your time than students who make easy progress learning to read. See the struggling readers more frequently and for longer blocks of time.

- Students who find it easy to read still need your attention but you only need to check in two or three times a week for shorter meetings.

Differentiating Tasks

Carol Connor and her colleagues have systematically studied what instructional tasks make the most difference for students who find it easy and those who find it difficult to learn to read. (Connor, Jakobson, Crowe, & Meadows, 2009). Their method involves observing teachers, recording how they teach reading, and then drawing relationships between their descriptions of classroom instruction and students' growth in reading. Connor categorized classroom instruction in the primary grades based on a 2 × 2 matrix (see Figure 4.3) (Connor Morrison, Schatschneider, & Underwood, 2007). Activities are either managed by the teacher or by the students. Student-managed activities take place when the students work independently or with partners. Students might be reading a book, engaged in partner reading with a friend, or writing a report. Teacher-managed activities can occur during whole-group time or small-group time and include direct instruction in decoding, comprehension, or writing. A teacher might model, explain, and guide students to use a strategy. A code-focused activity helps the student understand the alphabetic principle, develop phonemic awareness, identify and spell words. A meaning-focused activity engages students in the development of vocabulary, comprehension, or writing of extended text.

In the primary grades students who struggle to learn to read benefit from code focused teacher directed activity. Students who find learning to read easier need more meaning focused activities and they need less teacher directions. In the upper grades, good readers, those with strong oral reading fluency and vocabulary scores, demonstrate the most growth when they are engaged in student-managed, meaning-focused activities, whereas students with weaker comprehension skills benefit more from explicit teacher-directed instruction (Connor, Morrison, & Petrella, 2004). What this means is that good readers should spend more of their time reading independently, working in book clubs, and analyzing and responding to what they read. They do not need a great deal of teacher-managed instruction. Conversely, students with weaker comprehension and vocabulary skills benefit when they are engaged in more teacher-directed comprehension instruction. This instruction should focus on comprehension strategies, vocabulary instruction, text structure, and comprehension monitoring. The work of Connor and her colleagues is a clear demonstration of how teachers should differentiate time and tasks.

Within each of these broad categories there are some additional distinctions that should be made. At any level of instruction and for any area of reading

Figure 4.3 Instructional Activities

	Teacher Managed	Student Managed
Code focused	Phonemic awareness, rhyming, blending, segmenting Letter recognition Letter-sound associations Decoding strategies Spelling	Phonics games Phonics worksheets Writing and sorting spelling words
Meaning focused	Supported oral reading Comprehension strategy instruction Prior knowledge development Oral language development Repeated reading of text Writing compositions	Independent reading Partner reading Completing graphic organizer Independent writing and publishing

In the Classroom 4.2

Differentiating Word Study Tasks

A typical study task is sorting words. The child is given a set of words that consists of four or five examples of three or four phonics patterns. There may be short *a* words, long *a* words, and short *i* words. Often the teacher includes one or two words that do not fit in any of the patterns; these are the oddballs. The child's task is to sort the words into the three or four phonics patterns. Two completed sorts are depicted.

Sort A

CVCe side	VCC fight	CV sky	Oddball
ride	right	why	wild
mile	might	my	pint
nice	night	fry	
spice	light	dry	
twice			

Sort B

Long *a*	Long *i*	Short *a*	Oddball
play	might	chat	what
rain	write	had	
made	pint	can	
train	sky	plant	
lake			

In Sort A the student can concentrate on just the visual features of a word and perform the sort relatively easily. In fact, there is no assurance that the student actually needs to read the words to solve this code-focused task unless the teacher asks her to do so. By looking for *ight,* CVVe, or CV patterns the child can successfully complete the sort. Sort A is probably best used under teacher direction where the teacher can ask the students to pronounce the words and discuss their meaning after they have completed the task. Sort B cannot be solved by looking at just the visual features of the words. Each word must be pronounced. So the student has to work a bit harder to pronounce the word and isolate the vowel sound. If the student correctly completes Sort B you can be reasonably assured that she can pronounce the words.

MyLab Education
Video Example 4.3
Consider if this is a skills-based approach to independent work or a project-based approach. Is this an effective way to organize independent work?

some tasks provoke more thought or depth of processing than do others. Some tasks can be completed in a short amount of time whereas others may take days. Look at In the Classroom 4.2 to consider how the relatively simple task of sorting words can be made more or less challenging by varying the words that children have to sort.

Not all comprehension tasks are equal in complexity; not all lead to the same depth of understanding. Ample evidence exists that asking higher-level questions promotes more comprehension than lower-level questions (Hansen, 1981). Questions demanding that readers draw inferences, justify a conclusion with text evidence, and make judgments promote deeper understanding than do literal questions (Hansen, 1981; Taylor et al., 2003). When students have to explain, justify, and defend answers, they think more deeply than when answering literal questions. Different readers need different levels of comprehension instruction. Students who struggle to understand what they read need more support and guidance from the teacher than students who find the task relatively easy. There is little reason to teach comprehension strategies to students who comprehend well. All students need to employ the same comprehension strategies, but the teacher may vary how they are introduced, demonstrated, and practiced, as well as the amount of support provided. In the Classroom 4.3 illustrates two small-group discussions, one with considerable support and another with much less support.

In the Classroom 4.3

Differentiating Comprehension Instruction

Mr. Campbell organizes his fourth-grade students into three groups for guided reading, but the groups are not strictly homogeneous. One group has a predominance of students with comprehension problems, but in that group, he also places a few students who comprehend well. Mr. Campbell wants these stronger readers to act as a model for the weaker readers. The other two groups are also heterogeneous, students of mixed ability levels, but all are able to fluently read the texts he provides. The discussions are richer when the students do not think alike and the students who struggle can learn from those who are quicker to catch on. All the students will be reading and studying legends as part of a larger unit on Native Americans. The students must discover the problem solved in the legend, who solved the problem, and what this might reveal about one particular Native American culture. Let's consider the group with the weaker readers and then one other group.

Mr. Campbell wants to provide his weaker readers considerable support, so he meets with that group first. Students begin by silently reading a segment of the text and at each stopping point he explicitly focuses on reading strategies that help students understand the meaning of the legend. The students are asked to summarize what they read, consider what needs to be clarified, and look for cause-and-effect relationships—the focus strategy for the next couple of weeks. When students have difficulty, he prompts them to say more to expand their summary or to search for words like *because* and *since* that might signal cause-and-effect relationships. If the weaker students still have problems, he might model the task of summarizing himself or begin the task and then ask one of the students to complete the summary.

The stronger readers do not need the same support as the weaker comprehenders. They are given their legend and told to read it on their own, using a graphic organizer that guides the reading. They are to note the character in the legend, what the legend is trying to explain, and the message or moral in the legend. The students read and work independently. When finished they discuss their findings with the teacher in a small-group discussion. The students start by sharing what they recorded on the graphic organizer. When misunderstandings arise, the teacher may direct the students to reread portions of the text as a way to clarify a problem. The teacher focuses on strategies, summarizing or making inferences only when those strategies might clarify their misunderstanding. Most students understand what they have read, so teaching strategies would be counterproductive. If a particular paragraph is not well understood, Mr. Campbell will direct the students to reread it and summarize what they have learned. At times the teacher might simply ask the students what we have to do to clarify an issue. In this strong group the use of comprehension strategies is assumed and support is provided only as students need it.

Differentiating Texts

Teachers need to make many important decisions about the texts that students read. One size does not fit all. The texts that students read should be matched to their reading level, their interests, and their experiences. Let's unpack each of these ideas and see what they mean in terms of differentiating texts. It has been the fundamental principle of reading for decades that students should read texts at their instructional level rather than their grade level (Fountas & Pinnell, 1996). It is argued that that younger readers make more progress in developing decoding skills and oral reading fluency when they read texts at their instructional level and the research supports this conclusion (O'Connor et al., 2002). In the upper grades we should temper our concern for finding the "just right text" (Hoffman, 2017). Beyond reading level, many other factors determine the readability of a text. Teachers might consider the genre of the text, the background knowledge of the students, and the interest level of the text. When the text is fascinating, students are willing and able to read far above their reading level. We will consider the issue of text more thoroughly in Chapter 6.

Developers of core reading programs have recognized the need to have students reading at their instructional level and, therefore, created four levels of texts for each reading lesson. Core programs provide leveled texts for students reading above grade level, on grade level, below grade level, and one for English language learners. There is one problem with this system; the texts created for below-level readers are typically shorter and provide less reading practice than do the texts for on-level and above-level readers (Dewitz et al., 2010). Overall the weaker readers are shortchanged in the system. Teachers can and should obviously deal with this problem by finding additional texts for students to read at their instructional level.

A special case of instructional-level text is the need to have decodable text for beginning readers. Decodable text provides students the opportunity to practice phonics patterns in connected text that have been previously taught in a teacher-directed lesson. In such texts, a majority of the words are phonetically regular. Figure 4.4 shows examples of a decodable text and a text at the same level that is not decodable. Both are samples from a core reading program. Decodable text offers two advantages to the beginning reader. First, decodable text provides the student with an immediate rationale for all those phonics lessons and activities. By learning those phonics patterns, the students can now use what they have learned to read new words. To the first-grader, reading instruction makes sense and the child gains a sense of confidence. Decodable text provides a second benefit. Because the majority of words are phonetically regular, using patterns previously taught, the text schools the child in the left to right progression of reading—carefully decoding and blending letter-sound patterns as she moves across a word (Adams, 2009). When the children read decodable text they use their phonics skills in a more effective and facile manner (Juel & Roper/Schneider, 1985).

Selecting the right text in the upper grades is also an important instructional decision, one that demands careful differentiation. The teacher in the upper grades must ask what kinds of text are most likely to assist students to develop strong reading comprehension skills. In making these decisions the teacher needs to think about the knowledge of the reader and the structure and organization of the text. Fiction can be distinguished by the complexity of the plot, the use of time altering techniques such as flashbacks, and the manner in which the characters are developed. When students are reading in content areas where their knowledge is just beginning to develop, they benefit most from texts that are well structured, cohesive, and have unity; what has been called *considerate text* (Anderson & Armbruster, 1984).

In the upper grades, a teacher should keep genre, interest, and prior knowledge in mind when differentiating texts. These factors are more important than reading level. In many cases, a student can read well above his grade level if the book is engaging and the student has the necessary prior knowledge. Even if the book is difficult, the teachers can

MyLab Education
Click here to download a printable version of Figure 4.4.

Figure 4.4 Decodable and Leveled Text

Decodable Text	Below-Level Leveled Reader
Pat Can Help	*The Pond*
Pat has a cab.	This is a pond.
Jan has bags.	What animals live in the pond?
Jan has a cat.	Little fish live here.
Jan has a hat.	Ducks live here. They get their food from the pond.
Jan has maps.	This duck looks under the cold water.
Pat can help Jan.	Look! She sees a fish. The duck swims very fast!
Jan can nap.	The fish swims off? The duck will look for more food.

SOURCE: Beck, I., Farr, R. C., & Strickland, D. S. (2009). *Storytown Grade 1, Theme 1.* Orlando, FL: Harcourt, pp. T60, T77.

increase the scaffolding to make the book more accessible. Teaching vocabulary, using graphic organizers, asking guided questions, or having students engage in partner reading helps students reach beyond their grade level. A student's reading level should not be a ceiling, but merely a rung on a ladder. In the Reading Corner we present three differentiated units with text sets.

The Reading Corner

Books for Differentiated Thematic Units

In the upper grades, the concept of differentiated novel study has many advantages. Students of different reading levels can read different novels each considering a similar theme. Motivation is enhanced because all students are working on a related meaningful project. Finally, a differentiated novel study builds a cooperative spirit in the classroom. The following are some suggested units.

Unit 1: Exploring Friendship

Sharon Creech. *The Wanderer.* HarperTrophy, 2002. (For better readers.) A 13-year-old girl shows her bravery on a dangerous ocean voyage in a small sailboat. 320 pages.

Kate DiCamillo. *Because of Winn-Dixie.* Candlewick Press, 2000. (For average to above-average readers.) Through the help of a goofy dog, Opal learns to listen to the problems of others and, in turn, begins to feel part of a town where she once felt isolated. 182 pages.

Louis Sachar. *There's a Boy in the Girls' Bathroom.* Yearling, 1987. (For below-average to average readers.) The story of an isolated fifth-grader who, through the help of friends, learns to restore his self-confidence. 195 pages.

Unit 2: Survival

Ken Mochizuki. *Baseball Saved Us.* Lee and Low Books, 1993. (For below-average readers.) The story of how baseball saved the spirits and hope of Japanese Americans in an internment camp during World War II. 32 pages.

Gary Paulsen. *Voyage of the Frog.* Bantam Doubleday, 1989. (For average readers.) The story of a boy who inherits his beloved uncle's sailboat and then struggles to survive in a storm. 160 pages.

Johanna Reiss. *The Upstairs Room.* HarperCollins, 1972. (For above-average readers.) The story of two Jewish girls who survive the Holocaust hiding in a small room. 196 pages.

Unit 3: A Quest for Personal Identity

Edward Bloor. *Tangerine.* Harcourt Books, 1997. (For above-average readers.) The story of a nearsighted geek who, after moving to a new town, becomes a hero. 320 pages.

Beverly Cleary. *Dear Mr. Henshaw.* HarperCollins, 1983. (For average readers.) A new kid in town, with recently divorced parents, no dog anymore, and a lunch that gets stolen every day, writes in a journal and learns to cope with his feelings and gain confidence. 160 pages.

Jack Gantos. *Joey Pigza Loses Control.* HarperCollins, 2000. (For below-average readers.) The story of a hyperactive boy from a divorced, dysfunctional home who learns control and self-acceptance. 196 pages.

One simple truth captures the problem of differentiating instruction for English learners. What works for most students will work for English learners. The English learner must read books at their instructional level. They need to build their background knowledge, especially for American culture. They need clear modeling and well supported guided practice to learn strategies for decoding and comprehension. Above all, they need a steady focus on vocabulary development. The differentiated needs of the English learner mirror the needs of the English-speaking student. If phonics or fluency is a problem, those issues should be addressed in differentiated instruction. Likewise, if vocabulary or comprehension is a problem, the teacher should focus on those components of reading.

What is especially vital for the English learner is a strong focus on vocabulary. Teachers should focus on words necessary to follow directions, words that describe instructional concepts, and vocabulary terms necessary for text comprehension. Even when teaching basic decoding skills, the teacher should take extra time to focus on the meaning of the words used for modeling and practice of phonics patterns. Short CVC or CCVC words (*log, met, wig, fret, chat*) require definitions and discussions of their meaning.

Planning Small-Group Instruction

Teachers should differentiate instruction when working with small-groups of students, when meeting with individual students, or when the students are working independently. Barbara Taylor and her colleagues found that the most effective teachers in the primary grades spent approximately twice as much time in small-group instruction (up to 52 minutes per day) as the least effective teacher (Taylor et al., 2003). Effectiveness was defined as growth in students' reading ability. Small-group instruction allows the teacher to meet individual needs, provide scaffolding for difficult tasks, and encourage students who struggle.

There is no ideal number of reading groups, but there is a tradeoff between the number of groups and the amount of time that a teacher can work with each group. The total amount of time a teacher can spend on reading is fixed and limited by lunch, recess, specials, and the other major content areas. The research is equally clear that the most effective classroom teachers strike a balance between whole-group and small-group instruction. If a classroom teacher allocates 60 minutes for small-group instruction, three groups gives her 20 minutes to work with each group, four groups provides 15 minutes per group, and five groups provides 12 minutes per group not counting transitions between groups. The more groups you have, the more time will be lost to transition and the less that can be accomplished in that short span of time. Three, perhaps four, groups seem optimal.

In the Classroom 4.4 examines how a teacher might plan her small-group instruction for three groups of second-grade students. This example focuses on a typical week and does not break the planning down to daily activities and tasks. Each group is seen for a different length of time, with the below-level readers receiving more instructional time than the on-level or above-level readers. The above and on-grade level groups do not meet every day, while the students below level do meet every day. The below-level readers need to spend a larger proportion of their time on decoding while the on-level

In the Classroom 4.4

Planning for Differentiated Small-Group Instruction

Above-Level Readers	On-Level Readers	Below-Level Readers
Vocabulary (5 minutes)	**Decoding + Vocabulary** (5 minutes)	**Decoding** (10 minutes)
Introduce or review new vocabulary	Model decoding strategies	Segment and blend sounds
Apply structural analysis principles as needed	Review decoding strategies with new vocabulary words and review word meanings	Introduce or review phonics patterns
		Model decoding strategies
Read Leveled Book for Comprehension (15 minutes)	**Read Leveled Book for Fluency and Comprehension** (15 minutes)	Engage students in one decoding activity
Introduce new book or chapter and develop prior knowledge	Introduce new book or chapter and develop prior knowledge	**Read Leveled and Decodable Book for Fluency** (20 minutes)
Review reading comprehension strategies	Review reading comprehension strategies	Introduce new book or begin with echo reading
Read text silently and stop to discuss	Read text with partner or silent read, stopping to apply specific comprehension strategies	Read with one or more students to coach on word-identification strategies
Use strategies as needed when comprehension breaks down	Introduce or review independent assignment such as a graphic organizer	Use whiteboard to review and model decoding strategies for difficult words
Introduce or review independent assignment such as a graphic organizer		Reread text segments to work on oral reading fluency
		Have students retell the story, ask comprehension questions

and above-level readers do not. In fact, the teacher might only touch on a few difficult words with the higher group, focusing instead on vocabulary and comprehension. For those in the middle, some decoding work is appropriate because ignoring it leads to slower growth in reading.

The texts that the three groups are reading should be related in some way – similar themes, topics, or genres. If the teacher is following a core reading program, then the three or four leveled books are linked to each other and to the main anthology selection by a common topic or theme. If the theme of the main selection is about overcoming one's fears, it is desirable that all students read about the same topic or theme. At the end of the week, students in each group can contribute to the whole-class discussion, sharing their story and what they have learned about people and overcoming fears. This drastically reduces the isolation of weaker readers from the ongoing activities in the classroom.

The differentiation of tasks continues with the reading of the text. The above-level students engage in the application of comprehension strategies only as needed. If students comprehend well, it may actually be counterproductive to disrupt their reading by asking them to stop and clarify, predict, or make inferences. They should focus on meaning (McKeown, Beck, & Blake, 2009). For the on-level readers, who might not be monitoring their comprehension, placing the strategies more in the forefront may help them build greater comprehension. For the below-level students, thinking about decoding and comprehension at the same time might be challenging, because cognitive capacity is limited, but students still retell and discuss the story after they finish reading.

In the upper-elementary grades, differentiation can take on a different look. The teachers create instructional units that focus on common themes and knowledge development for all students while differentiating the texts and tasks. In the Classroom 4.5 is a snapshot of such a differentiated unit.

In the Classroom 4.5

A Differentiated Historical Fiction Unit

Mr. Hernandez wants to expose his fifth grader to the engaging and instructive qualities of historical fiction. The class will soon be studying the Civil War in social studies, he decides to build a reading/language arts unit around historical fiction. He feels that a unit focused on novels about the Civil War will deepen the students' interest in the period, create personal connections to the feelings of common people during the war, and provide an opportunity to teach comprehension strategies in a meaningful context (Guthrie, Van Meter, Hancock, Alao, Anderson, & McCann, 1998). Due to the wide range of reading ability in the class, he selects books that are appropriate to each student's reading level and plans to introduce the unit by reading a historical fiction picture book to the students. The texts are:

- *Pink and Say* (Polacco, 1994). A picture book about two teenage soldiers, one northern, the other southern, wounded, dazed, and in danger, helping each other to survive after a battle.
- *Civil War on Sunday* (Osborne, 2000). This book, part of the Magic Tree House series, is geared for struggling readers and tells the tale of two children who magically find themselves in Gettysburg and witness and aid people in that famous battle.
- *I Thought My Soul Would Rise and Fly* (Hansen, 1997). The book, selected for the average readers in the class, is set in the immediate aftermath of the Civil War and tells the story of a freed young slave's yearning for an education and struggle with her newly bestowed freedom.
- *Across Five Aprils* (Hunt, 1965, 2002). The book, selected for the stronger readers in the class, tells the story of families and communities living in southern Illinois and caught up in personal, economic, and political upheavals of the Civil War period.

(Continued)

Mr. Hernandez begins the unit by reading the picture book *Pink and Say* aloud. It is an interactive read-aloud and he takes every opportunity to build his students' knowledge of the Civil War. Before he begins, Mr. Hernandez discusses the basics of the war—who is fighting whom, for what reasons, and uses a map to explain the settings of the war. The setting is vital; it takes place in Georgia in Confederate territory. It is important that the students understand the goals of Union and Confederate sides of the war and the major issues—slavery, secession, and union. Mr. Hernandez also explains that many African Americans fought with the Union and a few for the Confederates. After reading *Pink and Say* the students and Mr. Hernandez develop a graphic organizer that lists the facts of the Civil War.

Each group has a similar goal: to read their novel and complete a series of assignments for each part of the book. The students develop a character list, infer the traits of each character, and describe the setting of the book and its importance. Later the students outline the plot as it developed and then work to determine the themes of the book. These assignments are explained and Mr. Hernandez uses the book *Pink and Say* to model the thinking he expects of his students. One activity is a story map the students will sort the fictional aspects of the novel from the historical information (see Figure 4.5).

During reading time over the next three weeks the students read independently and then work with a partner to complete the various assignments. The teacher meets with each group regularly but for varying amounts of time. Mr. Hernandez likes to see his below-level readers daily so that their small-group time can include work on decoding, vocabulary, and comprehension. The average readers, because there are many of them, have been split into two groups, and he sees these groups approximately every other day. He also meets with the better readers every other day.

The three or four groups do not work in complete isolation. The teacher holds whole-class meetings where themes common to all three books are discussed. The teacher might ask the students to consider who is brave in their novel and list the number of different ways that characters in the story express their bravery. Mr. Hernandez wants the students to understand that bravery is not always a physical act. Later in the unit, the class might discuss the concept of loyalty and what people can be loyal to. What happens to loyalty when there is a conflict of beliefs or values within a family? Students keep track of these big themes and write about them at length. At the conclusion of the unit, the students consider how reading a novel has expanded their understanding of the social studies content and which reading strategies have helped them understand their novel.

Figure 4.5 Mapping Historical Fiction

Title _____ **Author** _____

	Historical Elements	Fictional Elements
Setting ❑ Place ❑ Time		
Characters		
Problem ❑ Event ❑ Event ❑ Event ❑ Event ❑ Event		
Resolution		

Reflect and Apply

3. List as many ways as you can to differentiate teaching and learning in the classroom. Decide which would be easiest to implement and which would present the most challenges. As a beginning teacher where would you start?

4. In this chapter we have contrasted a more skills-oriented approach to differentiation to an approach that focuses on interests, abilities, and experiences. Would one of these approaches be more beneficial for upper-grade classrooms? Can you combine a focus on skills and interests and how would you do so?.

MyLab Education **Self-Check 4.3**

MyLab Education **Application Exercise 4.3:** Grouping for Instruction, but How?

Intervention for Struggling Readers

Even with well differentiated instruction it is likely that not all students will learn to read. When Juel (1988) studied students from first through fourth grades, she found that students who were struggling with reading at the end of first grade still struggled in fourth grade. She concluded that some form of early intervention is needed to prevent future reading problems. Despite the best efforts of classroom teachers, some children need extra help to learn to read. In most schools, it takes the combined talents and efforts of many professionals—classroom teachers, reading specialists, special education teachers, the librarian, and occasionally volunteers—to ensure that all children learn to read. The model most currently popular is response to intervention.

Response to Intervention

One factor influencing the whole conception of differentiation is the special education initiative called response to intervention (RtI), a process of providing increasingly more explicit and supportive instruction so that all students learn to read (Fletcher & Vaughn, 2009). The logic of RtI is quite straightforward. If children are having difficulty learning to read, then the school should provide increasingly more support through carefully crafted small-group instruction delivered during the regular reading time or as a supplemental instruction outside the regular reading time. If after this extra help the student still has difficulty learning to read, educators must conclude that the student has a disability and is, therefore, eligible for special education. Those students who respond well to extra instruction may not have had a learning disability; they just lacked good instruction (Fuchs, Fuchs, & Vaughn, 2008). RtI identifies struggling students early and provides them with help.

RtI also includes a system of assessments to determine who needs this additional instruction, and a means of measuring the benefits of this instruction. The first assessments are called universal screening and the latter are called progress monitoring. Universal screening assessments are given to all students in a school to determine who needs intervention. After it has been determined that a student needs additional help, a school can provide various levels of intervention or support, typically called Tier 1, Tier 2, and Tier 3. Tier 1 is defined as strong classroom instruction, the instruction that the teacher delivers to the whole class and to small-groups. Tier 2 is additional differentiated small-group instruction, provided by a reading specialist or a special education teacher typically within the general education classroom. The reading specialist pushes into the general education classroom and provides additional time in small-group instruction. Essentially, the students receive more small-group instruction, but the total amount of time for reading instruction may not be extended. In Tier 3, the students not only receive more time for reading instruction, but the instructional groups are smaller, and the work is more focused on the students' needs. The school may create a special intervention time during which selected students receive Tier 3 intervention. To find this additional time, the principal might reduce time in social studies, science, or mathematics instruction.

While intervention is taking place, student progress is monitored using regularly administered curriculum-based measures (CBM) (Deno, 1991). A CBM might be a 1-minute assessment of a student's oral reading fluency, an assessment of letter-name or letter-sound knowledge, or an assessment of short vowel patterns. CBMs are typically repeated every week or two and the results are graphed to determine whether the student is making progress. If progress is not apparent, then the teachers meet and revise the intervention plan. Progress monitoring assessments have the same pitfalls as any assessment system. The testing instruments can easily become the curriculum, with teachers teaching to the test and ignoring the transfer of skills. CBM assessments, which are more attuned to lower-level reading skills (phonemic awareness and phonics) than higher ones, can become so narrow that educators can lose sight of the larger goal of reading comprehension (Turner & Paris, 2010).

If the child continues to experience reading difficulties even with the extra support, then the staff concludes that the student may have a learning disability or be eligible for special education. Students who do not succeed at Tiers 2 and 3 and are referred for special education placement but likely to be taught by the same professionals who provided help at Tiers 2 and 3. What limits the effectiveness of the RtI model is the knowledge and skill of the classroom teachers, reading specialists, and special education teachers—all the people charged with assisting the students. It is likely that teachers will use the best instructional knowledge they possess at Tier 2 and may have no new ideas left for more severely disabled readers. Some schools purchase supplemental programs for Tier 3 intervention. Well-designed intervention studies regularly demonstrate that additional help improves students' reading ability especially for foundational skills like phonemic awareness, phonics, and fluency (Wanzek, Wexler, Vaughn, & Ciullo, 2010). Improvements in reading vocabulary and comprehension are more difficult to achieve.

In a larger national study involving over 20,000 students, the results of RtI were not promising (Balu, Zhu, Doolittle, Schiller, Jenkins, & Gersten, 2015). First graders who received special Tier 2 support actually made less growth than similar students who did not receive such support. For second and third graders there was no difference in growth between those who received intervention and those who did not. These were students with mild reading problems and the study did not address students with moderate to severe problems. None-the-less the findings are disturbing.

Apparently, the carefully controlled and implemented instruction that researchers designed is difficult to replicate by classroom teachers, reading specialists, and special education teachers. Because this study was conducted in 13 states, it is difficult to describe the instruction that these students received, but the results are troubling. When Wanzek and her colleagues conducted a meta-analysis of many different studies they reached the following conclusions about reading intervention (Wanzek et al., 2010).

1. Successful interventions take on several forms. Those that focus on just foundational skills (phonemic awareness, phonics, and fluency) tend to be more successful than those that also develop vocabulary and comprehension.
2. Interventions that include multiple components, especially comprehension, are more successful in the upper grades.

3. The size of the instructional group does not seem to matter a great deal. One-on-one tutoring is no more successful than working with students in groups of 4 or 5.

4. If the students' deficits are relatively narrow, like a problem with letter recognition or phonemic awareness, positive results can be achieved in a short amount of time—a few weeks or a month.

Intervention instruction might be provided by a reading specialist or special education teacher working within the students' classroom and taking this group of students for an extra 20 to 30 minutes per day. A volunteer might also provide the intervention, working with students after school. In either case the goal is to augment the amount of small-group guided instruction. Ultimately, the distinctions between a Tier 2 and Tier 3 intervention are not precise. All schools struggle to arrange time and human resources to meet the needs of all students.

Characteristics of Successful Interventions for Struggling Readers

The most successful interventions are geared to the youngest students; preventing a reading problem in first grade is easier than assisting a struggling reader in the upper grades (Wanzek & Vaughn, 2007). Yet there are successful models of reading intervention with older elementary students (Lovett, Lacerenza, Borden, Frijters, Steinbach, & De Palma, 2000; O'Connor et al., 2002). Successful interventions, especially those for older students, take time, at least half a year or more. Some students may need support in reading for many years. There is evidence that sometimes the underlying reading problem, such as the ability to manage and implement strategies, may be solved in terms of word recognition only to reoccur when a reader must manage comprehension strategies (Smith, Borkowski, & Whitman, 2008).

The actual instructional design of an intervention can vary widely and still be successful (Mathes et al., 2005), with some interventions having a strong emphasis on text reading and others stressing work on decoding skills in isolation. However, all interventions seem to embrace the following attributes (Coyne, Kame'enui, & Simmons, 2001):

- *Explicit strategy instruction.* Reading requires strategies for identifying words, determining a word's meaning, or understanding a text. In an intervention program, the teacher has to clearly explain the strategies and model them explicitly. It is not enough for students to know letter sounds; they must have a strategy or process to use that knowledge, just as they need a process for finding the main idea.

- *Mediated scaffolding.* The student needs support when learning new skills or strategies. Sometimes the support or scaffolding is provided by the sequence of tasks in a curriculum. Easier letters and sounds are introduced before more difficult patterns, or finding an explicit main idea in a paragraph is tackled before dealing with implied main ideas in longer passages. The teacher may also provide scaffolding through the hints, suggestions, or models he provides while students work out a reading task. Several researchers have documented the importance of moment-to-moment teacher scaffolding for both word recognition and comprehension (Piasta et al., 2009; Taylor et al., 2003).

- *Strategy integration.* Whereas curriculum and instruction break reading down into its constituent elements, students should always understand how the separate skills relate to the ultimate goal—constructing meaning. Phonemic awareness needs to be taught alongside decoding so that students understand that segmenting and blending sounds leads to ease in recognizing words. Decoding and fluency need to be taught along with comprehension of connected text, so that students understand that accuracy and speed are not the only hallmarks of a good reader. It is important for students to understand how the pieces fit together.

- *Priming background knowledge.* Students with reading problems often have memory deficits. What you think they learned on Monday is forgotten by Wednesday. Strong instruction requires that previous knowledge and skills be reviewed daily before new ideas are introduced. To spell, the student has to first segment the sounds in the word. Priming causes the student to think about segmenting before he begins to spell. Asking students to think about a topic before they read should prime the knowledge they need for comprehension.

- *Judicious review.* Students with reading problems need considerable review. Coyne and colleagues (2001) remind us that review needs to be cumulative, varied, and distributed over time. In a sense, we cannot assume mastery of a skill. That is one rationale for the use of word walls for decoding. The words on the wall are a running list of the patterns that have been taught and a reminder to the teacher and students that we should use these patterns every day. Effective teachers create daily review activities, so that the words on the wall and their phonics patterns are regularly reviewed. Similarly, with reading comprehension, teachers don't assume that summarizing has been mastered; it is a tool to be used whenever it might enhance comprehension.

- *Well-paced instruction.* Strong intervention is well paced. The teacher is organized and plans for several activities within the 30 to 40 minute block. Each of these activities should be well learned by the students, so that the focus of the instruction is on the content of the activity and not the steps in the procedure. Once students understand how to make words with letter tiles, only the phonics features change and not the rules of the activity. A well-paced lesson promotes students' interest, engagement, and attention.

- *Motivation.* Students need to be motivated. We can motivate students through the pace of the lesson, the engagement of the activities and text, and through their growing sense of efficacy. If students know they are moving up to harder books, or they are reading faster, they gain a sense of confidence and their self-image as a reader grows. An intervention program should regularly provide students feedback on how they are doing.

- *Curriculum Congruency.* It helps if the reading intervention program is aligned with classroom instruction. When the classroom teacher is assisting the students with short vowel sounds these students will do better if the teacher providing intervention can work on the same skill or strategy (Wonder-McDowell, Reutzel, & Smith, 2011). Congruency requires communication between the classroom teachers and those providing intervention. This can be difficult to achieve given the complexity of schedules in schools and the lack of planning time.

- *Motivational Discussions.* Recording progress is essential. Equally important is having a short discussion with the student. It is important that teachers work to change students' attributions. If the student is making progress, he reads more quickly or knows more sight words, he should be guided to attribute these results to his own efforts. The teacher should guide the students to notice progress ("Do you think your reading is improving?") and to clarify that progress ("How do you know?"). Then the teacher should ask, "Why do you think you are improving?" If the student does not attribute the progress to his efforts, then the teacher should do so. "You have been reading every night; that is why your fluency is much better." By changing student attributions, we change their motivation.

There are times when the classroom teacher alone can provide effective intervention. Remember that five minutes a day of extra help with phonics can provide a significant increase in decoding skills. Teachers should look for these opportunities. At the end of the day, pull a small-group of students to review the phonics principles that were taught earlier. While standing in line for lunch or recess, review the sight words for the day. Send books home every night for the students to read. One approach that is very successful is the autograph book. The student takes the book home and a sheet of lined paper with the word autographs printed at the top. Every person the student reads to signs the autograph sheet. Strive for five signatures per night. We have even had the family dog or cat sign the sheet with their paw print. In the Classroom 4.6 presents a powerful research-based approach.

Intervention programs can take many forms and there are too many to even attempt a review. Mathes concluded her study of two very different intervention programs by writing "that there is likely not 'one best approach' and not one right philosophy or theory for how best to meet the needs of struggling readers" (Mathes et al., 2005, p. 179). To elaborate on this important point we would like to consider two very different intervention programs, both of which have reported considerable success with struggling readers. Each of these programs has been evaluated by either the What Works Clearinghouse (http://ies.ed.gov/ncee/wwc) or the Florida Center for Reading Research (www.fcrr.org/Interventions/index.htm). Both of these organizations evaluate the effectiveness of reading programs and instructional procedures.

Reading Recovery, which was developed in New Zealand by Marie Clay (1993), is a one-on-one tutoring program for first-graders who are struggling to read. In a typical Reading Recovery session, the student reviews letter-sound knowledge using letter tiles, spells words with the same tiles, writes a short story, rereads old books to build

In the Classroom 4.6

Neurological Impress as Intervention

There are times when a classroom teacher will want to assist a struggling reader but the human resources are not available. In these instances, students in the class can assist each other. Lisa Brown and her colleagues conducted a study in which stronger readers read with weaker readers 15 minutes per day using leveled books that were two, three, and four grade levels above the reading levels of the weaker readers (Brown, Mohr, Wilcox, Barrett, 2017). The results demonstrate significant growth in reading ability for the weaker readers and continued growth for the stronger readers.

The process is based on an idea called neurological impress in which a weaker reader reads with a stronger reader trying to match her words to those of the teacher or parent (Heckelman, 1969). The voice and words of the skilled reader are impressed on the weaker reader. The process was quite simple and easily implemented in any classroom. Weaker readers are paired with stronger readers and they sit side by side sharing one book. One person tracks the print with his or her finger while the students read with two voices. They are urged to keep their eyes on the page and read not too fast or too slow. They have a piece of paper to write down "crazy" words—words that are hard to pronounce or words for which they do not know the meaning. As the weaker students improve in reading ability, the difficulty level of the text is ratcheted up, keeping the weaker reader engaged with challenging text.

The results indicated that the weaker readers made significant progress raising their reading level by a grade level or more. The actual results report growth of two grade levels or more during 95 days of instruction, suggesting that even greater benefits would accrue if the process were used for a full year. The students enjoyed the process and the parents reported more reading at home. Later in the book we will discuss the importance of reading volume. This process of dyad reading is just another way to increase reading volume, a very effective way.

fluency, and reads a new book as the teacher assists the student with word recognition strategies. The majority of the time in a session is devoted to reading connected text, and phonics skills are taught as needed. The teacher regularly checks the student's progress by taking a running record. Reading Recovery has been shown to be very effective for the students it serves but some educators have questioned the cost of the program and wondered if Reading Recovery teachers neglect the students with the most severe reading problems (Hiebert, 1992; Shanahan & Barr, 1995). Reading Recovery teachers go through an extensive training program that can last a year in which they develop strong coaching skills.

In sharp contrast to Reading Recovery is Early Reading Intervention (Simmons & Kame'enui, 2003). Early Reading Intervention (ERI) is a small-group intervention program designed for kindergarten and first-grade students who are struggling with phonemic awareness, letter-sound association, letter-name knowledge, blending, and word reading. A Reading Recovery teacher makes many instructional decisions, whereas ERI is a tightly scripted program and teachers make few decisions. In the span of 30 minutes, students will review letter names, isolate initial consonant sounds, write words, read regular words, segment words, and practice spelling words; later in the program the students will read simple sentences. Each of the seven lesson segments are timed and can be completed in 1 to 5 minutes. Whereas Reading Recovery emphasizes reading little books, the focus on ERI is letters, sounds, and words in isolation. ERI yields significant gains in reading because of explicit instruction, knowledge priming, careful scaffolding, and very regular review. The lessons are fast paced, challenging the teacher's skill, and the students' attention.

Intervention for English Learners

Students from all cultural and linguistic groups encounter problems learning to read and schools must respond. In the preceding sections we outlined the criteria for successful differentiation and intervention. How do these criteria change when working with students who speak Spanish, Urdu, Vietnamese, or Tagalog as their native language? The first answer is that most of what works with native English speakers will work with English learners (Lovett, De Palma, Frijters, Steinbach, Temple, Benson, & Lacerenza, 2008). These students will need work with letter-name knowledge, letter-sound knowledge, phonemic awareness, and decoding. They benefit from explicit, systematic instruction that is highly interactive, fast paced, and engaging. The same criteria we describe for intervention with students whose first language is English will apply to students who are learning to speak and read English at the same time (Mathes et al., 2007).

Yet the approach with English learners must be somewhat different. First, the vocabulary learning task for these students is daunting, so our efforts at differentiation and intervention should put a greater focus on vocabulary. Even the mundane task of decoding words must have a strong vocabulary focus. When students decode words, they know they are successful if the word they pronounce is in their oral or receptive vocabulary. If you are a native speaker of Spanish and you correctly read *hog, log,* and *bog,* your vocabulary knowledge tells you your efforts were correct. Words must be explained as they are being read and pictures help students make a connection between the English word and their native language equivalent. Bilingual students, if there are some in your class, can help to make the transition between English and the student's native language. During comprehension lessons it is important to focus on little words like *some, since, fewer,* and *therefore,* the words that connect one idea with another. Finally, the more students are asked to read and explain, the better; they should be encouraged to even use gestures to help them support their comprehension development.

Technology and Intervention

For students who have struggled with learning to read, computers can provide a motivation boost that can be part of an intervention program. When students are engaged on computers, playing an exciting game, their sense of learned helplessness diminishes. Caught up in the challenge of the game, they think less about the reading skills and more about winning the game. Computer-based reading games are effective for providing the practice students need to reach automaticity with decoding and sight word recognition. The following technology-based programs have received some research support from the What Works Clearinghouse or the Best Evidences Encyclopedia.

- The software in the RAVE-O Reading Program (http://ase.tufts.edu/crlr/RAVE-O/Home.html) helps students to develop automaticity in processing orthographic patterns. Students are presented with spelling patterns and are challenged to make as many words as they can in a fixed amount of time. The students can raise the stakes by making more words in the same span of time, or the same number of words in a shorter span of time.

- Earobics (www.earobics.com) engages students in games to work on skills such as phoneme segmentation and decoding.

- Lexia Learning(www.lexialearning.com) provides lessons for phonemic awareness, phonics, structural analysis, and vocabulary. The program is engaging and the research demonstrates growth in foundational skills.

- Oral reading fluency programs like QuickReads (Hiebert, 2002) and Read Naturally (Ihnot, 2004) use speech recognition software to track reading performance as the student reads on a computer. The programs report reading rate and accuracy and provide feedback on words that need additional practice. The computer prompts the students to set goals and provides feedback on progress in attaining those goals. Technology is an efficient and motivating way to supplement intervention and provide students with the practice they need.

Technology can provide a boost in reading achievement but we caution you to be wary of programs that look like worksheets on screen. These programs offer texts for students to read and questions to answer. They claim to gear the level of difficulty to the needs of the students with the computer adjusting the difficulty as needed. This is isolated practice that does not build general literacy skills. If the goal of reading is to build knowledge and enjoyment, these programs fall short. They are little better than the workbooks and worksheets of old.

Reflect and Apply

5. An important criterion of reading intervention is additional instruction time. Talk with a teacher or a principal you know and discuss their school's daily schedule. How do they find time to provide extra instruction in a tightly packed schedule? As part of this discussion, consider the problems in establishing an after-school reading program. What are the barriers you would have to overcome to create such a program?

6. Intervention is sometimes provided within the regular classroom and sometimes the students leave to go to the special education teacher or the reading specialist. Spend a day in a school and focus on one student. Bring a stopwatch and record how much time is spent in transition from one activity to another.

7. Discuss with your teacher or another student the merits of scripted programs versus programs that teachers create. Do you believe that scripted programs devalue teachers and reduce their importance?

MyLab Education **Self-Check 4.4**

Concluding Remarks

In this chapter we discussed the ways schools and teachers can meet the vast array of differences that students bring to school and to the task of learning to read. Many of these needs can be met within the general education classroom through differentiated instruction. For primary teachers who are concerned about students' development of word recognition ability, teachers can differentiate the skills that each group needs, they can use texts that match the reading levels of their students, and they can vary time, so that struggling readers receive more teacher-directed, code-focused instruction and stronger readers spend more time reading and writing independently on important tasks. We also illustrated how upper-elementary teachers can create units of study that consider the varied reading levels of their students and yet allow all students to study similar content, work with the same genre, and employ the same comprehension strategies.

Differentiated instruction will not ensure the success of all students. Some struggling readers need additional intervention. Intervention means small-group instruction by well-trained professionals over an extended period of time. Some students will require either more time in small-group instruction in the regular class and/or additional intervention time outside the regular reading block. We demonstrated that there is no single approach to intervention that is preferable, but there are a set of criteria common to strong intervention programs, including explicit strategy instruction, regular review, strategy integration, and pacing and motivation, among others. Even if a school crafts its own intervention program, teachers should stick to a script, by which we mean a regular pattern of instruction with set procedures and time parameters. Consistency is essential. If the students do not improve, then the teachers can modify the instructional plan. If the intervention is haphazard, with capricious instructional decisions, then the teachers do not know what should be changed in the intervention program if the results are disappointing.

Extending Learning

There are two important ways you can extend what you have learned in reading this chapter. First, you need to visit classrooms and interview teachers. Second, you need to do some more reading.

1. One means of increasing your understanding of differentiation is to locate schools and classroom in which teachers have been successful in differentiating instruction. Observe in these classrooms and then interview the teachers. Find out how they organized their students into groups. Ask how they determine when to move a student to a new group. Study their management system. How do the students know what to do? How effective are the transitions in the classroom? Take notes on how teachers organize the materials in their classroom.

2. When you talk to the teachers, ask how they plan. How do they determine the needs of each group? What skills and activities are essential for weaker readers but unnecessary for stronger students? How do these teachers meet the needs of the best readers in their classrooms?

3. Extend your understanding of differentiation by reading about classroom management. Two books by Fountas and Pinnell are useful: *Guided Reading: Good First Teaching for All Children* (1996) and *Guiding Readers and Writers: Grades 3–6.* The first book focuses on primary classrooms and the second on upper grades.

Children's Literature

Bloor, E. (1997). *Tangerine*. Orlando, FL: Harcourt Books. 320 pages.

Cleary, B. (1983). *Dear Mr. Henshaw*. New York: HarperCollins. 160 pages.

Creech, S. (2000). *The Wanderer*. New York: HarperTrophy. 320 pages.

DiCamillo, K. (2000). *Because of Winn-Dixie*. New York: Candlewick Press. 182 pages.

Gantos, J. (2000). *Joey Pigza Loses Control*. New York: HarperCollins. 196 pages.

Hansen, J. (1997). *I Thought My Soul Would Rise and Fly*. New York: Scholastic. 138 pages.

Hunt, I. (2002). *Across Five Aprils*. New York: Berkley Books, 173 pages.

Mochizuki, K. (1993). *Baseball Saved Us*. New York: Lee and Low Books. 32 pages.

Osborne, M.P. (2000). *Civil War on Sunday*. New York: Random House. 124 pages

Paulsen, G. (1989). *Voyage of the Frog*. New York: Bantam Doubleday. 160 pages.

Polacco, P. (1994). *Pink and Say*. New York: Scholastic.

Reiss, J. (1972). *The Upstairs Room*. New York. HarperCollins. 196 pages.

Sachar, L. (1987). *There's a Boy in the Girls' Bathroom*. New York: Dell. 195 pages.

A Day in the Life of Jenna LeBlanc and Her First-Grade Students

Jenna LeBlanc is in her first year of teaching in a first-grade class at Edgebrook Elementary School on the outskirts of Washington, DC. Her student teaching had been with older children, so she was not quite prepared for these squirmy 6- and 7-year-olds! Now, in mid-October, however, she believes she would never want to teach another grade. She says, "I have really seen these children emerge as readers and writers. I keep a portfolio on each child, and included in it are samples of their writing since the beginning of the school year. It's exciting to look back at these and see the progress—and to think I had something to do with it."

Jenna teaches 22 children of varied backgrounds and abilities. Most of her students come from working-class families representing a wide range of cultures. Several of her students have parents who recently immigrated to the United States. Among her students, there are eight different languages spoken at home. None of her students have problems communicating in English. But there is a considerable range in their knowledge of English vocabulary. Jenna tells us that, of her 22 students, three were already reading first-grade-level texts when they entered her classroom. Most of the others were not able to read conventionally and possessed quite a range of knowledge about print. Some children, for example, knew all the alphabet and some initial consonant sounds, whereas others had difficulty naming more than a handful of letters. All were eager to learn.

Jenna's school district uses a basal reading series that includes an anthology of children's literature and informational texts. Many of the selections are written by well-known children's authors and are grouped by theme. Within a particular theme, such as The World We Share with Animals, there might be a range of genres including predictable texts, narratives, poems, and informational texts. Every child has a copy of the anthology. The basal series also has about 200 "leveled books" (see Chapter 6). These leveled books range from 6 to 20 pages each, and each is a complete text. The 200 leveled books span a continuum of reading difficulty, from books with very predictable texts to some with well-developed stories. These leveled books are leveled readers. Some stress particular phonics patterns and are decodable books. Other leveled readers stress the repetition of sight words, and still others have less vocabulary control but are tied to the theme of the unit. Leveled books provide practice in reading words with the phonics features or sight words under study. Jenna has six copies of each of the 200 leveled books.

In one corner of Jenna's classroom is the library. This inviting place contains an old sofa, pillows, a rug, a few plants, and, most of all, numerous books, magazines, and other reading material. Many books are displayed with their covers showing, as children are drawn more to those than to books with only their spines showing. Jenna frequently displays books related to the theme that is the focus in the basal reading anthology. In choosing books, she tries to include a wide range of reading levels to match the wide range of reading experiences among her students.

"Children do best when they feel secure," Jenna reports. "That's why routines and a daily schedule that become familiar to the children are very important." Jenna's morning schedule looks like this:

8:30–8:50	Book check-in, calendar, morning message
8:50–9:20	Theme-related whole-class activity
9:20–10:40	Small-group guided reading, writing, and word study
10:40–11:00	Whole-class sharing of center activities
11:00–11:20	Recess

Let's join Jenna for her morning reading/language arts period.

8.30   Book Check-In, Calendar, Morning Message

As children enter the classroom, they pass a bulletin board that has a chart on it with each of their names printed on an individual library pocket. Each book in the class library has a check-out pocket with a library card in it. When the children leave at the end of the school day, they check out one or two books by putting the library card from the back of the book into the pocket with their name on it on the bulletin board. When they first arrive the next morning, they retrieve the card and place it back into the book they took home before returning the book to the class library.

After checking in their books and putting their personal items in their cubbies, the children gather on a rug in front of the whiteboard and large calendar. Jenna first goes over the calendar and has them locate the date and day. The amount of time spent on this activity varies from day to day. They talk about the season, the weather, birthdays, and other special events.

Every day, Jenna prints a morning news message on chart paper. Jenna asks for volunteers who would like to tell what special things are happening at home, in their lives, or in the world. She writes what is said on the chalkboard under the heading *Morning News*. Because it is relatively early in the school year, Jenna does most of the writing, but the children do participate. She asks the children how to spell individual words, what sound a word begins with, or what letter comes next. After the message is finished, individual students are asked to come up to circle specific words, find particular sounds, or add a period that might be missing. The morning message allows Jenna to review many of the phonemic awareness, phonics, and writing concepts that have been taught. If there is time, she then has children share information about the books they checked out and read at home.

8.50   Theme-Related Whole-Class Activity

The theme for the next few weeks is Animals Who Share the World with Us, and this is the first day of the unit. Jenna likes to start her theme-related work with a whole-class activity that develops the children's knowledge about the theme. In prior conversations with us, she emphasized that she likes "to start with what children know." We see that is the case, as Jenna begins the session today by engaging the children in a discussion about animals they have seen. She makes a language chart on a large sheet of butcher paper. After a child says something, she records the child's name next to what he or she says. As she records their words, she often makes comments—such as why she used a capital letter. Here's part of the language chart:

Jamal   I saw a horse with a policeman on it in DC!

Malt   I have a gerbil at home.

Kara   My dog Nick is black and white.

Tyron   I saw a black-and-white zebra at the zoo.

Cynara   There are lots of deer in the woods and I saw some.

Jenna steers the discussion to where the different animals were seen, and to the environments in which different animals live. She brings out a large piece of butcher paper on which the class will start a wall chart. The paper is divided into sections, with several headings printed across the top and room to the right to add additional ones, as shown below:

In the Water	On a Farm	In the Woods	In Our Homes	In the Jungle			
fish	horses cows	deer raccoons wolf snake owl	dogs cats	monkeys giraffe			

Jenna starts by asking the children where the animals they have mentioned live, and she records their responses under the appropriate categories. There is some discussion about where zebras might live if they weren't in a zoo and where horses normally would be found.

Next, Jenna brings out a big book version of *Hoot Howl Hiss* by Michelle Koch. She points to the illustrations on the cover. "Michelle Koch is not only the author, she is also the illustrator of the book," she tells the children. "The watercolor illustrations of animals are painted a lot like you paint in our class! Can you name any of the animals you see on the cover and tell where you might find them?" Jenna points to the title words as she asks which animal says *hoot*, which one *howls*, and which one goes *hiss*. They add the words *wolf*, *snake*, and *owl* to the In the Woods column on the wall chart. Jenna particularly emphasizes the sounds in the word *snake* as she prints the word on the chart. Jenna tells the children that when they are in the writing center, they will draw some of these animals, write about them, and paste their creations on the wall chart.

Jenna asks the children to think about where each animal mentioned in the book lives as she begins to read, "Deep in the woods, owls . . . hoot . . ." She pauses before *hoot*, and several children correctly anticipate it. *Hoot Howl Hiss* is a short book with a very predictable structure. The illustrations help the children identify the animal words. When she finishes reading the book, Jenna asks the children about the sounds various animals make, as well as where they live.

Small-Group Guided Reading, Writing, Word Study

9:20

There are four centers in Jenna's classroom: a reading center, a writing center, a science center, and a teacher center where Jenna provides direct instruction in word study and engages students in guided reading. She groups children by their reading level and their word study needs. She randomly divides the rest of her class into groups that rotate through the reading, writing, and science centers. Most days, the children rotate through all four centers. If children finish a center activity before it is time for the next rotation, they are free to return to their desks and read from their anthologies, little books, or books from the library.

The reading center is the classroom library. In that center, the children can either read to a buddy or read independently. Sometimes they have assignments; sometimes they do free reading. During the animal unit, they will find lots of books about animals prominently displayed on the low table in the reading center. Jenna requires some accountability for the students' work at the reading center. At the beginning of the year they complete a simple reading log, recording the title and author of the book and then drawing a picture. As the students grow throughout the year they will write longer responses to their books.

In the writing center, the children draw and write. They can draw a picture of an animal, write its name, and then paste their drawing on the wall chart. Before they paste it, they need to discuss with one other child which environment the animal lives in and whether its name is correctly spelled. The children are encouraged to check the spellings and animal habitats by looking at books in the reading center. Jenna tells us that she encourages the children to use invented spelling in free writing, but when the time comes to make the writing public, she wants the words correctly spelled. She says that she doesn't want the children to reread incorrect spellings on a permanent basis—and she intends to make use of the wall chart throughout the unit.

The science center is used both to promote understanding of science as well as children's reading and writing of expository text. Right now, the science center has 20 cups of radish seeds that are growing in various media—soil, wet towels, sand, and so forth. The children are to observe the growing plants and take notes. They have already practiced drawing growing plants and writing short captions. Also at the science center are many science books—such as *From Seed to Plant* by Gail Gibbons and *The Reason for a Flower* by Ruth Heller. The science center enables the teacher and students to continue a unit of study that began 2 weeks ago even though they have now moved on to the study of animals.

Each group that comes to the teacher's table will participate in different types of phonics instruction and engage in guided reading. The particular focus of the phonics instruction depends on the needs of students. One group of children is working on initial consonants, another on the consonant digraphs *ch* and *wh,* and a third group on short vowels. The basic format for each group, however, is the same. Jenna begins the lesson for each group by having the children chorally read *Hoot Howl Hiss.* The focus then shifts to a word or two in that story that contains the phonics feature under study. The consonant digraph group, for example, will focus on the words *chirp* and *whistle.*

After locating words with the phonic features in *Hoot Howl Hiss,* Jenna extends the phonics instruction to other words. This extension often involves four activities (described in Chapter 8):

- *Sorting* picture or word cards
- *Blending* and reading new words with new phonics patterns

- *Reading* a leveled book that contains several words with the phonics features
- *Writing* a dictated sentence with words that contain the target spelling pattern

Sorting

To develop phonemic awareness of initial consonant sounds, Jenna has the children do a group picture sort on a pocket chart. She calls out the name of a picture, and they help her place it under one of the word card headings *howl*, *lion*, and *quack*. She holds up a drawing of a hen and says "Hen, howl—hen, lion—hen, quack." The children agree that the hen picture belongs under *howl*. Then she takes out a drawing of a leg and says, "Leg— howl, —leg— lion, leg—quack, leg." The group continues in this manner with pictures of a queen, quilt, horse, and hat as well as pictures representing other words from *Hoot Howl Hiss*.

Blending

After the students have sorted words, it is important to try out their new letter-sound associations on other words. Sometimes this work is simply practice using the small whiteboard or a handmade flip chart. The teacher writes the word family pattern on the whiteboard—*at*, for example—and then changes the initial sound—*h* + *at* makes *hat*; *s* + *at* makes *sat*. The teacher first models the blending activity and then guides the students through it with a sliding hand gesture. Each group of students will practice making and blending words. Sometimes this will involve the use of letter tiles, other times the students will write the words on their personal whiteboards, and still other times the students will play a blending game.

Reading

To provide reading practice with the newly introduced initial consonant combination *qu*, Jenna uses a leveled book entitled *Quack!* by Matthew Benjamin. She gives each child a copy. "Can you read the word on the cover?" she asks. "The ducks are a good clue!" She has the children point to the letters that say /kw/ in *quack*. She tells the children that *Quack!* is about a mother duck and her three ducklings. Jenna reads the story as the children follow along, finger-pointing to the words as she says them. Then they all read it aloud together. After this rereading, Jenna asks them to go through the book on a word hunt. They are to find all the words that start with *qu* and read them to the child sitting next to them. There are lots of shouts of "Quack!" and "Quick!" and "Quiet!" as they locate these words in the story. Finally, all the students practice reading the story independently.

Writing

To end this word study session, Jenna reads simple sentences and has the children write them. She will later examine what each child has written to see which children might need some extra help. She is particularly interested in their spellings of the initial consonants. She hands out a piece of lined paper and tells them to write as best they can *Ducks quack. Lions roar. I hoot.* Here's what a few children wrote:

Wu	Dks quak. Lins r. I ht.
Kara	Duks quak. Lions rar. I hut.
Dustin	DS QUK LN RR I HT
Jamal	Duks quack. Lions ror. I hoot.

10:40 Whole-Class Sharing of Center Activities

The class gathers back on the rug in front of the calendar. Children bring with them any books they would like to share. Jenna begins by asking them to quack like a duck. Then she turns to the In the Water portion of the wall chart and asks if anyone put a duck up there. Several hands go up, and she has each child go over and point to his or her duck. She then asks for other children who drew animals that live in the water to come up and identify their pictures. There's a sea turtle and a whale among the group. Jenna does the same for the other categories.

With only a few minutes remaining until lunch, not everyone who has a book to share gets a chance to do so. But there's always tomorrow, and Jenna will make sure that any student who didn't get a turn today will get one the next day. Additionally, Jenna looks forward to the afternoon, when she and her students will be able to put their budding literacy skills to use in other curricular areas—science, math, social studies, art, and music.

Chapter 5
Classroom Assessment

 ## Learning Outcomes

After reading and studying this chapter you should be able to:

5.1 Describe the current assessment climate in the nation, it roots, and its consequences.

5.2 Develop a formative assessment program in your classroom that supports students and guides instruction.

5.3 Use an informal reading inventory and its various components to acquire a deeper understanding of how your students read.

5.4 Explain the strengths and limits of commercially developed assessments and how to prepare your students for high-stakes testing.

Classroom Vignette

The Check-up: It is early January and Ms. Aikens and her principal are concerned about the progress of her 28 fourth-grade students. Some clearly are reading well and enjoying it but six continue to struggle. Ms. Aikens is required by school district guidelines to assess the progress of her six students who struggle, but her principal is more concerned with the students on the "bubble." These are five students who might pass the state tests, or not, and they can make or break the reputation of the school and Ms. Aikens' evaluation. Ms. Aikens administers the Developmental Reading Assessment (DRA) to 11 of her students, the five students on the bubble and the six who are truly struggling with reading. The testing will consume most of the day and part of the next day. Because Ms. Aikens will be busy testing, an aide will be covering her class. This is the third time this year the students have taken the DRA.

The Test: 8:30 A.M., Thursday morning, early May. Ms. Aikens announces what does not need to be announced—that the reading test, Smarter Balanced, will begin with part I today and part II tomorrow. She asks two students to distribute the Chromebooks. Ms. Aikens briefly reviews the process for taking the online assessment, yet this is unnecessary; the student have been practicing taking computer assisted tests for months. Most students will spend the better part of the day taking the test. A few groans, a couple of questions, by 9:00 the 28 fourth-graders hunch in silence over screens, reading and selecting answers and occasionally writing out short answers. Some students take breaks, others push on until everyone stops at 11:00 for an assigned break. Some will finish part I by 12:00, others will continue well into the afternoon.

The Project: A month before, in early April. Ms. Aikens' students return from lunch for science. "Today is the A-team report on Mars. Eduardo, you're in charge. Bring up your group to tell us about your project." Eduardo and three classmates tape sheets of butcher paper with the headings *Place in the Solar System, Physical Characteristics*, and *Building a Habitat* on the front wall. Each sheet is a collage of graphics, photos, and notes from websites. For 40 minutes, the group describes the Red Planet and the books and websites they used as resources. Then they add their sheets to a huge "Planets" display being prepared for Parents' Night. Ms. Aikens prompts each group for accuracy and encourages them to check the understanding of the other students. But mostly she evaluates Eduardo's group and what it learned.

Our Perspective on Assessment

The first two scenarios capture the current assessment reality in most classrooms; the third reflects what we wish was more common. In this chapter, we will first describe the current assessment climate in the nation. Many of you will be teaching in schools that are dominated by high-stakes testing and many other assessments that prepare students for those tests. As current or prospective teachers we feel it is important for you to know what awaits you. Armed with knowledge you can become an advocate for your students and ameliorate some of the negative impact of assessment.

Next, we examine teacher-based strategies for classroom assessment, in which your role is to carry out practical research on student learning—collecting and analyzing data. We will walk you through this process because we believe that the data you collect from daily work in the classroom is more powerful and less disruptive to teaching and learning than standardized tests. At the end we will circle back to standardized assessments and how you can help students with these elephants in the room. We have updated many of the ideas and concepts in this book, but this chapter on assessment has gone through the most extensive revision.

The State of Assessment in Reading

In 2002, the No Child Left Behind legislation mandated that every third through eighth grade student be assessed in reading and mathematics. It was believed by policy experts and educational reformers that establishing universally high standards and holding all teachers and schools accountable for meeting these standards would raise students' achievement and close the gap between advantaged and disadvantaged students. This policy was enacted by President George W. Bush, strengthened by President Obama, and is largely intact with the Every Student Succeeds Act (ESSA, 2015). These are high-stakes tests because schools and teachers would be rewarded for strong performance and sanctioned for poor performance. Consistently poor performance over time could result in the firing of teachers and principals and reconstituting schools—in other words, starting over. The second policy mandate directed schools to regularly monitor the reading progress of students who had difficulty learning to read, so schools began to test some students every week or two.

High-Stakes and Benchmark Testing

School district administrators responded to these new testing mandates by asking two questions. Which students were likely to pass the high-stakes test and what were their areas of weakness? The district reasoning went like this. We know that the good readers will pass the test so they are not a concern. We also know that the students with the greatest weakness might not pass, so we can pay less attention to them. The schools sought to concentrate on the students on the bubble, those who could pass the test with extra help. Second, educators hoped to use the tests diagnostically and focus instruction on those skills, strategies, or standards that caused the students the greatest difficulty.

Thus began a barrage of interim or benchmark tests designed to predict and diagnose students' performance. The districts first designed their own interim tests, modeled after the state high-stakes tests, and later these tests were purchased from publishing companies who sensed a lucrative market. The interim tests were administered three times a year—November, January, and March. At the school level, the teachers and the administrators poured over the results, focusing on the students' areas of weakness. The teachers tended to forget that only some skills and strategies were assessed, ignoring what was not assessed. The reading curriculum narrowed.

Unfortunately, these diagnostic benchmark tests, sold as formative tests, became summative. Formative tests guide instruction. Summative tests assess the outcomes of instruction. District administrators compared the benchmark test results of one school to another and for the schools that performed poorly the principals were called on the carpet and told to submit remediation plans. When the principals returned to their schools they reviewed the test results by grade level and by teacher and those with low test scores had to design new instructional plans. This was accountability in action.

According to a series of research studies these benchmark tests had more negative than positive consequences (see Shepard, 2010). Time for reading instruction and independent reading was now spent preparing, giving, and analyzing tests. In one district in which one of us worked, over 65 days of instruction was devoted to these benchmark tests. Students reviewed before the tests, two days was devoted to taking the test, teachers were pulled from class to analyze the results, and then remediation took place. Time for other subjects, science and social studies, shrunk, so more time could be devoted to reading. The reading curriculum narrowed and teachers focused on tested items and ignored aspect of the reading curriculum that was not assessed. In many schools, teachers were teaching the test (Shepard, 2010). The instructional materials changed. Because students' comprehension was assessed with passages, reading was taught with passages; teachers avoided authentic novels, short stories, and non-fiction books.

These changes to assessment and instruction increased state test scores. But the increases were specious, what many called score inflation (Koretz, 2017). How do we know? Although students' scores on their state tests increased, for over a decade students' scores on the National Assessment of Education Progress (NAEP) did not change. If you look back to Chapter 1, you can see the differences between students' performance on their state test and on NAEP. In the worst cases the teachers and administrators cheated. They coached students and changed their answers. In a few school districts, teachers and administrators were indicted and a few served time in prison.

Teaching to the test, spending excessive time on test-taking strategies, and in rare cases cheating, (by teachers and administrators, not students), is an example of Campbell's Law. Don Campbell, a social scientist, wrote "The more any social indicator is used for social decision making, the more subject it will be to corruption pressures and the more apt it will be to distort and corrupt the social processes it was intended to monitor" (Campbell, 1979, p. 85). The recent VW diesel engine scandal is a good example of Campbell's law in action (Koretz, 2017). VW produced a very peppy, supposedly fuel-efficient diesel engine. Unfortunately, the engine, installed on many VW cars, polluted health impairing nitrogen oxides and failed to meet federal EPA gas mileage standards. The VW engineers solved the problem by installing a device on the car that gave acceptable pollution readings when the car was being tested, but turned off when the car was driving under normal conditions, polluting away. VW was fined billions for cheating.

Campbell's Law is in action across the country. It is in action when students practice taking tests, when benchmark tests consume time for reading instruction, when substitutes teach class so teachers can sit in the conference room to analyze test scores, when teachers spend excessive time on test-taking strategies and when schools cut short science, social studies, and recess (Caplan & Igel, 2015). The results of this high-stakes testing policy on reading achievement is summarized by Daniel Koretz in his detailed book *The Testing Charade* (2017).

> It's no exaggeration to say that the costs of test-based accountability have been huge. Instruction has been corrupted on a broad scale. Large amounts of instructional time are now siphoned off into test-prep activities that at best waste time and at worst defraud students and their parents. Cheating has become widespread. The public has been deceived into thinking that achievement has dramatically improved and that achievement gaps have narrowed. Many students are subject to severe stress, not only during testing but also for long periods of time leading up to it. Educators have been evaluated in misleading and in some cases utterly absurd ways. Careers have been disrupted and, in some cases, ended (p.191).

Response to Intervention and Progress Monitoring

High-stakes testing was not the only policy innovation that influenced assessment practices in elementary schools. The Reading First initiative (2002–2008), part of NCLB, was a larger Federal effort to raise reading achievement in high poverty schools in kindergarten through third grade. Reading First mandated that all primary students be screened early in the school year and the progress of those at risk be monitored throughout the year. Because of this mandate, Reading First schools, and many others, added another standardized test to screen students and determine who needed additional help. Four times a year or more, the progress of these students was monitored using assessment systems like *DIBELS Next* (Kaminski & Good, 2006) and *AimsWebPlus* (Pearson, 2011) which measured students' growth in letter-sound knowledge, phonemic awareness, phonics, fluency, and comprehension. These assessments were often administered individually to each student, taking time from instruction.

The mandate for progress monitoring introduced in Reading First was reinforced with the Individuals with Disabilities Education Act (2004) (IDEA) that provided a new means of identifying students for special education. IDEA proposed that students with difficulties be placed in an intervention program and their progress monitored. Those who did not improve in reading ability would be candidates for special education. In most schools, all struggling readers were progress monitored. Now every kindergarten through third grade student was screened for reading ability and those needing additional intervention were progress monitored, stopping instruction, as teachers gave one-on-one tests. Progress monitoring took its place alongside benchmark testing insuring that everyone was tested regularly.

The national results for Reading First (Gamse, Jacobs, Horst, Boulay, & Unlu, 2008) were negligible and those for Response to Intervention (RTI) were equally slim (Balu, Zhu, Doolittle, Schiller, Jenkins, & Gersten, 2015). A national evaluation of Reading First found that only first grades demonstrated modest progress in decoding, second and third grades made no growth, and no students improved in reading comprehension. There were isolated state efforts that painted a more positive picture (See *Journal of Literacy Research*, Vol. 42 (1) for individual state studies). The national evaluation for RTI demonstrated no significant growth for second and third grade students who received intervention, and, first grade students who received intervention actually showed less growth than similar students who did not receive extra help. We encourage you to think about why this happened.

All of these initiatives launched by NCLB, Reading First, IDEA, and RTI unleashed a flood of assessment practices in elementary and middle schools. Publishing companies began marketing assessment systems like *I-Ready* from Curriculum Associates and the *MAP* (Northwest Evaluation Associates) suite of tests that were directly linked to specific state standards, specific skills, and intervention activities. Administrators placed their trust in the data generated by commercial assessments and not teachers' observations and insights. We suspect that teachers began to question their own insight and judgment. These initiatives were encouraged by our thirst for, and embrace of, data.

Data Driven Instruction

The push for efficiency has been the goal of educators for decades. It began in the early decades of the 20th century when a more diverse student body entered our schools as millions of immigrants from Europe and six million African Americans who left the South sought a better life in the North, Middle West, and West. Schooling became mandatory and educators wanted an easy way to know the reading levels of their students. The standardized test was developed to meet this need and the first was the *Kansas Silent Reading Test* (Pearson & Hamm, 2005). When the standardized, multiple-choice reading test was coupled with the IBM 805 scanner, efficiency was at hand. Millions of students could be tested at a fraction of the cost.

Since these early times, the quest for efficiency has never left us. Education has always been pulled between a business efficiency model and a social humanistic model (Calahan, 1962). Most recently, educators have turned to products that assess students with computer adaptive software. The students spend 30 to 45 minutes in front of a computer screen taking a reading test. The test adjusts the type and difficulty of the questions to the student's responses using the fewest number of items to determine the student's reading level. The results report the students' reading level and attempt to "diagnose" the student's skills, his strengths, and weaknesses.

There are three problems with this approach to reading assessment. First, reading is both a cognitive and an affective endeavor, a product of skill and will. A computer adaptive testing program can report the student's knowledge of sight words, his ability to decode new words, and his reading fluency. It can assess his word knowledge and general comprehension, but it cannot measure his motivation to read. Furthermore, the computer testing program cannot tell how motivated the student was even to take the test, suggesting that for some students the reported scores are not an accurate reflection of their ability (Haladyna & Downing, 2005). The more frequently students are assessed, the less likely they take the assessments seriously. Assessment, like any activity in the classroom, required motivation and unlike other assignments, the motivation to take a test is based on extrinsic rather than intrinsic motivation. Seriously, how many of us look forward to regularly being assessed, labeled, and categorized?

The second problem with data driven instruction and the computer assisted testing is the uneven quality of such tests. Scott Paris (2005) divided reading into constrained and unconstrained skills. Constrained skills such as letter name knowledge and letter sound knowledge have few pieces of knowledge to teach and are relatively easy to assess. To assess a five-year-old's knowledge of letter names, a teacher needs 26 flashcards. Unconstrained skills such as vocabulary and comprehension are much more difficult to assess. A student's comprehension ability is heavily influenced by the passage, the student's background knowledge, and interest, making the assessment of comprehension tricky.

Computer adaptive testing uses the fewest number of test items to determine a reading level. As the number of items shrink, so do the diagnostic features of the test. If a test requires only 20 or so items it is difficult to gain reliable information about specific skills or concepts. Finally, as computer assisted assessment systems push into our schools, they tend to drive out other forms of assessment, those based on teacher observations and students' daily work. It is here we will continue our chapter.

Our View on Assessment

Assessments are divided into formative activities that teachers use in the classroom to monitor learning and summative events represented by the externally mandated

Figure 5.1 Comparison of Assessment for Instruction and Assessment for Accountability

	Formative Assessment Designed for Instruction	Summative Assessment Designed for Accountability
Purpose and Source	Designed by teachers for classroom decisions Several sources of information Strong link to curriculum and instruction	Designed by experts for policy makers Stand-alone, single indicator Independent of curriculum and instruction
Criteria	Valid for guiding instruction Profile reliability–strengths and weaknesses Sensitive to changes in performance	Predictive validity to other tests Total test reliability–one score Stable over time and situations
Pragmatics	Judgmental, quick turn-around, flexible Performance-based "real" task Continuously, as needed	Objective, cost- and time-efficient, standardized Multiple-choice "school" task Once or sometimes twice per year

standardized tests. Figure 5.1 represents the differences in these types of assessments. Summative tests come at the end of a course of study, when students become accountable for their achievement. Now, unfortunately, formative assessments are mandated and have taken on the aura of summative tests with all the pressures and anxiety they contain.

Assessments should be integrated into the curriculum. They should be natural, unobtrusive, and scarce. If students are making good progress learning to read and they enjoy reading, then all the teacher needs to know can be gleaned from their class work and the thoughts they share during groups discussions and reading conferences. It is only when students stumble that we need to take a closer look at their reading to determine what course of action might help them.

We have chosen to emphasize the left-hand side of the spectrum shown in Figure 5.1—teacher-based assessment—for three reasons. First, the teacher's role in standardized testing, both formative and summative, is often limited to management and reporting. Administrators select the tests, computers give them, and publishers score them and return results and interpretations. Our goal is to help you turn away from these mandated tests and encourage personal decision making, restoring teacher prerogative. So, we will start with true formative assessment, like students' written work and their thinking during discussions.

WHAT IS AN ASSESSMENT

At its roots, an assessment is as inference. Educators collect samples of students' behavior and thinking, and from those samples they infer how the students is reading, what his strengths and weaknesses are, and what instructional steps should be taken to help him improve. The quality of our inferences is determined by the reliability and validity of our data (Koretz, 2008). Reliability means that our data are accurate and consistent. From one test to another or from one work sample to another we are measuring the same thing. Validity means that we are measuring the true nature of things, in this case reading. If we ask a student to read a list of words and then conclude he is a good reader, that is not valid. There is more to reading than reading the words accurately. A valid assessment measures the right attributes of reading so that the inferences lead us to the right conclusions and actions.

This leads to the third reason for emphasizing teacher-based assessment: Authentic assessment of present-day literacy can never be completely "standardized" or completely reliable. Although prepackaged tests provide a rough index of achievement, the teacher is in the best position to monitor students' ability to use language, to think, and

MyLab Education
Video Example 5.1
In this video, the teacher demonstrates an alternative to the high-stakes testing and benchmark testing that is controlling many classrooms.

to communicate. Knowing that a student is at the 50th percentile in reading comprehension doesn't tell you what the student can and can't do. Picking the right answer to a multiple-choice question is less reflective of literacy than being able to explain the shift in the relationship between Charlotte (a spider) and Wilbur (a pig) over the course of E. B. White's *Charlotte's Web*. That is validity.

Reflect and Apply

1. Let's say you are looking for a teaching position in a particular district. The personnel director invites you to visit several schools. The district has a reputation for supporting thematic projects and literacy portfolios. You are curious about assessment in the district. What do you look for in classrooms and discuss with colleagues about the potential of projects and portfolios for assessing student achievement?

2. A parent approaches you because her third grade son has just scored at the 39th percentile on the I-Ready test. Yet, her son reads all the time, enjoys books, and talks at great length about what he reads. What would you say to the parent? How might you study this discrepancy?

MyLab Education **Self-Check 5.1**

MyLab Education **Application Exercise 5.1:** Coping with Benchmark and Other Interim Assessments

Formative Assessments in the Classroom

In this section, we will focus on formative assessments, tools, and procedures that can inform teachers and help them meet the needs all students in the class. Our approach to assessment is derived from the work of Wiliams and Black who laid out the foundations of formative assessment (Black & Wiliams, 2009). In this process, the teacher is not testing the student, but together the teachers and the students are exploring the learning and adjusting instruction to improve success. This ongoing process of assessment includes the following steps:

1. Clarifying and sharing with students the goals of instruction and criteria for success.
2. Engineering effective classroom discussions and writing tasks that elicit evidence of student understanding.
3. Providing feedback that moves the learner forward.
4. Activating students as instructional resources for one another.
5. Activating students as the owners of their own learning.

These five steps sound much like the process of scaffolding we outlined in Chapter 2 and a part of the gradual release of responsibility model (Pearson & Gallagher, 1983). Different sets of educators tend to develop similar concepts about teaching and learning but assign different labels. Think of Wiliams and Black's formative assessment process as the feedback loop that moves learning forward within the gradual release of responsibility model. We will focus our attention on the information a teacher can glean from the day-to-day activities in the classroom.

Learning about Your Students at the Beginning of the Year

At the beginning of each school year, the primary question for the classroom teacher seems simple enough: What do the students already know? How well can they read? At year's end, the questions are similar: What have the students learned? How have they grown as readers? Along the way, questions become more dynamic: How are students responding to various instructional activities? Who is getting it? Who is not? The foundation for these questions is the school or district standards and in most states, except for Texas, Virginia, Alaska, Indiana, Nebraska, Oklahoma, and South Carolina, those standards are based on the Common Core State Standards (NGA & CCSSO, 2010). The curriculum is the materials and instructional procedures a teacher employs to help the students meet those standards. The curriculum means much more than getting through the textbook or obediently following the district's pacing guide.

Let's consider this process from the point of view of two teachers, one teaching first grade and another teaching fifth grade. Except for kindergarten and first grade children, most students have an assessment history, previous test scores, and report cards from last year's teachers. This information provides a valid assessment of the students' reading ability.

First Grade. Our first-grade teacher begins her quest to learn about her students by consulting the foundational standards of the Common Core State Standards (NGA & CCSSO, 2010) and thinking about her experiences from previous years. She knows that her primary goal is to develop her students' word recognition skills, build their fluency, develop vocabulary, and begin the process of helping her students understand different genres of text. She needs to know the following about her students:

- Level of phonemic awareness,

- Knowledge of letter names, letter-sounds,

- Ability to decode short and long vowel words,

- Concept of word,

- The size of their sight vocabulary, and

- Ability to retell simple stories and informational text.

Much of this information can be learned by meeting with each student individually and administering a beginning reading inventory. We have included a beginning reading inventory and the Tile Test in the appendix of this book. These inventories take time, so it is important to establish a classroom routine that ensures that the students can work independently, giving you time to assess each student. While the students are engaged, call individuals up to your desk one at a time and administer the inventory.

Based on the data you collect you can form reading groups, but it is also important to listen to your students read. The running record procedure that follows will help you note the decoding skills of your students and estimate their reading level. Some first graders, with little reading experience, need to work on phonemic awareness and letter recognition, others might be ready for work with short vowels and the more skilled readers might be ready for work with long vowels. All of the students would be reading in a book that is geared to their level of development.

Fifth Grade. Our fifth-grade teacher begins to study her students by thinking about the curriculum standards in her district and how they are based on the Common Core State Standards. She does not need to assess their expertise with all of the standards, but she does need a place to start. She focuses on three standards. The other standards, such as integrating knowledge and ideas, using diverse media, and evaluating a written argument can come later as she move students to more complex text and into deeper analysis of those texts. At the beginning of the year, our fifth-grade teacher wants to know if her students can:

- Read closely to determine what the text says explicitly and to make logical inferences from it; cite specific textual evidence when writing or speaking to support conclusions drawn from the text. CCSS.ELA-LITERACY.CCRA.R.1

- Determine central ideas or themes of a text and analyze their development; summarize the key supporting details and ideas. CCSS.ELA-LITERACY.CCRA.R.2

- Analyze the structure of texts, including how specific sentences, paragraphs, and larger portions of the text (e.g., a section, chapter, scene, or stanza) relate to each other and the whole. CCSS.ELA-LITERACY.CCRA.R.5

She also wants to know something about the students' reading level so she can match students with the right level of text. She will have access to last year's test scores and that data is a reasonable way to initially form reading groups. To validate that data, she listens to each student read aloud, selecting a text that she typically uses at the beginning of the year. If the students oral reading performance coincides with previous test scores she has confidence in her decisions. She knows that groups are flexible and can easily be changed. In addition, it would be useful to have each student complete an interest inventory.

Many schools will require a standardized reading test, or the placement test from your core reading program at the beginning of the year. It gives you a quick impression of the distribution of skills and abilities in the room. For students new to the school and those a teacher wants to know better, she can administer a running record to assess reading level, accuracy, fluency, and comprehension. The process begins by selecting a text that you expect a student to be able to read. Pick a text from their core reading program, or a short selection from a book you expect most students in your grade to read early in the school year. In the Classroom 5.1 outlines the procedure for administrating and interpreting a running record.

Our fifth-grade teacher forms her reading groups and now the process of assessment and instruction begin to merge. The students are given a short fictional narrative; the teacher provides a brief introduction, and the students begin to read with a partner. By listening to their oral reading, she gains a sense of their decoding and fluency. After

In the Classroom 5.1

Running Records

Administration

To administer a running record, you will need a passage from a book that you believe your students should be able to read. Pick something that is between 100 and 300 words long, but shorter for first-and second-grade students. You will also need a means of timing the students and paper to take notes. Make sure your student is comfortable and relaxed. Tell the student what he will be reading about and give him some information about the selection. Say something like the following:

This is a story in which [theme-related statement]. Please read this story aloud for me. If you come to a word you don't know, try to figure it out, guess at it, or skip it. I will not be able to help you, so do your best. When you have finished I will ask you to retell what you have read.

Tell the student to begin reading and *turn on the timing device*. Record the student's response on a blank sheet of paper or on a copy of the text. If you are using a blank piece of paper place a check mark for each word read correctly and write down the errors the student made. Note the total time needed to read the passage. If you are recording directly on a copy of the passage, write the errors immediately above the words the student was trying to read and follow these guidelines. Figure 5.2 has an example of both types of scoring.

- Omission: Circle the words.
- Insertion: Add a caret and write in the student's response above the word.
- Substitution: Draw a line through the word and write in the substituted word over it.
- Repetition: Draw a box around the repeated words.
- Teacher help: Write a T above the word.
- Self-correction: Next to the miscue write SC.

Figure 5.2 A Sample Running Record with Two Note Taking Systems

The Story	Running Record on Blank Paper	Running Record on a Copy of the Story
My Hamster, Van	✓✓✓	My Hamster, Van *had*
I have a hamster.	✓ had ✓ have	I have a hamster.
His name is Van.	✓✓✓✓	His name is Va.
Van is tan and white.	✓✓✓✓T	T Van is tan and ~~white~~.
He has black eyes and a pink nose.	✓✓✓✓✓ -----✓ pink	He has black eyes and a pink nose.
I feed him.	✓ fed ✓ ✓✓✓ apple.	*fed* I feed him. *apple* I give Van a carrot.
I give Van a carrot.		
Total words = 32	Time = 45 seconds	

If the student becomes frustrated, reassure him that guessing is fine or he can skip the word. If he continues to pause and becomes upset, you should pronounce the word that is causing the difficulty. Mark that with a T, a teacher assisted word. When the student has finished reading, ask him to retell the story or article. If the student gives you very little information, ask the student to tell you more. Try to write down all the ideas the student includes in the retelling.

Analysis

Accuracy: Count the total number of oral reading miscues and record the total on a record sheet. Then divide this number by the total number of words read. (You will have to count the words in the passages.) This will give you the accuracy percentage. In the preceding example, the student read a total of 32 words and made 4 errors. That equals 28 words read correctly: 28 / 32 = 87.5% accuracy. Figure 5.3 presents the criteria for determining reading levels; we used the criteria from the Qualitative Reading Inventory – 5 and added our criteria for retelling (Leslie & Caldwell, 2011).

Fluency: On the retelling sheet or a copy of the story, write down the number of minutes and seconds the student spent reading the story. Use the following formula to calculate the reading rate in Words Correct per Minute (WCPM). Tindal and Hasbrouck's (2005) fluency norms will help you determine how well the students are doing (http://www.readingrockets.org/article/fluency-norms-chart-2017-update). Use the fall, winter, or spring norms.

Total Words Read – errors = total words correct
Total Words Correct / total seconds × 60 = WCPM [Record this number]
Total Words Read = 32 – 4 errors = 28 total words correct
Total Words Correct = 28/45 seconds = .62 × 60 = 37.3 Words Correct per Minute

Comprehension: The retelling score will be determined by using the following scoring guide. After the student reads his passage, ask him to retell everything he can remember. Then rate the retelling on the following scale and record the results on the student's score sheet.

(Continued)

Figure 5.3 Scoring Guideline for a Running Record

	Word Recognition Accuracy	Percent Comprehension Questions Correct	Retelling Score
Independent Level	98%	90% or better	4
Instructional Level	90–97%	67–89%	3 – 2
Frustration Level	Less than 90%	Less than 67%	1

Scoring Guide for Retelling

4 A reasonably complete retelling. The child mentions the main character or characters, the problem they confront, the attempts to solve the problem and the resolution or ending. In non-fiction the child lists the main ideas and several of the supporting details.

3 A partial retelling. The child mentions the main character or characters, one or more events in the story, and the resolution. In non-fiction the child mentions only one of the main ideas and a few of the supporting details. The retelling is not full or well formed.

2 An incomplete retelling. The child mentions a character from the story and one of the story's events or incidents. In non-fiction the child mentions just a few details from the passage.

1 The child mentions a few unrelated ideas from the story.

0 The child cannot remember any of the story even with prompting.

The running record provides considerable information but, because it takes time, it should be used sparingly. Much can be learned by simply listening to students read and asking them comprehension questions.

a few paragraphs, the teacher stops and the discussion is her assessment. She begins with the following questions:

- What type of text is this? What genre is it? (Genre knowledge)
- What typically happens in this type of story? (Knowledge of text structure)
- What has happened in the story so far? (Summarizing)
- Why did the main character do that? (Infer character motives). How did he/she feel about it? (Infer character feelings) What kind of person is he/she? (Infer character traits)
- What do you expect will happen next? (Predicting)

As the students discuss the questions and share their initial impressions of the story, the teacher takes notes. We recommend a simple checklist with the names of the students across the top of the chart and the types of information arranged vertically down the side. You want to note if the students understand the structure of a narrative. Can they discuss the characters, setting, and problem? Can they predict what might happen next? Figure 5.4 presents a checklist that should help you learn about your students.

The lesson continues as the students read the rest of the story with a partner. When the reading is completed the teacher continues the discussion and this allows her to learn more about their comprehension abilities.

When finished the teacher does the following:

- She asks the student to summarize what they have read?
- She asks a series of literal and inferential questions.

Figure 5.4 Checklist for Noting Students' Comprehension of Narratives

MyLab Education
Click here to download a
printable version of Figure 5.4.

	Students					
Characters						
• Role						
• Traits						
Setting						
• Importance						
Problem						
• Type of conflict						
Events – Rising Action						
Climax						
Theme						
Codes	O Failed to Recognize ✓ Student recognized ✓✓ Described					

- She asks the students about specific vocabulary words.
- They discuss the themes of the story and consider what might be the author's purpose.

Our fifth-grade teacher makes more notes on her checklist and begins to form an impression of the students in each group. She has some insight about their ability to extract information from the text, make inferences, determine the theme, and understand the structure of a narrative. From this information, she begins to understand what standards she needs to emphasize and in what areas the students are doing well. Based on these initial assessments she will adjust her groups.

Collecting Evidence During the School Year

Teachers can collect evidence from discussion, interviews, student work samples, scoring rubrics and teacher made test. These strategies overlap with good teaching practice, and instruction and assessment often intertwine. To assess your students in the classroom you need a plan, a process that will help you become systematic and that embeds assessments in the regular process of teaching and learning.

In Chapter 2 we introduced the gradual release of responsibility model as a framework for organizing reading instruction. The model has three phases. In the first phase, a new concept or strategy is introduced and modeled by the teacher. In the second phase, the students practice the strategy with support provided by the teacher and the other students. In the third phase, the students use the concept or strategy in their independent work. Each of these phases provides an opportunity to assess the students' understanding and use of the concept or strategy. Figure 5.5 illustrates the kind of evidence that teachers might collect to assess what the students know and can do. We will use as an example the development of inferential comprehension, but the process applies to any strategy or concept.

EXPLANATION AND MODELING

In the first phase of the gradual release model you want to check students' understanding as you teach and the best evidence is developed from questioning and classroom discussions. Here you can correct misunderstandings quickly and nip problems in the bud. Why wait for a computer assisted test to provide the information when all you have to do is listen to your students? Targeted questions, structured around Bloom's taxonomy (Anderson, 2000), help to check on their understanding and their application. Let's assume that you have introduced a process of making inferences that has the students: (1) consider what the text doesn't say, (2) search

Figure 5.5 Release of Responsibility Model + Types of Assessment Evidence

DIRECT INSTRUCTION			Oral responses from the students
	GUIDED PRACTICE		Oral responses & limited written responses
		GUIDED & COLLABORATIVE READING	Oral responses & short written responses
		INDEPENDENT READING	Written responses
As students move through the release of responsibility model, the teacher can collect different types of evidence on the use of strategies and concepts.			

for text clues, (3) think about what they already know, and then (4) construct an inference that fills in what the author left out. After modeling the process with a few short passages, you might engage the students in a short discussion to check on their understanding.

- What is an inference? (Knowledge)
- Why do we make inferences? (Metacognitive knowledge)
- When do we make inferences? (Metacognitive knowledge)
- How do we make inferences? (Knowledge of procedures)
- What do you think we can infer in this passage? (Application)
- Do you believe that _____'s inference made sense? (Analysis)

A class discussion does not give you precise information about each and every student, but you can gain a sense of the general level of understanding in the class. We suggest that you occasionally target your questions to students who are slower to pick up on new concepts and new strategies. When these students understand, then you can assume most of the class has a grasp on the new ideas. It is then time to move on to guided practice but provide more modeling and explanations for students who needs more.

GUIDED PRACTICE

Students will spend a long time in this phase of instruction, trying out new strategies, using new concepts. They will be doing so when they are reading with a partner or during small group instruction. It is important to have a plan for systematically collecting and evaluating evidence. The evidence should be part and parcel of instruction. Let's consider the evidence collection process from the point of view of our first- and our fifth-grade teachers.

First-Grade. Remember the first-grade teacher whose primary concern is the development of word recognition skills. She assesses her students as she listens to them reading aloud in small groups. Each day she selects one student to read to her, conducts a running record, while the other students read with a partner (In the Classroom 5.1 presents the process of conducting a running record). This organized system allows her to note if the students can retain sight words and recognize them in print, decode unknown words, and self-correct miscues. As the year progresses, she can listen for their phrasing and focus on the development of fluency. For students who are experiencing some difficulty, our first-grade teacher can have them read a preselected word list to assess if they can, for example, read short vowel patterns and which ones.

Fifth-Grade. Our fifth-grade teacher needs a system for noting her students' progress during the guided reading phase. She uses discussions during small group instruction and the students' written work to assess their progress. Student talk, when well-planned and managed, offers important opportunities to study students' thinking. In these exchanges, rich dialogues depend on three elements: why the questioner is asking the question, what kind of question is asked, and how the questioner handles the responses (Dillon, 1988).

1. *Why are you asking the question?* In school, most questions attempt to find out if the student knows what the teacher already knows. Outside school, a question is usually a genuine effort by one person to learn something from someone else. They have learned that school questions have a right answer, and the teacher knows it. "Real" questions seldom have one right answer. Listening to students answer questions reveals much about their thinking.

2. *What kinds of questions lead to rich discussions?* Try to ask questions that teach rather than questions that assess. Avoid yes and no questions and questions that have very specific answers. Begin the discussion with "What is the story about? What is the author trying to tell us?" Follow up with "What does the author mean here? Does the author explain it clearly?" "How does this connect to what the author already told us?" We will elaborate on this type of questioning, based on Questioning the Author (Beck & McKeown, 2006) in Chapter 12.

3. *How can you extend student responses to more fully reveal their thinking?* You can expand the discussion with simple statements or questions—"Tell me more." "Can you find support for that?" "How is your idea similar or different from Mark's?" "What evidence in the text supports your idea?"

During the discussion of the text, the teacher keeps track of the inferences that students make, whether they do so spontaneously or with her prompting. She also notes if the inferences were on track with the meaning of the text or simply flights of fancy. Finally, she notes if the students can support their inferences with evidence from the text. This requires a follow-up question. "Why do you think so?"

A structured form of note taking can be used to access the comprehension strategies that are the focus of instruction or any type of questions that might be asked during a discussion. Figure 5.4 can be adapted by changing any of the indicators on the left side of the chart. Based on what the teacher learns, he can intervene to support and guide students as needed.

The second stream of information that yields data during the guided phase of instruction are students' work samples. The more authentic the work, the more valid the data. Avoid worksheets. If the students care about what they are writing, then their products have validity; they reflect the thinking that went into the creation of the products. Work samples can be drawn from many sources.

- Response journals and dialogue. The latter is a written conversation between the teacher and a student or between two students. The teacher can analyze these products, looking for the students' ability to summarize, interpret, and infer the theme.

- The teacher can develop specific assignments to tap a particular skill or strategy the students are exploring. For example, the students can be given a few short pieces of text and asked to draw an inference. The written responses of the students can be scored to see how well the students were making sense of the text. Figure 5.6 shows an example of such work.

- During independent reading, students can be paired and, at particular points in a text, asked to discuss a passage and record their thoughts. These responses can be structured so that the teacher gains insight into the students' thinking.

Consider these examples from fifth graders reading *Earthquake Terror* (Kehret, 1996), the story of a family camping in Northern California when a massive earthquake hits. Abby, the youngest child in the family is partially paralyzed and needs help walking

Figure 5.6 Two Students' Responses to *Earthquake Terror* (Kehert, 2000)

Student 1 Response	Student 2 Response
When the text said *"Go ahead." Mr. Palmer said to his wife, "I'll help Abby."* I thought this was an important detail because it told me that the family all cared about each other. This makes me think that they, especially Jonathon was considerate.	When the text said *"Go ahead." Mr. Palmer said to his wife, "I'll help Abby."* I thought this was an important detail because dad helped Abby who could not walk very well. This makes me think that they have to help Abby.

and her mother has broken her ankle in a fall during the quake. That leaves Jonathan, the older brother, and the Dad to cope with a mounting crisis. At this point in the novel, the text reads, "Go ahead." Mr. Palmer said to his wife, "I'll help Abby." The students are given this prompt and paired to write a response, a typical classroom routine. *When the text said _____, I thought this was an important detail because _____. This make me think _____.* The prompt is asking the students to consider the thoughts and motives of the characters. Figure 5.7 shows two students' responses to this novel and this particular prompt.

From these two examples, it is clear that the first student is able to infer character traits for the whole family and for Jonathan in particular. The second student is merely restating what has happened in the text with little insight into the characters. This tells the teacher to bring some of these students together in a small group and do some additional work with them on character traits and how we use text clues to infer them. Some students only make these inferences when prompted, not when reading on their own.

INDEPENDENT PRACTICE

In the final phase of the release of responsibility model, the students are working on their own, applying what they have learned from the explanations, modeling, and guided practice. At this point in the instruction, the teacher can still engineer opportunities to assess the students' growth in reading comprehension. The assessments can take the form of conferences and the journals that we discussed earlier. We will explore conferencing with students as a form of assessment. Later in Chapters 11 and 12 we will share types of journals that a student might keep.

Observing

Often, the best information about student learning comes from looking and listening, or kid watching (Goodman, Goodman, & Hood, 1989). (For more information on observing, see Johnston, 1992; and Owocki & Goodman, 2002.) This job is easier said than done. Until you know how to look and listen, it can be hard to both instruct and observe. The classroom may seem a blooming, buzzing confusion. How can you make sense of student responses as you teach? What do you look for? How do you find out what's really happening in students' heads? The following questions offer a framework for looking and listening:

- When students are working independently, do they understand the purpose of the task, or do they seek clarification when they do not?
- When students are reading independently, do they read or do they wander the room looking for a book to read?
- How do students respond in small-group versus whole-group settings or working individually with you?
- How are the students responding? Are they attentive? Productive? Interested and engaged? What is their level of performance? Of social interaction?

Figure 5.7 Four Level Scoring Rubric for Narrative Writing

	4 Strong	3 Effective	2 Progressing	1 Developing
Ideas	• Strong control of topic • Relevant, accurate, specific details that support topic	• Writing stays on topic • Complete details given	• Topic too broad • Details are limited	• Topic undefined and/or difficult to follow • Details are unclear
Organization	• Has an effective beginning, middle, end • Powerful introduction/lead and conclusion • Effective transitions • Logical order/sequencing • Uses appropriate paragraphing	• Has an acceptable beginning, middle, and end • Includes a lead and conclusion • Transitions are used correctly • Mostly logical order • Mostly correct paragraphing	• Weak beginning, middle, and end • Has evidence of a lead, and/or middle, and/or end • Conclusion but missing elements • Transitions are used sometimes; some logical order • Most paragraphing incorrect	• Does not have a beginning, middle, and/or end. • Does not have a lead and/or conclusion • Transitions confusing and/or not present • Not written in logical order • No sign of paragraphing
Word choice	• Powerful and engaging words • Artful use of figurative language and/or sensory details	• Some active verbs and precise nouns • Effective use of figurative language and/or words that enhance meaning	• Generally correct words Attempt at figurative language and/or words convey general meaning.	• Vocabulary is limited/used incorrectly • No figurative language; words do not convey meaning
Sentence fluency	• All sentences are clear • Variety of sentence structure is used • Run-ons and/or fragments are not used	• Most sentences are clear • Some sentence variety is used • Run-ons and/or fragments are rare	• Some sentences are clear • Sentence variety used rarely • Some run-ons and/or fragments are present	• No sentences are clear • No variety in sentence structure • Frequent run-ons and/or fragments are present
Conventions	• Few errors in grammar, punctuation, capitalization, and/or spelling	• Errors in grammar, punctuation, capitalization, and/or spelling are present but don't distract from meaning	• Errors in grammar, punctuation, capitalization, and/or spelling are present and some distract from meaning	• Many distracting errors are present in grammar, punctuation, capitalization, and/or spelling
Voice	• Powerful connection with audience; purpose is clearly communicated • Maintains strong viewpoint (perspective) throughout entire piece • Writing is expressive, engaging, and has lots of energy	• Awareness of audience; purpose clear most of the time • Uses viewpoint (perspective) throughout most of the paper • Writing is pleasant, agreeable, and satisfying	• Shows beginning awareness of audience/purpose • Some viewpoint (perspective) used throughout the piece • Writing is distant, too formal or informal	• Not concerned with audience or purpose • No viewpoint (perspective) used • Writing is mechanical and lifeless
Presentation	• Handwriting is consistent and uniform • Overall appearance is pleasing	• Handwriting is mostly legible • Overall appearance is acceptable	• Handwriting poor • Overall appearance is distracting	• Handwriting unreadable • Overall appearance is unacceptable

These questions serve as a starting point, but we offer a couple of cautions. First, you can't simultaneously monitor all four questions for all students, and so for a particular observation you should pick a focus. Select those facets and students that fit a particular situation, and place everything else in the background. A clear purpose allows you to "zoom in." For instance, you might study how a particular student handles different situations with varying amounts of support. How does Sam handle summarizing in whole-class activities versus small groups? How does he do with and without a helping hand? On topics that are more or less interesting to him? When he is talking or writing?

Second, it's hard to observe while you are teaching, but you should create times when the students are working independently so you can watch them. While observing your class, don't limit your attention to academic work. You can informally assess students' motivation for reading or writing by listening to what they say and watching how they approach a challenging but doable task. For example, when Jim and Nanette begin the task of writing about life in a covered wagon on the Oregon Trail without hesitation, they are demonstrating a high level of self-efficacy. Their teacher, Mr. Edwards, has given them multiple opportunities during the year to brainstorm a topic and then organize their ideas in a concept web. When the teacher comments on the quality of their reports, the students attribute success to their decision to work hard this quarter on becoming better writers.

When David, on the other hand, hears the assignment, he spends the next ten minutes in avoidant behaviors. He rummages through his backpack, bothers the student next to him, and so on. Earlier, when the class was asked to read silently about the Westward Movement, he flipped dispiritedly through the history book—he wasn't especially interested in the topic. It seems to David that he has always had trouble understanding history. He thinks, "How can I handle the writing assignment when I know nothing about the topic? My writing is bad, so what's the point in trying?" These scenarios challenge a teacher to analyze his students' confidence and respond to their motivation as well as their performance. Doing so will help the student attribute success to their own efforts and build motivation. Observing on the fly can capture behaviors that are the starting point for more detailed inquiry.

MyLab Education
Video Example 5.2
Count the number of opportunities that the teacher in this video has for assessment. Can she gain information about both literal and inferential comprehension?

Reading Conferences

Conferences with students can take many forms; they can be quick and informal or longer and more thorough. It is useful to conduct a reading conference with every student in your class at least twice a month and spend 2–4 minutes discussing what they are reading. These conferences have three related purposes. First, you can judge, by listening to the students read aloud, if the book is at an appropriate level of difficulty. Second, the conference helps you explore the students' reading comprehension and growing vocabulary knowledge, especially for books they are reading independently. Third, the conference is the ideal way to explore and set reading goals and promote motivation.

A reading conference allows you to explore the comprehension of individual students. We recommend that you tailor your discussions to the structure of the book the student is reading and his progress in the book. If the student is reading fiction and has just read a quarter of the book, the questions should center on the student's understanding of the characters, the setting, the problem, and the beginning of the plot. In the next two quarters of the book, the questions can focus on the motives of the main character, his or her traits, and the rising conflict or action. In the last quarter of the book, questions should shift to theme and how it relates to the student's life.

When students struggle with comprehension, employ the funnel approach outlined in In the Classroom 5.2 which is an efficient strategy for collecting both broad and

In the Classroom 5.2

The Funnel Approach

The funnel approach begins with general queries and moves toward specific questions. Second-grader Martha has problems with story comprehension and can't seem to identify with characters. After reading *Nate the Great* by Marjorie Weinman Sharmat, a simple detective story that tells how Nate finds his friend Annie's lost picture, Martha expresses neither empathy nor interest. The teacher conducts a 1-minute interview using the funnel approach.

Teacher: Martha, what do you remember about *Nate the Great?*

Martha: It is about a boy who likes to be a detective.

Teacher: What can you tell me about that boy?

Martha: His name is Nate. I dunno. I guess I like the way Nate likes to solve problems.

Teacher: How do you think Nate feels when Annie tells him on the phone about her missing picture?

Martha: Happy, because he likes to solve mysteries and call himself "Nate the Great"! And Annie feels sad and mad, 'cause I think she really liked that picture.

Teacher: Very nice! What does the story tell you about why Annie likes the picture?

Notice how the teacher starts with a broad question designed to reconnect Martha to an earlier discussion about the story. She focuses Martha's understanding of the characters' feelings. "Why" and "How do you know that" questions delve into students' reasoning and explore their capacity to reflect and make inferences. Whatever Martha answers, the teacher will learn something from this exchange, which she will jot in her logbook.

focused information during an exchange. The key is to prepare yourself in advance with a collection of questioning such as the funnel approach.

When the student comes to a conference having read a non-fiction text, ask her what portion she has just read and begin with a very general question; "What have you learned about _____." Follow that with questions that probe the student's knowledge. "What topic are you reading about now?" "How does that connect with what you already know?" "What are some important things to remember about _____?" Have the student read a section of the text and then ask, "Does that make sense?" "How does it connect with what the author already told us?"

Quiocho and Ulanoff (2009) discuss the importance of conferencing with English language learners (ELLs) as part of an authentic assessment program. They share that, during conferences, teachers should ask open-ended questions and include much wait time to allow English language learners to formulate their thoughts. Moreover, Quiocho and Ulanoff encourage teachers to probe students' thinking. They recommend teachers ask students questions such as "Can you tell me more? What else do you remember? What happened next? What do you want me to know the most about what you are writing or reading? Arguably, these kinds of prompts are appropriate for any students who need scaffolding to express themselves, be they English language learners or not.

Student Portfolios

A writing portfolio can show a student's progression from early ruminations about a task to final publication (Farr & Tone, 1994). A writing portfolio can also reflect a change in competence and skill from the beginning of the year to the end of any academic period. Portfolios have multiple purposes. First, they enable the teacher to see growth. Standardized tests emphasize scores or levels of proficiency, but portfolios emphasize the details. Especially in writing we need to see the details. By comparing early products to late products, the teacher can see how a student has changed. Portfolios also benefit the student. They can examine and appreciate their growth. By asking the student to rate his own work, "Which is your best story?" we are helping her develop critical evaluation skills. Finally, portfolios are valuable for communicating to parents. Although school districts are pushing standards-based report cards, our educational jargon is often meaningless to parents. They don't easily understand what "key ideas and details" mean and how they differ from "craft and structure." A portfolio clearly illustrates that a student who could only write a paragraph in September can now write three pages in May. The student who was reading an easy 30-page book in October has moved up to a 150-page novel with strong comprehension in April.

Much of what we described in the Collecting Evidence section of this chapter can be placed in the students' reading/writing portfolio. At times, the teacher should designate which piece should be placed in the portfolio and at other times a teacher might suggest that students look through the work they have completed during the week and find two pieces to add to their portfolio. An extended writing task, one that takes a week or more, might include brainstorming notes or notes from researching the topic, a rough draft of the paper, revision suggestions, an editing checklist, and a final product.

Portfolios often include captions, brief comments by the teacher reflecting on the work and pointing out strengths and areas for improvement. Sticky notes allow the teacher to provide feedback and instructional guidance without marking up the original. Students can add their own sticky note captions, putting themselves into the assessment loop. In this way, a portfolio becomes a dialogue journal between the teacher and the student, a way to make suggestions and develop a students' insights about the texts they are reading and the compositions they are drafting. You will want to examine the portfolios to evaluate students' work, make instructional decisions, and assign grades.

Keeping a portfolio is the data collection phase, the next step is scoring and evaluating the work. We recommend scoring *rubrics*, a graduated scoring guide with criteria for each score level, something like a letter grade but without the letters, and with instructions about the meaning of each level on the scale. A large number of writing scoring rubrics are available on the Internet and most likely the department of education for your state has posted the rubric they recommend and use for their state writing assessment. Most large school districts either develop their own rubrics or use the one recommended by their state department of education.

The most commonly used rubrics are based on the 6-Traits +1 writing evaluation system (Culham, 2010) or those developed to align with the Common Core State Standards (NGA & CCSSO, 2010). The theory underlying both rubrics is similar, but the technical language is different. The six traits of writing are:

- Ideas—the main content and details of the message,
- Organization—the structure and logical flow of writing,
- Voice—the style and perspective of the writer; her orientation toward the readers,
- Word choice—variety and precision of language,
- Sentence fluency—a variety of sentence structure, and the rhythm and flow of the language,
- Conventions—spelling, punctuation, and grammar, and
- +1—presentation, layout, design, and other physical features.

The 6-Traits + 1 model defines the dimensions for evaluating writing but it does not specify quality ratings for each dimension. What are the criteria for exceptional, strong, average, and poor organization? Many rubrics specify six levels of quality for each dimension. We think this is excessive and beyond the discriminatory powers of many educators, especially those without extensive experience evaluating

MyLab Education
Video Example 5.3
Consider how a student's writing can inform the teacher about their reading ability.

writing. Therefore, we recommend four-point scales similar to the one in Figure 5.7. A separate score for each dimension allows teachers and students to identify specific strengths and areas that need work. Simpler rubrics are called for in the primary grades and might focus on just the following dimensions: Ideas, organization, vocabulary, and mechanics.

Rubrics are not complete without writing samples or anchor papers. It is very difficult to award a 4 for organization on one paper and a 3 on another without samples for comparison. Samples or anchor papers give life to the bland descriptions within a rubric. What is the difference in organization between a paper with "Mostly logical order" and "Some logical order?" In Figure 5.7 five criteria are listed for organization, but how are these applied unless the teacher has sample student papers for comparison? Working with your colleagues, develop anchor papers from the students that reflect a range of writing standards.

Analyzing and Summarizing Your Data

You will need to organize the information you collect into a coherent portrait for parent conferences and to fine-tune instructional plans for the rest of the fall. Students differ, and you must decide how to meet individual needs, how to organize students, and how to plan activities. It is time to assemble the evidence so that you can decide what it means and how to use it, for your own purposes and for feedback to others.

Teachers use a variety of strategies to handle data. Some rely on the computer printouts from district assessment systems and others keep notes and narrative journals. We believe it is vital to use multiple sources of information to make instructional decisions. It is not realistic to rely only on test scores or to put your faith exclusively on students' work in the classroom. These two streams of data should reinforce each other.

We recommend that you start with a simple note-keeping system, using recipe box or two and a large stack of 4" × 6" index cards. Place stacks of cards around the room so they are handy—one stack on your desk for reading conferences, another at the table where you conduct small group instruction, and still another where students congregate for small group projects. The recipe box should be organized alphabetically by the students' last name. Any time you note something of consequence write it down on a note card. Make sure you include the child's name and the date. On the note card, you can record comments during a discussion that suggest the ability to make an inference, ask a question, make a connection, or summarize. In a reading conference (note we provide a conference form in Chapter 11), note a student's fluency, decoding skill or problems, use of context clues, and comprehension. Keep accumulating these cards until it is time to consolidate your data and reach some conclusions.

In the middle and at the end of each marking period, you need to set aside time to evaluate the students' work, make instructional decisions, and arrive at a grade. We have created a Reading Record that will help you organize your data, see Figure 5.8. Note this record keeping system does not extend to writing, but you can expand. Begin using the chart after you have gotten to know your students. At this time, record the goals for each student on the top of the Reading Record chart. For students who read regularly and enjoy reading, your goals are limited to deepening comprehension or expanding their interests. For those students who have some difficulty, you might have multiple goals that consider decoding, fluency, vocabulary, comprehension, and motivation. As always, the goals should be aligned to the standards in your district but you can't meet every goal for every marking period.

The second and third columns of the chart are designed to help you think through test scores, observations, and the students' written work. Begin by recording the test scores in each area for which you have data: decoding/fluency, vocabulary,

Figure 5.8 Reading Record for a Fourth Grade Student–First Quarter of the Year

Student Russell Baker **School** William Gray Elementary **Grade** 4 **Marking Period** 1st x 2nd __ 3rd __ 4th __

Section 1: Reading Goals

- **Foundational** (Decoding/fluency)
  Russ is a strong reader. He decodes new words deliberately and is mostly fluent even though he does not enjoy reading aloud.
- **Vocabulary**
  Continue to build reading vocabulary and help Russ become more proficient in using word learning strategies, especially prefixes and suffixes.
- **Comprehension**
  Russ has adequate literal comprehension of narrative text but does not engage in any interpretations. With informational text, he needs to determine big ideas, make generalizations, and retain what he has read.
- **Motivation**
  Russ is not highly motivated to read. He reads what is assigned, will glance through non-fiction books, but has not yet found his passion.

Section 2: Results and Evaluations

	Test Scores	Observations	Written Work	Conclusions
Decoding/Fluency	Oral Reading Fluency 103 WCPM	Reads with few errors, generally proper phrasing but little intonation.	Demonstrates some spelling problems on multi-syllable words.	No work is needed in fluency. Review syllabication in small groups.
Vocabulary	MAP - RIT 185	Knows the meaning of most words, can't use context clues or word parts.	Does not use expressive words, word choice limited.	Work on context clues and word parts.
Comprehension: Narrative	Standards of Learning 3rd Grade – passing, 403 MAP - 193	Gives short answer to literal questions but not inferential. Can summarize plot, but no interpretations about characters.	Two or three sentence summaries, little elaboration. Reading logs are incomplete.	Work on inferential comprehension. Group will work with a variety of short stories.
Comprehension: Informational	MAP – RIT 182	Reading passage Russ reports little except when we hit an interest.	He is accurate with short, one-word answers. Can't describe a concept or list details that support it.	Work on helping Russ find the main idea and the supporting details. Needs work on text structure.
Interests/ Motivation	NA	Rarely picks up a book. During independent reading abandons many books. Can't identify interests.	Reading logs are incomplete and forges parents' signatures.	Work with Russ to find an interest and a book he enjoys. Talk to librarian.

Section 3: Next Steps

Motivation	Decoding/Fluency	Comprehension: Narrative	Comprehension Informational	Vocabulary
• Interest inventory. • Assist with finding books in the library. • Find a series book he might enjoy.	• No particular work needed on basic phonics. • Multi-syllable words.	• Inferential comprehension – character traits, motives, theme. • Writing a fictional narrative based on a TV character.	• Text structure and organization. • Determining importance.	Continue with regular classroom instruction. Stress and reward self-selected words.

comprehension, and motivation. You may not have test data on vocabulary and motivation, especially motivation. Sometimes students demonstrate greater insight in their class work, especially when they are motivated, than on their test results, where they had a lackadaisical attitude. In the observation column, note what you catch students saying during small group instruction, reading conferences, and work with their peers. The students' portfolios and the index cards provide the data for the column on written work.

At this point consolidate your impressions and your analysis of the students' work. Look for patterns across the data. If a student summarizes well during a small group discussion check to see that he does so in his written work. When the data align you have strong evidence that the student can summarize and get to the gist of what he reads. Note this observation in the conclusion column. Note the conditions when a student might not summarize well. When the data is inconsistent and especially when a student independent work is weak it suggests that you need to provide more instruction and more support during small group guided reading. The process is not precise, but it is valid. You are integrating data from several different sources.

In the conclusion column, you write down interpretations of this data. Analysis means combining information from many sources to create individual portraits and collective images over time. In the example in Figure 5.8, the student struggled with informational text on the MAP test and also in some of his small group work. However, he did write an interesting essay on the history of skateboards, a passion for Russ. This discrepancy suggests that his problem with informational text is caused by a lack of prior knowledge and interest and the two are closely linked. In Section 3 of the Reading Record jot down your instructional goals. You will now have to consider all 28 students in the class and begin to form groups.

Interpretation faces two challenges—consistency and persuasiveness, which are akin to reliability and validity. Reliability asks "Is the evidence dependable?" while validity asks "Can the evidence answer your question?" Standardized tests, covered later in this chapter, establish reliability and validity through statistics. Teacher-based assessment handles the issues through argument and debate. In the Classroom 5.3 shows a first-year, sixth grade teacher learning how to give meaning to evidence, to shape generalizations that lead to action.

Teachers in the primary grades face similar interpretation problems. When a first-grade student in the middle of the year struggles to read a level D or E text, a level typically encounterd early in the school year, the teacher must determine what is underlying his problems. An analysis of oral reading behavior using a running record may reveal that the student has a developing sight vocabulary but few independent word-identification strategies. Further probes with a phonics inventory will help to reveal what the student knows about letter-sound relationships and phonics patterns. It will even be useful to interview the student, stopping her while she is reading to ask how she goes about figuring out a new word. This will give you some insight into the student's understanding of the strategies necessary for decoding.

Assessments like these are subjective; they depend on informed judgment. How can teachers assure critics of the trustworthiness of such complex judgments? Our approach is to use multiple sources of evidence. You gather one piece of evidence from students' oral reading, another from class discussion, and still another from writing. This is called *triangulation*, and it provides evidence of consistency, the keystone of reliability (Fetterman, 1998). It also ensures validity. Another answer depends on

In the Classroom 5.3

Interpreting Evidence in the Sixth Grade

Jennifer Coombs, a new sixth-grade teacher, is assigned at the last minute to a school in a low-income, urban neighborhood. The previous teacher's notes and the principal's comments suggest that the students have limited experience and poor language skills. Working from Mr. Milton's lesson plans, Ms. Coombs greets her new class. The morning goes fine. After lunch, the students meet to read and discuss their social studies book, a chapter on the Federal government. After the students read a few pages, they stop to discuss.

Ms. Coombs: Can someone summarize what we have learned? What did the author tell us?

Students: [Silence.]

Ms. Coombs: What was one of the key ideas about the purpose of government?

Students: [Again, silence; clearly, there is a problem.]

Ms. Coombs: Let's start over and first preview the book. Let's look at the title, main heading, and subheadings. What do they tell us about the topic?

What does Ms. Coombs's experience reveal about the students? Several alternatives are consistent with the evidence but call for different courses of action:

The students are not able to summarize what they have read.

They feel uneasy with a new teacher and don't want to seem foolish.

They have little understanding about informational text and don't know how to use text features.

They really don't know much about government and have a limited vocabulary.

They really don't know much about government and don't care very much about the topic.

How can Ms. Coombs further evaluate these interpretations? As we noted earlier, inquiry is not a straight-line process. Validating an interpretation often calls for experimentation—for changing conditions and collecting new data. The teacher may have to model how to read informational text, develop prior knowledge of government, or even switch to a more familiar topic to unravel why these students are having problems discussing what they have read.

professional interaction. Ms. Coombs is still learning about interpretative processes. She is early in her career, with little time to consult colleagues, who are as busy as she is. But she is on the right path—she is inclined to experiment and to persist, not a bad beginning for the first week of school.

From Reporting to Grading

The Reading Record helps you collect your evidence, consolidate your thoughts, and reach conclusions about each student. Reports lead to grades which are often associated with testing. We will offer a few thoughts about this topic and then look at reports from a different perspective. Grading on the A-to-F scale is familiar to most of us. Some schools now use performance levels, linked to standards (Marzano, 2000; Nitko, 1996). Whatever the label, reports focus on competition (norm-referenced, grading on the curve) or preset limits (criterion-referenced, 90+ means an A). The goal is to summarize a complex portrait in a single index. Teachers view student achievement as a complex mix of effort and accomplishment. Joan's end-of-year compositions weren't as polished as Susan's, but Joan entered fourth grade barely able to finish a complete sentence whereas Susan was a budding author. No wonder traditional grades frustrate both teachers and students.

Standards-based tests, a newer version of criterion-referenced testing, offer an alternative to grading. Standards lay out what students should be able to do in a particular area at a particular grade level, using descriptions like those in Figure 5.9. They assign students to performance levels by combining information from a collection of work products. You will encounter labels like "Proficient: Meets the Standard," "Accomplished: Exceeds the Standard," and "Fails to Meet the Standard." On the surface, this approach looks different from traditional grading, but for practical purposes the two are much the same. They provide little guidance for instructional decisions like how to place students in groups or when the school can decide to retain a failing student or place him in an intervention program. In many schools the students now receive an individual grade for each standard, a process that is opaque for many parents.

Grades and other summative judgments serve as important indicators of students' progress. We think it makes sense to also provide a richer portrait of strengths and areas of need. The information on the Reading Report can be summarized in a short paragraph that students and parents can understand. The idea is to create a portrait that provides feedback to the students and parents about past efforts but also offers guidance about future decisions. Here is one we created about Russ.

> Russ reads accurately and fluently but he does not read often. During independent reading he rarely settles down and has difficulty finding something he enjoys. Because he rarely reads his vocabulary is not growing and his higher-level comprehension suffers. He can get to the gist of most texts we read in small groups but he finds it difficult to make inferences and interpretation. For Russ reading is an activity not yet a passion.

Preparing narratives or case studies for individual students may seem costly in time and effort, because teachers in the United States are accustomed to computer driven reports. However, written narratives are commonplace in other countries, including Great Britain, Australia, and Japan, where students are typically brought into the process. Once you have conducted a few such reviews, the blend of reporting and decision making is likely to "click" for you.

> **MyLab Education**
> Click here to download a printable version of Figure 5.9.

Figure 5.9 Sample Rubrics for Intermediate-Grade Literacy Standards

| Standard | Level of Proficiency | | |
	Exemplary	*Proficient*	*Developing*
Making Sense of a Story	Thoroughly understands complex stories Connects personal experiences to characters and themes Has multiple perspectives across stories	Understands most stories including some complex ones Makes some connections of personal experiences to characters and situations Has different perspectives on a story	Has limited and literal understanding of simple stories Extracts meaning but with little personal connection Describes events, people, and places factually
Using Tools and Strategies in Reading	Masterfully uses several strategies to deepen understanding Makes sophisticated analyses of plot and theme	Uses various strategies to understand story Uses rereading and rethinking to support understanding	Has limited range of strategies Uses some rereading to support understanding

Reflect and Apply

3. You are new to teaching and to the school district. In this district, test scores count heavily, and not just the end of year tests. How will you mitigate the influence of test scores in your classroom? How will you make students believe that the books they read and discuss daily and the text they write are more important than the test scores?

4. It is the middle of the school year, you are holding conferences with the parents, and you have asked them to bring their children with them. One of your students, Russ, has average to low test scores, but occasionally shows a spark of interest in reading, especially when it touches a personal interest. How will you present your results to his parents? How will you share your data? How will you encourage him?

MyLab Education **Self-Check 5.2**

MyLab Education **Application Exercise 5.2:** Administering and Interpreting Running Records

MyLab Education **Application Exercise 5.3:** Using Written Work to Evaluate the Development of Comprehension

Assessing Individuals—When More Precise Information Is Needed

When more precise information is needed about student's reading, teachers can consider running records, informal reading inventories, and assessment of phonological and phonics skills for young readers. Earlier in the chapter we presented information about running records (see In the Classroom 5.1). Now we will discuss informal reading inventories (IRI).

The informal reading inventory provides a systematic way to collect information about the reading ability of individual students. It is a tool to keep in your assessment kit. It is not necessary for every student in a class to take an IRI, nor is it necessary to use every part of an IRI to reach conclusions about a student's reading ability. IRIs consist of graded word lists, leveled passages with several at each grade level, questions, and retell procedures for assessing comprehension. From a thorough administration of an IRI, a teacher can gain insights into a wide range of reading factors. Figure 5.10 lists the components of a typical IRI and the information the inventory provides. It is important to remember that the use of an IRI can be tailored to the questions a teacher wants to explore. If you are confident of the students' listening comprehension skip to reading comprehension. If your primary interest is the student's reading comprehension skip a thorough analysis of her word recognition strategies. At times you might want to compare a student's comprehension of narrative and expository text.

There are several IRIs on the market and each has different properties. Although every IRI consists of passages there is considerable variation in the difficulty of the passages within a grade level and what one IRI considers to be a first-grade reading level another does not. Toyoma and her colleagues (Toyama, Hiebert, & Pearson, 2017) studied the difficulty of the reading passages in four popular informal classroom assessments—*The Basic Reading Inventory* (Johns, 2017), *Dynamic Indicators of*

Figure 5.10 Components of an Informal Reading Inventory and the Information They Provide

Components of an Informal Reading Inventory	Information Provided
Word Lists	• Sight word vocabulary • Decoding skills • Word recognition strategies and self-corrections
Reading Passages	*Word Recognition Accuracy* • Word recognition accuracy • Decoding—phonics • Word recognition strategies *Fluency* • Rate and Prosody *Comprehension* • Oral reading—literal and inferential understanding • Silent reading—literal and inferential understanding • Listening comprehension—literal and inferential understanding • Metacognition and strategy use

Basic Early Literacy Skills DIBELS Next (Good & Kaminiski, 2013), *Developmental Reading Assessment DRA2* (Beaver, 2011), and the *Qualitative Reading Inventory-6* (*QRI-6*) (Leslie & Caldwell, 2017). Toyama found considerable variation between and within inventories. A first grade *DIBELS* passage has the same Lexile score, or difficulty, as a second-grade passage on the *Basic Reading Inventory*. Second-grade passages on the *DRA2* range from a Lexile score of 200 to 800 spanning two grade levels. This variation clouds a teacher's judgment unless he understands the limits of his assessment tools.

These inventories also differ in their ability to assess reading comprehension. Keerman and her colleague compared four common reading tests (Keeman, Betjenan, Olson, 2008) but not the same tests that Toyama analyzed. Each of these tests requires print skills (decoding and fluency) and comprehension skills but in different proportions. The *QRI-6* and the *Gray Oral Reading Test* have strong focuses on reading comprehension and minimal focus on print skills. This is not true for *DIBELS Next* or the *Basic Reading Inventory* which are much more a test of word recognition than reading comprehension. Saying a student has a comprehension problem means something very different when considering his score on the *Basic Reading Inventory* versus the *Qualitative Reading Inventory*.

Administering and Scoring an Informal Reading Inventory

The typical administration of an IRI is outlined in Figure 5.11. The IRI is used to determine a student's independent, instructional, and frustration levels. This conception of reading levels was first established by Emmet Betts in the 1940s. To arrive at the student's reading level, the teacher considers both word recognition accuracy and reading comprehension. The independent level means that a student can read the text

Figure 5.11 The Typical Administration of an Informal Reading Inventory

1. Estimate a child's reading level.
2. Place the student in an appropriate level with the graded word list.
3. Student reads the graded word lists to determine instructional reading level (70 to 80% accuracy on the *QRI-6*).
4. Determine student's oral reading passage placement.
5. Student reads passages orally for word recognition, fluency, and comprehension until frustration is reached.
6. Determine student's silent reading passage placement.
7. Student reads passages silently for comprehension until frustration level is reached.
8. Teacher determines student's listening placement.
9. Students listens and answers questions for comprehension until frustration level reached.

successfully without any teacher support. The instructional level means that the students can read the text but requires some support from the teacher. Frustration level texts should probably be avoided—they are too difficult. Figure 5.12 presents the scoring guidelines for the *QRI-6*. Interest and motivation temper these guidelines. Often a students can read a text at his frustration level if he is interested in doing so.

The scoring guidelines are not fixed in stone. If a student is reading independently for word recognition, then the comprehension score determines his reading level (WR = Independent Level + Comprehension = Instructional Level = an Instructional Reading Level). However, a student might experience some difficulty with word recognition, read with 95% accuracy, and still have excellent reading comprehension with 90% of the questions correct. This still might place him at an independent level for this passage. If his oral reading miscues were trivial and did not affect the meaning of the passage, you might consider him to be reading at an independent level. Other factors should enter your thoughts. Not all fourth-grade passages in an informal reading inventory are of equal difficultly. The fourth-grade passage on plant structure, with a Lexile of 930, presents considerably more comprehension difficulties than the biography of Amelia Earhart with a Lexile of 500. The prior knowledge demands are different.

Interpreting the results of an IRI requires knowledge and judgment. We will discuss two issues—the interpretation of oral reading miscues and analyzing the comprehension results. Sometime in the 1980s, oral reading errors were relabeled miscues under the assumption that miscues were not random errors, but a reflection of the processing of the readers (Goodman, 1970). As the student is reading aloud, record the following miscues using this note taking system:

- *Omissions*—circle the word,
- *Insertions*—write a caret and then write the inserted words above the line,
- *Substitutions*—write the substituted word above the line,
- *Repetitions*—underline the words that were repeated,
- *Self-corrections*—after the error, write the code SC, and UC for an unsuccessful self-correction,
- *Punctuation*—if the reader omits punctuation, circle the punctuation mark.

Figure 5.12 Scoring Guidelines for the *Qualitative Reading Inventory-6*

	Word Recognition Accuracy	**Percent Comprehension Questions Correct**
Independent Level	98%	90% or better
Instructional Level	90–97%	67–89%
Frustration Level	Less than 90%	Less than 67%

Figure 5.13 Examples of Oral Reading Miscues

Jim a second grader is reading this passage to his teacher during an informal assessment.

Melwa

It was a hot, (hot) day, and Malawi the baby elephant was in a bad mood.

Melwa   jumped   pond

Malawi wanted everyone to know she was in a bad mood, so she stamped over to the water

threw

hole. She splashed and thrashed around in the water until it turned brown and muddy.

and

But it didn't make Malawi feel any better.

SOURCE: P. Dewitz, 2018.

When scoring miscues, the teacher should note the following issues:

- The total number of miscues: accuracy is a key indicator for reading ability.
- The number of miscues that change the meaning: If the student's miscues do not change the meaning it suggests that he is focused on the context or the meaning of the passage.
- The number of self-corrections: If half or more of the miscues are corrected by the reader it suggests that the reader is attending to context and he should be encouraged to do so.
- When the student substitutes one word for another note what parts of the word the student processes correctly and on which parts the student errs. Typically, students have more success with the consonant sounds than vowels, and more success with single consonants than with digraphs and blends.
- Note whether the student has success with one syllable words but struggles with two syllable words.

Study the examples in Figure 5.13. The omission of the word *hot* has no effect on meaning nor does the mispronunciation of the name *Malawi*. The latter error suggests that the student needs to work on phonics skills. Reading *jumped* for *stamped* and *pond* for *water* indicates that the reader is relying too much on context and not enough on the visual and phonological properties of the words. Note that in both miscues the reader maintains the meaning of the passage. Taking all the miscues together, the teacher should discourage the student from relying on context and each him to use phonics to identify words.

Interpreting Comprehension on an Informal Reading Inventory

Interpreting comprehension results is complex because of the many variables involved. From the students responses, the teacher attempts to understand how well the student comprehends the passages and what causes his misunderstanding (Dewitz & Dewitz, 2003). As we proposed in Chapter 2, several factors underlie reading comprehension. First, comprehension requires accurate and fluent reading (Hoover & Gough, 1990). Next, comprehension requires prior knowledge of the concepts in the passages and word knowledge. Graves (2016) estimates that, if the reader does not know 10% of the words in a text, comprehension will be impaired. Third, the reader must reason while reading. He must make a number of inferences and synthesize what he is reading. The reader is aided by his background knowledge and his use of comprehension strategies. Because the IRI is a relatively flexible diagnostic tool, it allows the teacher to use her clinical judgment in making sense of the student's comprehension processes. As we have said before, we cannot observe comprehension while it is happening, but from the students' answers and comments we can draw conclusions about how she thinks. These conclusions can help us make some instructional decisions.

In an informal reading inventory, the student can retell the selection and answer literal and inferential questions, allowing the teacher to determine if the student can extract meaning from the text and construct meaning. Some inventories provide an estimate of the students' prior knowledge enabling, the teacher to consider how much the student's prior knowledge, or lack of it, affected his understanding. Going a bit further, the teacher can determine what types of inferences caused the reader difficulty and where the reader's thinking process went awry. Finally, by having the student think aloud while reading, the teacher can consider what type of strategies she employs. We will examine each of these scenarios as we look at Mark, a fifth-grade student, in In the Classroom 5.4,

In the Classroom 5.4

Exploring Comprehension Responses

Mark read fluently at both a fourth- and fifth-grade level, but his teacher reports that he has intermittent difficulty with reading comprehension. Mark was given the *Qualitative Reading Inventory-5*. He read three passages silently and two orally. Before each passage was read, the teacher engaged him in a short discussion to estimate his prior knowledge and after he read he answered a series of literal and inferential questions. Mark's scores are presented in Figure 5.14. The figure lists the genre of the passages, their topics, and Mark's score for oral reading accuracy, prior knowledge, and literal and inferential comprehension.

Mark's word identification skills on the two passages he read orally are at an independent level indicating that word reading accuracy and fluency are not the source of his difficulty. His comprehension was weak for all but one of the passages—The Busy Beaver, the only passage for which he had adequate prior knowledge and the same passage on which he achieved an instructional level. On four of the passages he appeared to have adequate prior knowledge, but still struggled with reading comprehension. Prior knowledge was necessary for adequate comprehension but not sufficient. Something else was going on with Mark's comprehension processes. Mark had more difficulty with inferential questions than literal questions suggesting he was better at extracting information from the text but quite weak at constructing ideas.

Looking closely at some of Mark's answers to the comprehension questions we can gain a deeper glimpse into his thinking. Although we will only present two questions and answers we hope you will take our examples and use them to understand how students think. The following examples are taken from one fifth grade passage about Martin Luther King, Jr. and the Civil Rights movement, a topic the fifth graders had studied the past two years. Figure 5.15 presents the passage, the questions, and Mark's responses.

- Question 1 is asking Mark to draw a conclusion, to make a generalization. From the evidence in the text, Mark had to conclude that racial segregation was wrong and should be stopped. Mark, however arrived at a specific instance of racial segregation but missed the larger conclusion. He demonstrated skill at extracting information from the text, but was not able to construct a new insight.
- For the next question, Mark had to read a causal change of events that led to an effect. Some of the steps in the causal chain of events are spelled out but others must be inferred. This is possible only if the reader has the prior knowledge. Mark was able to link the first two ideas—Rosa Parks refused to give up her bus seat, people protested the bus company action through a boycott, the bus company lost money. Mark inferred that the bus company went out of business, but he could not make the final connection that the laws were changed. This required an inference that the bus company put pressure on the legislature.

If we look back to Mark's scores we realize that he did not have a deep well of knowledge about MLK, Jr., or an understanding of the purpose of boycotts and how they work. The lack of prior knowledge was as much of a problem as any specific issue with strategies or thinking.

Figure 5.14 Mark's Scores on the *Qualitative Reading Inventory* 5.

Text Type	4th Grade Passages		5th Grade Passages		6th Grade Passages	
	Narrative *Johnny Appleseed*	Expository *The Busy Beaver*	Narrative *Martin Luther King, Jr.*	Expository *The Octopus*	Narrative *Andrew Carnegie*	Expository *Predicting Earthquakes*
Reading Mode	Silent	Oral	Oral	Silent	Silent	Oral
Reading Accuracy	NA	Independent	Independent	NA	NA	Independent
Prior Knowledge	83%	83%	42%	75%	33%	67%
Explicit Questions	50%	75%	0%	25%	33%	75%
Implicit Questions	25%	24%	0%	0%	20%	75%

SOURCE: P. Dewitz & P. Dewitz (2003). They can read the words but can't understand: Refining comprehension assessment. *The Reading Teacher*, 56(5), p. 422–435.

Figure 5.15 *QRI-5 Martin Luther King, Jr.*

Question 1	Assessment Question and Answer
When Martin Luther King, Jr. was a boy, many laws would not allow black people to go to the same places as white people. Some people thought blacks were not as good as whites. Black children could not attend some schools and certain restaurants had signs that read "white only." Blacks could not sit in the front of a bus and if a bus got crowded, they had to give up the seat to a white person. Laws separating blacks and whites were unjust, and King decided to protest such laws. Finally, the United States Supreme Court agreed with King. The laws separating blacks and whites were changed.	Question: What was Martin Luther King's main goal? Answer: He wanted blacks to have seats on the buses as well as whites.
Question 2	
In Montgomery, Alabama, Rosa Parks, a black woman was arrested and fined for not giving up her seat to a white man on a bus. [Martin Luther] King led a movement to protest this action. Thousands of people refused to ride the buses. The bus company began to lose money. In time the law was changed.	Question. What happened when people refused to ride the buses? Answer: The bus company went out of business cause (sic) they lost money. Probe: What happened because of that? Answer: I don't know.

SOURCE: Dewitz, P. & Dewitz, P. (2003). They can read the words, but they can't understand; Refining comprehension assessment. *The Reading Teacher*, 56(5). 422–444.

The informal reading inventory is a powerful tool that should be used sparingly. Like all assessments, the IRI samples student's reading behavior and from this sample a teacher makes inferences about how a student reads, his strengths and weaknesses. These inferences are guided by the model of reading that resides in the teacher's head. Let's consider one example. If you believe that readers simply extract meaning (literal comprehension) or construct meaning (inferential comprehension) without considering the role of prior knowledge then you might infer that a student who has difficulty with inferential questions needs instruction and practice with inferential questions. By considering the role of prior knowledge, the problem is now re-conceptualized; the student lacks prior knowledge and this affects how he comprehends.

MyLab Education **Self-Check 5.3**

Commercial Assessment Systems

The odds are very high that you will work in a school that uses a commercially developed assessment system for summative and formative assessments. The market for commercial computer-based assessment systems has been growing steadily and is projected to grow well into 2020 (Molnar, 2017). Almost all state assessments are now administered on a computer as are 83% of formative assessments. While spending on state-level assessments is growing 18.4% a year, classroom or formative assessments are growing at a rate of 30% a year. These computerized assessment systems have largely replaced the tests that come with the basal reading programs and many basal programs now include digital tests and a digital platform for recording and interpreting test results. In this section, we will focus on two types of tests: those that are used for formative assessments and those for progress monitoring. These two categories clearly overlap, with the first set of tests typically used in the upper grades and administered on a computer and the second employed in the primary grades and administered individually. Our goal is to make you an informed user of these tests provide.

Computer Adaptive Formative Assessments

The computer adaptive formative assessment systems were designed to answer several important questions. Who will pass the end-of-year high-stakes assessment? Which students are making progress and which are not? What knowledge or skills are particularly difficult for the class or for individual students? The goal of these assessments is to assist with predictive, placement, and diagnostic decisions and there is some doubt that they can do all equally well. Before we review the efficacy of these assessment tools, we will describe how these tests work.

The major assessment tools being used around the country are *Star Reading 360*, (www.renaissance.com/products/assessment/star-360/star-reading-skills/) the *I-Ready Adaptive Assessment System* (www.curriculumassociates.com/products/iready/diagnostic-instruction.aspx) and the *MAP Reading Growth and Skills Test* (https://www.nwea.org/map-growth). Each of these tests employs a similar procedure. On a computer, a student begins to read a passage and answers a few questions. If she gets the item correct the computer selects a more difficult passage and more difficult questions. If she gets the item wrong the computer moves the student to an easier passage and easier questions. The fewest items possible are used to pinpoint the student's level of reading. These scores are correlated with past students' performance on the large statewide assessments like *Smarter Balanced Assessment Consortium (SBAC)*, *Partnership for Assessment of Readiness for College and Careers (PARCC)*, or any of the individual state assessments. That two reading tests are correlated is not remarkable. Underlying every reading test is the ability to read the words, do so with fluency, know the meaning of the words, and comprehend the language. When testing companies tout their ability to predict performance on state assessments, view the claim as unremarkable.

These computer adaptive tests also claim to offer diagnostic information to guide instruction and here we doubt what they can offer. The *I-Ready* website states, "I-Ready automatically provides individualized online and teacher-led instruction targeted to each student's unique needs." The reason we doubt this claim and that of similar assessment systems is the internal conflict between an adaptive test, seeking to administer the fewest test items possible, and a diagnostic test that hopes to examine multiple reading skills (Thorndike & Thorndike-Christ, 2010). Suppose a fourth-grader takes one of these adaptive tests and read three to five passages and completes 20 to 30 items. *Star Reading 360* measures 17 literacy skills, 21 informational text reading skills, and 11 language skills. *I-Ready* assesses five vocabulary skills, 13 informational reading skills, and 12 literary reading skills. Each of these skills or strategies cannot be adequately assessed with only one or two items. Suppose a student missed an item that assessed his ability to determine the theme of a short story. He might have difficulty with that particular passage, the vocabulary in the passage, or the ability to infer themes.

The research on these computer adaptive assessments suggests that they do not deliver the results that they promised. Although 32% of the users of these assessment systems generally believed that the tests were producing positive results, 45% thought the results were mixed and the rest had not seen positive results (Molnar, 2017). In a controlled study, researchers provided fourth-grade teachers with MAP reading data and trained them to use it. After two years of work the teachers using the MAP data were "not more likely than control group teachers to have applied differentiated instructional practices in their classes" (Cordray, Pion, Brandt & Toby, 2012, p. xii). Additionally, the students in the MAP classrooms showed no improvement in test scores compared to students in classrooms where teachers were not using computerized assessment data.

We suspect that computer adaptive testing, rather than supporting the classroom teacher, undermines them in subtle ways. To borrow a term from the arguments about basals in the 1980s, these computer adaptive systems "deskill" teachers. Rather than rely on classroom observations, discussions, and students' written work, the computer adaptive assessment system makes the assessment decisions easy, perhaps too easy, and teachers, especially administrators, conclude that what is assessed on the test is very similar to what the students do in class. Black and Wiliams (2009) are correct that the most useful formative assessment is a collaborative process with assessment embedded in instruction. Their research, and that of others, indicates that the formative assessment process, the one described in the first half of this chapter, has a positive effect on student learning, especially when it is supported with staff development (Kingston & Nash, 2011).

Progress Monitoring with Curriculum-Based Measurements

In many schools, spurred on by Response to Intervention (Fuchs, Fuchs, & Vaughn, 2008), teachers are being requested to collect progress monitoring data to determine whether a particular reading intervention is working. Children may be assessed every weeks on their ability to identify letter names; learning to segment words; decoding new words, typically nonsense words; or their oral reading fluency. These tests are administered one-on-one by the classroom teacher or special education teacher. Curriculum-based measurement may be designed by teachers or schools can use published assessment systems, *Dynamic Indicators of Basic Early Literacy Skills Next* (*DIBELS Next*; Good & Kaminski, 2002) and *AimsWeb Pro Reading* (Shinn & Shinn, 2002). By 2005 *DIBELS* was being given to over 2,000,000 children (Afflerbach, 2007).

Curriculum-based measures, the child has to name as many letters as he can or read as many words as he can in 1 minute. Reading comprehension is measured with the MAZE test. In a MAZE test a student reads a passage, encounters a blank, and must fill in the blank with one of three-word choices the test provides. The number of items successfully completed is his score. These tests come with norms and a child is evaluated on his progress in meeting these norms. For example, *DIBELS* expects the average student to read 90 words correct per minute by the end of second grade.

These curriculum-based measures are quick and easily administered assessments of discrete or constrained skills (Paris, 2005). We can measure letter-name knowledge, nonsense word decoding, and oral reading fluency, but *DIBELS Next* cannot assess vocabulary growth and it may be a poor assessment of reading comprehension. Some have objected to these tools because an undue emphasis is placed on speed and that may distort the reading process. When a child knows that he has only 1 minute to read he may read at a rate that sacrifices phrasing, expression, and comprehension.

Often the results of these curriculum-based measures do not provide rich details about the students' understanding of the curriculum. The letter-name fluency result tells you how many letters were named correctly, but the teacher must still comb the student's responses to determine which letters need additional instruction. The nonsense fluency test reports the student's general level of ability with nonsense words, but a phonics survey would still be necessary to determine which phonics patterns need further instruction and practice. Fluency results are often just a symptom, but they do not identify the underlying problem. Poor reading fluency may indicate problems with decoding, vocabulary, comprehension, or simply fluency. The MAZE test is a poor measure of reading comprehension because it is more a test of decoding and fluency than language factors (Muijselaar, Kendeous, de Jong, & van den Broek, 2017). The MAZE test does not assess factors like making inferences, interpretations, or determining the theme or big ideas of a text.

The danger in *DIBELS Next* or *AimsWeb* is confusing the assessment tool with the curriculum. These curriculum-based measures assess a small slice of reading and do so only at the earliest stages of learning to read. They are what they claim to be, a measure of progress, but not a deep dive into how a child reads. Relying on such narrowly conceived assessment tools can cause teachers and administrators to focus reading instruction on the wrong factors and ignore the development of vocabulary, comprehension, and motivation. If you do use these assessment tools, have a firm concept of reading in mind, consider what these tools are not assessing, and interpret the results with caution.

High-Stakes Tests

You are well educated, and so you know about tests. You have been there—college admissions, teacher certification, driver's license. In our world, the multiple-choice test is a fact of life. These instruments will be around for a while because they are cheap and efficient, offer a simple bottom line, and are "scientific" (Airaisan, 1994; Baumann, 1988; Koretz, 2009; Popham, 1999). They meet high standards of design and reliability. Test publishers produce technical manuals with detailed information about the standardization procedures, student samples, and lots of statistics.

Standardized tests fall into two broad categories, as shown in Figure 5.16: criterion-referenced and norm-referenced. Criterion-referenced tests include basal tests, progress monitoring tests, and high-stakes tests. The principle guiding these tests is that the student must meet a preset performance level. The class takes a 10-item test on vowels; students who are correct on nine items have "mastered" the objective and "meet the standard." Students who fall below the criterion are assigned additional practice on the objective until they attain a passing score. The two most commonly used high-stakes tests are the *Smarter-Balanced Assessment Consortium* (*SBAC*) and the *Partnership for Assessment of Readiness for College and Careers* (*PARCC*). After the Common Core (NGA & CCSSO, 2010) was enacted, most states employ one of these tests. Currently 16 states use *SBAC* and six use *PARCC*, with the rest using tests that resemble these two (Koretz, 2017).

Norm-referenced tests measure individual student's standing relative to others— "grading on the curve" (Koretz, 2008). Percentile scores show how many other students rank above or below a particular individual. Someone at the 50th percentile falls right in the middle; a person at the 99th percentile has performed better than 99% of

Figure 5.16 Norm-Referenced and Criterion-Referenced Scoring

Norm-Referenced Scoring	Criterion-Referenced Scoring
Performance Is Compared with Scores of Others	Performance Is Compared to an Absolute Standard
• Once the test is developed, it is administered to a norm group, and then each student's performance is described by how he ranks in comparison to the group.	• The test is developed with a goal in mind (students must read at a rate of 150 words per minute), or a fixed standard is assigned (80% of the answers must be correct).
Scores Represent a Norm Group	Scores Represent a Standard
• Percentile. The percentile gives the percentage of students whose scores fall below the particular student's score. It a student scores in the 60th percentile, then he outperforms 60% of the students in the norm group.	• Pass-fail. The score either meets or exceeds the preset value.
• Grade-level equivalent (GLE). The average performance of students at a given grade is used to convert a score into a comparative indicator. If a student scores at the average level for all students leaving third grade, he is given a GLE of 3.9, meaning "end of third-grade performance."	• Mastery of learning objective. In this approach, often linked to a curriculum sequence, students, by a given grade level, are expected to achieve a specific outcome. For instance, by the end of kindergarten, students should know all letter names, numbers 1–10, colors, and "common" words.
• Grading on the curve. In this common practice, grades are assigned based on the distribution within a particular class on a particular test. The teacher decides that the top 15% of the scores will receive A, and so on.	• Advanced, proficient, basic. This variation on pass-fail, similar to regular grades but not on a curve, is used by many state and federal assessment programs.

those in the norming sample. Stanines sort students much as percentiles do, but in ranges from 1 to 9. Normal-curve equivalents are another variation on percentiles. Scale scores place students on a statistical "growth curve," which lets you know how a student is doing on a developmental learning pathway. The grade-level equivalent, or GLE, also reports growth scores. The third-grader who scores 3.8 at the end of the year is doing about as expected; a score of 3.0, on the other hand, means that the student reads like an entering third-grader and so is in trouble. Assessment experts worry that GLEs can be misinterpreted (Nitko, 1996), but teachers still rely on GLEs because the concept makes sense to them and serves practical purposes. GLEs are most problematic at the extremes. A beginning third-grader with a score of 8.0 can't really handle Dickens's *A Tale of Two Cities*. He may be able to read most of the words in the novel but is unlikely to get much out of it and certainly will not understand the nuances of the narrative. In the middle ranges of a grade, the GLE provides a reasonable indicator of reading achievement.

The current high-stakes tests are criterion-referenced with the results reported as the percentage of students who are "proficient" readers. But what does "proficient" mean? What is the standard? Each state defines what it means to be proficient and this is frequently determined by a panel of experts. They do not look at test scores or at real students. The process begins by imagining a marginally proficient student in fourth grade should be able to do. In Nebraska "A student scoring at the 'Meets the Standards Level' generally utilizes a variety of reading skills and strategies to comprehend and interpret narrative and informational text at grade level" (Nebraska Department of Education, 2011). Then the panel is given, a list of 100 or so questions, and they have to determine how many the imaginary proficient students would answer correctly. That number becomes the standard or cut score. (For a much more detailed description see Koretz, 2017.) Koretz points out that there are different ways to set standards and each produces a different result. This process is also political because a number of people have a stake in the level of the cut score—legislators, the governor, and the state department of education. If they argue that education is improving, they want lower cut scores. If a crisis is a political advantage, a high cut score is useful.

High-stakes standardized tests have transformed schools and instruction. We described these changes in the beginning of the chapter. While discount the value of these test we can help your students cope with their demands and score well.

Preparing Students for Standardized Tests

The previous section cautioned against overreliance on standardized tests. This section offers suggestions about how to help students do their best on these instruments, so that you can use the results with confidence. How can you prepare your students for the tests without compromising validity? "Teaching to the test" may improve scores, but scores may no longer mean what they are supposed to mean. When your car runs low on gas, you can fiddle with the gas gauge to make it show "full," but you will eventually run out of gas.

The first word of advice is to connect the test situation with the best learning in your classroom. You and your students have spent most of the year studying various genres—realistic fiction, biography, nonfiction. Now you will approach a new genre, test taking. Standardized, high-stakes tests present unique reading tasks with passages unlike what we recommend and tasks somewhat different from what happens in class every day. The process of reading when taking a test is different from the process of reading when reading a novel, an article online, or implementing a new recipe. Reading comprehension is not answering multiple-choice questions in your head (Rupp, 2000).

The second word of advice is to help students see the test as a problem to be solved strategically and thoughtfully, a process that is consistent with best learning. What does strategic preparation look like? The first suggestion centers on the big picture. Why am I taking this test? What will happen if I fail? Who will find out how I did? Is it all right to guess? On your driving test, you had ideas about purpose of the test. You were taking the test so that you could get a driver's license. If you failed, you studied some more and retook the test.

Find out what your students think about tests, and set the record straight. In high-stakes tests, the students are not accountable, the teachers and principal are. Some kids will figure out that they don't have any skin in the game. They will go on to fifth grade no matter how they do. They know the test is important, but not why. The most logical way to approach motivation is to explain the reality of high-stakes testing. The test results tell the world about the quality of the school and their classroom. To motivate students to do well, you need to stress class and school pride. Win one for the Gipper!

The second suggestion centers on how to take the test. These tests present unique problems to solve. Tell your students we are going to think like a test maker. Set up a contest between the students and the test maker, a contest that they can win. We suggest that you teach five lessons on test taking, each with a specific goal. Some of the lessons can be taught once, others require repeated practice following the release of responsibility mode.

Whatever test your district or state uses, take the test yourself. You cannot help students negotiate a long and complicated test that you have never taken. A complete copy of our test taking unit is available at (www.readingbydesign.com.)

1. *Discuss students' understanding about test taking and clear up misconceptions.* How long is the test? Can we take breaks? Should students read the passage or questions first? (Read the passages first.). Can students guess? In most cases, guessing after you narrow the options helps.
2. *Build an understanding of assessment vocabulary.* Each test has a unique set of words, so teach those words. Make sure that students understand the meaning of the terms a *passage*, an *article*, a *story*, a *paragraph*, a *stanza*. Test authors use the phrases,

best summary, *mostly about*, *mainly about*, and *author's purpose* when they mean *main idea*. The best way to assemble these vocabulary terms is to take the test yourself, take notes, and list the terms you need to teach.

3. *How to read the passages*. We believe it is important for students to take a few notes while they are reading. Note taking focuses the mind and causes them to think a bit before rushing on to the questions. When they read a passage, they should write down the title, the genre, and a few thoughts about the beginning, middle, and end. Note taking helps students locate information when they answer the questions.

4. *How to answer the question*. We recommend a five-step process that students should follow for every question: (1) Read the question. (2) Highlight the key words in the question. (3) Determine whether the answer is in a sentence, a paragraph, or in the whole passage. (4) Determine what the question is asking you to do: locate information, make an inference, sort ideas, support inferences, and so forth. (5) Select the answer and go back to the text to support your answer choice. Sometimes you have to refute the wrong answer choice.

5. *Teach a few relaxation strategies*. High-stakes testing takes a long time and it is stressful. Learning how to clear your mind, take deep breaths, and take mental breaks helps performance. One teacher said to us:

> First of all, I make it clear to students that they are not really competing with one another. I encourage them: "Do your personal best. That's what really counts. That's what you should strive for." Second, I encourage them to support one another before the test—"Hey, good luck! I know you will do great." And after the test—"I bet you aced that puppy!" Third, I involve parents. I advise them to talk with their children in the days before the test, make sure they get a good night's sleep, and a solid breakfast on the day of the test, and talk with them about the test once it is over.
>
> —William Settlemeyer, fourth-grade teacher

Don't spend too much time on test preparation. The best preparation for a reading test is strong reading instruction (Guthrie, 2002). Students should read widely and often, volume matters. You should build their prior knowledge and their specific knowledge of texts and language. They should learn and use comprehension and word learning strategies and engage in guided reading. Guthrie suggests that no more than 10% of your time should be spent on test prep. If students are having difficulty determining the main idea, or using context clues to infer word meanings, you are not going to be able to "fix" these problems through test prep. Learning to use these strategies successfully requires a year of work and last minute efforts are doomed to fail.

Finally, what should you do when the test is finished? Testing is an important event for students, and you should learn from the event. You can develop your own "after-the-test" plan. Publishers handle scoring and reporting and typically you will learn the results quickly. You should deal with the experience as soon as the test is over. Ask students about their reactions. How did they do? How did they feel? What would they have done differently? Celebrate the event! Let students know you're proud of their efforts! Knowing that they all did their best is important in its own right.

Reflect and Apply

5. Think about the tests you have taken in your own education. Consider the stakes those tests made in your own life. How did you prepare for them? If you failed to pass what did you do next? How did your experience help shape your attitude toward test taking and test prep?

6. Your school places great emphasis on high-stakes test scores. Students in all grades will be tested in 3 weeks. Your sixth-graders are planning a skit about testing for the first-graders. The principal asks you to explain how the skit will help your students prepare for the tests and how it will help the first-graders. How do you respond?

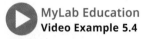

MyLab Education
Video Example 5.4
This is not your conventional educational video, but it does present another view on our assessment nation. https://www.youtube.com/ watch?v=J6lyURyVz7k

MyLab Education **Self-Check 5.4**

MyLab Education **Application Exercise 5.4:** Teaching Students to Take High-Stakes Tests

Concluding Remarks

Assessing reading, writing, and language is a tough job that calls for professional judgment. Effective assessment requires information from a broad range of sources, including standardized tests, classroom portfolios, informal observations, and student conversations. There is no substitute for the teacher's ongoing inquiries into student growth and accomplishment, which are essential for adapting instruction to individual needs.

This chapter began with a strong critique of the current state of assessment in the nation. We and others believe we are on the wrong track. Fifteen years of high-stakes assessment has not improved achievement but ratcheted up pressure and anxiety for students, teachers, and administrators. Ultimately, we assess what we value and our current assessments stress cognitive factors but ignore students' interests, motivation, social interactions, and self-confidence. What we ignore might be more important than what we assess.

Assessment captures the research side of the schooling endeavor, whether you are approaching classroom assessments or preparing for standardized tests. The inquiry approach involves asking the right questions, formulating a clear view of learning goals, determining the current status of the students, and deciding on a course of action. After the stage is set at the beginning of the school year, the process is continuous, an ongoing series of mini-experiments designed to inform you and your students about progress. Feedback is easy to handle when all is going well, but you also need to be honest with students about both limitations and strengths. The long-term prospects for genuine success are greater for all involved when you are candid with students, their parents, school administrators, and (of course) yourself. The ultimate aim of literacy assessment is to provide the ongoing information you need to guide each student to the highest possible level of present-day literacy.

Extending Learning

There is no substitute for involving yourself directly in assessment activities and the inquiry process. The two following exercises are designed to "get you into it."

1. Visit a school or district office, and talk with the teacher in a classroom. What tests are used? At what grades? Why? What happens to the results? Then study a couple of standardized tests and printouts of the results for a class or two. Think about what you can learn from these documents. After you have digested the

information, discuss your impressions with a principal, a teacher, and a couple of upper-grade students.

2. Informally assess a student's reading and writing knowledge and skills. Get your hands on one of the informal reading inventories that we described early in the chapter. Read the directions and then give the test to one or two students. Compare the scores of the IRI to those of the student's standardized test. Are they similar? What did you learn from the IRI that the standardized test failed to report.

Children's Literature

Dahl, R. (1988). *Matilda*. New York: Viking.
Kehret, P. (1996). *Earthquake Terror*. New York: Puffin.
Sharmat, M. (1972). *Nate the Great*. New York: Dell.

Sobol, D. (2005). *Encyclopedia Brown and the Case of the Jumping Frogs*. New York: Yearling.
White, E. (1952). *Charlotte's Web*. New York: Harper.

Chapter 6
Choosing Texts for Reading Instruction

 ## Learning Outcomes

After reading and studying this chapter you should be able to:

6.1 Understand why the purposes of reading in school are the same as reading out of school, for enjoyment, knowledge, and enlightenment.

6.2 Determine the difficulty of a text using a readability formula, a book leveling system, or the criteria for complexity outlined by the Common Core State Standards.

6.3 Understand the criteria necessary for selecting texts for beginning reading instruction.

6.4 Select appropriate texts for developing comprehension of fiction and non-fiction and help your students select appropriate Internet sites.

Classroom Vignette

The fourth grade has been working on comprehending non-fiction and Mrs. Nelson knew she needed a text for Monday that continued her work on amphibians. She and her colleagues are concerned about reading level and matching their students to just the right reading level. They have discovered that ReadWorks (http://www.readworks.org) is a useful website for finding passages for comprehension instruction. On that website the teachers can search by grade level, readability level, genre, and topic. The short passages come with comprehension questions and answers, questions that tap specific skills, and vocabulary words with glossary entries. The ReadWorks website has audio support so readers who struggle can listen to the passage.

On Monday, Mrs. Nelson's fourth graders sit down at her table in the back of the room for small group instruction. She hands out a passage, *Freaky Frogs*, about research that Japanese scientists have been doing on frogs. Last week this group read that the changing environment is endangering frogs. Mrs. Nelson begins the lesson by asking the students what they remember about frogs. A few students remember that the climate is changing and some frogs are dying. She then hands out the passage and the students read the title and the subtitle: *Will see-through frogs clear the way for frog research?* There is some discussion but no one really understands the subtitle. Next, Mrs. Nelson asks the students what they think will happen. What are your predictions? Josh offers that a large frog is going to eat the school. Mrs. Nelson ignores him and asks the students to read the article and then answer the comprehension questions.

MyLab Education
Video Example 6.1
Think about why text matters. Then read the next section of the chapter and see how your ideas develop.

The *Freaky Frog* passage is 328 words long with a Lexile level of 750 and it features a large picture of a pale frog at the beginning of the article. The passage is followed by a series of questions: nine multiple-choice comprehension questions, three short written response comprehension questions, 12 questions that explore the meaning and usage of the word *researcher*, and 11 questions that explore the meaning of the word *observe*. It will take the students two days to complete all of these questions.

The passage itself lacks coherence and voice. The first three sentences in the second paragraph read as follows: "Scientists in Hiroshima, Japan, have produced see-through frogs. Japan is a country in Asia. The pale frogs are the first see-through animals with four legs." In continues with a modest list of facts. The students take turns reading the article and then return to their desks to answer the 35 comprehension and vocabulary questions.

Why Text Matters

The short vignette is based on a lesson one of us observed last year in an elementary school. We will ignore the instruction for now and focus on the materials, the 328 words frog passage and 35 questions that follow. Text is a vital factor in developing students who can read and will want to read. The *Freaky Frogs* passage is short, poorly written, and unlikely to stir up any enthusiasm for the topic or for reading. It is just an activity, one of many activities that students complete and forget. It will make no lasting impression on the students.

In the first chapter of the book we introduced a model for thinking about reading comprehension that was developed by the Rand Reading Study Group (Snow, 2002). We reproduce this model in Figure 6.1. The first part of the model is the reader and we addressed many factors about the reader in Chapters 2 and 3, particularly the knowledge, the strategies, and the motivation the reader brings to reading. The second part of the model, the activities, we address in Chapters 7 through 14. The sociocultural context is part of motivation and instruction. So now we turn our attention to the text, what we ask students to read and what we hope they will select to read.

A fundamental question that we will attempt to answer in this chapter is how to select texts for reading instruction and how to match students to text. For many, that problem reduces to knowing the grade level or the readability of the texts and the reading level of the students. That is too simple because many other factors create a successful reading experience including the interest level of the text, its organization, style and the depth of the ideas within.

The Common Core State Standards (NGA & CCSSO, 2010) has pushed all educators to think about text difficulty and to gradually move students into more complex texts. The push for students to read more complex text, came from research developed by the American College Testing Service (ACT, 2006). They found that the students who were most successful in college were those who scored well on the complex texts within the ACT (ACT, 2006). In Figure 6.2 we present the results of the ACT research. You will note all students taking the test do quite well with uncomplicated text and more challenging text, but what distinguishes those with the highest scores from those with lower scores are the ability to read complex texts.

We can speculate why complexity matters and several reasons come to mind. First, complex text pushes a reader to think. Unraveling the syntax of complex sentences stretches the mind and forces the reader to think carefully to construct an understanding. As the reader moves through a complex text page by page the construction of meaning becomes more intricate or sophisticated. Complex text may also expose the student to more and varied words, and with exposure comes

Figure 6.1 RAND Study Heuristic for Thinking About Reading Comprehension

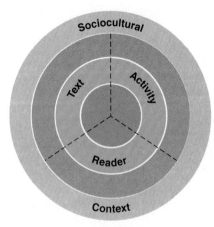

SOURCE: Based on RAND Reading Study Group. (2002). *Reading for Understanding: Toward an R&D Program in Reading Comprehension*, MR-1465-OERI. Santa Monica, CA: RAND Education. Copyright 2002.

Figure 6.2 The Effect of Complex Text on Reading Comprehension

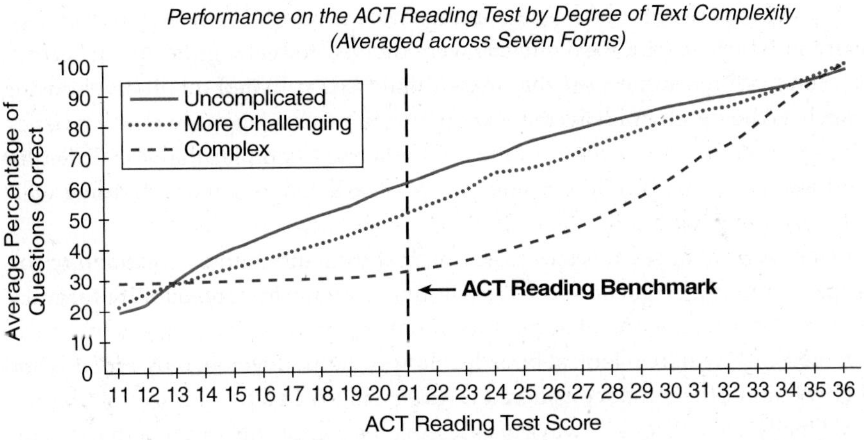

Performance on the ACT Reading Test by Degree of Text Complexity
(Averaged across Seven Forms)

[Line graph. Y-axis: "Average Percentage of Questions Correct" from 0 to 100. X-axis: "ACT Reading Test Score" from 11 to 36. Legend: Uncomplicated (solid line), More Challenging (dotted line), Complex (dashed line). A vertical dashed line at score 21 labeled "← ACT Reading Benchmark".]

SOURCE: Based on American College Testing, Reading Between the Lines: What the ACT Reveals About College Readiness in Reading. Iowa City, IA. Retrieved from: www.act.org/content/dam/act/unsecured/documents/reading_summary.pdf. August 24, 2018.

learning. Finally, complex text is an indicator that the students have been challenged, or have challenged themselves, with an interesting curriculum and have built a deeper knowledge base. But before we jump on the complex text bandwagon there is another position to consider.

Most of us became strong readers not through a diet of *War and Peace* and *Moby Dick*, but by reading incessantly easy and engaging books. The best readers raised themselves on *Nancy Drew*, *Baby Sitter's Club*, *Goosebumps*, *Encyclopedia Brown*, *Lemony Snicket*, or *Diary of a Wimpy Kid*—pick your decade. There is reasonable evidence that the volume of reading is important in developing reading skill and that students achieve the greatest growth when they are reading books at their grade level (see Allington, 2014). The findings of the ACT and the message about reading volume leave teachers with a difficult decision about texts. Teachers must encourage and create time for students to read a massive number of engaging books, and at the same time guide children to tackle ever more complex texts. We will divide our answer about choosing the right text into several questions. What are the right texts for beginning reading instruction? What are the right texts for teaching children how to comprehend literary texts and non-fiction? How do we go about selecting Internet sites and helping children select these sites? The world is changing and children rarely go the multi-volume World Book Encyclopedia, now they Google information. Before considering these topics, we will discuss how the readability of texts is measured.

MyLab Education
Video Example 6.2
This video introduces another concept, the Matthew Effect, and its importance. Consider why reading widely and deeply is important.

MyLab Education **Self-Check 6.1**

MyLab Education **Application Exercise 6.1:** Selecting Texts for Reading Instruction

Assessing Text Difficulty and Accessibility

The Common Core State Standards (NGA & CCSSO, 2010) are quite explicit that over the course of a student's schooling he should be reading increasingly complex texts. Previous standards mentioned that students should read only at grade level (Hiebert, 2014). The Common Core set the goal of increasing the complexity of text gradually from one grade to another and to increase complexity within a school year. The Common

Core defined complexity in three ways. First, text complexity can be determined with quantitative criteria. By that the standard meant readability formulas and specifically the Lexile scale (www.Lexile.com). The Common Core specifically referred to a staircase complexity in which specific Lexile levels were defined for each grade level. Second, the Common Core recommended that texts should be evaluated qualitatively using criteria such as the depth of ideas, the text organization, and language characteristics. Jean Fritz's *Shh! We're Writing the Constitution* is much less complex than the Federalist Papers. Third, educators should consider a reader-task analysis and determine what texts to use for what purposes.

There are several approaches to assessing text difficulty and the readability formula is the grandfather of the bunch. We will first examine how readability formulas work and consider which one of several formulas is best used for primary and more advanced texts. We will then look at book leveling systems, developed by Fountas and Pinnell (1999) and others that considered a wider range of factors for evaluating text difficulty. Finally, we will look at ways of assessing the complexity of a text that include the criteria recommended by the Common Core: level of meaning, structure, language, and knowledge demands.

Readability Formulas

Readability formulas are based on objective measures that consider two characteristics of a text and yield a grade-level equivalent score. Readability formulas considers are vocabulary difficulty and syntactic complexity. It is generally assumed that text with shorter words, words with fewer syllables, and shorter sentences with few clauses are easier to understand. When applied to a text, the formula indicates that the text is written at such and such a grade level. There are many different ways to calculate readability and there are many different formulas. For example, we calculated the readability of the text you just read—the last 1,000 words—and the results are presented in Figure 6.3.

According to the various readability formulas, the paragraphs you read in this chapter are written between an eighth and an eleventh grade level. We are writing sentences with an average of 19 words per sentence and 33 percent of the words have two or more syllables. According to the Lexile rating (we will get to the Lexile system later), this chapter earns a rating of 1300 to 1400 or an eleventh or twelfth grade level. By comparison, *The Firm* by John Grisham has a Lexile score of 680, *Harry Potter and the Sorcerer's Stone* a Lexile of 880 and *Hatchet* by Gary Paulson a Lexile of 1020.

Readability formulas are a good starting point for evaluating and picking books, but the formulas are not interchangeable or equally effective with all texts. The Flesch-Kincaid is useful for upper elementary through high school texts. The Dale-Chall is useful with text above a fourth-grade level, and Spache was designed for texts used in lower elementary grades. The Fry formula (Fry, 1977) is one widely used measure. It assesses word difficulty by considering the average number of syllables in the words of a text, and it assesses syntactic complexity by considering the average number of words per sentence. For example, when applied to Marion Ripley's *Private and Confidential: A*

Figure 6.3 Average Readability Rating for This Textbook

Readability Formula	Grade Level of Text
Flesch Reading Ease Score	60.0 (standard/average)
Gunning Fog	11.5
Flesch-Kincaid	9.7
The SMOG Index	8.4
Automated Readability Index	11.1
Fry Readability	10.3
Lexile	1300–1400

Story About Braille, the Fry formula indicates that the book is written at approximately the second-grade level. It would, therefore, appear to be appropriate for students reading at the second-grade level. However, both estimates of text difficulty and the reading levels resulting from testing students are approximations. Efforts to match students and texts must always be undertaken with the realization that the initial matches should be considered tentative and that you need to continually monitor students and be prepared to offer another book if the first one isn't right. In the Classroom 6.1 shows the procedures for the Fry formula and the graph used in applying the formula.

In the Classroom 6.1

Instructional Routines

Using the Fry Readability Formula

1. Randomly select three 100-word samples from the book, short story, chapter, or article that you want to assess, one each from the beginning, middle, and near the end of the selection. For longer selections, you may want to take additional samples. In counting the 100-word samples, do count proper nouns, initials, and numerals. Count hyphenated words as one word.

2. Count the number of sentences in each 100-word sample, estimating to the nearest tenth of a sentence, and average that count.

3. Count the number of syllables in each 100-word sample, and average that count. Syllables are based on sounds, not necessarily letters. There are as many syllables in a word as there are vowel sounds. Thus,

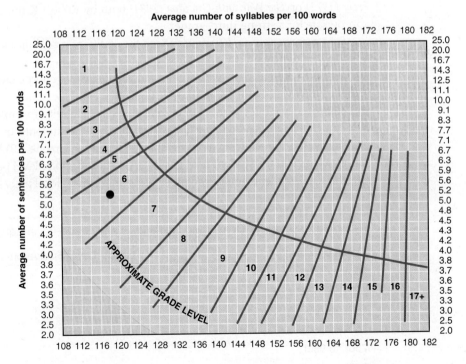

Graph for Estimating Readability—Extended
by Edward Fry, Rutgers University Reading Center, New Brunswick, NJ 08904

	Example	Example
First 100 Words	118	5.4
Second 100 Words	123	5.0
Third 100 Words	113	5.2
Average	118	5.2

Estimated Grade Level: 6th

(Continued)

want has one syllable, *stopped* has one, and *wanted* has two. When counting syllables for numerals, initials, and symbols, count one syllable for each symbol. Thus, *1945* has four syllables; *IRA*, three syllables; and *&*, one syllable.

4. Find on the Fry graph the lines corresponding to the average sentence length and the average number of syllables. Go to the intersection of these two lines to get the approximate grade level of the selection. An example is given below the graph.

SOURCE: Fry, E. B., Polk, J. K., & Fountoukidis, D. (2000). *The Reading Teacher's Book of Lists*. Paramus, NJ: Prentice Hall.

The second text difficulty tool we consider, the Lexile Framework for Reading (www.Lexile.com), is a multipart system that uses a complex formula of word difficulty and sentence complexity to determine the reading level of short texts and books. The Lexile website has a database that lists the levels for tens of thousands of books and an online tool for calculating the Lexile levels for text you input. Unlike the Fry formula and most traditional formulas, the Lexile formula yields a Lexile level, a score ranging from 200 to 1700, instead of a grade-level equivalent. Lexile levels can then be roughly equated with grade levels using the conversion chart shown in Figure 6.4.

A Lexile score can also be assigned to a student. When students take the Star Reading test, MAP Reading Growth Assessment, or any number of other tests, they can receive a Lexile score. When the students and the book are rated on the same scale, matching the students to the text is easy, or is it? A third-grade student reading at the 650 Lexile cannot necessarily read any book in the 600 range, nor should they avoid texts at the 700 or 800 level. For example, *The Firm* (Grisham, 1991) has a Lexile of 680, but I doubt most teachers or parents would expect their 8-year-old to negotiate a book about corruption, fraudulent legal practices, and the FBI. However, *Chocolate Fever (1972)* or *The War with Grandpa (1984)* both by Robert Kimmel Smith might be appropriate for a strong third-grader.

For years researchers have questioned the ability of readability formulas to predict how well students could read a passage. In several studies it was demonstrated that readability of the passages was not a good predictor of a child's oral reading fluency (Comptom, Powell-Smith, & Bradley-Klug, 2001). Two researchers went a step further and compared the effectiveness of eight different readability formulas to predict how well students might read a range of passages orally—the students' oral reading fluency rates measured the students' reading ability (Begeny & Greene, 2013). For example, it was expected that if a student read passage A, a second-grade level passage at a certain rate, that same student would read passage B, a third-grade level passage at a slower rate.

Figure 6.4 Chart for Converting Lexile Levels to Grade-Level Equivalents

Lexile Levels	Grade-Level Equivalents
200L to 400L	1
300L to 500L	2
500L to 700L	3
650L to 850L	4
750L to 950L	5
850L to 1050L	6
950L to 1075L	7
1000L to 1100L	8
1050L to 1150L	9
1100L to 1200L	10
1100L to 1300L	11 and 12

Only one readability formula successfully predicted students' change in performance—the Dale-Chall (1948) developed by Edgar Dale and Jeanne Chall. It was consistently more accurate at grades 1 through 7. Even the ubiquitous Lexile was only an accurate predictor for grades 3 and 4. The Fry formula was accurate at the lower grade levels.

The accuracy of the Dale-Chall formula in predicting students' oral reading fluency may be based on how that formula counts word difficulty. In most readability formulas, word difficulty is determined by the number of syllables in a word or the number of syllables per 100 words. The Dale-Chall formula considers the number of words outside a list of 3,000 basic words that every third or fourth grader should know. Thus, the Dale-Chall formula might be a more sensitive measure of vocabulary than the other formulas. It is important to remember that these studies used fluency as a measure of reading ability and not comprehension.

Readability formulas have their limits in matching students to texts. None of the formulas consider genre, topic, content, writing style, or the background knowledge and interests of the reader. All of these are important in selecting texts for students and in helping students select texts. We thoroughly disagree with the idea of telling students their Lexile score and then directing them to read books at that level. This practice brands students, leads to unnecessary comparisons among students, and limits choice in what to read. Matching students to texts is not a problem that can be solved through mathematical formulas. Because readability formulas are limited, some educators created book leveling systems that consider a wide range of factors.

Book Leveling

The book leveling approach, was developed as a way of ranking books for difficulty and accessibility by considering a number of factors beyond those considered by traditional readability formulas. Irene Fountas and Gay Su Pinnell (2006) and their colleagues have examined a large number of books and categorized them in levels ranging from Levels A and B (for children just beginning to read) to Level Z (for students reading at the seventh- and eighth-grade level). Among the many factors considered in Fountas and Pinnell's leveling process are the number of ideas in the book, size of the print, layout, correspondence between text and pictures, and sophistication and familiarity of the topics. The following excerpts are parts of their descriptions of Levels A and B books, such as Syd Hoff's *Barney's Horse*, and of Level M books, such as Jan Brett's *The Mitten*.

Levels A and B Books

Levels A and B books are very easy for young children to begin to read. Many of these books focus on a single idea or have a single story line. There is a direct correspondence between the text and the pictures, and children can easily relate the topics to their personal experience. The language, while not exactly duplicating oral language, includes naturally occurring syntactic structures. Teachers can use books at these levels to introduce children to word-by-word matching and locating known words.

Level M Books

Books in Level M are long, with lots of text per page, smaller print, and narrower word spacing. There is a wide variety of texts, but they all have complex language structures and sophisticated vocabulary. They are highly detailed and descriptive and present more abstract concepts and themes. The subtleties of these texts require more background knowledge. Many characters are involved in more complex and expanded plots; character development is a prominent feature. (Fountas & Pinnell, 2006, pp. 136, 142).

The relatively recent list of leveled books (Fountas & Pinnell, 2006) shows approximately 16,000 titles.

The Fountas and Pinnell book leveling system competes with several others. Reading A-Z an online source (www.readinga-z.com) ranks books from A to Z. Reading Recovery, the first group to level books continues to use a 1–40 ranking for books from emergent reading through fifth grade books. The Developmental Reading Assessment (Beaver & Carter, 2013) ranks text from A–1, for emergent readers, to 50 for sixth grade, and the PM Benchmark Assessment System (Nelley & Smith, 2000) ranks their texts from 1 in kindergarten to 30 at about fifth grade. Converting from one chart to another is relatively easy and the Internet offers a number of conversion charts so anyone can determine how one leveling system compares to another. Simply search for "reading level conversion chart." It is much more difficult to determine how books are leveled.

While the use of readability formulas is straightforward, book leveling is not. It is difficult to determine which criteria were used to level books and how the criteria were weighted. In the Fountas and Pinnell system the *Diary of a Wimpy Kid* (Kinney, 2007), a relatively innocuous book about middle school hijinks, receives a level of T–U, while a much more intricate and demanding text, *Lord of the Rings* (Tolkein, 1954) is ranked at R–S. Treat book leveling systems with some caution, especially in fourth grade and above.

Jim Hoffman (2017) wrote about the unintended consequences of leveling books and leveling students. Students take on a reading level as an identity and they should not. We have listened to children say I am a 40 and I can't read books that are a 50. Such an identity limits exploration and adventure. Levels limit teachers' decision making and cause them to think that students should be at their "just right" level. Instead, teachers should ask what kind of support does a student need to succeed with this book? There are many ways to support or scaffold reading and we will explore them throughout this book. Finally, Hoffman points out that book levels cause all educators to think of reading as a goal and not a tool. The goal of reading instruction is not to have all students in fifth grade reach a level 50. Reading is a tool for learning information, exploring the world, and escaping to unimagined worlds. Book leveling and readability formulas have a similar weakness. They reduce book choices to a single number. Because readability formulas and book leveling are only the beginning, the educators have sought other means to describe texts.

Qualitative Factors of Text

Many qualitative factors influence the complexity of text and they cannot be reduced to a single number. Teachers should consider an array of factors from psychological and linguistic research affecting the difficulty of text (Graves & Graves, 2003). Although this approach does not yield a single answer, such as a grade-level equivalent, Lexile score, or Fountas and Pinnell level, it does suggest that teachers should consider the following:

- Vocabulary
- Sentence structure
- Length
- Elaboration
- Coherence and unity
- Text structure

- Familiarity of content and background knowledge required
- Audience appropriateness
- Quality and verve of the writing
- Interestingness

The Common Core State Standards (NGA & CCSSO, 2010) propose four categories for examining the qualitative factors in determining a text's complexity. They are the level of meaning and purpose in a text, its structure or organization, the use of language conventions and clarity, and the knowledge demands on the reader. We tend to prefer a more expanded version developed by Hiebert (2014) because she explicitly addressed the concerns of teachers who need to make choices in selecting text. Hiebert's system includes seven criteria.

GOALS OF INSTRUCTION

Teachers should select text by first considering their instructional goals. Remember, reading is not a subject matter it is a tool. So, the goal might be to learn about frogs, develop some understanding of how to get along with others, or understand the rights of workers during the Industrial Revolution. Hiebert asks, "What will my students learn about the world with this text?" Later in Chapter 11 we outline a unit that begins with the novel *Shiloh* (Naylor, 1991). This novel was selected because its main character, Marty, has to make a complex moral decision about an abused dog. This text is used as a read-aloud, but the accompanying texts each continue the topic of dogs and the problem of making moral decisions. We recommend avoiding texts that were written specifically to teach reading. These include texts in workbooks and many intervention programs.

PRIOR KNOWLEDGE

Every reader brings to a text a body of knowledge with which he makes sense of that text. This is true for the youngest and oldest reader. The reader leaves that text with a new knowledge and sometimes new values. Despite the Common Core State Standard's goal of keeping the reader "within the four corners of the text" prior knowledge is essential for comprehension. It could be argued that after you have read paragraph one in a text that knowledge is now prior and used to make sense of paragraph two. The more knowledge a reader brings to the page, the better his understanding of that text.

The problem for the teacher is selecting a text for which the reader has the knowledge necessary for comprehension but not a text so commonplace that nothing is to be gained from reading it. This puts some books out of reach for the young reader, especially those that require considerable knowledge of history, science, or historical fiction. As teachers get to know their students they will gain a sense of what they know and for what text they are ready. When a text is out of reach, then the development of knowledge through discussions, video presentations, and read-alouds, builds a bridge between the students and the new text.

Another consideration is how a text builds knowledge. The science writer Gail Gibbons uses several techniques to assist the reader into a new and complex topic, building knowledge along the way. Consider these short examples from her book on *Bats* (1999). Gibbons typically starts with general statements, "Bats dive, and swoop and swerve through the night sky." Later in the text she is much more specific as she explains technical characteristics of bats. "Most bats are insect eaters and have a special way of 'seeing' in the night called echolocation." When she introduces new terms, she quickly defines the word before moving on. "These creatures are nocturnal, meaning they are awake at night and asleep during the day."

Finally, the teacher should consider that the knowledge demands of a text vary across the text. Novels are typically difficult at the beginning, there is much to learn, and it is often that a student abandons a book within the first quarter of the text (Collinge, 2013). In the first quarter, the student has to learn the characters, their relationship to each other, and develop an understanding of their traits and motives. The setting must be nailed down along with its role in advancing the plot. Finally, the reader is assembling the events of a story, striving to understand the conflict. The research suggests that, when students are given support and guidance in the early stages of a novel, they are much more confident and successful with the rest of the book (Dewitz & Collinge, 2019).

VOCABULARY

The complexity of a text is influenced by the vocabulary and it is important to understand how this works. Hiebert (2014) and others tell us that a small number of words, 4,000, account for 90 percent of the words in all texts, even in complex texts. It is the other 10 percent of the words that cause the most difficulty. These extended vocabulary words can be new concepts such as *invertebrate* and *longitude*, or new labels for old concepts such as *inept* and *indecipherable*. Typically, the extended vocabulary of non-fiction is introducing new concepts or complex idea such as *representation* or *impeachment* while the vocabulary in fiction often uses different terms for the same concept. In a paragraph, a writer can move from *horses*, to *mares*, to *stallions*, to *steeds*, with the labels changing more than the underlying concepts.

When helping students select texts for independent reading, it is best if the proportion of extended words is limited. Hiebert (2014) points out that, if a student reads 1,000 words and 6 percent of them are extended, he will encounter 60 difficult words. If the ratio increases to 7.5 percent, he will encounter 75 difficult words. Extend this out to a 40,000-word fourth grade novel and a student might encounter 600 new words while reading the novel. When selecting text for students to read, examine the frequency of extended or difficult words. Consider this excerpt from *Ramona Forever* (Cleary, 1984).

"Yes, where was Grandpa Day? Everyone worried, everyone *fussed*. His motel was called. No, his room did not answer. More worrying until Ramona, posted at the window, screamed, "Look!" There was Grandpa Day, arriving in a long black *limousine* driven by a real *chauffeur* wearing a real *chauffeur's* cap, just like *chauffeurs* on television (p.143)."

FIGURATIVE LANGUAGE

Similes, metaphors, and idioms add interest and delight, causing the reader to savor the language in the text as well as the ideas. These writerly techniques, along with dialogue, dialects, and colloquial expressions also make a text more difficult to read. Consider this short excerpt from *Chains* (2008) by Laurie Halse Anderson that includes a figure of speech, and a style of language and speech typical of the late 18th century.

> It was near a mile from the Tea Water Pump back down the island to the Lockton house, a long journey carrying heavy buckets that stretched arms into sore ribbons.
>
> I forgot the pain when Curzon stopped, pointed, and said,
>
> "There 'tis."

Teachers can help students comprehend figurative language and idioms. Treat idioms, *bite the bullet*, *hit the sack*, or *under the weather*, as new vocabulary words. The meanings of the individual words do not equal the meaning of the phrase. Therefore, idioms must be taught as are any other vocabulary words, but sometimes their meanings can be inferred from context. Idioms have one clear advantage, they tend to be fun to learn and use. Figurate language is using language as an analogy or a comparison, and after students catch on to that idea, comprehension is eased. As with vocabulary, try to estimate how much complex language your students can handle, and instruct on idioms and the process of making sense of figurative language.

SENTENCE STRUCTURE

The length of sentences and the number of ideas embedded within a sentence contributes to how easily a student can comprehend. According to the research, the sentence complexity contributes more to passage difficulty than does vocabulary (Hiebert, 2014). Basically, longer sentences with more clauses taxes memory, making it more difficult for the reader to assemble ideas. But that does not mean that shorter sentences are always better. When a long sentence with causal connections (*because, since, so*) are broken into shorter sentences without causal connections, then comprehension is impaired (Pearson, 1974). Consider these two examples:

1. The dogs collapsed on the floor because they were so hot and tired.
2. Dogs were hot and tired. They collapsed on the floor.

It is easier to comprehend the first sentence because the causal relationship is explicit. In the second example it is implied.

Despite what we know about sentence complexity, it is difficult to select books based on sentence structure alone. Typically, fiction shows a greater variation in sentence structure than non-fiction because the fiction writer uses many short sentences, particularly dialogue. Sentence length tends to be longer and more uniform in non-fiction writing when compared to fiction writing, because the non-fiction writer has some complex ideas to express within the span of one sentence—as was just displayed in the preceding 33 word sentence.

Although complex sentences do make a text more difficult to comprehend, there are tools for the teacher to make this process easier. First, teachers can explain how the syntax of a sentence works and, in some cases, this helps the students' comprehension. A fifth-grade student reading the sentence, "The mouth of the Mississippi River, its end, dumps into the Gulf of Mexico" may not be aware of how an apposition structure defines the meaning of a word or phrase. Explaining this could assist with comprehension. Most of our comprehension activities are directed at the paragraph level or higher. When a teacher suspects that complex sentence structure is affecting comprehension, it might be time to unpack the sentence, review the grammar in the sentence, and consider how signal words (*because, however, since, therefore*) affect the meaning.

PASSAGE LENGTH

In any elementary classroom there are students who balk at reading three pages, but across the room sits another student merrily reading through Harry Potter. Length as a feature of text can intimidate some students but not others. Currently it is popular to lament the lack of stamina among some readers, but we think stamina is a poorly chosen term more aptly applied to the problem of test taking and marathon running than the act of reading books for pleasure and information. The dictionary defines stamina as the physical or mental strength to withstand a hardship. Reading should not be a hardship and the concept of stamina is a poor replacement for interest, motivation and skill.

The inability to comprehend longer texts may be a product of how we teach reading and with what we teach reading. All basal reading programs and the guided reading approach (Fountas & Pinnell, 1996) focus on short texts. In basal book length selections are rare, less so in guided reading. Students need to be introduced early to longer texts, especially in reading aloud, so they develop the interest and confidence to tackle them.

Most approaches to reading instruction incorporate page-by-page questioning. On every page, the teacher stops the students, asks questions, and they discuss what has been read. In basals the pattern is the same for the first text in year and the last one. Reading instruction was not always so. Up until the early 1970s, it was common in reading programs to assign the passage, conduct some pre-reading instruction, and then direct the students to read the whole passage. Only when the students had completed the assignment did they come together to question and discuss.

Page-by-page questioning may affect the development of comprehension. In this style of guided reading, the student encounters the meaning of the passage twice, once when he is reading it and a second time when he is participating in the discussion. If the student fails to understand the first time, there is always the second chance when the teacher or the other students explain the passage and clear up his misunderstanding. Might this build up dependence on the teacher and the other students? It is possible that the attempt to build comprehension through page-by-page guided reading may undermine comprehension foster a lack of stamina. There is some research evidence to support this idea.

Van den Broek and Kramer (2000) set up an interesting study. They had third graders and ninth graders read passages and discuss the passage in three different ways. Some students were asked questions while they read, others were asked questions after they read, and some were not asked questions at all. The researchers then assessed their reading comprehension two hours after the passage was read. Although the comprehension of ninth graders improved when the teacher stopped to ask questions during the reading, this practice had the opposite effect with third graders. These students demonstrated greater comprehension when the teacher waited to ask questions after the passage was read or asked no questions at all. The researchers speculate that frequently stopping to ask questions of young students interferes with their ability to assemble ideas and make connections. The problem that students have comprehending longer texts may be a product of how we teach them to read.

One research finding is not cause for abandoning fifty years of practice, but it is cause for teachers to experiment with how much text students should read before we begin our discussions. In some cases, it might make sense to experiment and try having students read longer chunks of text before beginning the discussion. Over time, it might be useful to lengthen these text chunks before discussions, and, for younger students, it might be best to begin with longer chucks and shorten them to see how comprehension is affected.

Reading novels or non-fiction books in the classroom likely requires different instructional techniques than those developed for the short passages that abound in basal programs or are common in the guided reading approach. The reason that students might struggle with books is that we have not explained and modeled how to read these lengthy texts. We believe that each chunk of a text demands its own purpose and own set of thinking strategies (2013). In the first quarter of the novel the reader assembles the facts of the novel—character, setting, problem, conflict. Later in the books he considers character development, motives, and themes. We will explain much of this is Chapter 11.

TEXT AND ACTIVITY RELATIONSHIPS

We now turn to Common Core State Standards' final point, matching the students, the text and the instructional activity. Different instructional activities call for different texts. The text chosen for a read aloud can have a much higher level of difficulty than the text students will read independently. When your purpose is to improve fluency and you are using an approach in which students repeatedly read the same text, the text needs to be slightly challenging so that there is room for improvement across the repeated readings. Similarly, when you are working with the class or a small group, scaffolding their reading of a particular text, you will generally want to use texts that are a little challenging, ones that your students can succeed at because you are assisting them. Conversely, when students are doing independent reading and do not have your assistance, they should frequently read in texts that are not a challenge, ones that they find interesting and enjoyable but not taxing. When you are teaching a comprehension strategy, you want to use a text that is sophisticated enough to require the use of the strategy but not one in which decoding is a problem; students can hardly be expected to use a comprehension strategy if they cannot decode the text. Matching students and texts is important for all of the reading activities students undertake. We end with two lists for The Reading Corner which ranks books for sixth grade students from less to more complex.

The Reading Corner

Books that Reflect a Range of Complexity for Sixth Grade Students

The list here includes fiction and non-fiction and is ordered from the least complex to the most.

Fiction

Raina Telgemeier. *Drama.* Grafix, 2012. In this popular graphic novel, middle schooler Callie rides an emotional roller coaster while serving on the drama stage crew for the school's production of *Moon Over Mississippi.* 233 pages.

Sharon Flake. *The Skin I'm In.* Hyperion Books for Children; Revised ed., 2007. Uncomfortable because of her very dark skin, thirteen-year-old Maleeka meets a teacher

with a facial birthmark and makes some discoveries about how to love herself and what she looks like. 176 pages.

Lawrence Yep. *Dragonwings.* HarperCollins; 25th anniversary edition, 2001. Inspired by the story of a Chinese immigrant who created a flying machine in 1909, this Newbery Honor book touches on the dreams and struggles of Chinese immigrants in San Francisco. 248 pages.

Madeleine L'Engle. *A Wrinkle in Time.* Square Fish/Farrar Straus Giroux, 1st Square Fish 50th anniversary ed., 2012. In this Newbery Award-winning novel, a young girl and her friends become involved with unearthly strangers in their search for her father who has disappeared while engaged in secret work for the government. 236 pages.

Esther Forbes. *Johnny Tremain.* Graphia, 2011. After injuring his hand, a silversmith's apprentice in Boston becomes a messenger for the Sons of Liberty in the days before the American Revolution in this Newbery Award-winning book. 300 pages.

Louise Erdich. *Makoons. (Birchbark House).* HarperCollins, 2016. In this, Erdich's fifth book in the Birchbark House series, Makoons, named for the Ojibewe word for little bear, has a vision that foretells great challenges for his family. 158 pages.

J. K. Rowling. *Harry Potter and the Chamber of Secrets.* Scholastic, 20th anniversary ed., 2018. Just as Harry is packing his bags to get back to the Hogwarts School for Witchcraft and Wizardry, he receives a warning that if he goes back, disaster will strike. 341 pages.

Non-Fiction

Cece Bell. *El Deafo.* Henry Abrams, 2014. This memoir, a Newbery Honor book graphic novel, chronicles the author's hearing loss at a young age and her subsequent experiences with the Phonic Ear, a very powerful, and awkwardly large, hearing aid. 233 pages.

Stephanie Roth Sisson. *Star Stuff: Carl Sagan and the Mysteries of the Cosmos.* Roaring Brook Press, 2014. This illustrated book tells the story of Carl Sagan who, as a young boy, marveled at the universe and then never stopped trying to understand it better. 42 pages.

Joy Hakim. *A History of the US: From Colonies to Country: 1735–1791 A History of US Book Three.* Oxford University Press, 2007. Book Three in the History of the US series, this volume explores the making of a new, independent nation. 224 pages.

Candice Fleming. *Giant Squid.* Roaring Brook Press, 2016. This award-winning, non-fiction book explores the mysterious life of the elusive giant squid. 40 pages.

James L. Swanson. *Chasing Lincoln's Killer.* Scholastic Press, 2009. In this book, award-winning author Swanson describes the assassination of Lincoln and the pursuit and capture of his killer, John Wilkes Booth, and his accomplices. 194 pages.

Russell Freedman. *Freedom Walkers: The Story of the Montgomery Bus Boycott.* Holiday House, 2009. In this, one of his many award-winning non-fiction titles, Freedman provides captivating coverage of the events surrounding and including the Montgomery Bus Boycott, the end of segregation on buses. 114 pages.

Linda R. Monk. *The Words We Live By.* Hyperion, 2003. Monk gives readers an entertaining and informative look at the Constitution with discussions on new rulings and hot button issues such as gay marriage, gun control, affirmative action, and immigration. 288 pages.

Reflect and Apply

1. Think about the seven factors that Hiebert believes are critical to selecting texts for instruction. Get your hands on a current reading program for any grade and decide how many of those factors were considered when the texts for the reading program were selected or written.

2. Identify one widely used book you estimate to be at about the second-grade level and one you estimate to be at about the fourth-grade level. Look up each book in the Lexile Book Database at www.lexile.com, and convert the Lexile level into a grade-level equivalent using the conversion chart you can find online. Compare your estimates to those you got using the Lexile Book Database and the conversion chart, and jot down a comment on the agreement or disagreement between the estimates.

MyLab Education **Self-Check 6.2**

MyLab Education **Application Exercise 6.2:** Determining Reading Levels

Texts for Beginning Reading Instruction

For over 300 years, since the New England Primer, we have recognized that young children need special texts for learning to read. We just can't agree on their nature or structure and, there has been a great deal more heat than light shed on beginning reading texts (Hiebert, 2009). Despite a slowly growing body of research, this cloudy picture

Figure 6.5 Fun Wherever We Are: Third Pre-primer

Jane said, "Here, Puff.
Come here."

"Look!" said Jane
"Look here, Puff."

Jane said, "Puff! Puff!"
Look at this.
Come here and look at this".

SOURCE: Robinson, H. M., Monroe, M., Artley, A. (1962). Fun Wherever We Are. Chicago: IL: Scott Foresman and Company, pp. 5–8).

is developing some clarity. We will first take a quick historical survey of the changes in texts for beginning reading instruction and then consider how teachers might select the most appropriate texts for their students.

A Historical Look at Texts for Beginning Reading Instruction

The time from 1960 witnessed a number of changes to the text used for beginning reading instruction. In the early to mid-part of the 20th century, the texts in basal reading programs stressed the teaching of high frequency words through regular repetition of those words. The classic example of such texts was the Curriculum Foundation Series (Elson & Gray) commonly known as *Dick and Jane*. It is almost unnecessary to share an example of these texts but in Figure 6.5 we do so. Elson and Gray's method was to introduce the most commonly used words in the language and repeat those words at least 10 times every 100 words. The words were selected with no attention to the phonics patterns within the words. The Dick and Jane program was published from the late 1920s through the mid-1960s when it was replaced with a new program by its publisher, Scott Foresman.

The approach developed by William S. Gray and his successors was called the look-say method and it eventually came under tremendous criticism first by Rudolph Flesch in his book *Why Johnny Can't Read, and What You Can Do about It* (1955). But the most effective and lasting criticism came from Jeanne Chall in her book, *Learning to Read: The Great Debate* (1967). Chall analyzed a number of basal or core reading programs and the available research, and came to the conclusion that an approach and texts that emphasized phonics would be more successful. Chall's analysis was backed up by the First Grade Reading Studies (Bond & Dykstra, 1967) that also concluded that programs that emphasized phonics achieved stronger results.

Despite the research that put phonics in a positive light, change came slowly. The new edition of Chall's (1983) text concluded that through the 1970s the text for beginning reading focused on repetition of high frequency words with little attention to phonics elements. A new report, *Becoming a Nation of Readers* (Anderson, Hiebert, Scott, & Wilkinson, 1985), also concluded that children should be given the opportunity to apply phonics, but the texts in core reading programs changed little. The publishers did, however, include more phonics instruction in the teacher's manuals and in the workbooks.

The significant change in beginning reading texts came as a result of the rising whole language movement and its close cousin, literature-based reading. Jim Hoffman (1994) and his colleagues conducted a detailed analysis of first grade reading programs published in 1986/87 and in 1993. He examined the texts in the students' anthologies and the trade books that were sold alongside. In Figure 6.6, we present his results. A number of things changed in these new programs. First grade children read fewer words in 1993 than they did in 1986/87, but the number of unique words increased significantly. In 1986/87 children encountered 962 unique words, and six years later the

Figure 6.6 Word and Sentence Analysis of Texts in Basal Readers

	1986/87 Programs X (Range)	1993 Programs (without trades) X (Range)	1993 Programs (with trades) X (Range)
Total number of words	17,319 (16,865–17,282)	12,265 (6,629–17,102)	14,272 (9,569–22,728)
Number of unique words	962 (847–1,051)	1,680 (1,171–2,238)	1,834 (1,536–2,458)
Readability	1.00 (1.00–1.00)	(1.69) (1.28–2.14)	1.52 (1.22–1.96)
Syllables/word	1.117 (1.071–1.135)	1.20 (1.19–1.22)	1.195 (1.177–1.215)
Words/sentences	6.8 (6.5–6.9)	7.8 (7.2–8.4)	7.7 (7.2–8.2)

SOURCE: Based on J. Hoffman et al. (1994). So what's new in the new basals? A focus on first grade. *Journal of Reading Behavior*, 26(1), 47–74.

number increase to 1,680 to 1,834 words. With the number of unique words increasing and the total number of words declining, that means that the repetitions for each word declined. Children encountered more different words but had fewer opportunities to learn them. The data also suggests that the sentences grew longer and the readability of the texts increased. So far, the research on phonics had no effect on the books used to teach beginning reading.

Along with the rise of literature-based reading was the increased use of predictable texts. In these texts, some element of the sentence is repeated and only one word at the end of the line changes. Eric Carle's (1969) *The Very Hungry Caterpillar* uses elements of repetition (On Monday he ate … On Tuesday he ate …) and Bill Martin uses this structure throughout his book *Brown Bear Brown Bear What Do You See* (1967). The use of repetitive text was considered an important structure to help young children learn to read, especially by the developer of Reading Recovery, an early reading intervention program (Clay, 1985, 1993; Fountas & Pinnell, 1996; Pinnell, 1990).

It was argued that predictable text supported the beginning reader through the repetition of the words and phrases. The young reader could anticipate the words because the syntax was repetitive and they did not have to decode all of the words. Pictures provided the support needed for the words that could not be predicted or decoded. The advocates for predictable text argued that these texts would support students' use of the three main cuing systems—sentence structure (syntax), the message (semantics), and the letters (graphic cues) to identify words. As the students repeatedly read the same words, they would learn them much in the same manner that repetitions worked in the basals 70 years ago. Words were repeated within a book, but, unfortunately, not across books.

When James Cunningham and his colleagues studied these predictable texts, they found they did not meet expectations; they did not enhance children's word-learning abilities. These predictable books provided some support for learning high frequency words, but the repetitions of those words were not up to the standards that some experts have set (Hiebert, 1999). Cunningham and colleagues further concluded that these predictable books do not contain enough decodable words to help students learn the letter sound patterns. They found that over half of the 80 Reading Recovery books they examined contained 14 percent or fewer decodable words. While reading these books, the students do not have enough exposure to phonics patterns to learn them and apply them.

The change to more phonics-oriented text for early reading instruction finally began to emerge in the early 2000s. Hiebert and Martin (2015) argue that the change was precipitated by two causes. After California had switched to a literature-based approach to reading instruction, their students performed poorly on the next National Assessment of Educational Progress (1996). Second, legislation in Texas (Texas Education Agency, 1997) required that their new reading programs have a substantial proportion of decodable words. That meant that phonics patterns of the words had to have been introduced before the students read the story. It is a bit ironic that these changes began to emerge before the publication of the *Report of the National Reading Panel* (NICHD, 2000) that called for a strong focus on phonics instruction in kindergarten and first grade. These texts included many more decodable words, but Hiebert and Martin offered a caution. The publishers did not decrease the number of words that had to be learned nor was the number of repetitions of words increased.

This review of the texts for early reading instruction finds something lacking is most of them. The traditional basal neglected phonics, stressing the repetition of high frequency words. The literature-based instruction continued the neglect of phonics, as did predictable text. The current basal appear to introduce too many words too quickly. In the next section we will explore what type of books should be used for beginning reading instruction.

What Texts Should We Use for Beginning Reading Instruction?

This is a difficult question and we cannot provide a totally satisfying answer. The debate over what texts to use has suffered because teachers have been pushed to choose among three alternatives. Years ago, the recommended practice was picking texts that emphasized the repetition of high frequency words—the Dick and Jane model. Then, when whole language and literature-based instruction seized the center stage, we abandoned repetition for good literature and predictable text. Then, at the turn of the 21st century, decodable books were privileged and state adoption committees demanded a high percentage of decodable words in these texts.

We can draw a number of conclusions from the work of Hiebert, Cunningham, and others. First, we should not over focus on what Hiebert (1999) calls single criteria text. It is not repetitions of high frequency words, or phonics elements, or meaningful words that is the point. It is the use of texts that embrace all three criteria. Teachers should look for a balance of texts and, at times work with high frequency words, at other times with phonics patterns and decodable books, and at still other times with meaningful text. Dr. Seuss was on the right track when he wrote books that were engaging while providing considerable repetitions of words and phonics patterns. To meet these criteria, a school or the first-grade teacher might have to assemble a number of books from different series, so that different texts meet the needs of different students.

Second, Hiebert (2009) is clear that the current first grade texts are of sufficient difficulty that only 25 percent of first graders achieve success reading these books. Many of these books introduce new vocabulary at a rate that some students cannot handle. The texts in basal anthologies in particular do not provide enough repetition and this is true for the leveled books typically found in a guided reading program. The frequency of new words in Cunningham's research was approximately 1.2 to 1.4. That means within 100 total words a new word was repeated two or four times. Hiebert would argue that students who find it difficult to learn to read need words repeated 7 or more times per every 100 words.

If the texts do not provide the repetitions that teachers seek, then we suggest a change in the instructional procedures. Francine Johnson (2000) developed a lesson plan that insures that students learn more words. Her plan weaned the students from using the context and pictures as support for word recognition. In the Classroom 6.2 outlines that lesson.

Developing Comprehension with Beginning Readers

The texts you use to develop students' facility with decoding and high frequency words are not the texts you need to develop comprehension. In kindergarten, first, and second grade, many students' listening comprehension far outstrips their reading comprehension. Both the developmental theory of Jeanne Chall (1983) and the research on the development of fluency and automaticity direct us not to tackle the development of comprehension and the development of print skills with the same texts. According to Chall, the first grader's main task is to learn the code of written English and the books that assist with that process, the ones we have already discussed, do not contain the concepts and the vocabulary that will build comprehension.

This all suggests that the development of comprehension for young children must take place at a different time and with different texts than the development of word recognition. The shared reading experience, in which an adult reads a text aloud and engages students in an interactive discussion, builds vocabulary and comprehension (Shahaeian, Wang, Tucker-Drob, Geiger et al., 2018). When teachers and parents read aloud to young children, they favor narratives over information books (Duke, 2000;

In the Classroom 6.2

Building Lasting Word Recognition

Francine Johnson created this lesson so that children being taught to read with predictable books would receive more repetitive practice with some vocabulary words. The lesson plan also pushes the students to focus on the words and not the pictures or the context. The lesson plan is more useful for students who find it difficult to learn to read and who are not retaining high frequency words. The teacher selects a predictable book for the week, one that can be easily retyped onto one sheet of paper using a larger font.

Day 1
- Discuss title and cover of the book.
- Read book to the students and ask each child to read along with their copy (2 times).
- Ask students to read the book alone. Provide corrective feedback and encourage children to point to the words as they read.

Day 2
Create sentence strips from the text in the book. Try to write one line on each sentence strip. This can be done by typing the sentence into a word document, using a large font, and then printing the document on an 8½ x 11 piece of paper. Then cut the sentence strips apart. Create one set of sentence strips for each child.

- Chorally read the book with the students.
- Read the story from sentence strips on a pocket chart without picture support.
- Scramble the sentence strips on the pocket chart. As a group work to put the sentences back in the correct order and rebuild the story.

Day 3
Create a one-page typed copy of the story. On the back of the story print 5 to 10 lines and on the top write the word *autographs*. The students will be taking the story home to read to family and friends. You will also need a set of blank 3 x 5 cards.

- Chorally read the book with the students.
- Give each student a set of sentence strips from the story and have them arrange them in the correct order.
- Give each student a one-page copy of the story without illustrations and have them read it in the group.
- Have students underline the words that they know.
- Give students words they know on index cards to add to their personal collection.
- Students will take the autograph story home and read it to as many friends and family as they can. Each person who listens to the story has to sign on the back. This can include pets if they can write their name (paw prints allowed.)

Day 4
- Chorally read the book with the students.
- Have the students re-read the one-page copy of the story without illustrations.
- Have students underline the words that they know.
- While the children read the one-page story with a partner, review the words on their index cards.

Yopp & Yopp, 2006). Seventy-seven percent of what teachers and parents read aloud to young children are stories, 8 percent are information texts, and the rest are mixed genres like the *Magic School Bus* series. Parents and teachers alike believe, without foundation, that informational text is more difficult and enjoyed less than fictional stories. We offer the following suggestions about reading aloud and the texts for reading aloud.

- Read aloud to your students every day for 15 minutes or more.

- Keep a relatively equal balance of narrative and informational books. Your informational books should draw from the areas of science, history, and the arts. Your narrative texts should include a variety of genres—realistic fiction, fantasy, and folk tales.

- Select books that will build the vocabulary knowledge of your students. A picture book should have at least seven or more vocabulary words that appear to be outside the listening vocabulary of many students in the room. These words can be either new concepts or new labels for old concepts. Consider this short selection from *Dr. De Soto* by Steig (1982), the story of a mouse dentist who outfoxes a fox.

  > "Doctor De Soto was especially popular with big animals. He was able to work inside their mouths, wearing rubbers to keep his feet dry, and his fingers were so *delicate*, and his drill so *dainty*, they could hardly feel any pain.
  >
  > Being a mouse, he *refused* to treat animals dangerous to mice, and it said so on his sign. When the doorbell rang, he and his wife would look out the window. They wouldn't admit even the most *timid* looking cat."

- The books provide conceptual challenge. Young children can handle complex ideas and they should be led to actively construct meaning through the interactive read aloud (Beck & McKeown, 2001).

- Pair a fiction and a non-fiction text on the same topic. For example, on Monday and Tuesday you would read and discuss *Pocahontas* (Hudson, 2001) and then on Wednesday and Thursday the narrative *The Rough-Face Girl* (Martin, 1998). The two books share a common vocabulary. By the end of the week you will have built the conceptual and word knowledge of your students, and modeled many of the strategies readers use to grapple with the text.

In the Classroom 6.3 provides a weekly read-aloud plan.

In the Classroom 6.3

Reading Aloud to Develop Language, Vocabulary, and Comprehension

Plan your interactive read-aloud by selecting books that align with topics in the science, social studies or the reading/language arts curriculum. During the course of a month, you should read an equal number of fiction and non-fiction books. Good children's literature selections are your best choices especially books that offer some challenge and provide exposure to interesting vocabulary. The books should be above the students' reading level. Select stories that exhibit realistic event structure and some complexity to provide grist for children to build meaning. The non-fiction book should build on the fiction book. Diversity and multicultural connections are important. Select books written by African American and Hispanic authors and that reflect diverse themes. In the primary grades we recommend that you pair a fiction book with a non-fiction book that share a similar topic or theme (See Santoro, Edwards, Chard, Howard, and Baker, [2008] for a list of paired fiction and non-fiction titles.)

1. Select five or six words from each book. These words will be the focus of your vocabulary instruction. The words you pick should be important to the overall meaning of the story beyond the story. Do not pick sight words (*can, for, jump, and*).

2. The read-aloud lesson can be conducted during reading, science, or social studies, wherever it makes a good connection to the content.

3. The 4-day lesson plan

   - **Day 1**: Read the fiction book. Conduct some pre-reading instruction—develop prior knowledge and set a purpose for reading. Define and discuss the genre. Read the book and, as you read, stop briefly to define and discuss important words. At the end of the book, discuss vocabulary words and develop comprehension through discussion. Ask follow-up questions after reading the story. Add the new vocabulary words to a word wall.

- **Day 2**: Re-read and review the fiction book and the vocabulary words. Reread parts of the fiction book and discuss the characters, setting, problem, and plot. Review the vocabulary words by having the students try them out orally. Provide definitions for the words, synonyms, examples of how the word might be used and perhaps role play some of the words.
- **Day 3**: Read the non-fiction book. Discuss the genre, preview the book, and set the purpose. While reading, stop briefly to define vocabulary words, and ask comprehension questions. At the end, have the students discuss what they learned about the topic and how it relates to the fiction book. Write the new words on the word wall, and discuss their meaning and usage. Keep these particular words up for at least a week, better yet, a month.
- **Day 4**: Ro road and review the non-fiction book. Review concepts that have been learned. Review the vocabulary from both books. Discuss the meanings of the words on the wall. Have the students try out the words orally. Compare and contrast the fiction and non-fiction book.

4. At the end of the week review the books, the concepts, and the words that have been the focus of study. The children should discuss what they have learned about the topic and perhaps write about it. They should discuss the new words they have learned and use them in their writing. Encourage children to analyze words, and to compare and contrast similar words. Keep the word wall up for some time to draw attention to what the students have learned.

Reflect and Apply

3. Find a copy of any current reading program or guided reading book designed for beginning reading instruction and evaluate its words. Count out 100 words and then within those 100 words count how often any given word is repeated. You can also repeat the count and look for the number of repetitions of a phonics pattern—at, ing, ike, etc. Does your word count meet the criteria set out by Hiebert?

4. Building prior knowledge and vocabulary is the goal of reading aloud. Spend some time in the library of an elementary school or the children's section of a public library. Assembly a book set (a fiction and non-fiction book on a similar topic). You can also use the list provided by Santoro and her colleagues. Read both books and then look for vocabulary overlap—what words appear in both texts.

MyLab Education **Self-Check 6.3**

MyLab Education **Application Exercise 6.3:** Choosing Text for Beginning Reading Instruction

---

Texts for Developing Comprehension

What texts should we use for developing comprehension? The answer to that question depends on the purpose of reading instruction and the place of reading in the elementary and middle school curriculum. In the four-part model of the Rand Reading Study Group (Snow, 2002)—the reader, the text, the activity, the sociocultural context—the key factor for our discussion is the activity. Why do we read in school? There are two answers and perhaps more. Some would claim that we read in school to become better readers. School is about developing skills, realizing potential so that when we leave secondary schools we can use our skills for college and careers. Others would claim that we read in school for the same reasons we read outside school. We read for knowledge, entertainment, and insight.

In this section of the chapter we are going to take the position that we read in school for the same reasons we read outside of school: to learn from text and enjoy doing so. Unlike science, mathematics, or history, reading does not have its own subject matter laid down from hundreds of years of study. Reading is a tool we use to increase our understanding of the world and the people in it. As we consider the texts that teachers might use for developing comprehension, we will focus on texts that bring pleasure, knowledge, and enlightenment to our students. But first we will consider the more traditional view, text as a tool.

The Text as a Tool

For many educators, reading is a subject matter; there are things to teach about reading. We teach skills and strategies, concepts and words. The goal of the teacher is to help students find the main idea, or make an inference, or to summarize. We teach concepts like figurative language and text organizational patterns. We determine which words students need to know and explain them. From this perspective, the text is a tool, a vehicle to further students' capabilities as a reader.

Text as a tool is the assumption underlying many reading curriculums. The creators of several core reading programs first develop the scope and sequence of skills and strategies in the program and then find texts that fit well with specific skills (Dewitz, Leahy, Jones & Sullivan, 2010). If a particular lesson is focused on finding the main idea, then a text is found that has a clear main idea structure. Other core reading programs select the texts first and then fit the skills and strategies to them. In all programs the skills and strategies take precedence over what the students might learn or enjoy. These programs are organized into thematic units but often the selections are a hodgepodge with little rationale for why they were put together.

Many intervention or supplemental programs are constructed around the idea of text as a tool. The collections from Curriculum Associates, such as *Cars and Stars*, are organized so that each section of their workbooks is organized around a skill and the text is selected to support the learning of that skill. Online intervention programs such as ReadingPlus (https://www.readingplus.com/) select passages by level to build skills. The passages serve the skills. There is nothing particularly interesting or engaging about these texts. This structure is common in many supplemental materials and materials designed to support test taking. Websites such as ReadWorks (www.readworks.org), Reading A to Z (www.readinga-z.com/) and Newsela (www.newsela.com) are organized so that reading level, topic and genre the factors that help teachers select texts. A teacher could construct a set of texts from these sites that engages students and builds knowledge.

When comprehension strategy instruction first made the leap from the pages of research articles to professional books, several authors put the strategies first, and then suggested the texts that fit well. This is the case with *Super 6 Comprehension Strategies* (Oczkus, 2004) and *Strategies that Work* (Harvey & Goudvis, 2017). Both books are organized around teaching specific strategies, and the authors suggest books that fit well with each strategy. But in the appendix of *Strategies that Work* the authors develop content areas of study and suggest specific books the teacher can use to build units of study.

The Text as a Goal

In our approach to comprehension, the texts exist to promote learning, enjoyment, and escape, but not specifically to teach skills. The texts in school are read for much the same reasons that texts are read out of school. Novels, short stories, and poems, are a form of entertainment but also enlightenment. Newspapers, magazines, and non-fiction texts are read to build knowledge and insight, occasionally to solve problems. For many of us, the pleasure of reading an interesting biography or text about a current and vital scientific issue is as entertaining as reading a good spy thriller. The Internet is our third and increasingly popular source of information, both trivial and vital. In the sections that follow we will deal with literary texts, non-fiction texts and the Internet

We believe that teachers in all grades should design their units of study putting the texts and the ideas first. Even in kindergarten and first grade the read-aloud units should be organized around a theme. The teachers should think first about literature, science, and social studies and then consider what skills, strategies, and concepts the students will need to succeed with those texts. In such a system, students might study an author and her work. They might study a genre because it is interesting to learn how different authors write within the same genre. They might study topics within science or social studies that integrate the use of textbooks, realistic fiction, and online resources. We are confident that teachers can build fascinating units of study.

Selecting Literary Texts

We read literature for enjoyment, to develop our appreciation and skill with written language, to learn to think, and to foster our humanity. Literature is the product of the best writers wielding the best language. The vocabulary is rich and precise. A book like *Kensuke's Kingdom* (Morpurgo, 1999) offers up, on just one page, the following words for a student to learn—*apprehension, implications, dreadful, shimmering, extraordinary,* and *elated.* When we read literature, we learn to comprehend a 45-word sentence and appreciate the power of a three-word sentence. We recognize that language has rhythm, and we grasp the power of metaphor and analogy. It is no wonder that all good writers are good readers.

MyLab Education
Video Example 6.3
Consider the criteria that the teacher uses to select literary text in this video. After you read the next section of this text, see what criteria you might use to select text.

Books teach us to think. When the book stretches over 50 chapters and 150+ pages chronicling the lives of ten major characters and three intersecting plots (We are writing about *Holes*, by Lewis Sachar.) the reader has much information to integrate and construct. A reader must make many connections within the text and infer what the writer implies, drawing from prior knowledge. We much keep track of these ideas for weeks slowly creating a narrative rich with an intricate tapestry of actions, ideas, and thoughts. This is deep reading. It requires concentration and thought. With books, we develop our humanity and rehearse our lives.

We live in many worlds. We begin in the small world of our family and friends, move to the social world of school and activities, and then to the larger world of college and work. Ultimately, we have to understand the world of politics within and among nations. We also exist in an economic world in which Mom or Dad might lose their job or a depression strikes the nation. Only literature, fiction and non-fiction, can bring us into, and help us grapple with, these worlds. Books like *Poppy* (Avi, 1995) help us explore selflessness and confidence. *The War with Grandpa* (Smith, 1984) teaches us how to resolve disagreements peacefully, *Manic Magee* (Spinell, 1990) helps us learn about altruism, and *Streams to the River, River to the Sea* (O'Dell, 1986) helps us consider how we make decisions under difficult circumstances. Some texts afford us the opportunity to escape into the world of fantasy.

When selecting literacy texts consider theme, genre, structure and length. At any grade, select books and assist students to select books that explore themes that are consistent with the student's developing knowledge. Not all topics and themes can be addressed at all ages. Select books so that over the course of the year students experience a range of genres. All students can read fantasy and realistic fiction. Historical fiction, biography and autobiography might require a more knowledgeable reader. Consider structure when selecting texts for instruction. Some read are ready for intricate plots while others are not. Finally, keep length in mind. Young children are excited to read a 50 page chapter book but they are not ready for 200 pages.

Selecting Non-fiction Texts

Reading non-fiction is essential for studying science, history, geography, and the arts. Students will read the textbooks or non-fiction trade books to develop knowledge. Some of these books are considerably more readable than others. Years ago, researchers described these as considerate texts, books that convey information in an effective manner least disruptive to the reader (Anderson & Armbruster, 1984). We feel that this research is still applicable over 30 years later. We recognize that a textbook author is also trying to engage the reader and at times persuade them, but first we want to examine what makes a text considerate. Understanding the principles of a considerate text enables you to select good informative texts when given the opportunity and when stuck with less than ideal texts you can help your students over the rough spots. A considerate text has five characteristics. Note that we add one to the original list of four. They are structure, coherence, unity, audience appropriateness, and voice.

STRUCTURE

When students read texts that are well organized, they understand more and remember more (Anderson & Armbruster, 1984). Think of text structure as a roadmap; if you can follow that map, you will find what you want to know. The maps give you a clue to the organization of the information and structured information is easier to retain than random bits of knowledge. Authors use a variety of devices to structure a text and communicate that structure to the reader including topic sentences, and introductory paragraphs that alert the reader to the upcoming ideas, headings, subheadings, and other graphics that guide the reader through the content. The reader must recognize and use that structure.

Content information typically follows one of five different structures and, when the writer sticks to a structure and the reader is able to pick up on it, then comprehension is enhanced. The five structures are presented in Figure 6.7 along with a description of the structure and in what disciplines these structures are likely to be found. In most textbook chapters or informational tradebooks, authors typically mix two or more structures as their purpose changes. For example, in a book on butterflies, the author might begin with descriptive structure so the reader has a firm grasp on the anatomy of a butterfly. Then the author switches to a temporal structure to lead the reader through the life-cycle of the butterfly, and finally concludes with a compare and contrast structure to make clear the differences between the butterflies and moths.

The author uses several devices to signal the structure of a text and her purpose. A cogent topic sentence sets the stage for the subject and explains why it is important. Titles, headings, subheadings, and bold print words signal the organization and the hierarchy of ideas in the text. By skimming the text, the reader should have a decent sense of the topics that will be discussed by the writer. Consider two headings: *The Magic of Mexico* versus *Mexican Holidays and Celebrations*. The first gives the reader little information about the upcoming content, the second is explicit. The second heading suggests that the author will discuss many of the customs of Mexico.

Throughout a text, the author tends to stick with a consistent structural pattern even when the topic changes. For example, in a biology text about animals, the author might start with the prairie dog and discuss its anatomy, its environment, behavior, food source, and enemies. When the next chapter switches to the badger, the same sequence of topics is followed. This consistency helps the reader anticipate the ideas and easily compare one animal to another. When examining a text's structure, look for the following attributes:

- The author sticks to one text organizational pattern (problem-solution, description, temporal sequence, comparison-contrast, explanation) until his purpose is met.

- The structure matches the author's purpose.

- The author uses signal words to tell the reader what relationship he is describing among ideas. (See Figure 6.7.)

- The author uses topic sentences and introductory paragraphs to set a purpose and outline the scope of the topic. Conclusions recap what has been discussed.

- The author's headings and subheadings clearly signal the topic to come.
- The author uses the same sequences of structure when new and similar topics are introduced.

COHERENCE

When we examine a text for coherence we are evaluating the clarity of the writing. If structure refers to the overall organization of a text, coherence moves our lens closer and considers how the ideas stick together and whether there are gaps in the writing. The more information that the author leaves out, the more the reader has to work to build a complete understanding. When it is difficult to causally connect ideas, then the comprehensibility of the text is impaired. Text with low coherence pushes the reader to make more inference and that is possible only when the reader has a larger fund of knowledge. In the elementary grades where many children lack prior knowledge, incoherent text is a barrier to comprehension.

Consider the example in Figure 6.8 from a research study on the problems of understanding American history texts (Beck, KcKeown, Sinatra, & Loxterman, 1991). The original text does not explicitly state why the colonists were angry. The author omitted

Figure 6.7 Common Nonfiction Text Structures, Purposes, and Signal Words

Text Structure	Author's Purpose	Signal Words
Description/Definitions	• Define or describe an object or a concept • To list the features of an object or concept	This text is often not associated with signal words. Language included: is defined as means that is named, called, labeled that is, for instance, example of, such as, includes
Temporal Sequences	• Trace the development of a process or a series of events	then / later before / finally after / previously next / prior follows / afterwards earlier / first, second, third
Explanations (Cause & Effect)	• To explain the causes of something or the effects of something • Draw a conclusion or make a prediction • Hypothesize about something	causes / however affects / since leads to / because in order to / thus so that / as a result produces / consequently therefore
Compare & Contrast	• Compare and contrast to concepts or events • List the similarities or differences between two concepts or events	is similar to like likewise in the same way is different from however, but, yet, although, instead
Problem/Solution	• Explain the development of a problem and the solutions to that problem • Discuss how something became a problem	This text unit often does not use signal words. The author may say: the problem is the solution is

Figure 6.8 Examples of text with and without coherence

Lacking Coherence	Improve Coherence
Boatloads of tea were sent to America. Since it was cheaper than ever, the British thought that surely the colonist would buy tea now! They were wrong. Tea was burned. Tea was left to rot.	Since it was now cheaper than ever, the British thought that surely the colonists would buy tea! So, they sent boatloads of it to the colonies. But, because the tea still had a tax on it, the colonists were as angry as ever. To show their anger, the colonist burned some of the tea. They left some to rot.

SOURCE: Beck, I. L., McKeown, M. G., & Worthy, J. (1995). Giving a text voice can improve student's understanding. *Reading Research Quarterly*, 30 (2), 220–237.

the important information that the tax on the tea was still in place. The revised text ads one crucial detail and the motivation of the colonists was revealed. When you examine a text for coherence, look for the following characteristics:

- The relationship among ideas is clear and explicit. The motivation of historical figures and components in a scientific process are clearly spelled out. The author uses signal words (*because, since, however, next, last, however, but*) to help the reader track ideas and understand why things happen. When something is being contrasted, then it should be clear what two elements are under scrutiny.

- The pronoun references should be clear. The pronouns should be near their references and when there are two references the author should be clear which one he is writing about.

- Processes and events should proceed in just one order. When a writer disrupts the order, moves back in time to explain things and then moves forward again, comprehension becomes more difficult. Consider Figure 6.9 describing how a beaver constructs a dam. The sequence is disrupted. Putting the sticks together should come first, before the mud is used to cement the sticks.

Figure 6.9 How Beavers Build Lodges

> Beavers build lodges in the middle of ponds. First, they chop down trees with their sharp front teeth. They use mud to hold the sticks together. Then they swim with the branches to the building site. The beaver's family lives in the center of the lodge which is hollow. The lodge is made of piles of sticks.

UNITY

A text has unity when the author sticks to the subject and does not stray from her original purpose. Irrelevant information is kept to a minimum. Unity is important because readers can focus on a limited number of ideas at a time. The fashion for many elementary and middle school textbook authors is to clutter the page with many headings, multi-color boxes, and side-bars. The idea is that the richness of the design will keep the reader entertained. Perhaps writers and graphic designers are trying to emulate the flash of the Internet to the likely detriment of the reader.

- Each idea in a text should be related to the author's purpose. The writer should not wander among the ideas. Each subsequent idea should build upon a previous idea.

- When the author introduces ideas that are slightly related to the main content, they are set off with a box or presented in a different type face. In Joy Hakim's *A History of US* (1990), she sets the tangential ideas off to the side. On the first page she describes the scene of George Washington receiving a letter informing him that he has been elected President of the United States. Off to the side is a box that quotes the Constitutional procedure for electing our President.

AUDIENCE APPROPRIATENESS

A text is audience appropriate when the reader has the requisite knowledge to understand the ideas in the text. Judging whether a text is appropriate for an audience means considering the information in the text and what you know about the reader. A text

MyLab Education
Video Example 6.4
In this video, the teacher uses text structure in her instruction.

Figure 6.10 Two Texts that Reflect Different Levels of Audience Appropriateness

Text A High Audience Appropriateness	Text B Low Audience Appropriateness
Suppose you magnified a small square patch of a green leaf. The top surface of a leaf is made up of a thin layer of tough cells. These cells protect the softer cells inside the leaf. This is what your own skin cells do. The tough ones on top protect the cells deeper down inside you. Beneath the tough surface cells in the leaf is a layer of long cells. These long cells have a rich supply of chlorophyll. It is the substance that makes the green plants green.	A microscopic examination of a leaf cut crosswise reveals five major regions: upper epidermis, lower epidermis, veins, palisade region, and spongy region. 1. Upper epidermis. The upper epidermis of the leaf consists of a single layer of cells. These cells secrete a waxy protective coating.

SOURCES: Anderson, T. H. & Armbruster, B. B. (1984). Content Area Textbooks. (pp.193–226). In R. C. Anderson, J. Osborn – R. J. Tierney (Eds) *Learning to Read in American Schools*. Hillsdale: NJ. Lawrence Erlbaum Associates.

that is appropriate for a mature and knowledgeable audience might be inappropriate for a younger audience. Audience appropriateness is the flip side of the reader's prior knowledge. In Chapters 11 and 12 we will present ideas about how to develop reader's prior knowledge to improve comprehension. Teachers should select texts that are within the reach of the reader. If the text is too simple, there is little to learn; if the text is too complex, the reader is frustrated. Consider the two examples in Figure 6.10 from Anderson and Armbruster (1984).

Text A is appropriate for the sixth grade reader avoids most technical language and makes a clear analogy to the skin on our body. Few new terms need to be learned. For example, the word *cells* cannot be avoided, but the terms *epidermis* and *stomate* can because they are unnecessary at the sixth grade level of learning. Text B contains many terms that are not defined. When new vocabulary words are introduced, the author should either define the word within the text or provide a callout box in which the vocabulary is defined. Illustrations and labels go a long way toward clarifying the meaning of new words. Consider these three factors when examining a text for audience appropriateness.

1. Take what the students know into account when you select a text. The text should present enough information to help the reader understand the author's purpose, but not overwhelm them.
2. Technical or academic vocabulary should be introduced only if words are defined in the text or in a callout box.
3. The author uses analogies and metaphors when the referent is well known to the reader. Obscure analogies only compound the problem of comprehension.

VOICE

Graves (1983) has called voice the imprint of the soul. Many large textbooks and short non-fiction trade books, especially those that are part of instructional programs, are written by a committee. The style, verve, and feelings of an author have been replaced by a dull, computer-like voice conveying the facts and concepts in a monotone. The lack of feeling suggests that the author was not engaged in the book's creation nor will the reader be enthused to learn. These books tend to be authoritative but not necessarily engaging. As a good example of voice, we will draw upon a comparison of two texts by Beck and her colleagues. The first example is from an older textbook and the second was written by Jean Fritz, in her popular trade book, *Can't You Make Them Behave, King George?* (Fritz,1977). (See Figure 6.11.)

In a study, Isabel Beck and her colleagues took existing social studies/history books and added voice to them by changing the text in three ways. They added:

- Activity. They used more concrete actions and clearly described the feeling and reactions of historical characters.
- Orality. The texts include some real and imagined dialogue. The students can read what the historical characters were saying. The text has a conversational tone.

Figure 6.11 Voiced and Unvoiced Texts on Writing the Constitution

Voiced Text: Can't You Make Them Behave, King George (Fritz, 1977).	**Unvoiced Text:** Silver Burdett Ginn (1984)
England had been fighting a long an expensive war, and then it was over, the question was how to pay the bills. Finally, a government official suggested that one way to raise money was to tax Americans. "What a good idea! King George said. After all, the French and Indian part of the war had been fought on American soil for the benefit of Americans, so why shouldn't they help pay for it?"	The British lawmaking body was and still is called Parliament. The colonists were not members. The British started passing laws to tax the colonies. Britain thought the colonies should pay their share of the cost of the French and Indian War.

SOURCE: Beck, I. L., McKeown, M. G., & Worthy, J. (1995). Giving a text voice can improve student's understanding. *Reading Research Quarterly*, 30 (2), 220–237.

- Connectivity. When a text has connectivity, the author writes in such a way as to connect the reader to the text. The author might directly address the reader to point out specific and important ideas and highlight the emotional response of historical figures.

In the study, students read naturally occurring texts, that were improved by adding voice and coherence or both. Note that we described coherence previously. The results of the study indicate that when students are asked to read texts that are both more coherent and have an element of voice their ability to recall information and to answer questions about broad issues improves. When reading the texts enhanced by adding coherence and voice the students remembered more general issues but not specific details. It is important to note that a voiced and compelling text that lacks coherence is still difficult to comprehend and lacks utility for many students.

We leave this section about informational books with a few final thoughts. First, not all readers benefit from well-structured and coherently written text. The best readers in the room actually show stronger comprehension when challenged by more complex, less structured material (McNamara, Kintsch, Songer, & Kintsch, 1996). They are simply pushed to work harder and the payoff is worth the effort. One size does not fit all. Second, textbooks and non-fiction trade books can be used alongside historical fiction and biography. The non-fiction books provide the information and the concepts, the historical fiction and biography provide the context and the personal element.

Using the Internet for Information

By 2003, half the students in the United States were using the Internet to complete school assignments at home (National Center for Educational Statistics, 2006). Since then, high-speed broadband and Internet have penetrated deeper into our schools. Now, almost 100 percent of our public schools are connected to the Internet and the ratio of students to computers is 3.8:1 (Wells & Lewis, 2006). Approximately 72 percent of students are now using the Internet for school projects (NCES, 2016).

The Internet presents new opportunities and challenges for students and teachers as the reading of informational text moves from the textbooks and the non-fiction trade books to computer screens and tablets. Unlike books and traditional magazines, the information on the Internet is not filtered; anyone can create a website and post information. Students face three challenges. First, they have to know how to locate information. Second, they must determine if the information is readable, at their approximate reading level, and finally they must evaluate the trustworthiness and the usefulness of the information. We decided to approach these three issues from the perspective of the students, because they will be searching the net and using the information in reports and other school projects. Although teachers can screen and list desirable websites, they have to go through the same process as the students.

Many upper elementary and middle school students approach an Internet research task in the following manner. The starting point is *Google*, a noun and a verb. If the student knows her topic she types in a few key words, gets a list of websites and starts to click on them. Some look promising and others do not. The student opens a few websites, copies and pastes parts of different websites into a new document, adds a few pictures, and finishes up with a flashy font and colorful headings. The research paper is complete. The "research" process avoids the three big problems of the Internet—readability, trustworthiness, and usefulness. Two different sets of educators, Baildon & Baildon (2008) and Zhang, Duke and Jimenez (2011) attacked these problems in very similar ways.

As Leu and Kinzer (2000) have argued, students need to develop strategies for selecting and using information on the Internet. Much information on the Internet is difficult to read, unreliable, and inaccurate. Some of the information is harmful. So both research groups developed a set of strategies and taught them to their students. They used an explicit instructional model, by explaining *what* the strategy was, *why* it was important, *how* to use it, and *when* to use it. This approach is the first step in the gradual release of responsibility model that we presented in Chapter 2. After the direct explanation, the students tried out each of the strategies and reported on their use. We will first examine the problem of usefulness as that is the starting point for any research project: What do you want to know?

USEFULNESS

A student can judge the usefulness of a website only if he knows what he is looking for. Understanding how to use the Internet must begin outside the Internet by helping the students define their research questions. The teachers can begin, as with most research studies, by brainstorming possible topics, narrowing those topics until each student has arrived at a topic that is interesting to him and manageable. Once the topic is defined, it is important for the student to generate a specific set of questions. If a student decided to study hurricanes, his questions might include: How dangerous is a hurricane? How are they formed? Where are they formed? What were some of largest hurricanes in history?

After the students have generated their questions, they are ready to tackle the Internet. This process might be reciprocal. The student starts with a set of questions, but then, as she reads on the Internet, she refines the questions and writes more or revises some. Finally, the students need a set of questions to evaluate the websites they have located. Baildon and Baildon (2008) recommend these questions:

- Does the website have what I am looking for?
- Does it follow my research plan?
- Do I need it?
- Is this worthwhile, or am I wasting my time on this resource?

Shenglan Zhang and her colleague guide the students to ask this question. "Does this help meet my needs and how?" Without this question the students spend a great deal of wasted time on the Internet.

READABLE

Unlike books that are leveled and magazines that are written for specific age groups, the Internet offers little guidance about readability. Baildon and Baildon (2008) suggest beginning by printing off three different articles on the same topic but of different reading levels. For example, you might pick a *Ranger Rick* article, a very thoroughly illustrated non-fiction text by a writer like Gail Gibbons, and an article from an encyclopedia that typically has much fewer illustrations. The students as a whole or in small groups discuss the readability of each resource. The teacher helps the students refine their judgment as they evaluate the ease of reading each document. The students then develop the following list of questions (Baildon & Baildon, 2008, p. 641):

- Can I read and understand this on my own?
- Can I understand most of the words and not lose meaning if I have to skip words?
- Is it a 'just-right' read for me?
- Is the layout easy enough to follow?
- Can I stop and retell what I have just read in my own words? (A useful self-checking question)
- Are there pictures or charts that help me understand the text better?

Some are attracted to websites that allow the teacher or the students to control the readability of the selections. For example, www.readworks.com allows a student to search by topic, grade level, and Lexile level. The website www.newsela.com allows the teacher or the student to adjust the reading level of the articles. An article that was originally written at a 1150 Lexile level can be adjusted to an 840 Lexile or lower. These adjustments have consequences. We compared the 1150 article on *Brown v. Board of Education* to the 840 version. Information is lost and changed in the translation. For example, the 1150 passage states that the Supreme Court struck down a law permitting racially segregated schools, but the 840 version states that the Court created a new law. The 1150 version lists the states with segregated schools while the 840 version writes that the "states were mostly in the south and Washington, D.C." We would caution students and teachers to use the highest readability levels they can handle and avoid the loss and distortion of information.

TRUSTWORTHINESS

The most critical factor when using the Internet is trusting the accuracy and truthfulness of the information on the websites. We live in a world of "fake news" and the former mayor of New York City just proclaimed that "Truth is not Truth." Baildon and Baildon (2008) began their lesson by having the students study a fake photograph of a tsunami that was impossibly large. This led to a discussion of whether you can trust what you find on the Internet and how you can decide. Students began the discussion believing you can trust most Internet sites and gradually realized that not everything is believable. Zhang had the students begin by discussing who writes books, newspapers, and websites. The teacher introduced the concepts of editors and publishers and the regulation of information, and the lack of such on the Internet.

The next step for both research groups was to explore the criteria for judging the truthfulness of a website. Some teachers began the discussion by sharing a website and asking who wrote this. They point out that some articles have a listed author and others do not. Next, the students considered the author's credentials including her title, occupation, and affiliation. The students further discussed the URL extension for the website—.com, .org, and .gov. She wanted the students to realize that anyone can create a .com website, but .org websites are used by not-for-profit organizations and .gov are official websites run by the government. The students in the Baildon and Baildon (2008) study generated the following questions to help students critique websites.

- Do I recognize the author or creator?
- Is there an author or photographer identified with the source?
- Does the URL seem official or real?
- Have I found the same information in other books or websites?
- Does my gut feeling tell me that what I am reading and seeing is trustworthy?
- Does the information fit with what I might already know about the subject?

APPLYING WHAT WAS LEARNED

The teachers combined the three sets of questions about readability, usefulness, and trustworthiness into one anchor chart and students used it as a guide while they conducted Internet research. Eventually, the students internalized the criteria but it was still useful to provide a guide for the students as they conducted their Internet research. Figure 6.12 presents a note-taking guide that the students continued to use with the simple reminder R-T-U (Readable, Trustworthy, Useful). This helped students make decisions while they read.

Both groups of researchers evaluated the impact of teaching students to critically evaluate the readability, trustworthiness, and usefulness of the information on the Internet. The Zhang and Duke model used the acronym of WWWDOT (p. 152), standing for:

1. Who wrote this and what credentials do they have?
2. Why was this written?

Figure 6.12 Research Notes Using R-T-U (Readable-Trustworthy-Useful)

Research Question	Resources (two per Question)	It is	Details
		R	
		T	
		U	
		R	
		T	
		U	

SOURCE: Baildon, R., & Baildon, M. (2008). Guiding independence: Developing a research tool to support student decision making in selecting online information sources. *The Reading Teacher*, 61(8), pp. 637–647.

MyLab Education
Click here to download a printable version of Figure 6.12.

3. When was it written?
4. Does it help me meet my needs?
5. Organization of the site?
6. To-do list for the future.

In just four 30-minute lessons the students changed their views about the credibility of information on the Internet (Zhang & Duke 2011). The students were better able to judge the credibility of websites but the amount of change did not reach statistical significance, suggesting more practice and experience was needed. In the Baildon and Baildon (2008) study, students improved their ability to judge whether the websites were useful, trustworthy, and readable. Overall, the quality of their written work improved. Their reports were consistently written in their own words, better organized, and followed their research plan.

In this section of the chapter we chose not to list important or credible websites for students, rather we shared ways for students to discover and evaluate websites on their own. This is a tool, one that will serve them well throughout their school years and beyond. It gives these fourth and fifth graders a tool that many adults in our country lack and it furthers their ability to be independent learners.

Reflect and Apply

5. Locate a content area text book, either a science or social studies book. Then take the five criteria that were discussed previously—structure, coherence, unity, audience appropriateness, and voice—and evaluate the book. Does the book meet all of the criteria we outlined? Which were violated most grievously?

6. Locate a website and evaluate it as a student might do. You want to look for usefulness, trustworthiness, and readability.

MyLab Education **Self-Check 6.4**

MyLab Education **Application Exercise 6.4:** Judging the Considerateness and Motivational Properties of Non-Fiction Text

Concluding Remarks

The texts for reading instruction serve multiple purposes and, therefore, selecting them and helping students select them requires attention to a number of criteria. Many educators like to think that the right data will help them make the best decisions, but numbers alone will not solve all problems as we explored in Chapter 5. Early in this chapter we explored several readability formulas, including the dominant Lexile scales, and concluded that readability formulas provide useful information, but they do not solve all problems of matching students to text. Teachers must also consider the genre, the student's interests, and prior knowledge. Often a student can read several levels above his tested score if his knowledge and interest are high.

When we examined texts for beginning reading, we reached the conclusion that there is no one perfect type of text, no perfect program. Emergent readers need texts that help them learn the high frequency words of the language. At times, predictable texts help them get an early start in reading the lowest level books. They also need texts that stress and repeat phonics patterns so that they can master the code of the language. No one published series does all of this, so schools and teachers need to assemble multiple sets of books for beginning reading instruction.

When we discussed texts for the middle elementary grades and up we focused on the importance of selecting texts that motivate students. Motivation is critical for reading instruction, especially in an age where reading is not the first choice of many students who have many alternatives for entertainment and escape. Children and young adolescents are increasingly glued to electronic devices and, therefore, we must teach reading with texts that are gripping and informative. Interest and motivation have to come first as teachers design units of instruction and select text. Informational text should be chosen on the basis of their structure, coherence, unity, and audience appropriateness. We also believe that interest and voice is critical in selecting the right texts.

Finally, we turned your attention to the Internet, which is now the chief source of informational reading in many schools. We showed you a way to develop the critical eye of your students. They need to evaluate a text to determine if it is readable, trustworthy, and useful. That brought you back full circle. Selecting texts for reading instruction demands that we consider how they contribute to the growth of students' knowledge and motivation. Are these texts useful? The Internet adds a new problem, trustworthiness, something that is important for any consumer of information.

Extending Learning

1. A very useful way to extend your learning is to become familiar with some of the websites that are available for evaluating the readability of the texts. We recommend the following cite that allows you to input text online and use multiple readability formulas: http://www.readabilityformulas.com/free-readability-formula-tests.php.

2. For further information we also recommend www.textproject.org, a site developed and kept fresh by Freddy Hiebert who we have cited repeatedly in this chapter. Hiebert provides a wealth of resources including books lists, passages, and research on text and vocabulary development.

Children's Literature

Anderson, L. H. (2008). *Chains*. New York: Atheneum Books. Set during the America Revolution this is the fictional account of a young African America girl living in New England fights for her freedom. 299 pages.

Brett, J. (1996). *The Mitten*. New York, NY: G. P. Putnam. One by one, animals in a snowy forest crawl into Nicki's lost white mitten to get warm until the bear sneezes, sending the animals flying up and out of the mitten. The artwork will delight you. 38 pages.

Carle, Eric. (1969) *The Very Hungry Caterpillar*. New York: World Publishing Company. A richly illustrated and slightly romanticized account of the life of a butterfly. 37 pages.

Cleary, B. (1984). *Ramona Forever*. New York: William Morrow. Ramona and her older sister Beezus are finally old enough to stay home alone and the work hard to do so. This book is part of a continuing series.

Fritz, J. (1987) *Shh, We're Writing the Constitution*. Describes in a light humorous fashion how the constitution came to be written and ratified. An informative, interesting, and immensely readable account of the Constitutional Convention of 1787.

Gibbons, G. (1999). *Bats*. New York: Holiday House. A richly illustrated description of bats from their anatomy to their behavior to the habitat. 32 pages.

Hoff, S. (1990). *Barney's Horse*. New York, NY: Harpercollins. A very easy chapter book for beginning readers. First of the I Can Read series. 32 pages.

Kinney, J. (2012). *Diary of a Wimpy Kid*. New York: Amulet Books. The diary of a struggling put upon eleven-year-old who is struggling with slings and arrow of outrageous fortune, middle school. 226 pages.

Martin, B. (1967). *Brown Bear, Brown Bear What Do You See*? New York: Doubleday. A collection of endearing animals in this predictable text. 32 pages.

Madison, J., Hamilton, A., Jay, J. (1788). *The Federalists Papers*. A light persuasive romp through the United States Constitution by three writers who thought they had developed a good idea. Only time will tell. 448 pages.

Morpurgo, M. (1999). *Kensuke's Kingdom*. New York: Scholastic. Washed up on a small island in the Pacific, Michael and his small dog struggle to survive. 163 pages.

Naylor, P. R. (1991) *Shiloh*. New York: Dell Publishing. Marty encounters a Beagle being abused and decides to save it. This begins a complicated series of moral dilemmas. 144 pages.

Paulsen, G. (2006). *Hatchet*. New York: Simon and Schuster. Brian is in a small plane that crashed in the Canadian forest. He must survive for many weeks with a hatchet as his only tool.

Ripley, M. (2004). *Private and Confidential: A Story About Braille*. New York, NY: Dial. Laura discovers that her Australian pen pal is blind. She decides to learn Braille

Rowley, J. K. (2015) *Harry Potter and the Sorcerer's Stone*. London: Pottermore Publishing. The first book in the famous series. Harry Potter, a boy who learns on his eleventh birthday that he is the orphaned son of two powerful wizards and possesses unique magical powers of his own.

Sachar, L. (2000). *Holes*. New York, NY: Yearling. Stanley is unjustly accused of a crime and sent to a reform camp. Here is survives and deals with a age old family cures. 233 pages.

Steig, W. (1982). *Doctor De Soto*. New York, NY: Farrar, Straus and Giroux. A very clever dentist and his wife hitch up their bravery and treat a fox with a bad toothache. Excellent vocabulary. 36 pages.

Tolkin, J. R. *The Lord of the Rings*. An epic fantasy novel that follows the incredible journal of Bilbo Baggins a hobbit. 421 pages.

Chapter 7
Emergent Literacy

Learning Outcomes

After reading and studying this chapter you should be able to:

7.1 Describe how young children come to understand how our writing system works and implement classroom activities that spur this development.

7.2 Understand phonemic awareness, and discuss its importance and how it is necessary for spelling and reading words.

7.3 Describe how a young child's comprehension develops, particularly the understanding of text structure.

7.4 Implement a variety of instructional activities that assist young children in developing their knowledge of words, books, vocabulary, and writing.

Classroom Vignette

Lee awakened to find her favorite stuffed animal lying next to her—a teddy bear named Pooh after the character in *Winnie the Pooh*. At breakfast, Lee's mother asked her if she could read the letters on her cereal box to Pooh. After breakfast, Lee scurried off to watch "Sesame Street," naming the letters she saw on the screen to Pooh. Later that morning, Lee went to the grocery store with her mom, showing off her letter knowledge by naming print as they wheeled around the store and by helping her mom check off items on the shopping list.

On the way home, Lee was dropped off at an afternoon kindergarten. She put her gear in a cubby with her name above it. She noticed her name, too, on the list of helpers for the day. After settling in, the children gathered around their teacher to hear her read a folktale. Afterward, she asked the children to recall all the characters they could. As they named them, she put a picture of each character on a feltboard. Then she had the children help her retell the story, putting up the characters as they appeared in the story. When necessary, she prompted the children with questions such as "Then who came along?" If they weren't sure, she opened up the book and asked them to check.

At home again, Lee was eager to retell the folk tale. She told it first to her older sister and then to her mom and dad. As she snuggled into bed with Pooh, her dad began reading from James Marshall's retelling of *The Three Little Pigs*. "Once upon a time an old sow sent her three little pigs . . ."

From the time she awoke until the time she was tucked into bed at night, Lee's day was filled with literacy experiences and opportunities to learn about language.

Emergent literacy refers to "the reading and writing behaviors that precede and develop into conventional literacy," and when we talk about emergent literacy, we are ascribing legitimacy to "the earliest literacy concepts and behaviors of children and to the varieties of social context in which children become literate" (Sulzby & Teale, 1996). In other words, emergent readers are children who are in the process of learning what reading and writing are for and how to read and write.

For many children, these first steps begin at home and are refined in preschool and kindergarten. For some children, those that depend on school to learn to read and write, emergent literacy happens only at school. For all children, emergent literacy is a time of many discoveries about the sounds of language, the forms of words, and the purposes of books. In the emergent process, the child begins to learn how to recognize and spell words while exploring the alphabetic system. The child begins to learn about books and how they are structured and to gain information and enjoy stories. Finally, the child begins a journey of understanding, learning how to comprehend and produce written language.

Children enter school with wide differences, both in their exposure to text and in what they know about text. Some kindergartners know the alphabet; some know the sounds the letters make and can reproduce letters or even write a few words. Some have been read to extensively, as Lee has, and understand the basic structure of stories, but many have not. Some children enter first grade as readers, but most do not. Most children in preschool, kindergarten, and first-grade classrooms will need considerable help from you to become competent and independent readers.

In this chapter we will begin by exploring how children's first understandings about reading and writing develop. Next, we will discuss many types of activities that support and encourage the emergence of literacy. Finally, we will take you into one kindergarten classroom and explain how all of these factors are put together. Throughout this chapter we will take a balanced approach. In many cases, the children are encouraged to make discoveries about print and language, but often the teacher must directly and explicitly explain things to the students.

Emerging Knowledge about Word Structure

A typical class of entering first-graders, asked what they expect to learn in school that year, will almost always respond that they will learn to read. Despite high motivation and expectations, however, some children will experience considerable difficulty, frustration, and an early loss of self-esteem in the process of learning to read. Why does this happen?

Take a look at the following list of factors that predict children's success as readers (Share, Jorm, Maclean, & Matthews, 1984). Which ones do you think are the most important predictors?

- Phoneme segmentation ability (the ability to tell you the first sound of a spoken word, for example)
- Knowledge of letter names
- Kindergarten teacher's predictions of reading success in first grade
- Performance on the Peabody Picture Vocabulary Test (a measure of oral English vocabulary)
- Parents' occupational status
- Library membership
- Number of books the child owns
- Amount that parents read to the child

- Gender
- Amount that parents read themselves in their spare time
- Whether the child attended preschool

You may be surprised to learn that these factors are listed in the exact order in which they predicted the end-of-year reading ability of more than 500 Australian first-graders. The top two predictors (phonemic segmentation ability and knowledge of letter names) were significantly stronger than the others. No matter how much a child has been read to, then, that child must be able to *independently* identify many printed words in order to read on his own.

First-grade teacher Glenna Schwarze knows that reading independence means making sure her students get instruction in decoding skills:

> I am sure any first-grade teacher will tell you the same thing: At the heart of first-grade reading instruction is ensuring that children learn to decode words. Of course, we want children to be able to instantly recognize as many words as possible, but we also need to be sure they are equipped with strategies and skills to use when they don't instantly know a word. The beginning reader, of course, cannot instantly recognize many words. As teachers, however, we can help children identify words they don't know by helping them recognize the letters in the words and how to translate those letters into the sounds they represent.

> —Glenna Schwarze, first-grade teacher

Children need to acquire two insights about language in order to become successful readers: the alphabetic principle and phonemic awareness (Kim, Boyle, Simmons, & Nakamura, 2017; Snow, Burns, & Griffin, 1998). The alphabetic principle is the insight that spoken sounds can be represented by written letters. Phonemic awareness is the insight that spoken words are made up of a sequence of somewhat separable sounds, called *phonemes*. Children who have been read to have frequently heard the sounds in spoken words linked to printed words and letters, and this has helped them understand the alphabetic principle and gain phonemic awareness. Adams (1990) demonstrated that students with difficulty learning to read have problems with letter recognition and phonemic awareness.

Phonemic awareness develops from many experiences. Children may, for example, have attended to the sounds in the rhymes of Dr. Seuss's *There's a Wocket in My Pocket* and laughed at the silly sounds made by a change in the initial phoneme. Children who can take the next step and make this change themselves—transforming *basket* into *wasket*, for example—provide further evidence of phonemic awareness. Alliteration—the repetition of initial consonant sounds used in many nursery rhymes—also focuses attention on phonemes. In the Classroom 7.1 shows how one teacher helps his kindergartners make phonemic connections.

Mr. Felton emphasizes phonemic segmentation and alphabetic awareness in this lesson by reading aloud to his class. He realizes, as research suggests, that the potential for predicting success in reading based on a child's ability in phonemic segmentation and alphabetic awareness is not so straightforward; in fact, these two skills most likely have their origins in having been read to as a young child. So the importance of parents' reading to children, which appears fairly far down the list of predictors, is actually significantly higher than it might seem. In a British study that followed a group of children from ages 3 to 5, researchers found that children's knowledge of nursery rhymes at age 3 was closely related to their ability to perceive and produce rhyme and alliteration as well as to recognize letters and some simple words (Maclean, Bryant, & Bradley, 1988). In other words, children who had experienced a lot of nursery rhymes at an early age were better equipped with exactly the knowledge and understanding that enhance learning to read in school. It is not just nursery rhymes; children with larger vocabularies and more language experiences acquire phonemic awareness more easily (Snow, Burns, & Griffin, 1998).

In the Classroom 7.1

Kindergartners and the P Words

Mr. Felton's kindergartners, sitting in a semicircle on the floor, look quizzically at a large chart he has put on a stand. It is a poem that he has printed in large letters with a black felt pen.

"This is a poem, boys and girls," he tells them. "It's from a favorite book of mine called *Whiskers and Rhymes* by Arnold Lobel." He holds up his copy of the book.

"The poem is about a cat named George, who brushes his teeth!"

The children giggle.

"But guess what George uses for toothpaste? Pickle paste!"

The children roar with laughter as they consider toothpaste made from pickles.

Mr. Felton invites the children to come up and take a look at the book and the three pictures that accompany the poem. First, George squeezes a toothpaste tube labeled "Pickle Paste" onto his toothbrush. Second, he brushes his teeth, and green foam emerges from his mouth. Third, George smiles a big green-teeth smile. When the children sit back down, Mr. Felton reads the poem from the chart, pointing to each word as he reads.

Then Mr. Felton asks the children to find the letter *p* in the words. A child comes up and points to the *p* in *pickle*, and another child points to the *p* in *paste*. (When we write the sound of the letter *p* we use this convention /p/.)

Mr. Felton asks, "Which letter in *pickle* makes it say /p/?"

The children respond, "*p*."

He asks, "Which letter in *paste* makes it say /p/?"

The children respond, "*p*."

Mr. Felton says, "The letter *p* says /p/," emphasizing the /p/ as he says "pickle paste."

The children can't help giggling as they say "pickle paste" over and over.

Next, Mr. Felton shows the children a large tube of toothpaste cut out of construction paper—just like the one George had. It has "Pickle Paste" printed on the tube.

Mr. Felton asks the children if they can spot some other *p* words in the room to write on the tube. The children glance around at the books on the chalkboard ledge, most of which Mr. Felton has read to them. They find the *p*s in the title of Dr. Seuss's *Hop on Pop*, James Marshall's *The Three Little Pigs*, and Eve Rice's *Peter's Pockets*.

Mr. Felton carefully prints the following words on the tube as he emphasizes and underlines the letter *p*: *pig, Peter, pocket, hop, pop*. He then tells the children he is going to name some colors, and they should say "pickle" if they hear a /p/. He emphasizes putting his lips together as he pronounces the /p/ in this list of words: *pink, red, green, purple*. Following some discussion, Mr. Felton adds *pink* and *purple* to the tube. He tacks the tube to the wall for future reference and the addition of new words.

MyLab Education **Self-Check 7.1**

Phonemic Awareness and Alphabet Recognition

Of the two competencies we discuss here, alphabet recognition is the more straightforward: Students need to recognize letters and their distinguishing features in order to work effectively with print. Learning the names of letters is very useful. We discuss alphabet recognition more thoroughly in Chapter 8.

Phonemic awareness is a more complex matter. Although it is a competency that you mastered long ago, you are probably not familiar with the concept. Yet it is astonishingly important to the process of successfully learning to read. In a longitudinal study of learning to read and write in an elementary school in Austin, Texas, one of us found that development of phonemic awareness early in first grade was critical to children's successfully learning to read and write in first grade (Juel, 1988, 1994; Juel, Griffith, & Gough, 1986). As children learn to read, they also grow in phonemic awareness, but they have an easier time learning to read if they rapidly develop this proficiency (Bruck & Treiman, 1992; Ehri, 2015; Vandervelden & Siegel, 1995). That is, children need to perceive words as sequences of phonemes and link those phonemes to letters to begin reading words more efficiently. As Snow and colleagues (1998) note, "The theoretical and practical importance of phonemic awareness for the beginning reader relies not only on logic but also on the results of several decades of empirical research."

What Is Phonemic Awareness?

Phonemic awareness is the insight that spoken words are composed of somewhat separable sounds—sounds that can be played with (*dilly dilly silly Willy*), rearranged (*Connie Juel* becomes *Johnny Cool*), alliterated (*teeny tiny Tina*), and even used to create alternative languages (like pig Latin). Phonemic awareness is not synonymous with phonics; it is not knowledge about which letters represent particular sounds. Rather, it is an insight about speech—an attention to the sounds (phonemes) that reside within words. These sounds correspond to letters, but only roughly. For example, there are three phonemes in *cap*, but there are also three phonemes in *cape* and *shake*. Perceiving words as sequences of phonemes is important in learning to read and write because the link between phonemes and letters is the basis for alphabetic writing systems such as English and Spanish. Keep in mind that a child can be aware of phonemes yet still not recognize a single letter of the alphabet. Phonemic awareness is an awareness of the *sounds* of language, a metalinguistic insight; it is not a part of learning to understand or speak oral language.

Understanding phonemes is complicated by the fact that we rarely say them separately; instead, they run together. In speech, we actually begin forming our mouths to pronounce the upcoming phoneme as we are still saying the previous one. For example, in saying *cat*, we begin saying the /ă/ before we finish the /k/. It is almost impossible to say some phonemes in isolation. That is, it is almost impossible to say either the /k/ or /t/ in *cat* without adding a vowel sound, such as /ə/. It is this overlapping, called *coarticulation*, of phonemes that allows our rapid speech. But it is exactly this coarticulation that makes learning to read words so hard. A letter in a printed word does not map onto one clear, distinct sound.

Phonemic awareness does not come naturally. Achieving it demands that a child attend to the form or structure, rather than the meaning, of speech. This is difficult because our natural inclination is to attend to meaning. Thus, even those children who arrive at school with well-developed oral language may not have developed phonemic awareness. Phonemic awareness is not necessary for speaking or for listening, but it is vital to reading. Teaching phonemic awareness is thus sometimes quite difficult. Some children will need a good deal of assistance in gaining this abstract understanding. Fortunately, however, research very strongly indicates that phonemic awareness can be taught (National Reading Panel, 2000). In the Classroom 7.2 lists Common Core foundational standards for phonemic awareness for kindergarten children.

Why Do Phonemic Awareness and Alphabet Recognition So Strongly Predict Success in Reading?

Children must unlock the relationships between the sounds they use to say words and the letters they use in reading and writing words. The invented spellings of young children reflect their growing understanding of phonemic awareness and letter-sound knowledge. In English, consonants are the easiest phonemes to perceive in spoken

In the Classroom 7.2

Phonological Awareness

- Demonstrate understanding of spoken words, syllables, and sounds (phonemes).
- Recognize and produce rhyming words.
- Count, pronounce, blend, and segment syllables in spoken words.
- Blend and segment onsets and rimes of single-syllable spoken words.
- Isolate and pronounce the initial, medial vowel, and final sounds (phonemes) in three-phoneme (consonant-vowel-consonant, or CVC) words. (This does not include CVCs ending with /l/, /r/, or /x/.)
- Add or substitute individual sounds (phonemes) in simple, one-syllable words to make new words.

words. Children often represent consonants before representing vowels when they begin writing English. A child trying to spell *dog*, for example, tries to connect the phonemes he perceives to the actual letters. Initially, *dog* may be represented by just *D*, because the initial consonant is often the easiest for a child to attend to and attach to a letter. This is probably the earliest stage of invented spelling. Later, this child may spell it *DG* because he feels these two consonants in his mouth as he says the word. Still later, he may spell it *DAG*. These early spellings, or invented spellings, are perfectly natural for young children. This type of writing goes hand in hand with development of phonemic awareness (Juel, 2006). In stretching out *dog* (for example, *ddawg, dawguh, dawg*), a child notes changes in the tongue position, the lip movements, and how much the mouth opens as sounds are uttered. This feeling of sounds in the mouth is apparent to anyone watching young children as they write unknown words. Children literally move their mouths and exaggerate sounds as they try to link them to letters. In that parsing of sounds in the mouth, phonemes become more real because they are felt: The tongue pressed on the ridge in the mouth behind the front teeth and the brief holding of air on making the /d/ help children notice the sound of the letter *d*.

At the beginning of first grade, invented spelling plays an important role in Kay Hollenbeck's first-grade classroom, as she explains here:

Having the freedom to use invented spelling is essential for my first-graders. It allows them to be writers from day one. We call it "sound spelling" because they write words the way they think they sound, using the letters they know. This is a big accomplishment for them, and they are proud that they can "write" any word they can say.

For example, yesterday Mara wrote *Tuda iz mi brda i m 6*. When I read the words back to her—"Today is my birthday; I am six"—her face beamed; she was delighted that I could actually read what she had intended to say. I knew what she had written, both because she had chosen letters that approximated the sounds in the words she intended and also because I was able to use context clues. I knew that her concept of word was developing because she included spaces between her words. I knew it was her birthday, and the picture she had drawn was a give-away, too—a girl and a birthday cake with six candles! Although Mara was thrilled that I knew her exact words, she also was concerned that she hadn't "spelled the words right." So she asked me to "write them the *right* way." Which I did, of course, in her "word book"—a little booklet of pages stapled together that students keep on hand for me to write words they request. There is one page for each letter of the alphabet.

—Kay Hollenbeck, first-grade teacher

Of course, children like Mara will need to understand the connections between the approximately 44 phonemes of spoken English and the 26 letters that we use to represent them. This is one of the key tasks of learning to read, and it is not easy. As we all know, the English writing system does not reflect a consistent one-to-one relationship between letters and sounds; this is particularly true with vowel sounds. However—and this is a key point—words contain enough predictable correspondences to at least aid in word identification or spelling. In identifying the "irregular" word *come*, for example, the letters *c, m*, and the silent *e* reliably represent certain sounds. A child who can figure out which sounds these letters are likely to represent has a powerful tool for recognizing words, whereas the child who cannot figure out letter-sound correspondences will often be stumped when he comes to a word he has not previously learned to read.

Reflect and Apply

1. In her comment about empowering students to become independent readers, first-grade teacher Glenna Schwarze emphasizes that students need both decoding skills and the ability to instantly recognize many words. In your own words, explain why both of these skills are necessary.

2. Suppose you were reading a simple storybook to a kindergarten student and wanted to help him develop phonemic awareness. Describe three things you could do. (You can learn more from this activity if you focus on a particular storybook and give specific examples of what you might point out and questions you might ask.)

Learning to Spell and Identify Words

Children learn to identify words both through their own attempts to map sounds coming out of their mouth to letters in printed words and by receiving assistance and instruction from teachers and other knowledgeable adults. Here we first describe some of children's early understandings and then consider how they learn to connect letters and phonemes.

SOME EARLY UNDERSTANDINGS ABOUT PRINT

Children begin to read and write before they can identify or write all the letters of the alphabet and before they have developed phonemic awareness. Often, the first word children learn is their own name. Diane, for example, was 4 years old when her mother, a university student, came to the office of one of the authors. To keep her busy during the meeting, her mom handed Diane her notebook. Diane slowly and laboriously wrote her name and then wrote the message shown in Figure 7.1.

When Diane was finished, her mother asked her to tell what the message said and to also say the letters in her name. She easily told the message. It was about what she and her mom were going to do after they left the office—though she did not look at her paper as she "read" the message. However, Diane was unable to name any but the first letter, the *D*, in her name.

Diane treated her name as a visual unit, without distinguishing and naming individual letters as components. Quite frequently, the first letters children learn are those in their own names. Certainly, writing your name is an important step in declaring your identity (Bloodgood, 1999). Diane does know a lot about print. She knows that it moves left to right across the page, and there were clearly letterlike forms in her writing. Still, it was real work for her to write her name because she had to remember its visual form without fully understanding that it is composed of individual letters with particular shapes and names. At this point, the letter *d* is not linked to the sound /d/, the letter *i* is not connected to a long *i* sound, and so on.

Figure 7.1 Diane's Note

As children learn letterlike forms, these forms frequently start to creep onto the pages of their drawings. In Figure 7.2 another emergent reader, 5-year-old Jake, has drawn himself doing karate. Even an initial inspection of Jake's drawing makes it evident that he has reached a profound milestone in learning. He understands that the sounds that come out of his mouth as he speaks can be linked to letters, an important discovery about the alphabetic principle. The speech bubble coming out of Jake's mouth contains the letters *a* and *e*, which he says make the sounds he makes as he does a karate chop. This shows some fairly advanced understanding of letters and sounds.

Note that Jake's reversal of letters in his name does not indicate a problem; it simply illustrates that Jake perceives his name as a single visual unit. At this stage of development, Jake does not experience directionality as a relevant characteristic of his world. Until children begin working with print, virtually each thing they experience and learn to name retains the same name, regardless of the way it might be facing. Jake is still Jake whether he stands on his head or his feet. His dog is a dog whether he is coming or going.

Only in writing is this principle violated. Jake will catch on to the importance of directionality in writing as he writes and reads more. Also, once Jake learns the names of the letters, his task will become easier. When he knows that his name is made of the letter sequence *J-a-k-e*, he will find the spelling of his name easier to recall and to write.

In the Classroom 7.3 describes an activity that will help children like Jake further their understanding of letters and sounds.

Figure 7.2 Jake's Drawing

CONNECTING LETTERS AND PHONEMES: THE ALPHABETIC PRINCIPLE

The Common Core State Standards (2010) and most state standards today recommend that children segment words into phonemes and know the letters of the alphabet and their corresponding sounds by the time they leave kindergarten. What is important is not so much how many letters and sounds the child knows, but rather the *idea* that letters represent sounds. Yet in many schools, children are expected to know all letter-sounds by the end of kindergarten.

Once children learn letter names and possess some degree of phonemic awareness, they frequently use the names of letters to help them recall and spell words. They may be particularly dependent on the names of initial consonants for word recall. The name

In the Classroom 7.3

Instructional Routines

Using Letter Puppets to Help Children Understand the Connection between Phonemes and Letters

Purpose: To give students practice and feedback in recognizing the initial sound in a word and the letter that represents that sound.

Procedure:

- Purchase or make a set of puppets with alliterative names such as Pink Pig, Red Rooster, Jumping Jerod, Nice Nora, Mad Mike, and so on.
- Put on one of the hand puppets, such as Pink Pig, which has a big letter *P* on it. Introduce the children to it, saying "Pink Pig only likes things that start with a /p/, like her name, Pink Pig." Emphasize the /p/ as you talk, and point out the letter *P*.
- Walk around the room and ask the children what Pink Pig likes as the puppet touches the object. For example, "Does Pink Pig like pencils? Does Pink Pig like Peter? Does Pink Pig like Pasha? Does Pink Pig like red?" and so on.
- After you have touched several objects and the children have responded, ask, "What do you think is Pink Pig's favorite letter of the alphabet?"
- Students can take turns wearing the puppet and asking the same questions, and other puppets can be used to give practice with additional letters.

MyLab Education
Video Example 7.1
This video shows how the teacher develops the students' understanding of the alphabet principle.

of the letter *b* is the sound of the word *bee*, and the name of the letter *j* is part of the sound of the word *Jake*, for example, and this overlap may help children identify these words when they see them in a text (Ehri & Robbins, 1992).

In writing words, children often use letters whose names represent the sounds that they perceive in the words. Charles Read (1971) discovered that there is a logical development to children's invented spellings and the growth of phonemic awareness. At first, they may represent only the initial consonant or the most distinctive sound (for example, *b* written for *bee* or *l* for *elephant*). Even this level of processing represents a remarkable advance in understanding. To do this, children need both some phonemic awareness—to perceive the sounds represented by *b* or *l*—and knowledge of the alphabet. When children use this knowledge to spell, the result is invented or temporary spelling. These terms describe young children's attempts to spell words using their limited knowledge about letters and sounds. In the previous section, Diane engaged in invented writing, as do children who write entirely random strings of letters (for example, *czfdyxsy* for *this is my blue umbrella*). Invented spelling is a more sophisticated accomplishment.

The invented spelling of 5-year-old Jordan, displayed in Figure 7.3, shows how much this emergent reader has already learned about the code of written English. Jordan has encountered some common words frequently enough to have memorized their correct spelling (for example, *Jordan, and, in*, and *is*). He uses the sounds conveyed in the letter names in his spellings (for example, *im*). He more frequently represents consonants than vowels (for example, *kindrgrdin* and *grd*). He is actively working to link the phonemes he perceives to actual letters. For example, on one occasion he writes *grade* as *grd*, whereas on another he writes it as *grod*, adding a letter representing a vowel sound. He will, on occasion, reverse a letter or number; however, as with Jake, this is not a concern.

Jordan is not yet consistently writing silent letters. To do so requires instruction of within-word spelling patterns, something that should be taught directly to most children (Henderson, 1990). To acquire such knowledge, a child must have engaged in rather extensive reading, and, for many children, these spelling patterns must be isolated, explained, and discussed. Silent letters must be noticed, and often explained, to be learned. One of the most common within-word spelling patterns is the silent *e* marker, as in *grade*. As Jordan reads more, he will start to notice these patterns. Jordan is likely to progress from *grd* to *grad* to *grade* in writing *grade*. Notice that Jordan spells the last syllable in *kindergarten* with *in*. Jordan is from Texas, where *en* is pronounced /ĭn/. In many regions of the United States, both *em* and *en* receive short *i* pronunciations. That is, words like *pin* and *pen*, *tin* and *ten*, and *Jim* and *gem* have identical pronunciations. Sensitivity to dialect is important as we evaluate children's speech and invented spellings to plan instruction.

Figure 7.3 Jordan's Writing

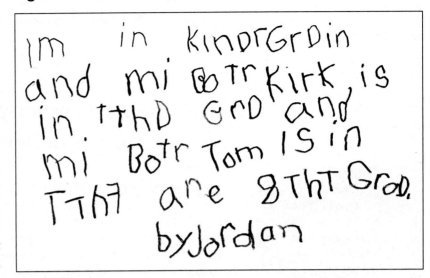

Children who enter kindergarten speaking a language other than English have some unique challenges learning to identify words. The orthographic structure, or spelling, of English is more complex than the structure of Spanish, so the research suggests that learning to read Spanish requires much less attention to phonemic awareness than does learning to read English (Goldenberg, Tolar, Reese, Francis, Bazin, & Mejia-Aranuz, 2014). When the Spanish-speaking child begins to read in an English classroom, there will be a few obvious points of interference between Spanish and English. The vowel sounds in Spanish and English are different and English has more spellings for a vowel sound than does Spanish. There are more than a dozen ways to represent the long a sound in English. Consider just these words: *play*, *made*, *maid*, or *eight*. There are sounds in English that are distinctly different, but not to the child whose first language is Spanish. /ch/ in *chin* and /sh/ in *shin* are almost identical to the Spanish-speaking child.

The development of phonemic awareness for the bilingual child proceeds more smoothly when you keep a parallel focus on vocabulary development and phonemic awareness. Consider the odd man out game. Which of these three words does not rhyme with the other two: *hat*, *pan*, *mat*. If these three words are first introduced with pictures that represent the meanings, then the discrimination task is much easier. The picture enables the children to hold the word in memory to conduct the comparison.

Reflect and Apply

3. One of us (Juel et al., 1986) once asked some first-grade children to read the word *rain*. Here are the replies of 14 of the children: "ring," "in," "runs," "with," "ride," "art," "are," "on," "reds," "running," "why," "ran," "ran," "ran." We also asked these 14 children to spell the word *rain*, and here are their spellings: *rach, in, yes, uan, ramt, fen, rur, Rambl, wetn, wnishire*, drawing of raindrops, *Rup, ran, ran*. Consider what understandings are suggested by each spelling and reading of *rain*. Also, consider what each child needs to learn to progress. Two other first-grade children correctly read the word, but one spelled it *raine* and another spelled it *rane*. What can you say about these two children's understanding of the code of printed English?

4. Explain the progress in perceiving words as sequences of sounds and connecting those sounds to letters, as well as learning common spelling patterns that a child is making as his spelling of *rain* moves from *R* to *RAN* to *RANE* to *RAIN*.

MyLab Education **Self-Check 7.2**

MyLab Education **Application Exercise 7.1:** Learning from Invented Spelling

MyLab Education
Video Example 7.2
This video will help you develop a list of the print that should be placed in a kindergarten classroom. Then, relate the video to what you are about to read.

Emerging Knowledge about Comprehension and Text Structure

As children learn about words and the alphabetic principle, they are also exploring comprehension and the process of constructing meaning. They have much to learn. Children who come from homes where they have been read a variety of books will understand the purpose of print and how books work. They will understand that print conveys information and enjoyment, an escape to the world of stories. They will understand that we read from left to right, that we turn the pages, and that the print conveys the ideas and pictures provide support. Over years of reading the young child may discern the boundaries between words and even begin to recognize a few words and letters. Shirley Brice Heath (1983) has found that children from middle-class homes may have had over 1,000 hours of experiences with print, whereas children from economically disadvantaged homes will have experienced only 50 hours of oral reading experience with a parent or another adult.

Comprehension Acquisition

When children are read to, they acquire some awareness of the process of reading comprehension (Smolkin & Donovan, 2002). Instructive adult readers will reveal the process of text comprehension as they read. Adults will stop to share the pictures, ask questions, point out important ideas, note comprehension problems, and reread to clarify misunderstanding. They will invite the child to enter into the process and encourage questioning and commentary. All of these behaviors during an interactive read-aloud school the child in the cognitive actions of a reader. The adult, parent, or teacher is not specifically teaching comprehension, but making the child aware that comprehension is a meaning-seeking process. Consider this interaction between a teacher and a child reading Tomie dePaola's *The Popcorn Book*. In this mixed-genre book, part of the book tells the story of two brothers making popcorn and the other half of the book presents information on the history of popcorn. The underlined portion in the following example is the actual text.

Teacher: <u>In 1612, French explorers saw some Iroquois people popping corn in clay pots. They would fill the pots with hot sand, throw in some popcorn and stir it with a stick. When the corn popped, it came to the top of the sand and made it easy to get.</u>

Child: Look at the bowl!

Teacher (providing an oral commentary on the "story"): Okay, now it's hot enough [for the brothers] to add a few kernels.

Child 1: What's a kernel?

Child 2: Like what you pop.

Child 3: It's a seed.

Child 3: What if you, like, would you think [of] popcorn seed? Like a popcorn seed. Could you grow popcorn?

Teacher: Oh, excellent question. Let's read and we'll see if this [book] answers that question, and if not, we'll talk about it at the end. (Smolkin & Donovan, 2002, pp. 145–146)

In this interaction the child poses a question and the teacher acknowledges the value of the question. The teacher instructs the student in how to answer the question—"Let's read." This construction of meaning, shared by the teacher and the students, helps the students understand the importance of actively asking questions and seeking answers by reading further in the text. This is just one of the several cognitive acts or strategies that teachers can model and students can try out during an interactive read-aloud. In addition to questioning, the reader can activate prior knowledge, monitor comprehension, and fix up misunderstandings (although in this example the child was doing the monitoring), generate questions, draw inferences, make connections, create mental images, use knowledge of text structures, and summarize. Although the children are not yet using these strategies independently, the interactive read-aloud is laying the foundation for future direct instruction in comprehension strategies.

The interactive read-aloud is an excellent way to build the vocabulary knowledge of English learners. During the interactive read-aloud, the students and the teacher discuss the story and the words. The pictures provide support for students to learn the words, and the discussion helps the students to pronounce them and clarify the meaning. Pick a book, fiction or nonfiction, that has five to eight important vocabulary words. Make these words the focus of your reading and the discussion. We suggest that you follow a 3-day plan: first focus on vocabulary, then comprehension, and then both.

Day 1. Read the book and stop at particular pages to discuss the particular vocabulary words. Ask follow-up questions after reading the story. Add words to a word wall. After you write the words on a chart, adding pictures will help ELL students learn and use these new English words.

Day 2. Read the book without stopping. Afterward, ask questions about target words in the book and refer to pages on which the words appeared. At the end, ask follow-up questions.

Day 3. Do not read the book again but ask targeted questions about the vocabulary words in the book. Have the students use the words in their responses. "Can someone use the word kernel in a sentence?"

Many of the books in the bibliography at the end of the chapter are suitable for an interactive read-aloud.

Text Structure Knowledge

The interactive read-aloud experience also builds knowledge of the world and of text structure in particular. The more prior knowledge you have about a topic, the easier it is to comprehend a text. This is equally true of text structures knowledge, the organizational patterns of the text. When you read a recipe, for example, you anticipate that it will begin with a list of ingredients and that directions will follow in a step-by-step format. You also know that you should probably read the whole recipe before you begin, so that you can estimate the time it will take and be familiar with the ingredients you will need. You have in your mind a schema or structure for recipes that allows you not only to comprehend what you are reading but also to write a recipe that others could follow.

Children who have been read to extensively have probably developed a similar schema for how stories like the ones they will encounter in school are put together. They can demonstrate this knowledge if asked. The stories they tell will imitate the stories they have heard; they will generally have a central character who must overcome an obstacle of some sort, and the resolution of that problem will generally develop through a chronological sequence of events. They know, for example, that the wolf is hungry and will blow down the houses of the three little pigs to get food—or, if they have been read a different version, that the pigs will succeed in protecting one or more of their houses from the wolf.

A knowledge of story structure, or story schema, helps a child in a number of ways. First, a story schema acts as a filing cabinet. As characters are encountered in a story, they are filed under the concept of characters or people. Ponds, mountains, and neighborhood are filed under setting. The filing compartments are stored in order. When the child is asked to retell the story, he follows the order of the files. Finally, the knowledge of story structure allows the child to make predictions. Once the characters are introduced we know that, sooner or later, a problem is going to arise.

Making up stories for wordless picture books helps young children understand the structure of text.

Instruction in story structure is very useful. Discuss with the students the elements of a fiction story. You might provide a graphic organizer that lists *characters, setting, problem, events, resolution* and *theme*. Read the story the first time with little discussion. Then go back and read it again and complete the graphic organizer with the class. At first you will be doing most of the work, but gradually the students will be able to identify the story elements on their own.

By the end of kindergarten most children have learned the distinction between a book that tells a story and a book that conveys information. When asked to write a story they will begin with the past tense as most stories begin and will use the present tense to craft an informational text (Donovan & Smolkin, 2002). Early on they learn other text structures beginning their stories with "Once upon a time" and employing some understanding of temporal sequence, "and then and then."

But, whether or not children have been read to before they arrive at school, you can provide experiences to help them understand the structures of texts and greatly increase their chances of becoming proficient readers. You can read to them in the classroom, and you can provide opportunities for them to understand story structure at the same time that they grow in vocabulary, ideas, imagination, and love of language and stories. In the Classroom 7.4 shows how one teacher does this in her kindergarten classroom.

MyLab Education **Self-Check 7.3**

Instruction that Facilitates Children's Growing Literacy

"Mrs. Cooper, you're going to teach us how to read, aren't you?" 6-year-old María asked.

Like María, most youngsters are eager to learn to read. That puts teachers of young children in an enviable position. Fortunately, there are many ways you can assist these eager learners in understanding the organization of text and the structure of words, developing phonemic awareness, and learning to identify words, all the while nurturing their interest, excitement, and desire to become readers.

Creating a Literate Environment

The starting point in fostering children's emerging literacy is to create a language-rich environment as described in Chapter 3—a classroom that abounds with opportunities to read, write, listen, and talk. A language-rich classroom includes:

- Walls filled with posters, signs, labels, and student work.
- A reading center with a library chock-full of books, comfortable chairs, pillows, stuffed animals, a rug, and anything else that will make it an enticing and secure spot for young readers.

- A special area designated for writing that contains paper of various sizes, textures, and colors, as well as a variety of pencils, pens, markers, crayons, alphabet strips, and the like.
- A science center where children can explore plants, insects, rocks, and animals, along with short simple books in which children can read about these topics.

In addition to having designated space and materials for reading and writing, children also need time and motivation. The activities you provide to these children on the threshold of literacy will focus on reading for enjoyment as well as reading for meaning; subsequent sections will highlight some of these literacy activities.

Reading Opportunities

Opportunities for children to read in the classroom are almost limitless. Here are some ideas you can try out and expand on in your classroom.

THE MORNING MEETING

The beginning of each school day is an ideal time to gather your students in a comfortable place and meet with them as a community of learners. The morning meeting can

---

In the Classroom 7.4

Using Wordless Picture Books in a Kindergarten Classroom

Seated in a chair with her kindergartners gathered comfortably around her on the carpeted floor, Mrs. Willey displays a copy of the mostly wordless picture book *Have You Seen My Duckling?* by Nancy Tafuri. Mrs. Willey tells the children that they are going to help make up a story about a mother duck who has lost her ducklings. She might remind them to draw on their knowledge of stories to help them make up their own story.

Mrs. Willey asks the children to close their eyes. "Think about the baby duck, a duckling we call it, that you just saw. Try to imagine what it feels like to be a duckling, to be so new, so small. What do you see? Now, open your eyes. Tell me, what did you see?"

"Grass!"

"Bugs!"

The children take turns suggesting what the world might look like from the perspective of a baby duck.

Next, Mrs. Willey has the children point to the mother duck on the cover illustration and count her ducklings. She opens the book and has them notice what happens on the opening page.

"There are eight ducklings in a nest. But one of them is climbing out!" Tamara volunteers.

Mrs. Willey smiles and turns the page. "Early one morning . . . ," she begins, and then she stops and asks, "What happens?"

Jason replies, "Early one morning, eight baby ducks got up."

"Ducklings!" Tamara corrects him.

"Well, okay, ducklings," Jason says. "They saw a butterfly, and one duckling got into the water and tried to swim after it."

"Then what happens?" asks Mrs. Willey, as she flips the page to uncover new illustrations.

Mrs. Willey continues to call on different children, who add to the story by considering the upcoming illustrations, their own imaginations, and their knowledge of stories, mothers, children, and ducks.

After Mrs. Willey and her kindergartners complete making up a story for *Have You Seen My Duckling?* the children divide into groups, and each group goes to one of three classroom centers. In one center, the children have a few additional copies of the book. Here they each get a chance to retell the story to a buddy.

In the art center, there are some black-and-white drawings of a duck and eight ducklings. The children cut out the drawings, color them in, and paste each one on a tongue depressor to serve as a puppet. Then they retell the story to each other, using their puppets to act it out.

In the library center are several wordless picture books, including *Do Not Disturb* and *Early Morning in the Barn*, two other books by Nancy Tafuri. The children take turns making up stories and telling them to each other as they turn the pages.

Frank Pedrick/The Image Works

The morning meeting is an excellent opportunity to engage students in a variety of literacy experiences.

develop and nurture a sense of belonging and purpose, engaging students in a variety of literacy experiences. The amount of time you spend, whether it is 10 minutes or 20, will depend on how long your students are able to focus without becoming restless. This time may be relatively short at the beginning of the year and increase as the year progresses.

During this meeting, many activities can take place. Here are some of the possibilities:

- *Attendance count.* Take attendance by showing name cards and having students respond to their names in print. The first word most children learn, because of interest and exposure, is their own name, so students are likely to be successful early on at reading their names.

- *Calendar.* Write the day and date on the board, reminding students of what day came just before and what day will come after (simultaneously teaching and reinforcing children's knowledge of the days of the week and the concepts of *before* and *after*).

- *Weather.* Talk with students about the weather, teaching words such as *rainy, sunny, cold, temperature, cloudy, warm,* and so forth.

- *Current events.* Have students share the events of their lives. This is an excellent way to build oral language skills and expand vocabulary.

- *Morning message.* Have students read your "morning message." This is a short message you write on the board to your class each day so that when they arrive, they know they will be reading a note from you. This message serves two purposes. First, it reinforces the notion that print conveys meaning. Second, it provides children with practice in tracking print as you read aloud. In fact, it is often worthwhile to read the message several times, drawing attention to the letters or words and having students come up to the board and circle the words they recognize. Later in the school year children should help you compose the message, because this allows practice in phonemic segmentation and spelling. You can start the message by writing Today is _____, and then ask the students; "What is the first sound in Monday? Can someone come up and help me write the word Monday? I will share the pen." Now the students are applying their knowledge of phonemic awareness and letter names.

- *The daily schedule.* Going over the day's schedule at the beginning of the day gives students a sense of what the day holds and, equally important, illustrates another use of print. The daily schedule should reflect what students will do in whole-group, small-group, and individual work.

FREE "READING"

Each day, students should have several opportunities to "read" books of their own choosing in any way they like. Some children might wish to share a book with a friend. They might do this by telling a favorite story that they have committed to memory, using the pictures as cues for turning the pages; if you model this activity for them, they will likely find it inviting. Others will silently look at books. Still others will want to be read to or listen to a book on tape or CD. As the year progresses children will want to reread the books they have read with you.

SELECTING BOOKS FOR SPECIFIC PURPOSES

At the beginning of this chapter, we talked about books as the heart and soul of reading. They also serve a host of specific literacy development purposes. Here we consider just three of the many purposes books can serve: motivating students, highlighting sounds, and enabling just-beginning readers to read. In the kindergarten classroom it is desirable to use big books, so the students can crowd around on the rug and see the print while you point to it.

Books That Motivate Children to Enter the World of Print.   As a teacher of young children, you will want to select books that develop their vocabularies, expand their knowledge of the world, connect to their lives, add to their knowledge of story structures, and increase their desire to read. Such texts can be well-known children's favorites, such as James Marshall's *The Three Little Pigs* (1989), or newer ones, such as Barbara Joosse's *Nikolai, the Only Bear* (2005).

Books That Highlight the Sounds of Language.   Because emergent readers need to attend to the forms of words, it is important to read texts in which the structure of words is particularly transparent, highlighting the sounds of words in order to foster phonemic awareness. You can choose texts with features such as word play, rhyme, and alliteration to accomplish this goal. One example is Jill Bennett's rendition of *Teeny Tiny* (1997). One kindergarten teacher, Jeff Baptista, extends this book to develop phonemic awareness. "After we have enjoyed the story, I will ask them, 'What letter in *teeny* makes it say /t/? What letter in *tiny* makes it say /t/? Can you think of other words that start with /t/, like *teeny tiny*?' Later my students can sort pictures that begin with /t/ and /s/, heightening their awareness of initial consonant sounds. Word-level instruction begins with a focus on meaningful text and then moves to words and letter-sounds. The link between meaning, words, and word parts should always be clear."

Books That Children Can Learn to Read on Their Own.   The books with predictable patterns that we described earlier in the chapter are purposely written so that children can remember them after hearing them a few times. The overall structure of the books is repetitive, and the picture clues are rich and informative. Books like Eric Carle's *The Very Hungry Caterpillar* fit this category. All in all, these books can make children "instant readers" after only a few readings by the teacher. The children should reread these books by themselves and with a partner.

Brian Wildsmith's *Cat on the Mat* exemplifies this repetitive structure and strong picture support. In this tale, various animals join a cat on the mat:

The cat sat on the mat. The dog sat on the mat. The goat sat on the mat.

As the child rereads the text and points to the lines and words after hearing it read several times, he can begin to gain insight into the conventions of print, such as the directionality of print from left to right. After rereading many predictable texts, a child may learn the printed form of some high-frequency words, such as *the*, and some high-interest words, such as *dog*; he may even begin to associate some letters with sounds. The teacher can highlight these connections.

You can encourage such understanding by using big books, which are large enough for the whole class or a group of students to see as you read. They allow you to replicate activities that parents or other caregivers carry out as they read to their children at home: point to the print, track the print as children speak it, and highlight words. Predictable text in big books or on charts can encourage children to follow along, echoing or chorally reading as you point to individual words.

To highlight words, letters, or text, you can frame words in a big book with your hand or cover a page with an acetate sheet on which you underline words, word parts, or letters. You can also ask questions or make comments about specific elements in the text; a few suggestions are listed here:

- Where do I start reading? What is the title? Who is the author?
- When I get to the end of the page what do I do?
- Point to where it said *goat.*
- Where does it say *cat?*
- Can you find a word that starts like Devon's name?
- I see some words that end with *at.* What are they?
- Here are some books that we have read before. Can you find *at* in the titles? (The books might include the Berenstains' *Old Hat, New Hat,* Dr. Seuss's *The Cat in the Hat,* and Carle's *Have You Seen My Cat?*)

In the booklists that we include throughout this text, we annotate a number of children's books suitable for reading aloud to emergent readers. A number of these titles are available in both big book and little book format. The following list provides a small sampling of big books.

Developing Phonemic Awareness, Letter Identification, and Word Recognition

Children should receive some of their instruction in flexible small groups. You should have a defined time for small-group instruction. These lessons should be short and fast paced, moving from books to words to sounds, whole to part, or other times from part to whole. Small-group instruction need not focus on just one skill, but may incorporate work on phonemic awareness, phonics, word recognition, and reading little books. Small-group instruction allows you to tailor instruction to the needs of students, as you observe their responses and provide corrective feedback. Membership in the skill groups needs to remain flexible, so as students make progress they can move to another group. While you work with one group, other children can be in the reading corner, creating their own book, engaged in literacy focused play, or—if you are fortunate—working with an instructional assistant.

The Reading Corner

Big Books

Pam Adams. *This Old Man.* Child's Play International, 1999. Ten old men in colorful outfits are featured in this traditional counting song in big book format. 16 pages.

Doreen Cronin. *Click, Clack, Moo: Cows That Type.* Scholastic, 2004. When Farmer Brown's cows learn to type, they send him a note demanding electric blankets. 32 pages.

Lois Ehlert. *Eating the Alphabet.* Harcourt Brace, 1994. Beginning with *apricot* and *artichoke,* this big book takes readers on an alphabetical tour of the world of fruits and vegetables. 32 pages.

Muriel Feelings. *Moja Means One: Swahili Counting Book.* Puffin, 1994. This counting book, which portrays the language and customs of Swahili East Africa, is beautifully illustrated by Tom Feelings. 32 pages.

Lorraine Jean Hopping and Meredith Johnson. *Today's Weather Is. . . : A Book of Experiments.* Mondo Publishing, 2000. Questions suggest various weather experiments students can do, and students can follow instructions to discover the outcomes of these experiments. 32 pages.

Myra Cohn Livingston. *Space Songs.* Scholastic, 1994. This collection of poetry contemplating space is accompanied by bold illustrations. 32 pages.

Bruce McMillan. *Time To . . .* Scholastic, 1996. This story follows a kindergartner through his day as he learns to tell time. 32 pages.

Ann Morris. *Loving.* Scholastic, 1996. This book about families around the world is richly illustrated with color photos. 32 pages.

David Schwartz. *How Much Is a Million?* Morrow/ Mulberry, 1994. Marvelosissimo the Magician uses his magic to help explain the concepts of million, billion, and trillion. 32 pages.

Kate Waters and Madeline Slovenz-Low. *Lion Dancer: Ernie Wan's Chinese New Year.* Scholastic, 1995. In this story, 6-year-old Ernie prepares for his first Lion Dance during Chinese New Year. 32 pages.

Audrey Wood. *Silly Sally.* Harcourt, 1994. Sally, a power walker, turns a stroll to the city into a rollicking adventure in this rhyming text. 32 pages.

Figure 7.4 Allocating Time for Small-Group Activities

	Below-Level Students	On-Level Students	Above-Level Students
Phonological awareness	5 minutes	3–4 minutes	2–3 minutes
Letter-sound association	10 minutes	5 minutes	5 minutes
Word recognition	3 minutes	5 minutes	5 minutes
Text reading	2 minutes	6–7 minutes	7–8 minutes

Students have different needs in kindergarten. Some may have developed the insights about language and words that are necessary for phonemic awareness; others may still struggle. Thus, some students will need more intensive instruction whereas others can move on to work on word recognition and text reading. Students in your class whose first language is not English will have their own set of difficulties. Figure 7.4 suggests how you might allocate time for these activities, depending on the needs of the students.

PHONOLOGICAL AWARENESS

Phonological awareness can be developed through a wide range of activities. Experts recommend that teachers begin by developing students' awareness of syllables and then move to rhyming (Adams, Foorman, Lundberg, & Beeler, 1998). Next students should develop an awareness of initial and then final sounds, moving eventually to full phonemic awareness and the ability to blend and segment words. The following activities are recommended for developing phonological awareness. They should be structured so that students respond to each task simultaneously. You will want to involve students in every aspect of the activity, with what are called pupil response activities. So if you are working on listening for initial sounds, you can ask students to raise the M card for words like *milk, mother,* or *mat,* and the T card for words like *tiger* and *tepee.*

- Students clap to indicate their awareness of each syllable in a word (*el/e/phant, ti/ger*).
- Students indicate with a thumb up or down whether two words rhyme.
- Students indicate which of three words does not rhyme (*hat, sit, fat*).
- Students sort words or objects by initial sound. Repeat later and sort by the final sound.

Elkonin Boxes

- Students use Elkonin boxes to represent the sounds in words according to the number of phonemes. They push in two markers for the word *at* and three markers for the word *keep.*
- Students sort pictures into categories by the number of phonemes (sea; dog, run; jump, cat, kite)
- Students blend phonemes into words. (What is /n/ /i/ /s/—*nice*)

Additional ideas for developing phonological awareness can be found in *Phonemic Awareness in Young Children* (Adams et al., 1998), *The Phonological Awareness Handbook for Kindergarten and Primary Teachers* (Ericson & Juliebo, 1998), and *Making Sense of Phonics* (Beck & Beck, 2013).

LETTER-SOUND ASSOCIATIONS

While children are developing phonemic awareness, they can also learn to identify letters, associate letters and sounds, and even begin to identify words once they are ready for blending. According to Neuman and Roskos (2005) it is best to teach these in a meaningful way, starting with real books and moving whole to part. These three skills reinforce one another. In a small-group lesson the teacher might begin with a phoneme awareness activity, sorting pictures for initial sounds, then move to some letter recognition activities, matching upper- and lowercase letters, and finally associating letters and sounds by having students hold up letter cards when they hear a word that begins with the target sound.

Although there is no perfect sequence for teaching letter names and letter sounds, there are some accepted guidelines. Only a few letters and sounds should be taught at one time. Teach the most common letters first—*m, t, s, r*, but not *x* or *z*. Teach letters that are least likely to be confused, so *b* and *d* should not be taught together, whereas *t, s,* and *m* are quite distinct. Uppercase letters that do not look like their lowercase equivalents (*aA, eE, qQ*) should be taught later in the sequence; *O, P,* and *S* can be taught earlier. The following activities are suggested for small-group instruction to develop letter-name and letter-sound knowledge.

- Students match pictures to letter cards.
- Students match upper- and lowercase letters.
- Teacher says a word and the students indicate by pointing at small boards with three spaces for beginning, middle, and ending sounds where the designated sound falls in the word. "Listen for /a/. Is /a/ at the beginning, middle, or end of *mat?*"
- Children sing the alphabet song while touching the letters on their individual alphabet strip.
- Students read and discuss alphabet books, focusing on just a few letters and sounds each week.

WORD RECOGNITION

Young children can begin word recognition with a very easy text—a predictable or patterned book. First, the teacher should read the book and then students should echo the teacher, repeating line by line what she reads. Next, the students should attempt to read the book in a choral fashion. After the book has been read and discussed, the teacher should focus on a few words in the text by highlighting or framing these words. The words can then be placed on flashcards and the students with the teacher can study the words. Together they can segment the words into sounds, sort words by beginning or ending letters, and practice reading them. The words can be used in games like Bingo and Concentration.

Although learning phonemic awareness and decoding is the primary goal, some sight words need to be taught. The most common words in the language, *the, of, are, saw,* and *are*, have irregular spellings and must be memorized. Without knowing these high frequency function words, reading and writing are near impossible. So it is important to teach some sight words, but keep the number small, no more than 50 during the whole kindergarten year. Students need to know that there are words that follow the rules, *cat, pan,* and *lump*, and there are words that do not. This is the suggested sequence for teaching irregular high-frequency words (Beck & Beck, 2013). Figure 7.5 presents a list of sight word with irregular spelling.

- Say the target word and tell the student that it is one of the rule breakers.
- Display a sentence in which the target word appears.
- Read and reread the sentence aloud.
- Indicate the target word and read it aloud. Ask the students to read it aloud several times.
- Point to each letter and ask the students to spell the word aloud. It is a good idea to occasionally ask students to write the words saying each letter.

Figure 7.5 High Frequency Words with Irregular Spellings

Sight Words that Should be on the Word Wall			
are	have	many	this
after	help	much	too
because	here	myself	two
don't	his	never	under
every	I	of	was
from	if	on	what
friend	into	one	who
goes	is	said	with
going	its	say	yes
has	little	the	you

- Point out that some of the letters in the word follow the rules. For example, in the word *said*, the *s* and the *d* are pronounced as they consistently do. Only the *ai* violates the rules.

Writing Opportunities

In order to become increasingly competent readers, children need to become message-makers and authors themselves. For this to happen, you need to create authentic writing opportunities for them. Some tried-and-true approaches are discussed in the following sections.

JOURNALS

When children write, they begin to internalize the notion that ideas can be represented symbolically. We know several kindergarten and first-grade teachers who have students keep journals, beginning on the first day of school. The journal need not be elaborate—several sheets of paper folded over to make a little book would be sufficient. In the journal, students are encouraged to express themselves in whatever way they choose. They can be given ideas to write about or write without prompts. Like most emergent literacy activities, journal writing should be modeled for children, who should be shown many ways to express themselves in writing: drawing pictures, making squiggles, writing letters, and combining several forms of expression. Thus, children can "write" even if they do not yet know the letters of the alphabet. They can then read back what they have written, which is easiest if they can do so right away. Another way for young children to write is to dictate a sentence or two that you or a classroom aide writes down. As children experiment with writing, they should be encouraged to get their ideas down in print even if they do not know some letters or spellings; urge them to use invented spelling.

Kindergarten teacher Sid Burns invites each child to work with a special word each day:

> As children are busy illustrating their "word," I circulate around the room and take down dictations. Each child has his or her own journal. One student tells me a word that is "on her mind" or special to her that day. (For example, *love* and *heart* were big last week—Valentine's Day fell on Friday.) I write the dictated word in the child's journal. She can then trace or copy it. Sometimes children discuss the word with me or with other children, draw a picture that illustrates the word, and dictate a sentence or two for me to write down regarding the picture. For example, Marta asked me to write, "I love my dog. Her name is Asta." As I wrote the sentences, I used the opportunity to comment on the form of print in a way that was appropriate for Marta. I pointed to the word *dog* and said to her, "dog," emphasizing

the initial sound, /d/. "What letter makes that /d/?" Then I asked her to reread the two sentences and point to the words.

—Sid Burns, kindergarten teacher

LANGUAGE-EXPERIENCE ACTIVITIES

Copying down children's dictation and then having them read their own words has been termed the *language-experience approach*. With this approach, the teacher or an assistant writes down the words of a story spoken by a student or group of students, using the students' language. When the story is read, students can easily read along. The vocabulary is familiar because students generated it, and they have prior knowledge related to content because it is based on their experiences. Because this approach is entirely student centered, it is particularly useful for meeting the needs of students who vary in ethnic background, English language competence, or educational needs. In fact, as we point out in Chapter 14, it is an extremely valuable procedure to use with students whose first language is not English.

SHARED READING AND WRITING EXPERIENCES

Another opportunity that encourages writing is the shared reading and writing experience, which we discuss again in Chapters 13 and 14. In the Classroom 7.5 shows first-grade teacher Connie Martinez combining reading instruction with an opportunity for students to compose a rhyme together. Although the children are not *physically* writing the words, they are participating in the act of composing; their teacher provides a sturdy instructional scaffold.

In the Classroom 7.5

Reading and Writing Rhymes

Sitting in a large rocking chair, Ms. Martinez holds a big book of Mother Goose nursery rhymes. The children gathered around her can see the words on the first two pages as she begins singing the rhyme:

Lavender's blue, dilly, dilly, lavender's green; when I am King, dilly, dilly, you shallbe Queen.

Ms. Martinez has the children take turns pointing to the color words they know. She helps them with *lavender* and has them tell each other what color this is close to (for example, purple). "Is anyone wearing lavender or blue or green today?" she asks.

Next, she asks them which word in the verse rhymes with green.

"Queen!" they chime in unison.

Ms. Martinez stands up and writes *green* and *Queen* directly underneath each other on the portable chalkboard next to her. She asks the children to name the letters in each word and which letters they share.

"E-E-N!" a couple of children answer.

Then Ms. Martinez remarks, "*Dilly* is a silly word!"

So she writes *dilly* on the board, with *silly* right underneath it. She asks them if they can think of some names of boys that sound like *dilly* and *silly*. She helps by saying, "dilly, silly, Billy?"

They shout, "Yes." Then she says, "Dilly, silly, Cassandra?" and they shout, "No."

Ms. Martinez tells the children they are going to write their own rhyme. She puts a large chart pad on a stand. The chart has part of a rhyme already printed on it. The children will suggest words or letters to complete it, and Ms. Martinez will print them on the lines. She begins by asking the children if they want to write about "Silly Billy" or "Silly Willy." They opt for Willy. Ms. Martinez prints *Willy* in the blank on the chart. The children alternate rereading the rhyme, as Ms. Martinez points to each word, and adding a word in the blank. The poem they wrote by filling in the blanks is shown in the accompanying illustration. Every so often during the week, the children recite this rhyme either as a class or in partner reading, always pointing to the words as they say them.

Silly _____

Silly, silly, ___Willy___,
Silly, silly, m_e_ ,
I fell down and scratched my knee.
I stood up and shook my head.
I stood up and this is what I said:
Silly, silly, ___Willy___,
Silly, silly, m_e_ ,
I fell down and hurt my head.
I think I should just go to ___bed___ .

By the end of our week, some of the children on the playground were reciting the poem as they jumped rope. "Silly Willy" made a perfect jumprope jingle. We wouldn't be surprised if the children thought up new verses to add over the days and weeks to come!

MAKING BOOKS

Children can be encouraged to take their language-experience stories or perhaps write their own stories and make them into small books with illustrations. Bookmaking can be as elaborate or as simple as you wish. Books can be laminated and bound with a plastic spiral or hand-sewn binding or simply stapled together. We recommend saving the more elaborate bindings for class books that can be saved and read over and over again.

Student-written and -illustrated books provide a wonderful opportunity to involve children actively in writing and reading.

MAILBOXES

A classroom mailbox system in which students can post one letter a day and have pen pals to correspond with reinforces print awareness and gives students motivation for writing and for reading their own writing (because, early on, they will probably be the only ones who can read their messages).

PLAY CENTERS

Many kindergarten teachers include play centers in their classrooms. In these centers, children act out real or imagined situations and events. They might act out what happens at a restaurant or events in a story they have just heard. Literacy activities can easily be included in such play centers. In playing restaurant, for example, a simple pad of paper can be provided for a waitress or waiter to write down orders, or a chart of recipes can be printed for the cook to follow. Similarly, in planning to act out a story, you and the children might together block out the sequence of the story, illustrating it with simple pictures and a few words and phrases.

Listening and Speaking Opportunities

Of course, listening and speaking are normal parts of the kindergarten and first-grade school day. Here we briefly mention some specific activities that enhance skills in these areas and, as you know by now, promote skills in reading and writing as well.

READING ALOUD

We cannot overemphasize the importance of reading aloud to all children, but it is especially important for emergent readers and doubly so for students who have not had the benefit of being read to at home. When you read to your class, you give students a chance to hear fluent reading and to develop the critical skill of listening comprehension. You also provide a rich opportunity to develop vocabulary knowledge. The books you read aloud to students should be above their grade level. We want them to stretch and hear words and concepts that are not familiar. Moreover, you give them the pleasure of hearing a good story and sharing enthusiasm for it. You should also read aloud nonfiction books to demonstrate the process of learning from text. The children will be eager to contribute and will actually ask more questions during an information read-aloud than when you read fiction.

Reading aloud to students also helps to develop the book handling skills and the concept of print. As you read aloud, especially using a big book, the students watch you turn the pages, read from left to right as you point to the print. They will realize that the print tells the story. If you stop, you can fame a word with your hands and point to the letters and the beginning and the end of the book, thus building the students concept of print.

To create an effective read-aloud experience, it is helpful to keep the following suggestions in mind:

1. Select a story or information book that interests you as well as your students. The book could tie into a topic in science, social studies, or something you are studying in reading. The book should offer some new words that can be the focus for a follow-up discussion.

2. Pick good stopping points for discussing the story and elaborating on the information.

3. Before reading, introduce the new words and concepts. Set a purpose for listening.

4. During reading, stop briefly to define the new vocabulary and model one or more strategies. You might ask a question, clarify something that is difficult to understand, make a prediction, or solicit questions and comments from the children.

5. Whenever possible, invite students to join in! If a word or a phrase is repeated or if you are reading a story students have heard before, encourage them to read along with you. Also, some stories lend themselves to gestures and simple movement.

6. After you have finished reading, elaborate on the new vocabulary, writing the words on a word wall, where we keep track of new exciting words. Discuss the story or the new ideas learned.

7. After two days with the book, find another book that links to it. For example, you might find a non-fiction books that builds on the first book, or another book of the same genre.

After reading, extend into a writing activity. If you have just read a fiction book, create your own story through an interactive writing experience. You and the class will construct your own story on chart paper. If you have just read a non-fiction book you might create a poster of what you have learned. As the students become adept with writing they can create an information book of their own. Staple several sheets of paper together. Have the students select a topic, an animal. On each page the students draw a picture and write a fact about the animal using their invented spelling. As the students gain skill you can add in a title page and a table of contents. The activity will last several days.

For more ideas on reading aloud and a host of suggestions on specific books to read aloud, we strongly suggest Jim Trelease's *The New Read-Aloud Handbook* (1995).

RECORDINGS

Recording stories yourself or having a classroom aide or older student do so can provide you with an inexpensive and useful resource. Today, recordings can be made with an iPhone, iPad, or other tablet devices. There are several apps that can be purchased that enable this. With recordings, a number of children can listen to stories at any time during the day, and you are freed to give attention to other students. Here are some Apps recommended by the National Association for the Education of Young Children.

1. Look and Learn: Animal Alphabet (Ages 0–3)
2. Kids ABC Letters Lite (Ages 2 and Over)
3. Read Me Stories (Ages 3 and Over)
4. iWriteWords (Ages 3–5)
5. Reading Raven (Ages 5 and Under)
6. Monkey Word School Adventure (Ages 5 and Under
7. Endless Alphabet (Ages 5 and Under)

A Kindergarten Scenario*

To show how a very skillful teacher engages her students in the meaningful literacy experiences we have just described, here, we give you a glimpse into a typical day in Jonni Wolskee's full-day kindergarten class. Ms. Wolskee will be the tour guide. The

---

* Jonni Wolskee, from Dover, Delaware, describes a typical day in her kindergarten class.

location is a small urban school where 75 percent of the students qualify for a free or reduced-price lunch. The class of 26 students consists of 15 African American children, 8 Caucasians, and 3 Hispanics. It is December, and the types of literacy activities you will read about here have been going on all year. We choose to focus on an all-day kindergarten because two-thirds of American children are now enrolled in a full-day kindergarten program (NCES, 2004).

8:20.   The students begin their day with a daily morning assignment that reinforces skills—initial sound sorts, rhyming activities, and so on that have previously been taught while also giving the students an opportunity to "warm up" for their day. This morning, my students will complete a phonogram picture sort where they will sort the pictures into columns for the phonograms *-at, -am,* and *-ap.* Once they have finished gluing the pictures into the appropriate columns, they will then write the word next to each of the pictures and circle the phonogram in each word. However, because the students are at different developmental stages, I always have some finish rather quickly, while others are dragging it out to the bitter end. To keep the above- and on-level students from having behavior issues due to boredom, I make sure that in the center of their tables is a book basket that is loaded with previously read books that those students may read.

9:00.   After the students have completed their morning assignment, they transition to a rather large carpet in the front of my room where we begin our calendar time, reviewing the days of the week, the month, and the weather. This includes work on math concepts such as pattern, place value, and money. Reading consists of skill instruction, a morning message, and an interactive read-aloud.

MyLab Education
Video Example 7.4
This video shows how the teacher develops both phonemic awareness and letter sound associations.

- *Skill instruction.* I always keep a basket of letters and high frequency words that we are learning. Each and every day the students are drilled on their letters and sounds: /m/ *m,* /s/ *s,* /r/ *r,* and so on. We then read our reading words and segment and blend each word: students say "is," then break it apart into /i/ /z/, and then blend "is." This is meant to be a quick 2- to 3-minute drill.

- *Morning message.* The morning message, *Kindergarten News,* is written on chart paper. The message is usually connected to the book for our read-aloud and provides multiple opportunities to reinforce the structure of words, concept of print, linking letters and phonemes, alphabetic principle, blending, and encoding. The message is already written on the chart paper in a cloze sentence format (a sentence with a blank): *I like to help _____ at home.* I give explicit instruction as to where the sentence begins and what it begins with. I also will draw a box around the beginning letter of the sentence. As time goes on, I have the students show me the beginning of the sentence and then they have to put the box around it themselves. The students volunteer to come up and circle high-frequency words that they know, highlight finger spaces, discuss the punctuation used and why, and fill in the blank with a response. When it is time to write the words, we stretch the words as we write them. Again, I start off with a lot of modeling, but with scaffolded instruction, over time, the students will begin to take this job over from me until they are independent.

- *Read-aloud.* This morning we are reading *Swimmy* (Lionni, 1973). I begin with reading and tracking the title of the text. I tell the students that the title is the name that the author has given the book and often can give a clue as to what the book is about. I begin my think-aloud by saying, "I see quite a few red fish swimming in the sea. I also see just one black fish swimming alone. I think that Swimmy is the name of one of the fish. I wonder why the black fish is swimming alone?" I then ask the students about a time that they have ever been alone and how they felt when they were alone. One of my students said that he felt sad and lonely. I then say, "I think that the black fish feels lonely and sad. Let's read on to find out."

During reading we soon come to the part of the story where Swimmy feels sad and alone because the big tuna had eaten up all of his brothers and sisters. I remind the students of the prediction we made about Swimmy feeling lonely. I ask them to give me a thumbs up if our prediction was correct or a thumbs down if our prediction was incorrect. Most of my class gives me a thumbs up. However, I had a few put a thumb down, so I take the opportunity to explain why our prediction was correct. I try to maintain eye contact with those who misunderstood our prediction during my explanation.

During a fictional story such as *Swimmy*, we come across key vocabulary words that I have highlighted in highlighter tape. The words I selected for this story are *creatures*, *marvel*, and *school*. When I encounter the word in context I give a brief explanation of what the word means and move on: " 'Then, hidden in the dark shade of rocks and weeds, he saw a school of little fish, just like his own.' A school is a large group of fish." When reading a nonfiction story to the students, I always preteach the key vocabulary words using explicit instruction, but again give a quick explanation when we come to the word in the text without breaking stride. The vocabulary cards are used throughout the week in simple and quick reinforcement activities to enhance their understanding of the word so that they own it for future use.

When reading narrative text, I save my vocabulary focus for the end of the text. I go back into the text and find the word *creatures* in the story. I explain how it is being used in the text. I never ask the students what they think it means because it reinforces the wrong concept to everyone if they are incorrect. "It says that the sea is full of creatures. The creatures are the jellyfish, lobster, anemones, and all of the different fish that he saw." I then show the word *creatures* on an index card with a picture of living things on it and explain that the word *creature* means any living thing that is not a plant. This means that the jellyfish, lobster, anemones, and fish are all living things. I give examples of other living things and nonexamples such as chairs, rocks, plants, and so on.

I ask my students to describe how Swimmy and all of the red fish felt at the end of the story. Many of my students said, "Happy because they were able to scare away the bad fish who tried to eat them."

9:45.   During this time, I teach three ability-based reading groups. Each rotation lasts approximately 20 minutes, but I do try to squeeze in an extra 5 minutes with my struggling students whenever possible. The rotations include instruction with a teacher, instruction with a paraprofessional, and independent practice at a differentiated literacy center. My groups are ability based, which means that my students are grouped based on teacher observations and informal assessments. The groups are fluid, which means students will be moved in or out of their groups based on growth or needed reinforcement.

- *Small-group instruction.* During the 20 minutes, the students are allotted time for phonemic awareness activities, phonics activities, word recognition, and reading little books. However, students are not given the same amount of time to practice each skill. Struggling students are going to need more instruction in phonemic awareness and phonics activities whereas above-level students spend more time with word recognition and text reading. As my students grow in reading ability their instruction will change.

The students from my below-level group come and sit on their assigned spot on the carpet. We are working on two- and three-phoneme words. I show them an Elkonin box and three chips and tell them that we are going to count the sounds in some words. When I model the activity, I say, "My turn." Then I say the word "sit." I break the word apart—/s/ /i/ /t/—and move a chip into a box for each sound in the word. I tell them that we are going to do this together. The students each have an Elkonin board with three boxes on it. They also have three chips. I say, "Our Turn," and I say the word "sit" and they repeat the word "sit." Then, together we move the chips. I watch for any confusion and make the corrections now. Then I say, "Your Turn," and watch the students complete this independently. The students now complete this activity independently with the following words: *am, was, dug, be, done, chair, flew, is, thumb, bird.*

Next, we move to our phonics activity. I hold up a flip chart of letters. The consonants are on the ends with the vowels in the middle. This is my real/nonsense flip chart. I begin by making the last two letters *a* and *t* for the *-at* word family. These letters will not be changed. I begin by flipping the first letter to *c* and make the word *cat.* The students read the word *cat* together. I then change the *c* to *p* to make the word *pat* and the students read the word *pat.* I run through all the letters in the alphabet for the beginning sound and the students read them together. If they make any mistakes, I offer them corrective feedback and we move on. As the year goes on and they master this skill, I will then keep the beginning the same and only change the final letter: *cat, cap, caj, cab, cag,* and so on. When they master the final letter, they will then manipulate the middle vowel sound. We always discuss real versus nonsense words and often this affords me an opportunity to teach the meanings of new words.

For our book reading I pass out the story "The Mat." I read the story to the students the first time around. Then the students echo read the story with me. The next day the students will read it chorally and then independently. I use many kinds of texts—leveled readers, patterned text, and many nonfiction expository books. The lessons for the other groups will emphasize more decoding and text reading and focus less on phonemic awareness and letter-sound knowledge.

- *Literacy Centers.* These centers are meant to reinforce the skills that have been taught in small-group instruction and provide opportunities for students to read and write. There are two rules for centers: (1) There should always be an accountability piece to show that the student has spent his or her time meaningfully. For example, if the students are sorting words by letters they draw two pictures for a letter and write the word next to the picture. (2) The students need to be able to complete this work independently. This means that the work needs to be at the student's ability level. There are five literacy centers that I use in my classroom:

  1. Word center: Students play word games, sort pictures and words, and make words using cards and dice.
  2. Reading center: Students read, individually or with a partner, leveled books, nonfiction books, and pattern books. They draw and write about what they read.
  3. Listening center: Students listen to previously read and new stories. Then they draw pictures about the stories and write about what they have heard.
  4. Writing center: Students write about pictures, complete simple story frames, or complete cloze activities from books they have heard.
  5. Computer center: My students use various commercial computer reading programs.

When students have completed each of their center accountability pieces, they will put them back at their tables for me to correct.

11:00. Lunch.

11:30. Math. I use a math series that utilizes a lot of manipulatives and hands-on learning. This provides an excellent opportunity for students to write and express how they come to a particular answer or concept. I have the students use a strategy called Picture, Answer, Word. My students always draw a picture to show what the problem is, then they compute the answer, and finally, they write how they came to the answer.

12:10. Recess.

Ms. Wolskee leads her kindergarten students in a word recognition activity.

Courtesy of Peter Dewitz

12:40. Special classes.

1:30. Writing. My students write in their journals every day. Sometimes I pick the topic and other times they choose. I regularly model writing and present mini-lessons on some aspect of writing. My students learn to use word walls and to stretch words to aid spelling. In the mini-lessons we talk about how to develop ideas, how to organize sentences, and how to spell words. When our writing time is up, each of my students shares what they have written and we all discuss some of the wonderful ideas and details their peers came up with in their writing. We also talk about common mistakes that we observed in their writing as well. By the end of the year, they are so meticulous about their writing that many do not want to misspell anything and completely embrace the word wall.

2:30. Social studies/science. The students are learning about pumpkins so I am reading the nonfiction text *A Day at the Pumpkin Patch* (Faulker & Krewesky, 2006). I begin with a KWL activity. K – What do you know; W – What do you want to know; L – What have we learned. I write on a KWL chart and the students tell me what they know about pumpkins: "They are orange. Pumpkins are round. You make them into jack-o'-lanterns." Then I ask my students what they would want to know about pumpkins and they reply with questions. "Do pumpkins grow?" "Where do pumpkins come from?" "What is in a pumpkin?" When I write their responses on the chart, I am always stretching the word out loud for my students to hear as I write it. I tell the students that we will read and look for the answers to their questions and hopefully learn some new interesting facts about pumpkins.

I will preteach the key vocabulary words to the students before I read the text. The words we are learning are *stem, ribs*, and *pulp*. I show the students vocabulary cards with the pictures and words on them. I hold up a picture of ribs and tell the students that the ribs of the pumpkins are the deep lines or ridges that run from the top of the pumpkin to the bottom. I ask the students whether our classroom pumpkin has ribs or not. They all give me a thumbs up. I continue in the same way with the other vocabulary words.

I read the text to the students and briefly discuss the vocabulary words as they come up in the text. I also make sure to briefly stop and discuss the questions from the KWL chart as we find the answers to them in the text. When I finish reading the text, I ask my students what they have learned about pumpkins from our book. They gave responses such as "Some pumpkins have ribs. There are seeds inside of pumpkins. Little pumpkins are green. Pumpkins grow in a pumpkin patch. Pumpkins seeds are planted in the spring and summer. Pumpkins have stems. Pumpkin blossoms are yellow." The next day we will read a fictional book about jack-o'-lanterns.

3:10 Dismissal.

Reflect and Apply

5. Jonni Wolskee is an outstanding teacher, and she does a terrific job developing her kindergartners' literacy skills. She engages her children in reading and writing experiences in which their understanding of books and print can be nurtured. She also provides direct explicit instruction in print concepts, phonemic awareness, and vocabulary. How important is exposure versus direct explicit instruction? Which children need which type of instruction?

Assessing Emergent Literacy Skills

We assess students' literacy development for several reasons. As a teacher you will need to know the students' current level of knowledge and skill so you can properly focus your instruction. At times you need to report your students' progress to parents or the administrators in your building. Finally, you might want to determine if your students have met the standards set by the school or the district. In this section, we will focus on informal or formative assessments that you can use in the classroom, but we start with a few standardized assessment systems that are widely used. These formal and standardized tools should not be used with the whole class or the whole school. In-depth diagnosis is only necessary when you have identified problems through more informal assessments.

Standardized Assessments

The Dynamic Indicators of Basic of Early Literacy Skills (DIBELS) is widely used in the primary grades to assess early reading skills. Included in the assessments are tests of letter names, letter sounds, phonemic segmentation, (dibels.org/dibelsnext.html) oral reading fluency (only for mid-first grade and beyond) and reading comprehension. All of the subtests on the DIBELS are administered for just one minute so the test measures the automaticity of the skills and some children's skills may be accurate but not yet automatic.

Aimsweb provides an Assessment of Early Literacy (https://www.aimsweb.com/) that is very similar to the DIBELS. Aimsweb provides subtests for assessing letter name fluency, letter sound fluency, phonemic segmentation fluency, and nonsense (decoding) fluency. Like DIBELS, all of the tests are administered for just one minute, so accuracy is confounded with automaticity. Teachers must be cautious not to over interpret the results and begin to teach these skills and knowledge stressing speed.

The Phonological Awareness Test-2 (https://www.wpspublish.com/) is a flexible instrument that allows you to assess letter names, rhyme detecting, and production, and the awareness of syllables, initial sounds, final sounds, and full phonemic segmentation. The test also has subtests for measuring letter names, letter sounds, and decoding. The test allows you to use as few or as many subtests as desired, depending on the age and development of the students.

Informal Assessment Procedures

Within your classroom there are a number of procedures that you can use to assess your students' progress with early reading skills. These informal measures can help you determine the students' knowledge of letter names, letter sounds, phonemic awareness, and early insights about their reading comprehension. As we stressed early in the chapter, phonemic awareness and letter name knowledge are the best predictors of students' ability to decode and learn to read. If you go to the website for this chapter you will find an emergent literacy inventory. As an alternative, here are some other means of assessing the students' knowledge.

Letter names. The easiest assessment of letter names is to print each letter, lower and upper case, on flashcards and test each student individually. Present the letters in a random order and ask the student the name of each letter. Develop a record sheet so you can mark which letter the student knows and which they do not. Analyze the results by considering these questions.

- How many letters does the child know?
- How many letters that you have taught does the child know?
- What letters does he confuse? Confusing b and d is common, confusing s and m is very uncommon.

Letter sound. Take the same flash cards and repeat the assessment but ask the students the sound that the letter makes. Present the flash cards in a random order.

You may want to know how many letter sounds the student knows or how many of the sounds that you taught the student is able to remember.

Phonemic Awareness. The Yopp-Singer Test of Phonemic Segmentation (Yopp, 1995) is a quick individual assessment of young children's ability to segment words. The test, while simple, is both reliable and valid and highly correlated with word attack skills and word recognition. We recommend this test be used during the second half of kindergarten through the second grade. The directions and the test items are presented in Figure 7.6. Children who score most of the items correct (80%) are considered phonemically aware. Those who score about 50 percent are demonstrating emerging phonemic segmentation skills. and those who score fewer than 30 percent of the items, or none at all, lack appropriate levels of phonemic awareness.

Reading Comprehension and Book Concept. This informal test was adapted from the work of Alison Paris and Scott Paris (no relation) to assess young children's knowledge of book handling skills and reading comprehension (Paris & Paris, 2003). The original task correlated well with other tests of reading comprehension and was a good predictor of students' future comprehension ability.

The students are given a short, easy picture book and asked to look through it, studying the pages, the illustrations, and talking about what they are "reading." We recommend a book like *The Bear's Toothache* (McPhail, 1980) that has two characters, a simple problem, three events, and a resolution. While the child is looking through the book, the teacher notes if the child holds the book properly, orients it, turns the pages right to left and moves through the book at a proper speed. Next, the teacher reads the story to the child. After the book is read, the teacher asks the student to retell the story, pretending that the teacher did not hear the story or did not understand it. The directions for the assessment process are provided in Figure 7.7.

As the student retells the story you can note if she understands who are the characters, the setting, the initiating event, the problem and resolution. Adding some inferential questions allows you to explore the student's ability to infer character feelings, causation, predictions, and even theme.

MyLab Education
Click here to download a printable version of Figure 7.6

Figure 7.6 Yopp-Singer Test of Phonemic Segmentation

Directions: Today we're going to play a word game. I'm going to say a word and I want you to break the word apart. You are going to tell me each sound in the word in order. For example, if I say "old" you should say /o/ - /l/ - /d/. Be sure to say the sounds, not the letters in the words. Let's try a few together.

Practice items (Assist the child in segmenting these items as necessary) ride, go, man.

Test items: (Circle those items for which the student offers correct segments: incomplete responses may be recorded on the blank line following the item.)

1. dog _____	12. lay _____
2. keep _____	13. race _____
3. fine _____	14. zoo _____
4. no _____	15. three _____
5. she _____	16. job _____
6. wave _____	17. in _____
7. grew _____	18. ice _____
8. that _____	19. at _____
9. red _____	20. top _____
10. me _____	21. by _____
11. sat _____	22. do _____

SOURCE: Yopp, H. K. & Singer, H.(1995). A test for assessing phonemic awareness in young children. The Reading Teacher, 49(1) 20–29

Figure 7.7 Assessing **Narrative Comprehension Picture Walk Task**

"We're going to look through this book together, and as we go through it I want you to tell me whatever you are thinking about the pictures or the story."

MyLab Education
Click here to download a printable version of Figure 7.7

Picture Walk element	Score Description	Score
1. Book-handling skills Orients book correctly, has sense of appropriate viewing speed and order (viewing errors may include skipping pages or speeding through pages)	Incorrectly handles book and makes more than two viewing errors	0
	Makes one to two viewing errors (e.g., skips pages)	1
	Handles book appropriately and makes no viewing errors	2
2. Engagement Behavioral and emotional involvement during Picture Walk, as judged by attention, interest in book, affect, and effort	Displays off-task behavior or negative comments	0
	Displays quiet, sustained behavior	1
	Shows several examples of attention, affect, interest, or effort (e.g., spontaneous comments)	2
3. Picture comments Discrete comments about a picture, which can include describing objects, characters, emotions, actions, and opinions as well as character vocalizations	Makes no picture comments	0
	Makes one picture comment or verbalization	1
	Makes two or more comments or verbalizations about specific pictures	2
4. Storytelling comments Makes comments that go across pictures and demonstrate an understanding that the pictures tell a coherent story—can include narration, dialogue, using book language and storytelling voice	Makes no storytelling comments	0
	Provides storytelling elements, but not consistently	1
	Through narration or dialogue, connects story events and presents a coherent story line	2
5. Comprehension strategies Displays vocalizations or behaviors that show attempts at comprehension such as self-corrections, looking back and ahead in book, asking questions for understanding, making predictions about story	Demonstrates no comprehension strategies	0
	Exhibits one instance of comprehension strategies	1
	Demonstrates comprehension strategies at least two or more times	2

Questions for Comprehension Assessment
Explicit Questions

1. [Book closed, characters]
   Who are the characters in this story? (replacement words: people, animals)
2. [Book closed, setting]
   Where does this story happen? (replacement words: setting, take place)
3. [initiating event]
   Tell me what happens at this point in the story. Why is this an important part of the story?
4. [problem]
   If you were telling someone this story, what would you say is going on now? Why did this happen?
5. [outcome resolution]
   What happened here? Why does this happen?

Implicit questions

1. Tell me what the people are feeling in this picture. Why do you think so? (Feelings)
2. Why did the _____? (Causal inferences)
3. What do you think the people would be saying here? Why would they be saying that? (Inference)
4. This is the last picture in the story. What do you think happens next? Why do you think so? (Prediction)
5. In thinking about everything that you learned after reading this book. What do you think the main character learned? What do you think you learned? (Theme)

Narrative Comprehension Task COMPREHENSION SCORING

We suggest that you assign the following points when you score the student's retelling.

Explicit information

Characters

- 2 points = response indicates who are the characters and their relationship to one another
- 1 point = response contains at least two of the story's characters
- 0 points = response provides only one character, or answer is inappropriate

Setting

- 2 points = response indicates an understanding of multiple settings
- 1 point = response provides only one setting
- 0 points = response is not an appropriate setting

Initiating event

- 2 points = response identifies the initiating event and links it with other relevant
- story information (e.g., with the problem)
- 1 point = response identifies the story element (e.g., the initiating event)
- 0 points = response fails to identify the initiating event

Problem

- 2 points = response identifies the problem and links it with other relevant story information (e.g., with the initiating action)
- 1 point = response identifies the story element (e.g., the problem)
- 0 points = response fails to identify the problem

Outcome resolution

- 2 points = response identifies the outcome resolution and links it with other relevant story information (e.g., the problem or the initiating action)
- 1 point = response identifies the story element (e.g., the initiating action)
- 0 points = response fails to identify the outcome resolution

Implicit information

Feelings

- 2 points = response indicates the inference of appropriate character feelings and connects the feelings to other pages or events
- 1 point = response indicates the inference of appropriate character feelings
- 0 points = response is not an appropriate inference of character feelings

Causal inference

- 2 points = response is an appropriate inference that is explained by using events from multiple pages
- 1 point = response is an appropriate inference that is derived at the page level
- 0 points = response fails to include an appropriate causal inference

Dialogue

- 2 points = response indicates the inference of appropriate character dialogue and connects the dialogue to other pages or events
- 1 point = response indicates the inference of appropriate character dialogue
- 0 points = response does not concern character dialogue or is not relevant

Prediction

- 2 points = response represents a prediction that used previous action or pages from the story
- 1 point = response indicates a prediction that could be made based only on the last picture of the story
- 0 points = response does not contain an appropriate prediction

Theme

- 2 points = response indicates the incorporation of multiple events in order to create a narrative-level theme
- 1 point = response is a simple theme that uses information from one aspect of the story
- 0 points = response does not indicate an understanding of any theme

SOURCE: Paris, A. N. & Paris, S. G. (2003). Assessing narrative comprehension in young children. *Reading Research Quarterly*, 38(1), 36–77.

MyLab Education **Self-Check 7.4**

MyLab Education **Application Exercise 7.2:** Describing a Print-Rich Environment

MyLab Education **Application Exercise 7.3:** Reading Aloud to Young Children

MyLab Education **Application Exercise 7.4:** Understanding Comprehension Development

---

Concluding Remarks

In this chapter on emergent literacy, we talked about the progression most children follow as they learn to read and the many and varied learning experiences they need in order to become readers and writers. In learning to read, at first children may rely on distinctive visual cues such as word length, initial or distinctive letters, and illustrations as the primary ways to access printed meaning. As children gain phonemic awareness and letter knowledge, they use their understanding that letters correspond to speech sounds as a means to recognize words. Using letter-sound knowledge is often difficult because reading requires an understanding of the rather abstract concept of phonemes. In fact, learning to read is much harder than learning to speak because reading requires a *conscious* awareness of phonemes that is not needed in speaking. The knowledge and competencies that children need to gain as developing readers include knowledge of stories, phonemic awareness,

alphabet knowledge, and a beginning understanding of how letters and sounds relate to make printed words.

The latter part of this chapter described instructional ideas for facilitating and nurturing children's growing literacy in the four modes of language—reading, writing, listening, and speaking. These included creating a literate classroom environment and providing a multitude of reading, writing, listening, and speaking experiences. Some of these literacy activities can revolve around the classroom morning meeting, morning message, and daily schedule. Other important experiences suggested were free reading and engaging students with a variety of books while providing activities that foster knowledge of how printed language works. Writing opportunities, also stressed in this chapter, are crucial to help children learn about the form and function of written language. Some ways to provide these opportunities include student journals, language-experience activities, the shared reading and writing experience, book-making, classroom mailboxes, and play centers.

Finally, listening and speaking opportunities for emergent readers were discussed. These included reading aloud, choral reading, audio recordings, and sing-alongs. The chapter concluded with a kindergarten scenario that described the many and varied literacy activities Ms. Wolskee provides for her kindergartners.

Besides the many practical and concrete ideas we hope you have gleaned from this chapter, what we also hope you will take away is the underlying message that our job as teachers of young children is to provide the kinds of literacy experiences that ensure, for all children, the strongest possible literacy footing on which to build lifelong reading and writing skills and a lifelong love of reading.

Extending Learning

1. Find an adult who reads to a young child at home or in a day care center. Carefully watch and listen to their story-book interactions. How does the adult keep the child's attention? What appears to interest the child? What does the child wonder about in the story? What does the child ask about? What is the child learning about the form or content of books and print in this interaction?

2. Observe a preschool or kindergarten classroom. Make a list of the kinds of literacy activities you see. Then explain how each of these activities helps children learn about books and print. Alternatively, or in addition, observe a preschool or kindergarten child outside of school, and make a list of the literacy activities the child is involved in.

3. In the latter part of the chapter, we mentioned using books with children for three different purposes—to motivate children to expand their knowledge of the world and their imaginations by reading, to highlight the sounds of language in words, and to engage students in reading right from the start by using books with predictable text and helpful illustrations. Go to a library, perhaps a public library, that has a good collection of children's books. Begin an annotated list of books that you think will motivate children to read and to expand their knowledge of the world, books that highlight the sounds of language in words, and books that contain predictable text and helpful illustrations that allow reading right from the start. Include five to ten books in each of these three categories.

4. Go to a kindergarten class to observe children's writing activities. Jot down the different kinds of activities you see them engaged in. Write a paragraph or so describing which of the writing opportunities presented in this chapter you would most like to try in your own classroom, and why.

5. Record samples of children's writing. Examine their spelling and see what their spelling reveals about children's knowledge of phonology and orthography.

Children's Literature

Bennett, J. (1997). *Teeny Tiny.* New York: Putnam. In this reprint illustrated by Tomi de Paola, a very small woman finds a very small bone and puts it away in her cupboard before she goes to bed. Illustrated. Also available in Spanish. 32 pages.

Berenstain, S., & Berenstain, J. (1970). *Old Hat, New Hat.* New York: Random House. Rhyming text poses the question of whether a new hat can really replace a perfect old one. 32 pages.

Carle, E. (1996). *Have You Seen My Cat?* New York: Simon & Schuster. A boy encounters cats of all sorts while searching for his own lost cat. 24 pages.

Cowley, J. (1990). *Dan the Flying Man.* Bothell, WA: The Wright Group. This book about a flying man is designed for group reading. 16 pages.

dePaolo, T. (1978). *The Popcorn Book.* New York: Holiday House. Two boys are at home making popcorn for a light snack. Interspersed into the narrative is the history of popcorn and the Native Americans who developed it. 32 pages.

Faulkner, M., & Krawesky, A. (2006). *A Day at the Pumpkin Patch.* Toronto: Scholastic. A nonfiction book that describes pumpkins and how they grow and gives instructions on how to carve a jack-o'-lantern. 32 pages.

Gibbons, G. (1993). *From Seed to Plant.* New York: Holiday House. A simple introduction to plants, discussing reproduction, pollination, seed dispersal, and growth from seeds. 32 pages.

Hall, J. (2000). *What Does Rabbit Say?* New York: Double-day. Rhyming text follows a boy and girl as they ask what sound their pet rabbit makes. 32 pages.

Hoban, T. (1988). *Look, Look, Look.* New York: Greenwillow. In this colorful book, photographs of familiar objects are first viewed through a cut-out peephole, then revealed in their entirety. 42 pages.

Hoban, T. (1973). *Over, Under, and Through and Other Spatial Concepts.* New York: Macmillan. Spatial concepts are illustrated with text and photos. 32 pages.

Jenkins, E. (2005). *That New Animal.* New York: Farrar, Straus and Giroux. The arrival of a new baby is told from two dogs' point of view. 32 pages.

Joosse, B. (2005). *Nikolai, the Only Bear.* New York: Philomel. Nikolai, the only bear of the 100 orphans at the Russian orphanage, finds the perfect family at last. 32 pages.

Keats, E. J. (1998). *The Snowy Day.* New York: Viking. This 1963 Caldecott Medal classic about a young city boy enjoying adventures in the snow, is now in board book format. Spanish text and CD available. 32 pages.

Lionni, L. (1973). *Swimmy.* New York: Dragonfly Books.

Lobel, A. (1985). *Whiskers & Rhymes.* New York: Scholastic. This collection contains short, humorous rhymes in the nursery rhyme tradition. 48 pages.

Marshall, J. (1989). *The Three Little Pigs.* New York: Dial. In this version of the familiar tale, one of the three pigs survives the wolf by using its head. 32 pages.

McPhail, D. (1980). *The Bear's Toothache.* New York: Enterprise. 31 pages.

Pomerantz, C. (1993). *If I Had a Paka: Poems in Eleven Languages.* New York: Mulberry Books. A collection of 12 poems incorporating words from 11 languages, including Swahili, Samoan, Yiddish, Indonesian, Vietnamese, and Dutch. Unnumbered.

Rice, E. (1989). *Peter's Pockets.* New York: Greenwillow. Peter's new pants don't have any pockets, so Uncle Nick lets Peter use his until Peter's mother solves the problem in a clever way. 32 pages.

Seuss, Dr. (1957). *The Cat in the Hat.* New York: Random House. Two children sitting at home on a rainy day are visited by a cat that shows them some tricks and games. CD available. 61 pages.

Seuss, Dr. (1963). *Hop on Pop.* New York: Random House. Pairs of rhyming words are introduced and used in simple sentences. CD available. 64 pages.

Seuss, Dr. (1974). *There's a Wocket in My Pocket!* This is a good book for developing phonemic awareness. New York: Random House. CD available. 24 pages.

Tafuri, N. (1987). *Do Not Disturb.* New York: Greenwillow. On the first day of summer, the forest creatures scurry about and make noise in this wordless picture book. 32 pages

Tafuri, N. (1983). *Early in the Morning in the Barn.* New York: Greenwillow. This almost-wordless picture book depicts farm animals along with some text showing the sounds they make. 32 pages.

Tafuri, N. (1996). *Have You Seen My Duckling?* New York: Greenwillow. This 1985 Caldecott Honor book, in which a mother duck leads her brood around the pond as she searches for one missing duckling, is now in board book format. 32 pages.

Wildsmith, B. (1982). *Cat on the Mat.* Oxford, UK: Oxford University Press. The cat liked to sit on the mat until the other animals wanted to sit on it too. 16 pages.

MyLab Education

Now go to the topics "Phonemic Awareness/Phonics" and "Emergent Literacy" in the MyEducationLab (www.myeducationlab.com) for your course, where you can:

- Find learning outcomes for the topics covered in this chapter along with the IRA standards that connect to these outcomes.
- Complete assignable activities in the Assignments and Activities section that show concepts in action to help you synthesize and apply strategies.
- Explore IRIS Center Resources—training enhancement materials that provide you with research-validated information and interactive materials to develop your skills in working with students.
- Apply and practice your understanding of the teaching skills identified in the chapter with the Building Teaching Skills and Dispositions exercises.

Chapter 8
Word Recognition

 Learning Outcomes

After reading and studying this chapter you should be able to:

8.1 Discuss why the process of learning to read words presents unique challenges to children who are already proficient oral language users.

8.2 Describe the structure of oral and written English and why understanding the alphabetic principle is the key to successful reading.

8.3 Discuss our position on phonics and learning to read and its implications for beginning reading instruction.

8.4 List the stages of learning to read and use this knowledge to understand a child's current level of functioning.

8.5 Understand the general principles of word study and be able to implement lessons that will develop the word recognition skills of young children.

Classroom Vignette

Six-year-old Anthony tries to read a page from the popular children's book *Rosie's Walk* by Pat Hutchins. He sits in a circle with other children around his first-grade teacher, Ms. Sullivan. Yesterday, Ms. Sullivan and the children read the story aloud together. The story is about a hen named Rosie, who takes a walk around a farmyard, blissfully ignorant of the fox that follows her. Along her way, Rosie walks

> across the yard
> around the pond
> over the haystack
> past the mill.

Ms. Sullivan has all the children point to the words as they read. Some children are better at this than others. Ms. Sullivan either has the entire class read a line aloud, calls on a few children to read, or calls on one child to read. She has just called on Anthony. He points to *around* and slowly says, "around the … ," stops, and looks up. Ms. Sullivan suggests that he look at the picture.

Anthony looks at the page and asks, "Tree?"

"Well," says Ms. Sullivan, "it does look as if she might walk around that tree, but what is the tree in front of? What is all this?" (as she points to the pond).

Anthony smiles and says, "Water."

"Yes," agrees Ms. Sullivan. "It is water. Remember, though, it is a special kind of water. Look at the word. What letter does it start with?"

"*P*," replies Anthony.

"*P*, puh—does *water* start with a puh?" asks Ms. Sullivan. "No. So it can't be *water*. Look at the letters. *P*, puh, and the *on* and *d*. You know the letter *d*."

"*D*, duh," volunteers Indigo.

"Yes." Pointing to the letters, Ms. Sullivan slowly says, "It's a puhond."

"*Pond*," declares Anthony.

The Importance of Recognizing Printed Words

For young children like Anthony and for most children, learning to recognize printed words is *the* big challenge on the way to becoming a reader. There are a lot of places Rosie the hen could walk around, and guessing words rarely works. Rather, the reader, like Anthony, must confront the print itself. Anthony is a typical 6-year-old native English speaker. He entered first grade with a command of spoken English that is nearly complete in terms of its underlying grammar and phonological development. He already has a vocabulary that would be the envy of any nonnative English speaker who, as an adult, is trying to learn English. And his emerging literacy skills are evident in his responses to Ms. Sullivan. Nonetheless, Anthony, like most first-grade children, will work hard at learning to recognize words and acquiring a basic reading vocabulary. Also, like most young children, Anthony will depend on his classroom teacher to help him acquire these reading skills.

Clearly, both spoken and printed English involve the same language. But the reason Anthony can't read, although he is already quite competent at speaking and understanding oral English, is that he does not yet know how to translate the printed word into the spoken word. The printed word is a barrier between him and the meaning of the text. He needs to learn how to get meaning from this printed form of language. To do this, he must, in a sense, get his eyes to do what his ears currently do for him.

The goal of both listening and reading is the same—to construct meaning, to understand. But it is easier to understand when listening than when reading, for several reasons. We will briefly look at six of these reasons and why Anthony's task as a reader is harder than his task as a listener.

Why Listening Is Easier Than Reading

Spoken language is characterized by a number of features that help speakers to communicate. These features are much less present in written language, as we will discuss.

SHARED BACKGROUND KNOWLEDGE

Conversational partners typically share background knowledge about topics. When talking with a friend, you most likely share a history of the people, places, and events the two of you discuss. You probably know which words, concepts, and topics your friend will easily understand and which will require more elaboration. This knowledge of your friend enables you to adjust your language as needed. There is typically much less shared background knowledge between an author and readers. For example, Pat Hutchins, who wrote *Rosie's Walk*, does not know if Anthony has ever seen a pond.

IMMEDIATE FEEDBACK

When you are listening to what a friend is saying and don't understand what she says, you can simply tell her so—"Wait a minute. What do you mean when you say to 'caramelize' the onions before I put them in the stew? How do I caramelize them?" In contrast, when you don't understand something you are reading in a book, you cannot ask the author what she meant.

VISUAL CUES FROM THE SPEAKER

A listener can see the speaker's features. Lips move as they shape sounds. The movement provides visual clues to the speech sounds being produced. In a noisy environment, these clues are especially useful. Additionally, speakers can enhance their message by exaggerating or adding intonation, facial expressions, vocal emphasis, tone of voice, repetition, and gesture. Body language can even override the speaker's words and send a different message than the words do.

MORE COMMON WORDS

Words used in spoken English are typically more common than those used in written English. For instance, in a conversation with a friend, you might say, "Last night, I just talked on and on about …" In penning your autobiography, however, you might write, "All evening, I chattered incessantly about …" Someone reading your autobiography will need to know what the words *chattered* and *incessantly* mean. If they do not, they will not understand your message. The more unfamiliar readers are with the words on a page, the more difficult the reading will be.

CONTEXTUALIZED MEANING

In a conversation, the listener benefits from the context created by the shared background knowledge, immediate feedback, visual cues, and more common vocabulary that are characteristic of spoken language. Conversely, when a reader reads, he must construct meaning without many of these supports. Without such supports, meaning is *decontextualized* (Purcell-Gates, 1989).

NO TRANSLATION NEEDED

Most important, the input modality in listening is primarily aural. A listener hears the words and immediately understands the message. In contrast, the input modality in reading is visual. To access meaning in printed language, a reader must essentially translate the printed words into their spoken forms. Thus, a child's basic problem in learning to read is learning to translate printed words into the spoken language she already understands.

Skilled Readers Automatically Recognize Words

Skilled readers recognize words automatically. They can identify words so quickly that they don't need to consider the meaning of the surrounding context (Adams, 1990; McConkie & Zola, 1981; Stanovich, 1991a, 1991b, 1992). For example, if you are reading "Kevin was walking his …" and then come to the word *dog*, you automatically—instantaneously and without conscious attention—process the letters in *dog*, even though in this case the word is fairly predictable. This seemingly obsessive processing of the letters in words actually makes word recognition faster than trying to predict upcoming words based on context, such as guessing the kind of animal Kevin might be walking.

Because young children cannot read many printed words automatically, we encourage them to use the context, any illustrations, and what they already know about language and the world to support their fledgling word recognition. However, as a child is taught specific ways in which letters relate to sounds, these letter-sound cues to word identification must take precedence over contextual and picture cues. Ultimately, letter-sound cues provide much more reliable information and a more efficient means to word recognition than do contextual cues or illustrations.

Your ability to reflect on, enjoy, and learn from a text depends on your thinking about the content as you read. Automatic word recognition enables a reader to think about content when reading. Still, automatic word recognition does not ensure good comprehension. It's what is called a necessary but insufficient condition. Even with it, a reader may lack the prior knowledge, conceptual background, interest, analytic skill, wit, and other factors required to understand a particular text.

The challenge you will face as a teacher of young children is to help them learn to recognize words without losing sight of the goal of reading—getting meaning. Children must learn how to rapidly pronounce *pond*, but they must also know the meaning. Accurate and automatic word recognition is the quickest route to a text's meaning. Explicit instruction in letter-sound patterns and relationships will be helpful for the vast majority of children.

Learning to recognize words is not an isolated skill but is linked to children's ongoing language development. We used to believe that word recognition and listening comprehension were the two major components of learning to read—the simple view of reading (Hoover & Gough, 1990). If you can recognize words, turning them into speech, then your listening comprehension skills would lead to reading comprehension. Recent research suggests that word recognition and comprehension are both influenced by students' vocabulary (Language & Reading Research Consortium, 2015). The link between vocabulary and comprehension is relatively obvious—if you don't know what the words mean, then comprehension is difficult. The link between vocabulary and word recognition is less obvious, and to explain this link, we turn to Charles Perfetti's Lexical Quality theory (2007).

We know that after a young child successfully decodes a new word, such as /b/ /a/ /t/ a few times, the word enters his reading vocabulary and with a bit of practice becomes a sight word, *bat*. Imagine the child lives in New York City and is sounding out the words *log* and *hog*. In NYC, people don't use *logs* to heat their apartments and *pork*, not *hogs*, are found in the grocery story. Perfetti and others argue that to know a word well means that the reader has a knowledge of the word's phonology (pronunciation), orthography (spelling), grammar, and meaning. When our child in NYC encounters *log* and *hog*, these words are not in his lexical or meaning vocabulary and, thus, become sight words with greater difficulty. Vocabulary supports word recognition in two ways. It enables the child to have a consolidated knowledge of words so that they become instantly available during comprehension. Second, a deep knowledge of words helps the child use what they know to figure out new words (Language & Reading Research Consortium, 2015). This is dramatically so for the English learner who struggles to sound out words for which they don't know the meaning. Consider these two French words, *je voudrais*. You could pronounce them, but without knowing their meaning, *I would like*, the words will not be retained as sight words.

In this chapter, we help you to build your understanding of the structure of spoken and printed words and of instructional procedures for teaching beginning readers how to recognize words. Without instruction in how to recognize words, most children will struggle with learning to read in first grade. And studies in several countries with different curricula and languages (Clay, 1979; Juel, 1994; Lundberg, 1984) have found that children who flounder with reading at this tender age have great difficulty catching up. Hence, it is critical for teachers of young children to be thoroughly competent in teaching beginning reading. Word recognition is a considerable focus of reading instruction in the early primary grades.

MyLab Education
Video Example 8.1
This video shows how a teacher helps students integrate orthographic, phonological, and semantic knowledge.

MyLab Education Self-Check 8.1

MyLab Education Application Exercise 8.1: Responding to a Parent's Concern: Why Their Brilliant Son Is Struggling to Learn to Read

The Structure of Spoken and Printed Words

Say your name out loud. You just created speech. You used your vocal system to modify the flow of air as you exhaled from your lungs. There are a limited number of ways you can affect this exhalation in your throat. You can modify it with your tongue and with your lips. You can change the direction in which the outgoing breaths are channeled and the length of time it takes the air to pass through the vocal system. Making a speech sound requires several simultaneous manipulations. You can build a puff of air behind your closed lips and let it suddenly burst out to make a /p/ sound; or, as you let out the burst, you can move your tongue up to touch the ridge behind your upper front teeth and make it a /t/ sound.

The Makeup of Spoken and Written English

The speech sounds that are used to distinguish one word from another in a particular language are called *phonemes*. In English, /s/ and /e/ are phonemes. Phonemes are a rather abstract level of language analysis, and what is perceived as a phoneme differs from one language to another. In English there are approximately 44 phonemes. By comparison French has 39 phonemes and Japanese 22.

PHONEMES: VOWELS AND CONSONANTS

Phonemes are divided into vowel sounds and consonant sounds. *Vowel* sounds are made when the air leaving your lungs is vibrated in the larynx but then has a clear passage from the larynx to outside your mouth. How you hold your tongue as the air passes by determines which vowel sounds you make. *Consonants* are speech sounds that are made when the airflow is obstructed in some way in your mouth. For example, the consonant sound /p/ is made by letting air build behind the lips before it is released from your mouth. Spanish and Japanese have five vowel sounds, but English has 12 with many different ways to spell them. Consider the long sound of /a/ in maid, made, pay, break, reign, they, and bouquet.

SYLLABLES, ONSETS, AND RIMES

In all languages, the basic phonological unit of speech is the *syllable*. At a minimum, a syllable contains a vowel. Most basic syllables contain an onset and a rime. The *onset* is the initial consonant or consonants, and the *rime* is the vowel and any consonants that follow it. In *sat*, the onset is *s* and the rime is *at*. In *smack*, the onset is *sm* and the rime is *ack*. In the two-syllable word *something*, *s* is the onset in the first syllable and *ome* is the rime; *th* is the onset in the second syllable and *ing* is the rime.

In speech, the syllable is the most noticeable unit. It is no coincidence that nursery rhymes and Dr. Seuss books are filled with wordplay involving the onsets and rimes of syllables. Onsets and rimes are naturally compelling sound units, and playing with them typically delights young children. They are likely to repeat lines such as "Jack and Jill went up the hill" literally hundreds of times, just for the fun of it.

Different languages have different rules about what sounds can precede and follow the vowel in a syllable. In English, an onset can be made up of a single consonant (such as *b* in *back* or *s* in *sit*) or a cluster of up to three consonants (*bl* in *black* or *str* in *strike*). Although most English syllables have an onset, they do not have to. Consider the word *about*. The first syllable is *a*. It has no onset. It has only the rime. A rime in English must contain a vowel, and a rime usually ends with a consonant or a consonant cluster. The *it* in *sit* and *ack* in *back* are examples. In English, the most common syllable structure is consonant-vowel-consonant (or CVC), as in *dog*, *cat*, or *pig*. CVC syllable units can be strung together to create multisyllabic words, such as *market* or *napkin*. English also allows several modifications of this CVC unit. For instance, two or three consonant sounds can occur together, as in *flat*, *split*, *blast*, or *splash*.

Figure 8.1 Six Common Spelling Patterns in English Syllables

1. Syllable that ends with a consonant: **CVC** (*sat, splat, **napkin***), **VC** (*at, up*); the vowel is usually short.
2. Syllable that ends with a vowel: **CV** (*me, **spider***), **V** (*a, **halo, baby***); the vowel is often long.
3. Final *e*: **CVC**e (*take, home, cup**cake***); the vowel is often long while the final *e* is silent.
4. Vowel team (for example, *ai, ee, ea, oa*), as in *team, green, lean, toad, **peanut***; in these particular pairs, the first vowel is often long and the second one silent, but that does not apply to many vowel teams.
5. Vowel plus *r: ar, ur, ir, or, er* (for example, *far, fur, fir, for, her*)
6. Consonant plus *le*, as in *little, purple, turtle, tre**ble***

Note: C stands for consonant, V stands for vowel.

There are six common spelling patterns for syllables in English, as shown in Figure 8.1. These are the consonant and vowel spelling patterns that readers usually encounter in words. As you look at Figure 8.1, remember that there can be up to three consonants on either side of a vowel in a syllable.

WORD FAMILIES AND PHONOGRAMS

Unfortunately, quite a few terms are used in discussing word study, and they are not always used consistently. (The problem of inconsistent terminology is not confined to word study but it is pervasive in reading education.) Many current instructional materials are likely to refer to onsets and rimes. Some materials refer to *phonograms*. Phonograms are rimes that share the same spellings. You will sometimes see the terms *rime* and *phonogram* used interchangeably. Words that share phonograms are called a *word family*. Thus *cat, bat, hat, flat*, and *mat* share the *at* phonogram (or rime) and belong to the *at* word family. Similarly, *same, game, tame, blame, fame*, and *flame* share the *ame* phonogram (or rime) and belong to the *ame* word family.

MORPHEMES

All languages use *morphemes* to represent the meaning level of speech. Morphemes are the smallest meaning units into which a word can be divided. Both words and parts of words can be morphemes. *Dog* is a morpheme, and the *-s* in *dogs* is also a morpheme; the *-s* has meaning by indicating that the word is plural. Figure 8.2 shows various ways of segmenting words.

Any word can be described at both the morphemic level and the phonological level. *Dog* is a one-syllable word with one morpheme. Its phonological structure is the common CVC syllable pattern: *d* is the onset and *og* is the rime. *Dog* is also called a *root word*, or *root*, because it can both stand alone and be combined with other roots to form new words. *Doghouse* is a *compound word* containing two root words, *dog* and *house*. *House* consists of the onset *h* and the rime *ouse*.

AFFIXES: PREFIXES AND SUFFIXES

Morphemes that cannot stand alone to form words are called *affixes*. There are two types of affixes. A *prefix* is placed before a root to form a word with a meaning different from that of the root. White, Sowell, and Yanagihara (1989) have produced a list of the most frequently occurring prefixes, shown in Figure 8.3. A *suffix* is placed after a root to form a word with a different meaning or a different grammatical function. There are two kinds of suffixes: inflectional and derivational. *Inflectional suffixes* make a word plural or indicate tense, as do the *-s* in *dogs* and the *-ed* in *snowed*. There are only a few inflectional suffixes, but they occur frequently. Figure 8.4 shows a complete list of inflectional suffixes taken from Rinsky (1993).

Figure 8.2 Various Ways of Segmenting Words

	PLANET	CATS
Morphemes	planet	cat s
Syllables	plan et	cats
Onsets and rimes	/pl-an-ət/	/k-ats/
Phonemes	/p-l-a-n-ət/	/k-a-t-s/

Figure 8.3 Most Frequently Occurring Prefixes

Prefix	Words with the Prefix	Prefix	Words with the Prefix
un-	782	*inter-*	77
re-	401	*fore-*	76
in-, im-, ir-, il- ("not")	313	*de-*	71
dis-	216	*trans-*	47
en-, em-	132	*super-*	43
non-	126	*semi-*	39
in-, im- ("in" or "into")	105	*anti-*	33
over- ("too much")	98	*mid-*	33
mis-	83	*under-* ("too little")	25
sub-	80	All others	100 (estimated)
pre-	79	Total	2,959

SOURCE: White, Thomas G., Sowell, Joanne, & Yanagihara, Alice. (1989, January). "Teaching Elementary Students to Use Word-Part Clues." *The Reading Teacher, 42*(4), 302–308. Copyright © 1989 by the Inter-national Reading Association (www.reading.org).

Figure 8.4 A Complete List of English Inflectional Suffixes

s (es)	plural	boys, brushes
's, (s')	possessive apostrophe	boy's, boys'
s	third-person singular	sings
ed	past tense	grabbed
ing	present participle	singing
en	past participle	has/have eaten
er	comparative	taller
est	superlative	tallest

SOURCE: Rinsky, Lee Ann, *Teaching Word Recognition Skills* (5th ed.), © 1993, and Peter Dewitz.

Figure 8.5 A Few Derivational Suffixes

Root Word	Part of Speech	Suffix	Affixed Word	Part of Speech
base	n.	-ic	basic	adj.
correct	adj.	-ly	correctly	adv.
fool	n.	-ish	foolish	adj.
allow	v.	-ance	allowance	n.
person	n.	-al	personal	adj.
attract	v.	-ive	attractive	adj.
clever	adj.	-ness	cleverness	n.
agree	v.	-ment	agreement	n.

SOURCE: Rinsky, Lee Ann, *Teaching Word Recognition Skills* (5th ed.), © 1993, and Peter Dewitz.

Derivational suffixes alter a word's meaning and its grammatical function. Common suffixes include *-ly* as in *lively, -ive* as in *selective,* and *-ment* as in *excitement.* There are a relatively large number of derivational suffixes, and most of them occur relatively infrequently. Figure 8.5, also taken from Rinsky (1993), shows a few derivational suffixes and illustrates their effects when attached to root words.

In sum, the structure of spoken and printed words is complex. To provide effective word recognition instruction, you need to be familiar with the structure of words and the ways that they can be analyzed.

The Alphabetic Principle

The basic principle underlying English writing is the *alphabetic principle*—phonemes are represented by letters. The three letters in *mad,* for example, correspond to the three phonemes /m/, /a/, /d/. The four letters in *dash* correspond to the three phonemes /d/, /a/, /sh/. The correspondence between letters and sounds in English is not perfect. There are only 26 letters to represent the approximately 44 phonemes. Many letters represent more than one sound. For example, *e* represents the sound you hear in *pet* and also the sound in *Pete.* Two or more letters sometimes represent a single sound.

For example, *ea* represents the sound you hear in *head* and also the sound in *meat*. And many sounds can be represented by more than one letter. For example, *booth, threw,* and *blue* all have the same vowel sound. Vowels are the most troublesome in this regard, but some consonants also represent more than one sound. For example, *c* can represent both /s/ and /k/.

Another difficulty with alphabetic writing systems is that phonemes don't exist as nice, neat, cleanly divisible units. They are only somewhat separable in words. For example, as you say the word *mad*, you actually begin forming your mouth to say the *a* while you are still saying the *m*; likewise, you begin to pronounce the *d* while finishing the *a*. As we shared in Chapter 6, this is called *coarticulation*, and it allows rapid and seamless speech. However, it also makes phonemes harder to hear. Moreover, some phonemes are even impossible to say in isolation without adding a vowel sound. For example, if you were to tell a child the sounds the letters *d* and *p* make, you would probably say something like "duh" and "puh." But there is no *duh* in *dad* and no *puh* in *pat*. Yet adding the schwa vowel to the consonants *d* and *b* makes the sound a bit easier for children to hear and aids blending (Murray, Brabham, Villaume, & Veal, 2008).

Devising a writing system to link letters and sounds required considerable insight and abstraction. Only relatively recently in human history were alphabetic writing systems invented—sometime between 1000 and 700 B.C. These systems are often considered to be among the most important human inventions. Their abstract nature is part of the reason that children have difficulty learning them: Being able to attend to a less-than-concrete phoneme in a spoken word, isolate it from the other sounds in the word, and attach it to a letter is quite a mental feat.

The Structure of Printed Words: The Good News

We are thus faced with the fact that the English writing system presents considerable challenges to children learning to read. The good news, though, is that many of the words with the strangest spellings tend to be the ones we see most frequently in print (e.g., *said, was, what, their, where, through*). Because of this, we have many opportunities to memorize them. The even better news is that despite glaring exceptions, there is a lot of regularity in English spelling. Even words with strange spellings include some letters that provide useful sound cues to their identity. Usually, the most reliable letters are the consonants.

Through years of reading, you have learned a lot about the structure of printed words even though you may not be able to articulate what you know. You also know intuitively that some letter sequences are much more likely to occur than others. For instance, you know that words are more likely to start with *pr* or *br* than with *rb* or *rp*—but just the opposite is true at the ends of words. You have this tacit knowledge because for years you have carefully looked at individual words as you read.

Even multisyllabic words, though they can be admittedly difficult, yield to analysis. Multisyllabic words are simply strings of syllables, and these syllables are composed of onsets and rimes. Though not perfectly consistent, there is a tendency in English to "chunk" words into syllables by placing, at a syllabic division, letter sequences that are less likely to occur next to each other within a syllable. For example, in the word *haystack* we have several clues as to where to divide the word. First, there are two morphemes, *hay* and *stack*. Second, each syllable is a common variant of CVC units and contains common onsets (*h* and *st*) and common rimes (*ay* and *ack*). Third, the letter combination *ys* is not likely to begin a syllable. Double consonants are also a common signal of a syllabic division. Only one consonant is actually pronounced, as you can see in *dinner* or *rabbit*.

A big part of what makes you an efficient recognizer of words is having read a lot. There is a lesson in this: *Wide reading is important for children to develop word recognition proficiency.* Most young readers will need instruction to develop their ability to recognize words, and all children need to read a lot to develop reading proficiency.

Reflect and Apply

1. Identify the onsets and rimes in *hen, past, back, mill*, and *time*. Then make a list of other words that share one of these rimes and thus belong to the same word family.

2. What are the morphemes, roots, and affixes in the words *haystack, dinner*, and *beehives*? What are some clues as to how to divide the words into syllables?

3. Skilled adults can read nonsense words almost as quickly as they can read their own names. See how quickly you can read these nonsense words: *zat, mig, unplick, kip, cleef, fand*, and *bufwixable*. The extent to which you read them quickly offers proof of the incredible sophistication skilled readers have in analyzing words and generating their pronunciations.

MyLab Education **Self-Check 8.2**

Our Position on Phonics Instruction and Related Matters

Phonics is an umbrella term for instruction about letter-sound correspondences. Acquiring phonics knowledge is critical to becoming an accomplished reader. Although a small percentage of children acquire phonics knowledge on their own, most children need direct teaching. This position is consistent with the findings of Jeanne Chall, a Harvard professor who reviewed the research on beginning reading instruction in a landmark book titled *Learning to Read: The Great Debate* (1967), and with most interpretations of Guy Bond and Robert Dykstra's first grade study (1967/1997), the most ambitious study of beginning reading conducted in this country. This position is also consistent with a host of research reports, syntheses of research, and position statements published over the past decade or so. These include special issues of the *American Educator* published in 1995 and 1998; the International Reading Association's position paper on phonics, *The Role of Phonics in Reading Instruction* (1997b); Elfrieda Hiebert and her colleagues' *Every Child a Reader* (Hiebert, Pearson, Taylor, Richardson, & Paris, 1998); Snow and her colleagues' *Preventing Reading Difficulties in Young Children* (1998); Burns and her colleagues' *Starting Out Right* (Burns et al., 1999); the American Federation of Teachers' *Teaching Reading **Is** Rocket Science* (1999); and the *Report of the National Reading Panel: Teaching Children to Read* (National Reading Panel, 2000). The *Common Core State Standards* reflect our position on word recognition outlining the phonological knowledge and phonics principles that all need to acquire (CCSSO & NGA, 2010). This position finally is consistent with the majority of research on beginning reading and with common sense. We are the enormously fortunate inheritors of an alphabetic writing system; we need to teach our children how to take advantage of that system.

The best evidence suggests that all young children benefit from phonics instruction, some more so than others (Snow & Juel, 2005). Conversely, there is no evidence that strong beginning readers are hurt by teaching them phonics (Connelly, Johnston, & Thompson, 2001). A focus on phonics instruction does not undermine the development of reading comprehension. The astute teachers will recognize which students are quickly catching on to the alphabetic principle, move phonics instruction to small groups, and decrease the emphasis for those student who do not need it.

Some children need less phonics instruction than others, and phonics instruction must always be kept in proper perspective—as a means to an end. Comprehension is the goal of reading, and reading, writing, speaking, listening, and being read to must form the heart of the literacy curriculum. But for readers who have not yet mastered the code of written English, learning to read words—which includes phonics—plays an absolutely essential role.

MyLab Education **Self-Check 8.3**

Learning to Read Words

Research suggests that children move through a series of overlapping developmental phases as they learn to read words. In these phases, children read words in different ways. We first will summarize the phases, and then describe the more general cognitive processes in which readers engage as they read words.

Developmental Phases in Learning to Read Words

Ehri (1998; Ehri & Snowling, 2004) has articulated a developmental theory of word reading that is grounded in two decades of research. According to Ehri, as children learn to read words, they form connections between the features of printed words and the sounds they represent. Children look at a printed word, pronounce it, and then analyze how the print represents the sounds in the word. This analysis helps children to store the word in memory. When children encounter a word in print, they draw on the connections they have formed for the word. Children form different kinds of connections as they move through four developmental phases: pre-alphabetic, partial alphabetic, full alphabetic, and consolidated alphabetic.

PRE-ALPHABETIC PHASE
Very young children read words based on visual but nonalphabetic features. For example, children might read the word *look* by remembering that the *o*s in the word look like "two round eyes" (Ehri, 1998, p. 19) or the word *camel* by remembering the two humps in the word (Gough, Juel, & Roper/Schneider, 1983). This kind of word reading is also known as visual cue reading (Gough, Juel, & Roper/Schneider, 1983) and logographic reading (Frith, 1985).

PARTIAL ALPHABETIC PHASE
In this stage, children are learning letter-sound correspondences and use what they know to form partial connections between letters and sounds in words and word meanings. Initial and final letters are often the letters used to remember and read words. For example, a child might use the *s* and *n* to remember and read the word *spoon* (Ehri, 1998). A problem for children in this phase is misidentifications that result when words have similar letters. For example, a child would identify *kitten* and *kitchen* as the same word (Gaskins, Ehri, Cress, O'Hara, & Donnelly, 1997). Similarly, a child would have difficulty distinguishing between *drop, drip*, and *damp* (Ehri, 1998).

FULL ALPHABETIC PHASE
In the next phase, children have well developed knowledge of letter-sound correspondences. They have formed what Ehri (1998) calls complete connections between letters and sounds in words and word meanings. For example, Ehri explains that a child in this phase would have formed connections between the *s, p, oo,* and *n* in the word *spoon* and would use them all to read the word. This kind of reading has been referred to as *alphabetic reading* (Frith, 1985) and sequential *decoding* (Marsh et al., 1981). Chall (1996) has described children who read words in this manner as "glued to print."

CONSOLIDATED ALPHABETIC PHASE

In the last phase, children consolidate the letter patterns that they see across words into larger units (Ehri, 1998). They connect these larger units to the spoken forms of words and their meanings. For example, Ehri explains, as children encounter words such as *nest, pest, rest, best,* and *test,* they consolidate the *e, s,* and *t* into the unit *est* (a rime). This consolidation enables children to read words more easily. As Ehri describes, a child in this phase would read the word *chest* using two units—*ch* and *est*—rather than the four letter-sound correspondences a child in the full alphabetic phase would require—*ch, e, s, t.* This kind of reading has been called *orthographic reading* (Frith, 1985) and ungluing from print (Chall, 1996). It is the type of word identification employed by adults.

Processes Involved in Reading Words

Ehri (1998) has emphatically stated "teachers need to understand the processes that their instruction is aimed at teaching and the behaviors that indicate whether students are progressing along the lines expected in learning to read. Teachers need this knowledge to evaluate and improve the effectiveness of their instructional efforts" (p. 4). We agree. Before we discuss particular instructional techniques, we summarize the cognitive processes at which word recognition instruction is directed. We draw on Ehri's (1998) and Thompson's (1999) articulations of these processes. Clear and succinct, they provide a useful framework within which to understand related instruction.

Ehri has identified four processes readers use to recognize words. These are *sight word reading, decoding, analogizing,* and *contextual guessing.* Thompson (1999) has described these processes as *recall* (sight word reading) and *generation* (decoding, analogizing, using context). When a child encounters a known printed word in text, he reads it as a whole unit from sight. That is, he recalls it from memory. When he encounters an unknown printed word, he needs to generate a pronunciation for it. This is accomplished through decoding, analogizing to known words, or using contextual information.

Decoding is the process of identifying letter-sound correspondences as well as larger units in a word and blending them to form a word. For example, a child who encounters the unknown word *drop* might map the letters onto individual letter-sound correspondences to generate a pronunciation (i.e., /d/ /r/ /o/ /p/) or might use the onset and rime to decode the word (i.e., /dr/ /op/). When the child uses onsets and rimes he is engaged in decoding by analogy.

Analogizing is the process of comparing an unknown word to a similarly spelled known word. For example, a child who is reading Peter McCarty's *Little Bunny on the Move* might read the word *bunny* by analogizing to the known word *sunny.* To identify *bunny,* the child has recalled from memory the known word *sunny,* identified the analogous word part *unny,* and replaced the *s* with *b.* Analogizing is probably the process that adults use when encountering a new and complex word.

When readers use contextual information, they draw on *semantic* cues (meaning cues) and *syntactic* cues (grammatical cues) to identify a word. For example, a child who doesn't know the word *bird* in a sentence could use an illustration of a bird on the page to correctly guess the word's identity. Similarly, a child reading the sentence "Sam was walking his dog" who didn't know the word *dog* would stand a good chance of correctly guessing the word from the sentence context. There are very few words that would make sense in the sentence and fit the grammatical structure.

A caution as you consider teaching children to use contextual information to support word recognition—research has shown that most words are not very predictable from contextual information (Gough & Walsh, 1991; Stanovich, 1980). Those that are tend to be *function* words—words that primarily express grammatical relationships, such as articles (e.g., *a, an, the*), prepositions (e.g., *of, to, in*), and conjunctions (e.g., *and, for, but*). These function words occur frequently in the language and are relatively easy to memorize.

Content words carry most of the meaning in a sentence. They aren't very predictable. We want beginning readers to use all of what they know to identify words, but we don't want to overemphasize the use of context. Research has shown that relying on contextual information to identify unknown words is a process that beginning readers and older weak readers rely on, which can easily become a bad habit (Nicholson, 1991; Stanovich, 1986). Context is useful only if the young reader can use letter-sound knowledge to identify words (Tunmer & Nicholson, 2011). Relying on context or even multiple cues as the current generation of whole language advocates (see Guided Reading) propose is simply not as efficient as decoding the words. Skillful readers recognize most of the words they read at sight; when they don't know a word, they generate a pronunciation for the word using their extensive letter-sound and orthographic (spelling) knowledge (Adams, 1990; Stanovich, 1991a, 1991b, 1992; Thompson, 1999; Tunmer & Nicholson, 2010).

MyLab Education **Self-Check 8.4**

MyLab Education **Application Exercise 8.2:** A Colleague Challenges the School's Approach to Reading Instruction

MyLab Education **Application Exercise 8.3:** Using a Child's Oral Reading Responses to Determine a Child's Stage of Reading Development

---

Word Study Instruction

Word study refers to instruction about words. Remember, any type of word study instruction is a means to an end—comprehension of text. We want to empower children with the knowledge and skills to unlock the meanings of printed words. Word study instruction can include a focus on high-frequency words, letter-sound correspondences, the larger units in words, and attention to the meaning elements in words (e.g., affixes and root words). You need to tailor your instruction to students, and research that one of us conducted suggests that different learners will need different emphases (Juel & Minden-Cupp, 2000). You want to keep word study instruction active as well, as in the following examples of active teaching and learning in word study:

- Children sort picture cards on the basis of the phonemes in pictured words.
- Teachers provide explicit instruction about which letters represent which sounds.
- Teachers explain and demonstrate how to blend individual phonemes to form words.
- Children sort word cards on the basis of letter-sound correspondences and other units in words.
- Children read text with repetitions of high-frequency words and common spelling patterns.
- Children write words that share common features (e.g., phonemes, rimes, affixes, roots).
- Children write dictated words and sentences with target spelling patterns or high-frequency words.

Six General Principles of Word Study Instruction

The word study instruction we recommend follows six basic principles:

1. Start where the child is.
2. Make word study an active process of classification.
3. Base word study on contrasting words with different sounds or spellings.
4. Help children understand how the writing system works.
5. Teach students how to develop a strategy for unlocking the pronunciations of unknown words.
6. Keep comprehension as the goal.

1. *Start where the child is.* Begin with concepts about words the child already understands and words the child can read. For example, if the child writes words primarily as initial consonants—*pig* as *p*, *dig* as *d*, and *big* as *b*—but stops there, then it is time to teach rimes such as *ig* and to help the child perceive and manipulate the letter sounds in *ig*.

2. *Learning occurs as an active process of classification.* Word study is based on this premise. Children learn about words by analyzing and classifying them on the basis of whether or not they share certain features, for example, a phoneme, onset, rime, affix, or root word.

3. *Word study instruction is based on contrasts.* That is, children learn to perceive short *i* by contrasting short *i* words with words that have another vowel. By contrasting *sit* with *sat*, *bit* with *bat*, *pit* with *pat*, and *slip* with *slap*, the child can begin to perceive which letters represent which sounds. By comparing words that have contrasting patterns, a child can focus on which features make which differences in words, but only if he pronounces the words while sorting them.

   Words can be contrasted in different ways. Sorting picture cards is one effective way to highlight contrasts in phonemes. A picture card is simply a card with a picture on it, such as a pig, rug, wig, or hug. Picture sorting for particular phonemes or rimes develops children's phonemic awareness—the ability to hear the somewhat separable sounds in spoken words. For example, children must determine whether the picture of a hug goes under the picture of a pig or under the picture of a rug (*hug–pig* or *hug–rug*). Does the word *hug* fit better with the sound /ug/ or the sound /ig/? To make these categorical judgments, children must engage in critical thinking rather than drill or memorization (Bear, Invernizzi, Templeton, & Johnston, 2015). However, these sorts can easily become mindless drill unless children are challenged to pronounce and justify their decisions.

4. *Children need to understand how the writing system works.* In learning to read and write, children need to understand how speech is written down. They need to perceive units of speech, such as phonemes and rimes. They need to learn which speech units are represented by which letters. Teachers of emergent readers will need to model how to segment spoken words into speech units and then how to connect these units to letters. They will need to help students perceive the units of speech that are represented in writing—words, syllables, and phonemes. And finally, they will need to help children learn how to represent these units in their own writing.

5. *Children need strategies to determine pronunciations of unknown words.* It is not enough to learn the patterns within a word; the students need a process to help them employ that knowledge. For example, a student might successively blend sounds to pronounce the word *splat* but use an analogy process to pronounce *banter*. (If I know *can* I know *ban*, and if I know *her* I know *ter*. Blended together the word is *banter*.) Ultimately, the reader has to use these strategies and know when to use them.

6. *Keep comprehension as the goal.* Children are learning to recognize words so that they can read stories, informational books, poems, and other texts.

Reflect and Apply

4. A child reads the word *clothes* as *color* in one part of a passage and a few sentences later reads it as *cold*. At what stage of word recognition is the child? How can you move this reader to a higher level of word recognition?

5. Explain two major reasons why the alphabetic principle is difficult for some children to learn. How is the English alphabetic system less than perfect?

Getting Started with Word Study: Building a Basic Reading Vocabulary

So where do you begin? Picture a kindergarten or first-grade classroom. The door opens, and suddenly the room fills with bright-eyed children eager to learn. However, these hopeful, energetic children may or may not be able to recognize or produce the letters of the alphabet, may or may not accurately track speech to print by finger-pointing to memorized text, may only be able to scribble letters or intersperse letters and scribbles in their writing, and may not be able to read any words. In other words, children with a wide range of proficiencies enter your classroom. One of your first tasks is to identify what individual children do and do not know and can and cannot do. Following this, your job will be to help every child become a competent reader and writer.

Differentiating Instruction for English Language Learners

PROXIMAL PARTNERS

- Bear, Helman, Templeton, Invernizzi, and Johnston (2007) remind us that English language learners must have opportunities to practice and ask questions when working on tasks. They suggest teachers assign "proximal partners" to English learners—someone to pair up with as they engage in learning tasks. Bear and his colleagues note that it is helpful when possible to pair an outgoing English language learner with a more reserved but more proficient native English speaker. This creates a balance of skills between partners. Such pairings can be used in a picture sort for short vowel sounds. Both children have their own cards to sort. As the children sort the cards, they say the name of the picture. Then they place the card with other cards representing the same vowel sound. Afterward, they explain their sorts to their partners. This allows the English language learner to practice using spoken English and to have an opportunity to ask questions and receive feedback.

- A major task of second language acquisition is learning the vocabulary. Bear and his colleagues note that concept sorts are a good way of helping English language learners with this task. Let's say that children are studying the weather as part of the science curriculum. During word study instruction, your English learners can engage in a picture sort of cards that represent weather-related terms (e.g., the sun, rain, snow, clouds, thermometer). Bear and his colleagues provide a set of such cards in their text *Words Their Way with English Learners*, but you can also make your own. Pair English learners with native English speakers and have them engage in and talk about their sorts. Here is an example of a sort where students classify words.

Storms	Precipitation	Clouds	Measurement
Thunder	Rain	Stratus	Thermometer
Hurricane	Snow	Cumulus	Barometer
Tornado	Hail		

We start by sharing how to help children develop a basic reading vocabulary. Then we discuss teaching children letter-sound correspondences and the larger units in words. Afterward, we discuss the importance of contextual reading to word recognition development. We conclude with our thoughts on the importance of wide reading to children's word learning.

BUILDING SIGHT VOCABULARY

Skilled readers have substantial sight vocabularies. Very likely, you have not needed to decode or otherwise generate a pronunciation for a single word that you have read in this text. You read the words automatically. Beginning readers have very limited sight vocabularies. A good way to develop children's sight vocabularies is to start with words they already know. Most children entering first grade can read their names and a few words, such as color words, names of family members, and kinds of household pets.

In many schools, kindergarten and first grade teachers begin word study instruction with sight words from the Dolch or Fry list of high-frequency words. These two lists were compiled from other word lists. The Dolch list of 220 basic sight words was first published in 1936 and is based on other lists of the time, estimates of words that children were reading in their school books. It is important to note that the Dolch list contains no nouns, but he did compile a separate list of 95 nouns. The Fry Instant Word list is based on the words in The American Heritage Word Frequency Book (Carol, Davies & Richmond, 1971). Both lists are very similar with only nine words on the Fry 100 not appearing on the Dolch 220 list. So either list provides a useful starting point.

The most important question is how many words to teach. Before we answer that question, it is important to note that many of these high-frequency words follow regular spelling conventions and are decodable—words like *and, can, go, me, not, play*, and *run*. Words like *saw, was, friend*, and *said* have some spelling irregularity, but parts of the word obey standard spelling rules. It is reasonable to teach 20 sight words in kindergarten and no more than 100 in first grade. At that point phonics instruction becomes the more important goal.

WORD BANKS

A word bank is a child's personal collection of words. Children work with these words regularly in class to cement them in memory. To create a child's word bank, print words on small cards. It is important that you—rather than the child—print the words because emergent readers are still learning how to form letters. The child keeps the cards in a small plastic bag or some other container.

The first word in a word bank can be a child's first name. Then add words the child already can read. Next, personalize the word bank by asking the child what other words she can read and adding them to the collection. You might also add a few words that the child volunteers she would like to learn. These might include a favorite food, the name of a pet, the name of a favorite friend, or a favorite activity. Add new words to the word bank each day. Both you and the child may select words to add. Good words to choose are those that the child will see a lot in print and use in daily writing. High-interest words are good choices as well. A child's word bank should grow until it has about 100 words. At that point, it becomes unwieldy. Figure 8.6 shows the word bank of a beginning first-grader.

Reviewing words and seeing them frequently in books and poems will help children continue to recognize them as new ones are added. Remember that young readers typically have incomplete knowledge of the letters in a word. They might recognize

Figure 8.6 Marcos's Beginning First-Grade Word Bank

Marcos	
cat	soccer
the	pizza
and	Luis
red	

a word by its initial consonant or by its length. As new words are added to the word bank, old words can be "forgotten." For example, a child who "knows" the word *cat* in her word bank because the first two letters are *ca* may fail to recognize it when the word *can* is added to the bank. The more times children look at their word bank words and compare them, the more likely they are to form connections between all the letters in the word and the sounds they make. This is what enables them to fully learn the words. First-grade teacher Gordon Scholander describes how he uses word banks with his emergent readers:

> My young scholars frequently enjoy sharing their word banks. They will sometimes read their word bank cards to each other, or, with a buddy, they'll sort their cards into categories—such as animals or words that start or end with a particular letter. Sometimes I'll have them spread out ten or so of their individual word bank cards on their desks or work with a buddy to try variants of a "pick-up" game. Here are some prompts I give them for the game:
>
> - Pick up all your animal words. Read your words to a buddy. Do you and your buddy have any of the same animals?
> - Pick up all your color words. Hold up the card with your favorite color on it.
> - Pick up all your words that start with /sssss/. Read them to a buddy.
> - Pick up all your words that start with the letter *b*. Read your *b* words to a buddy.
> - Pick up words that rhyme with *cat*. What do you have?
> - Pick up all your words that have three letters. Read them to a buddy.
> - Pick up your longest word and share it with a buddy.
>
> —Gordon Scholander, first-grade teacher

HIGH-FREQUENCY WORDS

High-frequency words are the most common words in printed English. Children will encounter them over and over when they read, including function words like *as, the, and,* and *of,* and content words such as *girl, blue,* and *little.* Some high-frequency words are very regular in their letter-sound correspondences. That is, they sound the way they look (e.g., *then, it, she*). Some are not very regular (e.g., *was, there, said*). It is difficult to read very much without knowing high-frequency words well. Along with letter-sound (phonics) instruction, high-frequency word practice will be helpful in getting beginning readers started. Many lists of high-frequency words are available, and most published reading series identify the high-frequency words that appear in their materials.

Teacher educator and former teacher Linda Allen (1998) has shared an effective instructional routine for teaching high-frequency words. Allen calls high-frequency words "core" words. In the instructional routine, rhythm and movement support learning. The routine is an enjoyable one that children find very motivating. Allen advocates grounding word study—core word and otherwise—in stories, informational books, or poems. We share Allen's instructional routine here.

A core word lesson typically involves about three new words. The teacher first presents the core words in a series of sentences from a text that children have read or will read with the teacher. If the sentences in the book are too long or not quite right for this step in the lesson, the teacher can modify them. The target core words in the sentences are highlighted in some way, for example, underlined or written in a contrasting color. Then each core word is analyzed apart from the sentences. The teacher points out the sound and visual features of each word. This helps children to notice the letters and sounds in the word and form connections between them. Next, children chant the spelling of each core word as they clap, snap their fingers, and write the words on a sheet of paper, on a small white board, or in a word study journal. Children then read new sentences containing the core words. Following the lesson, the words are placed on what is known as a word wall for future reinforcement and reference, as we will discuss shortly.

In the Classroom 8.1 shows a core word lesson. The book around which the lesson is built is Joanne Oppenheim's *"Not Now!" Said the Cow*. The book is a predictable text in which a crow finds a sack of corn seed on the ground. For each step in the planting and growing process, he asks various barnyard animals to help him. The language the crow uses to ask and that which the animals use to respond (in the negative) is a repetitive pattern. At the end of the book, the crow makes popcorn. All the animals wish to help him eat the popcorn, but the crow replies that he will eat it "all by myself."

WORD WALLS

Primary-grade teachers often have word walls. They typically set aside a bulletin board or a wall for this purpose. Word walls can be organized in two ways. Most teachers organize their words alphabetically by the word's first letter. Along the top of the word wall are the letters of the alphabet. Teachers place words under the letter with which they begin as children learn them. Generally, teachers add a handful of words

---

In the Classroom 8.1

Instructional Routines
Teaching High-Frequency Words

- *State the purpose.* "Our purpose today is to learn to read and spell three new core words. Core words are words we see a lot when we read and use a lot when we write. The core words we'll learn today are *who*, *said*, and *what*."

- *Show and read the words in sentences.* "Let's read these sentences together. Then we'll look closely at each core word."

  "Who will help me plant the seed?" *said* the crow.
  "Not now!" *said* the cow.
  Just *what* we need, a sack of seed!

- *Highlight the features in words.* "Let's think carefully about how each word looks and sounds."

  who: "In *who*, the *wh* sounds like /h/. The *o* sounds like the *o* in *to*—*who*."
  said: "In *said*, we hear the /s/ at the beginning and the /d/ at the end. The middle of the word doesn't sound the way it looks. It sounds like /eh/ as in *red*—*said*."
  what: "In *what*, the *wh* makes a /hw/ sound. The *a* sounds like /uh/. We hear the /t/ at the end—*what*."

- *Chant, clap, snap, write the words.* "Let's spell each word out loud three times. The first time, we'll clap as we say each letter. Then we'll snap our fingers as we say each letter. Next, we'll write each word. As we write each letter, we'll say it. Let me show you how we do this. Watch and listen to me once. Then we'll clap, snap, and write the words together." Model chanting, clapping, snapping, and writing one word. Then, start again and have children chant, clap, snap, and write all new core words chorally with you.

- *Practice words in new sentences.* "Now, let's read our new core words in these sentences. Let's read together."

  Do you know *who* will help me plant the seed?
  Cow and hog *said* they will not pull weeds.
  What will crow do?

- *Final review.* Remind students why core words are important. "Today we learned three new core words—*who*, *said*, and *what*. Core words are important to know because we see them a lot when we read and use them a lot when we write."

to the word wall each week. Cunningham (2009) notes that first-grade teachers typically begin word walls with children's names and then focus on high-frequency words. A word wall organized alphabetically assists students as they spell. A student who can't remember how to spell *friend*, segments the word and isolates the initial sound. Then he searches under the *f*s to find the word.

Word walls can also be organized a second way—by the rime or spelling pattern. These word walls have six sections for rimes beginning with *a, e, i, o, u,* and *y*. Thus, *cat, made,* and *rain* are all organized under *a*. This word wall facilitates the process of decoding by analogy. If the child encounters the word *remain* she can look at the word wall and find the word *rain* and the spelling pattern *ain* to help her read the word. If you teach analogy strategies, this type of word wall will be very useful.

Cunningham cautions that it is not enough for teachers to have a word wall; they must *do* word walls with children. This involves chanting and writing selected words and other reinforcement activities. Cunningham describes a favorite reinforcement activity, a game called *Be a Mind Reader*. A teacher thinks of a word on the word wall but keeps the word to himself. Children write down the numbers 1 through 5 as a list on their papers. Then the teacher gives the children five clues to the word that move from broad to narrow. As the teacher says each clue, children list the word they think the teacher has in mind. When the clues have all been given, the teacher reveals the word. By clue 5 most of the children have the word. The teacher then has the children share when they knew the word—after clue 4, 3, 2, or 1. A set of clues for the high-frequency word *every* might be as follows: (1) It's on the word wall. (2) It has five letters. (3) It begins with the short *e* sound. (4) It's a two beat (i.e., syllable) word. (5) In the word the *y* sounds like a long *e*. The high-frequency word *outside* might be given the following clues: (1) It's on the word wall. (2) It has seven letters. (3) It's a compound word. (4) It ends with a silent *e*. (5) It's the opposite of *inside*.

The word wall can be incorporated into other classroom activities. The more the word wall is used the better students will retain their words and learn their properties. Here is a short list of activities.

- As a warm-up in the morning, ask individual children to see how many words they can read on the wall. See who can read the most.
- When conducting any writing activity and a child asks how you spell *lamp*, direct the student by saying, "Is there a word on the wall that can help you?"
- When children write, expect that any word on the wall will be spelled correctly. This will encourage them to study the word wall.
- Later, tell the students that any word that rhymes with a word on the wall should be spelled correctly.
- When the student is reading in a small groups lesson and has difficulty with a word prompt the child by saying "Is there a word on the wall you can use to crack the pronunciation of the difficult word ____."

Teaching Letter-Sound Correspondences

Learning to read requires learning to understand the code of written language. In English, this is very much a matter of acquiring phonics knowledge—which sounds are represented by which letter(s). First-grade teacher Glenna Schwarze knows that reading independence means making sure her students get instruction in decoding skills.

> I am sure any first-grade teacher will tell you the same thing: At the heart of first-grade reading instruction is ensuring that children learn to decode words. Of course, we want children to be able to instantly recognize as many words as possible, but we also need to be sure they are equipped with strategies and skills to use when they don't instantly know a word. The beginning reader, of course, cannot instantly recognize many words.

As teachers, however, we can help children identify words they don't know by helping them recognize the letters in the words and how to translate those letters into the sounds they represent.

—Glenna Schwarze, first-grade teacher

Research has shown that phonics instruction most benefits beginning readers when it is explicit and systematic (National Reading Panel, 2000). This means that letter-sound correspondences are specifically taught to children with instruction that follows a pre-determined order (Beck & Beck, 2013). You will often see the following sequence recommended for teaching phonics elements: consonants, short vowels, long vowels, and vowels with other sounds. This order is likely because there is less variation in sounds that consonants make (Beck & Beck, 2013) and in the ways that short vowel sounds are represented in many primary-grade words. As Beck (2006) emphasizes, however, while we don't want to begin word study with complex vowel patterns, we also don't want to wait to teach some vowel sounds until all the consonants have been taught; vowels are needed to form words, and we want children forming and reading words right from the start.

In the Classroom 8.2 describes the major kinds of phonics elements for your reference. One difficulty in learning to teach beginning reading is developing an explicit knowledge of the units in words. At the end of the feature, we note the phonics elements that the New Standards Primary Literacy Committee (2004) states first-graders should know. This list is very close to the Foundation Standards of the Common Core State Standards (NGA & CCSSO, 2010).

Next, we share a number of instructional routines for developing phonics knowledge that involve manipulating letters, phonograms, or other word parts. Beginning readers find the hands-on nature of these activities engaging and motivating.

TEACHING CONSONANTS

Teaching consonants involves teaching individual consonants (e.g., *s, n, d*), consonant blends (e.g., *st, cr, spr*), and consonant digraphs (e.g., *sh, ch, th, ph*). Researcher and former elementary school teachers Isabel Beck and Mark Beck (2015) have developed a set of instructional routines for teaching letter-sound correspondences that we think makes pretty good sense, leading students through a series of steps to learn particular correspondences.

1. Develop the phonemic awareness of the target sound in the initial position. "I know a story with a character called Mary Mouse who drank lots of milk. The words Mary, Mouse, and milk begin with the same sound /m/. You say /m/."
2. Connect the printed letter with the letter's sound. "This is the letter m. The letter m stands for the sound of /m/ in Mary and Mouse. Say /m/."
3. Discriminate among words that begin with /m/ and those that do not. "I am going to say some words. If they begin with /m/ raise your hand: *mother, toy, move, mountain, run.*"
4. Develop phonemic awareness of the target sound in the final position. "What am I using to sweep the floor? Yes, a broom. Broom ends with /m/. These words also end with /m/ *jam, zoom, arm, hum.*"
5. Discriminate among words that end with /m/ and those that do not. "Raise your hand if you hear the /m/ sound at the end of the word: *jam, room, dog, pet, drum, farm.*"
6. Discriminate among words that have /m/ in the initial and final positions. Give each child a small pocket chart divided in half and several cards with the letter *m*. Then say the word and if it has the /m/ at the beginning put the *m* on the left side of the chart. If the /m/ is at the end of the word put the *m* on the right side of the chart.

Beck's instructional routines are precise and most often involve a pocket chart for demonstration purposes and small word pockets for children to use. A word pocket is simply a one-pocket pocket chart, easily created from construction paper or tag board.

In the Classroom 8.2

Common Letter-Sound Correspondences

Consonants

- Consonants are all the letters but the vowels (*a, e, i, o, u*, and sometimes *y*); *y* is a consonant when it is at the beginning of a syllable (e.g., *yes, yelp, yellow*).
- The following consonants have two sounds:

  - *c* ("hard sound" as in *coat* and *cake*; "soft sound" as in *city* and *cereal*)
  - *g* ("hard sound" as in *girl* and *gap*; "soft sound" as in *giant* and *gentle*)
  - *x* (can sound like /ks/ as in *text* and *x-ray* or /z/ as in *xylophone* and *Xerox*)

- Consonant blends are two or three contiguous consonants in which each consonant is heard.

  - Common two-letter blends: *bl, br, cr, cl, dr, fl, fr, gl, gr, pl, pr, tr, sc, sk, sl, sm, sn, sp, st, tr, tw, sw*
  - Common three-letter blends: *scr, spr, squ, str, phr, sch, thr*

- Consonant digraphs are two contiguous consonants that together form a new sound.

  - Common consonant digraphs: *sh* (*she*), *ch* (*chain, chef, chorus*), *th* (*these, think*), *wh* (*white, which*), *gh* (*laugh, ghost*), *ph* (*phone*), *ng* (*ring*)

Short and Long Vowels (*a, e, i, o, u*, and sometimes *y*)

- Short vowels are the sounds the vowels make in the words *bat, pet, sit, hot*, and *bug*.
- Long vowels are the sounds the vowels make in *cake, see, ride, so*, and *cube*. The letter *y* also serves as a vowel, representing the long *i* sound (*shy, crying*) or the long *e* sound (*baby, bumpy*).

Vowel Digraphs

- For digraphs with two contiguous vowels, you may have been taught the expression, *When two vowels go walking, the first does the talking*. This speaks to words in which the first vowel in the digraph is long and the second one is silent (e.g., *meat, boat, rain, cue*). However, there are so many exceptions (e.g., *eight, they, break, ready, again, laugh, eye*) that it's best not to teach it as a phonics rule.

Diphthongs

- Words with two contiguous vowels are pronounced with a gliding sound as one sound moves into the other. Common diphthongs include *oi* and *oy* (*coin, boy*), *ou* (*shout*), and *ow* (*how*).

R-Controlled Vowels

- Vowels change their sound when they are followed by the letter *r* (*car, her, sir, for, fur*).

Common grammatical endings

- Plural *-s* can sound like /s/ as in *cats* and *banks* or /z/ as in *dogs* and *cars*.
- The past-tense ending *-ed* can make three sounds: /ed/ as in *waited*, /d/ as in *yelled*, or /t/ as in *asked*.

Note. According to the New Standards Primary Literacy Committee (2004) and the CCSS, first-graders should know the following letter-sound correspondences: beginning and ending consonants; two-consonant beginning blends; consonant digraphs *ch, sh*, and *th*; short vowels; long vowels that follow the CVCe pattern (e.g., *cake*); and the vowel digraphs *ai, ee, oa*, and *ea*.

Simply fold the bottom inch or so of the paper or tag board up and tape or staple the sides together. The paper fold serves as a pocket in which letter cards sit and can be seen. The teacher will need large letter and word cards. Children will need small ones. In the book *Making Sense of Phonics*, Beck and Beck (2006) provide letter cards that teachers can reproduce. Another good source for letter cards (and much else) is Cunningham, Hall, and Heggie's (2001) *Making Words: Multilevel, Hands-On Phonics and Spelling Activities*.

In the Classroom 8.3

Teaching Single-Letter Consonants and Consonant Digraphs

- Say: "Yesterday, we listened to the book *Old Black Fly*. Old Black Fly had a very busy bad day. *Busy* and *bad* begin with the same sound: the /b/ sound. Watch my mouth /b/. [Children watch.] You say /b/." [Children respond.]
- Show children the large letter *b* card. Say: "This is the letter *b*. The letter *b* stands for the /b/ sound in *busy* and *bad*. Say /b/. [Children respond.] Each time I touch the letter *b*, say /b/." Touch the letter *b* card several times.
- Give each child a letter *b* card. Say, "If the word I say begins with the /b/ sound, hold up your card and say /b/. If it does not begin with the /b/ sound, shake your head no." Example words: *bit, bank, tack, buckle, something, bunny, table, bought, beautiful, room.*
- Say: "Old Black Fly might have gotten caught in something a spider spins. What is this?" When children have identified *web*, have them repeat it a few times. Then say: "The word *web* ends with the letter *b* that stands for the /b/ sound. I'm going to say some words that end with the letter *b*. Say them after me." Example words: *jab, tub, crib, bob, cab, grab.*
- Say: "I'm going to say some more words. If a word ends with the /b/ sound, hold up your *b* card. If it doesn't end with the /b/ sound, put your *b* card behind your back." Example words: *jab, come, sob, grab, ground, crib, track, crab.*
- Give each child a word pocket. Say: "I'm going to say some words that begin with /b/ and some that end with /b/. When a word begins with /b/, put your letter *b* at the beginning of your word pocket, like this [show children]. When a word ends with /b/, put your letter *b* at the end of the word pocket, like this [show children]." Example words: *batter, bump, tab, bottle, drab, banana, butter, mob, washtub.*

In the Classroom 8.3 shows a lesson that employs Beck's instructional routine and suggested language for teaching a single-letter consonant correspondence, in this case the correspondence *b* = /b/. We ground the lesson in Jim Aylesworth's text *Old Black Fly*. Grounding a phonics lesson in a text selection is not absolutely necessary, and at times it is not possible. However, like Linda Allen and many other educators, whenever possible we advocate connecting word study lessons to enjoyable experiences with books—the kinds of experiences that will motivate children to learn to read. Note that the same routine could be used for a consonant digraph. The only difference in the procedure is in the letter cards. When teaching a consonant digraph, the two letters that make up the correspondence (e.g., *sh*) should go on the same card. This provides children with an extra visual support for connecting the two letters with the single sound that they make.

You'll want to continually review letter-sound correspondences until children have learned them, as In the Classroom 8.4 demonstrates. We share how first-grade teacher Ms. Campbell helps a group of students review initial consonant sounds. The class has just listened to and discussed Michael Grejniec's *What Do You Like?* Now during center time, Ms. Campbell tells each student which center to go to, reminding them that they will spend 20 minutes rotating through each center. One group goes to the classroom library, where they can read with a buddy or read alone. Ms. Campbell has added a copy of *What Do You Like?* to the center. Another group goes to the writing center to write and illustrate "I Like" books. Another group of children will work with Ms. Campbell reviewing initial consonant sounds and reading leveled books that stress these sounds. They bring their word back to the center.

TEACHING VOWELS

Early literacy expert Leslie Mandel Morrow (2009) explains that vowels are challenging for children because they make so many different sounds. Often, short vowels are

In the Classroom 8.4

Reviewing Consonants: Ms. Campbell's Class

At the center, Ms. Campbell gives a copy of the read-aloud text *What Do You Like?* to each child. Ms. Campbell has them chorally read the text together. They point to each word as they read it. Then Ms. Campbell passes out a set of small word cards to each child showing *rainbow, like, love,* and *play.* Three of these words are high-frequency words, and *rainbow* is one that Ms. Campbell knows the children would like to learn. Ms. Campbell tells the children to find the page in their book that has *rainbow* on it, which they easily do. Ms. Campbell then says, "Find the word card that says *rainbow.* Check it to see if it is a match by putting it under the word *rainbow.*" She asks the children how they know the word is *rainbow.* Most say because it is long and starts with the letter *r.* Sara mentions that she can also hear an *a* in it. Because they have already learned the letter-sound correspondence for *b,* Ms. Campbell also has them put their fingers on the letter *b* at the beginning of *bow* and say the sound it makes (/b/).

Ms. Campbell next has the children put *rainbow* on their desk and search their word banks for other *r* words, which they line up under *rainbow.* Ms. Campbell asks them to read their list to the person sitting next to them. Ms. Campbell repeats this procedure with the words *like, love,* and *play.*

The final word center activity is called Writing for Sounds. Ms. Campbell gives the children pencils and blank sheets of paper, on which they write their names. Ms. Campbell has them write the letters *p, l,* and *r* across the top of the paper. Then she calls out words that start with one of these letters. When she calls out "play," she expects children to write it under the letter *p.* She doesn't expect them to necessarily write all of the word's letters, but she encourages them to write as many as they can. She tells them to write the sounds they hear. She emphasizes the initial consonant as she says the word, as this is the phonics element the group has been working on. Ms. Campbell will look at these papers later to check on how each child is progressing. Right now, she simply collects them because it is time for the children to rotate to another center in the room.

taught before long vowels. To review, short vowels are the sounds the letters *a, e, i, o,* and *u* make in the words *hat, let, bit, pot,* and *cup,* the CVC pattern. Long vowel sounds are easier to hear in words but have multiple spellings for the same sounds. This can be confusing for children. The long vowel spelling pattern that likely comes immediately to your mind is the CVCe (or CCVCe) pattern, as in the words *make, ride, mole, tube, shame, phone,* and *whine.* In this pattern, the *e* at the end of the word is silent and makes the first vowel sound long. The letter *y* acts as a vowel as well as a consonant. It can sound like a long *e* (*lovely, happy*) or a long *i* (e.g., *fry, my*). Other long vowel patterns include *vowel digraphs* and *diphthongs.* A vowel digraph is a single vowel sound represented by two letters. For example, the two vowels in *meat, pain, sheep,* and *day* are vowel digraphs. Diphthongs are also represented by two letters that have a glided pronunciation as one sound moves into the other (Venezky, 1999). The vowels in *boy* and *noise* are diphthongs. Beck (2006) notes that it isn't important for children to be able to label vowel digraphs and diphthongs as such. Rather, they need to learn the sounds that are associated with two-letter vowel patterns. *R*-controlled vowels are another kind of vowel. They are not short or long vowels but rather have their own *r*-influenced sounds. The *r* changes the sound the vowel makes. Read the following words to yourself. As you read, note how the vowel sound changes when *r* is added: *cat, car, put, purr, fit, fir, not, nor.*

As Morrow (2009) notes, there are many phonics rules but only three are consistent and thus worth teaching. Drawing on her work, we share these here.

1. In a consonant-vowel-consonant word (CVC) (e.g., *sun, man, pet*), the vowel sound is typically short.
2. In a consonant-vowel-consonant-silent *e* word (CVCe), the final *e* is silent and the first vowel is typically long (*same, hope, bike*).
3. A vowel that follows a consonant (CV) is typically long (*me, so, became*).

We highlight a number of instructional routines for teaching vowels. In the Classroom 8.5 summarizes Isabel and Mark Beck's (2015) instructional routine for teaching short vowels. We also describe how word sorting can be used to foster knowledge of vowel sounds. Word sorting activities are an integral part of word study instruction in many classrooms. According to Bear, Invernizzi, Templeton, and Johnston (2015), sorting words according to a particular feature requires children to closely examine the letters and larger units in words and thus fosters word learning and the development of spelling knowledge. Word sorts work better when the child has to pronounce the words before sorting them. The average child will sort *cat, rat, sat, chat, can, ran, fan,* and *span* without ever actually reading the words. Sorting *play, rain, made, make, day, slay,* and *gain* into a long vowel category and *pant, thank,* and *stand* into short vowels demands that the words must be read.

In the Classroom 8.5

Instructional Routines
Teaching Short Vowels

- *Lesson introduction.* "We're going to read Nancy Antle's book *The Good Bad Cat* together today. Before we start, we're going to learn the short vowel sound for the letter *a*." Point to the words *Bad* and *Cat* in the title. "The words *Bad* and *Cat* have the short *a* sound." Stretch the short *a* sound as you say the words, so children have an easier time hearing it [Baaaaaad ... Caaaaaat]. "Say the words with me."
- *Focus attention on the sound the short vowel makes at the beginning of the word.* "Let's look at these words. They begin with the short *a* sound." Have the following words in a pocket chart or on the board: *ant, apple.* "I'm going to say each word. Repeat it after me." Point to each word as you say it; children repeat it. "Say the short *a* sound /a/."
- *Connect the letter with the short vowel sound it makes.* Show children the large letter *a* card. "This is the letter *a*. The letter *a* stands for the /a/ sound in *ant* and *apple*. Say /a/. Each time I touch the letter *a*, say /a/." Touch the letter *a* card several times.
- *Discriminate between words that have the short vowel sound at the beginning of the word and words that do not.* Give each child a letter *a* card. "If the word I say begins with /a/, hold up your card and say /a/. If it doesn't begin with /a/, shake your head no." Say the following words: *at, am, bone, pickle, apple, bird, animal.*
- *Focus attention on the sound short a makes when it is in the middle of a spoken word.* "I'm going to say some words that have short *a* in the middle. Listen for the short *a* sound. I'm going to stretch it out so you can hear it. Then say each word after me. We'll stretch the sounds out together." Say and have children repeat the following words, making sure to stretch the short *a* sounds: *caaat, paaan, flaaag, jaaam.* "Now, we're going to say some more words. But this time we won't stretch the short *a* sounds. We'll have to listen carefully for the short *a*. I'll say each word first. Then you say it after me." Say the following words, without stretching the short *a* sound: *rat, tan, slap, glad, sat.*
- *Discriminate between words that have the short a sound in the middle of a word and those that do not.* "I'm going to say some more words. If a word has the /a/ sound in the middle, hold up your *a* card. If it does not have the /a/ sound in the middle, close your eyes. I'm going to stretch the sounds so you can hear them." Say the following words as children respond: *jab* [jaaab], *come* [cooome], *sob* [sooob], *grab* [graaab], *grip* [griiip], *crib* [criiib], *track* [traaack], *crab* [craaab]. "Now, I'll say some more words. This time, I'm not going to stretch the sounds. Listen carefully to the middle of the words. Hold up your *a* card when you hear the short *a* sound. Close your eyes when you don't." Say the following words without stretching the sounds: *hat, lamp, slip, shop, jam, chomp, past.*
- *Discriminate between words that have the short a at the beginning of the word and those that have it in the middle.* Give each child a word pocket. "I'm going to say some words that begin with short *a* and some that have short *a* in the middle. When a word begins with /a/, put your letter *a* at the beginning of your word pocket, like this [show children]. When a word has /a/ in the middle, put your letter *a* in the middle of the word pocket, like this [show children]." Example words: *apple, tap, ant, bad, sand, ask, rat, ash, man, last.*

SORTING WORDS: SHORT VOWEL SOUNDS

We are pattern seekers and sorting words helps children to develop their knowledge of spelling patterns in words. For example, Johnston, Bear, Invernizzi, and Templeton (2009) recommend a pattern sort for words with contrasting short vowel sounds. These sorts should be conducted during small group instruction so that you can ask the students to pronounce the words as they sort them and as review when their sorts are completed. Without this direction, students can sort words by visual features alone and never connect letters to sounds.

For the purpose of illustration, we'll focus on short *e* and short *u*. A teacher selects a set of one-syllable words with these short vowel sounds and writes them on word cards. Then she places the cards in random order in the lower pockets of a pocket chart. For a short *u* and short *e* sort, these words might include *sub, bet, fed, hum, men, nut, led, cup, bus, den, let, tub, pen, but, cut, shut, hen, tug,* and *sled.* Then the teacher has the children read the words together while focusing their attention on the vowel sounds in the words. Next she places the cards for *bug* and *red* in two top pockets of the pocket chart. Johnston and her colleagues explain that these serve as "header" cards for the sort. The teacher models reading *sub* and comparing it to the header word *bug.* As she models, she stretches the vowel sound: "suuuub, buuuug." Then she tells the children that the words have the same sound in the middle and so she places the word *sub* beneath *bug* in the pocket chart. She and the children engage in the same procedures for the word *bet,* and *bet* is placed underneath *red* in the pocket chart. The teacher next calls on individual children to identify where to place the other word cards. When all the word cards are placed, the teacher has the children read each list with her. She tells the children that, as they read, they are to think about how the words on each list are the same. When children have read the lists, the teacher explains that the words on the first list all have the short *u* sound and that the words on the second list all have the short *e* sound. Finally, Johnston and her colleagues explain, the word cards are removed from the chart, shuffled, and resorted.

In the Classroom 8.6 shares Beck and Beck's (2013) instructional routines for teaching long vowel patterns, diphthongs, and *r*-controlled vowels, following which we describe word sorting with these patterns. Word sorts for these patterns are particularly helpful to children as there are so many visual patterns that represent the long vowel sounds.

SORTING WORDS: LONG VOWEL PATTERNS

As we've discussed, word sorting is very useful for helping children learn the visual patterns in words. One kind of sort that Invernizzi, Johnston, Bear, and Templeton (2015) recommend for developing long vowel knowledge is a pattern sort. Children analyze and sort words by both their sounds and spelling patterns. The "header" cards are words that represent the spelling pattern the teacher wants children to notice and learn. For example, a teacher may want children to notice different spelling patterns that represent the long *a* sound. A sort might focus on consonant-vowel-consonant-silent *e* (CVCe) words and consonant-vowel-vowel-consonant (CVVC) words, for example, with header cards *race* and *main.* The teacher would then present children with a set of words to sort, such as *rain, cake, plane, train, plate, sail, cape, jail, grape, nail, vase, snail, gate, tail, skate, blaze, hail, pain, snake,* and *cane.* Children read each word, notice its spelling pattern, and place it under the appropriate header card. When the children have sorted the words, the teacher and children read each list and confirm that the words fit the pattern.

TEACHING BLENDING

In order to read, children must learn how to blend the sounds they're learning to form words. As Beck (2013) notes, many beginning readers find learning this very challenging. You'll need to model it many, many times and to engage children in many experiences with blending activities. In the Classroom 8.7 shows two variations of blending activities. In the first activity, initial blending, the teacher models how to blend the

MyLab Education
Video Example 8.2
This video shows a teacher teaching spelling patterns. Decide what spelling patterns the child is learning and how the teacher guides the student. What else do you believe she could do?

MyLab Education
Video Example 8.3
This video will cause you to think about the need to link meaning, phonology, and orthography. What would you add to this lesson?

In the Classroom 8.6

Instructional Routines

Teaching Vowel Patterns

The CVCe Pattern

- *Show children how adding an e to short vowel words they already know will change the vowel sound from short to long.* Put the letter cards for *c, a,* and *n* in a word pocket or pocket chart. Say: "Here is a word we know—*can*. In *can* we hear the short *a* sound. Read the word with me. [Children read.] Now, I'm going to add the letter *e* to the end of *can*. When I do, it changes the short *a* sound to the long *a* sound. The *a* now says its name. The new word is *cane*. Read the word with me. [Children read.] If I take away the *e*, we have the word *can* again."

c	a	n			c	a	n	e		c	a	n

- Say: "Let's do another word." Put the letter cards *c, a,* and *p* in the pocket chart or word pocket. Say: "Read this word with me." Now, add the *e*. Say: "Remember, when we add the *e*, the vowel changes from short to long. It now says its name. Say the long *a* sound for me. [Children respond.] Now, let's read this word (*cape*) together. [Children read.] Now, I'm going to take the *e* away. Read our short vowel word with me (*cap*)."

c	a	p			c	a	p	e		c	a	p

- Give children the following letter cards: *a, e, d, m, n, r, t*. Say "Line your cards up in front of you. Together we're going to spell and read some words. Follow my directions. The first word we're going to spell and read is *man*. Use three of your letter cards and make the word. Let's read it together—*man*. Now add your letter *e* to the word to change the vowel sound from short to long. Read the word with me—*mane*. [Children read.] Now, take away the *e* and read the word—*man*. [Children read.] Let's do some more." Lead children through the same steps for the following words: *rat, rate, rat; mat, mate, mat; mad, made, mad*.

Vowel Digraphs, Diphthongs, and r-Controlled Vowels

- *Connect the first two-letter vowel pattern with the sound it represents.* Say: "On our shelf today is a book I know you'll enjoy. It's called *Sail Away* by the author Donald Crews." Use your large letter cards to make the word *sail* in the demonstration word pocket. "This is the word *sail*. Read it with me." Children read. Pointing to the *ai*, say, "When we see an *a* and an *i* together in a word, they make the long *a* sound. This is the sound we hear in the middle of *sail*." Now take the *s* and *l* away. Say: "When I touch the *ai*, say the long *a* sound." Put the *s* and *l* back. Say: "Read the word with me: *sail*." Children read. Repeat this procedure a few times.

s	ai	l			ai			s	ai	l

- *Connect the second two-letter vowel pattern with the sound it represents.* Say: "Two other letters can make the long *a* sound." Make the word *say* in the demonstration word pocket. Say, "This is the word *say*. Read it with me." Children read. Pointing to the *ay*, say, "When there is an *a* and a *y* together in a word, the sound we hear is also long *a*." Now, take the *s* away. Say: "When I touch the *ay*, say the long *a* sound." Put the *s* back. Say: "Read the word with me: *say*." Repeat this procedure a few times.

s	ay			ay			s	ay

- *Connect the two two-letter vowel patterns with the sound they represent.* Put *sail* and *say* one on top of the other in the word pocket. Say, "As I point to each word, read it with me." Have children read each word a number of times. Each time you point to a word, underscore with your finger the two letters that make the long *a* sound.

s	ai	l			s	ay

- *Discriminate words that may compete with target two-letter vowel patterns.* Write the following words on chart paper or the board: *pay, nail, man, may, tan, tail, play, main, ran, ray, pan, stray*. Say: "Read these words. Pay careful attention to the vowels in the words."

In the Classroom 8.7

Blending Activities

Initial Blending

Say: "If I don't know what a word is right away, here's how I figure it out. First, I look at the word, and I find any parts I know. So let's pretend I don't know this word—*mat*." Write the word *mat* on the board. As you point to the *m*, say, "I know it starts with an /mmmm/ sound. Then I see the *at*." Point to the *at*. "I already know *at*. So I say /mmm/ /aaaaattttt/—*mat*. That makes sense. I can also say /mmmm/ /aaaa/ /tttt/—*mat*." Move your finger from *m* to *a* to *t* as you blend the sounds.

Successive Blending

- Place letters for the word you will blend in a pocket chart with spaces between (*r e d*). Then give each child a set of letter cards. Have children set their cards up in front of them with spaces between them.
- *Model.* Point to the *r* and *e* one at a time. Say: "/r/ [Pause] /e/."
- *With children.* Say: "Point to your letters as I point to mine. We'll say the sounds together." [Children respond.]
- *Model.* Slide the letter *e* over to the letter *r* (*re d*). Run your finger under the *re* and say, "/re/ /re/." Then separate the cards again.
- *With children.* Say: "Let's do it together. Slide your *e* over to your *r*. As we say the sounds, slide your finger under the *re*." [Children respond.]
- *Model.* Slide your finger under the *re*. Say: "/re/." Hold the sound until you point to the *d* and say, "/d/."
- *With children.* Say: "Together now. Slide your finger under your *re* and say /re/. Hold the sound until you point to your *d*." [Children respond.]
- *Model.* Move the *d* over to the *re* (*red*). Slide your finger under *red* and say, "/red/. This is the word *red*." Then separate the *d* from *red* again.
- *With children.* Say: "Together now. Move your *d* over to the *re* and read the word—*red*." [Children respond.]

beginning consonant (the onset) with the rime *at*. She then models how the rime *at* can be analyzed into its component phonemes and blended. The second activity is Beck's (2006) successive blending routine, with phonemes blended serially. You may use this following initial blending or begin blending instruction with it. Beck explains successive blending as follows: "In successive blending, students say the first two sounds in a word and immediately blend those two sounds together. Then they say the third sound and immediately blend that sound with the first two blended sounds. If it is a four-phoneme word, then they say the fourth phoneme and immediately blend that sound with the first three blended sounds" (p. 50). Beck explains that successive blending reduces the memory demands on children. With each successive blend, children must only hold in memory two sounds, and only two sounds are blended.

BODY CODA BLENDING

Bruce Murray and his colleagues have discovered that stressing the blending of the final sound onto the two initial sounds can be a great help to young readers (Murray et al., 2008). As we already discussed, a single syllable word can be divided into onset and rime (*m + op*). The word can also be divided into the body and the coda (*mo + p*) where *mo* is the body and the *p* is the coda. Blending activities should include practice changing just the final sound in the word. "Let's read *ba*; it's /ba/. Now let's add the letter *t*; what is the word? [Children respond.] Now let's change the ending letter." *bat* becomes *ban, bad, bam, bass, back*, and *bath*. Changing the final letter promotes flexibility in decoding and avoids the rhyming response children acquire when the teacher just changes the initial sound.

WORD BUILDING ACTIVITIES

Skillful readers see and use nearly all the letters as they read words (Adams, 1990). Thus, as teachers we must provide children with learning activities that foster close analysis of the letters in words. We share two techniques for word building, one designed by Beck and Beck (2015) and the other by Cunningham and Cunningham (1992). Both techniques involve students in building words while following the teacher's serial direction. Also, in both activities, each word the children create is different from the previous word by only one letter. What differentiates Beck's technique from that of Cunningham and Cunningham is the nature of the teacher's serial direction. In Beck's technique, the teacher identifies the letter children change to form the next word. In Cunningham and Cunningham's technique, called "making words," children must listen and decide for themselves which letter to change. Additionally, the children work toward making a "mystery word," a word that uses all the letters provided. In the Classroom 8.8 shows examples of each procedure.

In the Classroom 8.8

Word Building Activities

Beck's Word Building Routine

- *Demonstrate a word building.* Place the letter cards for *h, a,* and *m* in a pocket chart to make the word *ham*. Say: "This is the word *ham*. Read the word with me. [Children respond.] Now, watch what I do. I'm going to change the letter *a* to *i* and make a different word. Read the new word. [Children respond.] Now, it's your turn to build some words. I will tell you which letters to use. After we build each word, we're going to read the word together."

- *Lead students in word building.* Give each child a set of letter cards (*a, d, d, h, i, m, t*). Sequentially have the children build the words as directed. After children have built each word, write the word on the board in a list. Direct the children in the following way:

    "Put the letter *i* after the *h*. Put the letter *t* at the end. What's the word?" (*hit*)
    "Change the *t* to a *d*. What's the word?" (*hid*)
    "Change *i* to *a*. What's the word?" (*had*)
    "Change the *d* to *m*. What's the word?" (*ham*)
    "Change the *a* to *i*. What's the word?" (*him*)
    "Change the *h* to *d*. What's the word?" (*dim*)
    "Change the *m* to *d*. What's the word?" (*did*)
    "Change the *i* to *a*. What's the word?" (*dad*)

- *Read the words.* Say, "Read each word as I point to it." Have children read the listed words.

Making Words

Give the children letter cards for *n, t, r, s, p,* and *i*. Give them the following directions:

    "Take three letters and make the word *tin*."
    "Change one letter to make the word *tip*."
    "Change the letters around to make the word *pit*."
    "Change one letter to make the word *pin*."
    "Add a letter to make *spin*."
    "Change a letter to make the word *spit*."
    "Take away two letters and add a letter to make the word *rip*."
    "Add one letter to make the word *rips*."
    "Add another letter to make the word *trips*."
    "Now use all your letters to make the mystery word (*prints*)."

DEVELOPING A WEEKLY PLAN

At this point in the chapter we have introduced you to many activities and you have the tools or the components of word recognition instruction. We have not yet given you the overall plan. Now we want to show you what word recognition instruction looks like during a typical week of instruction. At the beginning of the school year, when the needs of the students are somewhat similar you can deliver the same instruction to the whole class. As the weeks go by the students will sort themselves into groups with some needing more direct instruction than others. By the middle of the year or sooner, we recommend that most word recognition instruction be delivered in small groups. In the Classroom 8.9 shows an example of a lesson plan where we introduce the short i pattern to a small group of students.

In the Classroom 8.9

A Weekly Lesson Plan

Learning Outcomes

By the end of the week the students will be able to

1. Discriminate words with short *i* patterns from short *a* patterns.

2. Decode new CVC, short *i*, words when reading them in isolation and in context.

Materials

- Letter cards for making words, individual sets of short *a* and *i* words for sorting, paper and markers or individual white boards for writing sorts, short grade level appropriate texts for reading practice

Week at a Glance for Small Group

	Day 1	Day 2	Day 3	Day 4	Day 5
Word Recognition	Introduce the short *i* pattern following the plan on page 39. Provide practice for students to decode short *a* and *i* words.	Sort and pronounce short *a* and *i* words (p. 20). Conduct a writing sort in which students spell several short *i* and *a* rhyme patterns.	Engage students in a making-words activity with letter tiles (p. 48). Students write and pronounce words they sorted.	Sort and pronounce short *a* and *i* words (p.20). Conduct a writing sort where students spell several short *i* and *a* rhyme patterns.	Provide an opportunity for students to read a random selection of short *a* and *i* words to assess their progress.
Text Reading	Re-read a familiar book to reinforce word learning. Introduce the first new book and preview the vocabulary. Add words to student's word bank.	Re-read a familiar book and ask students to retell the story. Read the first new book and coach on decoding problems. Review word banks.	Re-read a familiar book and ask students about story elements. Introduce the second new book and preview the vocabulary.	Re-read a familiar book to build fluency. Students individually read the book and coach on words. Review word banks.	Re-read the two books for the week. Discuss similarities and differences. Introduce the third new book and preview the vocabulary.

Teaching Larger Units in Words

To help children read words using the larger units in words—as opposed to individual letter-sound correspondences—we need to develop their knowledge of these larger units and their ability to recognize them in the printed words they encounter. Once children know some initial consonants (onsets), we can expand their word knowledge by teaching rimes and other units. Children then can use these units to decode by analogy.

TEACHING RIMES

Recall that a rime is the first vowel in a syllable and all the letters that follow it. In the one-syllable word *mat*, *at* is the rime. In the two-syllable word *backbone*, *ack* and *one* are the rimes. Remember, too, that rimes are also referred to as phonograms and spelling patterns. Sometimes you hear them called chunks, although the term *chunks* tends to apply to various kinds of larger units in words. There are many common rimes whose pronunciations are quite regular. Figure 8.8 toward the end of the chapter lists 37 rimes that occur in nearly 500 primary-grade words (Wylie & Durrell, 1970). Just by knowing a few rimes, children can use them to read and write many words that have them. For example, a child who knows the rime *ot* can use it to read *not, hot, rot,* and *dot*. The New Standards Primary Literacy Committee (2004) has noted that by the end of first grade, children should know word families ending in common rimes (e.g., *in, at, ent, ill, or, un, op, ing*). At the end of the chapter, we present these 37 rimes as a screening tool.

One way of explicitly and systematically developing children's knowledge of rimes is to teach them key words. This is called decoding by analogy or the compare and contrast method (Gaskins et al. 1997, White, 2005) A key word is a one-syllable word that has a common rime. Children are taught to use the key words to analogize to unknown words that share the rimes. In this way, the key words help children to "unlock" the pronunciation of the unknown words. For example, with the key word *cat* a child can figure out *sat, mat, rat, flat,* and *splat*. A number of studies have demonstrated the effectiveness of this strategy for helping children learn to recognize words (Gaskins et al., 1997; Leslie & Allen, 1999; White, 2005). Linda Allen (1998) has provided a lesson sequence for teaching key words. She refers to rimes as spelling patterns. In the Classroom 8.10 shows how a teacher might use Allen's lesson sequence. As you review the routine, note how the teacher cognitively models the thinking involved in the strategy. Following key word lessons, the key words are placed on the word wall for children's future use and reference.

In the Classroom 8.10

Decoding by Analogy

- *State the purpose.* Say: "Our purpose today is to learn to read and spell the key words *back, pig,* and *land*. Key words are words that have spelling patterns we can use to read and spell other words. The spelling pattern is the first vowel and all the letters that follow it. We can use words we know to pronounce new words with the same spelling pattern."
- *Introduce the key word.* Say the key word *back* and have the students repeat the word. Now segment the word. "How many sounds do you hear in the word?" Slowly segment the word saying each sound and raising a finger to represent each sound. Next write the word in a sound box | b | a | ck | representing each sound in the word. Students should see that the word has three phonemes but it is written with four letters. The *ck* makes one sound. Finally ask the students to think of words that rhyme with back. The word should then be placed on the word wall under the a column.

- *Word building.* Give each child a set of cards as follows: *back, ack, b, r, l, t, bl, qu.* Children will build each word using the onsets (*b, r, l, t, bl, qu*) and the rime (*ack*). Serially, give the children the clues below. As they build each word, copy it onto a blank card. Put the card in the pocket chart for later in the lesson. Or write it on the board or chart paper.

  "Spell the word that is the opposite of front." (*back*)
  "Spell the word that is something on which you'd hang your coat." (*rack*)
  "Spell the word *lack*. This word means you haven't got something." (*lack*)
  "Spell the word that would hurt if you sat on it." (*tack*)
  "Spell the word that is a color." (*black*)
  "Spell the word that is the sound a duck makes." (*quack*)

- *Cognitive modeling*

  Example 1: Put the following sentence on the board.
  Crow said, "Just what we need—a *sack* of seed!"

  Say: "Let's say I'm reading this sentence, and I don't know this word (*sack*). First, I look at the spelling pattern in the word. Then I think of a key word I know that has the same spelling pattern (*back*). I tell myself, if this word is *back*, then this word is *sack*. Then I reread the sentence to make sure it makes sense: 'Just what we need—a *sack* of seed.' Yes, that makes sense."
  Example 2: Say: "Let me show you another example."
  I will *pack* my suitcase.

  Say: "I see this word (*pack*) has the *ack* spelling pattern. I know the key word *back* has the *ack* spelling pattern. So I'll use it to help me read this word. I say to myself, if this is *back*, then this is *pack*. Now I read it again to see if it makes sense—'I will *pack* my suitcase.' Yes, it makes sense."

- *Reading and transfer.* Present new sentences for students to chorally read. They can be on chart paper, the board, or sentence strips.

  The train was coming down the track.
  I had a snack after school today.
  Mom told me not to smack my lips.
  I put my books in a stack.
  Don't step on the crack.

- *Onset/rime practice.* Using the pocket chart with word cards from earlier in the lesson (or from the words listed on the board), lead students through the following routine. For each word on the list, point to the onset and say, "First say—." Have the children say the sound the onset makes. Then point to the rime and say, "Then say—." Have children say the rime. When children have said the rime, say, "Put it together and you get—." Children then say the word. As they say the word, underscore the word from left to right with your finger. An example for the first word is below. Have children engage in the routine for the words *rack, lack, tack, black,* and *quack.*

  Teacher: "First say—"
  Children: "/b/"
  Teacher: "Then say—"
  Children: "/ack/"
  Teacher: "Put it together and you get—"
  Children: "back"

- *Final review.* Remind students why key words are important. Say: "Today we learned a number of words using the key word *back*. Key words are important to know because they help us read lots of words that have the same spelling pattern."

Technology that Assists Word Recognition

There are many programs available to assist with the development of the word recognition skills of young children, but few are very effective. However, there are resources available to help you select and evaluate instructional programs. We recommend two sites, one is The What Works Clearinghouse (https://ies.ed.gov/ncee/wwc/FWW/Index).

At this site search under the literacy programs and confine your search to K–2. The other site is the Best Evidence Encyclopedia managed by Johns Hopkins University (http://www.bestevidence.org/reading). Both of these sites report the number of studies used to evaluate reading programs, the quality of the studies, and the strength of the evidence—how much difference this programs made. Here are a few that we believe are worth considering.

- **Lexia Learning:** www.lexialearning.com. This is a computer-based program that assists students with phonemic awareness, letter recognition, and phonics. There is not a lot of evidence in support of the program, but exists in notable.

- **The Starfall** (www.starfall.co) has numerous activities to help early primary-grade children develop their word recognition skills. In the Learning to Read section of the site, a voice prompts children to build words using onsets and rimes. Children can build multiple words by dragging various onsets over to the rime. The computer voice provides support in this process. This website also provides opportunities for children to practice reading words in sentences and simple texts. The effectiveness of the program has not been determined.

- **Read Well:** http://www.voyagersopris.com/literacy/read-well/overview. This program has lessons in phonemic awareness, letter names, and phonics. The effectiveness of the program has not been determined.

- The International Reading Association's website (www.readwritethink.org) has a number of engaging online word study activities for children (as well as many resources for teachers).

- You might also consider one of the following apps. These can be used by parents to support their children's leaning.

AlphaTots Alphabet by Spinlight Studio

Interactive Alphabet by Pi'ikea Street

Simplex Spelling Phonics - Rhyming with CVC Words by Pyxwise Software Inc

Word Wizard by L'Escapadou

One caution—as you make decisions about instructional techniques to use with students, keep in mind the following. Research strongly suggests that working with rimes is useful only after children can analyze them into their component sounds (Ehri & Robbins, 1992; Gaskins et al., 1997; Vandervelden & Siegel, 1995). Because many poor readers cannot do this without explicit instruction (Juel & -Minden-Cupp, 2000), you want to make sure to still attend to individual letter-sound correspondences as you teach children to work with the larger units in words.

DECODING MULTISYLLABIC WORDS

As we've shared, the basic unit in speech is the syllable. All words have one or more syllables. As children become more advanced readers, they encounter increasing numbers of multisyllabic words, which can be intimidating for them. As teachers, we want to help children realize that multisyllabic words are simply strings of syllables comprising spelling patterns that they already know. Children need to examine long words and find familiar "chunks." These chunks can be onsets, rimes, affixes, or root words.

In the Classroom 8.11 shows two similar approaches to decoding multi-syllabic words. Both focus children's attention on chunks in words. In the first approach, the teacher focuses on locating and using multiple rimes to decode a multisyllabic word. The lesson is grounded in Bill Cosby's *One Dark and Scary Night*, a leveled text for younger readers. Teachers-in-training have regularly used this approach and lesson sequence with much success for many years in a university-based literacy center (Leslie & Allen, 1999). The second approach features an activity called "word detectives." In this approach, readers notice and use different kinds of chunks to recognize multisyllabic words. With either approach, you'll want to provide students with multiple examples

In the Classroom 8.11

Decoding by Analogy

Using Multiple Rimes to Decode

Ms. Sampson has written the following sentence on the board: *I tightened every muscle in my body so I couldn't move.* She thinks aloud as she cognitively models how to decode *tightened*.

Ms. Sampson: "Let's say I don't know this word (*tightened*). First, I look at all the parts of the word to see if there are rimes that I know. I see *ight* as in the key word *night*. And, I see *en* as in the key word *hen*. I also see the ending *ed*. I'm going to write the key words I know with those rimes above the parts of the big word that share those rimes."

night hen
I *tighten*ed every muscle in my body so I couldn't move.

Ms. Sampson: "Now, I tell myself, if this is *night*, this is *tight*. If this is *hen*, this is *ten*. I put the two chunks together and get *tighten*. Next I add the *ed* and put the three chunks together— /tight/ /en/ /d/. Now I read the sentence again to make sure it makes sense."

I *tightened* every muscle in my body so I couldn't move.

Ms. Sampson: "Here's another big word we'll read in the story (*tomorrow*). I see two rimes I know. The key words for them are *for* and *show*. So I say to myself, if this is *for*, this is *mor*. If this is *show*, this is *row*. I get *morrow*. I know the little word *to* that this big word begins with. Next I put the chunks together. I get *tomorrow*. Then, I read it again to see if it makes sense."

for show
Think about tomorrow, playing and having fun.

Word Detectives

Each day, Ms. Kenney writes a multisyllabic word on the board, talks about any clues to its identity that she can find, and lists these clues on the board. Then she writes another multisyllabic word on the board and asks the children to find clues to its identity. The following words and clues show some of the ways children have tried to figure out the words:

- *chipmunk*
  Karl noticed the rime *ip*.
  Marty said she got *unk* because she knew the word *skunk*.
- Tasha volunteered the pronunciation of the consonant digraph *ch*.
- *shameful*
  Katy said she instantly saw the affix *ful*.
  Ming said he knew the *ame* rime by heart.
- Tasha volunteered the pronunciation of the consonant digraph *sh*.
- *transit*
  Lily said she knew how to chunk it because she saw the familiar *an* and *it* rimes.
  Kyle added that the letter combination *ns* doesn't start a syllable.
  Mike volunteered the pronunciation of the consonant blend *tr*.

when they are first learning the techniques and then with scaffolding across time as needed. And when working with children on learning to recognize multisyllabic words, it's critical to emphasize that children are locating and using chunks in words as a strategy for figuring out how to pronounce large words. Without an explicit emphasis on the strategic nature of the technique, many children may not transfer it to other reading situations when they encounter unfamiliar multisyllabic words.

TEACHING MEANING UNITS IN WORDS: PREFIXES AND SUFFIXES

Many multisyllabic words contain prefixes and suffixes. Teaching students to be on the lookout for these can really help them with decoding. We discussed prefixes and

In the Classroom 8.12

Teaching Affixes

- Write two familiar words containing the affix you want to teach on the board. Ask students to define the words. Suppose you wanted to teach the prefix *un*. Most students know what *unhappy* and *unkind* mean, so these would be appropriate words to use for instruction.
- Underline the affix and note its spelling. Then, if the affix is a prefix with a concrete meaning, either elicit the meaning from students—if you think they know it—or give them the meaning. *Un*, of course, means "not." (If the affix is a suffix, it is usually best not to define it. The abstract definitions of suffixes are often confusing.)
- On the board, write a word that contains the affix but that students probably don't know. With *un*, you might use the word *unreal*. Ask students to use their knowledge of *un* and the root word (in this case, *real*) to figure out the pronunciation and meaning of the new word: *un* means "not," and *real* means "real." So *unreal* means "not real." (If the word part is a suffix, they will only need to figure out the pronunciation of the new word.)
- Tell students that they are likely to see the affix fairly frequently, and that often, if they cover it up, they'll recognize or be able to decode the root word. Then, if they add the affix back, they will probably be able to pronounce the complete word and understand its meaning.

suffixes previously in this chapter and listed possible prefixes and suffixes to teach in Figures 8.3, 8.4, and Figure 8.5. In the Classroom 8.12 describes a simple and straightforward routine to teach them. Note that there are many more prefixes and suffixes than you need to or *should* teach. Teach only those that are fairly frequent in the material your students read.

The Importance of Contextual Reading

READ, READ, READ

In this chapter, we looked at specific instructional ideas for increasing children's knowledge about how words are constructed and how to read them. We emphasized teaching high-frequency words, letter-sound knowledge (phonics), and larger units in words. However, we recognize that it is not possible to teach every phonic element and spelling pattern that children will encounter. They will acquire a lot of knowledge about words from wide reading. Moreover, we want to emphasize again how important it is for children to apply their developing word recognition skills during contextual reading (Juel & Roper/Schneider, 1985). Many teachers rely on core reading programs to teach reading and the most recent research suggests that there is not enough text in a core reading program for a child to become a fluent reader (Brenner & Hiebert, 2010). For most teachers we know, this is routine knowledge. Georgia Woods talks about how she has children read following instruction in the long *a* vowel sound.

I like to begin and follow up activities on spelling patterns for long *a* with reading books such as *Who Has a Tail?* (Level G) by Fay Robinson. This text has actual photographs of animals, and many of the words show spelling patterns for long *a*. For example, here are the lines from pages 3 and 4:

Who has a tail that shakes like a rattle?
The snake does. When this snake shakes its tail, the tail rattles. That way, other animals hear it. They stay away.

As you can see, this book gives students much practice reading long *a* spelling patterns in words such as *tail, shake, stay,* and *away*.

—Georgia Woods, first-grade teacher

The Reading Corner

Easy-to-Read Books

Most publishers of children's books have a series of leveled books dedicated to beginning readers. The difficulty of the levels, however, isn't consistent across publishers. For example, Level One books from one publisher may be simpler than another publishers' Level One books. However, the vast number of easy-to-read books available today gives teachers, librarians, and caregivers a wide array to choose from, making it possible to place the right book in a beginning reader's hands at the right time.

David A. Adler. *Don't Throw it to Mo! (Mo Jackson)* Level 2. Penguin Young Readers, 2016. Mo is a young African-American boy with a passion for sports but has "butter fingers" when it comes to catching the football. His coach, however, has a plan for turning Mo's small size into an asset for the team. Very simple sentences, no more than 3 lines to a page. 32 pages.

Ruby Bridges. *Ruby Bridges Goes to School: My True Story* (Scholastic Reader, Level 2). Cartwheel Books, 2009. The true story of Ruby Bridges, the first African-American child to integrate into a white New Orleans school—now with simple text for beginning readers. 32 pages.

Margaret Wise Brown. *I Like Bugs* (Step-Into-Reading, Step 1). Random House Books for Young Readers, 1999. The title says it all. The narrator likes bugs—black, green, fat, bubby bugs. It doesn't matter. With only a few words to each page, and most repeated, this is perfect book for the beginning reader. 32 pages.

James Dean. *Pete the Cat and the Tip-Top Tree House* (My First I can Read Book, Level One). HarperCollins, 2017. One of the many titles in HarperCollins My First I can Read Book series, this Level One easy-to-read book features the ever-clever Pete the Cat and his gang of groovy friends as they fix the problem of Pete's too-small-for-everyone playhouse. Level One books have simple texts with generally no more than 20 words to a page. 32 pages.

Jonathan Fenske. *A Pig, a Fox, and a Box* (Penguin Young Readers, Level 2). Penguin Young Readers, 2015. After pig finds just the right size box to hide in, a little fox tries to play some tricks on his bigger friend that don't exactly work out as planned. The simple dialog is written in comic strip type bubbles. 30 pages.

Wendy Cheyette Lewison. *Silly Milly* (Scholastic Reader Level 1). Cartwheel Books, 2010. *Silly Milly* is a rhyming easy reader where readers are invited to guess the riddle of why Miss Milly likes what she does. Answer: double letters. 32 pages.

Jennifer Liberts. *Go, Go, Trucks!* (Step Into Reading, Level 1). Random House Books for Young Readers, 2017. Readers will discover many kinds of different trucks in this very simple easy-reader with only 2–5 word sentences on each page. Rhyme and rhythmic text pared with picture cues help children decode this story. 32 pages.

Anna Membrino. *Big Shark, Little Shark* (Step into Reading, Level One). Random House Books for Young Readers, 2017. Big Shark and Little Shark are opposite in many ways except one—they are both hungry. *Big Shark, Little Shark* is one of several titles in Level One of Random House's Step into Reading Series. This level has a very simple text (usually only 4–10 words to a page) with most words repeated several times. 32 pages.

Jennifer Morris. *May I Please Have a Cookie?* (Scholastic Readers, Level 1). Cartwheel books, 2005. Alfie the alligator loves Mommy's cookies but learns a better way to get them than grabbing them out of the cookie jar. One to three simples sentences to a page. 32 pages.

Mo Willems. *Waiting is Not Easy* (An Elephant and Piggie Book). Disney-Hyperion, 2014. Gerald must learn to be patient after Piggie tells him she has a surprise for him. 64 pages.

COACHING WORD RECOGNITION

Coaching children to apply their developing word recognition skills during contextual reading is important and it helps them become more metacognitive and strategic readers (Taylor, Peterson, Rodriguez, & Pearson, 2002). They develop what Marie Clay (2001) has called a "self-extending" system: a system for recognizing words and understanding text that children will continually expand and refine over time. Accomplished teachers provide students with general and specific word recognition cues (Clark, 2004). General cues are nonspecific in nature. For example, when a child encounters an unknown word, the teachers say something like "How are you going to figure that out?" or "Look at the word and think about what you need to do." Specific cues focus children's attention on salient features of words. For example, the teachers offer suggestions like "Cover up the ending," "Use what you know about *r*-controlled vowels," or "Look for a chunk you know." To craft specific cues, the teachers consider such factors as the sounds the consonants make in the unknown word, particularly those that could represent more than one sound, like *c* (*cat*, *city*), *s* (*<u>say</u>s*), and *g* (*grand*, *giraffe*); the sounds the vowels make; the presence of blends, digraphs, or silent letters; and any rimes and affixes in the word.

Next we share a few excerpts from one of the teachers' small-group reading lessons. Elizabeth Fry, a veteran first-grade teacher, was among the most accomplished teachers in a nationally focused large-scale study of teachers that "beat the odds" in teaching children to read (Taylor, Pearson, Clark, & Walpole, 2000). In the first excerpt, Ms. Fry coaches a student as the group reads Kathy Dubowski's *Cave Boy*. Peter is having difficulty recognizing the word *always*. When he becomes stuck, Ms. Fry prompts him to consider his strategies. When he identifies a well-learned strategy, Ms. Fry positively reinforces his thinking. Peter then identifies the first two letters in the word. Ms. Fry knows that the *al* looks unfamiliar to her first-graders, so shares the pronunciation of the word part. Then she cues Peter to examine the vowel pattern in the word. He identifies it, and Ms. Fry prompts him to put the word parts together. Peter does, and he independently adds the *s*. Ms. Fry then has him reread to make sure it makes sense.

Peter: "Stop all that … banging. Stop all that noise. That is Chief Grump. He is a … a …"

Ms. Fry: What can you do if you're stuck?

Peter: Cover up the *s*.

Ms. Fry: Cover up the *s*. That's a good start.

Peter: There's an *al*.

Ms. Fry: Yes. The *al* sounds like the *al* sound in *ball*.

Peter: " … al …"

Ms. Fry: Now look at the vowel pattern.

Peter: *ay* … long *a*

Ms. Fry: Now, put the two parts together.

Peter: "… always … always …"

Ms. Fry: Exactly. Start again to see if it makes sense.

Peter: "He is always mad about something."

During the school year, Ms. Fry teaches students to coach one another (with her support), as the following two excerpts show. Children are reading Linda Hayward's *All Stuck Up*. In the first excerpt, Brady is stuck on the word *caught*, and Ms. Fry invites the others in the group to provide him with clues. Jake tells him to "throw the *g-h* away," a procedure that Ms. Fry has taught, modeled, and encouraged throughout the year. Jacinda focuses Brady's attention on the vowel pattern *au*, a pattern that students have studied and practiced in isolation and in context. Brady needs more help, so Ms. Fry has him think about the context. With these supports, Brady is able to recognize the word. Ms. Fry confirms his word recognition and affirms his effort.

Brady: "Brer rabbit is always thinking of ways to not get … kuh … kuh …"

Ms. Fry: Can we give him some clues?

Jake: Throw the *g-h* away.

Jacinda: The double vowel.

Ms. Fry: Think about the story and ask yourself what makes sense: "He's thinking of ways to not get …"

Brady: "kuh … caught!"

Ms. Fry: *Caught*, that's right. You worked hard to figure that out.

Next, Carrie is trying to figure out *pretty*. Betta offers a clue about the sound the *y* makes. Marcus focuses her attention on the consonant blend. These are helpful clues, and Carrie is able to decode the sounds in the word. However, she accents the wrong word part. So Ms. Fry has the students read the word with her.

Carrie: puh … er …

Betta: There's a *y* acting like an *e*.

Marcus: There's a *p-r*.

Carrie: pre-TUH-y

Ms. Fry: Let's read it together.

All: pretty

Carrie: "Pretty soon."

Coaching fosters children's knowledge of letters and patterns in words within the context of real reading. This makes the connection for children that learning letter-sound correspondences and the larger patterns in words is a means to an end—reading and understanding a text—and not an end in itself. These coaching exchanges also illustrate some important concepts that we have discussed. First, they show learning in children's zone of proximal development. The words were not too easy but not so hard that children could not be successful with support. Second, the coaching exchanges demonstrate supportive structures, or scaffolds, that teachers create to help children solve particular problems—in this case decoding words. Third, the exchanges show how children can serve as supports to one another given instruction and practice in specific techniques. Finally, we have talked about how important motivation, engagement, and a positive environment are to learning. Ms. Fry's practice of having her first-graders give clues about unfamiliar words to one another has resulted in high levels of motivation and engagement among children and created a supportive learning environment in the reading groups. Children readily participate both when it is their turn to read aloud and their turn to "whisper read" when a peer reads. Children all track the print as they read and are anxious to help one another with unknown words. When a reader stumbles on a word, everyone in the group works to think of clues to give. And because everyone in the group readily and positively provides support, children feel free to take risks and grow as readers.

We hope that the ideas we have presented for word study instruction will give you a good foundation on which to begin planning instruction for beginning readers. Remember to base word study instruction on the six principles we discussed at the outset of this chapter. Use your imagination, summon up your creativity, and have fun. Your enthusiasm will be contagious.

Reflect and Apply

6. Much word study instruction begins with sorting picture cards for sounds and follows that activity with sorting word cards based on their spelling patterns. Explain the rationale for this basic two-step process.

7. Let's say you are listening to a first-grader read the following line from a leveled text: *"Hello," said the firefighter*. The child struggles to read the word *firefighter*. Together with a partner, generate three to five coaching clues you could give the child. Base your clues on phonics elements and larger units in words.

About Wide Reading

Primary-grade children must do a lot of reading to develop accurate and automatic word recognition. Barbara Foorman and her colleagues examined beginning reading instruction in 107 first and second grade classrooms (Foorman, Schattschneider, Eakins, Fletcher, Moats, & Francis, 2006). They found that the amount of time spent reading connected text was the best predictor of the students' success. This is consistent with David Share's self-teaching hypothesis (Share, 1995, 2005). According to Share, instruction is necessary to help students develop phonemic awareness and learn the alphabetic principle. Then, after some phonics instruction, children go on to teach themselves the hundreds of letter-sound correspondences in English.

The best tools for this reading are leveled books. Select books that are at an appropriate level of difficulty but do not be rigid about matching children to text. This may come as a shock but a rigid adherence to reading level is not necessary (Shanahan, 2014). Leveled books are short books that use high-frequency words and words that repeat the phonics features that children are learning. These books provide children with contextual reading practice. Many reading series include leveled books as part of their materials. Another excellent resource is Irene Fountas and Gay Su Pinnell's *The Fountas & Pinnell Leveled Book List, K–8+* (2009). At a nominal cost for a classroom of children, teachers can also access downloadable and printable leveled texts online at the Reading A to Z website (www.readinga-z.com/index.php). To give you a flavor for texts at different levels, the following excerpts are taken from leveled books.

Robin Bloksberg's *The Hole in Harry's Pocket* is a Level I text. At the end of first grade, children are expected to be able to read most of the words in a Level I text.

> Harry liked to walk to the store. He liked to hop on the curb. He liked to look in all the windows and count cracks in the sidewalk.
> Harry got the milk. But when he looked for his money, it was gone! What could he do?

By the end of second grade, we expect children to accurately read most of the words in a Level L text, such as the popular Cam Jansen mystery series by David A. Adler (text from *Cam Jansen and the Mystery of the Stolen Diamonds*).

> Eric opened his eyes. "It's no use," he said, "I'll never have a memory like yours."
> "You have to keep practicing," Cam told him. "Now try me."
> Cam looked straight ahead. She said, "Click," and then closed her eyes. Cam always said, "Click" when she wanted to remember something. She said it was the sound her mental camera made when it took a picture.

By the end of third grade, we expect children to accurately read most of the words in a Level O text, such as the popular Ramona series by Beverly Cleary (text from *Ramona Quimby, Age 8*).

Ramona had reached the age of demanding accuracy from everyone, even herself. All summer, whenever a grown-up asked what grade she was in, she felt as if she were fibbing when she answered, "third," because she had not actually started third grade. Still, she could not say she was in second grade, since she had finished that grade last June. Grown-ups did not understand that summers were free from grades.

Book levels are not perfect, of course. But the levels can give you a feel for benchmarks in word recognition at the end of grades 1 through 3. Teachers need to have a large selection of leveled books available. These books should be linked to word study instruction and read and reread until children can accurately read them at appropriate rates. Plastic tubs full of leveled books are staples in most K through grade 3 classrooms. The movement is from predictable texts in kindergarten to chapter books by the end of second grade.

Assessing Word Identification

Many children readily succeed at word study and become accomplished readers quite quickly. Others struggle and will need additional instruction, support, and encouragement. For children who struggle, informal assessments can help to identify their difficulties. As we wrote in Chapter 5 we do not believe that in-depth assessments are needed for all children, nor is it necessary to track progress weekly for all students. We will now share some informal approaches for assessing the development of word identification skills.

Sight Words

A quick individual assessment of the words each child knows will help you to plan instruction. Your school may provide the assessment, or one may come with the set of published materials in use at your school. You can also use the word list shown in Figure 8.7, which includes both high-frequency function words and common content words. You can modify it by adding words that you are planning to have children read in books, on charts, around your room, or at home. To create a quick assessment if you don't have one, clearly print a set of words on a list with space between them. Make as many copies as you need to assess children in your class. Individually, have children read the list. On your copy, note (1) whether the child reads a word correctly and (2) the nature of any misreadings—write the word or word part the child says in response to the word on the list. This will give you information on how the child approaches reading words. You can build on the child's existing knowledge to further word learning.

Figure 8.7 A List to Use for a Quick Check on Words Children Know

the	dog	big	cat	run	is
at	like	see	can	to	dog
he	my	yellow	and	red	get
up	go	she	girl	bus	was

Phonemic Awareness

Research has shown that children with insufficient phonemic awareness will likely struggle with learning to read. The problem is that they cannot hear the somewhat separable phonemes in spoken words very well. If they can't hear the phonemes, they will have a terrible time trying to map them to print—something necessary in learning to recognize words.

One way to see if children can hear phonemes in spoken words is to have them sort picture cards. Start with a sort based on initial consonants (onsets). For example, you can have children sort picture cards that represent *s* words, *b* words, and *m* words. A more difficult sort would involve picture cards that represent one-syllable words that have either the short *a* sound or the short *i* sound in the middle.

It would also be useful to give these students a short phonemic awareness inventory. The Phonological Awareness Test (Robertson & Salter, 2007) or the assessments inside *Phonemic Awareness in Young Children* (Adams, Foorman, Lundburg, & Beeler, 1998) provide very useful information.

You can gain insight into how children hear sounds in words and link those sounds to letters by examining their spelling. A child who consistently and accurately uses initial (or other) consonants in her writing—spelling *rain* as *r* or *dog* as *dg*—signals a readiness to learn specific word families or rimes. A child who spells *rain* as *b* and *dog* as *x* will likely need instruction in initial consonants. A child who spells *rain* as *rane* will benefit from sorting words with *ain, ane,* and other long *a* patterns.

Word Identification—Phonics

There are a number of informal ways to determine students' level of word identification skill. You can determine your students' needs by looking at what they do when they don't instantly recognize a word in print. Bear in mind that if children are stumbling over many words, the text is probably too difficult. Children need to be able to decode most of the words in the texts they read (about 95–98%). At this level of accuracy, they can understand the text and enjoy reading. Children's attempts at words they cannot identify provides you with information for planning instruction. Do they guess randomly or focus on pictures for cues to the word? Do they look at initial letters? Do they look for patterns they recognize within words? Our job is to identify what our students know and plan appropriate activities to extend that knowledge.

Your can use the list of 37 rimes as a screening tool. Simply add a consonant sound to each rime, print the words on a list or flash cards and assess students individually. Portions of the Emergent Literacy assessment that is in the appendix can be used to assess word identification skill.

Another informal assessment is the Early Names Test first developed by Pat Cunningham and more recently revised and validated by Mather, Sammons, and Schwartz (2006). The child is given a list of 30 first and last names and asked to pretend they are reading the class roll. The names on the roll contain a representative sample of short and long vowel patterns, and 60 different rimes; for example, *Bob Hap, Pam Rack, Kate Tide, Brent Lake* and *Rod Blade*. The test comes with a scoring matrix and allows the teacher to determine where the student is experiencing difficulty—consonants, blends, digraphs, short vowels, or long vowels. By looking for patterns among children the teacher can target the needs of students in her individual groups.

Figure 8.8 Thirty-Seven Rimes That Occur in Nearly 500 Primary-Level Words

ack	ail	ain	ake	ale	ame	an
ank	ap	ash	at	ate	aw	ay
eat	ell	est	ice	ick	ide	ight
ill	in	ine	ing	ink	ip	ir
ock	oke	op	or	ore	uck	ug
ump	unk					

Concluding Remarks

This chapter has emphasized the importance of word recognition in learning to read. We began by discussing why it is so important for children to learn to recognize words early on. Then we discussed the structure of spoken and written words and how children come to recognize words. In the remainder of the chapter, we described specific instructional techniques to develop children's word recognition ability.

The topics in this chapter are particularly important to understand thoroughly because without the ability to read words, children will have difficulty with nearly everything else at school. Learning to recognize words may just be a piece of literacy instruction, but it is foundational to further literacy development. Without word recognition competence, attaining present-day literacy is extremely unlikely.

Extending Learning

1. Observe a first-grade classroom or, better yet, several first-grade classrooms at different times during the year. What kind of word study instruction do you see? What kinds of texts are the children reading? How are the children progressing?

2. Meet individually with several kindergarten and first-grade children. Have each child spell some words for you, such as *cat, run, jump, name, goat, van, arm, stripe, little, coat, rope, back, smash,* and *light.* What can you tell from the child's spelling about what he or she knows about words? What might you plan for word study instruction to help the child grow?

3. Individually, have several first-grade children read to you. Notice what happens as each child reads. Does the child look at the words? What happens when the child forgets a word? What can you infer the child knows about words from how he or she reads? What might you do to build on children's current knowledge?

Children's Literature

Adler, D. (Many titles in Cam Jansen series by this author). New York: Puffin Books. This is a staple for second grade.

Antle, N. (1996). *The Good Bad Cat.* Grand Haven, MI: School Zone. A rhyming story about cats. 32 pages.

Aylesworth, J. (1995). *Old Black Fly.* New York: Henry Holt. A fly annoys and meets his end. Audiocassette available. 32 pages.

Bloksberg, R. (1995). *The Hole in Harry's Pocket.* New York: Hyperion.

Cleary, B. (Many titles in the Ramona series by this author). New York: Avon Books. This is a staple for third grade.

Cosby, B. (2005). *One Dark and Scary Night.* New York: Scholastic. A boy searches for comfort during a thunderstorm. 40 pages.

Crews, D. (2000). *Sail Away.* New York: HarperCollins. A family's adventure on a sailing trip during a storm. 40 pages.

Dubowski, K. E. (1988). *Cave Boy.* New York: Random House. This Step into Reading book provides easy language and illustrations for a young reader. 30 pages.

Grejniec, M. (1992). *What Do You Like?* New York: North-South Books. Children discover they can like the same things and still be different. 32 pages.

Hayward, L. (1990). *All Stuck Up.* New York: Random House. A Step into Reading book about Brer Rabbit and Fox. 32 pages.

Hutchins, P. (1968). *Rosie's Walk.* New York: Macmillan. A hen unwittingly leads a fox into one disaster after another before arriving safely home from her walk. 32 pages.

Martin, B., Jr. (1992). *Happy Hippopotami.* San Diego: Harcourt Brace. In a lively rhyming story about a rollicking day at the seashore (with alliteration galore), hippos "board a beach-bound bus" and enjoy "swimming, sunning, and snacking." 32 pages.

McCarty, P. (2003). *Little Bunny on the Move.* New York: Henry Holt. An engaging little bunny has an important place to go. 32 pages.

Oppenheim, J. (1989). *"Not Now!" Said the Cow.* New York: Bantam, Doubleday, Dell. A beginning reading book based on the little red hen. Unnumbered.

Pikulski, R., et al. (eds.). Houghton Mifflin's Guided Reading collection. New York: Houghton Mifflin. This reading series has leveled books.

Robinson, F. (1996). *Who Has a Tail?* Boston: Pearson. This predictable text repeats *ay, ai,* and *a* consonant *e* patterns. It is one of many leveled readers in the Ready Readers series. 16 pages.

Zimmerman, A., & Clemesha, D. (1999). *Trashy Town.* New York: HarperCollins. This delightful tale of a trash man's job provides plentiful opportunities for pointing out alliterations, onsets, and rimes. 28 pages.

Chapter 9
Fluency and Independent Reading

 ## Learning Outcomes

After reading and studying this chapter you should be able to:

9.1 Define fluency and explain why it is an important underpinning of reading comprehension.

9.2 Describe how most children become fluent readers and list the classroom conditions that bring about fluent reading.

9.3 Select and implement individual and small group approaches to developing reading fluency.

9.4 Assess students' reading fluency and use data to make instructional decisions.

Classroom Vignette

His name was Jimmy Parker, and one of us went through eight years of grade school with him. It was a small school with only one classroom for each grade level, and, therefore, the same students stayed together over the years and got to know each other really well. Jimmy had blond hair, blue eyes, and a lot of freckles. He was a popular boy and did well on the playground, originally with games like dodge ball and tetherball, and later with football and basketball. But he was not good at reading. In fact, he was terrible at it. Round-robin reading was an almost daily activity in the school, and day after day, year after year, Jimmy would stand up and stumble with excruciating slowness through a passage in the basal reader. It was a terrible experience for Jimmy, for all of us listening, and probably for the teachers, too. But concepts like automaticity, fluency, and using appropriate texts were unknown to our teachers, and so Jimmy's pain and embarrassment continued year after year.

Jimmy had not learned to read well by the time we finished grade school, and it is unlikely that he ever became a fluent reader. It is even more unlikely that he became an avid reader, a person who made reading a significant and major part of his life. It is too late to change the experiences Jimmy had, but appropriate attention to fluency can change the reading experience for many other children.

Fluency and Its Importance

Fluency is the ability to read rapidly, smoothly, without many errors, and with appropriate expression. Fluency is often thought of as an oral phenomenon, and we assess fluency by asking students to read orally. But there is also such a thing as silent reading fluency (Pikulski & Chard, 2005). When reading silently, a fluent reader reads rapidly, without stumbling over words, and with good comprehension. You cannot, of course, hear fluent silent reading, but you can recognize it because the child reads relatively rapidly, without seeming to struggle, and with good understanding of what he has read. Our goal for all readers is fluency in oral and silent reading with comprehension.

Fluency should not exist without comprehension and the work of Melanie Kuhn and her colleague offers the best definition of fluency and it relationship to comprehension (Kuhn, Schwanenflugel, & Meisinger, 2010).

> Fluency combines accuracy, automaticity, and oral reading prosody, which taken together, facilitates the reader's construction of meaning. It is demonstrated during oral reading through ease of word recognition, appropriate pacing, phrasing, and intonation. It is a factor in both oral and silent reading that can limit or support comprehension. (p.240)

When Alexandra Spichtig and her colleagues (2016) compared the reading ability of American students today to those of 1960 they coined the term comprehension-based silent reading efficiency. They found that students today read significantly less efficiently than those in 1960. Even the eye movements of children today are less efficient than their counterparts sixty years ago. The fluency of today's eighth graders is comparable to fourth graders in 1960.

As Melanie Kuhn and Steven Stahl (2003) explain, when considering fluency and its importance, it is useful to think in terms of children progressing through several stages of reading development, a process described by Jeanne Chall (1996).

- Stage 0: The emergent literacy stage, occurs before formal reading instruction begins and is a period in which children begin to understand some very basic facts about reading: that print represents spoken language, that we read from left to right and from top to bottom, that words are separated by white space, that words are made up of somewhat separable sounds, and the like. They learn to recognize the letters of the alphabet and a few sight words.

- Stage 1: Children begin formal reading instruction, with the emphasis on decoding. They learn sight words, letter-sounds relationships and strategies for unlocking the pronunciation of new words. They learn how the alphabetic system works.

- Stage 2: In the third stage, children move from concentrating on decoding and slowly reading word by word to becoming automatic in their reading and thereby reading smoothly, accurately, and with expression. Many children enter this stage of fluency building in the early primary grades and continue to build fluency over time. It is important that their fluency increase steadily because, in the third and fourth grade, they are expected to read and learn from longer and increasingly difficult text. Other children, however, do not enter the fluency stage in the early primary grades, and these children need special help in becoming fluent readers.

- Stages 3–6: Building on fluent reading skills, children learn to comprehend increasingly complex texts and achieve deeper levels of understanding and critical thinking through high school and beyond.

MyLab Education
Video Example 9.1
This video shows the benefits of fluency and the types of fluency activities that engage the students.

Fluency is important because of the limited processing capacity of our brains. As David LaBerge and Jay Samuels (1974) noted in their pioneering work on automaticity, the mind's capacity to process information is limited. Basically, we can attend to only one thing at a time. If you believe you are multitasking you are really switching from one task to another, changing attention with each switch. Reading, however, demands that we attend to at least two operations. We need to decode the individual words, and we need to engage in a number of cognitive processes to comprehend what we are reading. If too much of our limited mental processing capacity is taken up with decoding individual words, we are left with no resources to comprehend what we are reading. The solution is for readers to become automatic in processing words. As defined by LaBerge and Samuels, an automatic activity is one that we can perform without conscious attention. If children can decode most of the words they encounter automatically, they will have the mental resources to comprehend what they are reading.

As LaBerge and Samuels (1974) also explain, the road to automaticity is quite straightforward. We become automatic at an activity by doing it repeatedly in nontaxing conditions. One of the best examples of an activity at which some of you reading this have achieved an appropriate level of automaticity is driving a stick-shift car. Driving a stick-shift car requires that you push in the clutch, let up on the accelerator, shift gears, let out the clutch, and press on the accelerator—all in a very brief period of time. Moreover, it requires that you do this while simultaneously watching the traffic, noticing brake lights, looking for debris on the road, and being alert to the possibility that someone will cut in front of you or engage in some other infurating behavior. If you are not automatic at the various steps involved in shifting, you will not have the mental capacity to monitor the traffic and respond to what might be a life-or-death situation. And how do you get to be automatic at driving a stick-shift car? You do so by repeatedly practicing driving and shifting in situations in which you don't have to worry a lot about traffic—perhaps in a parking lot or on side streets. You do it again and again, and eventually it becomes second nature, requiring almost none of your mental resources.

Fluency is more than just automatic, rapid word recognition; it requires prosoday, the ability to read with proper phrasing, intonation, and stress. Prosody is linked to comprehension but the relationship is complex (Kuhn, Schwanenflugel & Meisinger, 2010). As the child develops, she moves away from a staccato word-by-word method of reading to one that sounds more like natural oral language. Measurements of prosody predict reading comprehension beyond the predictions explained by measures of oral reading rate or word reading efficiency. At the moment, we do not know if reading with prosody leads to increased comprehension, if gains in reading comprehension lead to increased prosody, or if the relationship is reciprocal. We do know enough to stress that a focus on prosody is more critical for the development of comprehension than is the focus on reading rate (Calet, Gutierrez-Palma, & Defior, 2013; Veenendaal, Groen, & Verhoeven, 2015).

The road to fluent and expressive reading is based on a lot of reading in non-taxing situations. Fortunately, current research and theory allow us to make much more specific recommendations. For a number of years, fluency was a largely neglected area of reading instruction. However, that changed when the National Reading Panel (NICHD, 2000) identified fluency as one of the five cornerstones of reading instruction. It changed even more when fluency became one of the five components of Reading First, the federal program that has strongly influenced primary-grade reading instruction. Today, fluency is part of the foundation standards of the Common Core State Standards (NGA & CCSSO, 2010). In this chapter, we describe a number of approaches to building fluency, discuss ways of assessing fluency, and consider the sorts of fluency instruction different readers need.

Helping All Students Become Fluent Readers

The authors of the National Reading Panel (2000) left educators with incomplete and troubling information of the development of fluency. That report found evidence that the repeated reading of short texts was a proven path to improving fluency. The report also found limited evidence that designating specific classroom time for sustained silent reading was helpful. Teachers were discouraged from having a sustained silent reading (SSR) period or drop everything and read time (DEAR). So educators across the nation embraced various forms of repeated reading of short texts and ignored the need to motivate students to read widely and deeply from books.

As the research results began to build, many educators reached a conclusion opposite that of the National Reading Panel—the amount or volume of reading was vital to the development of fluency and to the building of vocabulary and comprehension (Allington, 2014). Kuhn and her colleagues compared the use of wide reading with the now traditional repeated readings. They found reading more, and reducing the time in repeated readings increased fluency faster, improved word recognition and comprehension more than an exclusive focus on repeated readings. (Kuhn, 2005; Kuhn, Schwanenflugel, Morris, Morrow, Woo et al., 2006; Kuhn, Schwanenflugel, & Meisinger, 2010). Other researchers learned that the volume of reading matters. Foorman and her colleagues found that in first and second grades the key instructional factor for growth in reading achievement was the volume of reading. The more children read the more their word recognition, vocabulary, fluency and comprehension grew (Foorman, Schatscheider, Eakins, Fletcher, Moats, & Francis, 2006). Shany and Biemiller (1995) found that when students spent more time reading, either with a teacher or with an audio-taped version of the book, they increased the volume of reading by two and a half times with gains in comprehension.

To close out this section we surmise that you are a fluent reader, and you became one by reading often and widely during your elementary school years and you probably still do. You spent hours engrossed in the *Baby-Sitters Club*, or the *Goosebumps* series. When you became older *Little House on the Prairie* and *Harry Potter* consumed your attention. Few of you engaged in repeated readings or remember doing so. So, we will begin our discussion exploring how to create fluent lifelong readers and then consider some specialized approaches for struggling readers. This is the proper focus because we are concerned with motivating children to read, especially those growing up in an age dominated by electronic screens of all sizes.

Reflect and Apply

We have just given an example of an activity that some people do automatically—driving a stick-shift car. Think of an activity you do automatically, and consider how you achieved this automaticity. Talk to some classmates about automaticity, the activity that you do automatically, and how you became automatic at it. Then ask your classmates about some activities they do automatically and how they achieved automaticity.

1. Think back to your elementary schooling and remember students who were not fluent in reading—students like Jimmy Parker, mentioned in the opening scenario. Journal your opinions about those students' attitudes toward reading, their attitudes toward school more generally, and whether they ever became real readers. If you cannot remember any actual students, journal about some imaginary ones.

MyLab Education **Self-Check 9.1**

Independent Reading: The Route to Fluency

As we have noted several times in describing the components of a comprehensive reading program, wide reading is a very important part of reading instruction—for all students. Wide reading builds automaticity, vocabulary, world knowledge, and the desire to read more. One of the ways you get good at reading—in fact, one of the ways you get good at anything—is to do a lot of it. If students are to make reading a habit, something that is a frequent and vital part of their lives, they must read and read and read. Wide reading both at home and at school is the basis of fluency development.

Remember that the road to automaticity and hence to fluency is to practice repeatedly in situations that are interesting, enjoyable, and non-taxing; wide reading certainly fits that description. In fact, for all children—those reading at grade level, those near grade level, or those reading below grade level—wide reading in interesting and enjoyable books is the primary road to fluency. We will say more later about who should engage in a focused approach to fluency instruction, in Choosing Among Approaches to Fluency. Jack Detmar is one teacher who recognizes the importance of both wide reading and other approaches to building fluency.

> I always hate to be part of a bandwagon, but I'm afraid that these days that's just what I am. I have always been a huge supporter of the position that students need to read a lot if they are to read well, and hence wide reading has always played a big part in my classroom. However, after I began reading about the National Reading Panel's emphasis on fluency instruction, read some articles about fluency, and went to an inservice of the topic, I have come to realize that some students need more direct help with fluency than wide reading provides. We currently do as much independent silent reading in my class as we ever did, and all my students have plenty of opportunities for wide reading, but I also use more direct approaches such as repeated reading for those students who struggle with fluency.
>
> —Jack Detmar, second-grade teacher

Independent reading, as we define it, means students' selecting their own material to read for their own purposes. These purposes may include pleasure, information, escape—whatever motivates those who love reading to pick up a book. If students are to become fluent and engaged readers who constantly choose to read for knowledge and pleasure, it is crucial that they be given many opportunities to do so. Some years ago, Dixie Lee Spiegel (1981) suggested several benefits of independent reading. These are still true today. Independent reading

- Develops positive attitudes toward reading.
- Gives students a chance to expand their knowledge.
- Provides practice in decoding and comprehension strategies.
- Helps develop automaticity.
- Develops and expands students' vocabularies.

More recently, Richard Anderson (1996) and Anne Cunningham and Keith Stanovich (2003) have summarized research that clearly demonstrates the rich cognitive gains that come from wide reading, including substantial growth in vocabulary and knowledge (A. Cunningham, 2005). Allington (2014), looking at recent research, concluded that basal programs provide only 15 minutes of reading daily; therefore, each classroom teacher must provide time and spur interest to create lifelong readers. However, two central questions remain. How much time should we provide for independent reading? How do we motivate students to engage in it?

Providing Time to Read

Common sense tells us that we get better at just about anything by doing more of it. Reading is no exception, and, as we just noted, research confirms this notion. In one study, for example, Anderson and his colleagues (Anderson, Wilson, & Fielding, 1988) investigated fifth-graders' activities outside of school and the relationship of those activities to reading proficiency. Not surprisingly, they found that students who spent

In the Classroom 9.1

Independent Reading with a Purpose

Jeanne Gateau plans her weekly reading assignments around the read aloud experiences. She picks a topic or genre for the week and reads those books to the students. When I visited her classroom, she was reading about bats, choosing *Stellaluna* (Cannon, 1993) for her fiction selection and *Bats* (Gibbons, 1999) for the non-fiction selection. She first read *Stellaluna* developing vocabulary and comprehension. Then she shifted to *Bats* to build more knowledge and to raise questions and record them on a chart. Ms. Gateau had also checked out from the school library 25 additional books about bats and several about birds. She then challenged the students to compare and contrast birds and bats and answer unresolved questions about bats.

The students' independent time for the week was now consumed with reading and writing about bats and birds. They read books, completed graphic organizers, wrote about bats and birds, and worked together. The students had to read at least five additional books during the week. All students were actively engaged and when they drifted from the task Ms. Gateau intervened to guide them back on tract. Friday was reserved for the students to report about what they learned. Ms. Gateau's students consistently had the highest reading scores in the second grade and the highest second grade scores in the school district.

time reading books made greater strides in reading than those who spent their time on other activities. Independent reading, therefore, has to be scheduled along with all the other activities we advocate—scaffolded or guided reading, vocabulary development, word study, and comprehension strategy instruction.

How much time should be set aside each school day for students to read independently for pleasure? When Michael Pressley and his colleagues looked at effective teachers, they reached the conclusion that about two-thirds of a child's day should be spent reading and writing real texts (Pressley, Wharton-McDonald, Allington, Bloch, et al., 2001). This means that students should be reading somewhere between 30 to 40 minutes a day, with some of this time reserved for independent reading instead of guided reading. Other research recommends at least 10- to 15-minutes. a day of independent reading (Fielding, Wilson, & Anderson, 1986). The amount of time spent in independent reading each day will depend on a number of factors—how often you schedule independent reading; what other opportunities for sustained reading students have in your classroom; the likelihood that students will read outside of school; and the age, interests, and maturity of students. As a rule of thumb, we recommend beginning with 5- to 10-minute periods for primary-grade children and 15- to 20-minute periods for older students. These times can, of course, be increased if your curriculum and students' interest and involvement allow it. All in all, the exact amount of time is not as important as making certain that there *is* a time set aside for pleasure reading on a consistent basis. Perhaps the easiest way to include independent reading is to make it part of the small-group rotations. So, every day, students read with the teacher, they work on projects, and they read independently. A second-grade teacher near Chattanooga, TN created a classroom structure that caused students to read widely every week. In the Classroom 9.1 describes on way to structure independent reading time.

Providing a Rich Array of Reading Material, the Incentive to Read, and a Place to Read

Motivating students to read requires attention and planning, but the secrets to motivating students are often found within your own experiences as a reader. Avid readers have patterns to their reading. Many enjoy the same author, so when James Patterson or Jodi Picoult publishes a new novel they rush to read it. Other avid readers peruse the bestseller lists in bookstores and newspapers. Oprah Winfrey set the reading tastes for many adults, then retired and left many without direction. Still others have interests or topics that they read with great depth. Finally, many readers exchange information at work, at parties, and over email about what they are reading and how they are enjoying it.

The secret to motivating independent reading is providing students with a steady source of information about good books and interesting authors. This is true for all students, but particularly for those who do not gravitate to reading and those whose home environment does not prompt and nurture reading. Students' reading material can come from a variety of sources—including their homes, their friends, the classroom library, classroom book clubs, the school library, and the public library. Types of selections can and should run the gamut from fiction to nonfiction, trade books, magazines, the Internet, even textbooks—the choice is up to the student.

We have found it extremely important for the classroom teacher to make reading materials readily available—in fact, to make them virtually unavoidable. The classroom teacher needs to regularly talk about and share books. One week he might feature the works of a well-known author, such as Richard Peck, and if the students conduct an author study, reading the works of that author over several weeks, we can guarantee that library check-out rates for that author will increase, spurred on by the interests of the students in the class and what they tell their friends in other classes. In many classrooms, teachers and students maintain a list of classroom and grade best-sellers. In some classrooms, students keep a large chart of their best-loved books and each student may rate a book by adding a gold star after the title on the chart. In other classrooms, the bestseller list is kept in a folder. In many of these classrooms, students regularly give book talks.

One absolute essential for stimulating independent reading is a well-stocked classroom library, a feature lacking in all too many schools (Allington, Guice, Michelson, Baker, & Li, 1996). A stimulating classroom library should do what a good bookstore does, entice you to browse, sit, and read. Your classroom library should have the following characteristics:

- A semiprivate focal area that is attractive and that communicates the importance of the library in the classroom
- Comfortable seating for four to six children
- A carpet
- At least five to six books per child in your classroom, probably much more
- Books that include a variety of genres, topics, and reading levels, as well as magazines, newspapers, manuals, and electronic text
- Shelving that holds books for display, preferably with the covers facing out
- Literature-oriented displays and props: posters, puppets, bulletin boards about the latest books, or book jackets
- To further student ownership of the classroom library, bulletin boards maintained by students to recommend specific books to classmates

Commercial book clubs, such as the Scholastic Book Clubs, Inc. (https://clubs .scholastic.com) make it very easy for you and your students to order books, and the extra points your students earn will help you stock your classroom library. We also suggest that you visit garage sales, browse eBay searching under book sets, and frequent used bookstores. You will also want to become thoroughly acquainted with your school library and local public library and the media specialists and librarians there, and you will want to introduce your students to these resources. Regular class visits to the school library and occasional field trips to the local public library are time well spent. For a young child, the first important legal document in his life is a library card.

One type of book may be particularly powerful for developing fluency—the series book. These books first appeared early in the 20th century with the Bobbsey Twins starting in 1904 followed by *Tom Swift* in 1910. For many years, the best-known series were the *Hardy Boys* starting in 1927 and *Nancy Drew* in 1930. There are many contemporary versions of the series book, including the *Baby-Sitters Club* (Martin, 1986) and all its variations,

Goosebumps (Stein, 2003), and the currently popular *Diary of a Wimpy Kid* (Kinney, 2007), *Dork Diaries* (Russell, 2009), *Stories from Sideways School* (Sachar, 2004), *Ramona* (Cleary, 1991), and *Captain Underpants* (Pilkey, 1997) series. Each generation of American children seem to thrive on the series book and they develop fluency in a number of ways (Mackey, 1990). If you are not sure what series to use, listen to your students. They know.

The series book is addictive and after reading one book many children are eager to read more. The books provide extensive practice that is not taxing, and the structure of the books makes reading relatively easy. According to Mackey (1990), the characters, setting, and problems are repetitive so the reader only has to concentrate on the plot. Many authors of series books include literary devices that guide school children in how to read a novel. Often, the author will speak directly to the reader, pointing out important clues and ideas and foreshadowing new plot developments. All of this makes reading easy and builds fluency as students continue through the series.

The impact of the series book can be seen in one case study of a young fifth-grade girl, Megan, whose score on an oral reading fluency test given at the beginning of the year was 70 words correct per minute, a score below the 25th percentile. About that time she went to New York City with her family and visited the American Girl store. Megan bought the Julie doll and the book about a girl living the counterculture life in the 1970s. She read the book, and then ordered another and another. By March she had read 15 American Girl books and other related works of historical fiction, also discovering the American Girl mysteries. Her fluency scores soared to 156 WCPM while she gained a growing knowledge of American history and its various cultural periods.

Assisting Students in Selecting Material

Helping students select the right material—material that they can read, will read, will enjoy, and will profit from—is tremendously important. Moreover, this task is particularly important and particularly difficult with less able and less avid readers, students who do not read much and are, therefore, less familiar with what's available and less skilled at selecting appropriate material. As you are thinking about matching students and texts—particularly matching less proficient readers with texts they can and will read—be sure to consider the information on text difficulty we presented in Chapter 6. In the Classroom 9.2 offers some guidelines for assisting students in selecting reading material they will enjoy.

In the Classroom 9.2

Guidelines for Helping Students Select Reading Material

- Give book and author talks. Regularly, introduce students to new authors by telling a little about them, giving previews of their works, and reading excerpts from their books, especially the blurb on the back.
- Read from a "big book" and then make multiple copies of the "little" books available.
- Read a chapter from a novel or chapter book and then make copies of that book available.
- Suggest that students use the "Goldilocks Principle"—choose a book that's not too hard, not too easy, but "just right."
- Invite students to give book and author talks in which they recommend books and authors they have enjoyed.
- Invite students to write previews, reviews, and testimonials and display them around the room.
- Invite your school media specialists or public librarians to talk about their favorite books and authors as well as give information on the public library's resources and how to locate materials.
- Invite other adults—parents, the principal, secretary, custodian, coach, nurse—to talk about their favorite books.

To motivate the English learner it is important to select books that resonate with her cultural background. Consider books with a Hispanic or an Asian theme, works by Pat Mora, Claudia Davilia, Judith Ortiz Cofer, Pam Munoz Ryan, or Alan Say. It is important that the English learner know that there are books written by people just like her. As one student said, "I didn't know that Hispanics wrote books."

Establishing and Maintaining an Independent Reading Program

There are two ways to schedule independent reading time in your literacy program. One is to establish a designated time for everyone to read—for example, the last 15 minutes before lunch or after returning from recess. The problem with this approach is that the demands of instruction, working on strategies, vocabulary study, and scaffolded reading tend to swamp this designated time and often it is sacrificed for other pieces of instruction. This is especially true in schools that live and die by their test scores.

The second approach is to make independent reading part of the students' everyday activities. So, during a typical day, a student might work with the teacher, read in a literature circle, complete a reading or writing assignment with a partner, and read independently. Independent reading is part of the daily activities all students complete but when they do so is up to each individual student. By incorporating an uninterrupted reading time into your daily routine, you will be not only contributing to students' growth in reading fluency but also sending several powerful messages. Among these are that reading books is important, that reading is something everyone can do, that reading is important to you, that children are capable of sustained thought, and that you believe they can and do comprehend what they read (McCracken & McCracken, 1978).

Encouraging Out-of-School Reading

Thus far, we have stressed the importance of in-school reading because it is the reading that you as a teacher have the most control over. However, anything you can do to encourage and support out-of-school reading is well worth your efforts. Students need to read a lot if they are to get really good at it *and* enjoy all the cognitive benefits reading provides. Students spend only about 14 percent of their time in school, with the rest of their time either sleeping (33%) or doing something (sports, eating, TV, hanging out) at home or in the community (53%) (Donovan, Bransford, & Pellegrino, 1999). Today, electronics of all types—cellphone, tablets, video games—dominate children's lives. Parents must set limits so children can and will read books. This being the case, out-of-school reading can, and if at all possible *must*, contribute hugely to the amount of practice students get.

Getting parents involved can greatly enhance students' out-of-school reading time. One way to do this is with book bags and home/school reading logs. Book bags are simply bags made of sturdy material, such as canvas or plastic bags. And book logs are small journals that fit into the bags. Students carry books to and from school in these bags. Parents and students use the logs to make comments about the books they read.

Here's how one teacher orchestrated an out-of-school reading program. Students and their parents in Roslyn Breslouer's first grade participated in a program called "We Love to Read Beary Much" (International Reading Association, 1997a):

> As part of the "We Love to Read Beary Much" program, my first-graders carry books home for their parents to read with them. Their parents sign a comment

sheet, and many include notes about their reading experience. I think something as simple as sending home a book or letter on a regular basis makes a big difference. I think parents just need that personal communication.

As part of the bear theme, all students have their own bear symbol on a bear bulletin board, and they get a bear sticker for every book that a parent has signed a card for. We have a big bear named Love-a-Lot that sits on a chair in the front of the classroom. Sometimes children read to Love-a-Lot or to Ted, the troll who sits on the bear's lap.

One of the keys to the success of this program is a classroom library well stocked with paperbacks. Another important factor is keeping parents involved. To do this, I hold "We Love to Read Beary Much" parties in December, March, and June each year. These parties often draw 15 to 20 parents, who sometimes bring along grandparents, aunts and uncles, and students' younger siblings. Students recite poetry to the group of parents, who then spread out and read to their own children (and sometimes others as well). They like the idea that they can read with the children and hear the children read and recite. I also hold after-school workshops twice a year to give parents advice on how to read to children.

It's especially enjoyable to me that the program gets the parents to spend quality time with their children to read and discuss books. By the end of the year, the kids love books. Books are an integral part of their lives.

—Roslyn Breslouer, first-grade teacher

One of the keys to a successful independent reading program is accountability, but the accountability tasks should not become routine or onerous. We suggest avoiding daily reading logs which quickly turn pleasure into an assignment. When the assignment becomes more important than the book, students cheat, and even parents cheat. Instead, vary your approach and give students a choice. One week they might give an oral public service announcement for their book and the next week create an advertising poster. The third week, have a short conference with each student and discuss what they are reading and what they plan to read next. Some weeks do nothing, just read.

The Accelerated Reader program is popular in many schools, but it too has pitfalls. In the program, students take tests on the books they have read and earn points. Frequently, teachers set point goals for individual students. The Accelerated Reader puts the emphasis on having read rather than on reading. If you do the AR program, be sure to go the extra mile to create interest in books authors and reading. Students who are motivated to read to earn points cease reading during the summer when the points are not available.

Thomas White and James Kim (2008) developed a program to motivate children to read over the summer. At the end of the school year, the students are assessed to determine their reading levels and interests. Then, each student is given a book to take home and read. After reading the book the student completes a response card and reflects on fluency and comprehension (see Figure 9.1). When the card is mailed to the school district, the student is mailed another book. This process is repeated throughout the summer, with the student receiving up to eight books. The response card provides a good way for students to reflect on their reading and a way for the teacher to maintain accountability, although it does require some instruction for students to understand the use of the response card. Systematic summer reading programs provide a strong benefit for children from low-income homes especially those who many not read over the summer (Kim & Quinn, 2014).

Ray Reutzel and his colleagues (Reutzel, Jones, Fawson, & Smith, 2008) advanced the concept of scaffolded silent reading. Key to their ideas was a brief reading conference with students. During the conference, the teacher takes a 1-minute reading sample and notes students' reading accuracy and reading fluency. She then follows this up with a short comprehension assessment. Students retell what they are reading and answer a few generic comprehension questions. For narrative text, students are

MyLab Education
Click here to download a
printable version of Figure 9.1

Figure 9.1 Student Response Card

1. What is the title of the book you read? _____
2. Did you finish reading this book?
   ❏ Yes ❏ No, I stopped on page _____
3. How many times did you read this book?
   ❏ 1 time ❏ 2 times ❏ 3 times or more
4. What did you do to better understand this book? (check all that apply)
   ❏ I reread parts of this book.
   ❏ I made predictions about this book.
   ❏ I made connections (text-to-text, text-to-self).
   ❏ I summarized parts of this book.
5. After you read this book, tell someone what the book was about. Pick a part of the book to read aloud two times. Ask him or her how you improved the second time you read the section and asked for his or her signature. (check all that apply)
   ❏ Did I read more smoothly?
   ❏ Did I read more words?
   ❏ Did I read with more expression?
   Signature
6. Write one comment about the book.

_____

_____

Motivating Struggling Readers

Using Graphic Novels

Graphic novels are often very appealing to children and in this way can motivate struggling readers. Former school librarian Elizabeth Haynes (2009) explains that graphic novels, like picture books and chapter books, are a format rather than a genre—graphic novels come in many genres. For those to whom the format is unfamiliar, Haynes shares that graphic novels are combinations of text and art. They tell full stories with beginnings, middles, and ends. School media specialist Allyson Lyga (2006) relates the many benefits of graphic novels. She notes that for readers who have difficulty visualizing events as they read, the art in graphic novels provides images. Furthermore, the successive images in the novels build understanding of plot development. Thus, they increase comprehension. Lyga shares that both boys and girls are interested in graphic novels and that there are many to suit each gender; boys may gravitate toward graphic novels like *Buzzboy* and *Adventures of Tintin*, whereas girls may prefer *Peanutbutter* and *Monkey vs. Robot*. Some graphic novels, Lyga notes, are connected with children's favorite television shows and in this way can spur motivation to read. Two examples she cites are *Lizzie McGuire* and *SpongeBob SquarePants*.

expected to talk about the characters, setting, problems, and events. Students reading expository text should discuss the main idea, supporting details, procedures, and explanations. At the end of the conference the student sets personal goals. He decides what he plans to read next, how much he plans to read before the next conference, and establishes a plan for sharing his book. We believe that the goal setting is vital for establishing and sustaining interest in reading. Here is a copy of that conference form in Figure 9.2.

Figure 9.2 Tracking Form for Individual Reading Conferences

MyLab Education
Click here to download
a printable version of
Figure 9.2

Student Name _____ Date of Conference _____

Title of book student is reading: _____

Part A: Fluency (Have the student read for one minute and rate the fluency)

❑ Level 4 Reads primarily in larger, meaningful phrase groups. Some or most of the story is read with expressive interpretation.

❑ Level 3 Reads primarily in three- or four-word phrase groups. However, the majority of phrasing seems appropriate, but little or no expressive interpretation is present.

❑ Level 2 Reads primarily in two-word phrases with some three- or four-word groupings. Some word-by-word reading may be present. Little or no expressive interpretation is present.

❑ Level 1 Reads primarily word-by-word. Occasional two-word or three-word phrases may occur, but these are infrequent and/or they do not preserve meaningful syntax.

Part B: Vocabulary (Ask the student the meanings of three new words from the book and discuss the meanings of those words.)

Word 1 _____ Meaning _____

Word 2 _____ Meaning _____

Word 3 _____ Meaning _____

Part C: Comprehension

Narrative Text

Ask the student to summarize the book up to the current point. Ask some of the following questions:

1. How is the main character changing?
2. How is one of the characters in the book similar to you?
3. What appears to be one of the author's themes?
4. What literary techniques or figurative language have you noticed in the book?

_____

_____

Informational Text

1. What are some of the main ideas in the book?
2. How does the author convince you that his ideas are important?
3. How do you know the facts in this book are true?
4. How does the author develop his ideas?

_____

_____

Part D: Goal Setting

1. When do you plan on finishing the book?
2. Where does this book fit between the best and worst book you have ever read?
3. What might you like to read next?

_____

_____

Reflect and Apply

2. Think about what you read for entertainment, escape, and insight. How do you choose what to read? What influences your reading habits? Create a concept map of how these influences affect what you read. Take what you have learned and think about how you will shape the reading behavior of your students.

3. Jot down a few reasons why it's important for students to do a lot of out-of-school reading as well as in-school reading. Prepare a pep talk on this subject to give to parents on "Back-to-School" night. Write out your pep talk, or give it orally in front of your classmates.

Individual Approaches to Developing Fluency

Developing strong independent reading habits is the backbone of reading instruction. But not all students will glom onto reading. By the time some students have reached second or third grade, they have experienced such little success learning to read that they avoid reading even when encouraged or required to do so. For these students, an excellent independent reading program may not be enough to insure fluency for all. For some students, a more direct or explicit approach is necessary and there are many instructional options from which to choose. Most of these options derive from the method of repeated reading, an approach developed by Jay Samuels in 1979. We will start our discussion with repeated readings and then move into its variations. Next, we will consider small group approaches to fluency and then discuss ways to put a fluency focus on the whole classroom.

The Original Method of Repeated Reading

Having developed the theory of automaticity, Samuels (1979, 2002b, 2006) decided to search for a practical application of the theory and found one in the method of *repeated reading*. Samuels began by suggesting that, in learning to efficiently recognize words, children go through three stages, much like those of Chall (1996) described earlier in the chapter:

- *The nonaccurate stage.* At the beginning, students have considerable difficulty in recognizing words, do so only with considerable time and effort, and are not always accurate. If you listen to these children read aloud, you will find that they misread a number of words, stumble and read slowly, do not use appropriate expression, and do not sound words, but understand some of what they read.

- *The accuracy stage.* At this stage, students are able to recognize words accurately, but doing so requires a good deal of attention, effort, and time. If you listen to these children read aloud, you will find that although they read accurately, they read slowly, haltingly, and without appropriate expression. They do not sound as though they understand what they are reading, and, in fact, many times they do not understand what they are reading.

- *The automatic stage.* Finally, students are able to recognize words accurately and instantaneously, and doing so does not require much attention, effort, or time. If you listen to children at this stage read aloud, you will find that they read accurately, at a good pace, and with appropriate expression. They sound as though they understand what they are reading, and indeed they usually do.

Samuels next wondered about other tasks involving slow, inaccurate, and stumbling efforts in the beginning before eventually becoming fluent and automatic. He thought of two—sports and music. In football, for example, a would-be offensive center may at first hike the ball over the quarterback's head, on the ground, or to his left or right. Eventually, however, the center learns to consistently hike the ball just where it needs to be, into the quarterback's outstretched hands. Moreover, the center then learns to accurately hike the ball while preparing to block the oncoming defensive center and carry out any other defensive assignments.

Similarly, a beginning saxophone player may initially be unable to make any sound on the instrument before moving to a level at which she sometimes plays the right notes and sometimes the wrong ones. Only then can she progress to a level at which she accurately plays all the notes but without expression and feeling, before finally achieving the goal of playing with feeling and grace, captivating an audience with her skill. In both cases, the route to fluency is similar. The aspiring athlete or musician repeatedly practices the tasks to be mastered in non-taxing situations, gets feedback on the performance, and eventually becomes automatic and, therefore, fluent.

These examples provided Samuels with the inspiration for repeated reading. He noticed that many less-skilled readers did not practice the same way that beginning musicians or athletes did. Instead of repeatedly reading a single passage until they got it right, most less-skilled readers instead faced a new and difficult passage each day, stumbling through it without success, and were often embarrassed by reading poorly in front of their classmates. Samuels reasoned that if students who were relatively accurate but non-fluent in their reading could repeatedly practice reading the same passage, with each successive reading they should become more automatic and, therefore, fluent. Moreover, just as musicians repeatedly practice a single piece with the goal of achieving greater skill with that piece and greater skill generally as musicians, students who repeatedly read the same passage should become more automatic and fluent in reading that passage as well as with other passages generally.

Samuels (1979) initially tested his hypothesis by providing individual repeated reading sessions for a class of students with intellectual disabilities. The results of this initial testing were very positive. In the Classroom 9.3 shows the original repeated reading procedure.

With each reading of a passage, reading speed increased, the number of word recognition errors decreased, and students read with more expression. Moreover, when

---

In the Classroom 9.3

Instructional Routines

The Original Method of Repeated Reading

Like other methods of repeated reading, the original method is used with students who are relatively accurate in their reading but not yet automatic. This original approach involves one-to-one instruction, but it can be employed with small groups.

1. Have the student select a book that she finds interesting and enjoyable. If you think the selection is either too hard or too easy, help her find a more appropriate text. The text should be at her instructional level. For English learners, help them find books that have personal appeal, books that reflect their heritage.

2. Mark off a half dozen or so 50- to 200-word segments in the selected book. Begin with 50-word segments and gradually lengthen them as the student becomes increasingly able to deal with longer texts.

3. Explain the nature and purpose of repeated reading to the student. She is going to read the same passage several times, trying to read it more smoothly and a bit faster each time. Note that she should not ignore comprehension but that her main goal is to read smoothly and fairly rapidly. It is important to explain the role of practice and make comparisons to music and athletics.

4. Have the student read the passage aloud and chart both her speed and the number of word recognition errors she makes.

5. At this point, the student returns to her seat and repeatedly practices reading the passage until she feels ready to read to you again. She should keep rereading the passage, sometimes to herself at her seat and sometimes to you, until she reaches a rate of 85 words per minute. This would be the goal for a second or third grade student. Although accuracy of word recognition is a goal, do not press the student too much for accuracy, and do not demand complete accuracy before moving on to another passage. Experience shows that too much stress on accuracy will make the student anxious and reduce her chances of meeting the rate goal.

6. Once the student reaches the target rate of 85 words per minute, show her the graph of her progress, and prepare to move to another passage, probably on another day.

Figure 9.3 Progress in Reading Rate and Word Recognition for a Student Using the Original Method of Repeated Reading with Five Passages

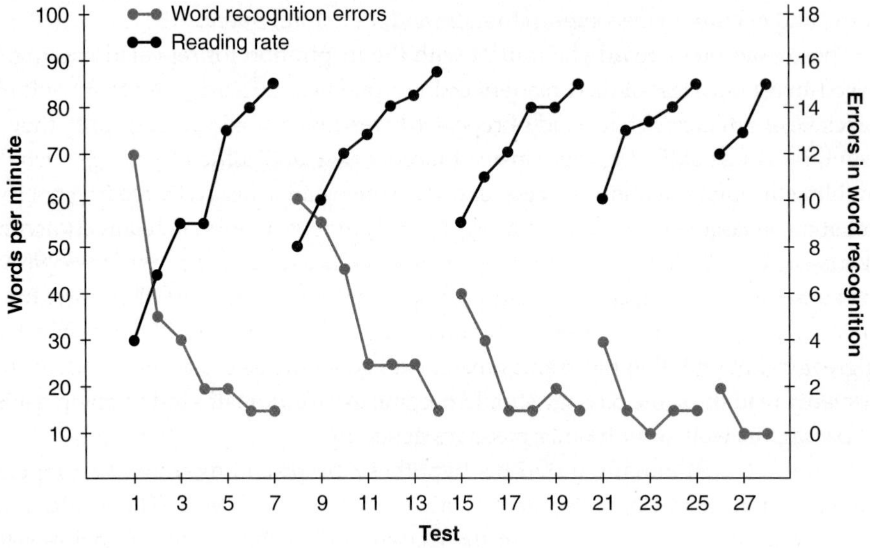

SOURCE: Samuels, S. Jay. (1979, January). "The Method of Repeated Readings." *The Reading Teacher, 32*(4), pp. 403–408. Copyright © 1979 by the International Reading Association (www.reading.org).

the students went on to a new section of a book, their beginning reading speed for that section was faster than their beginning reading speed for the previous section. That is, students' performance increased on both the texts they reread and the texts they were reading for the first time.

Figure 9.3 shows one student's progress in rate and word recognition using the original method of repeated reading on five passages. The student began the new passages with Tests 1, 8, 15, 21, and 25. The figure shows how, as the student repeatedly read each passage, speed increased and word recognition errors decreased. Moreover, the student's first reading of each successive passage was faster than the first reading of the previous passages, with fewer word recognition errors in the first reading of each successive passage.

The original method of repeated reading clearly does what it is supposed to—increase students' oral reading fluency. At the same time, it is costly in its requirement of one-to-one instruction. A teacher can employ the method of repeated reading in small groups by following these guidelines:

- On Monday select a passage for the students to read and model fluency and expressive reading.
- Time each student on the passage for one minute and record the number of words read correctly.
- Then, assign the students to practice the task with a partner for the next three days.
- On Friday, time the students again and record their new reading rate. Chart their improvement and discuss why they are improving. It is important for students to attribute their progress to their own efforts.

Simultaneous Repeated Reading and Neurological Impress

Simultaneous repeated reading is another one-to-one approach that has been used successfully (Heckelman, 1969). Its main difference from the original method of repeated reading is that the teacher or other competent reader and the student repeatedly read the passage together. The teacher (or other competent reader) at first takes the lead, reading in a strong voice, and then gradually reads more and more softly as the student takes primary responsibility. Like the original method of repeated reading, the teacher helps the student choose a book that is interesting and just a bit challenging, marks off passages of 50 to 200 words to read, explains the procedure and purpose to the student, charts progress in rate and perhaps word recognition, and shares the chart with the student to give concrete evidence of progress. As noted, simultaneous repeated reading calls for the teacher to read along with the student on each reading of the passage. The advantage of simultaneous repeated reading is that the student gets repeated models of fluent oral reading and receives sturdier scaffolding than when reading alone. The disadvantage is that it is labor intensive, requiring the teacher or some other adult to participate in every reading the student does.

In a variation called *neurological impress,* the student reads with another, better reader with the better reader tracking the print. We presented this idea in Chapter 6 as a way to make difficult text more accessible. The researcher who studied neurological impress found that the weaker readers could handle text two or three grade levels above their reading level. Their fluency and comprehension improved after 95 days of practice (Brown, Mohr, Wilcox & Barrett, 2017). As the weaker reader matched their voice with the better reader while looking at the print they were building the same fluency as does repeated readings. We will provide more information in In the Classroom 9.5.

Small-Group and Whole-Class Approaches to Fluency Development

The approaches described thus far have been shown to be effective and viable options. However, as one-to-one approaches, they have the disadvantage of taking a good deal of a teacher's or some other adult's time for each student. The approaches described next are group or whole-class approaches, making them feasible for teachers who do not have the time for one-to-one instruction.

Audio-Assisted Repeated Reading

At about the same time that Samuels was developing repeated reading, Carol Chomsky (1976) was developing a somewhat different approach to fluency. Chomsky's approach was to tape short books that students repeatedly listened to over a period of a week while also repeatedly reading them and comparing their reading to the tape. The children were third-graders with adequate decoding skills but poor fluency and with negative experiences in reading and, therefore, negative attitudes toward reading. They were also from homes in which books and reading were not prominent. Chomsky described their skills and attitudes toward reading.

> They hated reading, avoided it whenever possible, and consistently met the many opportunities for meaningful reading, adequately provided for in a lively classroom, with a total lack of response. … [They] couldn't so much as read a page of simple material to me. The attempt to do so was almost painful, a word-by-word struggle, long silences, eyes eventually drifting around the room in an attempt to escape the humiliation and frustration of the all too familiar hated situation.
>
> —Carol Chomsky (1976), researcher and reading tutor

Chomsky decided that students needed an opportunity to learn that reading was accessible to them in non-threatening, non-taxing, and non-embarrassing situations.

In the Classroom 9.4

Instructional Routines

Audio-Assisted Repeated Reading

Audio-assisted repeated reading can be set up in a number of ways. The following is one approach.

1. Select some books that are a bit of a challenge for the students you will be working with and for which recordings are available or which you can record yourself. Most laptop computers can record using the QuickTime program. You can also record with an iPad using the Voice Memo App. Select a book that will appeal to the interests and background of the students.

2. Tell students that they will be reading the books several times in order to improve their reading and that they should choose books that are interesting and present a bit of a challenge. Have students choose their own books, but monitor their choices and suggest other books if any are too easy or too difficult.

3. Have them listen to the book or a part of it repeatedly while silently or orally reading along with the recording. Tell students they should continue listening and reading until they can read smoothly and feel they are ready to read the text to you.

4. Have students read the book or passage aloud to you. Record reading rate and number of word recognition errors. Have them talk a bit about the book and also discuss it with them, both as an informal check on comprehension and as a reminder that comprehension is the goal of reading. Make charts showing each student's rate and number of word recognition errors over time to show students their progress.

And she realized that having children repeatedly listen to tapes until they had virtually memorized them and then work with her on the passage they had already mastered could provide this opportunity. She therefore got the five children she was working with tape recorders, made tapes of some short and easy books, had them read the books repeatedly over a period of a week, and then met weekly with them as a small group to work on skills, discuss what they had read, and do some writing. Today teachers could use an iPad and the voice mem app with the same results. The program, which extended over a period of four months, produced positive results for all five students. Both their overall reading scores and their word recognition scores went up. They read much more fluently. Equally important, their attitude toward reading became much more positive.

In a later investigation that involved taped reading, Michal Shany and Andrew Biemiller (1995) found that both repeated reading with teacher assistance and an audio-assisted repeated reading approach significantly improved the reading rates and comprehension of at-risk third- and fourth-grade children. Shany and Biemiller further found that with audio-assisted reading, students read through 2½ years of basal readers in 64 days. Volume matters.

In the Classroom 9.4 shows an approach to audio-assisted repeated reading based on the work of Chomsky (1978), Shany and Biemiller (1995), and Osborn and her colleagues (2003).

Partner Reading

Partner reading for neurological impress, is another approach that is less demanding on teacher time. In partner reading, more capable readers pair up with less capable peers and take turns reading to each other, with the stronger partner reading each passage first and the less strong reader following. It is important that partner reading be done

Motivating Struggling Readers

Goals Are Important

A key aspect of developing reading fluency is motivation. Some students thrive on knowing that their reading rate is increasing, and plotting their oral reading scores during repeated reading gives them a great sense of accomplishment. Audio-assisted reading can also be very motivating with the right hook. We believe that students should use the audio-assisted method to learn a book well that they plan to read to kindergarten or first-grade students. Set up the activity in the following way. Tell third- or fourth-grade students how important it is for kindergarten students to listen to good children's stories. The class project this year will be to read to the kindergarten students. To read well we need to practice the book several times before we go to the kindergarten class. This sets an important goal for the oral reading or fluency practice. Help the students select a good book to read to the kindergarteners and show them how to use the audio or tape recorder to practice. If recording equipment is not available, students might practice with each other until they are ready to read to the kindergarten students. Reading to kindergarten students is authentic, and students feel that they are accomplishing an important task. A reading comprehension element can be included in this activity. After reading the story, students can ask the kindergartners questions, and the act of developing the questions will boost their own comprehension.

on a regular basis, two or three times a week. Like all skill development, regular practice is essential. Like virtually all fluency approaches, partner reading can take place in different ways. In the Classroom 9.5 shows a slightly modified version of the procedures suggested by Osborn and her colleagues and is the also the neurological impress idea we introduced earlier. (2003).

In the Classroom 9.5

Instructional Routines

Partner Reading or Neurological Impress

Partner Selection Procedure

- The teacher uses fluency scores to rank-order the class from top to bottom.
- The teacher splits the class into two groups of equal size.
  Group 1: top to middle readers
  Group 2: middle to bottom readers
- The top reader in Group 1 is paired with the top reader in Group 2, and so on down the lists.

Partner Reading Procedure

- The Group 1 reader always reads first to set the pace and ensure accuracy.
- The Group 2 reader reads, attempting to match the partner's pace and fluency.
- The students keep a list of hard words they encounter and then review the decoding of these words during small group instruction.
- The teacher closely monitors fluency, moving around the room to listen to each set of partners, keeping partners on track, and providing feedback as needed.

Developing Fluency with Technology

Technology and fluency instruction are natural partners and each provides its own form of motivation. Children are intrigued with computers and their fascination grows with their expertise. Using a computer-based program, the students can select passages, reread them to build fluency, and receive a record of progress. Voice-activated fluency programs with recognition software can listen to children read, note errors, and provide a steady record of progress. A computer-based fluency program can do much of what a teacher can do and with a great deal of patience. These programs provide the motivation and the practice, plus they free up the teacher to work with other students.

Motivated by the same factors that gave rise to individual and small-group instruction several companies have developed prepackaged fluency programs. Fluency training is a rather straightforward matter, based primarily on modeling, repeated reading, and feedback; both taped programs and computer programs lend themselves well to providing instruction and practice incorporating these features.

READ NATURALLY

Read Naturally was one of the first companies to produce a fluency program. In fact, the company was founded specifically to provide fluency instruction. It published its first program in the early 1990s. The current basic Read Naturally program is titled Read Naturally®Live and is offered only online. While the student is sitting in front of a computer screen he works through the following sequence:

- The student clicks on a story he or she wants to read.
- The student reads key words and listens to their definition.
- The student makes a prediction about the story and writes it down.
- The student reads the passage one time to establish his reading rate. This can be done independently or with the teacher.
- The student reads along with audio support, typically three times. This is the teacher modeling part of the program.
- The student practices reading the story without audio support until able to read accurately with expression. He rereads the story 3 to 10 times.
- The student answers questions about the text. He may or may not focus on word meanings or decoding as options in the program.
- Finally, the student reads the story for the teacher to demonstrate that he has achieved his goals of reading rate, accuracy, and expression.

Read Naturally has been studied a number of times by the What Works Clearinghouse (https://ies.ed.gov/ncee/wwc/Publication), a service of the federal Department of Education. Five studies have been conducted to evaluate the program and, overall, the research suggests that Read Naturally has a moderate effect on reading achievement and an equivocal effect on fluency.

QUICKREADS

Pearson Learning's QuickReads is a fluency program developed by Elfrieda Hiebert based on her oral reading fluency research that stresses limiting the number of rare multi-syllable words when students work to improve reading fluency (Hiebert, 2005). The QuickReads program comes in both a paper-and-pencil and an electronic version. Expository passages are organized in sets of five around a common topic. The program includes science and social studies passages leveled for second, third, fourth, fifth, and sixth grades covering topics on dinosaurs, plants, American heroes, and celebrations. In the paper-and-pencil version, the students read a short passage several times, working to raise their reading rate. The teacher or another student times each reading and the results are recorded. To keep a focus on comprehension, students complete a short graphic organizer and answer a few comprehension questions. In the electronic version, students read passages into a computer equipped with voice-activation software. The computer notes oral reading errors and records the time. The students then reread the passage, trying to improve their reading times. The computer gives feedback on growth in reading fluency and identifies words that need additional attention. Both versions of QuickReads have been shown to increase students' reading ability (Hiebert, 2005).

Given the expense of many fluency programs, teachers must question whether commercial programs provide a benefit over and above many of the fluency practices discussed in this chapter. In one study, Melanie Kuhn (2004/2005) followed students who engaged in repeated reading, echo reading, and partner reading with the teacher providing positive feedback. She also observed another group engaged in wide reading, practices we stress. Both groups made gains, with the wide reading group making equal to or greater gains in both fluency and comprehension than the prescribed practices. Both of these methods avoided the expense of a commercial fluency program.

E-BOOKS AND E-BOOK APPS FOR BUILDING FLUENCY

E-Books and E-Book apps afford an opportunity to motivate students to build fluency that paper books and passages might not provide. For those eight- and nine-year-old's in the classroom who are turned off to books, the novelty of an e-book and the click of an app on an iPad might provide the motivation they need to restart reading and build fluency. When researching and selecting apps, teachers should ask themselves the following questions (Bates, Klein, Schubert, McGee, Anderson et al. 2016):

1. What knowledge, behaviors, or strategies do I want to develop in my students?
2. What kinds of texts are most likely to develop these behaviors?
3. How do the digital texts I am considering help to develop these behaviors?

The key challenge to the teacher is to use her knowledge of best practices when evaluating and selecting digital approaches to reading instruction generally and fluency in particular (Israelson, 2015). A digital approach to reading instruction should provide value above what can be achieved by more traditional means. It is quite likely that some digital texts can improve reading fluency and others might actually inhibit its growth. For example, many digital texts contain hot spots where students can click on a word and hear its pronunciation or read a short definition. While reading the text to build rate or expression these hot spots are an impediment and the best programs allow the teacher to turn them off. The text should be stable, not move on the screen, allowing the student to smoothly track the print while they read.

Israelson (2016) has developed a useful rubric for evaluating apps for developing literacy skills. The rubric guides the teacher to evaluate the features of the app, its literacy content, the ease of navigation, and the amount of interactivity. Can the app be modified to meet the needs of the students? Use Figure 9.4 to guide your evaluation of literacy apps.

Here are a few recommended e-book apps and sites for building fluency.

- *Who Can Read* developed by Pioneer Valley for the iPad. The program provides fiction and non-fiction leveled passages that the students can read or listen to. The student has the option of first listening to the narration of the passage and then reading it on his own. No pop ups interfere with reading and the development of fluency.

- *Raz-Kids* app, part of the Learning A-Z system, provides a large selection of texts spanning 29 levels. This free app is available for iPad, Android and Kindle Fire. The program offers narration for each story and the words are highlighted as the story is read. The students can also read the text on their own and record their readings. The teacher can then review the students' fluency.

Figure 9.4 App Map - A Framework for Evaluating Digital Activities

	1	2	3	4
Multimodal Features	**Distracting** Features only provide opportunity for games and entertainment	Features are mostly entertaining— some literary content	Features mostly engage with content—minimal distractions	**Engaging** Features will focus primarily on engaged instructional activities
Literary Content	**Inaccurate** Incorrect literary examples	Many literary inaccuracies that disrupt learning	Minor literacy issues with the content	**Accurate** Literacy examples are accurate and appropriate
Intuitiveness of Navigation	**Confusing** Numerous pop-ups; unclear how to proceed	How to navigate is not readily obvious	Generally intuitive but some aspects are confusing	**Intuitive** Tasks and options are easy to read and use: excellent examples
User Interactivity	**No Interactivity** No interactive tasks	The tasks are minimally interactive; user cannot change or alter tasks	Task is interactive and engaging, some opportunities for changing tasks	**High Interactivity** Content may be changed and altered to fit the needs of the student.

SOURCE: Israelson, M. H. (2016). The App Map. *The Reading Teacher*, 69(3) 339 – 349.

> **MyLab Education**
> Click here to download a printable version of Figure 9.4

- *PM E-Books* is part of Nelson Primary and contains digital versions of the 200 Rigby PM books that range from levels A–O in the Fountas and Pinnell (1995) system. Students can read the stories with full, partial, or no audio support. If they do not know a word they can tap on it, or listen to a whole page. The students can also record their own reading and the recording is available for the teacher to evaluate.

- *Unite for Literacy* offers 185 books all with narration in multiple languages. This is a plus for English language learners. The books are mostly non-fiction housed in an organizational system that allows students to find topics they want to read. The narration can be activated by the students to provide a phrased, fluent reading of the text.

All of these e-books can be woven into a fluency program either as part of independent reading or as a resource to be used with repeated readings. These digital resources can also enrich the after school and summer reading programs for all children (Kim & Quinn, 2013).

Developing Reading Prosody

When a child reads with prosody, she is reading with expression using appropriate phrasing, pauses, and rising and falling expression (Schwanenflugel, Hamilton, Wisenbaker, Kuhn, & Stahl, 2004). The current research suggests a subtle developmental pattern. First the child achieves some measure of word recognition accuracy and with practice word recognition becomes automatic. Reading quickly with few errors enables the children to read with prosody. Rate, accuracy, and prosody lead to greater comprehension. But comprehension also influences prosody because it is difficult to read a text with proper expression that you can't understand. The most current research indicates that instruction that focuses on prosody has a larger impact on comprehension than does instruction on reading rate.

Prosody is a new concept for most children so it must be introduced following the release of responsibility model, a model we will expand upon in the comprehension chapters of the book (Pearson & Gallagher, 1983). Concepts and strategies

MyLab Education
Video Example 9.2
This video shows a first grader reading fluently. Where is the borderline between great fluency and acting?
https://www.youtube.com/watch?v=fMkTp9TtyEM

are first explained and modeled by the teacher. The instruction is explicit. Next, the teacher releases responsibility to the students. They try out the strategy in a limited and safe context. Finally, after they have gained some proficiency, they practice on their own with decreasing amounts of teacher guidance and support. The two techniques that follow seem well suited to developing prosody—choral reading and Readers Theater.

CHORAL READING

Choral reading is a frequent activity in many classrooms, and it is a great way to get the whole class or a small group involved at the same time.

4. The teacher chooses a selection that will lend itself particularly well to oral reading—perhaps a humorous poem from Jack Prelutsky's *It's Raining Pigs and Noodles*—and explains the importance of reading the passage smoothly, with expression, at a good rate, and accurately.
5. When working with English learners, spend time on developing vocabulary knowledge. Make sure that the essential vocabulary words are explained. We will address this more directly in the next chapter.
6. Next the teacher reads a passage aloud as a model.
7. Then students read it aloud in unison several times. In this way, less fluent readers first have the scaffold of hearing the teacher read the passage and then can read the passage a few times rather quietly and perhaps lagging just a bit behind their more skilled classmates.
8. Finally, all students read it louder and more smoothly with the voices of their more skilled classmates acting as support.

This is just the sort of non-taxing situation students need to develop automaticity and fluency. Primary-grade teachers often use choral reading quite a bit, but it is also appropriate for older students who need to improve their fluency, and it is likely to be an enjoyable experience for all students. Choral reading, like all fluency practices, requires a goal for students, such as learning a piece to later read on their own to the class or to their reading group. The proof of the activity is the wonderful reading they deliver to their peers.

Readers Theater

Readers theater refers to the well-rehearsed reading of scripts, with feeling and expression, in front of an audience (usually the class), but without the memorizing of lines, costumes, prompts, scenery, make-up, and other time-consuming and sometimes expensive features of a full-blown play performance (Martinez, Roser, & Strecker, 1998). As an approach to building fluency, readers theater has several positive characteristics. For one thing, motivation is likely to be strong because the repeated reading that students do in order to master their parts takes place under the guise of preparing for the upcoming presentation and not as a fluency exercise. For another, both more skilled and less skilled readers can participate, thus avoiding any stigma that might be associated with being in a fluency group. The more skilled readers can be given longer and more difficult parts, with the less skilled readers assigned shorter parts, thus allowing all students to work at their own levels. Strive for parts in which all students read as much as possible. In the Classroom 9.6 shows an outline for a week-long readers theater exercise.

As with all fluency practice, students need to begin by observing you model fluent reading and then spend time practicing their piece for the performance at the end of the week. As we have noted in earlier chapters, students generally lack experience reading expository texts, so opportunities to read exposition are particularly welcome.

In the Classroom 9.6

Instructional Routines

Schedule for a Week of Readers Theater

Readers theater is the sort of activity that is best done occasionally, and a week is often an appropriate amount of time for a readers theater segment.

Select a script or several scripts, and make copies for each reader. If you are working with an entire class, you will have several different groups, so you can differentiate the reading levels. Each group of students can then read a script at their instructional level.

Monday

Introduce or review the procedure, stressing the importance of students' practicing their parts so that they can do really fluent presentations. Model some principle of prosody. You might focus on when and how long to pause, or how to convey emotions with your voice. Read that sentence again with anger or doubt. Make sure that the students imitate what you model.

Tuesday–Thursday

Assign parts, taking special care to assign each student only as much as she can handle. Have students practice their parts, both at home and at school. They can practice independently some of the time, but it is also important that they practice with a partner, with a group, and with you as their audience so that they get some assistance and feedback and are prepared for their class presentation on Friday. Of course, if students do not need 3 days of practice or their attention begins to wane, you can shorten the practice.

Friday

Have students perform their scripts for an audience, probably the class, but others should certainly be welcome. Be encouraging and supportive, and make this a festive occasion.

Fluency-Oriented Reading Instruction— Putting It All Together

Fluency-oriented reading instruction (FORI) is a whole-class program designed to build oral reading fluency (Stahl & Huebach, 2005). In FORI, the basal reading program is restructured to emphasize fluency, using a variety of techniques incorporating much of what we have already discussed. First, the reading selections in the basal are introduced and discussed with a strong emphasis on comprehension, because a focus on meaning builds word identification and comprehension skills (Anderson, Wilkinson, & Mason, 1990). Second, students read material at their instructional level when possible, although sometimes students will read more difficult material but reread it often. Third, students reread material often because research suggests that children do not read enough in school at an appropriate level (Allington, 2014). They echo read their basal materials, they reread their basal stories with a partner, they read their stories at home to their parents, and they reread the stories to themselves. Fourth, a specific time is set aside each week for partner reading, in which peers support one another in a format that provides more practice time than round-robin reading. Finally, students must read widely outside the basal reading program, both within the classroom and at home. Because evidence shows that basal reading programs do not provide enough text for students to become fluent readers (Brenner & Hiebert, 2010), students must read extensively from trade books, including non-fiction, chapter books, and novels. The research on FORI indicates that all children make significant gains. The child who

In the Classroom 9.7

Instructional Routines

MyLab Education
Click here to download a printable version of Figure 9.7

Fluency-Oriented Reading Instruction (FORI)

FORI requires the use of several fluency techniques during the week, including echo reading, partner reading, repeated readings, and wide reading at home and in school. This reading requires using a core reading program in a new and creative way. Following is the plan for the week.

	Day 1	Day 2	Day 3	Day 4	Day 5
Whole Group	Read main basal anthology story to the class, modeling fluent reading	Discuss the reading selection, focusing on story mapping or another comprehension strategy	Vocabulary instruction, journal writing, or other whole-class activities	Review comprehension strategies for the week	Vocabulary instruction, journal writing, or other whole-class activities
Small Group	Echo read the story and apply comprehension strategies	Introduce a second selection, model fluent reading, and echo read the book	Read and discuss the second selection, applying comprehension strategies	Introduce a third selection, model fluent reading, and echo read the book	Read and discuss the third selection, applying comprehension strategies
Independent Work	Partner read the basal anthology selection or readers theater for the selection	Independent reading of stories or informational books at school and at home	Partner read the basal anthology selection or readers theater for the selection	Independent reading of stories or informational books at school and at home	Perform readers theater or share a passage that students can read well

enters second grade reading at a primer level is likely to make two years progress and a child who reads at a third-grade level is likely to progress three years in reading ability. In the Classroom 9.7 provides a plan for implementing FORI in the classroom.

Kuhn (2004) did a study comparing fluency-oriented oral reading to wide reading, listening, and a no-treatment condition, and found that the fluency-oriented oral reading group outperformed the listening and no-treatment groups on tests of identifying words in isolation, number of words read per minute, and quality of oral reading. However, the wide reading group outperformed the fluency-oriented oral reading group on a comprehension measure. As we have noted, we recommend wide reading for all students, regardless of whether they are engaging in other fluency-building activities.

Reflect and Apply

4. For a while in our schools, fluency was all the rage and students were engaged in repeated readings, partner reading in an excessive manner. With our colleagues or with a teacher discuss the problem of balance. How much of the 90- to 120-minute reading block should be devoted to fluency, vocabulary, comprehension and the other components of reading.

5. Repeated reading or neurological impress while successful also have a downside. They can become boring. Re-reading passages for weeks is possible, but not for months. You does the teacher keep up the interest in the specific activities? When should the teacher shift the emphasis to independent reading?

Assessing Readers' Fluency

Good readers begin on their road to becoming fluent in the first grade. By the end of the second grade, they can read grade-level materials orally at something like 90 words per minute and are well on their way to becoming successful readers. Poor readers, on the other hand, may still struggle with fluency in the upper-elementary grades and beyond. For example, sixth-graders who are at the 10th percentile in fluency still read orally at something like 90 words per minute (Hasbrouck & Tindal, 2005). Because it is so important and because different students need different sorts of instruction and practice with fluency, assessment is vital for all students in the primary grades and all students whom you suspect may not be fluent readers in the upper-elementary and middle grades.

Although fluency is a straightforward concept, it has several components; if possible, each should to be assessed — accuracy, rate, expression, and comprehension. Time may not always allow you to assess all the components of fluency. Because assessing only some of them is definitely worthwhile, rate and accuracy are the first components to consider. Fortunately, there is a well-established, easy, and quick procedure for doing so. Called curriculum-based measurement (CBM), it was originally developed by Stanley Deno (1985). In using CBM, you simply select a grade-appropriate passage, have the student read orally for 1 minute, keep track of errors, and arrive at a word correct per minute (WCPM) score by subtracting the number of errors from the total number of words read. Rasinski (2003) has added a step of tallying the student's accuracy score, a useful addition. In the Classroom 9.8 shows a version of CBM that incorporates Rasinski's addition. This is very similar to the running record process we outlined in Chapter 5. Also review our discussion of Informal Reading Inventories. Once you have determined the student's rate and accuracy, you can compare them to the nationally accepted norms. Oral reading rate norms taken from the work of Jan Hasbrouck and Gerald Tindal (2005) are shown in Figure 9.5.

Students who are 20 percent or more below the reading rate norm for their grade level but at the independent or instructional level with respect to accuracy are likely to profit from instruction and practice on fluency. Students at the frustration level may need assessment of basic decoding skills. We discuss a variety of assessments and provide assessment tools in Chapter 5 and in the Appendix A.

As we noted, expression, sometimes called *prosody* in the current literature, is another component of fluency that deserves assessment. You assess expression by listening to students read orally and making a subjective judgment about their

Figure 9.5 Mean Oral Fluency Rates, 2018

Grade	Fall WCPM	Winter WCPM	Spring WCPM
1	—	23	53
2	51	72	89
3	71	92	107
4	94	112	123
5	110	127	139
6	127	140	150
7	128	136	150
8	133	146	151

SOURCE: Hasbrouck & Tindal, (2018). Oral Reading Fluency Data. www.readnaturally.com.

In the Classroom 9.8

Instructional Routines

Procedures for Measuring Rate and Accuracy

1. Identify a 100- to 200-word passage at the student's grade placement.

2. Ask the student to read the passage aloud in a normal way at a normal rate for 1 minute. If the student hesitates on a word for 2 to 3 seconds, pronounce it aloud. Audio record the reading, and mark the point in the text reached in 1 minute.

3. Mark any uncorrected errors the student makes. Mispronunciations, substitutions, reversals, omissions, and words that you pronounce for the student after a hesitation of 2 to 3 seconds are counted as errors.

4. Determine rate by counting the total number of words read correctly during the minute. For example, a student might correctly read 47 words in a minute.

5. Determine accuracy by dividing the number of words read correctly by the total number of words read. For example, a student might read 50 words in a minute and make 3 errors, leaving 47 words read correctly. Dividing 47 by 50 yields an accuracy score of 94 percent.

Figure 9.6 Oral Reading Fluency Scale

Level 4	Reads primarily in larger, meaningful phrase groups. Although some regressions, repetitions, and deviations from text may be present, these do not appear to detract from the overall structure of the story. Preservation of the author's syntax is consistent. Some or most of the story is read with expressive interpretation.
Level 3	Reads primarily in three- or four-word phrase groups. Some smaller groupings may be present. However, the majority of phrasing seems appropriate and preserves the syntax of the author. Little or no expressive interpretation is present.
Level 2	Reads primarily in two-word phrases with some three- or four-word groupings. Some word-by-word reading may be present. Word groupings may seem awkward and unrelated to larger context of sentence or passage.
Level 1	Reads primarily word-by-word. Occasional two-word or three-word phrases may occur, but these are infrequent and/or they do not preserve meaningful syntax.

SOURCE: U.S. Department of Education, National Center for Education Statistics. (1995). *Listening to Children Read Aloud, 15*. Washington, DC: GPO.

performance. The rubric shown in Figure 9.6, which was developed and tested by the National Assessment of Educational Progress (U.S. Department of Education, 1995), has proven to be an effective and easily used tool for rating expression. Simply have the child read grade-level material orally, and then rate the reading as Level 1, 2, 3, or 4. Students rated at Levels 3 or 4 are considered fluent in expression, whereas students at Levels 1 and 2 are not.

The final step in assessing fluency is to consider comprehension. If you assessed fluency with a 1-minute read, return the passage to the student and have them finish reading it. Then ask the student to retell the passage. A story map offers a simple system for scoring retelling of a narrative passage. During retelling, note whether the student names the characters, setting, goal, and problem, as well as the events and resolution. You might assign a point for each story element and then compute a percentage score. For an expository selection, look for main ideas and details.

Once you have assessed a student's fluency, it needs to be recorded so that you can monitor progress. It is generally recommended that you gather data at least

Figure 9.7 Class Fluency Record

Student	Rate			Accuracy			Expression			Comprehension		
	F	W	S	F	W	S	F	W	S	F	W	S
Malcolm C.	50			94%			3			30		
Jimmy V.	30			77%			1			10		
Mari R.	50			86%			3			22		
Hector A.	45			94%			3			15		

Teacher _____   Grade _____ 2   Year _____

three times a year. Figure 9.7 shows a form for describing all four aspects of fluency, with data entered for four second-graders' fall scores. Students with more severe fluency problems might be assessed more frequently.

Each of the four students presents a different profile and will require different sorts of attention. Malcolm is doing just fine. His rate, accuracy, expression score, and retelling score are all solid. He does not appear to need any special work in fluency. Jimmy, on the other hand, is doing poorly on all measures. He reads slowly, makes quite a few errors, reads without expression, and does not demonstrate good comprehension of what he reads. He appears to need special assistance in several areas, not just fluency. Mari presents a less even profile. Her rate is satisfactory, but her accuracy is low; her expression is good, but her comprehension is a bit low. She will need further assessment but will probably profit from work on word recognition and vocabulary as well as fluency. Hector presents yet another profile. His rate, accuracy, and expression are all satisfactory, but his comprehension appears to be quite low. Further assessment is definitely in order for Hector. In the next section of this chapter, we will consider what sorts of fluency instruction these and other students should receive.

Fluency instruction and fluency activities will not be the same for all students. Some approaches are appropriate for some students but not others. So, we group the different methods under three categories (see Figure 9.8). The first category contains only one approach—wide reading. For most students, those who are making good progress in fluency and are near or above the fluency norms shown in Figure 9.5, wide reading in material they find interesting, enjoyable, and occasionally a bit challenging is *the* major road to fluency. This is the primary method to use with Malcolm. The second category contains three approaches—choral reading, echo reading or neurological impress, and readers theater. All three can be used from time to time to celebrate, motivate, and improve oral reading. All students—including Malcolm, Jimmy, Mari, and Hector—will profit from using these approaches from time to time. Remember, though, that students who are struggling will need to take smaller, less demanding parts. The third category includes all the other approaches: the original method of repeated reading, simultaneous reading, echo reading, audio-assisted repeated reading, partner reading, and the use of commercial programs. Students who are not making adequate progress in fluency—those who are 20 percent or so below the rate norms for their grade or those who show an uneven profile across the four components of fluency we have described—are candidates for these other approaches. Mari, who seems to do well on everything but rate, clearly needs to use one or more of these approaches. Jimmy undoubtedly needs one of these approaches, but he needs other special work too. And Hector probably needs one of these approaches and may need other special work as

Figure 9.8 Three Types of Readers and the Fluency Needs

Student Types	Recommended Instructional Activities
Students making normal progress learning to read	Independent reading; reading conferences, finding books they can and will read
Students experiencing some difficulty with reading fluency	Activities like partner reading, readers theater, echo reading
Students struggling with fluency	The method of repeated reading, audio-assisted reading, some reading apps

well. Remember, if you adopt FORI, fluency-oriented reading instruction, many of these approaches will be incorporated into the students' daily work. However, there's no reason to limit your selection to one approach; using more than one approach provides variety and gives students some different opportunities.

For English learners who are still struggling to learn oral English, achieving fluency in English may be a real struggle. If such students are in true bilingual reading programs, it would almost certainly be best if they could become fluent in their first language initially and then work on attaining fluency in English. However, bilingual reading programs are rare and not the situation most students face. The alternative is to give English language learners as much support as possible and ensure that students have sufficiently easy English texts. Model fluent reading of text several times, allow students enough repetitions to truly master one passage before moving on to another, and be sure that students are not forced to read haltingly in front of other students.

Many English language learners, minority students, and children of poverty come to school with experiences and, therefore, background knowledge very different from those of middle-class students. It is particularly important to provide these students with texts for fluency instruction and practice that deal with topics they know something about and have some interest in. Talk to children about their experiences and interests, talk to their parents or other caregivers, and work with your school librarian and other professionals to get all students books that they will find interesting, enjoyable, and appropriate, given their experiences.

Reflect and Apply

6. It is important to consider how much assessment is enough. The advocates of progress monitoring that we discussed in Chapter 5 believe that students should be assessed every week or two. What happens to students when you assess too much? How does the frequency of assessment affect instruction?

7. What are some natural ways of assessing fluency what we might call embedded assessment? How do you know that students are making progress without stopping to give them a fluency test? What are the advantages of embedded assessments?

MyLab Education **Self-Check 9.4**

MyLab Education **Application Exercise 9.3:** Using Multiple Sources of Data to Make Instructional Decisions

The Reading Corner

Books to Build Fluency in Developing Readers

The following list includes books that Melanie Kuhn (2004/2005) used in investigating fluency-oriented oral reading, a few newer books similar to those she used, and some Spanish-English dual-language books, which may be particularly useful with Latino English language learners.

Barbara Bottner. *Pish and Posh* (I Can Read Book 2). HarperCollins, 2005. Wacky surprises occur when best friends Pish and Posh discover a book of fairy magic. 48 pages.

Betsy Byars. *The Golly Sisters Go West* (I Can Read Book 3). HarperTrophy, 1989. The singing, dancing Golly sisters, May-May and Rose, travel west by covered wagon, entertaining people along the way. 64 pages.

Betsy Byars. *Hooray for the Golly Sisters!* (I Can Read Book 3). HarperCollins, 1992. In these five amusing stories, May-May and Rose "cross the big river" and entertain folks with their zany variety shows. 64 pages.

Jack Gantos. *Rotten Ralph Feels Rotten.* Farrar, Straus and Giroux, 2004. When mischievous cat Ralph becomes ill after raiding garbage cans and is taken to the vet, he becomes lonesome for Sarah and makes his way home. 48 pages.

Lillian Hoban. *Arthur's Funny Money* (I Can Read Book 2). HarperTrophy, 1984. In this story, one of Hoban's many delightful tales of Arthur, his little sister Violet has a problem with math and Arthur is penniless, so they go into business and solve both problems. 64 pages.

Russell Hoban. *Bedtime for Frances.* HarperCollins, 1995. The endearing little badger Frances comes up with all sorts of delaying tactics to postpone her bedtime. 32 pages.

Jeff Kinney. *Diary of a Wimpy Kid.* Amulet Books, 2007. Part of a continuing first-person story of a middle school student who can't seem to get many things right but has a humorous view of the world around him.

Arnold Lobel. *Frog and Toad Together* (I Can Read Book 2). HarperTrophy, 1979. A collection of five tales about friends Frog and Toad, each a masterpiece of humor and sensitivity. 64 pages.

Herman Parish and Lynn Sweat. *Amelia Bedelia, Bookworm* (I Can Read Book 2). Greenwillow, 2005. When Amelia Bedelia helps out at her local library, she does everything by "the book," which, of course, gets her into a whole lot of trouble! 64 pages.

Shelley Moore Thomas. *Get Well, Good Knight* (Puffin Easy-to-Read). Puffin, 2004. When little knight's three dragon friends come down with awful colds, he sets off to find a healing potion. 48 pages.

Dual-Language Books in English and Spanish

Catherine Bruzzone. *Pupagesy Finds a Friend/Cachorrito encuentra un amigo.* Barron's Educational Series, bilingual edition, 2000. Pupagesy can't find anyone to play with until he meets a white mouse. 28 pages.

Susan Lowell. *The Three Little Pigs/Los tres pequeños jabalies.* Rising Moon Books, bilingual edition, 2004. In this southwestern retelling of The Three Little Pigs, three wild boars try to outsmart a hungry coyote. 32 pages.

Pat Mora. *Listen to the Desert/Oye al desierto.* Clarion, 2001. A brightly illustrated picture book that introduces readers to some of the desert sounds. 32 pages.

Pat Mora. *Uno, dos, tres/One, Two, Three.* Clarion, 2000. In this simple counting book, two little girls buy presents for their mother in a Mexican market. 48 pages.

Spanish Translations

Crockett Johnson (translated by Teresa Mlawer). *Harold y el lapiz color morado.* Rayo, 1995. In this children's classic, *Harold and the Purple Crayon,* he draws the world with a purple crayon. 64 pages.

Arnold Lobel (translated by Pablo Lizcano). *Sapo y Sepo son amigos.* Alfaguara, 2003. *Frog and Toad Are Friends* is a collection of five short stories about the friendship of a frog and a toad, another children's classic. 66 pages.

Concluding Remarks

In this chapter, we have defined fluency and described many different procedures for assisting students in becoming fluent. We began with wide reading, because that is how most of us became fluent reads. When students do not read widely there are other options to jump start the process—the original method of repeated reading, simultaneous repeated reading, neurological impress, audio-assisted repeated reading, partner reading, choral reading, readers theater, radio reading, fluency-oriented reading instruction (FORI), commercial fluency programs, and wide reading. We have also discussed ways of assessing fluency, suggested criteria for choosing among the many approaches so that students get the types of fluency instruction they need, and described several tools for assessing students and assessing texts in order to match students with appropriate texts.

In recent years, fluency instruction has been identified as a critical component of a comprehensive and effective reading program. All students must reach the goal of reading fluently if they are to progress from novices just learning to read to actual readers who can and do read for enjoyment, for learning, to become informed citizens, to investigate topics as diverse as health and hobbies, and for the myriad of other benefits one can gain from reading. You will need to select approaches to fluency that fit your students, your teaching style, and the overall context in which you teach. But one thing is certain: Fluency instruction should be a definite part of your curriculum.

Extending Learning

1. One excellent way to understand a phenomenon is to engage in a process in which you experience it. This works particularly well with the process of becoming automatic in reading because there is a very simple way of experiencing it. Find a fairly lengthy and complex sentence, and write it backwards. Here is an example with a very short sentence: "Bob had a cow" becomes "Woc a dah boB." Once you have written out your backward sentence—and remember that it needs to be a good deal longer and more complex than the example we have given—repeatedly read it aloud from back to front (right to left) until you can read it fluently. Time each reading, and make a note of how rapidly you move toward automaticity with the reversed sentence. This is a much simpler task than the one beginning readers face, so don't think their progress toward automaticity will be nearly as rapid. Still, the task will give you a good sense of what it means to move from consciously having to think about each letter as you read to becoming automatic in processing words.

2. Get together with a teacher who is working with some students on fluency (probably a second- or third-grade teacher or possibly a teacher in a higher grade with struggling readers), and volunteer to help with fluency activities for 2 to 4 weeks. Describe the fluency activity or activities you use. Keep a log book in which you chart student progress and keep a record of how each session goes, for you and for your students. Once you have completed your tutoring, write a brief summary of the experience. In the summary, explain what you did, how the fluency work was similar to or different from that described in this chapter, what your students gained from the activities, what you learned from them, and what you plan to do about fluency instruction in your classes.

Children's Literature

Brett, J. (1989). *The Mitten: A Ukranian Folktale.* New York: Putnam. A variety of animals are sleeping very snugly in Nicki's lost mitten—up until the bear sneezes, that is. 32 pages.

Dahl, M. (2002). *The Everything Kids' Joke Book: Side-Splitting, Rib-Tickling Fun.* Avon, MA: Adams Media. Offers jokes that upper-grade students will find hilarious and provides tips on how to tell jokes. 144 pages.

Hoff, S. (1987). *Barney's Horse.* New York: Harper & Row. Barney's horse becomes frightened by the new overhead trains he encounters in the city. 32 pages.

Kinney, J. (2007). *Diary of a Wimpy Kid.* New York: Amulet Books. This series tells the tale of an undersized weakling coping with middle school. 217 pages.

Maestro, M. (1997). *What Do You Hear When Cows Sing? And Other Silly Riddles.* New York: HarperCollins. A joke book to tickle primary-grade readers' funny bones. 48 pages.

Phillips, B., & Russo, S. (2004). *Fabulous and Fun Clean Jokes for Kids.* Eugene, OR: Harvest House. Just what the title promises, jokes that will please both students and the adults in their lives. 132 pages.

Pikley, Dav. (1997). *The Adventures of Captain Underpants.* New York: Scholastic. A tale of an elementary school superhero with a large bag of tricks. 121 pages.

Prelutsky, J. (2005). *It's Raining Pigs and Noodles.* New York: HarperTrophy. This wonderful read-aloud collection of humorous poems with "impeccable rhythms and rhymes" appeals to a child's sense of humor. 160 pages.

Ripley, M. (2003). *Private and Confidential: A Story About Braille.* New York: Dial Books for Young Readers. Laura finds out that her new pen pal is nearly blind and learns to use a braille machine to write to him. 28 pages.

Chapter 10
Vocabulary Development

 ## Learning Outcomes

After reading and studying this chapter you should be able to:

10.1 Explain why a multifaceted approach to vocabulary instruction is needed.

10.2 Describe the Frequent, Extensive, and Varied Language Experiences component of the approach in your own words, and note several activities that you would engage students in as part of that component.

10.3 Contrast the Teaching Individual Words and Teaching Word-Learning Strategies components, and discuss the strengths and weaknesses of each.

10.4 Define Word Consciousness, note some word-consciousness activities that you personally have engaged your students in in the past, and note some word-consciousness activities that you are likely to engage your students in in the future.

Classroom Vignette

At nine months, Julie spoke her first word. "Ba," she said with great gusto while pointing to the ball in her picture book. Over the next five months, Julie added another 50 words or so to her repertoire. After that, her vocabulary grew by leaps and bounds. Everyone in her family was an avid reader, everyone read to her a lot, and everyone talked to her a lot. By the time she started school, she had an oral vocabulary of several thousand words. Was Julie an unusual five-year-old wordsmith? Not really. Julie's vocabulary development is typical of many children, but not all children by any means.

After she began school, Julie, like many of her counterparts, began rapidly acquiring a reading vocabulary. Soon, both her reading and oral vocabulary grew impressively. Aided by her teachers—and, of course, by the reading she did and her growing understanding of the power of words—Julie acquired the vocabulary she needed to succeed in and out of school.

As noted, Julie's vocabulary development is not unique. But neither is it typical of all children. Children who grow up in homes where they are seldom read to, where they are not talked to a lot, or where English is rarely or never spoken are likely to have small English vocabularies when they enter school. And having a small English vocabulary is likely to adversely affect their success in school.

Fortunately, you as a teacher are in an enviable position. You have the unique opportunity to exert a powerful effect on the vocabularies of the students you teach. Teaching vocabulary can improve students' reading comprehension, their writing, their speaking, their success in school, and their success beyond school.

The Vocabulary Learning Task

Fortunately, because vocabulary is tremendously important to students' success, we currently know a great deal about how to create an effective vocabulary program (Baumann, Kame'enui, & Ash, 2003; Graves, 2016; Watts-Taffe, Fisher, & Blachowicz, 2017). Several considerations are particularly important to keep in mind as you begin planning a comprehensive and effective program. To begin, the vocabulary learning task is enormous! Estimates of vocabulary size vary greatly, but a reasonable estimate based on a substantial body of rigorous work (Nagy & Anderson, 1984; Snow & Kim, 2007; Stahl & Nagy, 2006; White, Graves, & Slater, 1990) suggests that the books and other reading materials used by schoolchildren include well over 100,000 different words. The average child enters school with a small reading vocabulary. Once in school, however, a child's reading vocabulary is likely to soar at a rate of 3,000 to 4,000 words a year, leading to a reading vocabulary of something like 25,000 words by the time she is in the eighth grade and maybe well over 50,000 words by the end of high school (Graves, 2016).

Quite obviously, each year students learn many more words than we can teach directly. This represents a tremendous learning achievement. They add to their vocabulary many words they do not know, and they deepen their understanding of words for which they have partial and incomplete meanings. Their partial and incomplete meanings often hinder full comprehension of reading materials containing the words and lessen their confidence in using them in speaking or writing.

Isabel Beck and her colleagues (Beck, McKeown, & Omanson, 1987) have distinguished three levels of word knowledge—unknown, acquainted, and established. Unknown words are, as the name indicates, completely unfamiliar. The word *repel* is likely to be unknown to most third-graders. A word at the acquainted level is one whose basic meaning is recognized, but only after the student gives it some deliberate attention. *Resident* would probably be understood by most fifth-graders but would require a moment's thought. At the established level, words are easily, rapidly, and automatically recognized. For most second-graders, the word *house* is at the established level.

Of course, students do not need to know *all* the words they encounter in reading at the established level—just most of them. Words that are not recognized automatically—not established—will thwart the process of comprehending text. Moreover, unless words are understood at the established level, students are not likely to use them in speaking and writing.

There is increasing evidence that the vocabularies of many children of poverty entering school are much smaller than those of their middle-class counterparts. There is also evidence that having a small vocabulary is a very serious detriment to success in reading. These two facts make it especially important to find ways to bolster the oral and reading vocabularies of students who enter school with limited word knowledge (Becker, 1977; Fernald, Marchman, & Weisleder, 2012; Hart & Risley, 2003; National Reading Panel, 2000; White et al., 1990). For similar reasons, bolstering the oral and reading English vocabularies of English learners is critically important (August, Carlo, Dressler, & Snow, 2005; Goldenberg, 2013).

A comprehensive and effective vocabulary program must respect these facts about children's word knowledge and how it grows, and the program we describe here does so. The program has four major emphases:

1. Provides children with frequent, extensive, and varied language experiences
2. Includes instruction in individual words

3. Provides students with instruction in learning words independently
4. Fosters word consciousness; that is, it builds students' interest in words, teaches them to value words, and gets them actively involved in building and honing their vocabularies

The program is consistent with the Common Core State Standards in that it ensures that students "acquire and use accurately grade-appropriate general academic and domain-specific words and phrases" and teaches word learning strategies such as the use of word parts and context so that students can "demonstrate independence in gathering vocabulary knowledge when considering a word or phrase important to comprehension or expression." The program is also consistent with the Common Core in that it gives attention to reading, writing, speaking, and listening and to content area vocabulary as well as to words students encounter in language arts materials. At the same time, it goes beyond the Common Core in directly dealing with fostering word consciousness.

Because the vocabulary learning task is large, it occupies many different places in the instructional week. A teacher should be reading to her students most of the days of the week. When new stories, books, or chapters are encountered in reading, social studies, science and math, the teacher will be spending time teaching word meanings and on other days students will practice with those words. During the week the teacher will introduce a new word learning strategy, or reviewing an old one, and the students will practice during small group instruction. From time to time a teacher might present a lesson or a unit on idioms, word origins, or slang to boost the word consciousness.

MyLab Education **Self-Check 10.1**

MyLab Education **Application Exercise 10.1:** Just how much time should we spend on vocabulary instruction?

Frequent, Extensive, and Varied Language Experiences

A variety of language experiences—listening, speaking, reading, and writing—are important for children's growth in learning. Listening is a child's earliest language experience; children begin to perceive speech sounds well before the end of their first year. Speaking comes next; most children utter their first word at about age 1. The most general statement that can be made about listening and speaking in the preschool years and beyond is that children need as much of both as possible. They particularly need to engage in real discussions—give-and-take conversations in which first caretakers and later teachers give young learners the opportunity to think and discuss topics of interest in an open, positive, and supportive climate. In summing up the major message of their longitudinal study showing the huge and ever-widening gap between the vocabularies of middle-class children and those of many children reared in poverty, Betty Hart and Todd Risley (1995) note that "the most important difference among families was in the amount of talking that went on." Anything that we can do to promote real discussions, both in school and out of school, is very worthwhile.

Of course, reading to children is also very valuable and extremely important (Cunningham, 2005). As teachers, we should frequently read to children, model our enthusiasm for reading, and do everything we can to get parents and other caregivers involved in reading to and with their children. Reading to children has been found to be effective in promoting vocabulary growth. We presented one of these approaches in Chapter 6 on selecting texts.

Reading to children is enhanced in an approach called *interactive oral reading*, in which an adult and a group of children focus on and discuss words that come up in the reading. Shown to be particularly effective (Beck & McKeown, 2004; Biemiller, 2003; De Temple & Snow, 2003; Zevenbergen & Whitehurst, 2004), interactive oral reading is designed for primary-grade students but it can be extended to the upper grades. It is particularly useful for students who come to school with relatively small vocabularies or who are English learners and, therefore, need special assistance to catch up with their peers. Interactive oral reading exposes children to words they are not likely to hear at home or find in their beginning reading books. The following characteristics of effective interactive oral reading are taken from De Temple and Snow (De Temple, Snow, 2003), our own experiences, and our reading of the literature:

MyLab Education
Video Example 10.1
Note the differences between direct and indirect vocabulary instruction in this video. In this text, frequent language experience forms the bulk of indirect instruction.

- Both the reader and the children play active roles.
- The book (or other reading selection) is read several times.
- The adult reader focuses the children's attention directly on words.
- The adult reads fluently, using an animated and lively reading style.
- The books are interesting and enjoyable and stretch children's thinking a bit.
- The books contain somewhat challenging words that children are likely to encounter in the future.

Of course, once students can read, they should be reading as much as possible in a variety of materials. Wide reading is important for a host of reasons, but it is particularly important to vocabulary growth. If students learn something like 3,000 to 4,000 words each year, it is clear that most of the words they learn are not taught directly. With a 180-day school year, teaching 3,000 to 4,000 words would require teaching approximately 20 words each and every school day. Obviously, this does not happen. Instead, students learn many of the words that make up their vocabularies from the reading they do (Anderson, 1996). We know that good readers encounter over 1,500,000 words a year and struggling readers less than 10,000 words (Anderson et al., 1988). Thus, if we can substantially increase the amount of reading students do, we can markedly increase their vocabularies. Moreover, wide reading will foster automaticity, provide knowledge about a variety of topics and literary forms, and leave students with a habit that will make them lifelong readers.

Unfortunately, many students do very little reading, and some do almost none (Anderson, Wilson, & Fielding, 1988). Richard Allington (1977) summed up the situation

Motivating Struggling Readers

Vocabulary Floods

Researchers Linda Labbo, Mary Love, and Tammy Ryan (2007) describe a vocabulary flood, a technique they designed for at-risk readers. During read-alouds, the teacher helps students to "notice" interesting words that an author uses. The teacher records the interesting words on a chart. The next day, the teacher and students revisit the read-aloud book, and the teacher has students make connections to the words—children note what visual images the words inspire, how the words relate to other words they know, and how the words connect to themselves. On the third day, the teacher creates a set of true/false sentences that use two to three of the words. Students answer the questions using a thumbs-up or down to indicate their responses to the questions. On the fourth day, students reenact the read-aloud story using the interesting words from the chart.

nicely in his memorable plea for students to do more reading—"If they don't read much, how they ever gonna get good?" The answer is clearly that they are not. Moreover, as Allington (2001) and a number of others have noted, a substantial amount of the reading students do needs to be easy enough that they can understand and enjoy what they are reading rather than struggle to decode it.

Finally, we need to recognize that writing is a powerful ally and aid to reading. From the very beginning, students need to engage frequently in activities in which reading and writing are paired, and some of these paired activities should focus on words.

Reflect and Apply

1. Based on the growth rates we suggest, give some estimates of the size of students' reading vocabularies at the end of grades 2, 3, 4, 5, and 6. Note that because we give a range of vocabulary growth rates, a range of answers will be correct.

2. Suppose that two concerned parents, fluent in both English and Spanish, come to you and say that they really want to help their daughter build her reading vocabulary but don't know just how to do that. Assuming that you do not want to suggest they do direct teaching of words, what might you suggest they do to help their daughter build her English and Spanish vocabularies?

MyLab Education **Self-Check 10.2**

MyLab Education **Application Exercise 10.2:** Overcoming the Findings of Hart and Risley

---

Teaching Individual Words

It is important to understand the various word-learning tasks students face and ways of identifying words to teach. We will consider teaching procedures for each of these word-learning tasks.

Word-Learning Tasks

All word-learning tasks are not the same, differing on matters such as how much students already know about the words to be taught, how well you want them to learn the words, and what you want them to be able to do with the words afterward. Here we list four of those tasks:

LEARNING A BASIC VOCABULARY

Many children arrive at school with substantial oral vocabularies, perhaps numbering 5,000 words. These children know the meaning of most words they are learning to decode. Some children raised in poverty, however, come to school with meager oral vocabularies, and, of course, some English learners come to school with almost no English vocabularies. For such children, building a basic oral vocabulary of the most frequent English words and learning to read the 1,000 or so most frequent words automatically are of utmost importance.

LEARNING TO READ KNOWN WORDS

Learning to read words that are already in their oral vocabularies is the major word-learning task of beginning readers. Words such as *surprise, stretch,* and *amaze* are ones that students might be taught to read during their first three years of school. By third or fourth grade, good readers will have learned to read virtually all the words in their oral vocabularies. However, this task will remain incomplete for many less able readers and for some English learners.

LEARNING NEW WORDS THAT REPRESENT KNOWN CONCEPTS

The next word-learning task students face is learning to read words that are in neither their oral nor reading vocabularies but for which they have an available concept. For example, the word *pant* would be unknown to a number of third-graders, but almost all students have seen dogs panting and know what it is like to be out of breath. All students continue to learn words of this sort throughout their years in school, and this is the major word-learning task for intermediate-grade students. It is also a major learning task for English learners, who, of course, have a great number of concepts for which they do not have English words.

LEARNING NEW WORDS THAT REPRESENT NEW CONCEPTS

Another word-learning task students face, and a very demanding one, is learning to read words that are in neither their oral nor reading vocabulary and for which they do not have an available concept. Learning the full meanings of words such as *equation, impeach,* and *mammal* is likely to require most elementary students to develop new concepts. All students continue to learn words of this sort throughout their years in school and beyond. Once again, learning new concepts will be particularly important for English learners. Also, students whose backgrounds differ from that of the majority culture will have probably internalized a set of concepts somewhat different from concepts of students in the majority culture. Thus, words that represent known concepts for some groups of students will represent unknown concepts for other groups. Students in rural Missouri have a clear understanding of the word *hog*, but in NYC it is *pork* and it comes from the supermarket.

Identifying Vocabulary to Teach

Once you have considered the word-learning tasks students face, you still must select specific words to teach.

Probably the source you will use most frequently in selecting words to teach is the texts students are reading or listening to. English, like all natural languages, consists of a small number of frequent words and a very large number of infrequent words. Once students acquire a basic vocabulary of a few thousand words, the number of different words you might teach is so large that frequency does not provide much of a basis for choosing which ones to teach. In most reading selections, you are likely to find more potentially useful vocabulary to teach than you have time to teach, and the challenge is to identify a relatively small number of the most useful words to teach.

The most widely discussed approach to selecting words from materials students are reading, and the one embraced in the Common Core, is based on Beck, McKeown, and Kucan's (Beck, McKeown, Kucan, 2003, Beck, McKeown, Kucan, 2013) concept of three tiers of words. According to Beck and her colleagues, words can be classified as belonging to one of three tiers. Tier One words are basic words, words like *clock, baby,* and *happy*. These, Beck and her colleagues believe, rarely need to be taught. Tier Three words are low frequency words usually found in specific content domains and usually best taught in content areas, words like *isotope, lathe,* and *peninsula*. Tier Two words, on the other hand, are "high frequency words for mature language users," words like *coincidence, absurd,* and *industrious*. These, Beck and her colleagues believe, are the words to focus on. Beck and her colleagues (2003, 2013) provide additional information on Tier Two words and how to select them, as well as providing more examples of them. So, too, do the following websites

- http://www.readingrockets.org/article/choosing-words-teach
- https://achievethecore.org/content/upload/Liben_Vocabulary_Article.pdf

- http://www.colorincolorado.org/article/selecting-vocabulary-words-teach-english-language-learners, gives suggestions for selecting Tier Two words for English learners

Several colleagues and I have recently developed an alternative approach to selecting vocabulary to teach termed Selecting Words for Instructional Text or SWIT. The basic belief underlying SWIT is that the principal goal of teaching vocabulary from a selection that students are reading is to support their comprehension of the selection. A detailed description of the SWIT procedure is given in Graves, Baumann, and colleagues (2013) and a shorter description is shown in the appendix for this book. Basically you list the words that you want students to learn and classify the words into three goups. First, are the words that are essential to understanding the text. Second, are valuable words. These are words that not essential to comprehending the text, but are interesting and important words. Finally, there is a group of accessible words. These are words that most students should know but the weaker students and the English learner do not know. These accessible words require additional attention for some students.

While the texts students are reading or listening to are likely to be your most frequent source of words to teach, word lists can sometimes be useful, particularly for identifying words that some English learners and some other students with small vocabularies may not know but absolutely have to learn. The list we recommend for this purpose is The First 4,000 Words, which is also available on the this website: https://michaelfgravescom.godaddysites.com. These roughly 4,000 words make up 90 percent of the running words students will encounter in almost any text they read, and if students do not know most of these words they will repeatedly stumble as they read.

Another source of words to teach is your students. It is quite useful to ask students to collect words from the books they are reading. They enjoy doing this and you will learn what they don't know. Informally testing your students or even simply asking them about which words they do and do not know can reveal a lot about words they do and do not know. We will discuss this and several other methods of testing students in the Assessing Vocabulary section toward the end of this chapter.

Methods of Teaching Individual Words

How might you go about providing instruction for each of the four word-learning tasks we have described? As you will see, the instruction needed for some word-learning tasks is much more complex than for others. Note, too, that some of these instructional methods will promote deeper levels of word knowledge than others.

TEACHING A BASIC VOCABULARY

As we have noted, building a basic vocabulary of very frequent words is crucial so that students don't repeatedly stumble over words they don't know. The first 100 words on the First 4,000 Words list account for about 50 percent of the words students encounter as they are reading; the first 300 words, about 60 percent of the words they will encounter; and the first 1,000 words, about 70 percent of the words encountered. As we have also noted, many students already have these words in their oral vocabularies, but some children of poverty and some English learners do not. We need to ensure that all students have these words in both their oral and reading vocabularies. Interactive oral reading, discussed earlier in this chapter, is the major approach we suggest for building a basic oral vocabulary. For building a basic reading vocabulary, we suggest that you identify ten or so words for instruction each week, define the words (unless they are function words like *the, and, of,* and the like), use them in context, and give students opportunities to contribute what they know about the words. Keep a list of words that have been taught and display them prominently in the room, perhaps pasting them to the classroom word wall. Word walls reflect the words we value and the words the class is learning. After the words are initially taught, help students review and rehearse them in a variety of ways.

Additionally, quiz students on sets of the words from time to time, give them feedback on how they are doing, remind them of the importance of learning these words, and talk to them about their perceptions of their progress.

TEACHING KNOWN WORDS

In learning to read known words, the basic task for the student is to associate what is unknown, the written word, with what is already known, the spoken word. To establish the association between the written and spoken forms of a word, the student needs to see the word at the same time that it is pronounced. Once this association is established, it needs to be rehearsed and strengthened so that the relationship becomes automatic. We have listed these steps to emphasize just how straightforward the process is:

Step 1. Look at the word.
Step 2. Listen to the word while looking at it.
Step 3. Rehearse and repeat that association again and again.

Repetition can take many forms from simple Lotto or matching games that students can complete with a partner, to word wall games. Post the words on a word wall and each morning challenge one or more students to read the words on the wall. The student who reads the most without making an error is rewarded with a prize. One very important point to remember when teaching these words is that there is no need to teach their meanings. By definition, these are words students already know and understand when they hear them; they simply cannot read them. Time spent "teaching" students the meanings of words they already know is time wasted.

TEACHING NEW WORDS THAT REPRESENT KNOWN CONCEPTS

Teaching new words representing known concepts is a relatively straightforward process. In the Classroom 10.1 shows a simple and straightforward approach to doing so.

LEARNING NEW WORDS THAT REPRESENT NEW CONCEPTS

As we have noted, learning new words that represent new concepts is often a challenging task. In the Classroom 10.2, based on a method developed by Dorothy Frayer (Frayer, Frederick, & Klausmeier, 1969), illustrates one very effective method to help students gain knowledge of new words that represent new concepts. Although the example is for primary-grade students, the procedure is appropriate for all grade levels.

In the Classroom 10.1

Introducing New Words Representing Known Concepts

Purpose

- To provide students with a basic understanding of a word's meaning and give them practice in using the dictionary.

Procedure

- In a handout, on a computer file, or on the whiteboard, give students a word in context—for example, use this sentence for the word *excel:*
  To get into the Olympics, a person must really *excel* at an Olympic sport.
- Have students read the word and the context-rich sentence and then look up the meaning of the word in a dictionary.
- Discuss the word and its meaning.
- Elaborate on the word, citing other examples of excelling and discuss what it means to excel.
- Ask students to use the word in context.

In the Classroom 10.2

Introducing New Words Representing New Concepts

Purpose

- To introduce second-grade students to the new word *globe* and the concept of globe.

Procedure

- Define the new concept, giving its specific attributes. For example,
  A *globe* is a spherical (ball-like) representation of a planet.
- When possible, show an actual globe or a picture illustrating the concept.
- Distinguish between the new concept and similar but different concepts with which it might be confused. It may be appropriate to identify accidental attributes that might falsely be considered definitive attributes of the new concept. For example,
  A globe is different from a map because a map is flat. A globe is different from a contour map, a map in which mountains and other high points are raised above the general level of the map, because a contour map is not spherical.
- Give examples of the concept, and explain what makes them good examples:
  The most common globe is a globe of the earth. Globes of the earth are spherical [display a sphere or spheres such as a ball or an orange] and come in various sizes and colors. A much less common globe is a globe of another planet. A museum might have a spherical representation of Saturn.
- Give nonexamples of the concept, such as a map of California or a map of how to get to a friend's house, and explain why they are not examples of the concept at hand.
- Present students with examples and nonexamples of the concept, and ask them to distinguish between the two. You might include an aerial photograph of New York (non-example), a red sphere representing Mars (example), a walking map of St. Louis (nonexample), and a ball-shaped model of the moon (example).
- Have students present examples and nonexamples of the concept, and explain what makes them examples and nonexamples. Give them feedback on their presentations.

Figure 10.1 The Frayer Model

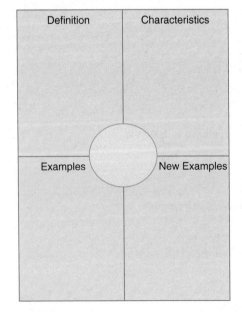

Words that represent new concepts can also be taught using the Frayer method but it will take a good deal of your and your students' time. The method also will require considerable thought from the students and you. However, for important concepts, the fruits of the labor will be well worth the effort, because with this method students can gain a new idea, another lens through which they can interpret the world. Adding words that represent new concepts to the word wall is also a useful way to help students retain these words. Figure 10.1 is the template to be used with the Frayer model. The teacher and the students fill in each quadrant as they discuss the new word.

Semantic mapping (Heimlich & Pittelman, 1986; Johnson & Pearson, 1984) is another effective method for teaching new concepts—if the concepts are not too difficult and if students already have at least some information related to them. We give an example of semantic mapping in the appendix.

Note that four of the approaches we have described for teaching individual words—all of them except the approach for teaching students to read known words—go well beyond simply providing students with the definition of the new word. As Steven Stahl (1998) points out, what we know about teaching individual words suggests using vocabulary instruction that "(a) includes both definitional and contextual information about each word's meaning, (b) involves children more actively in word learning, and (c) provides multiple exposures to meaningful information about the word."

Although the four approaches described here are certainly enough to begin your efforts in teaching individual words, you may eventually want to add others, such as those described in *Bringing Words to Life* (Beck, McKeown, & Kucan, 2013), *The Vocabulary Book* (Graves, 2016), and *Teaching Individual Words* (Graves, 2009b).

MyLab Education
Video Example 10.2
In this video, a teacher develops a content area word wall. Think about the efficiency of the system. What might you change?

Differentiating Instruction for English Learners

Because most of you will be teaching in classes with English learners, it is important to repeatedly consider what you might do for these students. An instructional intervention developed by Maria Carlo and her colleagues (Carlo, August, Snow, Dressler, Lippman, Lively, & White, 2004) included both English learners' and English-only students and is well worth considering. The 15-week intervention was organized around the theme of immigration, and each week's instruction focused on a single text. On Mondays, teachers provided their English learners with both written and recorded versions of the text in Spanish, the children's first language, as a preview. On Tuesdays, the teachers introduced the text and 10 to 12 target words to students in English. The students practiced using the context to infer the words' meanings. On Wednesdays, English learners and English-only students worked together in small groups to complete cloze activities, sentences in which the word is replaced with a blank and the student then completes the sentence with the correct word. On Thursdays, students engaged in word association activities, synonym/antonym tasks, and semantic feature analysis. On Fridays, they worked with cognates, root words, and multiple meanings of words. The study's results showed that both the English learners and the English-only students increased their knowledge of target words while enhancing their word analysis skills.

Chapter 14 in this book, Reading Instruction for English Learners, describes many other ways to assist English learners in building strong vocabularies as well as developing other aspects of literacy.

Reflect and Apply

3. Consider each of the four word-learning tasks we have listed, and explain how each of them requires a different sort of learning. It would be useful to work with a classmate in doing this, but after you have discussed your response, write it out. Writing your response will force you to really think it through, and it will give you a response on paper that you can examine and evaluate.

4. Identify a group of students. Select one word that is likely to be in their oral vocabularies but that they probably don't recognize in print, one that is a new label for a known concept, and one that represents a new concept. Choose an instructional procedure described in the chapter for teaching each word, create the materials you would need, and then explain how you would go about teaching each of them. If you have a few classmates available who could serve as "students," role-playing the teaching rather than explaining how you would do it is an excellent alternative.

Teaching Word-Learning Strategies

As we noted at the beginning of the chapter, students learn something like 3,000 to 4,000 words each year, many more than could be directly taught. Thus, even when instruction in individual words is as frequent and rich as possible, students still need to learn much of their vocabulary independently. In this section of the chapter, we consider three strategies that students need to become independent word learners: using context, using word parts, and using the dictionary.

Using Context Clues

It is almost certainly the case that we learn most of the words we know from meeting them in context rather than from being directly taught them (Anderson & Nagy, 1992; Cunningham & O'Donnell, 2012). No other explanation can account for students' learning 3,000 to 4,000 words each year. At the same time, gleaning a word's meaning from most contexts is not an easy task. However, wide reading exposes students to a huge number of unknown words. Given a typical amount of reading over a year's time, students with average skills in learning words from context might acquire over 1,000 words from meeting them in the context of their reading. Additionally, students learn a large number of words from oral contexts—conversations, lectures, films, and even television. Of course, students who have better-than-average skills in learning words from context will acquire more words this way than students with only average skills.

In this section of the chapter, we discuss teaching students to use context clues—the words, phrases, and sentences that surround an unknown word and provide clues to its meaning—to learn word meanings. Teaching students to use context clues requires a significant effort both for teacher and students, but research shows that it can be done (Fukkink & de Glopper, 1998), and several effective models of instruction have been described (for example, Baumann, Font, Edwards, & Boland, 2005; Graves, 2016). The method we describe here, which we call *balanced strategies instruction*, is our recommended approach for teaching students to use context clues, word parts, and the dictionary. In the Classroom 10.3 describes the basic components of balanced strategies instruction.

Balanced strategies instruction can be used at a variety of grade levels to teach students to use context clues. However, the ideal grades for in-depth instruction are the upper-elementary grades. In earlier grades, we would use less formal instruction. In the Classroom 10.4 describes an in-depth unit designed for fourth grade.

Using Word Parts

At the beginning of the Context Clues section, we noted that most words are learned from context, and that is certainly true. However, what we did not note is that there are two kinds of context, external context, the words and sentences that surround a

---

In the Classroom 10.3

Balanced Strategies Instruction

1. *Make motivation a prime concern.* Stress how learning and using the strategy will help students with their reading and learning in school and outside of school.

2. *Use prominent visual displays.* Before teaching the strategy, as you are teaching it, and after you have taught it, use posters, anchor charts, and the like to create interest in the upcoming instruction, highlight major features of the strategy, and remind students to continue to use it after the initial instruction.

3. *Follow the direct explanation/gradual release of responsibility model for the initial instruction* (Duke & Pearson, 2002; Duke, Pearson, Strachan, & Billman, 2011).

   - An explicit description of the strategy and when and how it should be used
   - Teacher and/or student modeling of the strategy in action
   - Collaborative use of the strategy in action
   - Guided practice using the strategy with gradual release of responsibility
   - Independent use of the strategy

4. *Provide substantial and long-term follow-up after the initial instruction.* Prompt students to use the strategy, review it periodically, and do everything possible to help students internalize and use it over time.

In the Classroom 10.4

Teaching Context Clues

Day 1: Introduction of Unit/Motivation

Because learning to use context clues is a demanding and challenging task, introduce the unit with a substantial motivational activity. For example, show a film that includes a lot of clues to the setting but does not directly identify it, and ask students to use clues in the film to infer where the film takes place. Next, suggest that figuring out word meanings from context is a lot like using clues in a film to infer where it takes place.

Day 2: Introduction to Using Context Clues and a Four-Step Strategy

Review the major points made on the first day and then introduce a strategy for figuring out the meanings of unknown words students come across as they read. The strategy entails four steps:

1. reading carefully and stopping when you come to an unknown word

2. reading slowly from that point forward, looking for clues to the word's meaning

3. going back and rereading the sentences preceding the term if necessary, and

4. selecting a word or phrase that seems to capture the meaning of the term and substituting it for the unknown word to see if it works.

After explaining the strategy, model the technique, explain when and where students are likely to use it, and let students try it out with some texts containing difficult words and particularly informative context clues. As students are working with the strategy, scaffold their efforts—provide additional clues as necessary, let them work in pairs if that is helpful, and answer any questions they have. At the end of the day, put up a large and colorful anchor chart listing the steps of the strategy, and leave the chart up throughout the unit and for some time after the unit is concluded.

Days 3–10: Additional Instruction, Practice, Encouragement, Increased Responsibility, and Transition to Increasingly Challenging Texts and Tasks

Over the next eight days, provide more detailed instruction on the four-step strategy, interrupt the hard work from time to time for games that employ the strategy. One particularly interesting activity is to write short paragraphs and include a nonsense word in place of the real noun, verb, adjective or adverb. Then have the students use context to determine the meaning of the nonsense word, engage students in guided practice in both narrative and expository texts, have them use the strategy with a variety of authentic texts, and assist them in making plans for how they will internalize the strategy and use it in the future. For example you might have them copy the steps of the strategy in their reading notebooks. Increasingly, the students should talk more and you talk less. They take more responsibility for the strategy and do more of the work, and they increasingly self-monitor and self-regulate their use of the strategy. At the same time, always be there to support students' efforts—providing encouragement, scaffolding, and feedback as needed.

word, and internal context, word parts. As Jeremy Anglin's (1993) study of elementary students' vocabularies indicates, about half of the "new" words that students meet in their reading are related to familiar words. Once students can break words into parts, they can use their knowledge of word parts to attempt to deduce their meanings—if, of course, they understand word parts and how they function. The three types of word parts to consider are prefixes, suffixes, and non-English roots.

We have already discussed prefixes and suffixes as elements that students need to deal with as they decode words, and we provided a brief procedure for teaching them when we discussed word recognition, another type of instruction advocated in the Common Core. Here we consider prefixes, suffixes, and non-English roots as elements

---

Figure 10.2 Why Prefixes Are Particularly Worth Teaching

- There are relatively few prefixes to teach.
- They are used in a large number of words.
- They are consistently spelled.
- They appear at the beginnings of words, where they are easy for students to spot.
- They generally have a clear lexical meaning that can be attached to the root word to yield a new meaning. For example, *predawn* means "before dawn."

---

students can use in gleaning word meanings. As we explain in Figure 10.2, prefixes are particularly worth teaching as an aid to deducing word meanings.

Suffixes are more complex than prefixes and present a different learning task for native English speakers than for English learners. As noted in Chapter 8, there are two kinds of suffixes: inflectional and derivational. Inflectional suffixes, the most common type, have grammatical meanings (for example, *-ed*, indicating the past tense) that are difficult to explain. Native English speakers already have a tacit understanding of the function of inflectional suffixes, and attempts to teach their meanings may cause confusion. English learners, on the other hand, do need to be taught their meanings, and we recommend using the procedure described in Chapter 8 for doing so. Derivational suffixes, most of which are less common, have abstract meanings (for example, *-ence*, indicating a state of being), and these too are often difficult to explain. Because they are uncommon and difficult to explain, we recommend leaving instruction in derivational suffixes for the secondary grades.

Non-English roots (for example, *anthro*, meaning "man" and appearing in such words as *anthropology*, *misanthrope*, and *philanthropy*) present teaching and learning problems not found with prefixes and suffixes. There is a much larger number of non-English roots, each used in relatively few words, compared to common prefixes and suffixes. They have a variety of spellings that often make them difficult to identify, and the relationship between the original meaning of the root and the current meaning of the English words is often vague. Recently a group of researchers published a list of 22 common and consistent Greek and Latin roots that can be taught in the upper elementary grades (Manyak, Baumann, & Manyak, 2018).

A list of the prefixes that appear sufficiently frequently to warrant teaching is shown in Figure 8.3 of Chapter 8, and In the Classroom 10.5 describes the use of balanced strategies instruction for teaching them.

MyLab Education
Video Example 10.3
In this video, a teacher reviews prefixes, suffixes, and base words. Based on the students' responses, how well do they understand these concepts? In what area could the teacher be more explicit? Hint: She does not distinguish inflected from derivational suffixes.

In the Classroom 10.5

Teaching Prefixes

Day 1: Introduction and Motivation

Introduce the concept of prefixes and the strategy of using prefixes to unlock the meanings of unknown words. Motivate students by stressing the value of using prefixes, and give students an overview of the unit. During the four-day unit, you will teach six of the most frequent prefixes.

Day 2: Introduction to the First Three Prefixes and the Prefix Strategy

Introduce the first three prefixes to be taught (*re-*, *in-*, and *un-*), and give their meanings. Describe the prefix removal strategy, which consists of

1. identifying and removing the prefix from the new word,
2. noting the meaning of the prefix and the meaning of the root word, and
3. combining the meanings of the prefix and the root word to infer the meaning of the new word.

Model the strategy yourself, let students try it out with your help and each other's help as needed, and have them practice using the strategy with a number of words containing the three prefixes. Put up an anchor chart that shows the prefixes you have taught, their meaning, and the prefix removal strategy.

Day 3: Reviewing the Prefix Strategy and Teaching the Remaining Three Prefixes

Review the prefix strategy, model it yourself, let several students model it, and answer any questions students have. Having the students model the strategy is critical because it helps them internalize the process. Then, teach the meanings of the next three prefixes (*dis-, en-,* and *non-*), and have students practice using the strategy with a number of words containing these three new prefixes. Add the three new prefixes to the poster.

Day 4: Reviewing the Information About Prefixes, the Prefix Strategy, and the Six Prefixes Taught in the Unit

Review everything you have done so far, take any questions students have, and have them practice using the prefix strategy with all six prefixes you have taught.

Beyond Day 4: Reviewing, Prompting, Guiding Students to Independence, and Teaching Additional Prefixes

From time to time, point out the prefixes you have taught when they appear in the selections students are reading, remind students of the value of using prefixes to infer word meanings, and briefly review the prefix strategy. Later in the year, teach a second set of six or so prefixes from the list in Figure 8.3, and later still teach another six or so.

Using the Dictionary

As George Miller and Patricia Gildea (1987) have convincingly demonstrated, elementary students frequently have difficulty using the dictionary to find definitions of unknown words. For example, after finding the phrase "eat out" in the definition of *erode*, one student showed her confusion in using the definition by composing the sentence *Our family erodes a lot.* Many students need help in using the dictionary effectively, and balanced strategies instruction can provide that help.

Begin by telling students that you are going to work on using the dictionary to define words, and tell them that the activity is worthwhile because using the dictionary sometimes isn't as simple as it seems. Then, put some guidelines, such as those shown in Figure 10.3, on a bulletin board, and leave them up over the coming weeks.

Don't ask students to memorize these guidelines, but talk through them, amplifying as necessary. For example, you should probably add to the third guideline by telling students that if they find that they still know nothing about an important word after considering context, looking for word parts, and checking the dictionary, they will probably want to ask someone about its meaning.

The remainder of the procedure continues to follow the balanced strategies instruction model shown in In the Classroom 10.3. Do some modeling; demonstrate how you

---

Figure 10.3 Guidelines for Looking Up Definitions in the Dictionary

When reading a definition, be sure to read it all, not just part of it.

- Remember that many words have more than one meaning.
- Be sure to check all the definitions the dictionary gives for a word, not just one of them.
- Decide which definition makes sense in the context in which the word is used.
- Often, the dictionary works best when you already have some idea of a word's meaning. This makes the dictionary particularly useful for checking on a word you want to use in your writing.

would look up the meaning of an unknown word. Think aloud, sharing your thinking with students as you come across the unknown word in a text. Show students how you look through a dictionary and find the word, locate the definition that seems to fit, consider all of that definition, and then mentally check to see if the meaning you chose makes sense in context. Then, gradually let students take over the procedure and model it for you and for each other. Finally, encourage students to use the procedure when they come across unknown or vaguely known words in context, and from time to time give them opportunities to model their thinking as they use the dictionary so that you can check their proficiency and give them feedback and further instruction as needed.

In addition to learning this general approach to using a dictionary, students need to learn about the particular dictionary they use, which for most students today is likely to be an online dictionary. There are many good online dictionaries available, but two student-oriented online dictionaries we have found particularly useful are *Merriam-Webster's Learner's Dictionary* http://learnersdictionary.com and the Wordsmyth beginners and intermediate dictionaries www.wordsmyth.net, both of which include audio pronunciations of words and other features that make them particularly appropriate for English learners.

In order to clearly and fully describe each of the word-learning strategies presented here—the use of context, word parts, and the dictionary—we have described them one by one. However, we conclude this section with a very important point emphasized by Wright and Cervetti (2016). Ultimately, students need to learn to use multiple strategies and to use them flexibly. Thus, in addition to teaching each strategy, we need to teach students to use the strategies in concert and flexibly as the situation dictates. The stages in this multiple strategy are:

1. Realize that you have encountered a word you do not know.
2. Seach for a prefix and use the prefix removal strategy to determine the meaning of the word.
3. If you can't determine the meaning think about the context around the word.
4. Use the context cue strategy.
5. Combine all that you know about the word and determine its meaning.

As with all strategy instruction, it is important to model the combined strategy several times, and follow the release of responsibility model. Students need opportunity to try out the strategy with the teachers guidance and feedback.

Reflect and Apply

5. In order to get a feeling for the extent to which context reveals word meanings, team up with a classmate. Each of you should independently select and photocopy a few passages of college-level material. Next, read, identify, and "white out" some difficult words in each passage. Then get together and discuss how and to what extent you can infer the deleted words' meanings from context.

6. Stop by the curriculum materials library at your university or a local public library, and examine the different levels of dictionaries found there. Note, for example, how dictionaries for younger students have fewer words, define words more simply, and are generally easier to use and, therefore, more appropriate for younger readers.

> **MyLab Education Application Exercise 10.3:** Making Instructional Decisions When Teaching Individual Words

Fostering Word Consciousness

The fourth part of a comprehensive vocabulary program involves fostering word consciousness. Word consciousness is a disposition toward words that is both cognitive and affective. The word-conscious student knows a lot of words, and she knows them well. Equally important, she is interested in words, and she gains enjoyment and satisfaction from using them well and from seeing or hearing them used well by others. She finds words intriguing, recognizes adroit word usage when she encounters it, uses words skillfully herself, is on the lookout for new and precise words, and is responsive to the nuances of word meanings. She also enjoys ideoms, jargon, slang and the origins of these terms. She is also well aware of the power of words and realizes that they can be used to foster clarity and understanding or to obscure and obfuscate matters.

Fostering such attitudes is a worthy goal across the elementary school years—and, of course, in the years beyond the elementary grades—and there are myriad ways to develop and nurture such positive attitudes. These include modeling and encouraging adept diction, promoting wordplay such as rhymes and puns, using wordplay books and playing word games, and providing intensive and expressive instruction in vocabulary. In Books About Words, we list a few word books and word games. In the remainder of this section, we consider some ways of modeling and encouraging adept diction and discuss approaches to intensive and expressive instruction. For additional suggestions on developing word consciousness, see Graves and Susan Watts-Taffe (2008), Camille Blachowicz and Peter Fisher (2012), and Graves (2016). For a detailed discussion of some cognitive aspects of word consciousness, see Nagy and Scott (2000).

Modeling and Encouraging Adept Diction

The starting point, we believe, in encouraging and nurturing word consciousness lies in our own attitude toward words and how we project it to students. We want students to feel that adept diction—the skillful use of words in speech and writing—is worth striving for. We want them to see that by using the right word themselves and recognizing the adept word choices authors make, they can both communicate more effectively and appreciate more fully an author's message. Focus on teaching one interesting word a day. Various conscious efforts can promote skillful diction. One is to model adept word usage in your classroom talk, deliberately using and perhaps explaining words that at least some of your students might not yet know. Thus, in describing how you were startled by a low-flying jet on the way to school, you might tell your fourth-graders that the jet made a *thunderous* noise and point out that *thunderous* is an excellent word for describing a really loud noise because it reminds us of the great booming noise of thunder.

A simple, widely used, and very effective way of focusing students' attention on words is to include a word-of-the-day activity in your daily plans. Appropriate for all ages, word-of-the-day activities can take a number of forms. In a first-grade classroom, word meaning can be linked to word recognition and general language facility by sharing with students a particular word of interest and paying special attention to the way it sounds, the way it looks, and what it means. The words of the day can be added to a bulletin board each day until, at the end of the month, the entire board is filled.

The Reading Corner

Books About Words

Ann Rand (author) and **Paul Rand (illustrator)**. *Sparkle and Spin: A Book About Words.* Chronicle Books, 2006. In this classic, recently reissued, Ann Rand uses rich rhythms, resonance, and pitch to entice readers to appreciate the power and music of the words they hear every day. This rich language, coupled with the colorful artwork of her husband, makes this a book to be read and enjoyed again and again. 40 pages.

Raold Dahl. *Oxford Roald Dahl Dictionary.* 2016. This is indeed a dictionary, but it is a unique dictionary because it includes only words and word play that renowned children's author Roald Dahl used in his books, and he used a lot of very interesting words. It is also easy to use, colorful, and has excellent definitions. 288 pages.

Fred Gwynne. *A Little Pigeon Toed.* Simon & Schuster, 1988. A marvelous collection of ambiguous phrases and amusing illustrations depicting the wrong interpretations of those phrases. Other similar books by Fred Gwynne include *Chocolate Moose for Dinner* (Windmill Books, 1976) and *The King Who Rained* (Simon & Schuster, 1970). 48 pages.

Richard Lederer (author) and **Dave Morice (illustrator)**. *The Circus of Words.* Chicago Review Press, 2001. Anagrams, palindromes, spoonerisms, and more from one of the leading wordplay artists. Lederer's *Pun and Games: Jokes, Riddles, Daffynitions, Tairy Fales, Rhymes, and More Word Play for Kids* (Chicago Review Press, 1996) is another choice young readers will enjoy. 144 pages.

Amy Krouse Rosenthal (author) and **Serge Bloch (illustrator)**. *I Scream! Ice Cream!: A Book of Wordles.* (2013). Wordles are phrases that sound the same but mean different things. This engaging word play book will have young readers thinking about words in a new way. 40 pages.

Marvin Turban (author) and **Giulio Maestro (illustrator)**. *Eight Ate: A Feast of Homonym Riddles.* (2007). Riddles unlike any you have ever seen before because the word being questioned and the answer sound just the same. 64 pages.

Words of the day can also be acted out, used in a game of charades, or illustrated. In addition, they can be made part of a song, riddle, pun, poem, or some other form of artistic expression. Fifth-grade special education teacher Bette Rochman explains how she uses word-of-the-day activities in her class:

> I teach fifth-grade and have several students with learning disabilities in the class. One vocabulary activity I have found to be quite successful is to pair up students to be responsible for coming up with a word of the day. After our morning announcements, the student pair responsible for that day's word writes it on the board and explains to the class what it means, why they selected it, and how to use it in a sentence. Sometimes the pair selects words they aren't too sure about and say something like, "We're not sure exactly how you use this word, but when we find out, we'll let you know!" I let the students know that such partial knowledge of the word is certainly okay, as long as students set their sights on gaining fuller knowledge. Of course, students always enjoy stumping me by presenting words that are new to me as well as to their fellow students!
>
> —Bette Rochman, fifth-grade special education teacher

Students can select words from any number of sources—books, newspapers, another classroom, their parents, and teachers, to name a few. Teachers can also suggest that students find their special words in particular sources in order to complement certain classroom activities. For example, during a unit on newspapers, the teacher might suggest that students find words in a newspaper; during a unit on weather, she might suggest that students choose "weather words." More often, however, it is worthwhile to let students find their words wherever they wish. Then, they tend to view the words as their own, take greater pride in sharing them, and more readily see learning new words as an enjoyable experience.

Another opportunity for recognizing and promoting adroit word usage comes from children's own writing. Thus, you might compliment a third-grader for describing banana slugs as *gigantic* and give some recognition to a sixth-grader who noted that the odds of winning the lottery are *astronomically small*. During writing conferences, you might also encourage students to rethink word choices in an effort to make their writing more colorful and precise.

Another approach is to encourage students to build their own vocabularies (Baumann, Ware, & Edwards, 2007) . Each week the students are responsible for finding new, interesting and unusual words. For the week they keep a list of words. At the end of the week they pick one or two words to study. Look up their definitions and origins in the dictionary and share their word with the class. These words are added to the word wall to celebrate what the children learned.

Providing Intensive and Expressive Instruction

Some very interesting and highly effective activities that can foster word consciousness have been developed and carefully researched by Isabel Beck and Margaret McKeown (1983) and by Ann Duin (Duin & Graves, 1988). The activities are quite similar, and both seek full and deep understanding of words; however, Duin's goal also involves children in using the words in writing. Developing and presenting these activities involves several steps, the first of which is to select a small set of words that are semantically related. For example, a set used by Beck and McKeown—*rival, hermit, novice, virtuoso, accomplice, miser, tyrant,* and *philanthropist*—contains words that refer to people; a set used by Duin—*advocate, capability, configuration, criteria, disarray, envision, feasible, habitable, module, quest, retrieve,* and *tether*—contains words that can be used in talking about space exploration.

The next step, the central part of the instruction, is for students to work extensively and intensively with the words, spending perhaps half an hour a day over a period of a week engaging in a dozen or so diverse activities—really getting to know the words, discovering their shades of meaning and the various ways in which they can be used, and realizing what interesting companions words can be. Beck and McKeown's activities, for example, include:

- Defining the words, asking students to use them in sentences, and

- Asking students to respond to words such as *virtuoso* and *miser* with thumbs up or thumbs down to signify approval or disapproval.

- Asking which of three actions an *accomplice* would most likely engage in—robbing a bank alone, stealing some candy, or driving a getaway car—and

- Asking questions such as, "Could a *virtuoso* be a *rival*?" "Could a *virtuoso* be a *novice*?" and "Could a *philanthropist* be a *miser*?"

Duin begins with defining the words and asking students to use them in sentences. Her other activities include asking students to discuss how *feasible* space travel might soon be, asking them how a space station could *accommodate* persons with disabilities, and asking them to write brief essays called "Space Shorts" in which they use the words in dealing with topics such as the foods that might be available in space. Reports from teachers on these activities indicate that students really get involved in them and do indeed become more word conscious (Duin & Graves, 1988).

The third step, only used when students are to use the words in their writing, is for students to write more extensive essays—using as many of the taught words as possible, playing with them and exploring their possibilities. Students appear to really enjoy this activity. As one teacher observed, "Students who were asked to write often and to use the words in written classwork showed great involvement in their writing."

Finally, we conclude with a fourth step—directly discussing with students the word choices they make, why they make those choices, and how adroit use of words makes speech and writing more precise, more memorable, and more interesting.

Duin found that students were very successful using the words in their writing, as this seventh-grader's essay—with the taught words italicized—demonstrates:

> I think the space program would be more *feasible* if we sent more than just astronauts and satellites into space. We need to send tourists and change the whole *configuration* of the space shuttle so that it could *accommodate* more people. While the tourists are in space, they could fly some of the manned-maneuvering units and *retrieve* stuff from space. They could maybe even see if our planets are *habitable* now. When the tourists would come back, they would have the *capability* of doing anything in space. They truly would be *advocates* of space. But, in order to make these special missions happen, we will need to add more *modules* onto our space station, so that we can store more equipment, supplies, food, and people! After about 10 years or so we would perhaps go back to the same old thing with astronauts and satellites until we found another new idea for the space program. My *quest*, someday, is to reach the stars. I hope to be not just an engineer, but a space engineer. We have to get more people interested since the crash. We have to try harder than ever.
>
> Seventh-grade space exploration fan (Duin & Graves, 1988)

Obviously, this student enjoyed the instruction, learned from it, and tried to do her best—managing to get 9 of the 13 unit vocabulary words into her essay. To be sure, some of the usage is a bit forced, but at this point in the student's writing career that is probably just fine. She is interested in words and in using new and different words in her writing. With practice, feedback, and encouragement from thoughtful respondents to her writing, we expect her to become a skilled and precise word user.

Reflect and Apply

7. Review a recent paper you wrote, looking at your word choices and asking yourself if you used appropriate, powerful, and perhaps even colorful words. If you did, consider how these helped make the paper strong and effective. If you didn't, try going through the paper and changing some of the vocabulary to make it more appropriate, powerful, and perhaps colorful. Then, look at your changes and consider how they affect the paper.

8. Get together with a classmate, identify a group of students, and brainstorm a set of brief and upbeat activities you might employ over a semester to foster their word consciousness.

Assessing Students' Vocabulary Knowledge and Skills

In order to decide which words to teach and which skills students need to improve, it is of course necessary to know something about what words your students know and what word learning skills they have. Here, we suggest three sources for gaining such information: standardized tests, teacher-made tests, and the students themselves.

STANDARDIZED TESTS: THE GATES-MACGINITIE VOCABULARY TEST

The Gates-MacGinitie Reading Test (MacGinitie, MacGinitie, Maria, Dreyer, & Hughes, 2000) is a group-administered, norm-referenced reading test that comes in a variety of levels from prereading through adult. The earliest levels do not include a test of reading vocabulary, but the tests for grade two and higher do, and the vocabulary test can be given by itself. Norms for the latest version of the test were developed in 2006 and appear to appropriately represent today's U. S. population. Scores available include normal curve equivalent, percentile rank, stanine, grade equivalent, and extended scale score, and these are available for the vocabulary subtest as well as for the other subtests and the total score. A sample item is shown in Figure 10.4. The test is easy to administer to a classroom size group and includes complete directions. Giving the vocabulary test takes about 15 minutes, and the results will give you an idea about your students general vocabulary development relevant to other students in the class and their peers around the country.

In closing our discussion of the Gates-MacGinitie, we want to note one very important limitation of them. As Pearson, Hiebert, and Kamile (2012) have pointed out, standardized vocabulary tests like the Gates-MacGinitie "provide teachers with scores that tell them how students perform in relation to other students (for example, percentiles or grade norms)." They do not provide information about students' knowledge of any specific body of words. To get that sort of information, you are going to need to rely on teacher developed approaches like those we discuss next.

TEACHER MADE TESTS

Here we consider two types of tests, multiple-choice tests and matching tests.

Multiple-Choice Tests.   Typically, you construct multiple choice tests for a specific group of words—for example, The First 4,000 Words (Graves, Sales, & Ruda, 2008), the potentially difficult words in an upcoming reading selection, or the glossary of a textbook you are using. This makes it possible to make conclusions such as "Almost all of my students can read all of the first 4,000 most frequent words," "Kimberly cannot read any of the words I identified as potentially difficult in Will Hobbs' *Crossing the Wire*," or "It looks like my class knows about half of the words that are glossed in our health text." In constructing such a test, we suggest making three-option multiple-choice items following these guidelines.

- Keep things simple and uncomplicated for yourself and your students. For example, make the question stem simply the word you are testing.

- Make the correct answer a clear and concise definition, doing everything you can to keep the words in the answer simpler than the word you are testing.

- Make the two distractors distinctly wrong. This is not the place for testing fine distinctions in meaning.

- While the distractors should be distinctly wrong, they should not be obviously wrong. All three alternatives should be about the same length and use the same syntax. Avoid alternatives that are silly or otherwise blatantly incorrect.

A sample item you might use with third graders and an item you might use with sixth graders are shown in Figure 10.5.

In addition to testing students on their word knowledge, you can use a multiple-choice test to check your knowledge of which words your students do and do not know. By constructing and giving a test with five words you are pretty sure most of your students know, five words you are pretty sure most of them don't know, and five you are uncertain about, you can readily find out how much you know about your students' vocabularies. If their performance squares with your predictions, great. If it does not, you need to work at learning more about their word knowledge. Only when you have a pretty good sense of the words your students are and are not likely to know can you effectively choose words to teach.

Matching Tests.   Matching tests are particularly useful, and less time consuming to prepare, when you have a number of items that can be

Figure 10.4 Sample Item Similar to Those Used in the Gates-MacGinitie Reading Tests

It was an interesting era.

- **a.** kind of food
- **b.** type of sport
- **c.** period of time
- **d.** way of talking

Figure 10.5 Sample Multiple-Choice Items for Grades 3 and 5

Grade 3
1. dignified
   - **a.** very hungry
   - **b.** important looking
   - **c.** often late

Grade 6
2. fanatic
   - **a.** very unreasonable
   - **b.** most acceptable
   - **c.** sometimes unhealthy

Figure 10.6 Sample Matching Item Testing Prefix Knowledge

un-	A. opposite of
re-	B. in
in-	C. again
dis-	D. half
sub-	E. under
	F. wrongly
	G. not

briefly defined. For example, matching test are particularly appropriate for testing students' knowledge of prefix meanings. Simply list the prefixes you want to test preceded by blanks in one column and randomly ordered definitions of the prefixes plus a couple of incorrect definitions preceded by letters in a second column as shown in Figure 10.6. Of course, you can also test words in this way, but matching tests are best suited to elements like prefixes.

QUESTIONING AND TALKING WITH STUDENTS

Less formal methods of assessing students' vocabulary knowledge and skills are also possible and can be very informative. If you want to find out about your classes knowledge of a specific set of words—again, something like the potentially difficult words in an upcoming reading selection or the glossary of a textbook you are using—simply create, duplicate, and hand out a list of words. Give students the list, and explain what students are to do and the purpose of the exercise. What they are to do is put a check mark beside the words they know. The purpose of their doing so—and it's really important to stress this—is for them to indicate whether they know each word so that you can teach those they don't know. It is not to give them a grade or in any way penalize them for not knowing some of them. In case you are suspicious of this approach, research by two colleagues and me (White, Slater, and Graves, 1989) showed that students are quite adept and truthful in identifying words they don't know in this way.

Another approach to identifying words that might be taught in an upcoming selection is to ask students to go through the selection and list words they don't know or are not sure of. A class discussion following this will give you and your students further insight into what sorts of words your students do and do not know. Additionally, such a discussion calls attention to words and their importance and may help to raise students' word consciousness.

Finally, there is the option of talking to students—individually, in small groups, or as a class—about various approaches they can use to learn words on their own. You might, for example, meet with a small group of students, ask them to read a short segment of text and identify any words they don't know, and question them about how they might use context or word parts to infer the meanings of the unknown words. Or you might discuss the use of the dictionary or the extent to which your students look carefully at their word choices when revising their writing.

MyLab Education **Self-Check 10.4**

Concluding Remarks

In this chapter, we have described the vocabulary learning tasks students face, noted the importance of wide reading, described four word-learning tasks and ways of selecting vocabulary to teach, and presented teaching procedures appropriate for each of the four word-learning tasks. We have also suggested approaches for teaching students to use context and word parts to unlock word meanings and ways of teaching them to use the dictionary effectively, and we have described methods of promoting word consciousness. Finally, we have suggested approaches to assessing students' vocabulary knowledge and skills using standardized tests, teacher-made tests, and less formal approaches.

Summed up this way, the task of teaching vocabulary appears to be a large one, and it is a sizeable endeavor. However, no single teacher is expected to accomplish all of the various tasks of vocabulary instruction. You can choose which word-learning task is most important at a particular point in your class, which level of word knowledge you expect students to achieve with particular words, which teaching plan will be most appropriate for the words in a particular selection your students are reading, and what specific words you wish to teach. Moreover, as we suggested earlier, not every teacher needs to take major responsibility for teaching students to use context, word parts, and the like. You and the other teachers in your school can work together to decide who will be responsible for these various tasks. We believe that the discussion and teaching procedures presented here will enable you to make appropriate decisions that will help your students gain rich and powerful vocabularies.

Rich and powerful vocabularies are, of course, an important part of present-day literacy. Students who have achieved the level of literacy necessary in today's world have vocabularies that enable them to use precise and appropriate words in their own speech and writing, to recognize and appreciate the skillful use of words in the literary selections they read, and to understand the sometimes subtle and often crucial meanings of words in the informational reading they do.

Extending Learning

1. Throughout the chapter, we have emphasized the importance of wide reading for developing vocabulary. Your ability to promote wide reading among your students will depend heavily on getting the right books into children's hands. As one step toward becoming more skilled in selecting books for children, imagine a particular grade level and group of students, and brainstorm possible topics that would interest this group. Then, using bibliographies, library card catalogs, electronic databases, or the advice of a librarian, select half a dozen books on this topic that are likely to be of interest to your students. If the students you are considering include less skilled readers or English learners, be sure to include some books appropriate for these children.

2. Identify a grade level and group of elementary students to whom you might teach vocabulary. If at all possible, this should be a real group of students you can actually teach. If possible, talk to the students' teacher and ask her or him to select half a dozen or so words to teach. If not, select a set of words yourself. Next, identify one of the procedures presented in the chapter that is appropriate for teaching these words, develop whatever materials you need, and prepare to do the teaching. If you haven't taught much before, it would be a good idea to rehearse with a classmate. Finally, teach the vocabulary, and then talk to students afterward to get their reaction to your instruction. If it isn't possible to work with a real class, simulate this experience using your classmates as students.

Children's Literature

Books

Arena, J. (2016). *Marta! Big and Small.* New York: Roaring Book Press. In this read-aloud book, children meet Marta, who is *una niña,* an ordinary girl, and encounter both English and Spanish words. 32 pages.

Freedman, R. (1993). *Eleanor Roosevelt: A Life of Discovery.* New York: Scholastic. In this rich and insightful photobiography of an admirable and courageous woman, photos appear on almost every page and fill some pages. 198 pages.

Hann, C. & P Páramo, P. (2014). *Danny Duck Tames the Lion: Danny Pato doma al León.* Malta: Lingolibros. Danny Duck is a very confident young duck who searches for adventure and finds more than he bargained for. 66 pages.

Tran, T. (2003). *Going Home, Coming Home/Ve nha, tham que huong.* San Francisco: Children's Book Press. In this English/Vietnamese book, a young girl from the United States visits her grandmother in Vietnam and learns that she has a home in both countries. 31 pages.

(Note that we have included several dual-language books here, certainly an important resource to use with English learners.)

Bibliographies

Book Links (quarterly, from the American Library Association, 50 E. Huron St., Chicago, IL 60611). This glossy magazine features annotated bibliographies, essays, reviews, and recommendations for using literature with children from preschool through eighth grade.

Children's Choices (annually). This annotated list is cosponsored by the International Literacy Association and the Children's Book Council and features fiction and nonfiction books that elementary and middle-school children have identified as among their favorites. Available in *The Reading Teacher* and at https://www.literacyworldwide.org/get-resources/reading-lists/childrens-choices-reading-list

Notable Children's Books (annually). This annotated list of recommended children's trade books is compiled by the Association for Library Services to Children. Available at http://www.ala.org/alsc/awardsgrants/notalists/ncb

Notable Children's Trade Books in the Field of Social Studies (annually). This annotated list of social studies oriented trade books for kindergarten through eighth grade is cosponsored by the National Council for the Social Studies and the Children's Book Council. All but the current year's list are available at https://www.socialstudies.org/publications/notables

Outstanding Science Trade Books for Children (annually). This annotated list of science-oriented trade books for kindergarten through twelfth grade is cosponsored by the National Science Teacher's Association and the Children's Book Council. Available at http://www.nsta.org/publications/ostb/

Teacher's Choices (annually). Sponsored by the International Literacy Association. This annotated list of fiction and nonfiction books features titles selected by teachers for readers ages 5–14. Available at https://www.literacyworldwide.org/get-resources/reading-lists/teachers-choices-reading-list

Trelease, J. (2013). *The Read-Aloud Handbook* (7th ed.). New York: Penguin Books. This rich source provides information on predictable books, wordless books, reference resources, picture books, short novels, novels, poetry, and anthologies.

Chapter 11
Teaching Reading Comprehension: Focusing on Narrative Text

 Learning Outcomes

After reading and studying this chapter you should be able to:

11.1 List the essential components of comprehension instruction and be able to include all of them when designing a comprehension lesson.

11.2 Select or design a reading curriculum that meets the needs of your students.

11.3 Compare and construct four frameworks for scaffolding or guiding students' reading comprehension and describe the strengths of each.

11.4 Help students respond to and discuss a narrative text using several different discussion formats.

Classroom Vignette

It was early in the school year and most of the students in Ms. Taylor's fourth grade room had settled into their independent reading routine. While Ms. Taylor was meeting with a small group of students, the rest of the class was reading independently or writing. This was true for most students except for Gabriel. The first week of school Gabe started reading the *Lightening Thief* (Riordan, 2000) but after a few days he abandoned that book. Next, he tried and abandoned *Wringer* (Spinelli, 1997). Currently Gabe is reading *Holes* by Louis Sachar. This complex book with many intertwining plots is about Stanley Yelnats, an 11-year-old boy carrying the family curse. At the beginning of the book Stanley has been unjustly convicted of stealing a prized pair of basketball shoes and has been sent off to a reform camp.

After a few days of independent reading, Ms. Taylor noticed that Gabe mostly wanders the room and rarely settles down to read, but he proudly carries *Holes*. She decided to confer with him the next day. At the conference, she learned that Gabe does not fully understand that Stanley did not steal the shoes. Gabe missed the plot because the events are not laid out in chronological order. He was mystified by "Camp Green Lake" and did not catch the irony of the name. Ms. Taylor asked Gabe to read a page or two and realized that he was an accurate and fluent reader who could define the important words in the passage.

While Gabe had strong foundational reading skills—decoding, fluency, vocabulary—he was not comprehending what he was reading. He could not construct a mental model of the text, a model that included the characters and their relationship to one another, the setting and its importance, or the problems faced by Stanley. Gabe was not putting ideas together. Additionally, he was not using what he knew to infer the cause of Stanley's problems, "the no-good-dirty-rotten-pig-stealing-great-great-grandfather."

Gabe is not alone. Despite years of emphasis on decoding and fluency, 32 percent of fourth grade students in the United States are reading at a basic level. Only 37 percent are considered proficient, able to demonstrate competence with challenging subject matter like *Holes* with its multiple intersecting plots. We want to improve Gabe's comprehension and that of the many students like him. To do so we need to consider the components of comprehension instruction.

A Model of Reading Comprehension Instruction

How do you teach reading comprehension? Or as Michael Pressley (2004) so elegantly phrased it, "What Should Comprehension Be the Instruction Of?" That is the question we will answer in this chapter and the next. In this chapter, we will first review our model of reading comprehension instruction, which has its base in the Construction-Integration Model of Kintsch (1998, 2004) that we presented in Chapter 2. Next, we will consider the comprehension curriculum. There are many parts to teaching reading comprehension and they have to be placed in some sensible order or structure—a curriculum. The basal reader is one such curriculum but we believe there are better ways to go about the task (Dewitz, Jones, Leahy, 2009). In the third section we will focus on teaching narrative text, primarily fiction, but also literary non-fiction such as biography, autobiography, and memoir. Next, we will consider the art and the craft of discussions. Much of what you do to develop comprehension will take on the form of a discussion with some led by the teacher and others by the students. We will address the task of assessing reading comprehension in Chapter 12.

Comprehension instruction requires four components—knowledge, strategies, metacognition, and motivation. We listed motivation last because we dealt with that extensively in Chapter 3. Models that explain how we read are not the same as models that guide our instruction. The purpose of our model is to ground your decision making and your thinking. As you construct a comprehension curriculum in your classroom and as you teach reading lessons consider how you will motivate your students, develop their knowledge, help them think strategically, and make them purposeful, reflective readers.

Developing Knowledge

Comprehension does not occur without knowledge. In the terminology of reading it is typically called prior knowledge or background knowledge, but it is knowledge. Numerous researchers starting with Anderson and Pearson (1984) and continuing until very recently (Kintsch, 2004) have documented that prior knowledge is related to comprehension and may be the best predictor of a student's ability to comprehend. This is true for all text, but probably more so for informational texts. The Christopher Paul Curtis novel, *The Watsons Go to Birmingham* (1900) requires knowledge of the

Civil Rights movement to grasp the theme of the story. According to the Construction-Integration Model, comprehension occurs when one idea in the text is linked to another or when the reader uses prior knowledge to complete what the author only implied. Consider this classic experiment from the early research into reading comprehension (Bransford & Johnson, 1972).

> The procedure is actually quite simple. First, you arrange things into different groups. Of course, one pile may be sufficient depending on how much there is to do. If you have to go somewhere else due to lack of facilities that is the next step; otherwise, you are pretty well set. It is important not to overdo things. That is, it is better to do too few things at once than too many. In the short run, this may not seem important but complications can easily arise. A mistake can be expensive as well. At first, the whole procedure will seem complicated. Soon, however, it will become just another fact of life. It is difficult to foresee any end to the necessity for this task in the immediate future, but then one can never tell. After the procedure is completed one arranges the materials into different groups again. Then they can be put into their appropriate places. Eventually, they will be used once more, and the whole cycle will then have to be repeated. However, that is part of life.

If this passage made no sense to you it is because we withheld the title, "Washing Clothes" and disabled your ability to apply prior knowledge to the comprehension task. You could not link the ideas in the text to your schema for doing laundry. Readers need several types of knowledge to understand a text. We will consider each.

CONCEPTUAL OR TOPICAL KNOWLEDGE

Conceptual or topical knowledge is what we know about science, history, economics, sports, the arts, and cooking. Building knowledge before students read has been a staple of comprehension instruction for over seventy years. This instructional move is more critical when reading non-fiction than fiction, but there are exceptions. The Gary Paulsen (1989) survival tale, *The Voyage of the Frog*, set in a small sailboat in a storm-tossed sea, is easier to comprehend if the reader can bring to the novel some knowledge of rigging and sailing a small sloop. The reading of science is easier if students can conduct experiments and observations before plunging into texts (Cervetti, 2006).

Teachers have two options before students read a text, developing and activating prior knowledge. Because some readers do not think to relate what they read to what they know, researchers have demonstrated that activating prior knowledge builds reading comprehension (Hall, 2015; Hansen & Pearson, 1981). Simply asking students to consider how they might think or behave in a situation similar to that in the text boosts understanding. If we ask students how they might feel moving to a new city, those feelings and thoughts are available to help the reader when reading about a child who has recently moved.

When activation is not enough, teachers are advised to develop knowledge that students need. The picture book *Pink and Say* (Polacco, 1994), a Civil War story, is not easily comprehensible unless the students have a grasp of the two sides of the war, what they were fighting about, and the setting of the war. Often in a prereading discussion you are activating knowledge for some students while building knowledge for others.

Quiocho and Ulanoff (2009) emphasize the importance of connecting reading activities to English language learners' lives. This is particularly important when children are learning to draw inferences. Quiocho and Ulanoff note that English learners benefit when teachers explicitly teach them to use their cultural beliefs and knowledge, along with information in the text and their general world knowledge, to support their inferential thinking. That is why the prereading discussions are so critical. As the discussion develops, the teacher can informally assess what the students know, and then broaden and deepen their knowledge by presenting new concepts and facts while drawing upon the experiences of others in the class. Knowledge is the foundation for making inferences (Elbro & Buch-Iverson, 2013).

MyLab Education
Video Example 11.1
This video explains how comprehension requires knowledge and builds knowledge.

Melanie Kuhn and Lesley Mandel Morrow (2003) have discussed how the Internet can provide a rich and motivating resource for building background knowledge prior to reading a selection and for extension activities following reading. As an example, Kuhn and Morrow describe how websites can support and extend children's experience of E. L. Konigsberg's *From the Mixed-Up Files of Mrs. Basil E. Frankweiler*. They suggest that teachers have children explore the Metropolitan Museum of Art, where the story is set, via the museum's website (www.metmuseum.org/learn). Another popular book for upper-elementary readers is Avi's ghost story *Something Upstairs*. Avi's website provides an intriguing introduction to the book (www.avi-writer.com). The website EyeWitness to History is a valuable resource for information to support both fiction and nonfiction reading. For example, upper-elementary and middle-grade students often read the "twin texts" *Fever 1793* by Laurie Halse Anderson and *An American Plague: The True and Terrifying Story of the Yellow Fever Epidemic of 1793* by Jim Murphy. At www.eyewitnesstohistory.com students can read about the Philadelphia yellow fever epidemic in 1793.

Reading comprehension not only requires knowledge it builds knowledge. This is true for the youngest and the oldest readers. Even when reading to children in kindergarten and first grade teachers need to develop knowledge before they read and select books that will help them build knowledge. We stressed this in the preceding chapter when we focus on the development of vocabulary knowledge. Building knowledge and building vocabulary are closely aligned.

GENRE AND TEXT STRUCTURE KNOWLEDGE
An understanding of genre and text structure enables comprehension by providing the reader with an understanding of how ideas are organized. When reading science fiction, a reader can anticipate real or imaginary characters trying to solve problems in a futurist setting far, far away. The experienced reader of science fiction might anticipate that even when the setting is on the planet Venus, as in Ray Bradbury's short story, "All Summer in a Day," the conflict and theme focus on contemporary problems like resentment and bullying. A knowledge of narrative structure facilitates the comprehension of stories.

When reading non-fiction, it is useful to know how text features—headings, subheadings, caption and graphics—facilitate comprehension. When reading on-line, it is equally important to know how to navigate links, use key words, and search for information. Knowledge of these text features facilitate comprehension. In a similar way, understanding a text's organizational patterns helps the reader set a purpose for reading and organizing what he is learning (Williams et al. 2003). Realizing that you are reading about an explosion on an oil rig in the Gulf of Mexico introduces the organizational structure of problem solution. The reader begins to search for a solution.

Comprehension and Metacognitive Strategies

Comprehension strategies are "conscious and flexible plans that readers apply and adapt to a variety of texts and tasks" (Pearson, Roehler, Dole, & Duffy, 1992). Accomplished readers use them in order to better understand, learn from, and remember what they read. One strategy, for example, is drawing inferences. This is particularly common when reading fiction and non-fiction narratives. Because authors are not always explicit, it is up to the reader to infer a character's feeling, traits, and motives. Moving further into a text we can infer the theme of a story, the author's message, and discern her point of view. The ability to infer is central to the comprehension of fiction.

As Michael Pressley (2000) has noted, and as his research with Peter Afflerbach (Pressley & Afflerbach, 1995) very clearly demonstrated, mature readers have a wide repertoire of reading strategies available, and they flexibly employ whichever strategies best fit each reading situation. This is something that all readers need to learn to do, including English language learners and students with special educational needs.

Unfortunately, research indicates that comprehension strategies instruction is not as frequent an activity as it should be (Pressley, 2006).

STRATEGIES ARE CONSCIOUS EFFORTS

At least when they are initially taught, strategies are conscious efforts that you ask students to deliberately use. For example, after teaching students how to make inferences, you will sometimes ask them to make inferences about specific aspects of material they are reading, and they will sometimes deliberately pause as they are reading and realize that they need to make an inference. With practice and experience, some strategies are likely to become increasingly habitual and automatic; for example, readers will frequently make inferences without realizing they are doing so. Nevertheless, even well-learned strategies can be brought to consciousness and placed under the control of the reader.

STRATEGIES ARE FLEXIBLE

Flexibility and adaptability are hallmarks of strategies. The very essence of teaching students to be strategic is teaching them that they need to use strategies in ways that are appropriate for particular situations. For example, the strategy of summarizing can be used in a variety of ways. Some students might compose a written summary at the end of a textbook chapter as a way of retaining the information. Other readers might stop in the middle of their reading and briefly summarize in their head what they have read as a means of checking their understanding. Ultimately, strategies should be used when necessary and appropriate, and teachers should refrain from insisting on deliberate use of strategies when students already understand what they read.

STRATEGIES LEAD TO HIGHER-LEVEL THINKING

The use of comprehension strategies takes the reader beyond the literal meaning of the text into deeper interpretation leading to the doorstep of judgments. When readers make inferences, determine importance, create graphic images, and monitor their comprehension, they are engaging in higher-order thinking. Strategic reading and higher-order thinking have much in common (Resnick, 1987). Each can be effortful and complex. Both involve self-regulation of thinking, the construction of meaning, and the search for structure in a text.

STRATEGIES HELP US REFLECT AND MONITOR

Good readers are metacognitive. They understand themselves as readers, they know the reading tasks they face, and they select strategies that help them complete these tasks. Before reading, they consider such matters as their purpose in reading, the difficulty of the text, how much they already know about the topic of the text, and how long they have to complete the reading. During reading, they monitor their comprehension, realize when understanding breaks down, and employ fix-up strategies like rereading if they do not understand. After reading, they self-check to see if they have what they want and need from the text. For example, realizing that the history chapter she has just read is crucial to the report she is writing, a sixth-grader might write a summary of it.

Being metacognitive is a more general strategy but the other strategies help to develop metacognitive thinking. When children ask questions or summarize, they are reflecting on what they have comprehended and they are being metacognitive. In an approach called reciprocal teaching, students continually use four strategies—predicting, clarifying, questioning, and summarizing. These strategies help readers become more metacognitive (Palincsar & Brown, 1984). Readers who are being metacognitive are asking themselves questions like these: Do I understand what the author is saying? What do I do if I don't understand what I am reading? What could I do better to understand what the author is saying? Can I do something to help me remember the material better? After initially teaching strategies, teachers need to encourage, and prompt students to use them over a considerable period of time, as sixth-grade teacher Ron Novack does in the scenario captured by In the Classroom 11.1

In the Classroom 11.1

Fostering Metacognition

To foster students' metacognition and help them thoroughly internalize and fluently use the strategies you have taught, it is important to repeatedly remind them of the importance of being metacognitive and employing the repertoire of strategies they have learned, which Mr. Novack is doing as he questions his students.

Mr. Novack: What does it mean to be metacognitive?

Felicity: To monitor your reading and do something when what you are reading doesn't make sense.

Doug: To think before you read something and have a good idea of why you are reading it and what you want to get out of it.

Artrell: To decide which of the comprehension strategies we know we should use in a particular situation.

Mr. Novack: What do you do when you are reading along and suddenly realize you don't understand what you're reading?

Amad: When that happens to me, I go back and read the same words again.

Mr. Novack: You mean you reread. That's a good strategy.

Ted: If I'm reading science or social studies, or something like that, and there are words I don't know, I'll look them up or ask somebody.

Mr. Novack: You consult another source. That's a good strategy, too.

April: Sometimes it helps me to look at the pictures or maps, if there are any.

Mr. Novack: You consider any graphic information. Good.

Doug: If something isn't making sense, I'll think about something I already know and see how it fits what I'm reading.

Mr. Novack: You connect what you already know with what you're reading. Excellent strategy.

Felicity: I try to picture in my mind what I'm reading, what the author's describing. I guess I'm always drawing pictures in my mind when I read.

Mr. Novack: You're imaging, and that's another very effective comprehension strategy.

Clearly, Mr. Novack encourages his students to do whatever is necessary to arrive at a satisfactory understanding of what they are reading. This, of course, is precisely what we want to prepare students to do.

Key Comprehension Strategies

Mature readers use a repertoire of comprehension strategies and metacognitive strategies. There is substantial agreement on the strategies that students need to use (National Reading Panel, 2000; Pressley, 2006; RAND Reading Study Group, 2002; Duke et al., 2011) but there is no agreement on the number of strategies that should be introduced at each grade level. A review of the strategy research suggests that a few might be just as beneficial as many (Willingham, 2006).

Our repertoire of strategies was based on reading print, but, as everyone moves deeper into the digital age of reading, some strategies take on greater importance because students are faced with more choices and distractions on the Internet (Afflerbach & Cho, 2009; Leu, Kinzer, Coiro, Castek, & Henry, 2017). The key strategies we recommend are shown in Figure 11.1 and discussed in the section that follows. Some strategies are more cognitive and have a stronger focus on the construction of meaning while others are more metacognitive helping us reflect on our progress while reading.

Figure 11.1 Comprehension and Metacognitive Strategiess

Strategies	Constructing Meaning (Cognitive)	Reflecting on Meaning (Metacognitive)
• Setting a purpose for reading/defining a question		✓
• Asking and answering questions	✓	✓
• Making inferences	✓	
• Determining what is important	✓	
• Summarizing	✓	✓
• Imaging and creating graphic representations	✓	
• Locating information	✓	
• Critically evaluating information	✓	✓

A few strategies take on special importance when reading digital text, especially the ability to define the purpose of reading, to locate information, to critically evaluate information, and to integrate information from several sources. We will discuss these strategies more completely in the next chapter where the Internet is a vital resource for informational reading.

Each of these strategies involves readers in actively constructing meaning as they read. These strategies are not distinct entities. To summarize you must be able to determine importance, and making inferences is impossible without using prior knowledge. When readers ask questions they are establishing a purpose for their reading.

SETTING A PURPOSE FOR READING

One of the first things a good reader does as she approaches a text is to establish a purpose for reading. That purpose will depend on the text, the reader, and what she needs from the text. How the reader reads—whether, for example, she takes notes, reads slowly or quickly, or rereads—will, in turn, depend on this purpose.

Sometimes the reader's purpose is to find a specific piece of information, perhaps the score of a soccer match or a critic's opinion about a current movie. Sometimes the purpose is to learn everything possible from the text, perhaps in preparation for a test. Sometimes it's to simply enjoy reading, as is often the case with a novel or short story. The goal is for the reader to identify the appropriate purpose for a particular situation and read in a way to accomplish that purpose.

This strategy becomes acute when reading on the Internet. A student may often be on the Internet with one purpose in mind and easily be seduced to follow an extraneous link. The ease of clicking from one article or video to another can lead the best reader to lose track of this initial purpose. Self-monitoring is critical on the Internet and purpose setting is an important tool to start that process.

ASKING AND ANSWERING QUESTIONS

When the reader poses questions before or while reading and then attempts to answer the questions, he virtually guarantees that reading will be an active process. It also serves to focus the reader's attention. A reader who has asked a particular set of questions will be particularly attentive to the information that answers those questions. This is particularly important when reading on the Internet because the ever-branching links can cause distractions.

Consider a sixth-grader preparing to read a chapter on nutrition in a health text. As the first step, he might survey the chapter and find these headings: *Nutrients and the U.S. RDA*, *The Seven Dietary Guidelines*, *Shopping for Groceries*, and *Preventing Disease Through*

Proper Diet. Then he might pose one or two questions about each heading: What are nutrients? What is the U.S. RDA? What are the seven dietary guidelines? Do I follow them in my diet? As he reads, the student will find answers to some of his questions, find that others are not answered in the chapter, and pose and answer additional questions.

MAKING INFERENCES

Readers can infer meanings by using information from the text and their existing knowledge of the world to fill in bits of information that are not explicitly stated in the text. No text is ever fully explicit, and thus readers must constantly make inferences to understand what they are reading. By teaching students to make inferences, you are helping them learn to use their existing knowledge along with the information in the text to build meaning. Readers also make inferences when they connect one idea to another. Making inferences is subtle and complex. Encouraging students to make inferences changes how they read, asking them to dig deeper in the text. In the Classroom 11.2 lets us look in as one teacher introduces making inferences to a fourth-grade class.

In the Classroom 11.2

Instructional Routines

An Introduction to Making Inferences for Fourth-Graders

An inference is hard to define, but somewhat easier to illustrate. Mr. Hernandez writes the following sentence on the whiteboard: *Mary looked at her menu carefully, trying to find the cheapest entrée, while John gazed lovingly in her eyes.* He then tells his students that they just made three inferences and they are not even aware that they made them. He further explains that an inference is something that the author did not tell us, but we can figure it out. We can dig deeper; we can read between the lines. He then explores the three inferences.

Mr. Hernandez explains that the author didn't tell the students where John and Mary are, but they can figure it out—they can make an inference. Students immediately raise their hands and offer that John and Mary are in a restaurant.

Mr. Hernandez asks, "What told you that they are in a restaurant?"

Robert responds, "They are looking at menus and you don't have menus at home."

Sarah says, "The word *entrée;* we don't talk about food at home like that, but a menu might have that word."

Mr. Hernandez explains that to make such an inference we use clues from the text, the words *menu* and *entrée*, plus what we know, that restaurants have menus, to figure out what the author did not tell us. Mr. Hernandez quickly sketches a chart on the whiteboard.

Clues from the Text	Prior Knowledge	Inference
Menu, entrée	Restaurants have menus so you can select your food.	John and Mary are in a restaurant.
Cheapest	When I don't have a lot of money I go for the grilled cheese.	Mary thinks John does not have much money.

Mr. Hernandez continues to explore the next inferences by asking what else the author implied. "What do we know about Mary? What are some important clues in the text?" The students talk about the words *cheapest* and *entrée* and make inferences that Mary is being cautious, this is a first date, and John is not wealthy.

Mr. Hernandez then draws the students' attention to the next inference, asking, "What do we know about John?" With some giggling, the students state that John likes or is in love with Mary. Mr. Hernandez wants to know how they made those inferences—what text clues were important. The students easily identify the word *lovingly*, but *gaze* takes some clarification. He also has the students consider what they know by asking how people behave when they are out on a date.

Mr. Hernandez will expand this lesson to larger pieces of text and then to full stories. Students will continue to ask themselves what the author implied that we can nevertheless infer. What clues did the author leave and what knowledge and experiences do I have that help me make these inferences?

DETERMINING WHAT IS IMPORTANT

Because most texts contain much more information than a reader can remember, determining what is important is a crucial and frequently required strategy. Using this strategy requires that readers understand what they have read and make judgments about what is and is not important. The task of determining importance takes a different form when reading fiction or non-fiction and when they are working with print or digital text. Informational texts include direct cues to what is important—overviews, headings, topic sentences, summaries, and the like. Fiction requires that the readers use what they know about narrative structure to focus on importance. Digital text presents its own problems and supporting a main idea is more difficult when reading digital text than print (Singer & Alexander, 2016).

MyLab Education
Video Example 11.2
This video notes the steps that the teacher takes to teach the students how to summarize. What would be her next step after she models how to write a summary?

SUMMARIZING

Summarizing requires students to first determine what is important and then condense it in their own words. To summarize, the reader must ignore the trivial and redundant, categorize details, search for an author's topic sentences, and fashion what remains into a cogent summary (Brown & Day, 1983) There are several ways to teach summarizing and how you do so depends on the type of text. When reading informational text, asking students to write one sentence summaries for each paragraph or section is helpful (Taylor & Beach, 1984). Narrative texts are best summarized by focusing on their text structure—characters, their problems, and the plot and including these pertinent elements in the summary.

DEALING WITH GRAPHIC INFORMATION

Readers can often improve comprehension by giving conscious attention to the visual information supplied by the author. Before youngsters learn to read, they are drawn to, and fascinated by, the visual material books offer. Teaching them when, how, and why to examine the illustrations, graphs, maps, diagrams, and other visuals that accompany selections will enable them to make optimal use of the visual aids texts often provide. History texts, for example, almost always contain maps that include a legend to the symbols they employ. Students need to learn that maps usually have legends, the kind of information legends normally contain, where legends are typically placed, and how to interpret them.

LOCATING INFORMATION

Locating information is important during any act of reading, but it becomes particularly vital when reading for information on the Internet. The relatively simple tools such as the table of contents and the index in a book become more complex on the Internet. Here a reader must know how to use key words, anticipate hyper-links, and be able to judge the usefulness of information. Given the multiple sources on the Internet, the reader must judge which ones might be useful and determine a sequence for reading them. We will address this strategy and the next in Chapter 12.

CRITICALLY EVALUATING INFORMATION

We live in an age when the truthfulness of what we read is questioned and questionable. Whether reading a textbook that presents the 18th and 19th century slave trade as a "pattern of immigration" that brought "workers" to southern plantations (McGraw-Hill, 2013) or an Internet site that claims climate change is a hoax, readers must critically evaluate all that they read. The reader must learn to assess the credibility of websites and the clarity of those sites. Then the reader must determine the relevance and utility of information that they read. This means weighing the new information read against what has already been read (Afflerbach & Cho, 2009).

The strategies described here—establishing a purpose for reading, using prior knowledge, asking and answering questions, making inferences, determining what is important, summarizing, dealing with graphic information, and being metacognitive—will help students reach the goal of understanding and learning from what they read.

These strategies will also promote deeper understanding of the stories and books that students read. By learning these strategies, students are internalizing an approach to reading and thinking that is active and reflective, an approach vital to literacy in the 21st century. But in the age of the Internet, students need more than these now traditional strategies. They must develop the ability to locate information, critically evaluate it, and synthesize what they have read.

MyLab Education **Self-Check 11.1**

MyLab Education **Application Exercise 11.1:** Teaching Students to Make Inferences

---

Planning and Selecting a Reading Curriculum

We have discussed the components of comprehension instruction but one critical question remains, how does a teacher pull all of these components together. How will the teacher weave together strategies, knowledge, motivation, and metacognition to construct a set of experiences that will create stronger and more motivated readers? When we look carefully at what it means to comprehend text, three factors are always involved: the reader (who is reading), the selection (what is being read), and the purpose or purposes for reading (why reading is being done). We cannot overstate the importance and interconnectedness of these three components in planning any classroom reading experience.

Reader, the Text, the Purpose

The readers will obviously be the focal point of your planning. This means considering the readers' needs interests, background knowledge, strengths and weaknesses as learners. When you begin planning reading instruction, you will want to take all of these factors into account. However, your students' background knowledge—what they know and have experienced—is probably the most crucial variable in their eventual success.

As you plan, your next consideration is the texts or the reading selections. Ideally, your students will be reading a wide range of materials that reflect a variety of cultures, including easy selections as well as some that are more challenging and that deal with topics that reflect the array of diverse interests your students have. In today's classrooms, it is particularly important to have materials that reflect our multicultural society. Figure 11.2 provides a short list of authors whose books illuminate a variety of cultures.

It is also vital to give students opportunities to read a variety of genres. Students should become familiar with narratives, informational texts, and poetry, as well as the many genres within these broad categories. By the time students leave middle school they should have had experiences with realistic fiction, historical fiction, fantasy, folk tales, biography, autobiography, and other expository text. We recommend making a chart of the genres to hang in your classroom, using it as a point of discussion when new texts are introduced.

Can you imagine reading something without motivation, without a purpose? As John Guthrie (Guthrie & Anderson, 1999) reminds us, "Reading is a conscious, deliberate act prompted by a plausible purpose." Purpose is what motivates us, helps focus our attention, and gives us something tangible to work toward (a goal). We read because somewhere in those combinations of symbols is something we need or want—information, escape, excitement, or knowledge. This is the message we want students to internalize from day one.

Figure 11.2 Authors Who Create Books Illuminating a Variety of Cultures

Alma Flor Ada	Virginia Hamilton	Jerry Pinkney
Joseph Bruchac	Minfong Ho	Faith Ringgold
Ashley Bryan	Angela Johnson	Allen Say
Floyd Cooper	Barbara Knutson	Virginia Driving Hawk Sneve
David Diaz	Jeanne M. Lee	Gary Soto
Leo and Diane Dillon	Julius Lester	Mildred Taylor
Arthur Dorros	Patricia McKissack	Joyce Carol Thomas
Tom Feelings	Walter Dean Myers	Yoshiko Uchida
Jean Craighead George	Lensey Namioka	Mildred Pitts Walters
Paul Goble	Ifeoma Onyofulu	Lawrence Yep
Eloise Greenfield	Brian Pinkney	Ed Young

Purposes motivate or give a reason for reading. Such motivation is missing when a teacher merely states, "Open your anthology and read the biography Martin Luther King, Jr. (Jones, 2006) and when you are done we will discuss it." "Why?" a student might ask—and rightfully so. In this chapter we will consider why we read literature and the answer is not simply entertainment. Literature enables us to consider what it means to be human. Through literature, whether it is fiction, biography, or poetry, we grapple with values and the problems of life. Through literature we consider the role of courage, the importance of love, and the need for community. Reading literature is entertainment, but it is also enlightening, puzzling, and disturbing. It is important to select and organize literature so that they provide entertainment and build knowledge about ourselves, others, and the world around us.

Three Comprehension Curriculums

The needs of the reader, the selection of texts, and the purposes for reading are typically formed into a curriculum. A curriculum includes learning standards or objectives, the texts that will be read, the instructional methods that will be used to help students achieve the standards, the assignments, and the assessments. Today, the dominant standards are the Common Core State Standards (NGA & CCSSO, 2010) and they articulate nine specific goals which are summarized into three broad goals. Figure 11.3 summarizes the Standards. Each reading curriculum attempts to meet the Common Core State Standards, but their structure and methods differ. There are two dominant curriculum structures in reading, basal readers and guided reading, and a third that should be, a thematic approach.

BASAL READING PROGRAMS

As of 2012, 74 percent of the school districts in the country used a basal reading program and about half of those followed it closely (Education Market Research, 2012). A basal is a sequence of texts and lessons that develop students' skills, strategies, and knowledge. In a typical week, a student will read one 10 page, reading selection and a shorter piece tied to it. Before reading, the teacher will develop prior knowledge, teach vocabulary, and introduce skills and strategies. While reading, the students will be guided to apply the skills and strategies as the teacher models and asks questions. After reading, the students will review the texts, engage in skill practice, and move on to additional skills. This cycle will be repeated thirty times across the school year. Figure 11.4 is the outline for one unit of fourth grade instruction from the *Journeys* program (Houghton Mifflin Harcourt, 2017) with some details omitted.

In the *Journey's* unit each student will read three texts a week, one primary selection, a much shorter follow-up text, and then a leveled book. The reading selections across the six-week unit do not hang together and build knowledge. The excerpt from *Because of Winn Dixie* develops few if any concepts that are useful for comprehending

---

Figure 11.3 College and Career Readiness Anchor Standards for Reading

Key Ideas and Details:

1. Read closely to determine what the text says explicitly and to make logical inferences from it; cite specific textual evidence when writing or speaking to support conclusions drawn from the text.
2. Determine central ideas or themes of a text and analyze their development; summarize the key supporting details and ideas.
3. Analyze how and why individuals, events, or ideas develop and interact over the course of a text.

Craft and Structure:

4. Interpret words and phrases as they are used in a text, including determining technical, connotative, and figurative meanings, and analyze how specific word choices shape meaning or tone.
5. Analyze the structure of texts, including how specific sentences, paragraphs, and larger portions of the text (e.g., a section, chapter, scene, or stanza) relate to each other and the whole.
6. Assess how point of view or purpose shapes the content and style of a text.

Integration of Knowledge and Ideas:

7. Integrate and evaluate content presented in diverse media and formats, including visually and quantitatively, as well as in words.
8. Delineate and evaluate the argument and specific claims in a text, including the validity of the reasoning as well as the relevance and sufficiency of the evidence.
9. Analyze how two or more texts address similar themes or topics in order to build knowledge or to compare the approaches the authors take.

Range of Reading and Level of Text Complexity:

10. Read and comprehend complex literary and informational texts independently and proficiently.

SOURCE: National Governors Association Center for Best Practices, Council of Chief State School Officers Title: Common Core State Standards. Publisher: National Governors Association Center for Best Practices, Council of Chief State School Officers, Washington, D.C. Copyright Date: 2010.

the biography of Martin Luther King, Jr. or the following non-fiction article about bringing books to developing countries. To create more coherence and build knowledge, a teacher could bring in additional readings about Martin Luther King, Jr. and the Civil Rights movement (Dewitz & Jones, 2013).

In these six weeks of instruction, a teacher would need to cover at least 17 skills, strategies, and principles of craft and text structure. The scope and sequence of instruction provides for little review with a different strategy and skill taught each week. In addition to the comprehension skills and strategies, the teacher has much to cover about vocabulary, word learning strategies, spelling, writing, and grammar. A teacher who knows her students well can decide which strategies should be taught now, which can be delayed, and which can be ignored. Except for brand new teachers who can benefit from the structure of a basal reading program, others should use it selectively and intelligently.

GUIDED READING

The second most common curriculum approach is guided reading (Fountas & Pinnell, 1996, 2001), which typically has three components; shared reading, guided reading, and independent reading. Or as the guided reading crowd likes to name them, "I do it, we do it, and you do it." Shared reading is whole class instruction in which teacher and students read the same text—it can be a short story, a poem or an excerpt from a novel—the teacher uses the experience to build word knowledge, text structure knowledge, or model comprehension strategies. It is during shared reading that all students work with grade level texts or texts that stretch them above their grade level. Shared reading can be considered the modeling phase of reading instruction.

Figure 11.4 A 6 Week Basal Reading Unit

	Lesson 1	Lesson 2	Lesson 3	Lesson 4	Lesson 5
Oral Language	Teacher read aloud: *Sideline Support*	Teacher read aloud: *The Troublemaker*	Teacher read aloud: *Bridging the Gap*		
Vocabulary	Target Vocabulary Prefixes, *re, in, dis*	Target Vocabulary Prefixes, *im, il, ir*	Target Vocabulary Using context	Target Vocabulary Prefixes, *non, mi,*	Target Vocabulary Reference materials
Text Reading	*Because of Winn Dixie* (Realistic Fiction)	*My Brother Martin* (Biography)	*My Librarian is a Camel* (Information)	*The Power of W.O.W.* (Realistic Fiction)	*Capitan Storm-along* (Tall Tale)
Comprehension Skills/Strategies	Story structure Summarizing	Author's Purpose Monitor/Clarify	Cause & Effect Visualize	Theme Analyze/Evaluate	Understand Characters Infer/Predict
Craft and Structure	Point of view Flashbacks	Explain historical events	Interpret visuals	Elements of drama	Point of View
Spelling Grammar Writing	Short & long a Sentence structure Descriptive paragraph	Short & long e Kinds of sentences Story writing	Short & long 1 Quotations Dialogue	Short & long o Sentence fragments Fictional narrative	Homophones Proper nouns Fictional narrative
Small Group Instruction	Reading a small leveled text Differentiated comprehension and vocabulary instruction	Reading a small leveled text Differentiated comprehension and vocabulary instruction	Reading a small leveled text Differentiated comprehension and vocabulary instruction	Reading a small leveled text Differentiated comprehension and vocabulary instruction	Reading a small leveled text Differentiated comprehension and vocabulary instruction

SOURCE: *Journeys*, Harcourt Houghton Mifflin, 2017.

The second component is guided reading, the heart of the matter, where the teacher works with small groups of students to develop their comprehension. Groups can be formed around genres, topics, themes, but in most cases groups are formed around reading level. The teacher develops a gradient of books, matching the texts to the reading level of the students. We discussed these various schemes for leveling text in Chapter 6. The teacher meets regularly with each group of students and guides them through the text with before, during, and after reading discussions. There is no scope and sequence of skills and strategies as in the basal system. Rather, teachers think opportunistically, helping students employ strategies as they are needed.

In guided reading, the teacher assists students to use a "network of strategic actions for processing text" (Fountas & Pinnell, 2013, p. 272). This network consists of strategies for thinking within a text, like word solving (identifying words), and searching for, identifying, and remembering information. The second set of strategies takes the reader beyond the text to infer, make connections, synthesize, and predict. The final set of strategies has the reader analyze and critique. There is no scope and sequence of skills and strategies in guided reading, although some experts suggest teaching one strategy a week (see Richardson, 2009). Rather skilled teachers make decisions that are responsive to the learner (Fountas & Pinnell, 2013, p. 279). Independent, self-selected reading is the final component of guided reading.

The two pitfalls to guided reading are the overemphasis on selecting books at just the right level and a somewhat haphazard approach to strategy instruction (Hoffman, 2017). When selecting books for instruction, teachers must consider the quality and characteristics of the literature, the interests of the students, and their background knowledge, not just reading level. The opportunistic approach to strategy instruction is problematic for students who struggle with comprehension. Many students require more sustained instruction than a bit of this and a bit of that approach. These students need a sustained focus with a strategy or strategies before they own it. Consistent practice with predicting, questioning, clarifying, and summarizing over 10 to 12 weeks creates students with better reading comprehension (Palincsar & Brown, 1994; Rosenshine & Meister, 1994).

A THEMATIC CURRICULUM

The third approach to the curriculum is a thematic approach in which the goals, the texts, the discussions, and the writing are integrated around a theme. As you think about what your students will read, think in terms of units of instruction, not individual selections. A unit might be organized to learn about a particular genre (e.g., fantasy), study a particular author (e.g., Roald Dahl), examine a particular topic (immigration), or explore a particular concept (e.g., justice). Some units might focus on just one genre whereas others might incorporate several different genres.

Thematic units that focus on generative topics are one way to build higher-order thinking (Perkins, 1992, 2004; Perkins & Blythe, 1994). Generative topics can be concepts, themes, procedures, historical periods, theories, ideas, and the like. For example, in the field of literature, plot is a generative topic. Plot is central to the study of literature, a critical element in many types of literature, and exists outside of literature as well. Historical episodes—for example, the Civil War period—basically follow a plot, as do our lives. As another example, consider cause and effect. Cause and effect is a concept central to much of history, and, to much of history and science. In fact, many, if not most, fields of study—science, humanities, and art, for example—deal with cause and effect. Some examples of generative topics and ideas generated from them for first-graders and fifth-graders are shown in Figure 11.5.

Figure 11.5 Some Generative Topics for First-Graders and Fifth-Graders

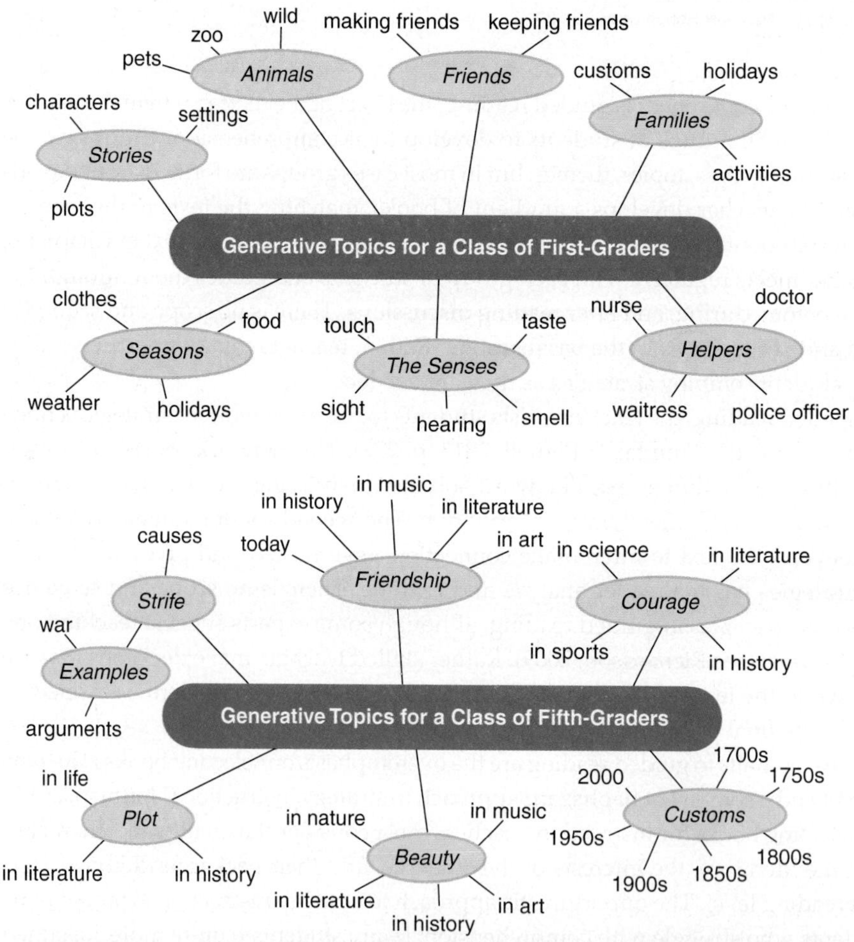

The units you create need to be differentiated—one size does not fit all. All students might be studying fantasy, but the text for students with weaker print and fluency skills needs to be selected for their reading level. In all cases we believe that you need to create units that will lead to higher-order thinking, units that will take students beyond the literal into a deep understanding of topics or themes.

One example of a thematic curriculum is the Read Side by Side reading program developed by Sarah Collinge (2010). Figure 11.6 is a thematically-based unit plan from that program (Collinge & Robinson, 2013). This thematic unit covers six weeks of instruction during which students read two novels and several related informational articles. The unit is focused on themes of animal rights, determining right from wrong in ambiguous situations, and coming to understand the concept of compassion. Students are introduced to the theme, text structure principles, and comprehension strategies through a whole class interactive read-aloud with the book *Shiloh* (Naylor, 1991). Students then apply those principles when they work in book clubs, a semi-autonomous form of independent reading. The strongest readers read *Shoeshine Girl* (Bulla, 1975), those with average skill read *Because of Winn-Dixie* (DiCamillo, 2000), and those needing the most support read *How to Steal a Dog* (O'Connor, 2007).

Strategies and text structure knowledge are sequenced within each book following a process called Collect-Interpret-Apply (C.I.A.). We will return to this later in the chapter. The instructional sequence follows the demands of the text, not a yearly scope and sequence. Early in a novel the students consider characters, setting, problems, and summarization. As they move deeper into the book they interpret character feelings and traits, making inferences. Toward the end of the book the students determine the theme and apply it to their individual lives.

Key to the success of building thematic units of instruction is selecting texts, and text selection requires a knowledge of the books' reading level and the text complexity. In the Reading Corner we offer a selection of novels that vary by complexity of plot structure and character development.

Curriculum is how we package all of the elements of reading instruction—vocabulary, text structure knowledge, strategies, and texts. Some curriculums are quite rigid or systematic like those in basal programs. Others, like guided reading, are quite

Figure 11.6 A Thematic Unit around the Novel Shiloh (Naylor, 1997)

	Week 1	Week 2	Week 3	Week 4	Week 5	Week 6
Themes	Animal rights, right versus wrong,					
Read Aloud Text	*Shiloh* (Naylor)					
Non-fiction articles		Protecting pets in your community		Document Animal Abuse		
Book Club Texts			*Shoeshine Girl* (Bulla) *Because of Winn Dixie* (DiCamillo) *How to Steal a Dog* (O'Connor)			
Text Structure	Narrative elements – characters, setting, problems	Character development – traits and motives Text features	Narrative elements – character, setting problems	Character development – traits and motives Text features		
Comprehension Strategies	Predicting Inferring	Summarizing Determining importance	Inferring	Summarizing Inferring		
Writing				Writing a persuasive essay		

SOURCE: Collinge, S. (2011). Raising the Standards. Seattle, WA: Peanut Butter Publishing.

The Reading Corner

Narrative Texts, from Simple to Complex Plots and Character Development

Engaging Novels with Less Complex Narratives

Jeanne Birdsall. *The Penderwicks at Last.* Knopf Books for Young Readers, 2018. This is the last installment of the adventures of a young girl and her five older siblings from *The New York Times* bestselling author, Jeanne Birdsall. 304 pages.

Christopher Paul Curtis. *Bud, Not Buddy.* Delacorte Books for Young Readers, 1999. Set during the Great Depression, 10-year-old Bud flees his foster home in search of the man he believes is his father, the famous bandleader, H. E. Calloway. 245 pages.

Kevin Henkes. *The Year of Billy Miller.* Greenwillow, 2013. This Newbery Honor book is a funny, fast-paced story about friendship, sibling rivalry, and elementary school. 240 pages.

Phyllis Reynolds Naylor. *Shiloh.* Atheneum, 1991. In this Newbery Award book, a young boy finds a lost beagle in the hills near his home in West Virginia and tries to hide him from his family and the dog's real owner, a mean old man known to mistreat dogs. 144 pages.

Grace Lin. *Dumpling Days (A Pacy Lin Novel).* Little, Brown Books for Young Readers, 2013. When Pacy, her two sisters, and their parents travel to Taiwan to celebrate Grandma's sixtieth birthday, the girls learn a great deal about their heritage. 261 pages.

Rachel Renee Russell. *The Misadventures of Max Crumbly 1: Locker Hero.* Aladdin, 2016. Max may not have the super powers like his favorite comic hero, but he tries his best to be the hero his school needs. 320 pages.

Engaging Novels with More Complex Plots and Character Development

Cynthia Kadohata. *Kira-Kira.* Atheneum Books for Young Readers, 2004. This Newbery Award winning book set in the late 1950s and early 1960s, chronicles the close friendship between two Japanese-American sisters growing up in rural Georgia and the anguish when one sister becomes terminally ill. 244 pages.

Chris Crutcher. *Losers Bracket.* Greenwillow Books, 2018. Skilled hoops player, foster child Annie Boots, feels like she's in the "losers bracket" when it comes to family until her nephew goes missing and she works with friends, her foster brother, and her social worker to help find him. 245 pages.

Alan Gratz. *Refugee.* Scholastic Press, 2017. This book chronicles the harrowing stories of three refugees—Josef fleeing Nazi Germany in 1930s, Isabel fleeing Cuba in 1994, and Muhmoud fleeing Syria in 2015. Although separated by continents and decades, surprising connections tie their stories together in the end. 352 pages.

Erin Entrada Kelly. *Hello Universe.* Greenwillow Books, 2017. This Newbery Award winning book is told from four alternating points of view by four misfits whose lives are intertwined when a bully's prank lands shy Virgil at the bottom of a well and three friends band together in a quest to find and rescue him. 313 pages.

Louis Sachar. *Holes.* Dell Laurel-Leaf Books, 2001. When Stanley Yelnats is sent to a hellish correctional camp in the Texas desert, he finds his first real friend, a treasure, and a new sense of himself. Newbery Award book. 231 pages.

flexible leaving most decisions up to the teacher. The thematic approach falls somewhere in the middle. None of these curriculums explain how the important knowledge and strategies are actually taught. That will be our task in the next section.

Reflect and Apply

1. Suppose you are teaching fourth-graders who come from a variety of backgrounds. Your literature curriculum includes *Number the Stars* by Lois Lowry, an award-winning middle-grade novel set in Nazi-occupied Denmark. The story revolves around 10-year-old Annemarie, who, with the help of her family, helps her best friend's family escape to Sweden. Are all of your students likely to succeed in reading this selection without help from you? Why or why not?

MyLab Education **Self-Check 11.2**

MyLab Education **Application Exercise 11.2:** Choosing a Curriculum

Four Frameworks for Scaffolding Students' Reading

In this section, we describe four frameworks that organize reading instruction with the purpose of guiding students into, through, and beyond the texts they read. The frameworks are the scaffolded reading experience (SRE), guided reading, close reading, and a process called Collect-Interpret-Apply (C.I.A). All the procedures have their origin in the directed reading activity (DRA) because its basic structure is generally repeated in all reading lessons. First described by Emmett Betts in 1946, the DRA procedure has five steps to guide students through a reading selection. First, the students are prepared for the selection, which the teacher does by creating interest, establishing purposes, and introducing new vocabulary. During the second step, students read silently. In the third step, the teacher checks students' comprehension in a discussion and also sometimes develops word recognition skills when necessary. In the fourth step, students read parts of the selection again, this time aloud, to focus on writing craft or to develop fluency. The fifth step involves postreading follow-up activities.

Although the procedure has been justly criticized as inviting a rigid, one-size-fits-all reading instruction approach and as being too teacher dominated, it is worth considering because it has served as the basis of so much reading instruction, quite possibly the instruction you or your parents received. Additionally, it is the precursor of the more flexible scaffolded reading experience, which we describe next.

Scaffolded Reading Experience

The scaffolded reading experience (SRE) takes students through the prereading, during-reading, and postreading phases of a text reading. Its simple, flexible design can easily be implemented in any reading situation at any grade level. The SRE is based on the notion of scaffolding, which, you will recall, is "a process that enables a child or novice to solve a problem, carry out a task, or achieve a goal [that] would be beyond his unassisted efforts" (Wood, Bruner, & Ross, 1976). The scaffolded reading experience (Avery & Graves, 1997; Clark & Graves, 2005; Graves & Graves, 2003; Graves, Graves, & Braaten, 1996; Watts & Graves, 1997) is designed to do just that—to ensure a student's reading success in whatever she is reading, for whatever purpose.

The SRE framework takes into consideration the three all-important factors discussed at the beginning of the chapter: purpose, selection, and reader. After carefully considering a purpose, a selection, and a group of readers, the teacher develops a set of prereading, during-reading, and postreading activities that supports students in achieving their reading goals.

The scaffolded reading experience lesson framework is well suited to supporting English language learners during reading lessons and content area lessons that involve texts. Fitzgerald and Graves (2004) note that reading in a second language involves more processes than reading in a first language, and that a significant additional process is that of translation. To support English language learners with this additional process, Fitzgerald and Graves recommend the following activities. During the prereading part of a scaffolded reading experience, preview the selection in English language learners' first language. To scaffold English language learners during reading, provide them with a list of major events or headings in their first language. To further support these students, Fitzgerald and Graves suggest, have them listen to an audio of the selection as they read. For postreading, have English language learners work in small groups with native English speakers to review the major events or outline important points depending on the nature of the selection (i.e., fiction/nonfiction). Then discuss the text as a whole class. Allow English language learners to use their first language to support their thinking and to express their ideas as needed during the discussion.

In the next three sections we discuss prereading, during-reading, and postreading activities of SREs. These phases demand considerable flexibility. Some texts require considerable prereading instructions and others do not. Some texts can be read quickly, others require considerable stopping and discussion before their message makes sense.

PREREADING ACTIVITIES

Prereading activities get students ready both cognitively and affectively to read a selection. Taking time to prepare students before they read can pay big dividends in terms of their understanding and enjoyment of what they read. Here are five categories of prereading experiences.

1. *Motivating and Setting Purposes for Reading.* Motivational activities incite enthusiasm, an eagerness to discover what the written word has to offer. As Kathryn Au (1999) notes, "It is students' interest that must serve as the starting point." In other words, motivational activities will draw on the interests and concerns of the particular group doing the reading.

2. *Activating Background Knowledge.* Having appropriate background knowledge is absolutely crucial to understanding text. When *activating* background knowledge, you help students draw on information they already have about a particular subject; when *building* background knowledge, you provide students with information they need to understand the text. For example, let's say a group of fourth-graders is going to read a biography of Martin Luther King, Jr. To activate their prior knowledge, you might have them talk about what they know or if you suspect they know little, share a film about the civil rights leader. By activating background knowledge, you seek to draw students into the text by helping them recall situations in their lives that are similar to those found in the selection. In the Classroom 11.3 shows a prereading activity that relates the text to students' lives and experiences.

3. *Building Text-Specific Knowledge.* Some activities should build text-specific knowledge. The most vital knowledge for comprehending fiction and non-fiction narratives is knowledge of narrative structure, structural devices such as flashback and foreshadowing, and the use of figurative language. In the Classroom 11.4 presents

---

In the Classroom 11.3

Instructional Routines

Prereading Activity Relating the Reading to Students' Lives

- *Selection:* Various biographies of Martin Luther King, Jr.
- *Readers:* Fourth-grade students, several of whom have parents who emigrated to the United States and four of whom recently moved to the United States from Somalia. All of these fourth-graders have experienced firsthand the concept of discrimination, owing to events that occurred in their community as a result of a large influx of Somalians.
- *Reading purpose:* To learn more about the life of Martin Luther King, Jr., and to understand and appreciate the purpose and results of his efforts to promote civil rights.
- *Goal of the activity:* To make connections with the topics and themes found in the biographies.
- *Rationale:* Having students write about times they felt discriminated against and later talk about them will help them understand the concept of discrimination, a central theme in the biographies of King and a topic that has become an issue in their community. This writing will also help build an immediacy and relevancy for the biographies students will read.
- *Procedure:* Before students begin reading biographies, ask them to write in their journals about a time in their lives when they felt that they were not treated as well as others, when they felt they were mistreated or treated unfairly. After students write, encourage them to read aloud or to discuss what they have written.

some specific ideas for developing students' knowledge of narrative structure. These activities are more valuable in the primary grades where students have not yet internalized an understanding of narrative or story structure.

4. *Preteaching Vocabulary and Concepts.* Teaching selected vocabulary and concepts before students read a selection can help them better understand and appreciate a

In the Classroom 11.4

Developing Text Structure Knowledge

Most well-written stories, whether simple or complex, have a fairly similar structure, and most children have a basic schema for this structure. Teachers can help students make this understanding explicit and give them a language for talking about stories. When teachers build on this schema, students' comprehension and enjoyment of narrative literature will be enhanced, as will their writing in this genre. Story grammars and story maps provide two ways to help students enhance their schema for stories.

Story Grammars and Story Maps

Story grammar is similar to sentence grammar in that it attempts to explain the various components in a story and how they function (Mandler & Johnson, 1977; Thorndyke, 1977). The story grammar we have found most helpful is a synthesis of those that both educational researchers and fiction writers have identified as consistent across stories. This grammar includes a setting with a character who has a problem to solve or a goal to achieve, the character's attempts to solve the problem or achieve the goal, the results of these attempts, and a conclusion. The conclusion and the character's attempt to solve the problem illuminates the story's theme. Story grammars can be applied through both guided questioning and the use of graphic organizers generally, called story maps.

A story map is a listing of the major ideas and events in a story, beginning at the starting point and moving through the story in sequential order. Beck and McKeown (1981) recommend that teachers create a story map to help identify the major structural elements, both explicit and implicit, in a story that students will be reading in class. Based on the map, the teacher then generates a question for the students to answer related to each major event. In the story map illustrated in Figure 11.7, based on the story *The Bear's Toothache* (McPhail, 1972), you will see that the left column gives the story event and the right column the corresponding question for students to answer. These questions, when answered, constitute the essence of the story and elicit information that is central to understanding it.

Figure 11.7 Story Map and Questions for *A Bear's Toothache*

The Story Map	Questions
Character: A boy lying in bed hears a loud moaning outside his window.	Who are the characters in our story?
Setting: A house, bedroom.	Where does it take place?
Problem: A bear with a bad tooth.	What did the boy hear outside his window?
Goal: Remove the tooth and alleviate the pain.	What did the boy try to do for the bear? Why do you think the boy wanted to help?
Event 1: Boy tries to pull the tooth.	
Event 2: Boy gives bear steak to eat to loosen the tooth.	What are some of the ways the boy and the bear tried to get rid of the painful tooth?
Event 3: Boy tries to hit the tooth with his pillow.	
Event 4: Boy ties a rope around the tooth and bear jumps out of the window.	How did they ultimately get the tooth out?
Resolution: The tooth popped out and the bear gave it to the boy to put under his pillow.	How do you know that the bear was pleased at the end of the story?

(Continued)

Figure 11.8 A Sample Story Map

Characters _____

Setting _____

Time _____

Problem _____

_____

Goal _____

    Event 1 _____

    Event 2 _____

    Event 3 _____

    Event 4 _____

Resolution _____

> **MyLab Education**
> Click here to download a printable version of Figure 11.8.

To create a story map, identify the characters, setting, and problem. Then list briefly the major events in chronological order, and then write a question for each element and event. Students should discuss the major elements of a story before they read and use them as they read to record their understanding of the story. Research by Dreher and Singer (1980) indicates that story maps are most useful for primary children or older students who do not have a decent concept of narrative structure.

As a postreading activity, teachers often have students complete a graphic organizer such as the story map depicted in Figure 11.8. Introduce the story map by reading aloud a very well-structured narrative, like *The Bear's Toothache*, and discuss its story elements. As you discuss the story, enter character names, setting, problems, events, and resolution into the story map. After completing a few story maps with the students, they will be ready to complete one on their own or with a partner. Story map and questions driven by story maps can improve students' existing schema for a story and improve their story comprehension. As Beck and McKeown note, however, story map questions are not the only questions to ask. Once students understand the essence of the story, then interpretive, analytical, and creative questions are appropriate and important. Once students can retell a story accurately it is time to discontinue story mapping and move on to more complex discussions of plot that focus on the types of conflict, foreshadowing, and flashbacks.

text. Chapter 10 discussed the various sorts of word-learning tasks and instruction needed to facilitate that learning.

5. *Prequestioning, Predicting, and Direction Setting.* Attention-focusing activities have the similar purpose of highlighting what readers should look for as they read and directing them to particular aspects of the text. With prequestioning activities, you and your students pose questions about the upcoming text that they would like to find answers to. After reading a bit of the text, students make prediction about the text and then read to find out whether their predictions are accurate. Direction setting reminds students about what to attend to while they read. You might say, "Read the next section of the story to find out how Donald solved his problem."

By now, you are probably aware that the possibilities for prereading activities are almost limitless. But there is a common thread to all of them—each builds a bridge from the students to the selection, connecting what students already know to what they will learn or meet in the text. Sometimes just one brief prereading activity will be sufficient. At other times, you may want to support students' efforts by using several activities. Don't overteach. You can undermine the pleasure of discovery and kill the anticipation by doing too much to get the students ready.

Reflect and Apply

2. In what kinds of reading situations are prereading activities likely to be unnecessary? In what situations are prereading activities essential? Why do you think relating the reading to students' lives is a useful prereading activity?

3. Do any of your college instructors engage their classes in prereading activities? If so, what activities? Do they help you better understand the assigned reading material? Explain.

DURING-READING ACTIVITIES

During-reading activities include both tasks that students do themselves as they are reading and actions that you do to assist them—activities that facilitate or enhance the actual reading process. You have two major considerations when planning during-reading activities. First, you need to consider how the students will read the text—orally with partners, silently by themselves, or some combination of these. The second consideration is how you will assist or scaffold their understanding. What questions will you ask? What support will you provide?

Reading the Text.   Beyond the primary grades, reading is carried out most efficiently through silent reading. Silent reading will be the most frequent during-reading activity done by middle- and upper-elementary students. But not all students have the endurance to read a long text silently, so you may need to break it into chunks. The goal for these students is to move them from supported reading to independent silent reading.

Oral reading provides support for younger readers and older students who are not yet confident of their silent reading skills. Three popular read-aloud activities are choral reading, readers theater, and buddy reading. In choral reading students read the text orally together guided by the teacher. Choral reading builds confidence, fluency, and automaticity as students respond creatively to a text. Readers theater, in which students take turns or assume roles in reading portions of text aloud, can be used effectively to interpret poetry, narratives, and even expository materials (Young & Vardell, 1993). In buddy reading, two people read the same passage aloud together or take turns reading. This kind of oral reading is particularly useful for younger students, English learners, and those who need extra support. It also does much to boost the reading skills and self-esteem of the older child who reads with his younger buddy (Brozo, 2002; Cunningham & Allington, 1999; Friedland & Truesdell, 2004). Buddies can be two peers, a parent and a student, an aide and a student, or a teacher and a student.

Guided Comprehension.   While students are reading, many will need help with the ideas in the text. Supported reading activities focus students' attention on certain ideas as they read, help them clarify what they do not understand, record main ideas, draw critical inferences, attend to graphic information, and summarize what they are learning. Supporting students' reading should lead them to higher levels of understanding.

In guided comprehension the students read a portion of the text and then stop to discuss it. At each stopping point the teacher works to guide their understanding by focusing on a few critical ways of thinking. Students should engage in three activities each time they stop to discuss: paraphrase what was read, clarify misunderstandings, and make inferences. Paraphrasing gives you insight into what students understand and it is a process that helps them integrate text ideas. Clarifying makes students aware of comprehension problems and causes them to work to fix them. Inferences are

Figure 11.9 The Process of Guided Comprehension

The students will read a portion of the text and then stop to discuss it. Use the following questions to guide the discussion.

SUMMARIZE OR PARAPHASE what has been read up to the first stopping point. You might say:

> What is the author trying to tell us? What is the story or passage about?
> What is the author talking about?
> Who can retell the story to us?
>> Probe: What else can you tell us about the story?
>> Probe: Who can add on to what _____ told us?

MONITOR COMPREHENSION to focus on text or comprehension problems.

> What problems did you encounter reading this section?
> Does that make sense? Is that said in a clear way?
> What questions do you think we need to ask?
> What words or phrases might be difficult for someone to understand?
> If none of the students encountered a problem, discuss one piece of the text that does present some difficulty. Think aloud about the difficulty you had and how you resolved it.

MAKE INFERENCES necessary to understanding the selection. You might use any of the following probes or queries.

> How does the character feel?
> What is the character's goal?
> How can we use what we know about _____ to understand the text?
> How does what the author said about _____ connect to what the author already told us?
> What clues led us to the author's main message?
> Can you visualize the character or the setting the author is trying to describe?
> What did you feel, smell, or see while reading?

PROBING DEEPER: Ultimately you want the students to think deeply about the text, search for information, and justify their answers. When the students answer your questions, ask one of these follow-up questions:

- How did you come up with that answer?
- Where in the text did you find your answer?
- What clues in the text led you to that answer?
- What strategy did you use?

essential for connecting one idea to another and connecting text ideas to prior knowledge. Figure 11.9 outlines the process of guided comprehension.

Another form of guided comprehension is a procedure called Questioning the Author developed by Beck and McKeown (Beck, McKeown, Hamilton, & Kucan, 1997; Beck, McKeown, Worthy, Sandora, & Kucan, 1996). QtA is designed for upper-elementary-age and middle schoolstudents. It is, as Beck and McKeown explain, "an approach to text-based instruction that was designed to facilitate building understanding of text" (Beck et al., 1997). In the Classroom 11.5 describes Questioning the Author.

Reflect and Apply

4. Briefly discuss, in writing or with a classmate, the purpose and function of supported reading activities. Discuss your personal philosophy about supported reading activities, including when they might be appropriate and when they might be inappropriate.

5. Identify a narrative or expository text you might use in the classroom. Design the support a group of average readers would need. Where would you stop to discuss? What questions would you ask to guide their thinking?

In the Classroom 11.5

QtA

The QtA procedure includes several steps. First, the teacher explains to children that texts are in fact written by ordinary people who are not perfect and who create texts that are not perfect. Consequently, readers need to continually work hard to figure out what the authors are trying to say. Once students understand this reality, the class reads a text together, with the teacher stopping at critical points to pose queries that invite students to explore and grapple with the meaning of what is written. The queries include initiating prompts such as "What's the author trying to say?" to get students started grappling with the text, follow-ups such as "What does the author mean by that?" to encourage them to dig for deeper meaning, and follow-ups such as "How does that connect with what the author told you?" to encourage them to integrate the information in the text. Importantly, queries are not scripted, and teachers are encouraged to modify those suggested and make up their own queries to fit the students and texts they are working with. A detailed description of the QtA procedure is included in the Appendix. Here are the recommended narrative queries for QtA discussion.

Beginning the discussion
- What is the author trying to say here?
- What is the author talking about?

Thinking about characters and their motives
- How do things look for this character now?
- Given what the author has already told us about this character, what do you think he is up to?

Focusing on the author's crafting of the plot
- How has the author let you know that something has changed?
- How has the author settled this for us?

POSTREADING ACTIVITIES

Generally, postreading activities encourage students to *do* something with the material they have just read, to think—critically, logically, and creatively—about the information and ideas that emerge from their reading, to respond to what they have read, and sometimes to transform their thinking into actions. These responses can take a variety of forms—speaking, writing, drama, creative arts, or application and outreach. Their joy and excitement should come from the reading itself. If you have to dress every text with an amazing artistic and dramatic activity, then you may communicate the message that it is not the reading that is motivating but what comes after.

1. *Questioning.* By encouraging students to think about the information and ideas in the material they have read, either orally or in writing, postreading questioning activities can promote thinking on a number of levels. They might help readers recall what they have read, show that readers understand what they read, or give readers an opportunity to apply, analyze, synthesize, evaluate, or elaborate on information and ideas. Questions might also encourage creative, interpretive, or metacognitive thinking and illustrate the various perspectives among readers. Questions can be of various kinds, but it is important that at least some of them give students the opportunity to engage in higher-level thinking (Beck & McKeown, 2001; Duke et al., 2011). In the Classroom 11.6 gives some sample postreading questions for the various types of thinking.

2. *Writing.* Writing is a powerful way to integrate what students know with the information presented in a text, as well as to find out what they really do and don't understand. Writing is powerful because it requires a reader to actively manipulate information and ideas. As a postreading activity, writing can serve to connect information and ideas in a logical way. Writing also provides opportunities for students to extend ideas and to explore new ways of thinking, doing, and seeing—to invent,

---

In the Classroom 11.6

Sample Postreading Questions for Various Types of Thinking

Here are some questions that teachers might ask students after they read *Shh! We're Writing the Constitution* by Jean Fritz. Our questions are based on the revised Bloom's Taxonomy.

- *Remembering:* How many delegates were supposed to attend the grand convention in 1787?
- *Understanding:* How did the delegates keep the proceedings secret?
- *Applying:* What are some things you might do to keep a meeting secret?
- *Analyzing:* Why did the delegates decide to keep the proceedings secret? What do you think might have happened if the public had found out what was going on in the meetings?
- *Evaluating:* Do you think it was a good idea to keep the meetings secret? Why or why not?
- *Creating:* What if the delegates had decided there should be three presidents presiding over the nation instead of one? What might have happened?
- *Thinking metacognitively:* Did you understand the author's description of the three branches of government on page 14? If you didn't, what might you do to make this explanation clearer to you?

---

evaluate, create, and ponder. Writing is discussed at length in Chapter 13, which includes many examples that can be used as postreading activities.

Fiction, nonfiction, and poetry can also spark many different kinds of personal and social action. For example, after reading Chris Van Allsburg's *Just a Dream*—in which a child dreams about a future wasted because of poor management of the environment—students might decide to write letters to state and local representatives encouraging them to support legislation that protects the environment, or they might develop an environment-related ad campaign for their school or their neighborhood.

3. *Drama.* As a postreading activity, drama, like writing, encourages students to extend existing meanings they have constructed with a text and to generate new ones. In the hands of a skillful, sensitive teacher, drama can become an enjoyable and highly motivating way to involve students in all of the cognitive tasks we listed at the beginning of this section—recalling, applying, analyzing, synthesizing, evaluating, and creating—through plays, skits, retelling of stories, pantomimes, and readers theater. In the Classroom 11.7 shows a list by multigrade teacher Harold Bulinski with several instances of how he uses dramatization as a postreading activity. These examples illustrate only a few of the great variety of possibilities for dramatizing text.

Art, music, and dance each represent a specialized language that can be used in response to printed and spoken communication. Numerous children's books can help connect students with the arts—for example, in *To Be an Artist* by Maya Ajmera (2004), photos and text reveal how children around the world express themselves through art. In her article "Music and Children's Books," Kathleen Jacobi-Karna (1996) gives an extensive list of children's books that suggest musical possibilities. In addition to responding to a selection through art, music, and dance, students can engage in other types of artistic and nonverbal activities. These include media productions, such as making audiotapes, videos, or PowerPoint presentations. Or students might enjoy creating visual displays, using bulletin boards, artifacts, models, and specimens.

4. *Reteaching.* Our last category, reteaching, is the safety net in the reading scaffold, a way to make sure students leave a reading selection with a sense of accomplishment, of a job well done. Reteaching is often necessary when students, after reading

In the Classroom 11.7

Students' Postreading Dramatizations

- Second-graders pantomime Indian tigers while listening to Ted Lewin's informational picture book *Tiger Trek* read aloud.
- Small groups of first- through third-graders prepare a dramatization of their favorite poem in Jack Prelutsky's *Tyrannosaurus Was a Beast*.
- Two fifth-graders play the parts of Gilly and Miss Ellis, Gilly's caseworker, and dramatize the opening scene in Katherine Paterson's *The Great Gilly Hopkins*.
- Two fifth-graders, after reading a chapter on the 1960s in their social studies text, portray Martin Luther King, Jr., and Lyndon B. Johnson. They carry on a conversation posing as these two historical figures. Later, their conversation is recorded on a video that is aired on a community cable station.

a selection and engaging in various activities of an SRE, have not reached their reading goals. Robert Dickenson, a fifth-grade teacher, discusses his reteaching approaches:

> I sometimes find it necessary to include reteaching activities in the scaffold I build to support my students' reading experience. This happens when my students have not reached their reading goals. These reteaching activities usually consist of a retracing of the steps of a specific activity *with* students, to see what went wrong and where—for example, if students had difficulty completing a reading guide or answering postreading questions. In these cases, my reteaching might include discussing with students the problems they had and why they had them, and then reviewing the purposes and steps involved in completing the guide or answering the questions.
>
> Alternatively, reteaching sometimes involves creating a totally different activity. I do this when the original activity was a disaster—something that happens more times than I'd like to admit, even though I'm a seasoned teacher.
>
> —Robert Dickenson, fifth-grade teacher

Reflect and Apply

6. What purposes do postreading activities serve? Do you think you will engage your students in postreading activities for most of the reading they do in your class? Why or why not?

7. Suppose you are teaching fifth-graders who have just finished reading biographies of prominent figures in U.S. history. What sorts of postreading activities might these students engage in and why? Now, suppose you are teaching first-graders who have just read a beginning chapter book on the theme of friendship. What sorts of postreading activities might these students engage in and why?

Guided Reading

Earlier in the chapter we introduced Guided Reading as one of three reading curriculums, but the heart of guided reading, the interaction of teacher, text, and students is also a means of developing comprehension (Fountas and Gay Su Pinnell, 1996, 2001).

(We chose to capitalize Guided Reading when referring to the whole approach, but for that part where students are guided through a text we will use lower case.) In guided reading, the teacher guides small homogeneous groups of students in their reading of texts that offer a bit, but not too much, of a challenge for them.

First, the teacher selects appropriate materials for students to read. Typically, students are assessed using an informal reading inventory or running record and then placed into a text at an appropriate reading level (See Chapter 5). There is evidence that young readers, those up through second grade, benefit by reading a text at the right level. The evidence is scant for older readers. In fact, there are instructional procedures such as paired reading that provide significant assistance. When weak readers are paired with strong readers and they read simultaneously they can improve their skills by two and three grade levels (Brown, Mohr, Wilcox, Barrett, 2016). Because level should not be the primary guide for selecting text, focus on genre, interests, and theme.

After the text has been selected, the students are given individual copies. The teacher briefly introduces the selection to the students, clarifying concepts or vocabulary that might prove difficult, prompting students to engage in certain reading strategies, and generally preparing the students for the reading. The amount of pre-reading discussion varies depending on the text and the needs of the students. Not every text requires a picture walk and often the development of prior knowledge is unnecessary.

Next, the students read either quietly or silently while the teacher observes them, guiding when necessary and encouraging the use of strategies to unlock meaning. Often the students are encouraged to whisper read, so that the teacher can provide support when needed. She can also stop individual students, prompting the use of appropriate word identification, vocabulary, and comprehension strategies. Here is an example of a teacher providing support to help students understand literary language (Fountas & Pinnell, 2001, p 234).

> Teacher: On page 8 the writer says the girls "stick together" like glue. What does she mean by that?

> Mike: They just do everything together and they're always with each other so nobody can even tell them apart.

> Kaya: It's like when you glue something it sticks tight and you can't pull it apart and they're like that. They're always together. If one does something the other one always wants to do it.

Students increase their decoding and comprehension depending upon how much and what kinds of support the teacher provides. "Teachers of student with higher outcomes were fully 8 times more likely than teachers with lower outcomes to prompt students to use sources of information that they were neglecting while trying to decode a word …" (Rodgers, D'Agostino, Harmey, Kelly et al. 2016). The same might be true for students struggling with reading comprehension.

After the students have finished reading a particular segment, they talk about what they have read, either recalling details of the selection or offering personal responses. This is a time to discuss any problem solving they did during the reading, focusing on vocabulary and decoding strategies. The teacher may also recommend that students reread the text at this time to increase their fluency or may use the text to teach a skill or concept. Extending the text through postreading activities, such as those discussed with the SRE, can also take place during this portion of guided reading.

Another important aspect of guided reading is teacher assessment and follow-up. While students are reading and after, the teacher makes notes and keeps a record of students' progress in areas such as strategy use, fluency, and self-monitoring. As with the SRE framework, guided reading is not meant to be the sole element of a literacy program. In contrast to the SRE, which can be implemented with any size group—whole class or small group, heterogeneous or homogeneous—guided reading is usually done in small homogeneous groups because the developers of the approach believe being at the right reading level is of prime importance. The most recent research has raised questions about the need to place students in just the right book (Shanahan, 2013).

Close Reading

The developers of the Common Core State Standards were concerned that in too many classrooms students were relying on what they knew and what the teacher told them to comprehend their texts. They believed that the overreliance on prior knowledge was leading students away from the ideas in the text. These developers wanted to make the text central to comprehension discussions. Thus was reborn the practice of close reading, new phenomenon that had its origins in literary criticism of the 1920s (see Richards, 1926).

In a close reading lesson, the teacher selects a short text that includes some challenging ideas but is readable by most students. The teacher avoids frontloading the lesson with the development of prior knowledge. The students read the passage for a specific purpose, looking for specific ways that writers express their thoughts. Typically, the passage will be read several times, students will annotate the text, making notes and the teacher will ask many questions causing the students to dig for the answers. The process is slow and thorough with the belief that students a close attention to the text will improve comprehension. According to Fisher and Fry (2012), the reading lesson will have the following characteristics.

- Students will read complex text that will challenge them to think.
- Students will examine the meaning and style of the text.
- Students will deliberately reread the materials trying to dig deeper for its meaning.
- Students will focus on central ideas, key details, word usage, and style.
- Students will reflect on the meanings of words and sentences.
- Students will assemble these understandings to comprehend the work as a whole.

Reading a text closely is one of several ways of reading. Reading closely is essential when studying a legal document about your insurance coverage or assembling the pieces of IKEA furniture. Reading closely is important when you question a character's motives in a novel and want to closely examine the author's language. Reading closely is not a good substitute for skimming a text for a single piece of information or kicking back with a book for a long pleasurable read on a flight from New York to LA.

There are a number of problems with close reading and the most critical is its assumption that we should or can ignore the students' prior knowledge. "There is a small but immitigable fallacy in the theory of close reading, ... and it applies to political journalism as well as to the reading of poetry. The text doesn't reveal its secrets just by being stared at. It reveals its secrets to those who already pretty much know what secrets they expect to find. Texts are always packed, by the reader's prior knowledge and expectations, before they are unpacked (Menand, 2015). As Kintsch (1998) and his Construction-Integration Model of comprehension have taught us, reading comprehension is based on making connections between what you know and what the text says and means.

Close reading is also likely to become tedious. Imagine reading and rereading text carefully and closely. The New York State curriculum, EngagedNY.org, offers many examples of close reading. In the fifth grade, the students begin a unit of study on human rights by reading the Universal Declaration of Human Rights and end the unit reading the novel *Esperanza Rising* (Ryan 2007). After reading and rereading the Universal Declaration of Human Rights for several days some students were heard to exclaim, "I hate human rights!" The method had undermined the content and the ideas. In a sense, the overreliance on text-based evidence diminishes the value of a students' knowledge, moral judgments, and social norms (Snow & O'Connor, 2013).

Close reading is an important tool, but it is just one of several important tools. If you want to motivate students to experience the joy of reading, close reading is not the

MyLab Education
Video Example 11.3
Thinking from the mindset of an educator who advocates close reading, in this video, what is the teacher on the floor doing wrong?

right tool, especially if you want to engage middle grade students whose self-efficacy is declining. "Close reading is an excellent technique for probing sentence structure, nuances of word meaning, subtleties of text organization and the structure of textual arguments. But it is not a technique for building background knowledge which is the bottleneck for many struggling readers" (Snow & O'Connor, 2013). Know how to conduct a close reading but use the technique sparingly.

Collect-Interpret-Apply—The C.I.A. Approach

Frustrated with students who wanted to read novels and chapter books but spent most of their time abandoning one book after another, Sarah Collinge (2011) developed the C.I.A approach. C.I.A. is designed to teach students how to read a novel or non-fiction narrative (biography and autobiography) and then transfer students' knowledge, skills, and attitudes to independent reading. The C.I.A approach is loosely based on Adler's (1972) concept of how to read a book, and the envisionment theory of Langer (1995). Each of these theories posits that a reader engages in a different type of thinking in each segment of a book. In C.I.A., instruction proceeds in two parts. First, the students participate in an interactive read-aloud with a complete novel, then they transfer what they have learned to another novel or non-fiction literary text working in book clubs.

In the read-aloud the teacher begins by dividing the text into four parts or quadrants. In the first quadrant the students collect information about plot, characters, setting, and problem. In quadrants two and three the reader moves into deeper interpretation, inferring character traits and motives. In part three the reader follows the author's line of thinking, searching for the themes of the book. In the last quadrant, as the writer wraps up the action, the reader reflects on the experiences and themes and applies what has been learned to his own life, evaluating the characters and the author's message.

The C.I.A. lessons follow an exact process. The students keep notes about the characters, their traits, they draw diagrams of the settings, they list the events, and they discuss new vocabulary using a modified Frayer Model. They regularly turn and talk to a partner about events and ideas in the text, draw conclusions about motivation and character traits and support their thoughts by noting evidence from the text. As the text requires, the teacher guides them to make inferences, determine importance, visualize, and predict. Periodically, the teacher has them stop and summarize in writing what they have read and with each quadrant the summaries become less literal and more interpretation.

These well-learned routines from the read-aloud are then applied in the book clubs. In the book club, students work with a partner to read another novel or non-fiction narrative that shares the same genre, themes, and topics as the read-aloud. There are typically three book club selections at various reading levels. Students follow the same instructional procedures, writing about their book and turning and talking with their partner. The teacher meets with the book clubs once per quadrant, or more frequently if needed. During the teacher meetings she guides the students' comprehension, but the process does not require the frequency of meetings as found in guided reading. The thinking procedures that students use are so well learned that they transfer easily from the read aloud to the book club and then to independent reading. Emerging research on the C.I.A process suggests that it provides a boost in comprehension, confidence and efficacy, and motivation (Dewitz & Collinge, 2018). Students learn how to read a book and with this knowledge and confidence they read more.

MyLab Education **Self-Check 11.3**

MyLab Education **Application Exercise 11.3:** Compare and Contrast Close Reading and Questioning the Author

Discussing and Responding to Literature

The reader is crucial to the literary experience as described by Louise Rosenblatt (1938/1995, 1975) in her reader-response theory. The reader doesn't come to the text empty, hoping to be filled, but brings meaning to the text. Reading is a transaction between the reader and the writer. Any reading of a text—particularly a literary text such as fiction and poetry—will produce an interpretation that reflects both the meaning intended by the author and the meaning constructed by the reader (Galda & Cullinan, 2006; Mills, Stephens, O'Keefe, & Waugh, 2004). The authors of the Common Core State Standards and Louise Rosenblatt would not see eye to eye. Discussion promote reader response and encourage students to make personal responses to literature, as Galda and Graves (2010), among others, recommend.

Classroom discussions are a prime technique for promoting reader-response and developing literal and inferential comprehension. When a teacher elects to discuss a text, he has several important decisions to make. Should he lead the discussion or should the students be more in charge? Some discussions take on an efferent stance where students concentrate on the information in the text, others are more aesthetic where students consider how a text made them think and feel. Questioning the Author, a technique we discussed earlier in the chapter, is a discussion technique where the teacher carefully selects the queries. Now we will present two more discussion techniques were the students assume considerable control.

Literature circles (Daniels, 2002) and Book Club and Book Club *Plus* (Raphael & McMahon, 1994) are instructional frameworks that center around students' reading and personally responding to literature. We discussed QtA earlier in the chapter but we need to point out that it is a more efferent stance focused on the meaning of the text. Literature circles and Book Club are more aesthetic and have reader response at their core but they have other goals and instructional objectives as well. Each seeks to develop an understanding of narrative elements, build vocabulary knowledge, and increase the students' use of strategies. These two instructional frameworks vary in terms of how often students work in groups, how much student choice is encouraged, and how much teachers engage in direct instruction. Each of these two approaches can be combined with what we have already discussed about the development of fluency, vocabulary, and comprehension strategies.

Literature Circles

A host of formats for postreading discussion groups designed to foster reader response emerged during the 1990s. One of those was literature circles (Daniels, 2002; Short & Klassen, 1993). Simply defined, literature circles are groups of students who come together to discuss a text they have all chosen to read. Before meeting in the discussion group, students read silently and develop responses they plan to share with their group (Spiegel, 1998). The response format is typically structured so that each student takes on a specific role during the discussion. For example, one student might be the leader and have the job of asking questions. Another student might focus on making connections between the text and other texts or other ideas. Other students might discuss new interesting vocabulary, or particularly interesting and poignant passages, or summarize what has been read. It is important to point out that these roles in a literature circle demand the same kind of thinking that we stressed when discussing comprehension strategy instruction. Each time the literature circle meets, the students change roles, so all practice multiple ways of responding to a text. Discussions are student led, and when students finish reading and discussing one selection, or one book, new groups are formed.

In the Classroom 11.8 describes how to set up literature circles in a fourth-grade classroom.

MyLab Education
Video Example 11.4
In this video you can study how the teacher assists students in a literature circle.

In the Classroom 11.8

Instructional Routines

Establishing Literature Circles in a Fourth-Grade Classroom

- Preselect a number of books and give a short talk about each book. For example, you might choose books by a single author such as Patricia MacLachlan and make available *Sarah, Plain and Tall; Skylark; Caleb's Story; Journey; Baby;* and *Painting the Wind*, which represent a range of interests and reading skills. After the students have familiarized themselves with the books, they select which book they would like to read, naturally forming groups. You can select books around a common genre (historical fiction, or science fiction) or theme. Share each title with your students and let them choose which books to read.

- Teach the roles students will assume during the discussion, which will require two or three lessons. Daniels (2001) suggests the following roles: Discussion Director/Questioner, Literary Luminary, Illustrator, Connector, Summarizer, Vocabulary Enricher, and Investigator. You will need to give everyone in the class a short text and then model each role, demonstrating how to ask questions, make connections, or summarize (a set of role sheets is available in the Appendix) . After you have modeled the role, give students the opportunity to try out the role with a short story and then give them feedback. We suggest starting with four students in a group and four roles.

- Once the groups have been formed, determine (with input from each group) how long the students will take to read the book, how many pages a day group members will read, when the group will meet, and who will assume which role. Remind students when the next meeting of their group will be, how many pages they will need to read, and what type of response will need to be completed before their next meeting.

- Students then need independent time to read their book and complete the role sheet. The Discussion Leader has to develop questions; the Literary Luminary has to find passages that are exciting, funny, moving, or puzzling; and the Investigator has to find background information about topics in the book.

- Meet periodically with each group—as a participant, not as a leader. Help each student complete his assigned role. Thus, if the Vocabulary Enricher hasn't located some words, point them out. If the Literary Luminary neglected a particular rich passage, point it out. Try to sit in with each group each week. Remind them to change roles, read the next chapters, and complete their new role sheets. Periodically, evaluate the literature circles, noting what went well and what could use improvement.

- When the group is close to completing the book, encourage them to discuss possible postreading activities, such as those listed in the SRE framework described earlier in the chapter.

- Form new groups with new reading material. This allows students the opportunity to work with other students and gain other perspectives.

Whatever their focus, literature circles put a premium on the element of student choice and on student-led discussions. These result in "critical thinking and self-reflection on the text and higher student engagement" (Galda, Ash, & Cullinan, 2000). Through discussion, students share their own understanding of what they have read, test it against what others have gleaned, and come to new insights and interpretations. As third-grader Chris puts it,

> In literature circles, everyone has a chance to give their opinion and even if you don't agree with that person, you keep on talking because you know that you will get more ideas. You aren't trying to figure out one right answer. In reading groups, when someone gave the right answer, we were done talking. In literature circles, we keep on going. We try to come up with as many different directions as possible (Short & Klassen, 1993).

Through this synthesizing process, readers come to a deeper understanding and appreciation of the literature they read.

In a review of research related to English language learners, Kris Gutierrez (2005) notes that when English language learners are not allowed to use their first language to explore and learn new content, their classroom experiences are impoverished. To prevent this from happening, a teacher in a St. Paul, Minnesota, fourth-grade classroom with many Hmong- and Spanish-speaking students organized literature circles in the following manner. Within each literature circle, she included multiple speakers of each language. At least one of the Hmong- and Spanish-speaking students in each group was able to speak English fairly well. This child could then translate as needed for peers who could not communicate as well in English. The students could also be paired up to complete their role sheets. In this way, the English language learners who were not able to communicate as well in English could share their thoughts with the group, ask and answer questions, and be privy to their English-speaking classmates' thinking via their better-English-speaking peer(s). Every child in these small groups, then, could enjoy and benefit from talking about the literature selections.

Book Club and Book Club *Plus*

Book Club and later Book Club *Plus* are both the results of a collaborative effort involving university-based and school-based educators (Goatley, Brock, & Raphael, 1995; McMahon, Raphael, & Goatley, 1995; Raphael, Florio-Ruane, & George, 2001; Raphael, Florio-Ruane, George, Hasty, & Highfield, 2004; Raphael & McMahon, 1994). According to Taffy Raphael (2000), one of the creators of the Book Club and Book Club *Plus* programs, in the initial planning of the Book Club program she and her colleagues searched for a theoretical model that would foster a high degree of student engagement and also provide opportunities for literacy instruction. What they discovered was a model called the Vygotsky Space (see Figure 11.10), which consists of two axes—the public/private axis and the social/individual axis. When these two axes intersect, four quadrants are formed.

Each of the quadrants provides opportunities for an activity or set of activities in the Book Club program. For example, quadrant 1, the public and social, is the whole-class setting where students learn literacy skills, strategies, and attitudes through teacher instruction and modeling. Quadrant 2, the social and private, represents opportunities for students to use what they have learned in quadrant 1 in the same way and for the same purposes. Working in this quadrant, third-graders might read about Gabrielle in *No Copycats Allowed!* (Graves, 1998) or fifth-graders might read about Angel in *The Same Stuff as Stars* (Paterson, 2002) and then write responses in their reading logs about times they have found themselves in new and challenging situations. Quadrant 3, the private and individual, is where students transform privately what they have learned and practiced. Here students make new discoveries and new interpretations. They are not just practicing the strategies that have been taught, but developing new insights. A student reading *Charlie Anderson* (Abercrombie & Graham, 1995), who realizes that the cat that has two homes is a symbol for the girls' lives after a divorce, has made a

Figure 11.10 The Vygotsky Space

	Public Space	
Individual	**Quadrant 4** Sharing and publications of new insights through discussions and writing.	**Quadrant 1** Whole Class – Learning about strategies and concepts
	Quadrant 3 Student make new interpretation and discoveries	**Quadrant 2** Personal independent reading to apply strategies and concepts
	Private Space	**Social**

SOURCE: Derived from Gavelek, J.R. & Raphael, T. E. (1996). Changing talk about text. New roles for teachers and students. *Language Arts*, 73(3). 182-192.

new interpretation and thus transformed the story. In quadrant 4, the individual and public, publication of private activity occurs. It is through publication—through student writing, book club discussions, or author's chair—that students' proficiency with conventional knowledge or transformation of that knowledge is revealed.

In addition to providing opportunities for students to work within each of these four quadrants, the Book Club program provides opportunities for students to be involved in four types of activities—reading, writing, book club discussion, and community share.

- *Reading* (10 to 20 minutes). The reading component of the Book Club program encourages students to respond aesthetically to what they read with evaluations, personal responses, comparisons to other texts, and the like. However, attention is also given to such matters as fluency, reading vocabulary, comprehension strategies, and genres of literature.

- *Writing* (10 to 15 minutes). The writing component grows out of the reading students do for the Book Club program and is designed to enhance their understanding of, and response to, what they read. Additionally, opportunities are provided for the kind of writing that requires planning, revision, and publishing.

- *Book clubs* (5 to 20 minutes). Book clubs are the student-led discussion groups for which the program was named. One of the goals of the Book Club program is for students to develop control over discussions and their own ways of preparing for them (Tierney & Readence, 2000). Another goal is for students to really learn to talk about books. In the Book Club program, the reading material is teacher-selected, high-quality literature based both on student interests and on various instructional objectives.

- *Community share* (5 to 20 minutes). The community share component is a time for teachers to meet with students as a whole class. Community share time can occur before or after students read a selection. Prior to reading, the teacher engages students in activities that will help prepare them for reading, such as building background knowledge or discussing the structure of the upcoming selection. Following Book Club discussions, students in different book clubs might share their thoughts on their books, debate issues prompted by their reading, or talk about confusing or disturbing aspects of their book that they have not been able to resolve in their individual book clubs. Community share time might also encompass mini-lessons, which can include any one or a combination of explicit instruction, modeling, and scaffolding.

The teacher's role in any of the four quadrants and during any of the four activities can be that of instructor, modeler, scaffolder, facilitator, or participant, depending on what the students or situation require. That is, the teacher does whatever is necessary to further students' competence.

Book Club *Plus* adds a skills-and-strategy instruction component to the Book Club program and is built around a theme for the year. For example, MariAnne George used "Our Storied Lives" as a theme for her third-grade class (Raphael, 2001). In George's classroom, the Book Club *Plus* instruction took place within three 3- to 8-week units—Unit 1: "Stories of Self," Unit 2: "Family Stories," and Unit 3: "Stories of Culture." The weekly instruction consisted of 3 consecutive days of Book Club, followed by 2 days of a literacy block. In the literacy block, the focus is on instruction and practice of skills and strategies. During this block, students work in guided reading groups and skills centers where they meet with the teacher. When students are not meeting with the teacher, they work independently to practice skills and work on theme-related writing, doing Internet research, journaling, and so on. See Figure 11.11 for a week's organization. The 2-day literacy block can occur at the beginning, middle, or end of the week.

Figure 11.11 How to Organize Your Week for Book Clubs

Day 1	Day 2	Day 3	Day 4	Day 5
15 – 30 Minutes Reading Aloud				
Book Club	Book Club	Book Club	Reading Block	Reading Block
• Opening whole group sharing • Reading (10 – 20 mins.) • Writing (10 – 20 mins.) • Book club meetings (5 – 20 mins)* • Closing whole group meeting (5 – 15 mins)			• Teacher guided reading groups • Independent reading • Internet research • Writing in response to reading • Writers workshop	

• Over time and experience the books club time will expand as students gain independence.

The Book Club and Book Club *Plus* programs both put quality literature at their core as well as providing space for teachers to impart conventional knowledge about text processing.

Independent Reading

Self-selected independent reading and response is crucial to students' reading development. Independent reading can be found in Guided Reading, it is at the core of the Reading Workshop (Atwell, 1998) and it plays an important role in the C.I.A. approach. Unfortunately it receives short shrift in basal readers. Without independent reading, students cannot read enough to develop fluency, build vocabulary and knowledge, and develop expertise with comprehension strategies. Consider just one point. If students don't read, the time spent teaching them word learning or comprehension strategies is a waste.

Students should spend 20 to 30 minutes a day reading independently. However, silent reading can be punctuated with several other activities, most frequently journaling. As they are reading their books, students keep a dialogue journal, in which they record their reactions, questions, and musings about what they are reading. These dialogue journals typically go to the teacher, who should periodically give a personal response to each student's thoughts. The teacher's response is critical. If no one is listening, most students stop writing. Dialogue journals can also be addressed to other students, so that there is student-to-student dialogue as well as teacher-to-student and student-to-teacher dialogues.

Another activity that takes place during the self-selected reading and response time is teacher conferencing. Periodically, the teacher meets with each student to discuss the book he is reading and to plan for the next book. Because teachers might have 30 students and conferences are spread out, most teachers try to see two or three students a day. Ray Reutzel and his colleagues (Reutzel, Jones, Fawson, & Smith, 2008) have developed a simple system for conducting a reading conference and learning about students' progress in reading. We have reproduced their form in Figure 11.12.

Consider the quadrant system of C.I.A. as a way to structure a reading conference. If the student is beginning a novel, focus on the characters, the setting, and the problem. If students are midway through a book, discuss how a character is changing and what is being learned about her traits. When students are at the end of the book, discuss the book's themes and how they relate to the student's life. Finally, consider what the students might read next. You might encourage the student to stick with the same author or genre and have specific suggestions ready for each student.

Figure 11.12 Tracking Form for Individual Reading Conferences

Student Name _____ Date of Reading Conference _____

Title of Book Student Is Reading _____

Part A: Fluency
Teacher Running Record of Student 1-Minute Reading Sample

Number of Words Read _____

Number of Errors _____

Words Read Correctly Per Minute _____

Part B: Comprehension
Student Oral Retelling

Narrative Text:
❏ Setting   ❏ Characters   ❏ Problem   ❏ Goals   ❏ Episode(s)   ❏ Resolution

Expository Text:
❏ Main Idea   ❏ Supporting Detail(s)   ❏ Use of Vocabulary Terms

Questions to Discuss
Narrative: Ask story structure questions about setting, problem, characters, etc.
Expository: Ask about the topic, main idea, supporting details, procedures, explanations, etc.

> **MyLab Education**
> Click here to download a printable version of Figure 11.12.

Part C: Goal Setting
Book Completion Goal Date _____
Goal for Pages to Be Read at the Next Reading Conference _____

Part D: Sharing the Book
Book Response Project Selected and Approved with Teacher _____

SOURCE: Reutzel, D. R., Jones, C. D., Fawson, P. C., & Smith, J. A. (2008). "Scaffolded Silent Reading: A Complement to Guided Repeated Oral Reading That Works!" The Reading Teacher, 62, 201.

Student sharing time is an important component of any reading program, a time when the class comes together to share what students have been doing. As in the writing workshop, which we describe in Chapter 13, not every student shares each day. Often it works best to have students sign up in advance to share, usually two to four students per session. The most common activity involves students' talking

In the Classroom 11.9

A Glimpse into a Classroom that Combines Instructional Frameworks

For Leigh Murray's students, each day begins with a whole-group activity that focuses on the important goals for the week. At the beginning of the week the whole-group lesson tends to be long as she uses the time to introduce new vocabulary or comprehension strategies and to model a new way of responding in their journal. Later in the week the whole-group time is brief as she spells out what they will be doing for the day, what groups she will meet with, and what students she will confer with.

The students then move to small groups. Each day Ms. Murray tries to see two groups, meeting with her struggling readers more frequently than the better readers. The small-group format allows the students time to practice reading strategies as she provides support and guidance. The students who are not meeting with Ms. Murray are reading on their own in texts that she has selected and then responding to their reading, journaling, or engaging in other writing activities. Some of the students will use this time to work in a literature circle they have organized themselves, deciding how often their literature circle will meet and how much they need to read. During the independent time, the students will complete the assigned readings and accompanying assignments or prepare for their literature circle. The small-group time typically lasts 30 to 40 minutes.

The class then shifts to a reading workshop. At the beginning of the school year, the lessons center on the organization of the classroom: behavioral expectations, choosing books, checking out books, how to complete dialogue journals, grading, and earning extra points. Ms. Murray frequently introduces books and authors that she thinks the children will like. Once students know her expectations and organization, she devotes more lessons to topics such as narrative voice, point of view, author's purpose, theme, and specific reading strategies, such as focusing on important words.

When she finishes the mini-lesson, students begin reading. A few students choose to sit on the cushions in the reading area. One or two pull their chairs to isolated corners of the room. Students do not use the period to look for books in the library unless they happen to finish a book during class. From time to time, students go to the shelves to get their reading dialogue journals. They add the title of the book they just started to a list of previously read books at the back of the journal. They then turn to the correspondence section of their journal, write the date, and begin a letter to the teacher or another adult. All students have to write a minimum of once every 2 weeks, telling Ms. Murray the title and author, sharing their opinions of their books, and relating the books to their lives in some way. Ms. Murray responds in writing to each letter, expressing her own ideas and encouraging students to try books and authors new to them.

about what they have been reading and sharing their experiences and suggestions for good reading.

Literature circles, book clubs, Questioning the Author, and independent reading are all instructional frameworks designed to stimulate students' interest in reading, to promote wide reading, and encourage interpretative response to literature. These classroom procedures share much in common. In all of these procedures students are expected to read widely and deeply. They reflect on what they read, write about it, and share it with others. Literature circles concentrate on small-group discussions and can be seen as an extension of comprehension strategy work. Book clubs promote both individual and small-group work, whereas independent reading is centered on the individual. All of these frameworks should be combined with explicit instruction in vocabulary and comprehension. In the Classroom 11.9 takes you into a classroom where both direct instruction and frameworks for response to literature have been combined.

Reflect and Apply

8. In this section, we described the story map. Why might this procedure be helpful with a group of primary-grade students reading a folktale? For which age groups is the use of story mapping inappropriate.

9. Skim through this section, we describe several ways to discuss a text. Which discussion technique would be most valuable if you wanted to the students to concentrate on the author's technique and use of language? Which discussion technique would be most dissimilar to close reading?

MyLab Education **Self-Check 11.4**

MyLab Education **Application Exercise 11.4:** Launching Literature Circles

Concluding Remarks

This chapter has focused on the basics of teaching reading comprehension. We demonstrated the importance of prior knowledge, comprehension strategies, and metacognition. In an earlier chapter we stressed the importance of motivation and returned to that when we wrote that having a strong purpose for reading is vital for comprehension. The bulk of this chapter then focused on teaching narrative text. We discussed three basic curriculum structures—basal readers, Guided Reading, and a thematic approach. We then presented four frameworks for assisting students to comprehend a text. The four frameworks—the scaffolded reading experience (SRE), guided reading, close reading, and the Collect-Interpret-Apply approach—provide ways to ensure that students are successful with the texts they read and to nurture their competence and confidence as readers. Finally, we considered the important role of discussions that build reading comprehension. Frankly, we find it hard to distinguish between the dialogue in a SRE or a Guided Reading lesson from the discussions in literature circles and book clubs. What is essential is that students talk about what they read, take ideas from the text and from one another and refine their thinking with the help of the teacher. In the next chapter we will look at teaching informational text, especially digital text.

Extending Learning

1. Visit an elementary school classroom, and take notes on the kinds of supports the teacher provides for students as they read a selection. Using the same selection for the same group of students, design your own plan for helping them understand and enjoy the selection. Try out your lesson on your target students, or share it with your classmates.

2. From the children's section of your library, select a narrative text that you think would interest students at the age level you would like to teach. Create a scaffolded reading experience especially for those students and that text. Give your plan to a classmate to get his or her feedback. We recommend the following four books to help you select appropriate titles: *From Biography to History*, edited by Catherine Barr (1998); *Kaleidoscope: A Multicultural Booklist for Grades K–8* (4th ed.), edited by Nancy Hansen-Krening, Elaine M. Aoki, and Donald T. Mizokawa (2003); *Books Kids Will Sit Still For: 3*, by Judy Freeman (2006); and *Adventuring with Books: A Booklist for Pre-K–Grade 6* (13th ed.), edited by Amy A. McClure and Janice V. Kristo (2002).

Children's Literature

Brown, M. (1998). *Arthur's Mystery Envelope*. Boston: Little, Brown. Arthur thinks he's in trouble when the principal asks him to take home a large envelope marked CONFIDENTIAL. Audio CD available. 58 pages.

Compestine, Y. C. (2001). *The Runaway Rice Cake*. New York: Simon & Schuster. The Chang family learns about the power of sharing during this Chinese New Year celebration. 32 pages.

DiCamillo, K. (2000). *Because of Winn-Dixie*. Cambridge, MA: Candlewick Press. This is a poignant and well-told story of a young girl who must build a new life after her mother leaves and she and her father move to Florida—with, of course, a little help from her dog, Winn-Dixie. 182 pages.

Duncan, A. F. (1995). *Willie Jerome*. New York: Macmillan. No one but Willie's sister appreciates his jazz trumpet playing until she finally gets their Mama to really listen to Willie play and let the music speak to her. Unnumbered.

Freedman, R. (1987). *Lincoln: A Photobiography*. New York: Clarion. In photographs and text, this Newbery Medal–winning book traces the life of the Civil War president. 150 pages.

Fritz, J. (1987). *Shh! We're Writing the Constitution*. New York: Scholastic. The author gives a humorous behind-the-scenes account of how the Constitution came to be written and ratified. 64 pages.

Graves, B. (1996). *The Best Worst Day*. New York: Hyperion. In this chapter book, second-grader Lucy struggles to prove herself "best" in order to win the friendship of Maya, the new girl in class. 64 pages.

Hallworth, G. (1996). *Down by the River*. New York: Scholastic Cartwheel. This is a collection of Afro-Caribbean rhymes, games, and songs. 32 pages.

Houston, J. (1977). *Frozen Fire: A Tale of Courage*. New York: Atheneum. Determined to find his father, who has been lost in a storm, a young boy and his Eskimo friend brave windstorms, starvation, and wild animals on their trek through the Canadian Arctic. 149 pages.

Johnson, L. L. (2002). *Soul Moon Soup*. Ashville, NC: Front Street. Written in free verse, this poetic chapter book tells the story of the homeless Phoebe Rose, who, after being banished by her mother to live in the country with her grandmother, learns family secrets and hopes for her mother's return. 134 pages.

Lewin, T. (1990). *Tiger Trek*. New York: Macmillan. Informative narrative tells of the preying habits of the Indian tiger and the numerous animals that live on a hunting preserve in central India. Unnumbered.

Lionni, L. (1984). *Swimmy*. New York: Pantheon Books. Through teamwork and cooperation, Swimmy the fish and his friends triumph over the "big" fish. Videocassette available. 32 pages.

Lionni, L. (1985). *Frederick*. New York: Pantheon Books. Frederick, an apparently lazy mouse, has a special surprise for the mice who thought he should have been storing up supplies for the winter. 32 pages.

Lobel, A. (1970). *Frog and Toad Are Friends*. New York: Harper & Row. The five stories are about the friendship of Frog and Toad and their adventures in the woods. 64 pages.

Lobel, A. (1979). *Days with Frog and Toad*. New York: Harper & Row. This classic beginning chapter book with five humorous stories stars best friends Frog and Toad and dramatizes universal truths about life and friendship. 64 pages.

Lowry, L. (1989). *Number the Stars*. Boston: Houghton Mifflin. In 1943, during the German occupation of Denmark, 10-year-old Annemarie learns about courage when her family shelters a Jewish family from the Nazis. 137 pages.

McPhail, D. (1972). *The Bear's Toothache*. Boston: Little, Brown and Co. The story of a little boy's attempt to help a bear in distress. The perfect book for introducing the concept of narrative structure to young children. 20 pages.

McWhorter, D. (2004). *A Dream of Freedom: The Civil Rights Movement from 1954 to 1968*. New York: Scholastic. In this history of the modern Civil Rights movement, the author focuses on the monumental events that occurred between 1954 (the year of *Brown v. the Board of Education*) and 1968 (the year that Dr. Martin Luther King, Jr., was assassinated). 160 pages.

Paterson, K. (1978). *The Great Gilly Hopkins*. New York: Crowell. This novel portrays feisty 11-year-old Gilly, a foster child who, in her longing to be reunited with her birth mother, schemes against all who try to befriend her. Spanish text available. 152 pages.

Prelutsky, J. (1988). *Tyrannosaurus Was a Beast: Dinosaur Poems*. New York: Greenwillow. Poems celebrate 14 dinosaurs in rollicking rhyme and illustration. 32 pages.

Simon, S. (1991). *Earthquakes*. New York: Morrow. This text, illustrated with colorful photos, describes how and where earthquakes occur, how they can be predicted, and the damage they cause. Unnumbered.

Van Allsburg, C. (1990). *Just a Dream*. Boston: Houghton Mifflin. A young boy has a dream about the environment that causes him to wake up to his indifference. Unnumbered.

Chapter 12
Comprehending Informational Text

 Learning Outcomes

After reading and studying this chapter you should be able to:

12.1 Explain why prior knowledge is vital for comprehending informational text and how to develop its several components.

12.2 Understand the role of comprehension strategies in understanding informational text and the instructional procedures that help students acquire and employ these strategies.

12.3 Discuss the importance of multiple strategy instruction and understand how to implement it within the classroom.

12.4 Understand the importance and difficulties of reading digital text and how to assist students to make the best use of these new literacies.

Classroom Vignette

In Mrs. Pearson's fifth grade class the students are studying the late colonial period and the origins of the American Revolution. The next topic will be the French and Indian war, so Mrs. Pearson has them all turn to their textbook and begin reading. The following passage from the school's textbook was particularly difficult for the students.

> In 1763 Britain and the colonies ended a 7-year war with the French and Indians. As a result of this war France was driven out of North America. Britain would now rule Canada and the other lands that had belonged to France. This brought peace to the American colonies. The colonists no longer had to fear attacks from Canada. The Americans were happy to be a part of Britain in 1763. Yet a dozen years later, these same people would be fighting the British for independence, or freedom from Great Britain's rule. This war was called the War for Independence, or the American Revolution. A revolution changes one type of government or way of thinking and replaces it with another (Silver Burdett, 1984).

After the students read the passage Mrs. Pearson began the discussion with two questions: "Who was fighting against whom in the war?" "Why was the war fought?" Few students were able to answer the questions. Robert thought that the French were fighting the Indians, while Maria felt it was colonists fighting the Indians because they had fought before. Few could speculate on the cause of the war but one student believed that the Indians were threatening the colonists.

Mrs. Pearson, remembering the concept of close reading, had her students reread the first three sentences and ask them to think about the meaning of the third sentence: *Britain would now rule Canada and the other lands that had belonged to France*. She asked, "If Britain would now rule Canada what were they fighting over?" A few students guessed they were fighting over Canada but they didn't know how the Indians got into this mess. For most students the passage remained clear as pea soup.

At this point Mrs. Pearson stopped the discussion and decided to provide some of the explanation that the text lacked. First, she explained the setting of the war and pulled down the map of North America and discussed the disputed territories, just west of the original 13 colonies. Next, she explained that Britain and France were fighting each other not just in America but all over Europe. Because the Colonies belonged to Britain they fought on the same side. Many Indians fought on the same side as the French.

This vignette is based on a research study conducted by Isabel Beck and her colleagues (Beck, McKeown, Sinatra, & Loxterman, 1991). In the study, the researchers took segments of a poorly written history textbook, revised them to improve coherence, had students read the text and then measured their comprehension. The study showed that the students' comprehension improved when the text was coherently written but gaps in their learning persisted. Reflecting on their work, the researchers concluded that well written texts are necessary but not sufficient to improve content area learning. Students still need prior knowledge, knowledge of text structure, strategies to think through a text, and the motivation to engage in some difficult reading.

The Challenges of Informational Text

In this chapter we will focus on comprehending informational text because much of what we read in our daily life is information. We are living in the information age dominated by websites that vie for our attention. In school, students read information in science, history, economics, mathematics, health, and probably physical education. The only place that students can avoid information is in English, but even that is rare because the Common Core State Standards have mandated that 50 percent of fourth graders' reading should be from informational text and by twelfth grade that rises to 70 percent. Many middle school English teachers believe they should create units of instruction that focus on informational topics because their colleagues in the hard sciences and social sciences continue to believe that teaching reading is not their job, despite decades of pestering by the "reading in the content area" crowd.

At home we read news, reviews, recipes, and directions for assembling toys. We hunt for consumer information and for the right contractor to repair the roof. We scan sports scores and the latest entertainment industry gossip. The overall consumption of news is up, but adults are increasingly shifting from print to digital sources. At work we read reports, memos, and emails, often in a digital format, as businesses attempt to go paperless, a goal that is unrealized because the consumption of paper at work is projected to steadily increase (Sellen & Harper, 2002).

If we want our children to be college and career ready, then they must have the knowledge and the skills necessary to read informational text. However, there is a more important reason for building the interest and skill with informational text— the demands of citizenship. If we want to preserve our democracy and live in a just, equitable, and peaceful world, then our students must learn how to find information, comprehend it, and make decisions about its validity. The dominance of the Internet should shift the focus of our schools toward the need for critical reading.

Informational text is more difficult for students to comprehend than narrative for several reasons. Informational text requires more and deeper prior knowledge. The sports fanatic brings much prior knowledge to the sports section of the paper, but she is likely stumped reading chemistry or physics. As children enter the middle grades, they have likely read more fiction in school than non-fiction; thus, they have less experience with both the structure and the ideas in informational text. Informational text comes in several different structures compared to the relatively consistent story grammar of fiction.

This chapter will be organized much as the previous one with one exception, a focus on digital text. We will first review the basic components of reading comprehension instruction—knowledge, strategies, and motivation, but we will focus on how those components change when reading informational text. After that, we will showcase techniques for developing students' knowledge for reading informational text. Next, we examine the strategies necessary for reading informational text. While the list of strategies remains largely the same, some are more important in the context of reading information. Digital text demands its own consideration. Finally, we will conclude with a look at multiple strategy instructions which are activities very close to discussion techniques.

Building Knowledge

When we read information text, knowledge is crucial. You probably understood the opening paragraph about the French and Indian War because you have the background knowledge that ten-year-olds lack. Because most teachers will not have access to the well-crafted text that Beck and her colleague created, they must build their students' knowledge (Beck et al., 1991) or employ discussion techniques like Questioning the Author that compel students to think their way through the text. The amount of prior knowledge the reader brings to the page improves word identification, fluency, and reading comprehension (Cervetti & Hiebert, 2015).

There are three types of knowledge that students need to comprehend informational text. They are word knowledge, content or domain knowledge, and text structure knowledge. Word knowledge or vocabulary and content knowledge are closely linked and together explain a significant amount of students' success reading informational text (Leibfreund, 2015). When a student is reading about the early 19th century in the United States, words like *industrial, manufacturing, factory, apprentice,* and *cotton* are both vocabulary words and concepts specific to the changing economy in the country. When reading informational text, teaching vocabulary and developing prior knowledge are often the same thing. Most of the words that need to be taught are Tier 3 words, domain specific words necessary to understand a specific content (Beck, McKeown, & Kucan, 2013). These words are best taught not as isolated terms, but as part of building content knowledge (Nagy & Townsend, 2012).

Building Conceptual Knowledge

To build conceptual knowledge teachers must determine what knowledge students need and then decide how to develop that knowledge. A teacher must provide enough information so that the text is accessible, but not so much information that the reading of the text is redundant. These are our recommendations derived from the decisions that Beck and her colleague made when revising difficult text (Beck et al., 1991). These directions will make you think through the demands of the text and the knowledge your students need.

- Read your proposed text carefully and search for places where comprehension will be difficult.

- If the basic structure or schema of the text is obscure, make it prominent in your pre-reading discussion. For example, if the text is about a war, make sure the students understand that a war has two sides, it is fought over an issue or land, and there is typically, but not always, a winner.

- Consider how many inferences a reader will need to make. If there are many, provide the knowledge necessary to make those inferences.
- Consider the density of the text. If the readers have too much information to learn, consider presenting some before they read.
- Does the text help the students make connections to their own knowledge and experiences? If not, help them make those connections.
- Make sure that the knowledge you provide is germane to the text and avoid taking the students off on a tangent.

Teachers can build students' prior knowledge in several different ways. At times, a teacher might choose to impart the information directly through lecture, discussion, video, or reading aloud. At other times, the teacher might use the process of brainstorming to assemble what the class knows and then slip in additional ideas that the students lack. All of the methods we list presume that you will organize the reading of informational text into topical units of instruction.

Reading aloud is an excellent way to develop the students' knowledge and while doing so the teacher can model fluent reading, develop vocabulary, and model comprehension strategy use. In the Reading Corner, we recommend the Russel Freedman book, *We Will Not Be Silent* about the Hitler resistance movement. A great way to introduce that book is to read aloud the picture book *Rose Blanche* (Gallaz & Innocenti, 1985) that portrays the militarization of a small town in Europe.

Watching and discussing a video is another way to build students' knowledge. If your students are about to plunge into the book *Streams to the River, River to the Sea* (O'Dell, 1999) a fictionalized account of Lewis, Clark, and Sacajawea you might start with this video. The video will provide the historical and geographic background necessary to understand the text.

Brainstorming is the process of asking students to share what they know about a topic, with the expectation that each student will prime the pump of other students. We encourage you to view brainstorming not as a random flood of information but as an activity that has two benefits. First, as students share what they know about a topic you are actually assessing what they know and this helps you make decisions about what further knowledge you need to develop. Second, a brainstorming session allows you to organize what they know into categories. As students come to understand how ideas are organized you are developing and deepening their conceptual knowledge.

The K-W-L procedure is a commonly used routine for developing prior knowledge and setting a purpose for reading. It is so well known it is hackneyed, so use it sparingly. K-W-L stands for what you Know, what you Want to know, and what you Learned. The K-W-L procedure, developed by Donna Ogle (1986), is a three-part process designed to motivate and guide readers in acquiring information from expository texts. Despite the K-W-L's ubiquity it is often presented incorrectly. In the Classroom 12.1 illustrates how this procedure is put into practice in a California classroom with a group of fourth-graders who are reading the trade book *Earthquakes* by Seymour Simon.

Building Text Structure Knowledge

Good readers understand how a text is organized, how the ideas are put together. This leads to improved comprehension and learning from text. Narrative text has one overriding structure, a story grammar but with variations like flashbacks, foreshadowing, and intersecting plots. Informational text comes in at least five different structures—description, sequence or chronological order, comparison-contrast, cause & effect, and problem-solution. Readers who have a sense of a text's overall structure approach the ideas with a purpose. looking for the relatedness of ideas, while readers without this knowledge approach reading as a search for loosely related ideas (Ray & Meyer, 2011).

In the Classroom 12.1

Using K-W-L

- Fourth-grade teacher David Scott writes the title *Earthquakes* on the chalkboard. Underneath that title and to the left, he writes the heading *What Do You Know?* He then asks students to tell what they know about earthquakes and jots down their responses under the heading, as shown here.
- Not all of the students' responses are accurate, despite Mr. Scott's questions during the brainstorming session to help them consider the correctness of their statements, such as "How did you learn that?" or "How could you prove that?" Later, during the postreading discussion, he and his students will clear up the remaining misconceptions.
- After Mr. Scott's students give a variety of responses, he shows them the cover illustration of *Earthquakes*, has them page through the book, and asks them to think about the kinds of information that might be included in the book. He then writes their suggestions underneath where it says categories of information that might be included.
- Next, Mr. Scott reminds his students that informational books such as *Earthquakes* are written to provide knowledge that we might need or want. He then asks students to think about what they would like to know about earthquakes—things they don't already know or aren't quite sure of. He records these responses in the middle column—*What Do You Want to Know?* Mr. Scott has his own questions prepared in case students do not zero in on the important purposes for reading the book. He will add his questions to the students' questions.
- On the chalkboard to the right of the previous two headings, Mr. Scott writes *What Did You Learn?* He explains to students that this is the last part of the K-W-L procedure. He says, "You have already completed the first two steps—thinking about and writing down what you know about earthquakes and what you would like to know. The last step is to record what information you do learn as you read."
- At this point, Mr. Scott gives students their own K-W-L charts and tells them, "In the first column, record what you *know* about earthquakes; in the second column, what you *want* to know. Then, as you read, write what you *learned* in the third column." He also reminds students that not all of their questions will be answered in the text. Later, they will talk about where they might find answers to those questions.
- The K-W-L procedure is very useful for dealing with informational material, both in hard copy and websites (Pritchard & Cartwright, 2004). The three phases of the procedure—brainstorming, establishing purposes through questioning, and finding answers to those questions—virtually guarantee that students will be actively involved in their learning.

MyLab Education

Video Example 12.1

In this video, two teachers employ a K-W-L strategy. Note that the strategy has limits, especially when the students know very little about the topic of coral.

EARTHQUAKES

What Do You Know?	What Do You Want to Know?	What Did You Learn?
Can cause damage Are unpredictable Are scary Happen in California Not all are the same Shake the earth Don't happen at night Are getting worse	What causes earthquakes How earthquakes are measured What places have earthquakes What was the worst earthquake When most earthquakes happen What we can do about earthquakes	

Categories of information that might be included:
How earthquakes happen • When they happen • What we can do about them • How much damage they do • Why they happen • Descriptions of some of the worst earthquakes

SOURCE: Heimlich, Joan E., & Pittelman, Susan D. (1986). Semantic Mapping: Classroom Applications. Copyright © 1986 by the International Reading Association (www.reading.org).

TEXT FEATURES

To develop students' text structure knowledge, it is important to explain the graphic features of a text and then its underlying organizational pattern. The graphic features are easier to grasp, while the organizational patterns are subtler and employed in multiple combinations. Authors typically provide a map through an informational text by using text features. The most prominent features are titles, introductory paragraphs, headings, subheadings, bold print, pictures, charts, captions, and conclusions. A lesson on text features should begin with a text or a textbook that has many of these features. (Note there are a few nonfiction writers who do use these features, most noteworthy is Seymore Simon.) In the Classroom 12.2 presents a lesson for teaching students about text structure.

TEXT ORGANIZATIONAL PATTERNS

Writers typically organize their ideas into one of five organizational patterns—description, sequence or chronology, compare & contrast, cause & effect, and problem-solution. More than one pattern can be found within a chapter or an article. The research demonstrates that explicit instruction in organizational patterns can help students improve their knowledge of these patterns and their reading comprehension (Ray & Meyer, 2011; Meyer & Ray, 2017). We illustrate these patterns in Figure 12.2

In the Classroom 12.2

Teaching Text Features

MyLab Education
Click here to download a printable version of Figure 12.1.

Begin the lesson by explaining that authors organize and label informational text to help readers search for and understand ideas. Explain that if we understand how the text is organized we will improve our understanding of the ideas. This is a strategy we can use whenever we are reading science or social studies text.

- Every student will need a copy of a text that contains most if not all of the important text features. If possible, use the science or social studies text currently being read in the classroom or a common website. You will be teaching a reading and context lesson simultaneously.
- The students will also need a features and purpose chart, see Figure 12.1, and you should display a large copy of that chart in the front of the classroom.
- Slowly identify and discuss each of the features in the non-fiction text. Begin by asking the students, "What is this called (pointing to the title)? Why does the author use a title? How does that help us as readers?" Write the text feature on the left side of the features and purposes chart and on the right side make notes about its purpose. The title identifies the topic of the chapter or article.
- Work through the text stopping to discuss each of the text features and their purpose. You will want to discuss the title, chapter introduction, headings, subheadings (note the relationship of headings and subheadings as this is a clue to their importance), bold print, pictures, captions, graphs, diagrams, and chapter summary.
- Repeat the process with a second text but in this round have the students point out the features and discuss why they are useful. For example, the title and the headings should help us anticipate what the whole text and the individual segments are going to be about.
- When you sense that students can identify and describe the purpose of the many text features make a point of using them during your class discussions. In a guided reading lesson have the students preview the text by reading all of the text features. Ask them what they expect the text will be about.

Figure 12.1 Features and Purposes of Informational Text

Features and Purposes Chart

Features	Purpose

SOURCE: Harvey, S. and Goudvis, A. (2000). *Strategies that Work: Teaching Comprehension to Enhance Understanding.* York, ME: Stenhouse.

MyLab Education

Video Example 12.2
In this video, the teacher introduces the concept of text features. Could she have been more explicit?

Figure 12.2 Five Text Organizational Patterns for Informational Text

Text Structure	Signal Words	Graphic Organizer
Description	for example for instance characteristics include specifically, in addition	
Sequence or Chronology	before, in the beginning, to start, first, second, next, during, after, then, finally, last, in the middle, in the end	
Compare & Contrast	similar, alike, same, just like, both, different, unlike, in contrast, on the other hand	
Cause & Effect	since, because, if, due to, as a result of, so then, leads to, consequently	
Problem Solution	problem, issue, cause, consequently, therefore, as a result, because of, leads to, due to, solve, so, then	

along with the clue words that help readers identify the pattern and a sample graphic organizer. While it is tempting to teach all of these organizational patterns in a school year, the research suggests that this is not a wise course of action. It takes 7 to 10 weeks working two days a week for students to identify a text's organizational pattern and use this knowledge to improve their comprehension (Williams, Hall, Lauer, Stafford, Laner, Sesisto, & deCani, 2005; Williams, Pollini, Nubla-Kung, Snyder, Garcia, Ordynans, & Atkins, 2014).

Knowledge of expository text structure is not complete by middle school and there is some evidence that high school students are still learning about text organizational patterns. Even college students' comprehension improves when they learn the organizational pattern of a research article (Samuels, Tennyson, Sax, Mulcahy, Schermer, & Hajovy, 1988). Therefore, instruction in text organizational patterns can begin as early as second grade and continue through post-secondary education. Even in law school appellate court rulings have distinct structure. In the primary grades, students can begin to identify text structure patterns within sentences and then as students mature they can move to paragraphs and longer pieces of text. This calls for an organized curriculum.

Instruction in text organizational patterns typically takes place with the following activities and materials.

- Trade books or website that introduce the topic students will study—animals, types of weather, etc.

- Short, very well-formed passages that illustrate one particular type of text structure.

- Identification and discussion of clue words that signal a text's organizational pattern (see Figure 12.2).

In the Classroom 12.3

Teaching About Organization Structure—Compare and Contrast

The lesson on text organizational patterns begins with identifying an interesting area of study, because the first goal is to capture the students' attention and stimulate motivation. For example, select a few short books on animals—lions, crocodiles, eagles, sharks, and frogs. Identify the key vocabulary – *warm-blooded, cold-blooded, hair, feathers, oxygen*—because these concepts are essential for making the comparisons among the animals.

Day 1

- *Reading and clue words*. The first lesson begins with a short passage that compares lions and eagles. The teacher introduces the clue words (*alike, both, and, compare, but, however, than, contrast*) and asks the students to use each word orally in a sentence.
- *Vocabulary instruction*. The teacher introduces the vocabulary words, explains them, discusses examples and helps students generate sentences with these words. "*The eagle is covered with white and black feathers.*"
- *Reading and Analyzing Paragraphs*. The students read a short passage about eagles and lions first to themselves and then the teacher rereads it while the students follow along.

  Lions and eagles are interesting animals. Both lions and eagles are warm-blooded. Lion's bodies are covered with hair, but eagles' bodies are covered with feathers.

- The students are then guided to analyze the text with the goal of looking for the similarities and differences between the two animals. The students label the parts that are similar with an **S** and the differences with a **D**. Finally, the students take turns orally generating paragraphs that describe how the two animals were similar and different.
- *Graphic Organizers*. Next, the students use a graphic organizer to compare and contrast the two animals. They use check marks to identify the specific features of each animal. Later the graphic organizers can be expanded to include more animals and more features.

Animal	What type of body covering does the animal have?			
	Hair	Scales	Smooth	Feathers
lions	✓			
eagles				✓

- Finally, the students create a well-structured comparison sentence using the information in the graphic organizer and one of the clue words.
- *Comparison-Contrast Questions*. The teacher introduces three questions that help students organize the information from the graphic organizer and the books. *What two things is this paragraph about? How are they the same? How are they different?* Students then write their sentences within a T-Chart. On the left side they write about how the animals are similar and on the right side how the animals are different.
- *Summary*. Finally, the students write a summary of the information from the books, the T-chart and the graphic organizer. Because summaries are difficult, the students are provided with a writing frame.
- *This paragraph is about _____ and _____. In some ways they are the same _____. In other ways they are different _____.*
- *Lesson Review*. The lesson ends with a review of the animals, the concepts, and the clue words.

Days 2–14

The previous lesson is thorough and the concepts are reviewed many times. In the days that follow the basic plan is repeated. Each day begins with a review of the vocabulary and then the reading of two or more books. Each book focuses on two of the five animals in the study. The students read the texts, label what is the same (S) and different (D) and then organize this information on a graphic organizer. The students generate questions for the T-chart and then write a summary of the days' work. Over time, the text becomes longer and more complicated.

- Discussions that analyze the relationship among ideas in the paragraphs.
- Graphic organizers that diagram the relationship of the concepts.
- Sentence/paragraph frames for writing about the concepts and their relationships.

In the Classroom 12.3 presents a lesson for introducing the compare and contrast structure to second graders (Williams et al, 2005). A similar procedure would be used for other text organization patterns. In the upper grades the teacher can lessen the amount of support that the students receive.

When students follow the instructional procedure for learning about comparison-contrast, they build their content knowledge of animals and they are able to read other texts with the same structure with greater comprehension. Their knowledge of text structure transfers. That does not mean they can transfer what they have learned to a cause and effect or problem-solution structure. Each of those structures would need to be specifically taught. Instruction in text structure improves recall, identification of the main idea, and learning of content area information (Meyer & Ray, 2011).

We classified teaching about text structure as building knowledge and strictly speaking it is building an understanding of how a text is organized. With that understanding students can read strategically. When a reader intuits how a text is organized he begins to look for specific information. The organizational structure helps the reader retain, recall, and summarize the information. Instruction in text structure promotes strategic thinking and learning.

In the Reading Corner we present a few informational books that could form the basis for building units of study. Consider what other books, articles, and websites could be added to create an enticing unit of study.

Reflect and Apply

1. Because prior knowledge is critical to the development of comprehension, spend some time considering what that means for designing a reading curriculum. Should skills and strategies necessary for the comprehending of informational text be taught during the reading/language arts portion of the day or during science and social studies instruction?

2. Examine a basal reading program. How is the curriculum in this program designed and organized to develop prior knowledge?

The Reading Corner

Informational Books, a Sampling

Non-Fiction Books Recommended for Readers at the Second Grade Level

Gail Gibbons. *Hurricanes.* Holiday House, Reprint edition, 2010. In this book, young readers will discover how hurricanes are formed, how they are named and classified, and what to do if a dangerous storm is coming their way. 32 pages.

Kathleen V. Kudinski. *Boy, Were We Wrong About Dinosaurs!* Puffin Books, 2008. This book offers insight into certain theories about dinosaurs and how they sometimes were proved or disproved. 32 pages.

Vaunda Micheaux Nelson. *Dream March: Dr. Martin Luther King, Jr. and the March on Washington* (Step into Reading). Random House Books for Young Readers, 2017. One of the titles in the Step into Reading Biography series, this inspiring biography introduces young readers to the civil rights movement, Dr. Martin Luther King, Jr., and the 1963 historic march on Washington. 48 pages.

Isabel Sanchez Vegara. *Frida Kahlo (Little People, Big Dreams).* Francis Lincoln Children's Books, 2016. A childhood accident prevented Frida Kahlo from pursuing her dream of becoming a doctor, but from her bed she began a distinguished career as a painter. 32 pages.

Non-Fiction Books Recommended for Readers at the Fourth Grade Level

Margriet Ruurs. *My Librarian Is a Camel: How Books Are Brought to Children Around the World.* Boyd Mills, 2005. Celebrating books, libraries, and readers, this book describes unusual mobile libraries around the world. 32 pages.

Malala Yousafzai. *I Am Malala: How One Girl Stood Up for Education and Changed the World* (Young Readers Edition). Little, Brown Books for Young Readers, 2016. In this Young Readers Edition of Malala's inspiring memoir, readers learn of her courageous fight for the rights of girls and women to an education. 256 pages.

Seymour Simon. *Our Solar System: Revised Edition.* Collins; Updated edition, 2014. One of many of Seymour Simon's outstanding non-fiction books, this title takes readers on an interplanetary tour from the sun to Mars, and then, thanks to the Voyager missions, to the planets beyond. 48 pages.

Melissa Sweet. *Some Writer!: The Story of E. B. White.* HMH Books for Young Readers, 2016. This illustrated biography of E. B. White, author of the beloved Charlotte's Web and "the man who loved words," is the winner of National Council of the Teachers of English 2017 Orbis Pictus Award, among many other awards. 176 pages.

Duncan Tonatiuh. *Separate Is Never Equal: Sylvia Mendez and Her Family's Fight for Desegregation.* Henry Abrams, 2014. This book tells the story of eight-year-old Sylvia Mendez, who played an instrumental role in the landmark segregation case of 1954—Brown v. Board of Education. 40 pages.

Non-Fiction Books recommended for Readers at the Sixth Grade Level

Russell Freedman. *We Will Not Be Silent: The White Rose Student Resistance Movement That Defied Adolf Hitler.* Henry Abrams, 2016. This book is an inspiring account of Austrian born Hans and Sophie Scholl who helped form the White Rose, a resistance campaign against Hitler and the Nazis. 112 pages.

Mary Losure. *Isaac the Alchemist: Secrets of Isaac Newton, Revealed.* Candlewick, 2017. This engaging narrative gives us a glimpse into the life of the "father of physics" a boy in an apothecary's house, observing, reading, and experimenting with alchemy and recording his observations of the world. 176 pages.

David Macaulay. *The Way Things Work Now.* HMH Books for Young Readers, 2016. Through text and numerous detailed illustrations, Macaulay introduces and explains the scientific principles and workings of hundreds of machines. 400 pages.

Jim Murphy. *The Great Fire.* Scholastic Paperbacks, 2010. This story, based on eye-witness accounts of the great fire that destroyed Chicago in 1871, describes the countless acts of foolishness and bravery of its citizens as well as the courage they found to rebuild their city. 144 pages.

MyLab Education **Self-Check 12.1**

MyLab Education **Application Exercise 12.1:** Teaching Compare and Contrast: The Link Between Writing and Reading

---

Comprehension Strategies

In Chapter 11 we introduced eight comprehension strategies. Most of these strategies are important for reading narrative and informational text, and a few are vital for reading digital text. We will first discuss the relative merits of the strategies for reading informational text and for narrative text. Then we will present lessons for teaching students to determine importance, summarize, and self-question. Strategies need not be taught one at a time; they can be combined as a suite of cognitive moves and we will consider one multiple strategy approach—reciprocal teaching. In a separate section, we will move on to digital text and the strategies vital for reading on-line.

Strategies are mental acts, plans that a reader can employ flexibly to solve comprehension problems, develop understanding, and learn from what they read. As Michael Pressley has pointed out, "The evidence is overwhelming that upper-grade elementary students can be taught to use comprehension strategies, with substantial improvements in student comprehension following such instruction" (2002). Actually, Pressley need not have limited his claim to upper-grade students because one of the best studies—by Brown and her colleagues (1996) and the work we already discussed about text structure—clearly shows that children as young as second-graders can profit from strategy instruction.

Figure 12.3 presents the same list of comprehension strategies from Chapter 11 but this time we have categorized them by their utility for comprehending informational and narrative texts. Most strategies are applicable for all types of texts, but some are more important for narratives (marked with ✓✓) while others are more important for informational text. Making inferences is critical for comprehending narrative text. A reader has to infer character traits and motives, the character's goal, often the physical and emotional response to an event, and the theme. When reading informational text, the major inferences are causal and determining importance.

Reading informational text requires setting a clear purpose and sustaining that purpose, sometimes over the course of many reading selections. Determining importance is critical with informational text because memory is limited and the reader should retain the critical information. The strategy of determining importance is very similar to summarizing. It is impossible to summarize without determining importance. Each of these strategies drives the other. Finally, when reading informational text, dealing with and creating graphic images is vital because few graphics appear in narrative text.

We do not know how many strategies need to be taught in a school year, but probably fewer than the full list of eight (Willingham, 2006). Most schools and districts have had their view of curriculum shaped by basal programs that present one strategy a week with occasional review. Work by Rosenshine and Meister (1994) suggests that students improve their comprehension by working with as few as two strategies—perhaps one to set a purpose and one to focus on importance. In the multiple-strategy routine reciprocal teaching (Palincsar & Brown, 1984), students are taught just four strategies, questioning, clarifying, summarizing, and predicting and the students' comprehension improves. It is best to teach a few things well and insure that students use and benefit from the strategies.

The extensive body of theory and research on comprehension strategies instruction has shown two approaches for teaching strategies to be extremely effective: direct explanation of strategies following the release of responsibility model (see Chapter 2) (Duffy, 2002; Duke et al., 2011) and multiple strategy instruction (Brown, Pressley, Van Meter, & Schuder, 1996; Pressley, El-Dinary, Wharton-McDonald, & Brown, 1998). Direct explanation is explicit with the teacher and students working with one strategy at a time, gradually phasing in new strategies. Multiple strategy instruction, with reciprocal teaching (Palincsar & Brown, 1984) and transactional strategy instruction (Brown, Pressley, van Meter, & Schuder, 1996) or collaborative strategic reading (Klingner, Vaughn, & Schumm, 1998) embeds strategy instruction in the ongoing discussion of the texts.

As we have repeatedly noted, a balanced literacy curriculum is for all students—more accomplished readers, less accomplished readers, students who come less prepared to school, and students who do not speak English as their native language. This is as true for comprehension strategies as it is for other parts of the curriculum. One danger is that capable readers who comprehend well might actually be confused by

Figure 12.3 Comprehension Strategies for Narrative and Informational Text

Strategies	Narrative Text	Informational Text
• Setting a purpose for reading/defining a question	✓	✓
• Asking and answering questions	✓	✓
• Making inferences	✓✓	✓
• Determining what is important	✓	✓✓
• Summarizing	✓	✓✓
• Imaging and creating graphic representations	✓	✓
• Locating information	✓	✓
• Critically evaluating information	✓	✓

attempts to replace already functional strategies with a new one. The solution here is to know your students and their capabilities well, find out what strategies they already have, check periodically to see if they view the new ones as useful, and avoid imposing new strategies when they are unnecessary.

With less proficient students, on the other hand, comprehension strategies are likely to be particularly welcome. You need to be especially careful to introduce them at a rate slow enough to prevent frustration yet rapid enough to avoid boredom, to give students plenty of time to apply them in class, and to deliberately structure students' work and the assessment system you use to reward their use of strategies. Over the past two decades, Donald Deshler (Schumaker & Deshler, 2003) has conducted more than a dozen studies clearly indicating that at-risk students can successfully learn to use comprehension strategies—if they are properly instructed. English language learners can be introduced to comprehension strategies but they will require considerably more support than native speakers (Gutierrez, 2005). For students from certain cultures, the group work involved in learning strategies may be particularly facilitative and comfortable. With these students, you might let the group work continue for some time, gradually building in independent assignments and explaining to students that they will often need to use strategies in situations in which their classmates are not available, such as with work done at home.

In the balance of this chapter we will explore four strategies, enough to improves students' competence with informational text – setting a purpose, determining importance, summarizing, and question asking.

Setting a Purpose for Reading

Reading should be an intentional activity, something we do for fun, escape, information, and enlightenment. Ideally, the reader should be setting the purpose for reading, but in school, especially in the early grades, the teacher sets the purpose. Setting a purpose is important for several reasons. First, purpose and genre are intimately linked. Purpose, structure and language are all characteristics of genre (Pare & Smart, 1994). Think what happens to fiction when the teacher approaches it as an information gathering activity. A follow up lesson sounds like this: What was Bob wearing? How did he get to school?

Purpose also defines the strategies we use while reading. Reading closely, rereading, looking for important ideas is critical with nonfiction, while fiction leads us to make inferences, speculate about characters, and imagine their future. We make considerably more inferences when reading fiction than we do when reading nonfiction (van den Broek, 2002.) A few of the approaches we have already mentioned help readers set a purpose.

1. The question generation with K-W-L is a purpose-setting activity.
2. When we engage students in a study of text organization patterns, such as compare and contrast, we are setting a purpose for reading.
3. Examining text features sets a purpose for reading. When students note the title, headings, and subheadings, they are setting up an expectation, a purpose for reading.
4. The most important purpose comes from the curriculum. If the topics of study are interesting or can be made interesting, then the students' purpose is set, but it must be specifically aligned to every text that is read.

Determining What Is Important

To illustrate direct explanation, we show how to introduce the strategy of determining what is important. This strategy overlaps with summarizing, so we will illustrate how to move students from determining what is important to summarizing. Although instruction will vary somewhat with different strategies, different students, and different age groups, the general plan being presented is widely applicable. The critical parts of the plan follow the gradual release of responsibility model:

- Explain the strategy, what it is, how to do it, and when and why to employ it.
- Model the strategy several times.
- Gradually have the students try out the strategy taking on more and more of the task.
- Provide support with graphic organizers, partner work, and verbal guidance.
- Help students use the strategy when independently reading and studying.

In this illustration, the students are third or fourth-graders, and the strategy is determining what is important. To capture students' attention and build interest, strategy instruction must be embedded in a meaningful area of study (Guthrie et al., 1998). Students do not have a natural passion to find the main idea or make an inference, but they do like to learn about violent weather, snakes, and volcanoes. If strategy instruction is a tool that will take them to deeper understanding, they will work with you. Ask students about the reading they have been doing in science and social studies and discuss some of the challenges they face. One of the challenges likely to come up is that these books cover a lot of information, and it is hard to remember all of it. Explain that the strategy they will learn—determining what is important—will help them to better understand and remember what they read. In the Classroom 12.4 outlines our approach.

In the Classroom 12.4
Determine What Is Important

The strategy lesson begins with an analogy. Students are introduced to the idea that there are objects and they can fit under categories. We have chosen fast-food restaurants, sports that use balls, and sports that don't use balls. Write the word sets on the board underneath unlabeled umbrellas illustrated in Figure 12.4. Tell students that these words are examples of more general ideas. Have them guess what those more

Figure 12.4 Word Sets for Motivation and Interest Building

What idea covers all of these?

McDonald's	tennis	swimming
Burger King	soccer	track
Wendy's	football	gymnastics
Arby's	basketball	weightlifting
Taco Bell	broomball	archery

general ideas are and write them in the umbrellas above the sets of examples. Explain that determining a general idea or label for words and phrases is just the beginning; next they will determine important ideas in paragraphs and longer selections.

Tell students that knowing how to determine what is important can make understanding and remembering what they read much easier. Sometimes the author provides clear clues as to what is important and sometimes he does not. As a class we are going to walk through some examples and discover the rules for determining what is important. While doing this we will create a chart that lists the guidelines.

- Project the following paragraph on the whiteboard and ask the students what is the main idea? Don't give any hints.

    The bald eagle is known to make very large nests. One nest found in Ohio was twelve feet deep. It was over eight feet across. The nest weighed as much as an automobile. A bald eagle's nest found in Florida was even larger than the one in Ohio.

Some students will say that the paragraph is about eagles or nests. Tell them that they have identified the topic, but the main idea is more than the topic. The main idea tells us something about the topic. Ask, what have we learned about eagles and nests? Engage the students in a discussion and guide them to understand that the main idea is about the size of eagles' nests. Then ask them where this idea is stated. Many students will point to the first sentence but if they don't then you point it out. Then ask if the rest of the sentences expand upon or support the idea that bald eagles make very large nests. On an anchor chart record these three guidelines that the class discovered:

The topic is often the most frequently written word or concept.

Look at the first sentence or the topic sentence to find the main idea.

Ask if the rest of the sentences support the main idea.

Figure 12.5 illustrates the completed anchor chart. You might want to repeat these steps with several other paragraphs.

- Now project the following paragraph on the whiteboard and continue the discussion about determining the main idea.

  One bird keeps warm by burrowing under the snow to sleep. One city bird sleeps near electric signs. The signs keep it warm on the coldest days. Birds take up sleeping positions that seem strange to humans. Birds are clever.

Figure 12.5 Anchor Chart for Determining Importance

How to Determine Importance

- Examine the title, headings, subheadings, bold print, and pictures.
- Think about the topic. What is the author mainly writing about? What is the author's purpose?
- Search for topic sentences. Look at the beginning of paragraphs.
- If there is no topic sentence, try to infer one—make one up.
- Let's check. Do the other ideas, the details, support the main idea we found or invented?

- Lead the students to discover that in this paragraph the main idea is at the end, a summative statement. Discuss the possibility that the main idea or topic sentence can be at the beginning, end, or embedded within a paragraph. Add these guidelines to the chart.
- Now project the following paragraph on the whiteboard and continue the discussion. Some students will quickly realize that the paragraph does not contain a main idea statement, a topic sentence.

  The heads of sharks are sometimes made into glue. The flesh of some sharks is used as food. Sometimes the flesh is used to help make the soil better for crops. Oil is gotten from the liver. Leather is made from the hide.

- Pose the question, "What do we do when the text does not have a topic sentence, a stated main idea?" Some students will suggest that we can invent one. Then ask the students to do so and you will get responses like: *Sharks can be used for many purposes. You can use sharks in many ways.* On the chart add this guideline. *"If we can't find a clear main idea statement we need to invent one."* Each time consider the final rule. "Do the rest of the sentences support the main idea?"
- Sometimes the main idea can be a synthesis of two or more paragraphs. The following sample is taken from *Scaly Babies: Reptiles Growing Up* by Ginny Johnson and Judy Cutchins (p. 24):

  For many people, the word *reptile* describes an ugly, slippery, and sometimes dangerous animal. But reptiles are not slimy, and most are not dangerous. There are nearly six thousand different kinds of these scaly-skinned animals in the world today. It is true that some are large and scary-looking and a few are venomous, but most reptiles are harmless to humans. Like many wild animals, reptiles may strike or bite to defend themselves. But they rarely bother a person who has not disturbed or startled them.

- Ask students what the paragraph is mainly about (reptiles). Next, ask them how they determined this (everything in the paragraph is about reptiles). Ask which of our guidelines helped? What is the main concept the author is trying to tell you? The students might say several sentences seem important. Suggest that they combine sentence. Perhaps they will come up with; *Although many people think reptiles are dangerous most are not*.
- Continue to have the students practice with a few more paragraphs until you have some evidence that they can reliably determine the main idea of a paragraph.

When we read, we do not determine importance one paragraph at a time. We read larger chunks of texts and we use much more than the repeated words, the topic sentences, and our own intuitions to determine what is important. Determining what is important requires a more complex thinking process, especially when reading passages with multiple paragraphs or a section from the social studies or science textbook. To determine what is important, students need to combine what they know about text features, what they learned about paragraphs, and their prior knowledge.

Several researchers indicate that there are two routes to finding the main idea, a text-based strategy and a reader-based strategy (Afflerbach & Johnston, 1986; Afflerbach, 1990). When we read a familiar topic, we use our prior knowledge as a filter to focus on the important ideas. Because we know a great deal about reading instruction, we are able to quickly focus on what is important and ignore trivia. Lacking this background knowledge, the young reader relies more on a text-driven strategy using text features and topic sentences to find the main idea. In the Classroom 12.5 walks you through this process.

In the Classroom 12.5

From Determining Importance to Summarizing

Instruction in this strategy begins with the work you have done with paragraphs and combines that thinking with students' knowledge of text features. Review the guidelines you developed with your students that you posted on the anchor chart (see Figure 12.5). Explain that we rarely approach determining importance one paragraph at a time, so now we will look at a passage that is several paragraphs or more in length. Also review with the students what they know about text features. Draw their attention to the *Features and Purpose* (Figure 12.1) chart and review the role of titles, headings, subheadings, and bold print. Leave graphics, pictures, and captions for another day.

- Distribute a copy of the following passage to the students and place a copy under the document camera.

> *Get Some Sleep!*
>
> **Are you tired during the day? Do you have trouble focusing in class? Do you feel like a grouch? If so, you might not be getting enough sleep.**
>
> *On weekday mornings, Vanessa Louie, 10, does what most kids her age do. She rolls out of bed at 7:00 a.m., brushes her teeth, and gets dressed. Some days, she watches a little bit of TV. Then she hops on the bus to P.S. 124 Yung Wing School, in New York City.*
>
> *Vanessa gets about eight hours of sleep each night. Waking up in the morning isn't always easy for the fifth grader, though. "My mom has to pull me out of bed almost every day," Vanessa told TFK. "I get really tired. Sometimes, I almost fall asleep in class."*
>
> *Vanessa's not alone. Studies show that kids across the nation aren't catching enough z's. Experts say children ages 5 to 12 should get 10 to 11 hours of sleep each night. But according to a poll by the National Sleep Foundation, kids are only snoozing an average of nine and a half hours a night. An extra 30 minutes of slumber may not seem like a lot, but it can make a huge difference for kids. (V. An. Time for Kids, January 2007).*

- *Modeling.* Read the title, the subtitle, and the series of four questions that follow. Sleep is the most frequently repeated word or concept. The topic of the article is sleep, specifically whether kids get enough sleep. In the first paragraph, the author is discussing the schedule of Vanessa and what she does every morning. In the next paragraph, the author quotes Vanessa saying that she does not get enough sleep. In the third paragraph, there seems to be a topic sentence, but it is not the first sentence in the paragraph, *"Studies show that kids across the nation aren't catching enough z's."* Then the author expands and advises how much sleep kids should get.

- *Explanation.* To determine what is important, use the title and the subtitle. Note that the writer started with many details but in the third paragraph he summarized these details using a topic sentence. We should add these new guidelines for determining what is important to our anchor chart. The revised chart will include the suggestion that we examine the title, headings, subheading, and bold print.

- *Guided practice*. Give the students another short passage to read and have them work with a partner to find the main idea. Encourage them to follow the guidelines on the anchor chart. After they have finished reading and discussing, pose two questions. "What is the author's main point?" "How did you determine that?" You want the students to point out the specific text elements and the type of thinking that lead to their conclusions.
- *Application*. Now the strategy moves to the reading of textbooks, articles, newspapers, and other informational material. The most important instructional element is purpose. Build interesting units of study. Remember, thinking or determining what is important is difficult mental work and the students need a strong reason to engage in this work. The texts you select and the purpose you set for reading are critical. It even helps if the topic is controversial, a topic where students can take a stand.

Teaching Students to Summarize

The students will now be incorporating all they have learned about determining importance as they read, take notes, and summarize. They will do so using the Determining Importance–Summarizing Guide (see Figure 12.6). Two things have been added to build a global strategy that students can use independently while reading:

- Students will first think about what they know before they begin reading and jot down some notes.
- Students will take notes while reading by writing down key words or key phrases.

Note that the note-taking guide has a small version of the anchor chart to remind students to apply what they have learned.

Figure 12.6 Determining Importance–Summarizing Guide

Determining Importance–Summarizing

Name _____ Date _____

Title of Reading Selection or Chapter _____

What do I already know about this topic? _____

Titles, headings
Topic sentences
Bold print
Repeated words

Key Ideas & Words	Main Idea Statement/One Sentence Summary

Write a summary of the most important things you learned from reading this selection.

MyLab Education
Click here to download a printable version of Figure 12.6.

Explain that today we are going to read a chapter and write down the important ideas plus the details, evidence, and reasons that support and extend those ideas. To help us, we will use the Determining Importance–Summarizing guide (see Figure 12.6). Explain that one step has been added to the guide, thinking about what you already know about the topic. Think about what you know; this will help you determine what is important. Walk the students through the steps in the guide first noting the title of the chapter. Next, have them write a few notes about what they already know. Then, they can begin the note taking process. In the left column write down important words found in the headings, subheadings, bold print, or topic sentences. In the right column write down the main ideas, evidence, and reasons that support the main idea. If they locate a topic sentence they can write it in the "main ideas" section. The determining importance guide can be used whenever the students read.

Once students have a basic understanding of the strategy, they need a chance to practice it in pairs because students working together support each other. You want to ensure that students achieve and feel successful at this point. They have worked only with short passages and now they are applying all that they know to longer passages or chapters. After students have had an opportunity to use the strategy in pairs, they should share their work with the class. Call on pairs to present the important information they found in the passages and discuss how they determined that this was the crucial information. Monitor their responses carefully and provide feedback and clarification as necessary.

You will note that this process includes an array of scaffolds that help students learn to determine importance. It began with short paragraphs where the main idea was obvious then to paragraphs with implied main ideas. It moved to longer and more complex text. Each time the teacher modeled the thinking and then the students tried it out with a partner. An anchor chart and a note taking form was provided to guide the students' thinking. Finally, the teacher's questions, comments, and suggestions provide further support as the students engage with the comprehensive strategies.

Question Asking and Answering

There is a long history of research that demonstrates that asking and answering questions improves reading comprehension (Rosenshine, Meister, & Chapman, 1994; Joseph, Albers-Morgan, Cullen, & Rouse, 2016). When students are asked questions, it focuses their attention on the text with questions asked before, during, and after reading having different effects (Anderson & Biddle, 1975; Reynold & Anderson, 1982). Questions asked before students read determine their purpose for reading. Questions asked while students read causes them to attend more closely to the ideas the questions tap, and questions asked after reading helps students reconceptualize what they have read.

When students generate questions, they learn more (Rosenshine, et al., 1994), likely more than when the teacher asks the questions. Isidor Rabi, a physicist was asked when he was awarded the Nobel Prize, who was the greatest influence on his thinking. The interviewer, expecting an answer like Einstein or Bohr, was startled when Rabi responded that it was his mother. "Every day when I came home from school my mother would ask me, so Itsak did you ask any good questions today." Self-questioning sets a purpose for reading. It focuses students' attention on the content, particularly important ideas, and self-question fosters metacognition. When students read to answer a question, locating the answer is a signal that their reading has been successful.

Although there are several instructional procedures that guide students to ask questions, we will focus on Question Answer Relationships (QAR), an approach that has stood the test of time (Raphael, 1982; Raphael & Wonnacutt, 1985; Raphael & Au, 2005). In the QAR procedure, the students are taught four types of questions that are

Figure 12.7 Question Answer Relationships

Location of Answer	Question Type	Source of Information	Clues
In the Text	Right There	Answer is in the text	What, where, when
	Think and Search	Answer is in the text but the reader must think, search, and infer	How and why
In Your Head	The Author and Me	Answer is not in the story, but the author gives you clues you can use to think of an answer	What and why
	On My Own	Answer in your head	Suppose, what if

distinguished by the sources of information needed to answer the question. Some answers are in the text and others are primarily in your head. Figure 12.7 illustrates the four types of questions. *Right There* questions can be answered by finding specific information within a sentence or two; the answer is in the text. *Think and Search* questions cause the reader to search the text putting information together or comparing and contrasting two ideas. *Author and Me* questions are inferential. The author has supplied a clue but the answer is typically in the reader's head. *On My Own* questions are answered from information in the reader's head. These are questions, based on information in the text, that call for judgments, evaluations, and speculations. In the Classroom 12.6 provides a guide for helping students use the QAR process.

In the Classroom 12.6

Question Answer Relationships

Question Answer Relationships (QARs) help students learn to ask good questions, to understand the thinking needed to answer questions, and to understand that reading demands searching for information, making inferences, and using prior knowledge. To introduce this strategy every student will need a short text and a copy of the QAR chart. The instruction proceeds in two stages. First, the students learn to identify and answer the four types of questions. Then they learn to ask the questions.

- *Introducing the Strategy*. Start by asking students: "Do you ever ask yourself questions when you read?" Explain that you often do. "Questions help keep me on track. When I ask questions, I read to find answers. Asking questions puts me in charge of my reading. I have a clear purpose. Questions cause me to clarify things that I do not understand."
- *Model the Strategy*. Introduce the concept of Question Answer Relationships. Using the following QAR chart, explain the four types of questions, and how they differ (see Figure 12.7). Questions differ by where you, the reader, go to find the answer. Give the students something very simple to read and then ask four questions, one of each type. Discuss the answers, the source of answers, and label each question.

Passage	Questions
The team boarded the school bus and started out for the big game. If they won this game they would be champions! Suddenly, fifteen miles from the site of the game the bus broke down. There they sat, waiting. Nobody seemed to know what to do, and it was getting closer and closer to game time.	How was the team getting to the game? *(Right There)* What happened on the way to the game? *(Think and Search)* How did the players on the bus feel? *(Author and Me)* What would you have done if you were on the bus? *(On My Own)*

(Continued)

- The first question is obviously right there because in the first sentence it states that the team was on the bus. The second question is a bit ambiguous because students could answer that the bus broke down (*Right There*) or the bus broke down on the way to the championship game (*Think and Search*). The latter answer is *Think and Search* because it requires putting ideas together. The third question is *Author and Me* because the reader must infer the feelings of the team members. The last question is *On My Own* because the reader relies on his own knowledge to fashion and answer. This process should be repeated several times with different passages. Arguments about labeling questions is desirable because the differences between *Think and Search* and *Author and Me* is subtle. You want the students to discuss why a question is *Think and Search* because the discussions push them back to the text to justify their answers.
- *Guided Practice*: Repeat this process several times, reading short passages and having the students label the questions. The students will want to answer first and label second but resist the urge. Labeling the questions helps students understand how they need to think to answer them. Do they search the text, or bring what they know to bear on the question? If you think back to Chapter 2, you are giving the students a short course in the construction-integration model of reading. *Right There* and *Think and Search* questions address what the text says and *Author and Me* and *On My Own* questions address what the text means.
- *Apply the Strategy*. Now it is time to change the focus and have the students begin to ask the questions. Because they understand different types of questions, they should be able to generate questions. Give all the students a passage (it should be something they are currently reading) and have them generate questions. At first, this will be difficult and they will feel overwhelmed. Start by making the task simple and then increase its complexity. The first time, ask students to write just one question, a *Right There* question. Stop, have the class label the question and answer it. Gradually require more questions, perhaps a *Right There* question and an *Author and Me* question. You will need to provide guidance and feedback. As you continue this process, the students will be leading the discussion, asking and answering the questions. You have released responsibility to the students.

Instructional Units

The students have learned the text features of non-fiction and its organizational patterns. They can determine what is important, summarize, and ask and answer questions. These strategies have been slowly added to their repertoire as they continue their content area studies. As each piece has been added to their repertoire they have read with more purpose and success. As the students become more proficient with the strategies, the instruction should change in the following ways:

- Strategies are used with authentic tasks.
- Instruction becomes less concentrated each week.
- Texts become longer and more challenging.
- Students do more of the work.
- Students are encouraged to use the strategies as an aid to learning from text.

As students become more adept at determining importance and summarizing, the strategies will be used alongside the other strategies like asking good questions. A colorful bulletin board such as that shown in Figure 12.8, or the anchor charts, can serve as a reminder for students to use the strategies they've learned or reviewed during the year and as a refresher on how to use them.

One of the most successful approaches to developing comprehension has been Concept-Oriented Reading Instruction (CORI) developed by Guthrie, Wigfield, and Perencevich (2004). CORI situates the development of reading comprehension within the study of science as students pursue topics like animal survival over a series of weeks. Students collaborate, make choices, and set goals for learning. CORI places a premium on motivation. A group of students might decide to study what soil produces the best plant growth. They, with the teachers help, assemble readings, design experiment,

Figure 12.8 Strategy Bulletin Board

CAN'T FIGURE IT OUT?
Try using the strategies we've learned!

THINK
about what you know
about the subject!

If you are reading
about sharks, think
about what you already
know about sharks,
fish, and the ocean.

LOOK
at pictures, graphs,
charts, and maps.

ASK QUESTIONS
before you read and
while you read.

If you are reading
a story, ask, "What
will happen next?"

How will Cinderella get to the ball?

Cinderella

Or, if you are reading about sharks and
the author writes, "Sharks have gotten
a bad reputation," ask,

Why SHOULDN'T sharks have a bad reputation?

ASK YOURSELF,
"Am I Understanding
What I'm Reading?"

Self, do you understand this?

record results, and write what they have learned. The results of the study are presented to the class using a PowerPoint or other means.

Students are engaged in reading and writing daily for 60 to 90 minutes. They read a range of text. The teacher works to build disciplinary and text structure knowledge. To meet the needs of the students, the teacher introduces strategies when they are useful. If a group of students has many texts to read and much to learn, then it makes sense to teach the students to summarize. By summarizing the students can remember what is important. Strategies work as tools to enable the students to learn from text and to complete their projects. The results of CORI suggest that strategies are learned more thoroughly in this embedded context than when strategies are presented in isolation. For more information on CORI go to www.corilearning.com.

Reflect and Apply

3. Although we all read strategically, few of us can remember specifically learning strategies. In your class or with a colleague discuss how you became a strategic reader. Do you believe you might be a stronger reader if you had more direct instruction in comprehension strategies?

4. Think about the curriculum in your school, your district, or in your instructional materials. Are you asked to teach too many skills and strategies or too few? Think about how many strategies students actually need to become successful readers.

MyLab Education **Self-Check 12.2**

MyLab Education **Application Exercise 12.2:** Can You Determine Importance?

MyLab Education **Application Exercise 12.3:** How Question-Answer Relationships Illuminate the Reading Process

Multiple Strategy Instruction— Reciprocal Teaching

When researchers were first exploring comprehension strategy instruction they tended to study the impact of teaching one strategy at a time. Other researchers explored the impact of multiple strategy instruction and from that work three prominent instructional routines were developed. They are transactional strategy instruction (Brown, Pressley, Van meter, & Scheder, 1996), reciprocal teaching (Palincsar & Brown, 1984), and collaborative strategic reading (Klingner, Vaughn, & Schumm, 1998). Reciprocal teaching developed as a procedure in which students and a teacher work together to improve students' understanding of complex informational texts and at the same time improve students' general ability to monitor their comprehension. The extensively researched procedure has produced very positive results with first-graders (Palincsar & David, 1991), sixth- and seventh-graders (Palincsar & Brown, 1984), and even college students (Fillenworth, 1995). Reciprocal teaching also benefits English learners, especially when linked to cooperative groups or cross-aged tutoring (Klingner & Vaughn, 1996). Studies show that students who work with reciprocal teaching increase their group participation and use strategies to increase their learning when reading independently. The studies also demonstrate that the procedure can be used in various settings and that students maintain the comprehension gains they achieve.

The procedure employs four strategies: generating questions, clarifying issues, summarizing, and making predictions. Each of these strategies serves one or more definite purposes. Questioning focuses students' attention on main ideas and provides a check on their current understanding of what they are reading. Clarifying ensures that students are actively engaged as they are reading and helps avoid confusion. Summarizing requires students to attend to the major content of the selection and determine what is and is not important. And predicting requires students to review what they have learned thus far and approach the next section of the text with some expectations of what is to come.

Initially, reciprocal teaching is teacher directed. At first, the teacher serves as the leader of the group, taking the primary role in carrying out the strategies and modeling them for the students. One central purpose of reciprocal teaching, however, is to get students actively involved in using the strategies—that is, in doing the questioning, clarifying, summarizing, and predicting themselves. Thus, from the beginning, the teacher increasingly hands over responsibility to the students in the group. As soon as possible, the teacher steps out of the leadership role, and each student in the group takes her turn as group leader. It is, in fact, when students have the leadership role that they do some of their best learning. The teacher, however, continues to monitor the group as much as possible and intervenes when necessary to keep students on track and to facilitate the discussion.

In the Classroom 12.7 shows the four steps of the procedure and very briefly illustrates the responses they might prompt for fifth-graders reading Bradley Cruxton's *Discovering the Amazon Rainforest*.

In formal studies of reciprocal teaching, students who have usually worked with reciprocal teaching for 12 to 16 sessions spread over a month or more, produce the gains described earlier. To give you a more concrete indication of what those gains look like, we present a transcript of a seventh-grader's work with the procedure. In the Classroom 12.8 (pp. 372–373) presents the student's discussion of several texts (summarized

---

In the Classroom 12.7

Reciprocal Teaching

The session begins with reading a short segment of text, typically a paragraph or so. The leader reads it aloud or students read silently. The four steps of reciprocal teaching then follow.

Questioning

Once the segment has been read, the leader or other group members generate several questions prompted by the passage, and members of the group answer the questions. For example, after reading the opening paragraph of Cruxton's *Discovering the Amazon Rainforest*, a student might ask, "What does a rainforest look like?" Another student might respond, "Very tall trees, lots of plants and animals, not much light under the tall tree branches."

Clarifying

If the passage or questions produce any problems or misunderstandings, the leader and other group members clarify matters. For example, in continuing with *Discovering the Amazon Rainforest,* a student might wonder what the phrase "sun umbrella" means. Another might point out that the only plants that can grow in the rainforest are those that can grow with little light like mushrooms, because the branches of the giant trees act like a sun umbrella and block the light. Typically, clarifying focuses on words and sentences that are difficult to understand.

Summarizing

After all the questions have been answered and any misunderstandings have been clarified, the leader or other group members summarize the segment: "A rainforest is a place of giant trees, lots of rain, many different kinds of plants and animals, with little change in temperature, day to night, season to season."

Predicting

Based on the segment just read, segments that have preceded it, and the discussion thus far, the leader or other group members make predictions about the contents of the upcoming section: "I think in the next section we will learn about some of the different kinds of living things—plants, animals, and people—that reside in the rainforests."

The sequence of reading, questioning, clarifying, summarizing, and predicting is then repeated with subsequent sections but now the students take the lead in using the strategies and the teacher provides support. Eventually the students should be able to sustain the discussion on their own.

from the work of Brown & Palincsar, 1989) and illustrates the student's improving self-questioning.

As the example from In the Classroom 12.8 illustrates, the student progressed from being unable to phrase an appropriate question to phrasing a very clear and concise one. As the student became increasingly competent, the teacher gradually turned over responsibility for generating questions to her. On day 1, the teacher had to phrase the question for the student. On day 4, he provided substantial scaffolding to assist the student in phrasing a question. On day 7, he needed to use much less scaffolding. On day 11, when the student produced two good questions, he reminded her that the procedure called for only one. And on day 15, he simply praised the student, as she was able to produce a clear, concise, and appropriate question without the teacher's assistance.

In the Classroom 12.8

Instructional Routines

Increasing the Questioning Ability of a Seventh-Grade Student

Day 1

- *Text:* The water moccasin, somewhat longer than the copperhead, is found in the southeastern states. It lives in swampy regions. It belongs, as do also the copperhead and the rattlesnake, to a group of poisonous snakes called pit vipers. They have pits between their eyes and their nostrils which, because they are sensitive to heat, help the snakes tell when they are near a warm-blooded animal. Another name for the water moccasin is "cottonmouth." This name comes from the white lining of the snake's mouth.

  Student: What is found in the southeastern snakes, also the copperhead, rattlesnakes, vipers—they have. I'm not doing this right.

  Teacher: All right. Do you want to know about the pit vipers?

  Student: Yeah.

  Teacher: What would be a good question about the pit vipers that starts with the word *why?*

  Student: (No response)

  Teacher: How about, "Why are the snakes called pit vipers?"

  Student: Why do they want to know that they are called pit vipers?

  Teacher: Try it again.

  Student: Why do they, pit vipers in a pit?

  Teacher: How about, "Why do they call the snakes pit vipers?"

  Student: Why do they call the snakes pit vipers?

  Teacher: There you go! Good for you.

DAY 4

- *Text:* Spinner's mate is much smaller than she, and his body is dull brown. He spends most of his time sitting at one side of her web.

  Student: (No question)

  Teacher: What's this paragraph about?

  Student: Spinner's mate, How do Spinner's mate …

  Teacher: That's good. Keep going.

Student: How do Spinner's mate is smaller than … How am I going to say that?

Teacher: Take your time with it. You want to ask a question about Spinner's mate and what he does, beginning with the word *how*.

Student: How do they spend most of his time sitting?

Teacher: You're very close. The question would be, "How does Spinner's mate spend most of his time?" Now, you ask it.

Student: How does Spinner's mate spend most of his time?

DAY 7

- *Text:* Perhaps you are wondering where the lava and other volcanic products come from. Deep within our earth there are pockets of molten rock called magma. Forced upward in part by gas pressure, this molten rock continually tries to reach the surface. Eventually—by means of cracks in the crustal rocks or some similar zone of weakness—the magma may break out of the ground. It then flows from the vent as lava, or spews skyward as dense clouds of lava particles.

Student: How does the pressure from below push the mass of hot rock against the opening? Is that it?

Teacher: Not quite. Start your question with, "What happens when?"

Student: What happens when the pressure from below pushes the mass of hot rock against the opening?

Teacher: Good for you! Good job.

DAY 11

- *Text:* One of the most interesting of the insect-eating plants is the Venus flytrap. This plant lives in only one small area of the world—the coastal marshes of North and South Carolina. The Venus flytrap doesn't look unusual. Its habits, however, make it truly a plant wonder.

Student: What is the most interesting of the insect-eating plants, and where do the plants live?

Teacher: Two excellent questions! They are both clear and important questions. Ask us one at a time now.

DAY 15

- *Text:* Scientists also come to the South Pole to study the strange lights that glow overhead during the Antarctic night. (It's a cold and lonely world for the few hardy people who "winter over" the polar night.) These "southern lights" are caused by the Earth acting like a magnet on electrical particles in the air. They are clues that may help us understand the Earth's core and the upper edges of its blanket of air.

Student: Why do scientists come to the South Pole to study?

Teacher: Excellent question! That is what this paragraph is all about.

SOURCE: Brown, Ann L., & Palincsar, Annemarie. (1984). "Reciprocal Teaching of Comprehension-Fostering and Comprehension-Monitoring Activities," *Cognition and Instruction, 1*(2), pp. 138–139.

As the transcript further shows, the leader's role is crucial. Skilled leaders can keep the discussion on track, constantly assess students' strengths and weaknesses, and provide just enough scaffolding to challenge students while ensuring that they succeed.

Because reciprocal teaching is consistent with the principles of effective teaching, is strongly supported by research, and assists students in understanding and learning from challenging expository material, we recommend using it in your classroom as yet another procedure for fostering your students' increasingly sophisticated literacy.

Reflect and Apply

5. In Chapter 11 we presented several discussion techniques—questioning the author, literature circles and book clubs. Consider the similarities of these techniques to reciprocal teaching. Consider the similarities of several discussion techniques including questioning the author, literature circles, and book clubs when compared with reciprocal teaching.

6. In all of these discussion techniques who is leading the discussion? Does it matter who is leading the discussion?

MyLab Education **Self-Check 12.3**

MyLab Education **Application Exercise 12.4:** Implementing Reciprocal Teaching

Reading with Digital Text

How we read in our information saturated and digital environment is changing rapidly. Email is already twenty-five years old, as are Internet search engines—remember Netscape and Yahoo Search? Google appeared twenty years ago and the first Tweet was sent in 2006. By 2012, there were 100 million Twitter users. Much of this change is driven by young people because some of us older folks have yet to Tweet. A survey of American adults in 2012 found that 48 percent of those ages 18 to 29 read lengthy text online and the percentage is expected to increase rapidly (Zichuhr, Rainie, Purcell, Madden, & Brenner, 2012). These are New Literacies, growing outside of the classroom more quickly than inside them.

How the Digital Environment Might Affect Reading

Because the way we read is rapidly changing, so must our approach to comprehension instruction. Many adults read fiction on their Kindles and tablets, but the focus of our concern is reading for information on the Internet. We suspect that reading a novel on a Kindle is not markedly different from reading the same novel as a paperback book, but some researchers have found differences in the two mediums. The LCD screen may make the perceptual process of reading more difficult. The screen resolution, backlighting, contrast, and the refresh rates might contribute to visual fatigue (Benedetto, Drai-Zerbib, Pedrotti, Tissier, & Baccino, 2013; Mangen, Walgermo, & Brennick, 2013).

The most likely factor that undermines comprehension on the Internet is scrolling. When the reader has to scroll frequently through a text or has to move from one link to another cognitive demands increase. At the simplest level the imposition of ads within an Internet text causes the reader to lose his place and attention is disrupted (DeStefano & LeFevre, 2007). Print text allows the reader to see and feel where the ideas are located on the page, how much more they have to read, and it is even possible that physical location of ideas on the printed page provides a clue to remembering the information (Mangen 2006, 2013). All these factors make the process of comprehending different and more taxing on the Internet.

The effects of the digital environment are not all negative. People who own an e-reader tend to read more than people who stick to print (Zickuhr et al., 2012). The amount of time people spend reading electronically is increasing at the expense of print reading. The e-reader is more portable, can hold dozens of volumes and provides quicker access to books. However, it is likely that the e-reader promotes increased reading among people who are already readers. Our real concern is not the impact of the e-reader on the volume and desire to read, but how the Internet is influencing reading for information. It is likely that the digital environment will have minimal effects on the reading of fiction, but profound effects on the comprehension and learning from text.

The most serious issue on the Internet is truth and the need to develop critical readers who can sort fact from fiction. Before the Internet, news and information was edited. The reader knew that a series of editors reviewed what was published. With knowledge and experience, a reader understood that one source, such as the *Wall Street Journal*, might slant right while *Mother Jones* would slant left. Today, when news and information is available on the Google homepage or Facebook it is much more difficult to know what is fact and invention.

At the primary levels, the accuracy of information is rarely an issue because teachers can select the websites that students will be using. However, teachers in the upper grades will need to discuss the characteristics of websites that can be trusted for the accuracy of the information. *The New York Times* website offers the following questions to start the discussion about the veracity of news sources. When visiting a news site ask these questions and then try to determine the answer.

- Who made this?
- How was this made?
- Why was this made?
- When was this made?
- What is this missing?
- Where do I go from here?

The New York Times also has an excellent set of guidelines for evaluating new websites and for teaching students to evaluate websites: https://learning.blogs.nytimes.com/2015/10/02/skills-and-strategies-fake-news-vs-real-news-determining-the-reliability-of-sources/. The *Newslit* website also has useful resources for teachers: https://newslit.org/services/

Comprehension on the Internet

Comprehension and learning on the Internet involves many of the factors that we have previously discussed; knowledge, strategies, motivation, and metacognition, plus some new and different concerns. The environment of the Internet is more complex than the print word. The information on the Internet includes print, images, animation, audio, and video each linked to one another in a complex way, what was previously called hypertext. The Internet is expanding, with more links between information being added every day, making the navigation between sights increasingly difficult. The reader is forced to make many more decisions.

Reading information on the Internet requires two distinct types of prior knowledge. All readers still benefit by having specific knowledge of the topic they are reading, they also need to understand how the Internet works. Internet specific knowledge includes how to use search terms, how the home page and menus work, links to related topics, how to evaluate the information, and how to synthesize from several websites. There is evidence that topic knowledge and knowledge of how to use the Internet have different effects on young adolescent readers (Corio, 2011). Readers with low levels of online reading skills benefited from having higher amounts of specific topic knowledge. But for readers with strong skills in managing the Internet, topic specific knowledge mattered less.

The classroom teacher who is introducing a research project must be concerned about what students know of the topic and also what they know about using the Internet, because the Internet requires new strategies and heightens the importance of some old strategies.

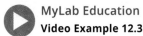
MyLab Education
Video Example 12.3
Here is a contrarian view of the effects of the Internet. Compare the perspective of this speaker to the one voiced in the chapter.
https://www.youtube.com/watch?v=Q3yUjgY8NKY

The process of comprehension on the Internet requires strategies that are different from the set we presented at the beginning of the chapter. When researchers examined how experienced readers read on the Internet, they discovered readers had to (a) identify and learn text content, (b) evaluate that content, and (c) monitor their reading. But the task of identifying and learning content is more complex on the Internet because there is more text to read and what is learned from each must be assembled as the pieces of a puzzle are interlocked. The reader has to determine the most fruitful path among the available information sites and then piece that information together. Thus, the construction and integration process that we outlined in Chapter 2 is more complex in the shifting Internet environment than with a static chapter in a history text. Reading on the Internet requires locating, evaluating, synthesizing, and communicating information.

Some digital text environments provide benefits for English learners because support can be embedded within the text. In one study, researchers documented that when definitions are one click away, embedded in the text, English learners read with greater comprehension and build vocabulary knowledge. While reading in the text, the students click on an unknown word, hear it pronounced, and retrieve its definition (Proctor, Dalton, & Grisham, 2007). The hypertext environment can also prompt readers to engage in a comprehension strategy, a prediction, and provide feedback.

Teaching Comprehension with the Internet

As we researched and wrote about comprehension on the Internet, we were struck by the many studies that theorized about reading in a complex digital environment (Briancarosa & Griffith, 2012; Leu, Kinzer, Coiro, Castek, & Henry, 2013) and the relatively few studies that described how readers read on the Internet (Corio & Dobler, 2007; Zhang & Duke, 2008). There were even fewer studies that evaluated programs and practices for helping students improve their comprehension of Internet text. The recommendations that follow are based on the insights we drew of how elementary and middle school students read on the Internet. We drew heavily on the work of Corio and Dobler (2007) and Afflerback and Cho (2009). We are going to look at four issues—purpose setting, prior knowledge, inferential thinking, and self-regulation or metacognition.

SETTING A PURPOSE

The Internet was designed to store massive amounts of information but it also distracts users from their appointed task. The Internet provides the reader with a much larger informational space, one that is tricky to navigate; therefore, setting and sticking to a purpose is critical (Zhang & Duke, 2008). Previous research indicates that we set different purposes depending on the genre of the text. The purpose we set for fiction, enjoyment and empathy, are different from reading a textbook or a website (Pare & Smart, 1994; Kucan & Beck, 1997). The Internet provides the reader with a great sense of control but it demands responsibility and a great sense of purpose.

Slatin (1991) argues that we enter the Internet for three specific reasons. At times, we use the Internet to search for specific pieces of information. After finding the number of Tony's awarded to *A Chorus Line*, nine, we leave the website. We use the Internet to answer *Right There* questions. The second reason we use the Internet is to create new understandings. We assemble ideas from one or more websites and refine our conceptual knowledge. We are answering *Think and Search* and *Author and Me* questions. We might look at Wikipedia to start our study of Thomas Jefferson, because that site pops up first, and then continue to website for Monticello to learn more about his home. The third use of the Internet is browsing or finding information that you are not looking for. The browser, "wanders rather aimlessly (but not carelessly) through an area, picking things up and putting them down as curiosity or momentary interest dictates (Slatin, 1991,p.159)." We are *On our Own*. We hope you notice the similarities between our previous discussion of questioning and reading on the Internet.

Zhang and Duke's (2008) interviews with adult readers suggest a three-step process we might teach to students. First, set a purpose or goal. I want to find out if goldfinches migrate south in the fall. This takes you to a search engine, search terms, and results. Next, evaluate the search results and decide which website will likely have the information you are seeking. You are evaluating the usefulness and the authenticity of the site. Finally, read the information on the site and decide if your purpose has been satisfied. Goldfinches do migrate south and winter in Mexico.

PRIOR KNOWLEDGE

Students draw upon several types of prior knowledge when they are reading on the Internet. They use general or conceptual knowledge, knowledge of informational text structures, knowledge of Internet text structures, and knowledge of Web-based search engines. Like our previous recommendations, it is useful to review what students know about a topic before they begin their Internet reading and it is useful to return to the topics like text features and text organizational patterns. Consider what one student said about the usefulness of text structure knowledge:

> Textbooks are divided into units, and then in chapters and then to lessons and sections. So you could see on the website that we visited that we started out with just the homepage, and then you'd pick something on the side and that was basically your unit, and then you had like five choices there, and that was a chapter and then you went in there and pick from like 10 or so there and that was like a lesson or a section. So it was similar to a book (Corio & Dobler, 2007, p. 230).

The competent reader on the Internet has a familiarity with website structure and the purposes of the various links on the homepage. For example, in Figure 12.9 the students grasp that the links at the top of the page guide you to either specific topics or general opinions (blogs) and current studies (Collections). One sixth grade student demonstrated considerable understanding. "Yeah, these [links in the left frame] are a little bit broader , . . but once you get to the page [pointing to the right frame], see it will bring you to a page that will be more in-depth so you can actually find what you need easier" (Corio & Dobler, 2007, p.231).

Figure 12.9 Navigating Menus on a Science Website

The Internet reader also needs a knowledge of search engines and keywords and how to formulate searches. Employing the right search terms helps to narrow down the information needed. Students need to know when to use a broad search term such as *environment* or a narrow one like *landfill*. They need to know that environment will bring lots of extraneous information when they are really trying to learn more about waste and recycling. Students also need to know that this is a trial and error process and that if the first search terms do not work they need to think of alternatives that will yield the results they are seeking.

Early in the chapter we introduced a lesson on the text features of books. Equally important are lessons on features of search engines and webpages. Knowing how these features work will help your students navigate with search engines and find information on a webpage. A lesson on digital text features should include the following:

- Search engines like Google and Chrome
- How to select terms and try alternatives
- Evaluating websites and Domains (.com, .org, .gov)
- Home pages and menus
- Navigation and Links

Overtime we suspect that a lesson on digital text features will replace the lesson on text features as students do most of their informational reading online.

INFERENTIAL REASONING

On the Internet, much is hidden and the reader does not know what she might find under the next link. Because of that, readers make predictions anticipating what they might find. Predictions, forward inferences anticipating what will happen next, are typically associated with reading fiction, while reading non-fiction seems to be associated with backward inferences, explaining a causal connection or support for an observation (Graesser, Singer, & Trabasso, 1994; Murry, Klin, & Myers, 1993; Leon, Escudero, & van den Broek, 2000). On the Internet students make predictions. For example, when looking at the results of a web page search one student said, "Now, I'm going to read the subtitles and a little information about it to see which one to choose … and I'm going to look here for what tiger parts are used for, (Corio & Dobler, 2007, p. 234.)." Readers know how to read the results of a web page search and predict which links are likely to provide the most useful information. Another student reported,

> I'm going to choose "Weather for hurricanes and typhoons" [click on link] and now I'm going to read the list of sites and information about them to see if they're good. And this looks like a good site 'cuz it says [after the hyperlink] "See how hurricanes are formed" and it might have information on hurricanes losing power.

Printed text, magazine articles, and chapters allow the reader to flip through the pages and preview the content. Just reading the headings and subheadings give the students a good sense of what the text will be about. Previewing is not as easy on the Internet, so educated guesses or predictions seem to take their place. Internet reading seems to require more inferring and evaluating choices.

These findings suggest that an appropriate lesson is to project a website on a whiteboard or smartboard and model how to search among the links within that site. Much like any other comprehension lesson, the teacher needs to explain the purpose of the lesson, how to use keywords to conduct a search, how to read the results, and how to make inferences about which results are likely to yield the most useful information. Engaging the students in these or predictions will sharpen their skills when they are conducting their own web page searches. This could be extended to conducting two web page searches, one more general and the other more specific and then evaluating the results of each search.

SELF-REGULATED READING

When we consider the research of Zhang and Duke (2008) and Corio and Dobler (2007) it is clear that the Internet compels and requires a considerable degree of self-regulation or metacognition. On the Internet, readers engage in some traditional form of self-regulation, the same type of thinking that occurs when reading print. Readers set goals, monitor, ask themselves does it make sense, reread when it does not, and at times try to repair breakdowns in comprehension. One student in the Corio and Dobler study said. "I'm going to try (search for) landfills again. I'm going to see if I didn't read something that maybe I should have. (p. 235)."

On the Internet, readers engage in a four step, self-regulated process, similar to the planning process we discussed a few sections back. Readers:

1. *Plan*. They ask themselves question like: What do I need to find out? Where should I begin? Where do I want to go?
2. *Predict*. They try to anticipate which website will lead to the best results. What website will provide answers to their questions?
3. *Monitor*. The readers monitor the choices they have made. They wonder if they are in the right place. Should I skim or read carefully?
4. *Evaluate*. Does what I am reading meet my goal? Is this the information that I need? Is this information trustworthy? What criteria can I use to judge this information? At this point the reader is back to step 1.

Like all strategies this one needs to be modeled by the teacher as she projects a website on the screen or Smartboard. The students need to follow along as they read the same text on their laptop computers. The teacher can then engage in the same type of guided practice that we have outlined in previous chapters. Eventually students will be ready for independent work on the Internet.

Reflect and Apply

7. The Internet presents new challenges and new opportunities to elementary and middle school students. Based on what we presented in this chapter, discuss with your colleagues how you will incorporate reading on the Internet in your classroom.

8. Can the Internet be used with routines like guided reading or the scaffolded reading experience or reciprocal teaching?

MyLab Education **Self-Check 12.4**

Assessing Reading Comprehension

Assessing reading comprehension is tricky because we can't observe comprehension as it happens (Pearson & Hamm, 2005). Somewhere deep inside the mind the reader is constructing an understanding of the text, a mental model. And a 'click' happens when the text makes sense and a 'clunk' when it does not. When we assess comprehension, we are looking at the product—the number and type of questions answered correctly, the information recalled or summarized and the writing the student completes in response to reading. Compared to decoding and fluency, which we can actually observe, comprehension is a messy task.

In Chapter 1 we introduced The Rand Reading Study Group comprehension model and that is the best starting point for considering how to assess reading comprehension. In the Rand model, comprehension arises from an interaction among the reader, the text, and the activity within a social context. To assess comprehension, we first need to look at the reader. Can she decode accurately, read with fluency, and bring a reasonable amount of vocabulary and prior knowledge to the page? Does the reader employ cognitive and metacognitive strategies and is the task we ask her to perform reasonably motivating? Next, we consider the text, its difficulty, its genre, and its coherence. There is ample research to suggest reading narratives is easier than informational text. Finally, we must consider the activity. Asking a child to retell a story he has just read is a vastly different activity than answering a string of multiple-choice questions. These three variables exist within a social content. A child who sits in front of a computer for three to four hours (yes it can take that long) answering a string of multiple-choice and open-ended questions is in a far different context than the child who comes to the teacher's desk to report on the novel she is currently reading.

With these cautions in mind, here are some suggestions for assessing reading comprehension in the classroom. We are not going to delve into standardized reading assessments; those we covered in Chapter 5. Your assessment should consider the reader, the text, the activity, and the context.

The Reader

1. Distinguish between comprehension problems and decoding or fluency problems. Can the students you are assessing read grade level texts with reasonable accuracy and fluency? You might want to start your comprehension assessment with a one-minute fluency test to determine basic skill level.
2. It would be valuable to know something about your students' vocabulary or language skills, but it is unlikely that a classroom teacher would have the time to administer these tests. If you believe that language is interfering with comprehension, check with the speech/language specialist or school psychologist.
3. Are the students motivated to read? In Chapter 3 we suggested a survey instrument that explores what motivates students to read.

The Text

1. Text selection is critical in assessing reading comprehension in the classroom. Select texts that are close to the students' reading level. Recognize that the match between the level of the text and the student's reading level is always imperfect.
2. The students should have some prior knowledge of the content. Chose a short piece of realistic fiction and a nonfiction article for which the students have some prior knowledge.

The Activity

There are many activities that assess reading comprehension and each changes the construct of comprehension in some way. Teachers have the option of creating multiple-choice tests, open ended or constructed response tests, cloze texts, and oral or written summaries. Each of these testing formats measures something different about the reading process and about comprehension specifically (Rauch & Hartig, 2010; Pearson, Garavaglia, Lycke, Roberts, et al., 1999). First, teachers have to decide what they want to know about their students' comprehension, because different types of text yield different answers.

Let's briefly examine these several types of assessments before making recommendations. Cloze tests or maze tests (we discussed the differences in Chapter 5) measure local comprehension, specifically vocabulary and the relationship between sentences. For assigning higher-level thinking they are inadequate (Shanahan, Kamil, & Tobin, 1982). Multiple-choice tests can assess both lower and higher levels of comprehension but they are more difficult to construct and there is some evidence that students engage in few strategies and less intertextual thinking than they do with open-ended test items (Pearson et al., 1999). Oral and written summaries tell the teacher something about the students' ability to remember and recall main ideas and details, with summaries producing more main ideas. Summaries limit insight into the students' inferential skills unless additional open-ended questions are asked.

Recommendations

We believe it is important for teachers to establish a routine system for assessing students' growth in reading comprehension. It is best to rely on homemade measures because the individual teacher or the grade level team can control the content and structure of these assessments. If you have been focusing on helping your students draw inferences, then the tests you design can focus on various types of inferences.

1. Select passages in which the content or the situations are reasonably familiar.
2. Write multiple choice questions to assess the students' understanding of the text-base or the literal information.
3. Write a few open-ended questions to assess higher order thinking—drawing inferences, interpretations, reaching for themes.
4. Avoid assessing too many skills or strategies within one test. If each skill (main idea, cause & effect) has its own item, then it becomes impossible to know if the students are having difficulty with the skills or the test items.
5. From week to week or month to month try to keep the tests reasonably similar so you can note changes in performance.

Concluding Remarks

In this chapter, we focused on teaching students to comprehend information text. To do so the students need prior knowledge, vocabulary, comprehension strategies, and motivating purpose to engage in these activities. Informational text presents some challenges not found in narratives. Students are typically reading information to learn; hence the demands of prior knowledge are greater. Informational texts are written with different structures than is fiction and students benefit from learning these structures. Strategies help and a few, such as determining importance, summarizing, and questioning, seem to be particularly important. Finally, it is important that all of this work is embedded within units of instruction that grab students' interest and motivate them to think deeply about issues that are important to them.

Your work with informational text should be aligned with your district or state standards. In almost all schools, students will be assessed on these standards starting in third grade. Our curriculum suggestions will help students meet the four basic goals of the Common Core State Standards. Using strategies, students will understand what the text says and what it means, locating information and making inferences. Our focus on text structure will help students understand how the craft and structure aid comprehension. Embedding all work in rich units of instruction will help students integrate and build knowledge. We trust your instructional units will expose students to increasingly challenging and interesting text.

Finally, we recognize that digital text presents new challenges for all teachers. We do not fully understand how best to use these texts in the classroom, but we have tried to give you a few suggestions and a few cautions. Digital texts offer great hope for building knowledge but the distractions inherent on the Internet suggest that the hopes of its creators might be difficult to realize.

Extending Learning

1. One excellent way to better understand and appreciate the nature of good comprehension instruction is to observe a teacher who is doing an excellent job of it. We suggest that you locate an effective teacher, observe her teaching, and afterward talk to her about it. Potential sources for locating teachers are your university instructor, your cooperating teacher, other teachers you know, and your classmates.

2. To really come to understand teaching informational text, it is useful to study successful programs. Earlier we presented Concept-oriented reading instruction, a reading program, a science program, likely both. We also recommend you examine Seeds of Science/Roots of Reading (Cervetti, Pearson, Bravo, & Barber, 2006), a program designed to promote the integration of science and reading. This program, like CORI, is built on the premise that strategies and text structure knowledge work best when they are tools of learning and not ends in themselves.

Children's Literature

Cruxton, B. (1998). *Discovering the Amazon Rainforest.* New York: Oxford University Press. This book in the Discovery series describes the tropical rainforest of Brazil and examines plans for saving the rainforest. 64 pages.

Fleischman, J. (2002). *Phineas Gage: A Gruesome but True Story About Brain Science.* Boston: Houghton Mifflin. This fascinating and admittedly gruesome book tells about Phineas Gage, who, having survived a hideous brain accident in the mid-19th century, provided doctors with valuable information about how the brain functions. 85 pages.

Guest, E. (2004). *Iris and Walter and the Substitute Teacher.* San Diego, CA: Gulliver/Harcourt. When Iris's beloved teacher becomes ill, her grandfather steps in as substitute, with mixed results. 44 pages.

Jackson, D. (2005). *ER Vets: Life in an Animal Emergency Room.* Boston: Houghton Mifflin. A behind-the-scenes look at the animal-saving drama of a veterinary ER room. 96 pages.

Johnson, G. & Cutchins, J. (1988). *Scaly Babies: Reptiles Growing Up.* New York: Morrow. This informational book has four chapters of descriptive text and color photographs highlighting snakes, lizards, crocodiles, turtles, and their young. 40 pages.

McPhail, D. (2002). *The Teddy Bear.* New York: St. Martin's Press. A young boy's lost teddy bear ends up being found by a homeless old man who learns to love it as much as the boy did. 32 pages.

Ritchie, R. (1999). *Mountain Gorillas in Danger.* Boston: Houghton Mifflin. This is a short book that features classic photographs of mountain gorillas while the text presents the threat they face. 32 pages.

Sellen, A. & Harper, R. (2002). *The Myth of the Paperless Office.* Cambridge, MA: The MIT Press.

Sendak, M. (1963). *Where the Wild Things Are.* New York: Harper & Row. When Max is sent to bed without his supper, he imagines a world where he is king of the "wild things." 32 pages.

Stanley, D. (2002). *Saladin: Noble Prince of Islam.* New York: Morrow. This picture book relates the life story of Saladin, a 12th-century Muslim hero who held off the crusaders and united his people. 48 pages.

Woolridge, C. (2001). *When Esther Morris Headed West: Women, Wyoming, and the Right to Vote.* New York: Holiday House. This inspiring nonfiction picture book tells about the life of Esther Morris, a trailblazer for women's rights. 32 pages.

Chapter 13
Writing and Reading

Learning Outcomes

After reading and studying this chapter you should be able to:

13.1 List and understand the classroom components that will create a climate where students will write and enjoy it.

13.2 Describe how writing boosts reading ability and select writing activities that will enhance reading comprehension.

13.3 Compare and contrast the writing process and a genre approach to writing how each enables students to construct extended pieces—stories, compositions and essays—and understand the skills that are part of each process.

13.4 Explain why revising, responding, and publishing are necessary to create strong and willing writers.

Classroom Vignette

Sixth-grader Derrick sits at his desk, his social studies book propped open in front of him, jotting down words in a notebook.

> Bryce glances over Derrick's shoulder. "What are you doing?" he asks.
> "Writing stuff."
> "Why?" Bryce asks.
> "So I remember it. We have a test tomorrow . . . in case you've forgotten."

In the third-grade room down the hall, Jasmine plops into a beanbag chair and starts reading a story her friend Brianna wrote. It's a story featuring the characters in a book the class just read. Next to her, Brianna giggles as she reads Jasmin's story.

Next door, two fifth graders, Mark and Diego, are working together to construct a concept map of the ideas in a science chapter on geology. They debate which concepts to put on the maps, how to arrange, and how to connect them.

In the first grade, the students are making and writing Mother's Day cards. Sasha carefully writes, "I hope you have a great day. Love, Sasha.

Each of these writers is using writing for a different purpose—for learning, for understanding, for communicating, and for just having fun with words—as this chapter will illustrate. Equally important, each of these writers is improving his or her reading ability. Working on spelling, sentence structure, writing about ideas, and constructing complete stories has a strong effect on reading ability and, surprisingly, the effect of writing on reading ability is as strong as the techniques we have shared about teaching reading (Graham & Hebert, 2010).

The Reading-Writing Connection

As you know, we write for a number of different reasons and audiences, and *how* we do it—the *process*—is different for each. But no matter what the reason, the audience, or the process, what we write is usually meant to be read, either by ourselves or by someone else. And, quite obviously, anything we read has to have been written by someone. Writing and reading, as Bernice Cullinan (1993) has noted, are two sides of the same coin. Like speaking and listening, they are two complementary components of a communications process (Pearson, 1990) and depend on similar cognitive structures and strategies (Snow, Griffith, & Burns, 2005).

Although there are similarities between reading and writing, viewed from another perspective they are substantially different, especially in their execution, and each process requires a very different brand of instruction. To understand the differences, consider this imaginary dialogue between Margaret Mitchell and an unknowing reader in 1942 at a cocktail party in Atlanta. "I just read the most amazing book, *Gone with the Wind*." "I wrote *Gone with the Wind*." Writing and reading *Gone with the Wind* are starkly different mental activities that differ in intent, planning, execution, and rewards.

Even though this reading-writing connection might appear obvious, these two language arts have traditionally been taught as separate subjects in U.S. classrooms. Today, however, virtually all educators agree that combining reading and writing in the classroom makes a great deal of sense, both theoretically and practically (Atwell, 1987, 1998b; Graham & Hebert 2010; Moore, Moore, Cunningham, & Cunningham, 2003; Olson, 1996; Routman, 2003, 2005). Fifty years ago, John Carroll (1966) suggested that reading and writing be experienced as parallel and reciprocal processes, in much the same way that their own speaking and listening are parallel and reciprocal to younger children. We will even step back 400 years and quote Francis Bacon: "Reading maketh a full man; conference a ready man; and writing an exact man."

Regularly engaging students in all types of writing improves reading ability (Graham & Hebert, 2010). Integrating the results of 57 studies, Graham and Hebert showed that when students write about the text they read, their comprehension improves. The effects of writing on reading ability are as great as developing reading fluency and directly teaching comprehension.

> Having students write about a text should enhance reading comprehension because it affords greater opportunities to think about ideas in a text, requires them to organize and integrate those ideas into a coherent whole, fosters explicitness, facilitates reflection, encourages personal involvement with texts, and involves students transforming ideas into their own words (Graham & Hebert, 2010, p.13.)

Sounds much like Francis Bacon. Throughout this chapter, we explore this reciprocal process of reading and writing, focusing on a variety of writing forms, purposes, and procedures. We will stress writing activities that improve reading ability. But before we can begin that discussion, the stage must be set. The reading-writing classroom—what does it look, sound, and feel like?

A Positive Reading-Writing Environment

"I write because I have something important to say, and I think people need to hear it!" says Brandon, a fifth-grader. Brandon's heartfelt, if somewhat boastful, comment succinctly captures in one sentence at least three critical truths about writing that will greatly affect your own thinking about the writing opportunities you provide for students:

- Students should write for important purposes.
- What students write should be valued by themselves, by you, and by the others in your classroom community.

- Writing should function to communicate or to foster the writers' own learning, understanding, or appreciation.

If literacy is to prosper in our classrooms, we need to create an environment in which children view themselves as writers. Writers flourish in an atmosphere in which written words are used and valued and writers are encouraged to take risks while being supported in their attempts. This environment involves both the intellectual climate of the classroom and its physical attributes.

The Intellectual Climate

The intellectual climate of the ideal reading-writing classroom conveys this message: "We are all readers and writers. Together we are all learning to be better readers and writers." The intellectual climate will be reflected in the number of children seen reading and writing at any given moment and their engagement in their writing tasks. It will be reflected in the students' writing displayed throughout the room—student-made books, posters, bulletin boards. It will be reflected in the faces and voices of students meeting to read and respond to each other's writing.

In a positive classroom writing environment, students write often and for a variety of purposes and also feel free to take risks. Writing across the curriculum provides extended opportunities for students to write, and when they do so, their comfort level increases (Spandel, 2005). Students need to be given opportunities to write without fear of criticism. One very effective way teachers can help establish this risk-taking atmosphere is to become writers themselves. Doing so helps teachers understand the arduous process involved in transforming thoughts into words and to appreciate what it is like to have those words evaluated. Another important element in the intellectual climate of a classroom is the teacher's role as modeler. Writing in front of students, showing them what you are doing, and talking about what you are doing and why provides students with concrete examples of how writers work (Dyson & Freedman, 1991; Graves, 1991; Routman, 2005; Temple, Nathan, Temple, & Burris, 1993).

The Physical Environment

Students need *time* to write, a *place* to do it, and *materials* to write with. The physical environment of a productive reading-writing classroom will reflect the attitude "This is a great place to read and write!" Joanne Hindley, a teacher at the Manhattan New School, has developed this kind of environment. This is what she had to say about the writing environment of her classroom (Hindley, 1998, reprinted with permission).

> I think carefully about how the room needs to look in order to allow comfortable working space for the whole group, small-group, paired, and individual working situations. Materials need to be clearly labeled and organized so that it is easy for children to use and take care of them. This not only promotes good "housekeeping" in the small space we share, it also ensures that the room belongs to all of *us* and not just to *me*. It is much easier for 30 people to take on the responsibility of caring for our home than for one person to do it for the other 29.
>
> When we as teachers think about ourselves as learners, we are able to envision what our students need in terms of support from us and from the environment. Creating an atmosphere that encourages students to interact, feel independent, and take pride in the upkeep of their classrooms is critical for everything we do throughout the year.
>
> —Joanne Hindley, elementary teacher

The main goal is to provide a place where students feel safe and comfortable exploring ideas on paper. In the Classroom 13.1 gives you suggestions for creating such an environment.

In the Classroom 13.1

Guidelines for Creating a Positive Writing Environment

- Establish a predictable writing time.
- Create a writing center equipped with writing necessities—writing materials, dictionaries, a thesaurus, and books on the writer's craft.
- Provide opportunities to write throughout the day in all the subject areas for a variety of purposes and audiences.
- Provide enough computers or tablets so all students can research, compose, and revise.
- Become a writer yourself and share with your students your writing and the struggles you experience in writing.
- Provide students with guidance and constructive feedback.
- Stock the classroom library with texts in a variety of genres—magazines, picture books, biographies, informational books, novels, beginning chapter books—that reflect a wide range of interests and readability levels.
- Read aloud quality literature—fiction, nonfiction, and poetry—that can serve as models of good writing.
- Model writing forms and techniques.
- Guide students to write about topics that are important to them—writing that has a genuine purpose and a real audience.
- Provide opportunities for students to share their writing with their peers and receive constructive feedback from them.
- Provide direct instruction on matters of mechanics—grammar, usage, spelling, and punctuation—and the writer's craft—dialogue, characterization, voice, engaging beginnings, and so on—as the need arises.

The Writing Workshop

One way to create the physical and intellectual environment we advocate is the writing workshop. The writing workshop is a designated time during the school day when children write individually or collaboratively on topics of their own choosing, for their own purposes. This writing may take place several times a week or, in some classrooms, every day. As Charles Temple and his colleagues (Temple, Nathan, & Temple, 2012) point out, the writing workshop provides a setting in which children's "own interest in life, coupled with their desire to express themselves," motivates them to write. Additionally, it provides a predictable structure and routine in which students feel comfortable taking risks, "collaborate with their peers, and take control of their own learning" (Hindley, 1998).

Over the past 25 years, educators have discovered that when students know they will have a chunk of time to write, a time in which they will be actively involved in writing for reasons that are important to them, they really develop as writers. Donald Graves (1991) suggests that it takes at least 3 hours a week for this habit of mind to take hold, and students begin "rehearsing off stage" what they will write about. The writing workshop—a concept developed by Nancie Atwell (1987, 1998b) and a number of other teachers and researchers—is designed to provide your writers with that sort of time.

In the writing workshop, both teacher and student have equally important roles. The teacher's role is that of facilitator, coach, and guide—establishing a community of writers who interact and support one another through all the phases of the writing process. The student's role is to write and encourage and support other writers. Students who confer with their classmates provide a sounding board and offer suggestions.

A typical writing workshop has a number of key components and activities, with student writing at the core, as shown in Figure 13.1. Instruction takes place through mini-lessons, demonstrations, and shared writing activities, as shown in Figure 13.2. These activities usually occur before students begin their own writing in the workshop setting. The writing workshop is coupled with assigned and wide independent reading. Reading provides the writer with ideas to write about and the opportunity to learn about genre and text structure. When students have frequent opportunities to discuss their reading they begin to read like a writer noticing the structures and language that writers can employ.

Students who find writing a challenge, who speak and write in a dialect other than standard English, or whose native language is not English may profit from extra support and extra time. The following suggestions offer such students help with writing tasks; some were recommended by Robin Scarcella (1996), director of the ESL program at the University of California at Irvine:

- Keep directions simple, and check to be sure students understand them.
- Have a model of the completed writing task available.
- Demonstrate or model the writing activity.
- Guide the students through the activity.
- Have needed writing supplies readily available.
- Provide feedback that is both comprehensible and constructive; conference often.
- Show respect for students' home languages and cultures.

Figure 13.1 Key Components of the Writing Workshop

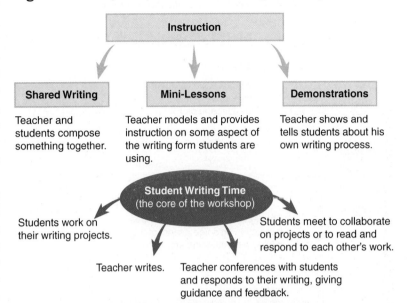

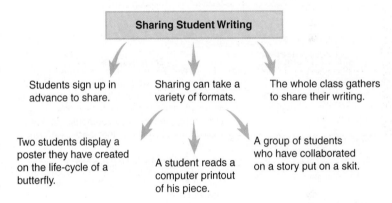

A writing activity that shows respect for students' home languages and cultures encourages students to write about stories, songs, or customs from their home cultures or in their own languages (Canney, Kennedy, Schroeder, & Miles, 1999). *Salsa Stories* by Lulu Delacre, in which characters from several South American countries tell stories of their customs and holiday traditions, would be a good read-aloud springboard and model for this writing activity. Should students be allowed to write in their own dialects as well as their home languages? As educator Lisa Delpit (1988) has eloquently argued, students of color need and deserve to become adept at writing in standard English, and teachers need to assist them in doing so. However, in some situations, such as writing stories that are based on the writer's personal experiences and reflect his cultural heritage, dialect is definitely appropriate, especially if the writer includes dialogue. Three questions can serve to guide both you and your students with regard to whether dialect is appropriate and effective in a piece of writing: What is the purpose for writing? Who is the audience? Who is talking in the story?

MyLab Education **Self-Check 13.1**

MyLab Education **Application Exercise 13.1:** Writer's Workshop in Second Grade

Figure 13.2 Three Types of Writing Workshop Instruction—Mini-Lessons, Shared Writing, and Demonstrations

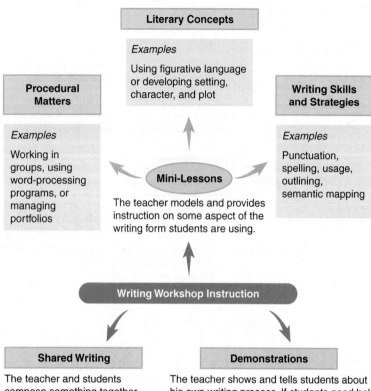

Literary Concepts

Examples

Using figurative language or developing setting, character, and plot

Procedural Matters

Examples

Working in groups, using word-processing programs, or managing portfolios

Writing Skills and Strategies

Examples

Punctuation, spelling, usage, outlining, semantic mapping

Mini-Lessons

The teacher models and provides instruction on some aspect of the writing form students are using.

Writing Workshop Instruction

Shared Writing

The teacher and students compose something together.

Example

Students supply words and punctuation for a letter to an author whose work they are reading while the teacher writes these on the board or large newsprint.

Demonstrations

The teacher shows and tells students about his own writing process. If students need help in any particular area (such as writing a paragraph), teachers can demonstrate how *they* go about writing in that particular form.

Example (for formal letter writing)

Using an overhead projector, talk through the decisions you made regarding word choice, format, and tone in writing a formal letter.

Writing to Learn and to Understand

Typically, a student does informal writing for his own purposes—to learn from his reading, to better understand ideas, and to explore or personally engage with what he is reading. This writing will take the form of notes, lists, diagrams, journals, summaries, and the like. In this section, we take a look at some of the types of writing elementary and middle school students are likely to find most useful. Graham and Hebert (2010), in their extensive review of the literature, note that responding to reading, summarizing, writing notes, and writing questions and answering them in a written form all increase reading ability, particularly comprehension. It is important to consider when, why, and how each type of writing should take place.

Often, we use writing as a vehicle to learn about something or to more fully understand it. When students write to learn, they are using written language to help them wrestle with information, ideas, feelings, and intuitions. Reading done in subject matter areas such as science, social studies, and literature offers rich opportunities for this kind of writing, which fosters comprehension and personal response. In this kind of writing, students are actually "thinking on paper" or perhaps on a computer screen. In other words, they are using written language to discover, clarify, refine, expand, or reflect on meaning. They are in Bacon's term develop an exact mind.

James Britton and his colleagues (1975) have noted that this type of writing is closely related to talk, and Richard Vacca and Wayne Linek (1992) point out that such writing can serve as a catalyst for reading and studying content area material. In fact, many of the writing-to-learn activities we discuss are often accompanied by small-group discussion centered on the topics students are writing about.

What kinds of writing can students do to help them better learn, understand, and personally respond to the information and ideas in the texts they read? To enhance their ability to "think on paper" and actively integrate new knowledge into old? To prepare them for more formal genres such as reports and stories? We discuss note-taking, brainstorming, quick writing, summarizing, semantic mapping, Venn diagrams, and personal response journals in this section. We described several of these procedures in Chapters 11 and 12 when we talked about helping students comprehend the various texts they read. Here, we focus on the writing component of these endeavors.

Note Taking

Although note-taking is perhaps the most traditional of all the activities we discuss in this section, students do not pick it up naturally. To help students learn how to take notes, Regie Routman (1995) recommends using demonstration, participation, practice, and sharing in a variety of note-taking situations. These situations include taking notes from texts, oral presentations, films, and videos. To be successful at note-taking, students not only need repeated practice in the skill but also need to have it demonstrated to them again and again throughout the school year. In the Classroom 13.2 shows a sample lesson adapted from a procedure Routman and third-grade teacher Julie Beers used with a group of third-graders who were getting ready to begin research reports on animals.

Routman offers the following suggestions for additional work on note taking:

- Have students work in pairs instead of groups, with one acting as scribe and the other giving suggestions and feedback.
- Allow students to take notes on their first reading of the material with their books open.
- Repeat note-taking sessions throughout the year, demonstrating and working with various genres and contexts.

Brainstorming and Quick Writing

When brainstorming, students quickly jot down single words or short phrases that come to mind in response to a topic. For example, before a group of third-graders read Steve Parker's *It's a Frog's Life! My Story of Life in a Pond*, they brainstormed words and phrases that the word *pond* brought to mind and came up with this list:

water	frogs	pollywogs	weeds	woods	forest
ducks	green	slime	mud	turtles	

And before sixth-graders read *Sparks Fly Upward*, Carol Matas's historical novel about a Russian immigrant family in 1910 trying to adapt to a new culture and new circumstances, they wrote down words and phrases in response to the word immigrant. Brainstorming can be done individually, as a small-group activity, or as a whole-class activity, either before or after reading. However it is done, brainstorming generally leaves students with some raw material that they will employ as they read or write.

In the Classroom 13.2

Instructional Routines

Sample Lesson on Note Taking

1. Make a copy of the first page of the selection students will be reading and leave the other half of the page blank. (For example, Routman and Beers made a transparency of the page on alligators and crocodiles from *Zoo Books 2* [Wildlife Education, 1986].) This transparency will be used on an overhead projector to demonstrate note taking. (This activity works best with an old overhead projection and transparencies. If you don't have one around you can adapt it to the document camera or a computer image projected through an LCD projector.)

2. Slowly read the passage aloud, highlighting key phrases and important information by underlining them with a yellow marker. Verbalize the thought processes you go through in deciding what to highlight. Demonstrate to students how to turn these key phrases into notes by writing them on the right side of the transparency. The process shares much in common with determining importance, which we outlined in Chapter 12.

3. Review with the students how titles, headings, bold print and topic sentences are good placed to being note taking. Demonstrate the process several times with additional pages from the text, inviting students to participate in choosing the notes to write down.

4. Have students form small groups. Give each group a photocopied page from the book they will read, a blank transparency, and two pens—a yellow highlighter and a black marking pen for writing on transparencies.

5. Tell students to place the blank transparency over the article and underline key phrases and important points with the yellow marker (as they did earlier as a whole class) and then write their notes on the right side of the page with the black marking pen.

6. Invite each group to come up to the overhead projector with the completed transparency. Ask members to place it over a transparency of the text they have just read, and encourage them to discuss their notes. Give feedback and guidance on their note taking, and invite other students to give feedback as well.

In contrast to brainstorming, quick writing—a technique popularized by Peter Elbow (2006)—is a way of very quickly getting down connected sentences and phrases on a topic without stopping to correct or analyze them. Simply stated, quick writing is jotting down thoughts on a topic as quickly as they come to mind. Because the students are not worrying about mechanics, structure, or communicating their ideas to someone else, they are free to generate many thoughts and ideas, and they gain confidence and fluency in writing. The following quick write was done by a fifth-grade student after reading an excerpt from *Strange Plants* by Howard Halpern and thinking aloud with a partner (Armbruster, McCarthey, & Cummins, 2005).

> I'm writing about stinging nettles. Stinging nettles have sharp needles that have acid in it, and, if you get a needle in you, you will get a read warm rash that stings and hurts very, very, very badly. It will sting for 2 hours or, if its very bad, it will last for a day or even more. I would hate to run into that plant because I've gotton poked by a needle really hard, and it hurts!

Like brainstorming, quick writing is a strategy students can use as a prereading or postreading activity. Quick writing before students read a text can help them relate the reading to their lives and activate and build schemata, bringing ideas from the subconscious level to the conscious level. For example, before third- or fourth-graders read any one of Joanna Cole's Magic School Bus books, they might do a quick write on what they know about the topic of the book—the human body, for example. Or as a postreading activity after reading Russell Freedman's *Eleanor Roosevelt*, sixth-graders could quick write on the most memorable moments in the biography.

Both brainstorming and quick writing are excellent strategies for generating ideas before or after students read a particular text. Both can also be very effective strategies for gathering thoughts and ideas in the beginning stages of formal writing.

Semantic Mapping and the Venn Diagram

Semantic mapping and Venn diagrams make use of brainstorming to some degree but take it a step or two further by organizing the brainstormed ideas in a specific way. As we discussed in Chapter 10, and provide examples in the Appendix, semantic mapping (also called clustering or webbing), words generated in brainstorming are linked to a nucleus word, which reflects a main idea. This nucleus word functions in much the same way as the main idea in an outline or a topic sentence in writing a paragraph.

Semantic maps can have one nucleus idea or several and can be used with both narrative and informational texts. Students can develop them individually or as a small- or large-group activity, and they can be used either as a prereading activity to activate prior knowledge, as a postreading activity to recall and organize pertinent information, or as both when students update the map after reading a text (Heimlich & Pittelman, 1986). As a postreading activity, semantic mapping can also serve as a helpful prewriting technique preceding more formal writing such as reports, stories, or biographies. Figure 13.3 shows a semantic map developed by first-graders after reading "Kate and the Zoo," a story from a basal series.

Figure 13.3 Semantic Map Used with First-Graders After Reading "Kate and the Zoo"

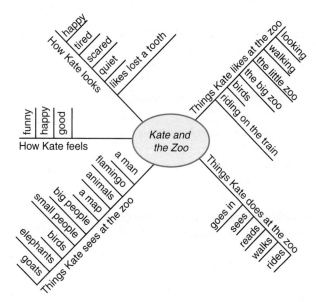

SOURCE: Heimlich, Joan E., & Pittelman, Susan D. (1986). *Semantic Mapping: Classroom Applications.* Copyright © 1986 by the International Reading Association (www.reading.org).

A variation of the semantic map is the star organizer (Poindexter & Oliver, 1998/1999), which can help primary-grade students in the prewriting stages to organize their thoughts when writing a description. The framework can be used as a map for writing a paragraph describing an object. Figure 13.4 shows a star organizer for writing a paragraph about a friend.

Like the semantic map, the Venn diagram is a way to organize ideas and present them graphically. However, in a Venn diagram, two or more topics or ideas are contrasted. Consisting of circles that intersect, the diagram highlights the similarities and differences between topics. The differences are indicated by words or phrases written in the nonoverlapping parts of the circles, whereas the similarities are written in the space created by the intersection of the circles. Figure 13.5 shows how one group of fifth-graders used a Venn diagram to compare and contrast the planets Earth and Venus after reading *The Planets in Our Solar System* by Franklyn Mansfield Branley.

The Venn diagram is a particularly effective device for students to use when reading informational texts in which two or more topics are being compared and contrasted or when reading narratives and two characters can be compared. It can also be used to compare and contrast books that explore a similar theme or topic, such as Ann Martin's middle-grade novel *Belle Teal*, a fictional account of desegregation, with Ruby Bridges's photobiography *Through My Eyes*, a personal account of the author's own experiences with desegregation. It can also be used with characters in the same story, such as Prince Brat and Jemmy in Sid Fleischman's *The Whipping Boy* or Princess Elizabeth and Iris in Jane Resh Thomas's *The Counterfeit Princess*.

Figure 13.4 Star Organizer for a Five-Sentence Paragraph

> She has brown hair and blue eyes.
> She likes to play soccer.
> My friend Chantelle
> She is funny.
> She makes me laugh.
> She is my best friend.

Writing Summaries

Summarizing is an activity that improves both reading comprehension and writing ability. There are multiple ways of teaching students to summarize and the research suggests that all are effective. We have discussed summary writing for informational text in Chapter 12, but here we will consider summary writing for narrative text. When students read a novel, they have multiple opportunities to write a summary. Before the students attempt any of these summaries, the teacher should model the process on a white board or use a document camera. Point out the important elements of the summary—note they will change depending upon where the students are in the text. For example, an early summary would include characters, their traits, the setting, and the problem.

Here are a few suggestions.

- After reading the first few chapters, the students can summarize the text focusing on the characters and the setting.

- Later in the novel the students can summarize what they know about the main characters focusing on his or her traits.

Figure 13.5 Venn Diagram Comparing and Contrasting Venus and Earth

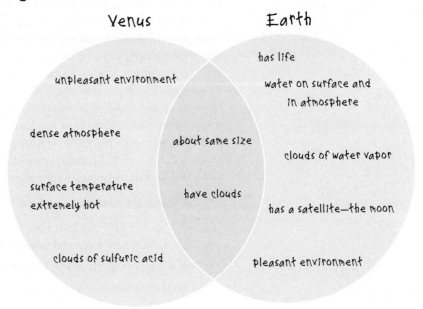

Venus | Earth

unpleasant environment

has life

water on surface and in atmosphere

dense atmosphere

about same size

clouds of water vapor

surface temperature extremely hot

have clouds

has a satellite—the moon

clouds of sulfuric acid

pleasant environment

- Midpoint through the novel the students can describe the climax of the story and the events that turn the action.
- At the end of the novel the students can summarize the themes and consider how these themes relate to their own lives.

Journals

Perhaps you have used journals yourself, either for personal reasons or as a learning tool in academic classes. If so, you're probably not alone, for journal writing is a widely recommended procedure. Chris Anson and Richard Beach (1995) view the journal as a genre in its own right and a "significant tool for learning." Toby Fulwiler (1987) suggests that journaling engages the writer in a vast range of cognitive activities—observing, questioning, speculating, becoming aware of oneself, digressing, synthesizing, revising, and informing. Routman (1991) describes the journal as a "nonthreatening place to explore learnings, feelings, happenings, and language through writing" and of significant benefit to both teacher and student. The following list shows some of the specific benefits Routman highlights:

- Promotes fluency in writing
- Provides opportunity for reflection
- Validates personal experiences and feelings
- Provides a safe, private place to write
- Promotes thinking and makes it visible
- Promotes development of written language conventions
- Provides a vehicle for evaluation
- Provides a personal record for students

Four types of journals—reading logs, learning logs, double-entry journals, and dialogue journals—are particularly effective for developing reading-writing connections and promoting thinking and learning.

READING LOGS
Sometimes called *response journals*, reading logs are journals in which students record personal responses to the literature they read. Before students write in their journals, you will want to talk about some of the topics they might write about and model how you write responses in your own reading journal. In the Classroom 13.3, which shows one way to introduce primary-grade students to response journals, is based on an approach used by first-grade teacher Barbara Werchadlo (Wollman-Bonilla & Werchadlo, 1995).

As good teachers always do, you will want to reflect on the success of the journaling activity and make adjustments if necessary. After Werchadlo's first experiences with response journals, she decided to provide more modeling of varied responses and give prompts that were even more open-ended. She did this in order to help children view journals not as a place to simply retell or predict what might happen in a text, but rather as a place to react personally. The following is a list of possible open-ended questions:

- How does the story make you feel?
- Does anything puzzle you? If so, explain.
- Do the characters seem real to you? Why or why not?
- Are you enjoying the story? Why or why not?
- Are there words that you particularly like? What are they, and why do you like them?
- Does anything in the story remind you of your own life?
- Is anything the author says particularly meaningful to you? Why?

In the Classroom 13.3

Instructional Routines

Introducing the Response Journal to Primary-Grade Students

- During the first week of school, read aloud a chapter a day from an engaging book such as *James and the Giant Peach* by Roald Dahl.
- For the first few days, model how to write a response by expressing a few ideas while thinking aloud. Then write a sentence on the board such as *James is very sad because his parents are gone* or *James does not like living with Aunt Sponge and Aunt Spiker.*
- When you think the children are ready, perhaps on the third day, give them their own journals. These can be made by stapling story paper (blank on the top and lined on the bottom) between manila or cardstock covers that the children can decorate.
- Ask students to write in their journals about the story. Give them writing prompts such as "What did you like about this chapter?" or "What do you think will happen next?"
- Invite students to illustrate their responses when they have finished writing or before they write. Sometimes drawing first, especially for young students, provides a stimulus for writing.

Figure 13.6 provides a sample entry in a fifth-grade student's reading log, written after he had read the first chapter of *Baby* by Patricia MacLachlan.

In a study of English language learners' comprehension development, researchers William Saunders and Claude Goldenberg (1999) found that certain kinds of literature log prompts benefited students. For each chunk of a reading selection the teacher assigned, students were given the following kinds of prompts: "write about a personal experience (related to the story); elaborate on something that happened in the story (e.g., assume the role of the character); or analyze/interpret some aspect of the story or theme." These kinds of prompts are open-ended and enable students to express their ideas as they are able. Following writing, students in the study most often shared and elaborated on their responses and thinking in small groups with the teacher. Called instructional conversations, students shared their understanding of the story and its theme(s) and their personal experiences related to the story. They used their literature log entries to support their discussion.

LEARNING LOGS

In contrast to reading logs or response journals, learning logs are generally oriented to subject matter rather than personal response and are used in content areas such as science, mathematics, and social studies. They can include a variety of entries—questions to the author, summaries of the material, explanations of problems solved, or recording of observations as in an experiment. As Stephen Koziol, Brad Minnick, and Kim Riddell (1996) observe, one important function of learning logs is to enable students to select, connect, and organize knowledge in ways that allow them to better understand what they read. They have suggested three types of questions for learning logs: questions that elicit prior knowledge, questions that encourage students to interact with the text, and questions that ask students to respond retrospectively to what they have learned. Figure 13.7 shows a question and a response for each of these three types, relating to the book *California Condor: Flying Free* by Bonnie Graves.

To support these learning logs, teachers should keep a word wall at the writing center. On this wall, teachers place the content words that students need for their writing. For example, when students write about a personal experience that is related to a story, they need words to express the emotions reflected in

Figure 13.6 Reading Log Entry

Chapter One: I like the characters, but they are kind of wierd. I mean like there names. The grandmother is called Byrd. The main character is Larkin (a girl) and her friend (a boy) is Lalo.

Grandmother (Byrd!) wears fancy sox (black ones with jewels!) and Larkin's father dances on the coffee table!!

Figure 13.7 Three Types of Learning Log Questions and Responses

Anticipatory Question	Reactive Question	Retrospective Question
What do you want to know about the, California condor?	*What didn't you understand about the California condor?*	*What information did you learn about the California condor that was the most interesting or important?*
I'd like to know why they almost became extinct	I didn't understand why Topa's parents abandoned him or why he couldn't survive on his own.	I learned that it has taken a long, long time to bring only a few more condors back. It has taken a lot of work. I hope I get to see a condor fly sometime. They're huge!

the narrative. The teacher posts words like *anxious, nervous, elated, cautious*, and so forth. Before students begin to write, these words are reviewed. If the students are writing about the weather then the word wall contains words like *tornado, precipitation, low-pressure,* and *wind.* Sometimes a picture beside the word helps the students remember its meaning.

DOUBLE-ENTRY JOURNALS

Double-entry journals are two-column journals that can be used when reading any type of text. In the left column students might write a quotation or a selected passage from the text, and in the right column their comments, questions, or responses to the quotation or passage. Or instead of writing quotations or passages from the text in the left column, the student might write about events, characters, or settings in the left column and then make personal comments on them on the right side, as illustrated in the example in the Classroom Portrait in Chapter 14.

DIALOGUE JOURNALS

In a dialogue journal, a teacher and a student or two students carry on a written conversation over a designated period of time. As you can see from the following example, the entries in a dialogue journal look very much like informal letters. These entries are written by a fourth-grader and her teacher. They are dialoguing about a book the teacher recommended, *The Tiger Rising* by Kate DiCamillo.

> Dear Mrs. G,
>
> I'm on chapter 8 of *The Tiger Rising*. It's a good book so far. I'm not sure if the tiger is real or if Rob just imagined it. I can't imagine finding a caged tiger in my neighborhood!!! I wish Rob could make some friends. But I think he will, probably, I hope. What was your favorite part of the book? So far the tiger is my favorite!!
>
> Dear Andrea,
>
> I'm glad you like *The Tiger Rising*. It's interesting that you think the tiger might be imagined. I'm not going to give away if you are right or not! You'll just have to keep reading to find out, also to find out if Rob does make friends. After you finish reading, I'll tell you my favorite part. I don't want to give anything away!

The dialogue journal can be used to help students become more aware of the power of language (Mode, 1989) and of audience (Wollman-Bonilla, 2001), to help students become more comfortable about writing and more willing to write (Britton et al., 1975; Hannon, 1999), to assist students from varied backgrounds in learning to write (Fulwiler, 1987), and as a means for individualizing instruction (Werderich, 2002).

All types of journals—from reading and learning logs to double-entry and dialogue journals—can be used successfully in classrooms from kindergarten through middle school. However, a word of caution: Do not overuse them. All writing forms have a

In the Classroom 13.4

Instructional Routines

Guidelines for Journal Writing

- Read and comment on students' journal entries as often as possible. Doing so not only gives you the chance to offer encouragement and feedback but demonstrates to students that you value this activity.
- Make the purposes for journal writing explicit. Students need to know *why* they are writing in their journals and *how* it will benefit them. For example, students might be using their journals to generate ideas for an extended writing project.
- Use journals purposefully and carefully, or, as Regie Routman (2005) advises, "Make sure the writing children do in response to their reading is worth their time." Misuse or overuse could cause students to view journaling as trite, boring, or a waste of time.
- If and when students become bored with the repetitive aspect of journal writing, drop the activity for a while.

time and a place. Variety is the spice of the student writer's life. To ensure that journals are useful and not viewed by students as busywork, In the Classroom 13.4 offers some worthwhile suggestions by teacher Raymond Philippot.

In this section—Writing to Learn and to Understand—we have highlighted just a few of the many ways writing can be used to help students read, understand, respond to literature, and learn subject matter, as well as prepare them for writing to communicate to an audience what they have learned. Whatever the writing form students use, the primary goal is to get them to think about what they are learning, to try to make sense of the reading experience, and to discover meaning for themselves and their lives. This, of course, is what gives learning its real purpose.

Reflect and Apply

1. Think about the term *writing to learn*. What does it mean to you? Discuss your response with a classmate or classmates.
2. In addition to journal writing, six other writing-to-learn activities were discussed in this section. Give an example of an appropriate reading situation for using each of these six techniques. For example, when might it be appropriate for students to take notes? To quick write? To keep a journal?

MyLab Education **Self-Check 13.2**

MyLab Education **Application Exercise 13.2:** Dialogue Journals

Teaching the Process and Skills of Writing

There are several approaches to teaching the skills of writing and the process of writing. All of these have a positive but moderate effect on reading ability (Graham & Hebert, 2010) In this section, we will feature two approaches to developing students' writing ability, a process approach and a genre approach. We will then consider various genres of writing—letter, biographies, narratives, and informational reports.

MyLab Education
Video Example 13.1
This video shows how one teacher introduces the writing process to her class.

A Process Approach to Writing

In recent years, a particular approach to teaching writing—the process approach—has been widely explored, and evidence indicates that students in classrooms that include more elements of the process approach indeed become better writers than those in less process-oriented classrooms (Persky, Daane, & Ying, 2003). We think this evidence is convincing, and we strongly endorse the process approach as a method of teaching writing. However, a good deal of the writing students create in relation to their reading is less planned, less lengthy, less polished, and less formal than that for which the process approach is appropriate. As Gail Tompkins (1996) has pointed out, effective reading teachers give students plenty of opportunities to do both process writing and informal writing.

For some writing projects and in some situations, the writer goes through several stages of writing, particularly when writing formal pieces. With the release of Janet Emig's (1971) study of twelfth-graders' composing process and Donald Graves's (1975) observations of 7-year-old writers, educational researchers began focusing on the process involved in writing and its implications for classroom instruction. The result of this research has been a shift of emphasis away from the end product of writing toward the process involved in the writing.

Step into a third-grade classroom for a moment, and witness a reading-writing event:

> Gabbie, wearing gray sweatpants, high-top sneakers, and a wide grin, is sitting in the "author's chair," reading her story "The Noise in the Laundry Chute." You are impressed that a third-grader could write so well. You notice, however, that Gabbie's face, her body language, and her whole demeanor are speaking even more eloquently than her words: "This is good. I like this and am proud of my story."

Gabbie didn't get to this moment of accomplishment and satisfaction in one quick leap but went through several stages before arriving at the author's chair to read her "finished" product. First, she engaged in *prewriting* activities, which helped her generate ideas. With the teacher acting as a recorder, the whole class had brainstormed "scary moments" together on the chalkboard. As a second prewriting activity, Gabbie did a quick write to let her own thoughts run free and then capture them on paper, discovering what she knew and how she felt about the frightening moments in her life. Next, her teacher directed her thinking to the audience for her story, her purpose for writing it, and the form she would use. She decided she would write and illustrate a picture book for her younger brother and two older sisters, one that would be funny and scary at the same time.

During the next stage, *drafting,* Gabbie wrote a rough draft of her story, trying to keep her audience and purpose in mind. Gabbie went through three drafts before she felt ready to share her story with classmates to get their feedback. When she did read her story to a small group of classmates, they responded to what she had written, giving her positive feedback on some aspects of her story and suggesting what she might think about for her next revision.

Revising the story—reviewing it in light of the comments she received from her classmates and rewriting it—was the next stage in the process. Here, Gabbie reworked her composition by adding, deleting, changing, and moving around words, sentences, and even whole sections. During this stage, Gabbie's main interest was in making the story "work." Did it make sense? Was it scary *and* funny? Would her brother and sisters like it?

After Gabbie was satisfied that she had done what she could to tell the story she wanted in the way she wanted, she began *editing* the piece. Here she focused on mechanical elements such as grammar, punctuation, and spelling. This proofreading process required that Gabbie hunt word by word for errors, a different focus from that of the revising stage, in which she concentrated on the meaning she was creating. Because

MyLab Education
Video Example 13.2
This video teaches a number of techniques for the pre-writing stage of the writing process.

young writers like Gabbie are not usually critical readers, it can be helpful to provide suggestions for revising and editing. Teacher Marilyn Blackley (Five & Dionisio, 1999) finds an editing list, such as the one shown in Figure 13.8, helpful for her students. Using colored pencils, her third-graders work in pairs to edit their own writing.

MyLab Education
Click here to download a printable version of Figure 13.8

The last stage of the process, *publishing*, involved a sharing or "celebration" of the work. To prepare her story for sharing, Gabbie keyed her story into a word processor, printed it, cut it into sections, and pasted the sections in the pages of a booklet. Then she drew pictures to accompany her text. Other types of publishing possibilities are discussed later in this chapter.

A focus on the writing process can begin early in a child's education. In kindergarten and first grade a student does not move through all the stages of the writing process but planning and drafting are certainly in order. In Mrs. Hoffman's kindergarten class, the students were asked to write about something strange or funny that happened last week. The class began with brainstorming their experiences as the teacher wrote and classified them on the board. Next, she had the students draw a picture of the experience on a piece of paper and leave the bottom half empty to write their caption. Cole reported that his grandpa slipped and fell in the sewer water while walking their dog. Cole's work is show in Figure 13.9.

To review, the five major steps in the writing process are as follows:

- Prewriting
- Drafting
- Revising
- Editing
- Publishing

Figure 13.8 Form to Help Third-Graders Edit Their Writing

NAME: _____ DATE: _____

Steps to Editing

⟵——————————————————⟶

THE TITLE OF MY PIECE IS _____.

MY EDITING PARTNER WAS _____.

I read my story to a friend to see where to **STOP** for

       periods ·   _____

       question marks ?   _____

       exclamation points !   _____

I took out extra words that I didn't need (and, then) _____.

I checked for capital letters

      at the beginning of each sentence _____

      for the first letter of a name   _____

      for the word I   _____

I circled words that may be misspelled.   _____

Example: I (plade) with my dog.

SOURCE: Five, C. L., & Dionisio, M. (1999). "Revisiting the Teaching of Writing," *School Talk, 4*, 3. Copyright 1999 by the National Council of Teachers of English. Reprinted with permission.

In most schools today, the students have access to computers and tablets and many have received rudimentary instruction in word processing. Word processing is a valuable tool for composing, revising, editing, and publishing with one caveat (Graham, McKeown, Kiuhara, & Harris, 2012). Students can employ the power of the computer only if they have some keyboarding skills—so teach typing. Computers aid students in composing, revising, and editing. In a few cases, with the right software, the computer can aid with the prewriting process (Englert, Zhao, Dunsmore, Collinge, & Wolberts, 2007). Those computers can help, but they cannot take the place of the modeling and feedback that the teacher can provide.

A word of caution is in order here. The preceding description gives merely the highlights of what is, in reality, a very complex and recursive process. Writers don't simply move lockstep from one stage to another; they repeatedly move back and forth between the processes involved in prewriting, drafting, revising, and editing, as the writing task dictates. Different writers, different topics, different purposes, and myriad other factors will affect the writing process. No two writers approach writing in exactly

Figure 13.9 A Kindergarten Personal Narrative

Grnd gr
rellinWAter

SOURCE: Cole Williams, kindergarten, Mariners Elementary School. Newport Beach, CA. Reprinted by permission of Peter Dewitz

MyLab Education
Video Example 13.3
This video shows how one teacher uses a writing conference to assist the editing process.

the same manner, and the same writer writes differently at different times. The scenario describing Gabbie's story presents a general characterization of the writing process. Virtually all formal and polished writing is the product of a relatively lengthy and multifaceted process that involves thinking, drafting, and revising.

A Genre Approach to Writing

In a genre approach to writing, students and teachers work to develop an explicit understanding of how language works so they can grow as readers and writers. This approach, called systemic functional linguistics, an Australian export, engages the class in a close study of the various forms and characteristics of genres (Derewianka, 2000). When students use language to speak, read, or write they do so for specific purposes and must, therefore, select a text that will help to achieve those purposes. Writing begins by exploring a particular genre such as biography or fantasy, by reading and studying its structure. From these reading comprehension lessons the students and teachers move to creating their own texts in the same genre.

Gail Williams's classroom decided to explore the environment around the school, looking for litter and other pollutants. After collecting their data, they needed to report their findings to the principal and other school authorities. The students decided to write a report to share what they discovered and perhaps mount a campaign to persuade the bordering manufacturing companies to change their ways. Reporting and persuading are specific language functions and each requires a specific text organization and employs specific language features.

The curriculum cycle for using the genre approach, presented in Figure 13.10, begins with building knowledge of the topic, similar to the prewriting step in the writing process. Mrs. Williams' students did this through direct observation and extensive reading about pollution. Their next step was to learn how to write a strong persuasive argument; they needed, therefore, to learn about this specific text type. The class began by studying other pieces of persuasive writing. The students read several examples and examined the structure and characteristics of persuasive writing. They learned that their writing must begin with a thesis statement. Both logical and emotional language should be used to amplify this statement. Next, the students noticed that their thesis statement needed to be supported with well-defined arguments or reasons. Each argument must have evidence and not just opinion. They also learned that a good piece of writing must conclude with specific recommendations. Beyond structure, they also noted that writers use emotional words, they write in the present tense because this is an ongoing problem, and they use signal words to connect their arguments—*first, second, finally.*

Next, the teacher creates a persuasive essay' modeling the process of composing an argument while the students participate. The teacher might start the composing process and then seek ideas from the students. She can accept, modify, and mold the ideas of the students. This shared process affords the teacher the opportunity to engage in guided practice. Here the students are taking what they have learned about persuasive writing and putting it into practice. In the functional linguistics approach, students need both models of good writing and demonstrations in which they see the process modeled. These steps are not typically part of the traditional writing process, but they could be.

Once the modeling is completed, the students begin to apply what they have learned about the structure and language of the genre to their own writing. The teacher purposefully leaves a copy of the group's persuasive essay in the room with its parts and language features clearly labeled. The students can use it as a resource to make sure they have included the same elements in their own writing. As the students continue to write, they are engaged in the drafting portion of the writing process. After drafting, the students continue on to revise and consolidate what they have written. Again, the structure of persuasive writing helps to guide the revision process. The students can consult the model hanging in the classroom to see what they might have left out. At the end of the process the students reflect on the text type they have been studying and how its structure helps them compose and comprehend.

By engaging students in a deep study of genre and text characteristics, the functional linguistic approach to writing may provide greater support to the young writer than does the traditional writing process. As students read models of good writing they learn how texts are organized and the purposes of the various genres. The evidence strongly suggests that knowledge of text structure supports reading comprehension and an understanding of genre helps the reader set a purpose (Armbruster & Anderson, 1984; Duke & Pearson, 2002; Slater, Graves, & Piche, 1985).

Figure 13.10 Curriculum Cycle for Writing with a Focus on Genre.

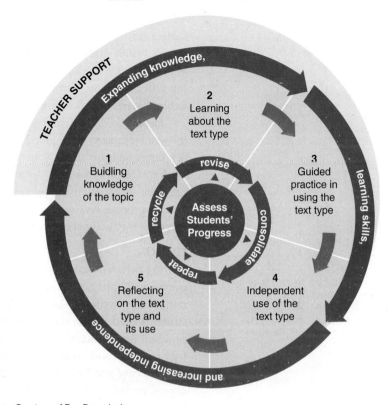

Courtesy of Bev Derewianka.

The second advantage of the functional linguistic, or genre, approach is the construction of an integrated reading and writing units. A teacher who seeks to explore realistic fiction or mystery can do so by both reading stories and writing stories. What students learn through reading stories will support their own compositions. The teacher can take the functional linguistic approach down to an even finer level. For example, to learn to find the main idea it is often a good idea to learn how to construct well-crafted paragraphs. So, the strategy of finding the main idea that we developed in Chapter 12 can be paralleled with lessons on writing strong paragraphs. Last, the functional linguistic approach used the same lesson structure that we advocated for teaching reading comprehension—direct instruction, guided practice, and independent practice.

Reflect and Apply

3. We have discussed reading and writing as being reciprocal and parallel processes, or "two sides of the same coin." Explain what this idea means to you. Think specifically about the functional linguistic approach.

4. Think about your own writing experiences in elementary school. What did you write? For which audiences did you write? Did any of your writing take you through the various processes we talked about in this section? What sorts of informal writing did you do? At this point, jot down the types of writing elementary students might do that illustrate both the process approach and informal kinds of writing.

Teaching the Different Genres

The writing process and the genre approach to writing can be applied to several different writing tasks. When we talk about writing as communication, four interrelated factors are always involved—audience (who), purpose (why), content (what), and form (how). When students write to communicate, they need to be aware of these factors. Very often, it is the audience, purpose, and content that determines the form the writing will take. Four particularly useful forms to used in conjunction with reading are fictional narratives, biographies and autobiographies, reports and letters.

Here is the time to merge the functional lingusitic or genre approach to writing with the writing process we outlined previously in the chapter. Students need to tackle one genre at a time and learn about its text organization and language features. *Exploring How Texts Work* by Derewianka (2000) is an excellent resource for teaching various text structures. Once the structure on and purpose of the genre is studied the students move through the writing process. As Courtney Cazden (1991) notes, "Children would not learn to speak a language they do not hear; so how do we expect them to learn the forms they do not read?"

FICTION

Writing fiction or narratives provides opportunities for students to express themselves in creative ways and to explore a topic and a genre by giving their imaginations free rein. Fiction writing is one avenue in which to use the genre approach to writing. As students read fiction they are learning about its basic structure—characters, setting, problem or conflict, rising action, climax, and resolution. At each stage of the book, they can stop and write short summaries and this process will help them learn about the structure and language characteristics of writing fiction. Figure 13.11 is a graphic organizer that students can use to plan their fiction writing.

Narrative writing can take many forms at various grade levels. For example, at Beauvoir, the National Cathedral Elementary School in Washington, D.C., first-graders wrote and recorded their own stories about "If I Was a Sled Dog" as part of their study of the Inuit Indians, and second-graders wrote German folktales after reading and listening to stories by the Brothers Grimm. Fifth- and sixth-graders in Anchorage, Alaska, created their own imaginary creatures and wrote about them after a unit on how various species adapt to their environment. Their teacher, Diann Stone, had them select an environment with which they were familiar—in this case, their own neighborhoods—and create a creature who would dwell in that environment. Along with drawing a map

MyLab Education
Click here to download a printable version of Figure 13.11.

Figure 13.11 Story Map for Planning Narrative Writing

Story Map

Characters
Setting
Place:
Time:

Problem/Conflict
Event
Characters' Feelings and Reactions
Event
Characters' Feelings and Reactions
Event
Characters' Feelings and Reactions

Resolution—How was the problem solved?

of the creature's environment, students wrote a fictional report that included what this creature would look like, what it would eat, and what its habits would be.

BIOGRAPHIES AND AUTOBIOGRAPHIES

Biographies and autobiographies are a type of narrative, a narrative that is true or largely so. The structure of a biography follows that of fictional narrative with a few modifications. Biographies and autobiographies typically have a central point, a theme. We write biographies to celebrate an individual's accomplishments—Jackie Robinson, Marie Curie, or Indira Gandhi. Autobiographies are written to celebrate the writer's life because he or she presumes their life is worth celebrating. Or, as Ambrose Bierce said, autobiography is the highest form of fiction. The structure of both forms typically begins early in life, moves through growing up and education leading to their early attempts to a launch their career. Finally, the narrative focuses on their major trials, accomplishments, and what we can learn from this life.

Biographies and autobiographies are a popular genre with children because they enjoy reading about real people and because biographies and autobiographies often represent fairly easy reading, following as they do the basic narrative form children are familiar with. Biographies written expressly for young readers range from picture books such as *Dr. Martin Luther King, Jr.* and *America's Champion Swimmer: Gertrude Ederle*, both by David Adler, or *The Amazing Life of Benjamin Franklin* by James Giblin and *Revolutionary John Adams* by Cheryl Harness to in-depth portraits of noteworthy figures such as *Behind the Mask: The Life of Queen Elizabeth I* by Jane Resh Thomas, *Free to Dream: The Making of a Poet: Langston Hughes* by Audrey Osofsky, and *Pocahontas* by Joseph Bruchac.

Read one or more of these books with your class. If you have the resources, have the students select the biography, organizing the students into groups by their interests. As you and the students read the books, study the life and contributions of the individual. Also consider the structure of the biography so that students can learn how to create their own. Figure 13.12 is a graphic organizer that can be used to record the

Figure 13.12 Graphic Organizer for a Biography

EXAMINING A BIOGRAPHY

The famous person is _____

What were his or her major accomplishments?		
	What were the important events in this person's life?	Why were these events so important?
Childhood		
Education		
Adulthood		
Death		
What can we learn from this person's life?		

MyLab Education
Click here to download a printable version of Figure 13.12.

events and accomplishments of an individual or it can be used by the students to plan the biography they plan to write. This assignment will lead the students to new books and the internet as a research tool. This website is a good place to begin (https://www .ducksters.com/biography/).

REPORTS

In general, reports represent a more challenging writing and thinking task than do biographies or letters, primarily because they usually do not follow the chronological, narrative structure children are so familiar with and because they often require students to use several sources of information. On the other hand, we are fortunate today that an ever-increasing number of excellent models of informational writing are becoming readily available. More and more informational books and periodicals—which include everything from why animals have tails to the mechanics of spaceflight—are being written expressly for elementary-level students. Many of these informational materials are intriguing, relevant, and expertly crafted; they provide excellent models for students' own writing of reports. The Reading Corner on page 403 contains a list of a few such authors and titles.

As we discussed in Chapter 12 much of the information that students now seek is on the Internet. The first problem students face is finding that information. The Internet is a blizzard of websites that provide good information, websites that are poorly constructed, and website that list and evaluate other websites. The search process is complex. It is also important for teachers and students to study how that information is organized and presented on the Internet. Students are unlikely to find a well-structured five paragraph essay. The Internet provides many more illustrations and graphs supported by extended caption that found in textbooks. Information is presented in short written bites and supported with visuals and video. This makes the task finding, noting, and synthesizing information demanding.

Writing a good report requires many skills, from research and note taking through composing, revising, and editing to publishing. Beverly Derewianka (2000) counsels that reports can refer to several types—from news reports to science reports to weather reports. In school, students typically write reports to discuss the classifications of things, to examine the components of systems, or to describe processes. So a report on snakes might begin with looking at their classification in the animal kingdom, move on to a description of their anatomy and habitat, and then look at their life cycle. To write a strong report a student will need training in all of these structures. As we have stressed before, learning about text structure through writing also enhances reading comprehension.

As Shelley Harwayne (1993) so aptly states, in addition to having numerous opportunities to read the sorts of materials they are asked to write, students also need to "develop the same hunger for learning and communicating what they find out" that professional writers demonstrate. Harwayne suggests three lessons we can learn from professional nonfiction writers that we would do well to pass on to our students:

- They take learning about their subject seriously.
- They want to claim the information as their own by offering their own slant or perspective on it.
- They know their options and their audiences.

Spending time communicating these truths to students through the reading-writing opportunities you provide will pay off in their enthusiasm for writing and the quality of their products.

As defined here, reports include a range of informational writing that generally serves two purposes—to learn about a topic and to communicate that information through written language. A report can take any form—a paragraph on table manners, a science notebook capturing a series of pictures and notes on the metamorphosis of a

Figure 13.13 A Second grader's notes about her caterpillar study

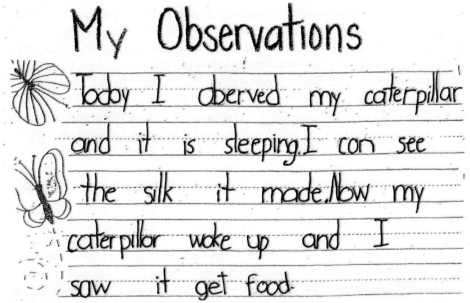

SOURCE: Presley Williams, 2nd Grade, Mariners Elementary School, Newport Beach, CA. Reprinted by permission of Peter Dewitz

caterpillar (see Figure 13.13), or a multimedia research report on natural disasters. We offer the following recommendations for developing students' skill in writing reports:

- Read informational books and websites and study how they are organized. Make this part of your basic reading curriculum.

- Brainstorm with your students possible topics that they could write about. Encourage students to choose their own topics.

- Model the process of conducting research. Review and share possible resources. Model note taking or double-entry journals.

- Help students develop and outline their report and make connections to what they have learned about the structure of a report. Make sure to consider what text features to include—headings, pictures, captions, and so forth.

- Allow students ample time for drafting, revising, and meeting with you.

- Conduct mini-lessons when common problems occur with students' writing, such as crafting an engaging lead.
- Generally follow the writing process and develop a means for publishing the students' work.

LETTERS

Letters are a wonderful way to highlight the reading-writing connection. Students can write formal letters to request something, express thanks, issue a complaint, or express a point of view. They might be addressed to businesses, government employees, authors and illustrators, or pen pals across the seas. Letters actually incorporate many different genres. Letters that inform friends and family about personal experiences are actually personal narratives and require a study of that genre. Other letters require a study of persuasion or argument as in letters to the editor. Before students can write a strong letter they must study the genre essential to their purpose. As we wrote earlier, this requires reading models of good letters. Books that feature letters, such as *Dear Mr. Henshaw* by Beverly Cleary, *The Ballad of Lucy Whipple* by Karen Cushman, *Nettie's Trip South* by Ann Turner, and *Dear Papa* by Anne Ylvisaker can provide good models of this form. Next, you must model the process, composing a letter in front of students (either on an overhead transparency or on the board) and explaining the thought processes you go through. Beyond the text structure in the body of the letter, all letters have unique conventions—date, inside address, salutation, body, closing, and signature.

Formal letters are likely to go through several stages—drafting, revising, and editing. Informal letters, however, may or may not require revision and editing. Students who have had plenty of experience writing letters can often pen a friendly letter just once before sending it off. Students can write informal letters to classmates, friends, relatives, and pen pals; in these letters they can deal with reading-related topics such as stories, story characters, and other aspects of stories that they are particularly interested in. Teacher David Carberry has his fifth-graders write letters to first-graders, a writing task his students find particularly appealing. "The kids are very aware of taking their audience and purpose into account," Carberry says.

Students can also write simulated letters to or from fictional characters or to or from real people whom they encounter in reading true narratives or informational books. In the Classroom 13.5 provides some examples.

Children love receiving letters and are, therefore, motivated to write them. Now, however, we live in an age dominated by email and we want to take advantage of this exciting mode of communication. Email is an informal letter stripped of many of its traditional conventions, but with the addition of new ones. The date is still there, supplied by the computer; the inside address is the email address, and the salutation remains. The subject line is a new feature, but the body may resemble a traditional letter in an informal style. Email still requires concise clear writing with proper spelling, punctuation, and grammar. Email also permits abbreviations such as LOL (laughing out loud) and emoticons (the smiley ☺). Email exchanges between students within the same school or with students in other schools combine the excitement of letters with the power of electronic communication. Just as you would model letter writing, you also need to model the writing of email. Make sure that you monitor this process carefully, because the rapid nature of email does not allow for much reflection and revision.

Teachers might set up email exchanges within the school or across schools among students studying the same topics. Mary Kreul (2005) recommends telecollaborative projects in which teachers and students connect via the Internet to work on specific activities. There are websites where teachers may advertise their specific projects and seek collaborators outside the school or look for existing projects their students might join. Global Schoolhouse (www.globalschoolnet.org) and Pen Pals of the World (http://www.studentsoftheworld.info) offer suggestions, projects, and pen pals in other countries.

In the Classroom 13.5

Instructional Routines

Writing Letters to or from People Students Read About

- After reading a biography, invite students to write a letter to that person.
- Have students assume the role of a character in a story and write a letter to one of the other characters. For example, in the following letter, a student is assuming the persona of Miata in Gary Soto's *The Skirt* and is writing to Miata's friend Ana:

> Dear Ana,
> What is my mother going to say when she finds out I lost my folklorico skirt? She is going to be so mad! You've got to help me out!
> > Your amiga,
> > Miata

- Suggest that two students take on the roles of characters in stories and write letters to each other about novel situations those characters might face. For example, after reading Nancy Carlson's *Arnie and the New Kid*, one student might write a letter from Arnie's perspective and the other student from the perspective of Philip, the new kid in a wheelchair.

> Dear Philip,
> I wish they had given me a wheelchair like yours instead of these dumb crutches. Can you believe I broke my leg falling down some steps?
> > Your friend,
> > Arnie

> Dear Arnie,
> Sorry you broke your leg, but now I can do some things faster than you. Ha! Want to come over and play some video games?
> > Your friend,
> > Phillip

The Reading Corner

Books by Exemplary Nonfiction Children's Book Authors

Science

Aliki. *Wild and Woolly Mammoths*. HarperCollins, 1998. This fascinating delineation of the woolly mammoth and the Ice Age is a "model of interesting factual writing for children" (Horn Book). 32 pages.

Gail Gibbons. *Dinosaur Discoveries*. Holiday House, 2018. Author-illustrator Gibbons is an expert at depicting complicated subjects in a clear and simple style. In this book, one of many she has written on a variety of science-related topics, she answers questions young readers might have about dinosaurs. 32 pages.

Sandra Markle. *What If You Had Animal Eyes?* Scholastic, Inc., 2017. Another imaginative book by Sandra Markle in the What If You Had series, this one explores what would happen if you looked in the mirror and saw a pair of animal eyes instead of your own. 32 pages.

Laurence Pringle. *Scorpion Man*. Macmillan, 1994. In a text accompanied by photographs taken by the subject—Gary Polis, the "scorpion man"—Pringle describes the fascinating work of this biologist and the creatures he studies. 42 pages.

Millicent Selsam. *How to Be a Nature Detective*. HarperCollins, 1995. In this text, Selsam shows readers how anyone can be a nature detective by learning to recognize clues, especially footprints, that tell which animals have been around. 32 pages.

Seymour Simon. *Exoplanets*. Harpercollins Children's Books, 2018. Award winning science writer Seymour Simon explores the farthest reaches of space, examining the planets outside our solar system and uncovering what makes them potentially inhabitable. 40 pages.

(Continued)

Social Studies

David A. Adler. *A Picture Book of Cesar Chavez.* Holiday House, 2018. One of the many books in Adler's Picture Book Biographies series, this title covers the labor leader's life from birth to death but mostly focuses on Chavez's later fights for better wages and safer working conditions. 32 pages.

Russell Freedman. *The Voice That Challenged a Nation: Marian Anderson and the Struggle for Equal Rights.* Clarion Books, 2004. In this chronicle of the acclaimed singer's life—with a special emphasis on the historic 1939 Easter concert at the Lincoln Memorial—Freedman illustrates how a person's life is molded by its historical and cultural context. 128 pages.

Jean Fritz. *Alexander Hamilton.* G. P. Putnam's Sons, 2012. The award-winning author brings her talent for bringing history to life once again to this biography of Alexander Hamilton, one of America's Founding Fathers. 144 pages.

James Cross Giblin. *Good Brother, Bad Brother: The Story of Edwin Booth and John Wilkes Booth.* Clarion, 2005. In an engaging narrative, Giblin intertwines the tale of the two Booth brothers with accounts of their families, friends, the Civil War, and 19th-century theater. 256 pages.

Milton Meltzer. *Hear That Train Whistle Blow! How the Railroad Changed the World.* Random House, 2005. In this nonfiction text, illustrated with numerous archival photographs, Meltzer presents the myriad ways in which the railroad affected almost every aspect of modern civilization. 176 pages.

Andrea Davis Pinkney. *Martin Rising: Requiem for a King.* Scholastic Press, 2018. The final months of Martin Luther King, Jr.'s life are conveyed by author and illustrator in a rich embroidery of visions, musical rhythm, and powerful emotion. 127 pages.

Figure 13.14 Second-Grade Student Poetry Sample

Nimbostratus
by Lucy Hooper, second grade

Yuckey!
Nasty!
Dismal!
Nimbostratus clouds
are like a witch's huge black
hat with spiders' webs all over it.
Dismal!
Dreary!

POETRY

Poetry can be written in response to anything children read, and like any genre it must be read first, discussed and analyzed. Since poetry can take many forms from simple couplets, to haiku and to longer forms students need to read study the forms before they can imitate them. A good place to start is one of two books by Kenneth Koch. *Wishes, Lies and Dreams* (Koch, 1999) presents very simple forms of poetry that are easily imitated by young children. *Rose, where did you get that red* (1990) introduces students to famous poems and then has the student mimic their structure. Children can imitate the simple poems of William Carlos Williams and the complex poetry of William Blake. Compare the poem by Williams on the left to that of a elementary student on the right.

William Carlos Williams	8-Year-Old Girl
This is Just to Say I have eaten the plums that were in the icebox and which you were probably saving for breakfast Forgive me they were delicious so sweet and so cold	This is Just to Say That the dog tore your shoes in to little pieces and I let him do it. It was quite amusing.

Once students understand the form or structure of a poem they can write poems about any many topics. For example, after reading about the Gold Rush, students could write poetry about some aspect of that particular slice of U.S. history. After reading about the weather, they could write a cloud poem, as second-grader Lucy did (Figure 13.14). Or they could write either jump rope rhymes after reading Afiodelia Scruggs's *Jump Rope Magic* or a variation of the Japanese tanka on the horse, as fourth-grader Julie did (Figure 13.15) after reading several of Marguerite Henry's horse stories.

In the Classroom 13.6

Instructional Routines

Writing Poems around a Theme

- Read aloud to students several poems that relate to a theme or unit of study, such as weather.
- Choose a particular poem on which to concentrate, such as "A Week of Weather" by Lee Bennett Hopkins and talk about the words that the poet has chosen to describe the weather.
- Have students perform the poem as a choral reading.
- Together, as a shared writing activity, write a poem that reflects the week's weather in your town.

You will find wonderful examples of poetry on almost any subject imaginable to read to your students, which will inspire them to express themselves in this special form as well. In the Classroom 13.6 illustrates one type of poetry writing.

Rachel Weiss, a third-grade teacher, used the three forms of writing in one integrated unit. The students began with a content unit about animals. They read informational books and learned about the structure of these books. Next, each student selected one animal to research with the goal of writing his or her own informational book. As the students worked through this process, they learned a great deal about their animals. With that knowledge in hand they next had to write a piece of fiction that featured their animal. Much like Roald Dahl (2007) did in *Fantastic Mr. Fox*, they incorporated all that they learned about their animal's behavior characteristics in the fiction. Finally, they had to feature that animal in a poem, again highlighting its physical characteristics.

An intrinsic feature of each type of writing we have discussed in this and the previous sections is that it is meant to be read. The writer creates a letter, biography, report, story, or poem with an audience and purpose in mind—to inform, entertain, persuade, evoke feelings, or tickle or challenge the imagination. As you read to your students, occasionally ask them to identify the intended audience (Olness, 2005) and purpose. Additionally, as with any writing students do, sufficient scaffolding must be provided before students begin the writing as well as during the writing process. Careful motivation, preparation, modeling, encouragement, coaching, and feedback are crucial to success.

Figure 13.15 Fourth-Grade Student Poetry Sample

HORSES
by Julie Graves, fourth grade

Swift, gallant
great flowing manes
and large flying tales
beautiful!

Reflect and Apply

5. Think of a piece of writing you have done recently, and briefly answer these four questions about it: Who was the audience? What was your purpose? What was the content? What form did you use?

6. Think of a piece of writing you have done that went through several stages before you finished the piece. Briefly describe the process you went through. Compare your process with the description on the writing process we presented earlier in the chapter.

7. If you wanted to ensure your students' success in writing reports on a topic they had been reading about, what steps would you take to guide them? Be as specific as possible in your explanation.

MyLab Education **Self-Check 13.3**

MyLab Education **Application Exercise 13.3:** Pre-Writing in Sixth Grade

Revising, Responding, and Publishing Writing

Revising may be the heart of the writing process, at least it is a vital element. Unfortunately, most students believe that once they lift their pen from paper they are finished and nothing feels better. Barry Lane devoted a whole book to revision, *After THE END* (2015), making the claim that the true craft of writing comes in only after the first draft is completed. Some writers revise along the way, alter sentences and paragraphs as they go. Other, like Stephen King revise after they have completed a first draft of the story. King claims that he does not know what or where the turning point of a story is until he completes his first draft (King, 2000).

Teaching students to revise is actually teaching them the craft of writing. It is best to tackle revision one topic at a time. Begin by teaching students how to create an enticing beginning or lead. Start with a story of your own and model different types of leads for that story. Start one lead with a rich description, another with an anecdote, and a third with a question. After modeling have the students return to their draft and create at least two or three different leads. Not one lead, but a few. Students need to learn to play with language and be flexible. Have them share their leads with the class and reflect on what makes an exciting one.

Here is a partial list of the revision topics that can be introduced during the school year. For additional sources we recommend Ralph Fletcher's books *Craft Lessons* (2007) and *The Writing Teacher's Companion* (2017).

- Exciting leads
- Leading with a question
- Creating a setting
- Playing with time—foreshadowing and flashbacks
- Precise words—strong verbs and concrete nouns
- Sensory words
- Adding dialogue
- Creative endings

Responding to Writing

To grow as readers and writers, students need to receive feedback on their writing and what it reveals about their reading. Here we present a handful of suggestions on how to respond to students' writing in ways that will help them evaluate their own success at achieving their writing goals.

- *Be positive.* Emphasize what works in a piece more frequently than what doesn't— "Wow, you really got my attention with that great opening sentence!" Recall the emphasis we placed on success in Chapter 03, and realize that writing is for most of us (authors, teachers, and students alike) an area in which we are very vulnerable to criticism.

- *Respond to only some of what students write.* Students don't need your feedback on everything they write. In many cases, they will profit from feedback by their peers. They will also profit from their own self-criticism, which they can use to decide what writing they want you to look at.

- *Respond to only a few matters at any one time.* It is simply a waste of your time and energy to respond to many things at once. Students will attend to only a limited number of comments.

- *Comment primarily on works in progress rather than final drafts.* Comments after a final draft is completed get very little attention and often produce frustration.

- *Give feedback during brief conferences with students on their works in progress* (Graves, 1996). A typical conference between a teacher-writer and a student-writer might begin with "Tell me about your piece" or "How is it coming?"

- *Observe students as they write.* Asking questions or making statements can lead students to solve their own writing dilemmas.

- *Deal with content first and mechanics later.* It is not that mechanics are unimportant, but the content of students' writing should take priority, especially as it reflects and promotes students' proficiency in reading.

- *Praise correct spelling, but also encourage invented spelling* (especially with primary-grade writers). If your student's goal is to have someone else read his writing, then spelling is an important means to that end, and correct spelling is something to strive for.

- *Make peer response an integral and frequent part of your reading and writing program.* There is probably no better way to learn something than to teach it—which is part of what peer reviewers are doing. However, students must be taught how to be effective peer respondents. The ReadWriteThink (http://www.readwritethink .org/professional-development/strategy-guides/peer-review-30145.html) website provides an excellent plan for teaching peer editing. They recommend three logical steps—Compliments, Suggestions, and Corrections. Provide the students with sentence starter templates such as, "My favorite part was —— because ——." And "A suggestion I can offer for improvement is ——." Teach the students how to give constructive feedback by focusing on very specific aspects of the text and contrast it with vague feedback so they know the difference. This will educate both the writer and the reviewer. Before you begin any of this, model all parts of the process. The website provides many good resources.

- Finally, in addition to following these suggestions for responding to students' writing, like virtually all current writers on writing, we recommend that you have students keep portfolios of their writing—ongoing and cumulative records and examples of their work. Items to be included can be selected by both you and your students. A major strength of these portfolios is that students can use them to evaluate their work and growth as writers. You and the students can use these portfolios as a tool for evaluating their writing and deciding where future efforts might be directed, sharing with parents, and determining and agreeing on grades.

Publishing Writing

There is something universal in the appeal of a book with good-quality paper and a hard cover, something that we hope will continue to live alongside the Kindle and other electronic books. And sometimes good paper and a hard cover will be just the right format for kids' published works. However, charts, posters, articles, and radio or TV scripts can also be "published."

Publishing means making a work available to some "public" audience. This audience might be the writer's classmates, students in another class, the entire school, a broader audience such as readers of a newspaper or magazine, or perhaps even a blog. The Students of the World website (www.studentsoftheworld .info) provides a place for students to create their own blog about a topic or add on to other blogs. Publishing highlights the importance of considering an audience while writing, and writing intended for publication is usually the result of the full writing process—brainstorming, drafting, revising, and editing. Although the larger audiences just mentioned are certainly possibilities, in many cases publishing will be accomplished simply by posting the work in the classroom. Whatever audience it reaches, published work is generally produced with the aid of word processors, spell checkers, computerized dictionaries and thesauruses, and, in some cases, desktop publishing programs.

MyLab Education
Video Example 13.4
This video shows one way of publishing students' writing. How does the interaction assist the writer?

One such publishing program is Story Jumper (https://www.storyjumper.com), with which children's original works can be published as bound books. This is a school-based publishing program that is built on the efforts of students, teachers, parents, and school principals (Chihak, 1999). Another highly successful publishing effort is that of Cheri Cooke's seventh-grade reading classes. Each year, they produce a bound volume of reviews of their favorite books (Cooke & Graves, 1995). Lauretta Beecher's second-graders celebrate their writing in yet another way. They host a party and invite parents and other adults in the school to listen to their stories and poems.

Reflect and Apply

8. Identify a grade level at which you would like to teach and consider for a moment the mini-lesson component of the writing workshop. Name some topics you might choose to cover early in the year, some you might choose to cover in the middle of the year, and some you might choose to cover late in the year. Now consider what surprises you might find in your students' writing and how these would affect your plan.

9. We listed nine suggestions for responding to students' writing. Rank these in order from most important to least important and ask a classmate to do the same. Then get together and discuss the similarities and differences in your rankings, trying particularly to understand any large differences and what those differences suggest about your views of writing instruction.

MyLab Education **Self-Check 13.4**

MyLab Education **Application Exercise 13.4:** Peer Revising and Editing

---

Assessing Writing

We have two overlapping tasks when it comes to the assessment of writing because in this chapter we have featured two types of writing—writing to learn and writing to create complete texts following the writing process. In both cases we are assessing both the content and the form of writing, content is more important in writing to learn activities, with content and form being equally important in extended writing projects such a stories, biographies, informational reports, and essays.

Assessing Writing to Learn

In writing to learn activities we are more concerned with the content of what the students have written than the form or the mechanics. Although teachers should remind students to use proper punctuation, capitalization, and spelling, it is what students are writing that counts. We want to know if the summaries that students create are truly summaries, if their notes reflect the important points in the text, and if their journals capture their thoughts and feelings as they are reading a novel. Figure 13.16 is a rubric for scoring the summaries that students write while reading a novel or a piece of non-fiction. This rubric works best if it is accompanied by anchor papers, examples of strong, average, and weak student writings. Anchor papers, or examples, give some real context to the statements in a rubric.

Another form of assessment is the reading log, or in this case a diary. While her students were reading the novel *Hatchet* (Paulsen, 2000), Mrs. Rodriguez assigned a learning log. The students were to pretend that they were Brian, the main character. At the end of every two chapters, the students had to write a journal entry in Brian's voice, a first-person account. In each entry, they had to summarize what had happened, how

Figure 13.16 Rubric for Scoring Students' Summaries

4	**Narrative** The summary includes *three elements:* character development, plot, and theme. The major characters are described, including their relationships to other characters, traits, and motives. The plot line of the story is clear, containing major events, and the causal links between events are clear. The summary identifies one of the themes in the story. **Information** The summary identifies the topic, the importance of the topic (i.e., the main idea), and provides some supporting details. The ideas are described using the appropriate content vocabulary. Student conveys an overall understanding of the topic.
3	**Narrative** The summary includes *two of the three major elements*—character development, plot, and theme. The summary includes some mention of the character's traits, the plot has some of the significant elements, in an appropriate sequence, but the links between events are not stated. The theme is stated, but there is little development. **Information** The summary identifies the topic and why the topic is important—the main idea. Few facts are offered to develop the main idea. The student uses some of the context vocabulary but some are omitted.
2	**Narrative** The summary includes *characters and plot* but neither is developed. Character descriptions may include relationships to other characters ("his sister") but no attributes or traits. Plot elements or events are few, incomplete, and disjointed with no clear logical development. **Information** The summary is mainly a list of facts with a mention of the topic. The student does not state a main idea or broader concept. The summary includes little of the content vocabulary.
1	**Narrative** The summary is very incomplete with one or two events and the student does not seem to grasp the development of the story. The student does not state any causal links in the plot. One, perhaps two characters are mentioned, typically using pronouns ('He then did'). No explanation of character's relationships or traits. **Information** The summary is just a list of facts or events. With no overarching main idea or topic. The student does not use content vocabulary.

Brian was thinking, and then predict what he might do next. Each entry captured both the student's understanding of the content and their ability to engage in three reading strategies—summarizing, inferring, and predicting. Figure 13.17 shows how we might score this diary or learning log project.

Assessing Extended Writing

The assessment of extended writing, narratives, informational reports, and persuasive essays should all be done using rubrics. Rubrics are typically created using a set of criteria by which the piece of writing will be scored. We introduced rubrics and the 6 Traits + 1 (http://educationnorthwest.org/traits/trait-definitions) scoring system in Chapter 5. This system provides the teacher and the students with a shared vocabulary about each of the traits vital to strong writing. The six traits + 1 are:

- *Ideas*—the main messages and the development of those ideas
- *Organization*—the internal structure of the piece

Figure 13.17 Scoring Learning Logs

A Character Diary as Response to Literature
Select a novel and read with the class the first chapter or two. Then identify the main characters in the novel. Ask the students to pick one of the main characters as the focus of their diary.

The students are to pretend that they are that character and that character keeps a diary. At the end of every chapter or two the students are to write a diary entry in the voice of their character. The diary must include the following three parts:

- A summary of what has happened in the last chapter or two.
- Inference or conclusions about how the character feels or his/her motives.
- A prediction about what will come next.

At least four times during the course of reading the novel the students must turn in their diary entry for your response and evaluation. The student may also respond to the diary entry of another student.

Scoring Diary Entries
Summary

4	The summary includes the main points of the narrative, it is well formed and concise.
3	The summary includes some of the main points of the narrative, but it has too many smaller details. The summary is organized but a bit rambling.
2	The summary includes mainly details that are unimportant and poorly organized.
1	The response focuses just on incidents in the chapter with no integration of ideas. The writing is very poorly organized.

Inferences—Character Motives and Feelings

4	The reader makes clear inferences about the main character that are consistent with and can be supported from the chapter.
3	The reader makes inferences about the main character that are logical but cannot be fully supported from the chapter.
2	The reader makes inferences about the main character that are not logically derived from the story. The reader relies on prior knowledge and not text information.
1	The reader fails to make any inferences about the main character's motives and feelings.

Predictions

4	The predictions are logical extensions of the text and can be justified with the text.
3	The predictions are logically related to the plot but rely more on the reader's knowledge than on the text knowledge.
2	The predictions are not logically related to the developing plot.
1	The reader does not make any predictions.

- *Voice*—the personal tone and feeling of the author's message
- *Word Choice*—the precision of the vocabulary a writer chooses to convey the meaning
- *Sentence Fluency*—the writer's skill in employing different types of sentence structures for different effects
- *Conventions*—spelling, grammar, punctuation, and capitalization
- *+ 1 Presentation*—how the writing looks, including printing or the use of electronic publishing

The six traits system lends itself to the use of rubrics, a system for evaluating several traits at a time. The rubric introduced in Chapter 5 is an example of a rubric that was designed around the criteria used in the Common Core State Standards. You can find 6-Trait +1 scoring guidelines at the National Educational Association's website (http://www.nea.org/tools/lessons/59760.htm). Like any scoring system, you need to identify anchor papers, papers that reflect excellent, strong, average, and weak writing. It is best to do this with your colleagues because the discussions you have will clarify what you mean when you state that a paper "Organizes ideas and information in an incomplete paragraph structure" versus "Organizes ideas and information into logical, coherent paragraphs that are clear to the reader." These are subtle differences that can only be clarified by consistently studying students' work.

When you first begin to evaluate students' writing, begin with one are two traits. Explain what these traits mean and share examples of them. Show the students what a 4 or 3 means for organization or sentence fluency. Then, after students have written a paper they should work with a partner and decide if they would give themselves a 4 or a 3 for organization. It is interesting to note that students are typically rigorous when evaluating their own writing. This process of self-evaluation is a lesson in good writing and it makes your writing conferences much more efficient.

Concluding Remarks

The value of developing a literate environment and establishing a curriculum to help students grow as writers in concert with their reading has been the overriding theme of this chapter. That means providing a classroom atmosphere, both physical and intellectual, that is safe and nurturing as well as inviting, fun, and challenging. It means providing opportunities to write for real purposes and for real audiences, purposes that include writing to learn for oneself and writing to communicate with someone else. It means providing students with opportunities to improve their writing and thinking skills through all sorts of writing—informal writing, such as brainstorming, quick writing, and journaling, as well as formal writing, such as reports and storybooks that require the process approach. It means giving students every benefit possible—providing daily time to write, publishing their works, and giving them constructive feedback. In short, your reading-writing environment and curriculum will help and inspire students to write more often and more effectively. It will encourage them to use writing as a thinking tool to learn more about themselves and their world and as a communicative tool to share their knowledge, feelings, and insights with others, both of which are essential for living successfully in today's world.

Extending Learning

1. Get together with several classmates and develop a set of interview questions that you can use with teachers to learn how they use writing in conjunction with reading in their classrooms. Limit yourselves to five or six questions that can be answered rather briefly. For example, you might ask how often their students write in conjunction with the reading they're doing. Once the questionnaire has been developed, try it out first on one teacher, and modify it as necessary. Then, each person in the group can interview two teachers and record their answers. Finally, get together with your classmates, share the results of your interviews, and discuss to what extent the writing you learned about is consistent with the principles and techniques recommended in this chapter. After your group meeting, you might consider presenting the results of your project to your university class.

2. Observe the reading and language arts periods of an elementary class for at least 1 week (2 weeks, if possible), and keep a detailed record of the writing the students do. Then, as a writing-to-learn activity for yourself, write a description of the class and the teacher, the writing you observed in the 1- or 2-week period, and the extent to which the writing you observed is and is not like that recommended in this chapter. Next, write an evaluative statement on the quality of the writing activities you observed and the extent to which they seem to support and extend the reading experiences students had during the period. Finally, if you believe that what you observed could be modified to better support and extend students' reading, briefly describe the modifications you would suggest.

Children's Literature

Adler, D. A. (2001). *Dr. Martin Luther King, Jr.* New York: Holiday House. This short biography tells the story of Dr. Martin Luther King, Jr.—his life, his accomplishments in the civil rights movement, and his impact on U.S. history. 32 pages.

Adler, D. A. (2005). *America's Champion Swimmer: Gertrude Ederle.* San Diego: Gulliver Books. This picture book biography covers the life of Gertrude Ederle, highlighting her world-record-breaking long-distance swims in the late 1920s, when women were thought to be "the weaker sex." 32 pages.

Branley, F. M. (1998). *The Planets in Our Solar System.* New York: HarperCollins. Part of the Let's Read and Find Out series, this book takes a quick look at the nine planets in our solar system using photographs and color illustrations. 32 pages.

Bridges, R. (1999). *Through My Eyes.* New York: Scholastic. In this photobiography, Ruby Bridges recounts the story of her involvement, as a 6-year-old, in the integration of her school in New Orleans in 1960. 63 pages.

Bruchac, J. (2005). *Pocahontas.* San Diego: Harcourt. Although the book is a historical novel, not a true biography, Bruchac goes to great lengths to present a historically accurate depiction of the relationship between the Virginia colonists and the Powhatans as seen through the eyes of Captain John Smith and the 11-year-old daughter of the Powhatan chief. 192 pages.

Carlson, N. (1990). *Arnie and the New Kid.* New York: Puffin. In this picture book, Arnie begins to better understand the new kid in a wheelchair after he falls and becomes temporarily disabled himself. Unnumbered.

Cleary, B. (1983). *Dear Mr. Henshaw.* New York: Morrow. In this Newbery Medal book, 10-year-old Leigh writes letters to his favorite author that help him to cope with his parents' divorce and a new school and to find his place in the world. Audiotape and filmstrip available. 134 pages.

Cole, J. (1989). *The Magic School Bus Inside the Human Body.* Ms. Frizzle takes her class via the magic bus inside the human body to look at how the body parts work. Spanish CD available. 40 pages.

Cole, J. (1992). *The Magic School Bus on the Ocean Floor.* Ms. Frizzle takes her class to the ocean floor aboard the magic school bus, where they learn firsthand the mysteries of underwater life. Spanish CD available. 40 pages.

Cushman, K. (1996). *The Ballad of Lucy Whipple.* New York: Clarion. While stuck in a California gold-mining town with her adventurous mother and siblings, Lucy pours out her heart and frustrations in a series of letters written to the folks she left behind in Massachusetts, where she longs to return. 195 pages.

Dahl, R. (1961). *James and the Giant Peach.* New York: Scholastic. Young James experiences madcap adventures as he enters a peach as big as a house and encounters new friends. Audio CD available. 128 pages.

Dahl, R. (1970). *Fantastic Mr. Fox.* New York: Puffin. A very resourceful fox saves his family from three disgusting farmers. 90 pages.

Delacre, L. (2000). *Salsa Stories.* New York: Scholastic. In a notebook Carmen Teresa receives as a holiday present, guests fill the pages with their colorful stories from a variety of Latin American countries. 144 pages.

DiCamillo, K. (2001). *The Tiger Rising.* Cambridge, MA: Candlewick. After Rob's mother dies and he and his father move to rural Florida to get their lives back together, Rob finds a way to come to terms with his mother's death through the help of a friend and a tiger. 116 pages.

Fleischman, S. (1986). *The Whipping Boy.* New York: Greenwillow. In this Newbery Medal book, Prince Brat and his whipping boy, Jemmy, run away from the palace, end up trading identities, and have many adventures together. Audio CD available. 90 pages.

Freedman, R. (1993). *Eleanor Roosevelt: A Life of Discovery.* New York: Clarion. This photobiography portrays the first wife of a president to carve out an influential career of her own. 198 pages.

Giblin, J. C. (2006). *The Amazing Life of Benjamin Franklin.* New York: Scholastic. In a concise, readable style, this biography presents a realistic, unsentimental portrait of the famous inventor, statesman, and diplomat, including his contributions and his challenges. 48 pages.

Graves, B. (2002). *California Condor: Flying Free.* Des Moines, IA: Perfection. Through the story of the capture of TopaTopa, the first California condor in the condor recovery program, the reader learns facts about this endangered bird and efforts to save it from extinction. 62 pages.

Halpern, M. (2002). *Strange Plants.* Washington, DC: National Geographic Educational Service. From the Windows on Literacy series, this brief text discusses meat-eating plants. 24 pages.

Harness, C. (2006). *Revolutionary John Adams.* Washington, DC: National Geographic Children's Books. This appealing and informative book is about the life and contributions of the second president of the United States, John Adams, who is often overshadowed by the more colorful Washington and Jefferson. 48 pages.

Hopkins, L. B. (Ed.). (1995). *Weather: Poems for All Seasons.* New York: HarperCollins. This collection of poems by well-known as well as lesser-known poets describes various weather conditions. 64 pages.

MacLachlan, P. (1993). *Baby.* New York: Delacorte. This exquisitely crafted short novel tells of a family learning to deal with the death of their own infant son after a baby girl is left on their doorstep for them to care for. 132 pages.

Martin, A. (2001). *Belle Teal.* New York: Scholastic. In 1962, fifth-grader Belle Teal faces the challenges of sticking up for Black students in her newly desegregated school in Coker Creek, Tennessee, as well as sorting out problems at home. 214 pages.

Matas, C. (2002). *Sparks Fly Upward.* Boston: Houghton Mifflin. In 1910, 12-year-old Rebecca and her Russian immigrant family try to adjust to a new culture while maintaining their traditions and faith. 192 pages.

Osofsky, A. (1996). *Free to Dream: The Making of a Poet: Langston Hughes.* New York: Lothrop, Lee, and Shepard. This is a biography of the Harlem poet who gave a voice to the African American experience in America. 112 pages.

Parker, S. (1999). *It's a Frog's Life! My Story of Life in a Pond.* Pleasantville, NY: Reader's Digest Children's Publishing. This is a look at the busy life of an English pond from a frog's viewpoint. 32 pages.

Paulsen, G. (1987). *Hatchet.* New York, NY: Simon & Schuster. The story of a boy's survival in the Canadian wilderness after the plane he is riding in crashes and the pilot dies. 181 pages.

Scruggs, A. (2000). *Jump Rope Magic.* New York: Blue Sky Press. Shameka and her crew, who love to skip rope to the music of the jump-rope beat, make even Mean Miss Minnie a believer in "jump rope magic." David Diaz's colorful illustrations add to the warmth and fun. 40 pages.

Soto, G. (1992). *The Skirt.* New York: Delacorte. After fourth-grader Miata accidentally leaves her folklorico skirt on the bus, she tries desperately to get it back before her parents find out. 74 pages.

Thomas, J. R. (1998). *Behind the Mask: The Life of Queen Elizabeth I.* Boston: Clarion. This biography of Elizabeth I, daughter of Henry VIII and Anne Boleyn, describes how she takes a personal misfortune and turns it around to make a difference in the world. 196 pages.

Thomas, J. R. (2005). *The Counterfeit Princess.* Boston: Clarion Books. This book is set in 16th-century England, as the young King Edward nears death and various factions vie for control of the throne. Fifteen-year-old Iris, who is trained as a spy for Princess Elizabeth, acts as the princess's double in an effort to save the country from the Duke of Northumberland. 176 pages.

Turner, A. (1987). *Nettie's Trip South.* New York: Macmillan. Based on the actual diary of the author's great-grandmother, this picture book tells about the cruel realities a 10-year-old girl encounters when she visits Richmond, Virginia, and witnesses a slave auction. 32 pages.

Wildlife Education. (1984). *Zoo Books 2: Alligators and Crocodiles.* San Diego: Wildlife Education. This series of books depicts a variety of zoo animals.

Ylvisaker, A. (2002). *Dear Papa.* Cambridge, MA: Candlewick. One year after her father's death in 1942, 9-year-old Isabelle begins writing him letters, which are interspersed with letters to other family members, relating important events in her life and how she feels about them. 184 pages.

Chapter 14
Reading Instruction for English Learners

 Learning Outcomes

After reading and studying this chapter you should be able to:

14.1 Describe the number of English learners in the United States, the percentage of U.S. classrooms that include English learners, and the reading proficiency of English learners compared to that of English-only students.

14.2 Describe what research says are the major approaches for educating English learners in general education classrooms.

14.3 Explain and apply the general principles of working with English learners including issues of teaching children who come from economically disadvantaged backgrounds.

14.4 Discuss and implement some specific instructional techniques for developing word recognition and comprehension with English learners.

Classroom Vignette

Cynthia studied her incoming class of third-graders and once more thought of the increasingly daunting task she faced. She had chosen to teach in a large urban district because she wanted to help the children who most needed her help, and she had never regretted that decision. But each year there seemed to be more challenges, including preparing students for the ever-increasing and ever-more-critical annual state testing and working with more and more students who did not speak English as their first language.

The latter challenge, working with English learners, was for her the most daunting one. She had completed her teacher education program a decade ago in the Midwest, where no attention had been given to working with children who did not speak English as their first language. This year, almost 30 percent of her students were English learners. A few of them spoke no English. Two of them did not have any sort of formal schooling. Others had received excellent instruction in their homeland schools and could read and write very well in their native languages.

What could she do? Her task, she knew, was to lead all of her English learners as well as her students who spoke English as their native language toward a level of literacy that would enable them to succeed in school and beyond. She knew a lot about good teaching, and she was convinced that good teaching is effective with all students. But she was constantly on the lookout for approaches that would prove particularly effective for English learners.

Learning to Read English as a Second Language in the United States

As Cynthia realizes, addressing the needs of English learners is a significant challenge. As we will note repeatedly in this chapter, good teaching is effective with all students. All students, including English learners, will benefit from more traditional instructional practices as well as practices motivated by constructivist and sociocultural theories. We presented these in Chapter 2 but we will briefly summarize them in In the Classroom 14.1. This is not to say that applying generally effective instructional practices is all that we can do for English learners. There are many more techniques we can use, and later in the Teaching Word Recognition and Comprehension we will present some of these techniques that are particularly effective with English learners.

Before we describe those techniques, we want to present some current information about English learners in U.S. schools. In the remainder of this introductory section, we consider linguistic diversity in U.S. schools, note the numbers of English learners in U.S. schools, present data on their reading proficiency, and note why mastering English is particularly important at the present time.

Linguistic Diversity in U.S. Schools

U.S. schools have always been populated with children from diverse linguistic backgrounds, and teachers have had to confront the challenges and opportunities of linguistic diversity for many years. The apparently opposing forces of the home language and

In the Classroom 14.1

Traditional and Constructivists Instructional Principles

- Focus on academically relevant tasks. Concentrate on important topics, skills, and strategies that students really need to master.
- Employ active teaching. From the construstiviest point of view it is important to follow the gradual release of responsibility model. Begin instruction with a rich explanation and modeling, then allow the students to take over the tasks. As students progess they can take on more and more of the tasks as you and other students support them.
- Use direct explanation. In teaching strategies, (1) give students a description of the strategy and when, how, and why it should be used; (2) model it; (3) work along with students as they use the strategy; (4) gradually give students increased responsibility for using the strategy; and (5) have students use the strategy independently.
- Provide instruction in students' zone of proximal development. Instruct students at a level that challenges them but allows them to achieve with effort and your assistance. While doing so, scaffold students' efforts. Provide students with the temporary support they need to complete tasks they could not complete independently. This will move them to higher levels of achievement.
- Foster active learning. Give students opportunities to manipulate and grapple with the material they are learning.
- Distinguish between instruction and practice. Instruction consists of teaching students knowledge, skills, and strategies. Practice consists of asking students to use the knowledge, skills, and strategies that they have already been taught.
- Provide sufficient and timely feedback. Whenever possible, respond to students' work with immediate and specific feedback. Ensure that students contextualize, review, and practice what is learned. Real learning takes time, effort, and a lot of practice. Feedback and scaffolding is what moves the students from explanation and modeling to independent work.
- Teach for transfer. Transfer seldom occurs automatically. If we want students to take what they have learned in one context and use it in a new context, we need to show them how to do so.

English have been at issue since the birth of the United States. Benjamin Franklin, John Adams, and Noah Webster, for example, all argued that a common language was a key element in promoting social unity (Simpson, 1986). Indeed, throughout the development of the U.S. public school system during the 19th and early 20th centuries, the concept of one people/one language was central (Higham, 1988). The world wars, particularly World War I and its aftermath, marked by southern and eastern European immigration, solidified this belief in the minds of many Americans, a belief that some still hold. In fact, three U.S. states have recently passed legislation that severely limits the use of English learners' home language in school (Goldenberg, 2015).

Yet other Americans have always viewed ethnic pride as a hallmark of American freedom and the suppression of language and culture as contradicting the American spirit. They argue that the strength of America lies in the diversity of culture, beliefs, and perspectives of persons who flock to the United States seeking a better life (Tollefson, 1995). This tolerance for diversity is certainly reflected in major studies of reading instruction for English learners, including Robert Slavin and Alan Cheung's *A Synthesis of Research on Language of Reading Instruction for English Language Learners* (2005), Diane August and Tim Shanahan's *Developing Literacy in Second Language Learners* (2009), and Claude Goldenberg and Rhoda Coleman's *Promoting Academic Achievement Among English Learners* (2010).

We agree with this latter group, and our position is simple: It is absolutely crucial that all students become proficient in English. This does not, however, mean that students should abandon their native language.

English Learners in Today's Schools

According to the National Center for Educational Statistics' *Conditions of Education 2017*, in 2014–2015 there were 9.4 million students, 9.3 percent of all students enrolled, participating in programs for English learners (McFarland et al., 2017, https://nces.ed.gov/pubsearch/pubsinfo.asp?pubid=2017144). This figure has increased every year and will continue to increase for the foreseeable future. As shown in Figure 14.1, the vast majority of English learners, 77 percent of them, have Spanish as their home language. No other home language accounts for more than about 2 percent of English learners. Although all states have some English learners, the percentages of them vary hugely by state, with California, the state with the highest percentage enrolling 22 percent English learners and West Virginia the state with the fewest English learners, enrolling just 1 percent English learners (McFarland et al., 2017). Yet "Nearly 3 in 4 American classrooms now includes at least one English-language learner" (Sparks, 2016, https://www.edweek.org/ew/articles/2016/05/11/teaching-english-language-learners-what-does-the-research.html).

Figure 14.1 Most Common Home Languages of English Learners

Home Language	Number of English Learners	Percentage of All English Learners in the U.S.
Spanish	3,707,818	77.1
Arabic	109,165	2.3
Chinese	104,279	2.2
Vietnamese	85,289	1.8
Hmong	37,432	0.8
Somali	33,713	0.7
Russian	32,493	0.7
Haitian	31,428	0.7
Tagalog	28,547	0.6
Korean	28,530	0.6

English Learners' Reading Proficiency

According to the most recent elementary level National Assessment of Educational Progress report (2018), the average score for fourth-grade English learners on the reading assessment was 189, while that for English only-students was 226. This is a substantial difference. It means that the average English learner scored at the Basic Level, which NAEP defines as "partial mastery of prerequisite skills," while the average English-only student scored at the Proficient Level, which NAEP Defines as "competency of challenging subject matter." The results for eighth grade students were similar: ELs scored markedly lower that English-only students.

The Critical Importance of Mastering English in Today's World

We know that in the past most immigrant families became English-dominant in less than two generations, so why is there anything to be concerned about? We know that the children in our classrooms will more than likely become speakers of English. Isn't it a simple case of waiting until this happens? The answer is no! Research indicates that it takes English learners at least five years to reach the oral skill level of their English-speaking peers (Cummins, 2001). Waiting five years to begin reading instruction would mean delaying literacy learning for many children until they are adolescents. This would be educationally and morally absurd. We know that all children need to begin literacy learning as early as possible in order to become effective readers and writers.

But there is more to be said about the current situation. Several other considerations make English learners' mastering English even more crucial at this time. The level of literacy needed to succeed in the United States has increased dramatically over the past decades and continues to do so. While a person can get a low paying service job with rudimentary English skills, getting a good job that pays enough to lead a comfortable life requires advanced levels of literacy and in most cases advanced schooling, which itself requires advanced levels of literacy. Also, with the advent of the Common Core and its provision that all students, regardless of their English language skills, read challenging material, undertake sophisticated tasks, and demonstrate sophisticated understanding of that material, it has become even more critical that English learners become proficient in English. Although the Common Core requires that students attain these high levels of competence and understanding, it provides very little information on how schools and teachers are to accomplish this task (Coleman & Goldenberg, 2012).

Finally, there is the issue of the importance of more Americans mastering more than one language. As Goldenberg put it in an open letter to the U.S. Congress, "Congress: Bilingualism is Not a Handicap" (2015). Supporting this position, recent reports from the American Academy of Arts and Sciences (Commission on Language Learning, 2017) and the National Academy of Sciences (2017) emphasize "the benefits of second language learning for all, the need to encourage language study, and the contributions of dual language and heritage language learners and their communities to U.S. multilingualism" (Arias, 2018).

Reflect and Apply

1. Listen carefully to the radio or television or examine several magazines or newspapers. What kinds of attitudes toward nonnative speakers of English do you find in these media?

2. Imagine a 10-year-old student who has just arrived in the United States after growing up in Iraq. Brainstorm a list of just a few of the myriad topics familiar to virtually all 10-year-olds

who grew up in the United States but probably unfamiliar to this student from Iraq. Now brainstorm a list of a few topics you expect are familiar to 10-year-olds who grew up in Iraq but are probably unfamiliar to U.S. students.

MyLab Education **Self-Check 14.1**

What the Research Says About Teaching English Learners

Prompted by the huge increase in English learners in U.S. schools, a good deal of research has focused on how to best help ELs develop their English literacy skills. A number of sources published over the past two decades provide excellent summaries of this research. The research focuses on instructional issues (Gersten & Baker, 2000), the effects of languages used for instruction (Slavin & Cheung, 2005), and other issues (August & Shanahan, 2009). Claude Goldenberg and Rhoda Coleman (2010) a present and brief and readable review. Goldenberg and Coleman's work has had the greatest influence. However, if you are looking for a concise summary of the book, we recommend Goldenberg's "Unlocking the Research on English Learners" (2013), which is available at http://www.aft.org/periodical/american-educator/summer-2013/unlocking-research-english-learners.

We now turn to practical application of what we have learned from the research of others, what we have learned from our own research, and what we have learned from our own teaching and learning over the years. Your own situation will, of course, be unique. You may have a class in which only one language other than English is spoken, or you may have a class in which several different languages are spoken. You may have only one or two nonnative speakers in your classroom, or you may have many. Whatever your specific situation, the following guidelines and principles, will lead you to ask appropriate questions and work toward effective classroom instruction.

Effective Practices Are Likely to Be Effective with English Learners

Nearly a century of research on teaching provide evidence on what sorts of instruction is likely to result in improved student learning. We presented this list In the Classroom 14.1. Moreover, you will also see many of them repeat in recommendations we outlined at the beginning of the chapter. This is important. There is a lot of agreement here! Additionally, most of them make good common sense. It is a big plus when research, theory, and common sense coincide. So here are the effective practices Goldenberg lists in Figure 14.2.

As a check on their making good common sense, try stating the opposite of each of them and see how much sense that makes. For example, do you think that having unclear goals and objectives or failing to provide learners with feedback are likely to promote learning?

English Learners Require Additional Instructional Supports

Of course, English learners require additional support. They are faced with the dual tasks of learning the language and learning the content being taught. Additionally,

Figure 14.2 Instructional Practice That Work for All Students Including English Learners

• clear goal and objectives	• informative feedback to learners
• appropriate and challenging material	• application of new learning and transfer to new situtations
• well-designed instruction and instructional routines	• practice and periodic review
• clear instruction and supportive guidance	• structured, focused interactions with other students
• effective modeling of skills, strategies, and procedures	• frequent informal assessments, with releaching as needed
• active student engagement and participation	• wee-established classroom routine and behavior norms

some of them are faced with a new and challenging situation, learning to get along in the United States and in U.S. schools. Goldenberg's recommendations here again echo other parts of this chapter and make good common sense. He groups these under the heading of sheltered instruction. The goals of sheltered instruction are to promote both English language development and content learning.

- Building on student experiences and familiar content, then add on material that will broaden and deepen students' knowledge.
- Providing students with necessary background knowledge
- Designating language *and* content objectives for each lesson. Decide what students will learn about the content and about the English language.
- Using graphic organizers (tables, web diagrams, Venn diagrams) to organize information and clarify concepts
- Making instruction and learning tasks extremely clear
- Using pictures, demonstrations, and real-life objects
- Providing hands-on, interactive learning activities
- Providing redundant information (gestures, visual cues)
- Giving additional practice and time for discussion of key concepts
- Using sentence frames and models to help students talk about academic content
- Providing instruction differentiated by students' English language proficiency

As Goldenberg notes, these aspects of sheltered instruction do not have as strong a research base as the generally effective practices listed in Figure 14.2. Nevertheless, these make good sense and are activities we definitely recommend. A lesson plan with a number of sheltered instruction components is shown on the Appendix.

The Home Language Can Be Used to Promote Academic Development

We fully agree with Goldenberg when he says that the home language can be used to promote academic development. In fact, we would say "can and should be used." However, as Goldenberg notes and as you have almost certainly learned from the news media, this is a hotly debated issue. There are really two issues here: (1) whether to provide students with some sort of dual language education and (2) whether to use the home language to support students in an otherwise all-English classroom by means of activities like giving students directions in their home language. Figure 14.3 lists some of the many types of dual language programs available in the United States. Goldenberg asserts that "reading instruction in the home language can be beneficial," and we absolutely agree. However, we do not discuss dual language education or debate its merits in this chapter because whether or not you use dual language education is unlikely to be your decision; it will be up to your school, district, or state. We will, however, suggest opportunities for providing home language support that is useful regardless of what sort of classroom you teach in.

Before moving on to discuss principles and instructional activities suggested by other authorities, we want to mention a valuable resource that Goldenberg has created. As part of a project that will allow teachers, supervisors, and researchers to assess the quality of the instruction that takes place in elementary classrooms that include English learners, Goldenberg has assembled a set of more that 60 short videos (generally, 2–10 minutes) in which skilled teachers demonstrate the effective practices and additional instructional supports described above. For example, one video shows a teacher explicitly stating an objective, another shows two teachers soliciting students' prior knowledge, and a third shows a teacher as she teaches student to visualize from a verbal description. These are free of charge, require no registration, and are a terrific resource. They are available at https://people.stanford.edu/claudeg/cqell in the Observational Protocol section.

Figure 14.3 Some Types of Programs for English Learners

- **Two-Way Immersion/Dual Language.** Native English speakers and English learners are taught academic content in both languages for an extended period of time with the goal that both groups develop academic proficiency in both languages.
- **Transitional Bilingual Education.** English learners receive academic instruction in their first language for part of the day. For the remainder of the day, they receive some ESL instruction and spend some time in regular classes.
- **ESL Pullout.** English learners attend mainstream classes for much of the day and also meet separately in small groups with an ESL instructor who focuses on language development.
- **Content-Based ESL.** English learners receive ESL instruction, taught by an ESL teacher, in preparation for grade-level content instruction in English. The emphasis is on language development, but attention is also given to academic vocabulary and content area concepts.
- **Sheltered English Instruction.** English learners are taught academic content in English by a regular teacher. However, the English language used by the teacher and the activities students engage in are adapted to the proficiency level of the students. While the instruction focuses on content, sheltered English instruction also promotes English language development.
- **Structured English Immersion.** English learners are taught subject matter in English by a licensed teacher who is also licensed in ESL or bilingual education. The teacher is proficient in the first language of the student. Students may use their native language for clarification, but the teacher uses only English. No ESL instruction is provided in this model.
- **Heritage Language.** English learners are taught literacy in the language the student and his or her parents regard as their native, home, or ancestral language.

MyLab Education **Self-Check 14.2**

MyLab Education **Application Exercise 14.1:** Supporting English Learners in the Regular Classroom

Teaching Economically Disadvaged Students

Not all English learners live difficult economic lives, but many do, especially in our cities and rural areas. Lisa Delpit is, an African American educator who has worked extensively with urban children, many of whom come from homes that struggle with difficult economic conditions. Through her work, she has identified many of the factors that help raise their motivation and achievement. Her principles extend what we have already presented about English learners. Here we discuss and interpret those of Delpit's principles that we see as most important for working with English learners.

DEMAND CRITICAL THINKING

Often, we fall into the trap of thinking that students who speak a different language are not as bright as other students. Consequently, we often reason that they cannot handle critical thinking. No judgment could be more debilitating to students' growth. The goals of a high level of literacy and the literacy curriculum that we discussed throughout this book are just as appropriate for English learners as they are for any other students. For example, teaching for deep understanding—using techniques like Text Talk and Questioning the Author—is absolutely crucial to second-language learners.

ENSURE ACCESS TO THE BASIC SKILLS

We sometimes begin teaching nonnative speakers with less emphasis on skills than English-only students typically receive. This will not work. We are not suggesting that you teach only basic skills. As we just noted, a high level of literacy is the goal. But do remember that although not all children come to school with the same skills, all students need to master the building blocks that lead to literacy. Students from higher income homes are more likely to have had reading instruction at home, or at least they have been read to. These students are also more likely to have attended preschool and received instruction in basic skills.

As a teacher, you want to be certain that your students acquire whatever skills they need to be successful in school and in later life, something Timothy Hayden, a third-grade teacher, makes a very conscious effort to do:

> One thing I really try to work on with my Puerto Rican students is mastery of basic skills, such as standard usage and spelling, while still giving them plenty of chances to engage in critical thinking. This is a tough decision to make because I know that in many cases my kids know more than their English skills show, and so in some sense I'm slowing them down to work on the basics. Yet I also know that if they can't read when they leave school or use poor grammar or spelling when they're looking for a job, they won't get very far. That's why I feel that I have to balance attention to basics with attention to higher-level stuff.
>
> —Timothy Hayden, third-grade teacher

EMPOWER STUDENTS TO CHALLENGE RACIST VIEWS OF THEIR COMPETENCE AND WORTHINESS

Racism and classism often extend to children who are nonnative speakers of English. You must support your English learners' egos and help them build the sort of self-worth that will lead them to persevere when they encounter challenges. All students need the support and skills that will enable them to meet challenges, be successful, and realize that success is something under their control. Creating an "I can do it!" attitude in your ELs and conveying to them that you as their teacher hold an "I can help you do it!" attitude are crucial. In the Classroom 14.2 shows how sixth-grade teacher Ann Beecher provides reading experiences that promote positive attitudes.

In the Classroom 14.2

Using the Shared Reading Experience in a Sixth-Grade ESL Class

Ann Beecher teaches sixth grade in a public school in a Los Angeles suburb. The majority of the students in her class speak Spanish as their primary language, with a sprinkling of students speaking a variety of other languages. Ms. Beecher has found that the shared reading experience—students and teacher reading aloud and discussing the text together—is a highly effective technique for developing confidence and building on students' skills in reading and speaking English. "My English learners are often reticent to risk being wrong or making mistakes when it comes to speaking or reading in English," Ms. Beecher says. "So I need to think of ways to create a safe environment that will support their learning. One of those ways is the shared reading experience. It's a risk-free way for them to use oral language." Here are the steps Ms. Beecher usually follows in preparing a shared reading experience:

- Choose a selection. Ms. Beecher always chooses a short selection, something like one of the 50 brief selections in Tracy Kelly's *50 Things You Should Know About American Presidents* or a poem from their literature text. One of the class favorites is 'The Shark' by John Ciardi. They enjoy reciting the colorful words Ciardi uses to describe the shark, such as *gulper, ripper, snatcher,* and *grabber*. "The key is choosing something that will engage students, something that they will really enjoy and can relate to and something that builds what we study in science, social studies or language arts." Ms. Beecher says. "One of the values of using the shared reading experience is that the students are reading 'at grade' materials. This is a big boost to their confidence. It gives them a real sense of accomplishment."
- Set up the document camera, and make copies of the selection for each student.
- Prepare and motivate students for the selection. "This usually takes very little effort," Ms. Beecher says. "When the kids see the document camera, they know it means we're going to read something together. It's one of their favorite things we do. Like singing or reciting jazz chants, they enjoy the rhythm of the language and the community experience of speaking the same words together."
- With expression and enthusiasm, read through the selection once or twice, and then invite students to read along in unison.
- Focus on a particular reading skill or strategy. "If we are reading rhyming poetry, usually I will circle the rhyming words on the chart or document camers and have students do the same on their copies. I then talk about certain words and check for students' understanding. Also, sometimes when I first read the piece through, I will stop occasionally and have students predict what will happen next."
- Follow up the reading with a variety of activities. Use art (illustrating the shark gulping, ripping, snatching, grabbing, for example), writing, or evaluating: "How did we do? Did you like the piece? Why? What did you like about it? Is there anything we should do differently next time? What's your favorite new word you learned?"

BUILD ON THE STUDENTS' PRIOR KNOWLEDGE

Using metaphors and experiences from the children's world is another technique good teachers use instinctively. We know the importance of background knowledge. As Delpit suggests, instead of insisting that all children have the same background knowledge at the beginning, deal with the knowledge and background students have and use that as the basis of teaching. This means you will need to learn something about your students' cultures. For example, if you are teaching about the destructive power of tornadoes and have Vietnamese children in your class, you can use their knowledge of the awesome power of typhoons as a bridge to understanding the power of tornadoes.

CREATE A SENSE OF FAMILY AND CARING

For some students, school can seem a distant place, unwelcoming and perhaps even frightening. ESL teacher Lillian Colon-Vila knows how crucial it is that all students feel that they are a valuable part of the class and will be supported in their efforts by both the teacher and the other students in the class:

> To welcome my English learners, I always begin the semester by telling a story. It's usually a simple one to welcome them to the United States and particularly to my classroom. Because I use the students' names and their native countries, I invent the stories on the spur of the moment. I use puppets, pictures, flash cards, or the whiteboard to draw pictures as I go along.
>
>> I make it a point to share my own first day of school, too—how I stuttered, mispronounced the teacher's name, and wished for the floor to swallow me. The students laugh and relate to my experience. The iceberg between us breaks, and I can begin to teach.
>
> —Lillian Colon-Vila, ESL multigrade teacher

In the terminology we used earlier in the book, your classroom must be a literate environment for *all* students.

MONITOR AND ASSESS STUDENTS' NEEDS

Effective teaching cannot be done without careful assessment and evaluation of what students know and learn. Teachers need to be vigilant and prepared to discontinue teaching techniques that prove inappropriate for some students. Students can often benefit from a different teaching strategy when the one initially attempted did not work. Such choices require careful reasoning based on data gathered in assessing the students. As we emphasized in Chapter 5, assessment does not simply mean formal assessment. You will need to use a wide range of techniques to gauge students' strengths and weaknesses and then create ways to build on their strengths. These techniques are likely to include the use of formal tests, but they will also include talking to students, carefully observing them as they work at school tasks, and seeking insights from parents and others in your students' home communities. Figure 14.4 illustrates how a drawing can show a student's understanding of a story.

HONOR AND RESPECT CHILDREN'S HOME CULTURES

It would be difficult to imagine anything seemingly easier than honoring and respecting children's home cultures, but unfortunately honor and respect are too often lacking in classrooms. Knowledge that has been gained in children's home cultures constitutes a strength that can be brought into the classroom and used as the basis for learning to read about all manner of ideas and topics. Besides, changing children's cultural orientations and allegiances is not really an option. Children come to school having spent a huge amount of time within their cultures and their families, and once they begin school, they will continue to spend far more time at home than in the classroom. You cannot win against such odds. It is just not possible to instill in children a totally different culture in a few hours a day—it may even be impossible to do so in a lifetime. Your goal must be to support students' attempts to maintain their cultural identities and to support them in becoming successful in the mainstream culture represented by the school. One small step toward doing this might be taken during birthday celebrations. Inviting English learners to share their birthday traditions with the class gives status to those traditions and adds to other students' store of knowledge about different cultures.

Another and more significant step toward demonstrating and fostering respect for children's home cultures is to provide students with literature that accurately and fairly represents a variety of cultures, including literature involving Hispanic figures such as *Cinco de Mayo* by Linda Lowery, *Portraits of Hispanic Heroes* by Juan Filipe

Figure 14.4 Maria's Drawing of *Island of the Blue Dolphins* by Scott O'Dell (1960) Reveals Her Understanding of the Story

Herrera, *Napí* by Antonio Ramírez, and *Esperanza Rising* by Pam Munoz Ryan. The last story deals with the combined issues of immigaration, economic displacement, and second language learning.

Reflect and Apply

3. Think about attitudes toward English learners that you have observed. Have you encountered attitudes that might negatively influence the ways in which teachers interact with students? How might you guard against allowing those attitudes to negatively affect your classroom style?

4. Consider your own family traditions. Can you think of any holiday celebrations you and your family enjoy that are not widely observed? Do you think they are any less valuable because they are not more widely observed? How might you use these holiday celebrations when you are teaching students?

MyLab Education **Self-Check 14.3**

MyLab Education **Application Exercise 14.2:** Assisting Children from Economically Disadvantaged Backgrounds

General Instructional Techniques for Working with English Learners

There are a number of instructional techniques that assist English learners as they learn to read, write, listen, and speak. Michael Kamil and Elizabeth Bernhardt (2004) have developed a set of techniques specifically for working with English learners. Here we present a slightly modified and shortened version of their recommendations. Like Kamil and Bernhardt, we have placed these techniques in an order reflecting their utility. Thus, you should probably attempt to implement these principles in the order given. Also, you are likely to have a good deal more success if you employ a number of the suggestions rather than just one or two of them.

Take Advantage of the 20 Percent Rule

Recognize that although languages are different there is considerable overlap between them. In fact, the overlap between languages can be as much as 20 percent. Thus, your task in teaching literacy in a second language is far easier than if there were little or no overlap. You do not have to start at the beginning with English learners; rather, you can consider yourself as being one-fifth of the way to success.

Figure 14.5 shows the 20 percent rule in action. In this graphic display of the generation of electricity, there are 17 Spanish words used. Three of the words—*natural, vapor,* and *magma*—are identical to the equivalent terms in English. Another seven words—*turbina, generador, uso, energía, geotérmica, producir,* and *electricidad*—are almost identical and certainly recognizable. Words that have a very close spelling in both languages are called cognates. It is also useful when words share common roots across languages—*vapor, turbine, magma*. This simple example illustrates the overlap between English and Spanish and reminds us that children do possess substantial information that they can draw on for reading second-language texts.

Of course, as we all know, there is never a free lunch, and this rule holds true for the 20 percent dividend. The percentage will be different for each language. In some languages, the overlap may be greater than 20 percent, but in others considerably less.

When students in your classroom have some native-language literacy and are able to work with content, have them conduct Internet searches on topics you are covering in current events. For example, major new geologic discoveries, such as finding the bones of an ancient mammal, are often reported in magazines like *Scholastic News* or *Time for Kids* (which are available in both print and digital form) or in books that children naturally gravitate to. Such findings are almost always discussed in the Internet press. Have your students read something about these findings in their native-language press and report on any differences between reports in English and what they have read. Such an activity reinforces using their first language to support their learning of the second. It also enhances their critical thinking skills by asking them to compare and contrast information presented in an array of sources and boosts their self-esteem by demonstrating to their peers that bilingualism actually provides greater access to information than monolingualism does. Newsela.com provides some new articles in Spanish and on Readworks.com the students can hear the informational and fiction articles read aloud.

Figure 14.5 Graphic Display of Overlap Between Spanish and English Vocabulary

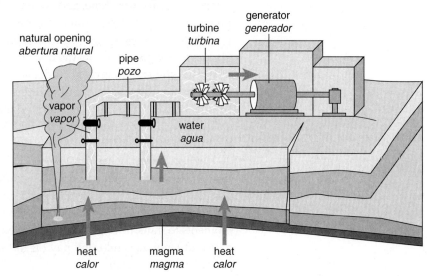

The use of geothermal energy to produce electricity
El uso de la energía geotérmica para producir electricidad

SOURCE: *Ciencias* by Mallision, Mallision, Smallwood, & Valentino. Copyright © 1985 by Silver Burdett Ginn, Simon & Schuster Elementary. Used by permission.

Give English Learners and Yourself Plenty of Time

It is important to remember that children who do not speak English as a native language will, in all likelihood, not be as automatic as native speakers at completing any English-language task, including, of course, reading. Figure 14.6 provides an example of the very different amounts of time it would take students reading at three different rates to complete a typical intermediate-grade book, in this case Gary Soto's *The Skirt*. If children are reading a longer book, something like Sara Brierley's *Lion: A Long Way Home*, the amounts of time needed vary even more: To complete this book, Maria would need about 5 hours, Carlos would need about 8 hours, and Chen would need over 20 hours. The instructional implication of these illustrations is straight-forward: Provide English learners with extra time to complete the linguistic tasks you ask them to do.

Figure 14.6 Times Required for Three Students, with Varying Reading Rates, to Read Gary Soto's *The Skirt*

Student	Reading Rate (Words per Minute)	Chapter One (1,000 Words)	Whole Book (8,000 Words)
Maria	250	4 minutes	32 minutes
Carlos	150	7 minutes	53 minutes
Chen	50	20 minutes	2 hours, 40 minutes

Following this simple suggestion can minimize what is perhaps the greatest difficulty teachers face in multilanguage classrooms. The question, of course, is how you can provide this extra time, and we have several suggestions. Students who need the time can be given opportunities to complete their work as part of free-choice activities. Or they might be allowed to take home work that isn't completed during class. Or you might give students the questions you will ask ahead of time during reading lessons, being sure to give *all* students sufficient time to do the reading and thinking necessary to answer them. Still another option is to shorten some of the selections students are asked to read by summarizing parts of them. In the Classroom 14.3, for example, includes a summary of the first half of Pegi Deitz Shea's *The Whispering Cloth: A Refugee's Story.*

To be an effective teacher of English learners, you also need to give yourself extra time, particularly when making day-to-day informal assessments of their progress. You will have to train yourself to perceive their progress in different ways, as that progress will not look or sound the same as progress for native speakers. The extra moments to think through whether you have made the right instructional decision for a second-language child will pay off in the end, both for the child and for your self-confidence as a teacher.

In the Classroom 14.3

Summarizing Part of a Selection

The Whispering Cloth: A Refugee's Story is a touching story of a young Hmong girl, Mai, who learns to create embroidered tapestries—pándau in the Hmong language—while in a refugee camp in Thailand. The book is beautifully illustrated with both watercolors and reproductions of the pándau Mai creates. Although the book is not a long read for students who read fluently, for students beginning to read English it constitutes a formidable task. Summarizing the first half of the book would simplify that task considerably, particularly for Hmong students, coming as they do from a culture that does not have a written language.

Introduce the book in a fashion that you and your students will be comfortable with. You might tell children that it is the story of a young Hmong girl in a refugee camp in Thailand, show children the location of the refugee camp and the Hmongs' homeland in northern Laos, and briefly discuss the situation that forced the Hmongs to become refugees. Then explain to children what embroidery or pándau is, show a sample of embroidery (actual Hmong pándau, if possible), and explain that pándau plays an important part in the story. You might also tell children that the main characters in the story are Mai and her grandmother, who is simply called Grandma.

Finally, tell children that you are going to summarize the first half of the book for those who would like it summarized and that they can either listen to your summary or begin reading on their own. After children have made their choices, perhaps with some guidance from you, students who want to hear your summary can gather around you as you read or summarize it, perhaps saying something like this:

> As *The Whispering Cloth* opens, we learn that Mai lives in a refugee camp with her grandmother and that Mai can remember little of her life outside of the camp. She knows, though, that many people leave the refugee camp and some of them go to America, and it seems that she would like to go there, too. Partly to give her something to do and partly to provide the family with some income, Grandma teaches Mai to make pándau. Mai learns very quickly and is soon very good at making this beautiful "flowery cloth." One day, Mai begins to work on a pándau in which she tells a story that is filling her head with thoughts.

After reading the summary, introduce the reading itself, saying something like:

> As you read the rest of the book, you will see pictures of the pándau that Mai stitched. Now read the rest of the book to see the pándau and what it meant to Mai and her Grandma and what they decided to do with it.

Use the Rosetta Stone Technique

We have all heard about the wonder of the Rosetta Stone. This tremendous discovery, shown in Figure 14.7, contains the same text in Egyptian hieroglyphics, Egyptian demotic script, and several ancient Greek languages. The discovery of the Rosetta Stone allowed linguists to decipher Egyptian hieroglyphics, which they did not know how to read, based on their knowledge of ancient Greek, which they could read.

One useful vocabulary technique for working with a class that includes English language learners is based on this approach. If you make a chart of everyday English words in one column, your students who speak other languages can contribute the equivalent words from each of their languages in other columns. Alternatively, your English language learners might periodically put words from their native languages on the chart and solicit the equivalent English word and words in other languages represented in your class. Or as you encounter words in a content lesson, you could use them as the entries to the Rosetta chart and have students add the equivalent words from their languages, creating a multilingual word wall.

The Rosetta Stone word wall can be used to build vocabulary and as a source of words for writing. It supports both word choice and pronunciation. Whatever the specific source of words you put on the chart, be certain to practice pronouncing both non-English and English words with English learners as well as with the entire class. In this way, all students will be able to do well at some parts of the task. Also, not only will your English-only students begin to learn some vocabulary in another language, they will also begin to appreciate the challenges some of their classmates face. And they will be able to see that ELs know a great deal that native English speakers do not know.

Involve Parents, Siblings, and Other Speakers of the Children's Languages

Often, parents, siblings, or other relatives can help in translating between the native language and English, or vice versa. Sometimes all it takes is a bridge between languages to get children started. Translating the first page or so of a text they are going to read or making a graphic organizer of what they are going to read, such as the example shown in Figure 14.8, can be extremely helpful. Moreover, such a bridge can work both ways. As students become more proficient in English, many times they assume the role of translator for parents who are not quite as proficient. This will give students a reason for wanting to learn more English and may encourage the parents to learn more English as well. In addition, as students become increasingly competent in English, they will be motivated to become still more competent.

Siblings can sometimes be particularly helpful in the classroom. Older brothers or sisters who may be reluctant to participate in their own class because they are not as proficient as their English-only classmates may work extremely well with their younger brothers or sisters. An added bonus here is that, when tutoring these younger students, the older siblings may very well realize that they know more English than they thought and consequently feel encouraged to attempt to read when they would have otherwise been reluctant to do so.

Use Peers as Tutors

Older students who speak the same languages as your students and are somewhat more proficient in reading English than your students can be a great benefit. Again, sometimes the older students may realize that they know more English than they thought and be encouraged to

Figure 14.7 The Rosetta Stone—Showing Greek, Demotic, and Hieroglyphic Scripts

Figure 14.8 Graphic Organizer in English and Spanish for a Section of Lynn Rosenblatt's *Monarch Magic!*

attempt more challenging reading tasks themselves. They may also be motivated to learn more because they begin to realize what they do not know yet or because they wish to do a better job in helping the younger students.

Of course, students who are the same age as the tutees but have somewhat more advanced English reading skills can also serve as classroom tutors. And as is the case with cross-age tutors, peer tutors are likely to benefit from the teaching they do. As we have noted before, the research strongly demonstrates that students tutoring other students is a true win-win situation in which both tutor and tutee benefit markedly (Cohen, Kulic, & Kulic, 1982), and recent research indicates that this can be particularly true with English learners (Marieswari & Prena, 2016). Finally, students are not the only people resources that may be of help in your classroom. Aides, volunteers, college students preparing to be teachers, and sometimes even administrators and maintenance personnel can perform a variety of helpful tasks with English learners.

Bilingual teacher Margaret Thayer suggests one powerful way to motivate students and foster interactions between English learners and English only students—establishing a buddy system:

> One of the most successful things we have done in our classroom is to set up a buddy system in which we deliberately pair our native English speakers with our English language learners. We do this at the beginning of the year or whenever an English language learner enters the class, and from that time on, the two students do many things together. They work as a pair doing in-class assignments, talk about what they have read, and work together on homework. Of course, in many cases, the native speaker serves more often as the tutor and the English language learner as the learner. But whenever possible, we try to get the English language learner in the teacher's role. Often, for example, the English language learner teaches his English-speaking buddy some things about his language or culture. And, in many cases, the pairing doesn't end at the school. Buddies often visit each other's homes, share holidays, and pal around together. As I said, the buddy system has been a real success. Also, it does not take up a lot of the teacher's time, always an important consideration when you are trying a new approach in the classroom.

Margaret Thayer

Fifth-grade teacher

Give Students the Freedom to Choose the Language in Which to Respond

Research tells us that students often demonstrate greater abilities when they are given the option of responding in the language in which they feel most comfortable. This is particularly true, of course, when the text is in English and the students are not fluent in English.

Although allowing students to respond in their native languages is a very easy change for you as an instructor to make, it can pay big dividends. In addition to demonstrating better understanding when using the language of their choice, students may also be able to remember more of what they have learned in their native language. Also, students' language preference may vary for different reading materials. For example, a reading passage about a student's native country might be best responded to in the student's native language. In reading a passage about American history, however, a student might choose to use English. The key is to allow the student to choose the appropriate language in which to respond.

One concern some teachers have about this technique is that they may not be able to understand and assess what the students wrote or said. However, even if you cannot understand the language the student chooses, all is not lost. The easiest way to handle the situation is to have the student respond in his native language and then have him do the translation into English. Note the terrific practice this gives the student. He is, in effect, using the language-experience approach—writing down his own words and then translating them. Note also that allowing students to do this is one way of providing the extra time we have recommended. Alternatively, if the student cannot read what he wrote back to you or translate it into English, you might obtain the assistance of a sibling, parent, or other speaker of the language in the class to do the translating.

In addition to giving students the opportunity to respond in the language they choose, you can sometimes give them the opportunity to read in the language of their choice. Bilingual books, a growing set of children's books in which the same book contains both English and another language, make providing this option very convenient. A small sample of the books in this growing genre is shown in The Reading Corner. If you, aides, parent volunteers, or other volunteers speak the home languages of your students, you have still other opportunities to tap their native-language skills. You can give directions for classroom work and homework in both English and the students' native languages. This can be a huge help to students in doing their class work, and it can be a tremendous help to parents in assisting their children with homework.

We will conclude our general section about teaching English learners with a brief discussion of the SIOP model. Echevarria, Voigt, and Short's Sheltered Instruction Observation Protocol (SIOP) model (2016) was developed over the course of a 7-year research project and is the most widely used approach to sheltered instruction. The SIOP model is specifically designed to promote English learners' English language skills and their academic literacy in content areas. Echevarria and her colleagues' book, *Making Content Comprehensible for English Learners: The SIOP Model*, now in its fifth edition, provides a detailed description of the approach and is certainly worth reading for those who will be working with English learners in content areas. Here are the major tenets of the model:

- Identify the language demands of the content course
- Plan language objectives for all lessons, and make them explicit to students
- Emphasize academic vocabulary development
- Activate and strengthen background knowledge
- Promote oral interaction and extended academic talk
- Review vocabulary and content concepts
- Give students feedback on language use in class

The Reading Corner

Books Available in Bilingual Formats

Books with text in two languages, usually on facing pages, provide an outstanding opportunity for English learners to practice reading in both their own language and English. Moreover, the text in their stronger language acts as a scaffold for reading the text in their weaker language. The books listed below are a sample of the many books available. Searching sites such as Amazon with the terms bilingual books and dual-language books will yield hundreds more. Additionally, to locate books for Spanish-speaking students, Isabel Schon's *Recommended Books in Spanish for Children and Young Adults: 1991–1995* (1996), *Recommended Books in Spanish for Children and Young Adults: 1996-1999* (2001), *Recommended Books in Spanish for Children and Young Adults: 2000-2004* (2004), *Recommended Books in Spanish for Children and Young Adults: 2004-2008* (2008) are very useful.

George Ancona. *The Piñata Maker/El penatero.* Harcourt, 1994. With full-color photos and text in both Spanish and English, this book provides a glimpse into the art of piñata making. 40 pages.

Rebecca T. Anonuevo. *Ang Mahiyaing Manok (The Shy Rooster).* Pan Asia Publications, 2000. In this English/Filipino book, a shy young rooster who cannot crow as well or as loud as the other roosters proves his worth. 32 pages.

Enebor Attard. *Ali Baba and the Forty Thieves* (Bilingual Book in English and Hindi). Basking Ridge, NJ: Language Lizards, 2011. Colorfully illustrated version of this classic tale. 32 pages. This is available in English and over 20 other languages.

Eileen Browne. *Handa's Surprise* (Somali–English Bilingual Edition). Mantra Publishing, 1999. In this African tale, Handa puts delicious fruits in a basket to take to her friend in another village and passes several animals who find the fruit very inviting. 24 pages.

Fred Burstein. *The Dancer/La bailarina.* Bradbury, 1993. As a father accompanies his daughter to her ballet lesson, the sights they encounter—a horse, a flower, a fish, and more—are given in English, Spanish, and Japanese. 32 pages.

Lois Ehlert. *Moon Rope/Un lazo a la luna.* Harcourt, 1992. In this adaptation of a Peruvian folktale, Fox and Mole try to climb to the moon on a rope woven of grass. 32 pages.

Janet Halfmann. *Good Night, Little Sea Otter* (Arabic/English Edition). Cambridge, MA: Star Bright Books, 2016. A bedtime story in which Little Otter must say good night to all the creatures before finally going to sleep. 24 pages.

Diana Dávila Martinez and Gabriela Baeza Ventura (translator). *A School Named for Someone Like Me/Una escuela con un nombre como el mio* (Bilingual Edition). Piñata Books, 2004. This inspiring biography chronicles the life of Jaime Dávila, a role model and a hero in his Hispanic neighborhood in Houston. 63 pages.

Eduardo Mendez. *Bilingual Children's Stories: Cunetos Infantiles Bilingues* (Kindle Edition). Boulder, CO: Micro-mango Publishing, 2016. The stories in this collection take place in Peru and the Caribbean.

Patty Rodriguez and Ariana Stein. *The Life of/La Vida De Selena: A Lil' Libros Bilingual Biography* (English and Spanish Edition). Lil'Libros, 2018. Best-selling biography of Selema Y Los Dino, the late "Queen of Tejano Muiic." 22 pages.

Roser Ros. *Musicians of Bremen/Los músicos de Bremen* (Spanish–English Bilingual Edition). Chronicle Books, 2005. Retold in both Spanish and English, the universally loved story will delight early readers and older learners alike. 32 pages.

Developing Word Recognition and Comprehension

In the chapter we have presented a number of general recommendations for teaching English learners. Now we want to focus on some specifics for teaching word recognition, vocabulary, and comprehension. It is important to keep in mind that the more support you provide, the better the students will grasp the new skills and concepts. The set of ideas and strategies we present here was developed by the American Educational Research Association (AERA, 2004), the major educational research association in the United States. In the Classroom 14.4 lists these ideas and strategies.

Beginning Reading Instruction with English Learners

Many of the instructional recommendations we have discussed thus far in this chapter apply primarily to students who have mastered the rudiments of reading in English.

Now look at beginning reading instruction for English learners. In this section, we briefly present a way of looking at beginning reading based on our experience in schools with significant numbers of ELs.

An English learner has to learn to decode written English and acquire the alphabetic principle. In several ways, teaching the young English learners to read is similar to teaching monolingual students, but with some added complications. When a child is learning to read in his first language, word recognition problems are a bit simpler. Once the child has decoded a new word, sounded it out, his existing vocabulary provides a point of recognition and lets him know that the task was successful. In many cases, the student only has to produce an approximation of the word before the mind completes the task of pulling a known word from the child's oral vocabulary. When an English learner decodes a new word, that rich vocabulary is not available. So when the student gets close to the correct pronunciation there is no moment of recognition, there is no "aha" experience. The English learner often does not know that he has correctly identified the word. Lacking a rich English vocabulary, the student is hampered in both word recognition and comprehension. So word recognition for English learners must proceed carefully and supported concurrent vocabulary instruction.

Another set of problems confronts English learners just learning to read English, because there is often a mismatch between the phonemes in the student's first language and the sounds of English. While the teacher is diligently trying to get the students to pronounce one sound, the students are hearing another. A few common language interference problems are presented in Figure 14.9. Being aware of these potential language interference problems, the astute teacher can minimize language confusions by careful pronunciation and by guiding students in the proper mouth movements.

Given the problems associated with teaching phonics to English learners, the teacher must craft phonics lessons that ameliorate potential difficulties. In the Classroom 14.5 presents a phonics lesson you might use with a mixed group of English learners and English-only students. The integration of phonics and vocabulary development is essential for the development of decoding skills and vocabulary. Students will fail to benefit from the phonics unless their English vocabulary builds at the same time. For the English-only students in the class, the extra emphasis on vocabulary helps to ground the decoding work in a meaningful context, making the work much less abstract. The lesson in In the Classroom 14.6, which is based on one developed by Isabel Beck and reflects the same structure for phonics lessons we presented in Chapter 8. The lesson is also consistent with some principles developed by Russell Gersten and Scott Baker (2000) and the work of Robert Jimenez (2000). This work presents only a few new ideas.

- *Build and apply vocabulary as a curricular anchor.* Vocabulary is crucial to understanding content and to becoming proficient in English. Increasing English learners' vocabularies should be one of your major goals.

- *Provide visuals to reinforce concepts and vocabulary.* Visuals are helpful to all students, but they are particularly helpful to students who have yet to achieve sophisticated verbal skills in English.

- *Draw on both languages when and where they are needed.* Use the students' first language, when possible, to explain concepts that might be difficult in English. Directly teach and use English to help students build their English skills.

- *Validate Spanish speakers' language.* Provide students with Spanish-language texts, invite Spanish-speaking volunteers into the classroom, encourage the use of Spanish during cooperative learning, and learn and use Spanish vocabulary.

As with any learners the process does not stop with phonemic awareness, learning letter sounds and blending. The students have to apply and practice their new skills in context. Two concerns stand out – text selection and guided practice. When selecting text we believe the guidelines developed by Hiebert in Chapter 6 apply equally well to the English learner. Select texts where students can practice the phonics patterns they

In the Classroom 14.4

AERA's Recommendations

Like several of the other sets we have presented, AERA's recommendations are grouped under several headings.

Word Recognition

- Emphasize decoding skill early. Like other children, English learners can learn to decode words relatively quickly—in two years or so.
- Provide systematic training in phonemic awareness.
- Give students lots of practice reading.
- Provide explicit instruction in phonics.
- Use frequent in-class assessment to find out where students need assistance, and then provide that assistance.

Comprehension

- Allot a substantial period of time to building sophisticated language skills. Engage students in substantive reading, writing, and discussion on academic topics.
- Provide in-depth instruction in both oral and reading vocabulary, and be sure to teach a significant number of words using powerful approaches.
- Provide instruction in learning from text.
- Provide comprehension strategy instruction.

have been taught in isolation. This helps to insure transfer. Second, select texts where the phonics patterns and the individual words are repeated often so that the students have a sufficient amount of practice. This means that reading level should not be the only criteria used to select text. Examine the texts closely and determine if the phonics patterns you have taught receive a generous amount of practice.

Figure 14.9 Sources of Sound Confusion Between English and Spanish

English		Spanish
Sounds	*Words*	*Problems of Recognition*
"u" schwa	fun	Spanish has no schwa. The closest would be the "aw" in *fawn*.
"a" There are eight basic ways to pronounce *a*.	cat, about, play	Spanish has one sound for "a." The nearest sound to short *a* in Spanish would be the "e" in *hen*.
"i" There are four basic ways to pronounce *i*.	pig, till, bike	It is difficult for the Spanish ear to hear the short sound of *i*. The Spanish speaker will hear "ill" as "eel" or "ell."
"ch" The digraph is pronounced with a high volume of air.	chair, church,	"sh" and "ch" are very similar in Spanish because Spanish is spoken with a low volume of air, making the sounds similar.
"wh"	why, what, where	The "wh" does not occur in Spanish and it will be perceived as "gwai," "gwhat," and "gwear" in Spanish.
"sc," "sp," or "st"	scan, speak, stick	In Spanish the "s" at the beginning of a word is followed only by vowels. So these words will be perceived as "escan," "espeek," or "esteek."

In the Classroom 14.5

Phonics Instruction for English Learners and the Rest of the Class

Phonics instruction for English learners follows the same general lesson plan that would be used with English-only students. As noted, it is based on one developed by Isabel Beck. In teaching the lesson, it is best to work with small groups of four to six students composed of both English-only students and English learners. Begin the lesson by developing phonemic awareness and then move to letter-sound associations and finally decoding practice. The lesson should weave in words from Spanish, if that is the English learners' home language, and English words. As noted, there should be a heavy focus on vocabulary, so that words are not just decoded but the meanings explained and discussed.

Phonemic Awareness

Develop phonemic awareness by focusing attention first on the initial sounds in words. The major differences between the sounds in English and Spanish are the vowels. While Spanish has five vowel sounds English has twelve. Additionally, there are sounds in English like the diagraphs *sh* and *ch* that are difficult for Spanish speakers to distinguish.

The English learner will be more successful if teachers keep it simple and begin with initial consonant sounds. Students might conduct a picture sort and then isolate the initial sound in the word. Use words like *dog* /d/, *perro* /p/, *cat* /c/, and *gato* /g/. After each picture is sorted, the students name the picture and identify the initial consonant sound. The activity can be repeated to identify the final sound in each word using both English and the child's first language.

Connect Letters to Sounds

Show students a large letter card and explain that this is the letter *m* and it makes the /m/ sound as in Maria, Michael, Miguel, mother, and milk. Say something like, "Each time I point to the letter you say the letter sound." Using the students names grounds the lesson in the familiar. Next show the students several words that contain an m and have them point to and say /m/ as in *man*, *ham*, or *jamón*. Always use a visual so that the English learner can make the transition between his first language and his second.

Discriminate Sounds

Students will now discriminate among words that contain the /m/ sound and words that do not. "If the word I say begins with the /m/ sound, hold up your *m* card and say /m/. If it doesn't begin with the /m/ sound, shake your head no." Then say words like *milk, leche, money, dinero, mother, madre,* and so forth. After the students respond, discuss and define the word or share a picture. Vocabulary is being developed alongside phonics.

Blending/Decoding

The last step in the lesson is to build words with the letter-sound associations that have been introduced. The students will be decoding English words, but the lesson must stress the meanings of these words. After each word is decoded, define the word or share a picture. English learners are building both decoding ability and vocabulary.

Place the letters *h a m* in a pocket chart and give each student the same set of letters. Point to the letters one at a time and say the sounds of each letter. Then have the students repeat the process. Slide the letter *a* over to the letter *h* and say /ha/. Slide your finger under the *ha* and pronounce it and hold it until you point at the letter *m* and say /m/. Have the student repeat what you say with their letters. Move the *m* over to the *ha*. Slide your finger under *ham* and say /ham/. Have the students repeat the process. Discuss what ham is and when you might eat it. Say it in Spanish: *jamón.* The process continues as students sound out additional words—*ham, him, hit, hid, had,* and *dad.* With each word make sure the students understand what it means and have them try it out in an oral sentence. You can have the students work together to develop a sentence for each word with English-only students assisting English learners.

Much of the students reading practice will come during small group guided reading and it is during that time that the teacher can provide support and guidance in the use of word recognition strategies. Mary Avalos and her colleagues recommend that the ideal time to assist English learners with word recognition problems is after they have read the passage (Avalos, Plasencia, Chaves, & Rascon, 2008). The instructional routine might look something like this:

- After a student finishing reading ask if they encountered any difficult words.
- If the student identifies a difficult word discuss the process of decoding the word. Ask the student how she identified or figured out the word. If not, model a strategy for the group.
- It is best to help the students to identify chunks within the word that they already know. Especially for English learners we recommend the decoding by analogy strategy that we presented in Chapter 8. By using this strategy the English learner does not have to deal with the complexity of the English vowel structure and can decode the word as syllables. The word *advertise* is best decoded as *ad*, as in *had*, *ver*, as in *her*, and *tise* as in *size*.
- After the student has decoded words from the text, have them try a few similar words. For example after the word advertise have them try *advertisement*, *likewise*, and *downsize*.
- A bit of practice with each student each day will help to improve their decoding skills. But remember to do as much of the work in context as you can.

The English learner, like all students needs to build their reading fluency. In Chapter 9 we stressed the importance of both wide reading and specific practice like repeated readings or neurological impress. For the English learner who is not ready to read widely for long periods of time we recommend repeated readings. This will give them the fluency practice to build their reading rate and their prosody. These activities can begin in the guided reading group and then continue with partner work. Pair an English learner with a stronger English speaker and reader so they can provide assistance. Follow the same instructional routines we presented in Chapter 9 but with one modification. Review some of the vocabulary words before the students begin their repeated practice.

Developing Comprehension

Much of what we have written about the development of reading comprehension applies to the English learner, so here we will dwell on some of the differences. As with all students, comprehension is a product of knowledge, strategies and motivation. The English learner comes from a different culture with different funds of knowledge. Much of what she knows may not be useful in comprehending texts in our country. So comprehension requires ways to bridge cultural divides. We will focus on four issues developing vocabulary, building background knowledge and reading fiction and informational text.

VOCABULARY INSTRUCTION

In Chapter 10 we introduced a procedure call SWIT and we elaborated on it in the appendix. That process will help you choose words for English learners. In the process new words in a text are classified as either essential, valuable or accessible. The English learner must, like all students, learn the words that are essential for comprehending the text, but the teacher should also focus on the accessible words. These are words that most of the class might know, but the English learner might not. The SWIT process guides you in the selection of vocabulary words to teach.

The process we have outlined for teaching word meanings in Chapter 10 works well for English learners with one addition. Use as many visual images as possible.

The young students can then use the pictures to connect the concept to the word. When explaining word meanings, it important to use many examples. Examples, non-examples, rich discussions are much more valuable than learning the definitions of words. A definition is in many respects an abstract statement where examples are much more concrete and easier to grasp.

BUILDING BACKGROUND KNOWLEDGE

Building knowledge before students read is important for many comprehension activities and we discussed how to do this in Chapters 11 and 12. With the English learner knowledge development is vital since the stores of knowledge they bring to the text are different from what English only students possess. The English learner is likely to have difficulty with cultural differences, the idioms of English and figurative language, expecially metaphors and similies. Imagine reading; *The dude hoofed it over to the hoosegow*. This means that fiction, especially realistic fiction or historical fiction, with long passages of dialogue might be more diffiucult for the English learner than non-fiction where concepts of science and some social studies concepts are universal.

READING FICTION

When reading and studying fiction we recommend the C.I.A. process that we described at the end of the Chapter 11. In C.I.A. the students' knowledge and understanding is carefully built during a read-aloud of a chapter book where the teacher carefully models the process of reading a book. The class develops character lists, draws the setting, outlines the plot, considers the conflict and develops themes. Each section of a book is specifically supported with a graphic organizer. Students work with a partner for additional support. All that is learned is transfer and applied during a book club where students replicate the same process. Each students has a book club partner and for the English learner this is essential. Consider the value of having a buddy. The structure and support in the C.I.A. process suits the need of the English learner.

Ocassionally during comprehension the English learner encounters difficult grammar or syntax and these problems deserve some attention by the teacher. Because English grammar differs from Spanish or Arabic grammar, it is important to stop during a guided reading lesson to unravel a complex sentence. Consider this short sample from an essay about Martin Luther King, Jr. written for sixth graders.

> King had a dream of equality for all and hope for the poor. And even though prejudice and poverty still exist, the important lesson that King taught, Branch told TIME, was that "first, we have to believe we can do something about this."

This paragraph is complex for a number of reasons. First, the subject of the sentence follows an introductory clause. "And even though prejudice and poverty still exist ..." and the predicate of the sentence follows the embedded idea that the someone else, Branch, is reporting this information. There are several ideas embedded in this one sentence and it helps to unpack them. Sometimes during guided reading our attention and support should be at the sentence level.

READING INFORMATIONAL TEXT

In the past, informational texts were not used in our schools for reading instruction, but this is changing with the Common Core State Standards that require 50 percent of instruction be conducted with informational text (Cummins, 2013; Duke, 2004). We strongly recommend that you use informational texts with English learners for three reasons. First, students can read informational texts to find out things that they can use in their lives outside of the classroom. This may be a greater motivation to learn to read in English than anything else you can do. It will give students a reason to work as hard as they can to understand texts in English. The task can be as simple as reading a recipe for making chocolate chip cookies or as complex as reading a science article on hibernation. Being able to read informational texts may also contribute to the stature of a child, as the new skill can be taken home and used to help others in his family.

Second, informational text benefits the English learner is one elegant way. Narrative fiction is full of slang, idioms, similes, and metaphors, the language that brings stories to life, but makes comprehension more difficult for the English learner. The language of informational text is concrete. In any language a volcano, a vertebrate, and the moon is the same concept. Most can be illustrated with pictures, so the English learner has quicker access to the meaning. Non-fiction writing tends to avoid slang, making the prose much more crisp. Most adult English learners will say that reading science and social studies material is much easier than reading fiction.

Third, it is possible to find informational texts dealing with topics that English learners have a lot of background knowledge about and that do not demand background knowledge specific to U.S. culture or to English, such as Taro Gomi's very simple picture book *Spring Is Here/Llegó la primavera* or Gail Gibbons's *Dinosaur Discoveries*. Knowledge of basic facts about common animals, for example, is independent of the language and culture in which those facts were learned. Conversely, in stories written for U.S. children, there is often a good deal of cultural knowledge assumed that some English learners may not have.

Informational text can expand opportunities for home–school connections (Duke & Purcell-Gates, 2003). Some parents, older siblings, and relatives of English learners seldom have the time or interest to read fiction. These same people, however, may welcome opportunities to work with their children in reading and understanding newspapers, magazines, and other non-fiction texts that deal with real-world topics. As we noted earlier in this chapter, involving parents, siblings, and other speakers of students' native languages can be a huge benefit for all parties.

A note of clarification is needed here. We are not advocating the elimination of narrative texts from the reading curriculum. We are, however, recommending that exposition be used as a major component in reading instruction. In one study (Kamil & Lane, 1997), approximately 50 percent of reading instruction in first grade employed expository text, while the remaining 50 percent employed narrative text. This seems like a reasonable balance of these two different and important text types. Of course, some books—for example, Bonnie Graves's *The Whooping Crane*—both tell a story and provide a good deal of information on a topic.

One important concept to keep in mind when giving English learners informational texts is not to require them to learn large bodies of new knowledge in English. English learners need plenty of scaffolding, through teacher guided questions, working with a peer and well structured graphic organizers. Expecting ELs to learn large amounts of new information by reading English texts without sufficient scaffolding is simply an invitation to failure.

In addition to the teaching suggestions and the descriptions of informational books provided throughout this book, Sunday Cummins', *Close Reading of Informational Texts: Assessment-driven Instruction in Grade 3-8* (2013), Nell Duke and Susan Bennett-Armistead's *Reading and Writing Informational Text in the Primary Grades* (2003), and Rosemary Bamford and Janice Kristo's *Making Facts Come Alive* (1998) can be very useful.

Reflect and Apply

5. Think about reading activities that are not specific to a particular language. For example, the process of using a table of contents in a book is the same, regardless of the language used. What other reading tasks are similar across different languages?

6. Create your own Rosetta Stone chart, with words or phrases that you know in English and in one or two other languages. For example, you might already know that mesa is the Spanish word for "table." If you cannot construct much of a chart by yourself, get together with classmates who speak other languages and create a chart together.

MyLab Education **Self-Check 14.4**

MyLab Education **Application Exercise 14.3:** Developing Vocabulary Knowledge

MyLab Education **Application Exercise 14.4:** Developing Word Recognition with English Learners

Assessments for English Learners

Two of the major themes of this chapter are that (1) English learners may require additional support and (2) students' home languages can and should be used where appropriate. These themes are at the center of our recommendations for assessing ELs. Here, we consider some types of modifications and supports that can be useful in assessing ELs, make some recommendations for using modifications and other supports, and provide some examples of what modifications and supports might look like and how appropriate they might be in assessing students' motivation and in assessing their vocabulary knowledge.

Types of Modifications Useful in Assessment

Probably the easiest type of modifications you can provide for English learners during assessments is to give them more time to complete the assessment. The additional time can range from giving students a few minutes to letting them work until you think they have done as much as they can or are willing to do. Another relatively easy type of modification is having students complete the assessment in a place where they are particularly comfortable and likely to produce their best work. This might be the front of the classroom near you, in a quiet corner of the classroom, or in a separate room where there will be as few distractions as possible. A third, and probably more challenging logistically, type of modification is to give the assessment at a time of day when students are likely to be at their best. The optimal time of day will vary from student to student and from situation to situation, but in many cases this might mean mid-morning. It probably does not mean first thing in the morning, just before or just after lunch, or late in the school day. A fourth, and definitely more demanding in terms of resources, modification is to pair the student with an adult, probably an aide, who can keep him on track, encourage him, or perhaps answer questions.

The next type of modifications to consider are supports to provide before the actual assessments take place, systematically preparing students to take assessments. The first step here might be to explain upcoming assessments and their purpose. Another step might be to give students test-taking tips such as completing items they understand and can readily respond to in their first pass through the test and then circling back again to work on more problematic items, being sure to complete all items on the test, and keeping the time allotted in mind and proceeding at an appropriate pace. Next, you might have students take a practice test that mirrors the format and content of the upcoming assessment. Finally, it would be useful to debrief students after they have taken the practice text, helping them to understand what they did well, what they did not do as well, and how they can improve their test taking skills.

Another type of modification, a very different one and one you will want to use with care, is reading some or all of the test to the student. Obviously, the more of the text you read to the student, the more the assessment becomes a listening test rather than a reading test. We will say more about this concern as follows.

Still another type of modification, and one that may not be easy to accomplish, is using the student's home language. There are a number of options here: You could give the directions in the student's home language. You could allow the student to answer questions in his home language. You could read the possible responses in the student's home language. You could read the entire test in the student's home language. Or you could present the written test in the student's home language.

Some Recommendations for Using Modifications and Supports

Our first recommendation is to fully realize how you are changing the assessment and how its results are affected by your using these modifications and supports. We are not talking about giving the matter some casual thought. We are talking about thoroughly considering how your supports or modifications affect the assessment outcome. Our second recommendation is closely related to the first. Make a written record of your support or modifications so that both you and others who look at the results of the assessment will understand just what was and was not being measured. This is particularly important when using standardized assessments, because the norms for standardized assessments will be affected by any changes you make to the standard procedures. However, it is important for all assessments, because all assessment results need to be interpreted in light of just what modifications and supports you included. Finally, use only as many and as powerful modifications and supports necessary to get the information you need. Remember that the major purpose of reading assessments from a teacher's perspective is to find out what students can and cannot do so that you can assist them in becoming better and better readers. Students in U.S. schools need to become more proficient in reading English, so the more your assessments reflect their skills in reading English, the more they will help you help your students.

SOME EXAMPLES OF MODIFICATIONS AND SUPPORTS

Here we consider the appropriateness or inappropriateness of modifications and supports for assessing motivation and for assessing vocabulary. We provide the examples here to give you some idea of what to consider as you look at possible modifications and supports.

Motivation is probably the area in which modifications and supports are most appropriate and do the least to change the intended purpose of the assessment. Consider, for example, the set of questions on reading attitudes we presented in Chapter 3:

- Do you like to read? Why or why not?
- Are you reading anything for fun at this time? What is it? Why do you like it?
- Do you have any favorite authors or titles? Why are these your favorites?
- Is there a certain kind of text that you prefer—books, magazines, fiction, nonfiction, or some other format?
- How do you choose what to read when you go to a library or book store?

- What do you do if what you are reading is too hard or too easy for you?
- What makes a good reader?

The first thing to consider when using this assessment with English learners is to note whether you are asking about reading in English, reading in the students' home language, or both. Once you have clarified this point, you could include such modification as reading the questions to students, letting them respond in their home language, or presenting the questions in the students' home language. With any of these modifications, you would clearly still be assessing students' reading attitudes and interests, just what the original assessment was intended to assess.

The situation with vocabulary and a standardized test is quite different. Consider the situation with the vocabulary section of the Gates-MacGinitie Reading Test (MacGinitie et al., 2000), a test we discussed in Chapter 10. Here is a sample test item with four answer choices.

Sample questions:

a. kind of food
b. type of sport
c. period of time
d. way of talking

Gates-MacGinitie is norm referenced, and any modifications you make will affect the norms. Consider one of the easiest modifications we have suggested, having a student complete the assessment in a place where he is particularly comfortable, perhaps in a room by himself or with just an aide. You would make the modification because you believe the student might score better without the distractions of the typical classroom, and he might. He might score higher, and this higher score might be a truer indication of his vocabulary knowledge. But you could not compare his score to the scores of students in the norm group, who took the test in a classroom setting. The same applies to giving the student more time to complete the test. The results might be a better representation of what the student is capable of if given enough time, but you could not compare this students' score to the scores of students in the norm group.

Now consider a very different modification, reading the test items themselves to the student. Now you are no longer using the Gates-MacGinitie Reading Test, you have created a "Gates-MacGinitie Listening Test." You are not testing reading at all, you are testing listening. And while your test will provide you with some information about the student's listening skills, it tells neither you nor any other teachers who see the results of your assessment anything about the student's reading skills. You might think that the student's score on a listening test would be higher than his score on a reading test. However, some English learners have stronger written English skills than oral English skills, so it is very difficult to make a conclusion about the student's proficiency with reading vocabulary based on a listening test.

Our general message about providing extra support or modifications when assessing English learners can be summed up this way: Supports and modifications can certainly be useful, but before you use them you need to carefully consider what you are assessing and what effects the supports and modifications are likely to have on students' scores. Additionally, you need to keep a written description of your supports and modifications so that you and other teachers who might look at students' scores in the future can interpret them correctly.

Concluding Remarks

In this chapter, we began by considering linguistic diversity in the United States, the number of English learners in today's schools, and the reading performance of ELs. Then, in the major portion of the chapter, we described a number of instructional approaches that can be used with ELs and some modifications to consider when assessing ELs. In concluding the chapter, we want to emphasize six points, three from Goldenberg and three from other sources.

First, practices that are generally effective are likely to be effective with English learners. Good teaching is good teaching in a variety of context and with a variety of students.

Second, English learners will profit from, and in many cases require, additional instructional supports. Good teaching by itself is not sufficient.

Third, using students' home languages will help promote English learners' success.

Fourth, with English learners, as with all children, it is not merely low-level literacy or the rudiments of literacy that we must assist students in reaching. The goal is full literacy in English—the ability to use the English language as a vehicle for thinking, for problem solving, and for communicating—in other words, the ability to use English in a way that makes possible full and productive participation in our society.

Fifth, vocabulary instruction was stressed in many of the sets of suggestions we have discussed throughout this chapter. Vocabulary is absolutely crucial to English learners. Take advantage of the many techniques for vocabulary instruction we described in Chapter 10. Also, you may want to consider the fuller discussion of vocabulary instruction one of us presents in *The Vocabulary Book* (Graves, 2016).

Finally, the task of assisting English learners in reaching the level of English literacy sufficient for success in the 21st century is clearly a challenging one. Yet, it is a task we can and must accomplish.

Extending Learning

1. Visit a school with English learners. You might volunteer to work with some students whose first language is not English. If you cannot find such a school, many social service agencies, religious organizations, and other nonprofit groups have programs that target reading for English learners. Volunteering to work in these settings, or even simply observing, will allow you to see how the principles in this chapter play out in real life.

2. Study the instructional recommendations made throughout this chapter. There are over 40 of them, many more than you can implement at one time. Identify half a dozen or so that you see as particularly useful and as steps that you definitely could take in your present or future classroom. Explain in writing why you selected each of these recommendations and in what order you are likely to implement them.

Children's Literature

Brierley, S. (2017), *Lion: A Long Way Home.* New York: Puffin Books. In thus remarkable true story, Saroo Brierley recounts how he used Google Earth in traveling half way around the world to find his mother. 272 pages.

Ciardi, J. (1975). "The Shark." In *Fast and Slow: Poems by John Ciardi.* Boston: Houghton Mifflin. This poem provides a colorful and engaging description of a shark. 1 page.

Gibbons, G. (2005). *Dinosaur Discoveries.* New York: Holiday House. In simple language, Gibbons provides details of the most recent theories about the history of dinosaurs, along with amazing facts about dinosaur discoveries. 33 pages.

Gomi, T. (2006). *Spring Is Here/Llegó la primavera.* San Francisco: Chronicle Books. In this colorful, dual-language picture book, a winsome calf provides the backdrop for the story line, which follows the cycle of the seasons from one spring to the next. In spare text, the author conveys the underlying themes of renewal and growth. 34 pages.

Graves, B. (1997). *The Whooping Crane.* Des Moines, IA: Perfection Learning. While on an airplane ride from Texas to Maryland, a young girl sits next to a biologist transporting a whooping crane chick to the Patuxent Wildlife Research Center and learns about this endangered species. 64 pages.

Herrera, J. F. (2014). *Portraits of Hispanic American Heroes.* New York: Dial Books. Well crafted biographies of Hispanic Americans who have made their mark in the United States. 96 pages

Kelly, R. (2016). *50 Things You Should Know About American Presidents.* Blanchester, OH: QEB Publishing. This informational book presents 50 succinct chunks of information about presidents from George Washington to Barak Obama. 80 pages.

Lowery, L. (2005). *Cinco de Mayo.* Minneapolis, MN: Lerner. This colorful book honors the joyful holiday that celebrates Mexico's victory over the French army at the Battle of Pueblo in 1862. 48 pages.

O'Dell, S. (1960). *Island of the Blue Dolphins.* Boston: Houghton Mifflin. By using her wits and the resources at hand, a young Indian girl survives alone on an island for several years. Newbery Medal winner. Audio- and videotapes available. Spanish text also available. 154 pages.

Ramírez, A. (2004). *Napí.* Toronto: Groundwood Books. A Mazateca girl, who lives beside a river in Oaxaca, describes her home and village at different times of the day. 32 pages.

Rosenblatt, L. (1998). *Monarch Magic!* Charlotte, VT: Williamson Publishing Co. Simple text and colorful photographs depict the life cycle of a monarch butterfly, from egg to caterpillar to chrysalis to butterfly. Includes 40 butterfly activities. 96 pages.

Shea, P. D. (1995). *The Whispering Cloth: A Refugee's Story.* Honesdale, PA: Boyds Mills Press. A young Hmong girl in a Thai refugee camp creates a *pándau* (embroidered tapestry) that tells her own story. Includes glossary. Illustrated by A. Riggio, with reproductions of *pándau* by Y. Yang. 32 pages.

Soto, G. (1994). *The Skirt.* New York: Bantam-Doubleday. When Miata leaves the skirt she is to wear for the folklorico dance performance on the school bus, she must use all her wits to get it back before her parents find out. Illustrated by Eric Velasquez. Audio CD available. 74 pages.

Yumoto, K. (1999). *The Spring Tone.* New York: Farrar, Straus and Giroux. Resenting the changes in her life and resisting growing up, Tomomi joins her younger brother in taking revenge against the neighbors with whom her family is battling. 166 pages.

Bibliography

Schon, I., (2008). *Recommended Books in Spanish for Children and Young Adults: 2004 through 2008.* Lanham, MD: Scarecrow Press. This and the older Schon bibliographies listed below are well done and very useful. Unfortunately, this is the most recent version available at the present time, Summer, 2018.

Schon, I. (2004). *Recommended Books in Spanish for Children and Young Adults: 2000 through 2004.* Lanham, MD: Scarecrow Press.

Schon, I. (2001). *Recommended Books in Spanish for Children and Young Adults: 1996 through 1999.* Lanham, MD: Scarecrow Press.

Schon, I. (1996). *Recommended Books in Spanish for Children and Young Adults: 1991–1995.* Lanham, MD: Scarecrow Press.

A Day in the Life of David Weiss and His Fifth- and Sixth-Grade Students

David Weiss has been teaching fifth- and sixth-graders at Oak Grove Intermediate School for 10 years. Oak Grove, which includes grades 4 through 6, is located in a southern suburb of Minneapolis. Most of the children at Oak Grove come from middle- to lower-income families; the majority are European Americans, with a sprinkling of Asian Americans, Native Americans, and African Americans.

David works in a team with three other teachers, which is fairly typical of many upper-elementary classrooms. Before the school year begins, the team meets to make program decisions and to discuss matters such as scheduling and curricular responsibilities. The four classrooms in David's team each have approximately 30 students, equally divided between fifth- and sixth-graders. When the sixth-graders move on to junior high school, 15 fifth-grade students take their place, so students are with the same homeroom teacher for 2 years.

When we asked David to describe the literacy program he and his colleagues have developed, he spoke of the diverse range of student abilities.

> The literacy program we have developed over the years reflects the unique challenge we face as upper elementary teachers. Differences in reading ability are extreme in students in grades 5 and 6. For example, one of my students, 11-year-old Kelly, reads at an 11th-grade level and devours John Grisham novels during her free reading period. Tommy, also 11 years old, struggles with anything beyond second-grade materials. He finds it difficult to read even short, episodic stories. This disparity presents a critical question for my teammates and me: How do we meet the needs of students, given such a huge range of ability? My team has developed a plan we think best meets the needs of our students.

On the following pages, David describes in his own words his team's plan for organizing the fifth-/sixth-grade curriculum to emphasize reading and writing instruction throughout the school day and to meet the wide range of needs in their classes.

Every district has a list of goals and objectives or learning outcomes. At the beginning of, during, and following the school year, my colleagues and I sit down and figure out what to teach. Our team looks for connections within all the language arts and within broad themes as well. As a starting point, we choose a broad theme that will connect all the students' learning experiences to their knowledge and experiences. The theme we choose is determined by a number of factors, including appropriateness of topic, access to resources, our own talents and failings, and district and state standards. Typically, we choose three themes over the course of the year.

Although each day has a particular focus for instruction, I have found it useful to teach content that will serve the students in a variety of settings throughout the school year. Over the years, I have become more and more convinced that the teaching of comprehension strategies makes for more powerful readers. I choose strategies that are flexible and widely applicable. I will ask the students to use them in their content area classes and when using self-selected materials, as well as in my class. My suggestion to a beginning teacher—or any teacher—is to develop a small number of them (five to six) throughout the year. The students' repertoire of strategies will grow through the year, so by the end they will successfully employ multiple strategies.

At the beginning of the year, I note several strategies I think would be helpful for my students. One of my favorites is teaching students to create advanced story maps (see Chapter 10). Although story maps were introduced to most students by second grade and have been reviewed in subsequent grades, now my students are ready for a more in-depth analysis of narrative structure. My first goal is to review the story mapping strategy in such a way that all students will recall previous concepts. For this reason, I choose content that is familiar to all students and that they do not need to read. For example, I may ask them to recall the story "Little Red Riding Hood" as a text to use in doing their story mapping. I let students know that they will be learning a more sophisticated version of the strategy designed to help them understand the reactions and motives of the characters. Then I model the activity in a large-group setting. I begin by listing the elements of a story map and then ask the students to assist me in identifying the characters, setting, problem, and events:

Story Elements	Little Red Riding Hood
Characters	Little Red Riding Hood, Grandmother, the Big Bad Wolf
Setting	The forest, Grandmother's house
Problem	Little Red Riding Hood wanted to bring food to her grandmother
Events	Red begins her journey to Grandmother's house and encounters a wolf

After creating their first map, we begin to deepen our understanding of narrative structure by considering two new elements in the story grammar or story map, character motives and reactions. I pose the following questions: "Why was Red -visiting Grandmother's house? How did she feel when she encountered the wolf?" I want the students to understand that there is more to the narrative than a simple listing of the literal elements in a story. We review the entire fairy tale, discussing the motives and reactions of each character and adding them to the story map. I use a read-aloud for the next one; again, my interest is minimizing the effect of reading ability as a critical factor in acquiring the strategy. I've found picture books to be an excellent vehicle for this, as they are nonthreatening to the listener—short, full of illustrations, and appealing. Following whole-group instruction, the students will use this strategy in small groups and individually later in the day. The students have learned a strategy that may be applied to a variety of texts; have had an opportunity to integrate reading, writing, listening, and speaking; and have created responses to share with the other groups in the class. One student's map for *The True Story of the Three Little Pigs* by Jon Scieszka is shown in the figure on the next page.

Name: Coltrane, B.

Title of book: The True Story of the Three Little Pigs

Author of the book: Jon Scieszka

On the left side of the page, list the important events in the story (choose between 3 and 12 events). On the right side, describe how the main character felt at the end of the event and what caused him to take the actions he did. You may write from the point of view of the wolf or the three little pigs.

1. The wolf was sick and wanted a cup of sugar.

   The wolf loved his grandmother and wanted to make her a cake even though he had this rotten cold.

2. The wolf sneezed and blew down the first pig's house.

   The wolf thought the pig was stupid for building his house from straw.

3. The wolf ate the first pig.

   The wolf's diet is small animals and he didn't want the dead pig to spoil, so he ate it up.

4. The wolf sneezed and blew down the second pig's house.

   The wolf's cold is not getting any better and he felt it was stupid to build a house of sticks.

5. The wolf ate the second pig.

   Again, ham is part of the wolf's diet and he didn't want the dead pig to spoil.

6. The wolf went to the third pig's house and sneezed, but nothing happened.

   The wolf felt the third pig was rude and selfish because he would not loan him a cup of sugar for his cake. The wolf was hurt that the pig insulted his grandmother.

7. The police came and thought the wolf was trying to blow down the pig's house.

   The wolf felt framed by the pig and angry that the reporters changed the story to make the wolf look bad.

8. The police took the wolf to jail.

   The wolf felt justice went awry and sad that his grandmother did not get her cake.

Two aspects of our team approach are particularly important to our use of a -language arts block. First, the language arts block provides time for focusing on and inter-relating all of the language arts. Second, we use both flexible grouping and -student self-selection of reading materials. I regularly introduce new books and stress the genre of the books. This encourages students to read widely across many different genres. The students may read individually or in self-selected groups or literature circles. The literature circles are particularly important because they promote independent reading, strategy use, and group responsibility. The students respond to the texts in a variety of ways, sometimes determined by the instructor and sometimes determined by the students.

A literature-based approach is particularly attractive to fifth- and sixth-grade students. Meeting to discuss what they read in literature circles (see Chapter 12) helps students develop rich, engaging schemata. The students really get into a piece of writing when they are sharing the experience with others. I find it easy to model and be enthusiastic about appropriate literature circle behaviors, as I am able to relate my own experiences in a book club. Literature circles and other literature-based approaches encourage deep understanding of texts. The circles have an advantage over whole-group instruction in that participants find it difficult to check out of the discussion. Students who are eye-to-eye and knee-to-knee and responsible for developing meaning have a greater chance of experiencing the "aha" -phenomenon—gaining a perspective that they hadn't considered before. An additional advantage to literature-based approaches is that students are able to self-select their groups. The teacher, for example, may select four texts—differing in length, type of characters, and so forth—that all relate to a broad, general theme. Emily may be ready for Lynne Rae Perkins's *Criss Cross*, a complex Newbery Medal–winning story, while James may prefer a book made up of short, easy-to read episodic stories like Donald Sobol's *Encyclopedia Brown and the Case of the Jumping Frogs.* Allowing student choice increases the likelihood that students will read an engaging book at their level of reading competence.

Our approach to reading instruction does not ignore basic skills. As I said at the outset, six of our students are still struggling with basic print skills and they read between a second- and third-grade level. I make it a plan to meet with these six students every day. During our 20-minute small-group lessons we are working on decoding by -analogy and oral reading fluency. Each week the students are introduced to four or five key words that contain a common and useful rime. The students then practice using that rime to decode increasingly complex words. The figure shows that today the students worked on words with the spelling patterns in *rain* and *hide*. For oral reading fluency the students are working on a readers theater project that they will present to the whole class. The six students are organized into groups of three and each is learning and practicing a short play.

There are five important features in our organization of time, curriculum content, space, and students. First is the concept of the homeroom, second is scheduling large blocks of time for students to be in one place with one teacher, third is centering instruction around a broad theme, fourth is working with students to acquire some of the decoding and fluency skills they still lack, and fifth is selecting reading comprehension strategies and procedures to teach throughout the year that are flexible and broadly applicable. Here is what our typical schedule looks like:

8:30–11:00	Homeroom—Reading/Language Arts	
8:30	Independent silent reading, journal writing, reading conferences	
9:00	Whole-group morning meeting, knowledge development, strategy instruction	
9:30	Teacher guided small-group instruction, literature circles, process writing	
11:00	Mathematics	
12:00	Lunch and recess	

Key Words	rain	hide
Words to Decode	gain	ride
	main	side
	pain	slide
	plain	snide
	slain	tide
	strain	wide
	abstain	bedside
	disdain	confide
	obtain	reside
	remain	provide
	restrain	coincide

12:45	Special subjects: Physical education, art, music
1:30	Social studies, science, health
3:00	Homeroom and school logs
3:15	Dismissal

As the schedule shows, each homeroom stays intact for over 2 hours in the beginning of each day. For example, fifth- and sixth-grade students in my homeroom stay with me from 8:30 to 11:00 and then move to another teacher for mathematics. Heterogeneous groups made up from each of the four classrooms within our team comprise the classes for instruction in social studies, science, art, and health.

Large blocks of time have a number of advantages. To begin with, the students have less downtime between classes. They spend less time moving from room to room. Lengthier time periods also allow for greater depth and breadth of instruction. We have greater opportunities to go into detail on a given topic, or we can use the extended time to develop connections to other curricular areas. Another advantage of large time blocks is greater flexibility for everyone involved, making it easier to schedule special education services, computer lab time, and guest speakers.

Independent Silent Reading, Journal Writing, Reading Conferences

Homeroom begins with one of two different activities—independent silent reading or journal writing, which I alternate throughout the school year. Having a structured activity ready for the students helps them warm up for school and establishes a healthy working culture for the classroom.

Independent Silent Reading

Independent silent reading (see Chapter 12) is an important part of any elementary-level reading curriculum. I've found it helpful to ask the students to have their books out and ready to read the moment class begins. I think it is good practice to feature sustained reading of student-selected texts as a primary feature of the classroom, rather than an adjunct to the "real work" of the day. If students are asked to do silent reading only when their other assignments are done, this almost guarantees that the least successful students will get the least amount of time to read independently and the least opportunity to develop fluent, success-oriented reading practice. My students are especially interested in a pre-set quiet reading time, as this gives them time to complete the response log, which is a required part of their independent reading. During independent reading I confer with three or four students every day. During this time we assess their oral reading, comprehension, and vocabulary knowledge, plus we discuss what they might like to read next.

Journal Writing

I have tried all sorts of journal writing, both structured and nonstructured. I have responded at length to students' writing and have enjoyed it, although it is terrifically time-consuming. However, having students write to a real audience is powerfully motivating. Lately, I have found it particularly productive to have students share their writing thoughts with two or three others. I may suggest a topic for a journal entry, or the students may choose their own. The small group that develops as a result of this journaling activity is asked to respond to what each member of the group writes. Some of the students are writing to each other via the school email system. Conversations between students develop in print, similar to what happens in dialogue journals (see Chapter 13). I like to introduce this activity by modeling my own journal writing and students' responses, sharing these on an overhead projector. The figure shows two journal entries by students reading *Matilda* by Roald Dahl.

Working in small groups not only provides students with a real audience but also allows me to give feedback quickly and efficiently. To give this feedback, I ask each group of three or four students to come up to my desk, where I respond orally to their writing.

9:00 Whole-Group Morning Meeting, Knowledge Development, and Strategy Instruction

Morning Meeting

Just about every teacher I know sets aside time during the beginning of the day to do the routine chores that are part of every classroom. Here, we talk about the day's schedule, important dates, current events, and the like. I list on the board which groups I will be meeting with and what tasks they should have finished before small-group time.

The time required for our morning meeting varies day by day. It is common practice in my classroom to use this time to assign ad hoc student committees designed to solve problems. For instance, we may have a party coming up. Following a list of guidelines, a student committee is formed to submit their written recommendations as to treats, activities, and the like. A committee may be responsible for cleaning and putting fresh water in the iguana cage or figuring out a way to get homework to absent students. In almost all cases, students are asked to submit a written plan, which I will review. These authentic language arts experiences allow students to have an impact on their world, and they really work well with fifth- and sixth-graders.

Knowledge Development

I will use for our whole-class lesson a selection in the basal taken from *Call It Courage,* Armstrong Perry's Newbery Medal–winning story about a shipwrecked boy searching for courage. This selection will serve to introduce the theme of the sea, develop prior knowledge, and review some comprehension strategies. Purpose and selection, of course, are two of the three factors of the scaffolded reading experience (discussed in Chapter 10). The third is taking into account the readers. So next, I consider what each of my students will be reading. I have four groups in the classroom with some reading well above grade level, and one group struggling to read the basal story.

I begin developing a reading scaffold by thinking of my prereading activities, asking myself what sort of background knowledge will be required for the students to understand the story. One advantage of using a story out of a basal text (which is usually highly illustrated) is that all students have access to a powerful cue—illustration. Illustrations are one way to tap into the students' existing knowledge. I ask them to look at the pictures and to write predictions of what they expect will happen in the story. The illustration for *Call It Courage* shows the character Mafatu on a beach, apparently making something out of bamboo. He appears to be alone, but for a seagull and a dog. Students might predict that he is alone on an island and that he is intent on building a shelter, which they will later find to be the case. Analyzing illustrations is also a helpful way to introduce semantic mapping to further activate background knowledge. Besides activating background knowledge, mapping serves an additional purpose. Inevitably, important vocabulary will surface; or you, as the instructor, can make it surface. My colleagues and I have found that the key in vocabulary instruction is picking out critical terms or concepts and giving the students repeated exposure to them, using a variety of techniques. Students need to hear and use critical vocabulary in a variety of contexts.

Strategy Instruction

At this point in the instruction I will review the current strategy, story mapping with the focus on character motives and reactions, plus other strategies that the students will be using in their small-group discussions. Some students will be working on self-questioning, others on predicting, summarizing, or comprehension monitoring. I will continue to model these strategies with the basal text from *Call It Courage*. Because the text is difficult for some students, I will read a portion of it aloud. Then, when whole-group instruction ends some of the students, will read the text independently while others might read it with a partner. They have to finish the story so we can discuss it in whole group tomorrow. Next the students will move to small-group instruction. I have already written the assignments for each group on the assignment board so that students know what to do next without having to get my attention.

9:30 Teacher Guided Small-Group Instruction, Literature Circles, and Process Writing

Teacher Guided Small-Group Instruction

I meet with my lowest group of students first, so that I have ample time to explain and scaffold their work. In addition to partner reading the basal story, *Call It Courage*, this group will read one of the leveled readers that accompanies the basal story. Because many of the students in this group read 2 years below grade level, we will also review strategies for decoding words focusing on decoding by analogy (see Chapter 7). In our comprehension discussions about *Call It Courage*, we consider characters' motives and reactions, the strategies for the week. While I meet with the struggling readers, the rest of the class will be reading independently or working with their literature circle.

The strongest readers will be meeting with their literature circle discussing *The Great Wide Sea* by M. H. Herlong. The book continues the theme from the basal story and students will be able to apply their newly developed knowledge. The book should also challenge those reading above a sixth-grade level. As they discuss the story the members of the literature circle will focus on summarizing, questioning, clarifying, predicting, and character motives and feelings. After they finish their discussion they will work on their book poster, which includes a short plot outline. Our work on story mapping should help with this task. They are also responsible for finding new vocabulary words and sharing them with the class. After I finish with the lower group I will meet with this group.

The next group will also be working in their literature circle. They had chosen the book *Voyage of the Frog* by Gary Paulson, another survival story but well matched to their reading ability. Like the other groups, my *Voyage of the Frog* people will be focusing on the same comprehension strategies——summarizing, questioning, clarifying, and character motives and feelings. This group will also complete a book poster and search for new vocabulary words.

Notice that the entire class is engaged in parallel activities but at their instructional level and each has an opportunity for teacher feedback. I allocate about 90 minutes for small groups, literature circles, and independent work. It is important to see the below-level readers everyday. After I see the below-level readers, the reading specialist comes into the room and continues with them for another 20 minutes, working on decoding and fluency. Before or after the students meet with me, they work on a number of independent projects. Some will be working in literature circle books, others will be working on their readers theater project, and all will be completing a story map based on what they have been reading. Again, there is an implicit appeal here for integrating language arts—students are reading, writing, speaking, and listening. Furthermore, now that the students have demonstrated facility in creating story maps, each is able to use this strategy with his or her own content. Students are able to use the procedure to take notes for their posters or generate discussion questions, which they will share when they next meet with me.

At the end of the small-group time I bring the whole class together so they can share what they have accomplished. Each group discusses how story mapping has helped them today. This builds a common purpose and a sense of community among the groups as well as providing a transition to writing.

Writing Instruction

Because we have been reading about survival stories and studying story maps, the students are also working on their own survival stories. We started several days ago and considered how a story is organized and how the plot is developed. I gave the students the task of creating a story map or plot for the story they plan to write. I ask each of the groups to share some interesting points of conflict from the plot of their story. As the students are working I meet with individual students and help them organize their stories. Tomorrow we will focus on leads, or interesting ways to start a story. We are following the writing process and by the end of the week the students will be editing and getting ready to share what they have written.

`11:00` Mathematics

As I said earlier, our team is made up of four classrooms, each serving two grade levels. My teammates and I are always looking for ways to connect with our theme. For example, I know through team meetings that the science teacher will be using whales to illustrate content in a unit on oceanography. I have an opportunity to illustrate mathematics in an engaging way, which will enrich their understanding of our theme, by having my students make cutout re-creations of whales. In doing so, the students work from a pattern, grid out an image, and convert their numbers, using the concept of scale in creating paper or chalk models. In a variety of ways, my students will develop a better sense of number and demonstrate facility in the use of ratios and estimation, while further developing a rich and engaging schema that will serve them in other content areas.

`12:00` Lunch and Recess

The themes here are eating and playing!

12:45 Special Subjects: Physical Education, Art, Music

Our district uses specialists to teach these three content areas. The students alternate classes on a 3-day rotation. I can't always integrate physical education, art, or music with common themes, as these teachers have their own scope and sequence. Integration requires meeting with these teachers to plan our curricular content together, which, although it is a challenge, I occasionally do with music. For example, a music teacher developed a score for a play that my classroom was working on.

1:30 Themes: Social Studies, Science, and Health

As I mentioned earlier, my team—Nancy Eller, Troy Miller, and Suzy Neet—uses a thematic approach to interrelate our classes. Our goal is to find a way to connect the disciplines of science, social studies, art, and health, given available curricular materials, district outcomes, and teacher expertise. Nancy and Suzy's area of expertise is social studies. Troy's is science. The students attend two of the three classes each day.

Social Studies

Nancy has a pretty good background in ancient civilizations. For the present unit, she's going to focus on the Roman Empire's movement throughout the Mediterranean region. She plans to focus in part on trade routes, commerce, and the transmission of Greco-Roman culture throughout the Mediterranean. Social studies requires a good deal of expository reading by the students, which is particularly difficult. It would be appropriate for all team members to use a comprehension procedure—for instance, K-W-L (discussed in Chapter 10)—in the language arts setting.

Science

Troy has decided to do a unit on oceanography. The content fits with our district outcomes in that he will explore relationships between a marine environment and all sorts of creatures. There are many opportunities to connect with mathematics, including graphing the ocean floor via echo sounding and determining the speed of sound in various environments.

Health

Connecting health to other content areas has always been a stretch for our team. Suzy has agreed to do health the past several years. Sometimes she is able to make connections, but in this case the topic of the sea fails to inspire her. As her colleagues are at a loss to make thematic connections between health and the sea, she will be out of the loop this time around. She will likely have greater success when we pursue other themes—challenges, for example.

In trying to find connections between theme and subject areas, we have learned something that Sean Walmsley (1996, p. 54) stresses: "Don't try to integrate every subject area into every theme." Sometimes there are important connections, and sometimes not.

We try to concentrate on connections that really make sense. Walmsley offers some other tips about theme teaching that I'd like to pass along:

- When you teach a theme, tuck the skills inside it.
- Balance teacher-generated and student-generated themes.
- Avoid cutesy treatment of themes.
- Draw themes from a variety of arenas—concepts, content areas, current events, people, the calendar.
- Make sure your themes are the right size.
- Approach year-long and schoolwide themes with caution because you may simply run out of energy.
- Bump up your own knowledge of the themes you're preparing.
- Borrow theme ideas from others.

Although writing thematic units can be hard work and time-consuming, we have found the process of planning together to be fruitful and stimulating and the results rewarding. Resources such as *The Complete Guide to Thematic Units* (Meinbach, Rothlein, & Fredericks, 2000), which provides 20 comprehensive units that can be adapted to fit any classroom, can help you with valuable and time-saving information on teaching strategies and books to use.

3:00 Homeroom and School Logs

All of our students have school logs. At the end of each day, I ask students to write down what happened over the course of the day. The purpose of the activity is to give them an opportunity to reflect on learning, to have a written record to communicate to parents, and to note any assignments or other tasks that will be due. This can be difficult unless you really make it a vital part of your everyday activities.

3:15 Dismissal

Appendix A

Table of Contents

Assessment Tools

Lesson Plans and Materials

Assessment Tools

Emergent Reading Inventory

Name_____

Date_____

Alphabet Knowledge

____/26 Upper case letter recognition

____/26 Lower case letter recognition

____/26 Written production of letters

        Score ____ /78

Letter Sound Association

____/ 21 Consonant sounds

        Score ____ /21

Phonemic Awareness

____/10 Rhyme Detection

____/12 Blending

____/12 Segmenting

        Score ____ /34

Concept of Word

____/8 One-to-One correspondence

____/5 Counting words on a page

        Score ____ /13

Spelling Inventory

____/5 Initial consonants

____/5 Final consonants

____/5 Vowel inclusion

____/5 Correct short vowel

        Score ____ /20

Word Recognition

____/10 Decodable words

____/10 Sight words

        Score ____ / 20

Total Weighted Benchmark Score _____ /186

Alphabet Knowledge

Have the children name the upper- and lower-case letters in random order using the alphabet cards. Mark all errors below and record substitutions.

A B C D E F G H I J K L M N O P Q R S T U V W X Y Z

____/26

a b c d e f g h i j k l m n o p q r s t u v w x y z

____/26

Have the student reproduce the alphabet as you dictate each letter in random order. A form is provided for the student to write each letter. The student can write either the upper- or lower-case form of the letter. Call the letters of the alphabet out in this order:

E H F C S Q J P W A I N B Z G K R V T L X D M O U Y

____/26

Concept of Word

Using *Animal Homes* or *Animal Babies* or other short emergent literacy book.

1. Have the student look at the pictures and tell you about them.
2. Read the book to the student, pointing to each word as you read it.
3. Read the book chorally with the student, pointing to each word as you read it.
4. Have the student read the book independently, pointing to each word as it is read.

Score one point for each page that the student accurately demonstrates one to one correspondence.

____/8

Ask the student how many words are on the first page. If the student answers the correct number, they score five points. If incorrect, they score 0 points.

____/5

Spelling Inventory

Administer the first ten words of Neva Viise's "form B" word list (a form is provided for the student).

1. lap
2. fit
3. cop
4. bag
5. hen

Score one point for each word with the correct initial consonant.

____/5

6. rap
7. fun
8. mad
9. wig
10. hot

Score one point for each word with the correct final consonant.

____/5

Count the number of words in both lists which include any vowel (* see scoring below).

____/5

Count the number of words in both lists which include a correct short vowel in the correct vowel position (* see scoring below).

____/5

* Scoring key: 10 = 5, 8–9 = 4, 6–7 = 3, 4–5 = 2, 2–3 = 1, 0–1 = 0

Word Recognition

There are two sets of word cards provided, decodable and sight words. Mark each of the following words read correctly with a check mark. Score one point for each correct response.

DECODEABLE	SIGHT
____sad	____look
____ran	____little
____set	____have
____red	____the
____cut	____do
____sun	____you
____pig	____see
____fit	____and
____hot	____come
____top	____my
____/10	____/10

Phonemic Awareness

Rhyme Detection

"Rhymes are words that sound the same at the end. *Bat* rhymes with *cat*; *man* rhymes with *can*. Does *ball* rhyme with *tall*? Yes, *ball* rhymes with *tall*. Not all words rhyme. Does *book* rhyme with *cup*? No, *book* and *cup* do not rhyme because *book* ends with <u>ook</u> and *cup* ends with *up*. Does *like* rhyme with *lost*? No, *like* and *lost* do not rhyme because *like* ends with <u>ike</u> and *lost* ends with <u>ost</u>. Does all rhyme with tall? Yes! Now I am going to say some words, and I want you to tell me if they rhyme."

One point is awarded for pair judged correctly. Make a √ mark if the response is correct. Leave it blank if the answer is incorrect.

day - play			page - paint	
me - he			cold - sold	
moon - jump			not - got	
go - no			went - when	
bag - bat			make - rake	

Total correct ____ / 10

Blending

"I'm going to say some words in a secret code, spreading out the word until the sounds come out one at a time. I will be stretching the word. Guess what word I'm saying. For example, if I say *h-a-m*. You say *ham*. Let's try one more. If I say *p-i-g* what would you say? That's right *pig*."

One point is awarded for each word pronounced correctly. Make a √ mark if the given response is correct. Leave it blank if answer is incorrect.

h - e			sh - i - p	
g - o			ch - i - n	
t - e - n			wh - e - n	
b - a - g			s - t - o - p	
d - ay			t - e - n - t	
d -i - d			f - a - s -t	

Total Correct _____ / 12

Phoneme Segmentation

Directions: Today we're going to play a word game. I'm going to say a word and I want you to break the word apart. You are going to tell me each sound of the word in order. For example, if I say **cat,** you should say /c/ /a/ /t/. Let's try a few together.

> **Practice items:** (assist in segmenting, if necessary) **ride (3) go (2) man (3)**

Test items: Make a √ mark if the word is fully and correctly segmented. Incorrect responses are recorded on the blank line following the item.) Please note if the child is able to just segment the initial letter. This is important information, but does not count in the scoring. (Yopp-Singer, 2003).

Answer Key

Practice Items: ride (3) go (2) man (3)

1. **dog** (3) _____   7. **lay** (2) _____
2. **keep** (3)_____   8. **race** (3) _____
3. **fine** (3) _____   9. **zoo** (2) _____
4. **no** (2) _____   10. **top** (3) _____
5. **she** (2) _____   11. **job** (3) _____
6. **wave** (3)_____   12. **in** (2) _____

_____ ____ / **12**

Letter-Sound Associations

Using consonants from the lower-case letter deck, ask the student to say the sound that the letter says (one point for each correct response).

b c d f g h j k l m n p q r s t v w x y z   (a e i o u)
                                         (no points for short vowels)

____/**21**

Written Production of Letters

1. _____	14. _____
2. _____	15. _____
3. _____	16. _____
4. _____	17. _____
5. _____	18. _____
6. _____	19. _____
7. _____	20. _____
8. _____	21. _____
9. _____	22. _____
10. _____	23. _____
11. _____	24. _____
12. _____	25. _____
13. _____	26. _____

<u>**Word Feature Spelling Inventory**</u>

A B C D E F G H I J K L M N O P Q R S T U V W X Y Z

a b c d e f g h i j k l m n o p q r s t u v w x y z

1. _____

2. _____

3. _____

4. _____

5. _____

6. _____

7. _____

8. _____

9. _____

10. _____

Tile Test
Directions

Grade Level: Kindergarten–Second Grade
The Tile Test is designed to quickly assess students' understanding of letters, sounds, words, and sentences. Metalinguistic questions encourage students to talk about the strategies they use when decoding and spelling words.

General Procedures

1. Start with a collection of letter tiles, not just one card.
2. Allow sufficient time for each response.
3. Provide general positive feedback to encourage students; do not correct mistakes.
4. Write the students' responses to each item:
   a. Correct response is marked + or ✓.
   b. Incorrect responses will be recorded in full.
   c. No response will be recorded as DK (doesn't know).
   d. Self-correction is marked SC and counted as correct.
   e. Segmented words read without blending sounds will be marked with slashes between sounds (e.g., /t/a/p/).
5. Administer all components.
6. Stop rule: If a student is unable to respond to any word of the first four items, use teacher judgment to discontinue this segment and move to the next. If a student is unsuccessful in reading the word tiles at all, do not proceed to sentence reading.

Letters and Sounds
Begin with a collection of letter tiles [m, a, p, i, f, s, t, d, n].

1. Have students point to the letter you name.
2. Ask students to tell you the *name* and *sound* of each letter.

Words

Add the following letters to the collection of letter tiles [h, e, w, c, k, v, u, l, s, o, d, d, b, r, p, g].

1. Manipulate individual letters to build the words in the directions on the recording sheet. The teacher builds, and the student reads. Follow up with the Metalinguistic (ML) and the following articulation questions.
2. Ask the student to use the letter tiles to build the words you read. Follow up with Metalinguistic (ML) and Articulation questions. Record student responses. Observe and record strategy use (e.g., orally articulating sounds) and behaviors.
3. Use the word tiles provided on page 452 to assess word reading. Leave word tiles on the table for use in the next section.
4. In the Word section of the test it is useful to make up the following flash cards: *I, is, cat, sat, run, me, at, big, fat, the, look, map, sit, a, dog, can, on.*

Metalinguistic (ML) and Articulation Questions

Following the reading of "pat" and "sat" and the building of "tan" and "tad," ask how the student knew to make the change(s) he or she made. After the successful reading or building of the most difficult word, ask the student what his or her mouth did to say the first sound of the word. Then ask how he or she knew to read/build the word that way. Record student responses. Provide and document probing questions as necessary (e.g., "What were you looking at?" "I noticed your mouth moving; how did that help you?"). Score the ML questions using the Tile Test Metalinguistic Rubric.

Sentences

Use the collection of tiles to create sentences. Record student responses.

1. Using the word tiles, build each sentence and have the student read.
2. Ask the student to use the word tiles to build sentences you read. Then ask the student to read the sentence he or she built. Record student responses.
3. Hand the student the sentence on a separate sheet and have the student read it. Record student responses.

Metalinguistic Rubric

0	No response; "I don't know."
1	"I know it;" "My mom taught me;" "I'm smart."
2	Recognition of letters: "I looked at the letters."
3	Recognition of sounds: "I sound it out;" "I listen to the sounds."
4	Partial linking of sounds to letters: "It starts with a *P* /p/, then *a* /a/." Partial analogy: "Pat is like cat."
5	Explains spelling of each sound. Full analogy: "Pat is like cat, but it starts with a /p/."
6	Explains how sounds are articulated: "It starts with /p/. My lips are together and the air pops out; my tongue is resting in the middle of my mouth. … "

Recording Sheet

Student _____ Teacher _____ School _____ Date _____

Letter Identification
Lay out letter tiles [m, a, p, i, f, s, t, d, n].

"Here are some letters. I'll say the name of a letter and ask you to point to the letter. Point to the card that has the letter *m*." *(Record, continue procedure.)*

"Now, I'll point to a card and you'll tell me two things about the letter. First, the *name* of the letter, and second, the *sound* that it makes." *(Record.)*

	Identification	Name	Sound			Identification	Name	Sound
m					s			
a					t			
p					d			
i					n			
f								

Words
Add these letter tiles to the previous tiles: [b, c, d, d, e, h, k, l, o, r, r, s, u, v, w].

"Now let's put some letters together to make words. Some of the words are real words and some are pretend words. I'll go first and make a word, and then I'll ask you to read it for me." *(Manipulate only necessary letters, stop after sat and ask the first ML and articulation questions.)*

↓pat		vute	
*sat		flass	
sam		lodded	
hin		wembick	

*ML: "I noticed that you said 'sat' *(or repeat what the student said if different)*. How did you know to change it that way from 'pat' *(or repeat what the student said)*?" _____

_____

_____

Articulation: "Tell me what your mouth did to say the first sound in _____ *(repeat the most difficult word the student read correctly)*." *(Record verbal responses and behaviors.)*

ML: "How did you know to say _____ *(use the most difficult word decoded correctly)* that way?"

_____

_____

"Now, I'll say a word, and you make it for me." *(As you dictate, clearly articulate by "stretching" each sound. Example: tan = /t/ /ă/ /n/. Stop after tad and ask the first ML and articulation questions.)* You will be reading down the first list and then down the second list.

↓tan		plat	
*tad		mape	
tap		pridder	
leb		radmin	

*ML: "How did you know to change [the 'n' to a 'd']?" *(Use the letter changes the student has made.)*

_____

_____

Articulation: "Tell me what my mouth did to help you spell _____ *(repeat the most difficult word they spelled correctly).*"
(Record verbal responses and behaviors.)

ML: "How did you know to spell _____ *(use the most difficult word spelled correctly)* that way?"

_____

_____

Words
Lay out the collection of flash card that you have made.

"I'll show you some words, and you read each one." *(Record, and if incorrect, say the right word.)*

I	_____	me	_____	the	_____	a	_____
is	_____	at	_____	look	_____	dog	_____
cat	_____	big	_____	map	_____	can	_____
sat	_____	fat	_____	sit	_____	on	_____
run	_____						

Sentences
"I'll make a sentence with some words, and you read the sentence for me."

I can run. _____

Look at me. _____

I sat on the cat. _____

The map is big. _____

Sit the dog on the fat cat. _____

"Now I'll say a sentence, and you can make it for me." *(Have the student read the sentence after building it. Record sentence made and the student's read of it.)*

I can sit. _____

The dog is fat. _____

Look at the map. _____

A dog can look at me. _____

The big cat sat on the dog. _____

"Now I want you to read one sentence for me." *(Give the student the sheet with the sentence printed on it. Record the student's reading.)*

General Observations: _____

_____

_____

_____

_____

Word Tiles

Copy this page. Cut out and laminate each tile for use in word and sentence reading segments.

I	.	at	me
look	the	dog	a
cat	is	big	A
map	on		can
run	sat		Look
fat	Sit	sit	The

Name _____ School _____ Grade _____

Teacher _____ Age _____ Are you a girl or a boy? _____

Motivation for Reading Questionnaire

	A lot like me	A little like me	A little different from me	A lot different from me
1. I read because books and stories are often fascinating.	4	3	2	1
2. I read in order to get better grades in school.	4	3	2	1
3. I read because I know that my friends also read a lot.	4	3	2	1
4. I read because it is important to me to understand things better than other students.	4	3	2	1
5. I read when I am angry and need to calm down.	4	3	2	1
6. I read in order to avoid being bored.	4	3	2	1
7. I read because sometimes I can forget everything around me.	4	3	2	1
8. I read in order to cheer me up when I am in a bad mood.	4	3	2	1
9. I read if there is nothing better to do.	4	3	2	1
10. I read because it's exciting to see what happens to the main characters in a story.	4	3	2	1
11. I read because it helps me when I am angry.	4	3	2	1
12. I read because that is how I can learn something new.	4	3	2	1
13. I read because it is important to me to be among the best students.	4	3	2	1
14. I read because I want to perform better than others in my class.	4	3	2	1
15. I read because that is how I can learn more about interesting things.	4	3	2	1
16. I read because it helps me do better in school.	4	3	2	1
17. I read when there is nothing interesting on television or my tablet.	4	3	2	1
18. I read because it is fun.	4	3	2	1
19. I read because it helps me do well in some subjects.	4	3	2	1
20. I read because I like it when other people think I am a good reader.	4	3	2	1
21. I read because my parents think that it is important that I read a lot.	4	3	2	1
22. If the teacher discusses something interesting I might read more about it.	4	3	2	1
23. I read because it is important to me to always be the best at reading.	4	3	2	1
24. I read because other people say it is good for me to read a lot.	4	3	2	1

Survey of Reading Amount

	Almost every day	Once a week	Once a month	Never or almost never
How often do you read books all by yourself in your spare time?	4	3	2	1
How often do you read books all by yourself at bedtime?	4	3	2	1
How often do you read books by yourself during school vacations?	4	3	2	1

Survey of Reading Interest

My favorite book is _____

_____

My favorite author is _____

_____

My favorite genre is _____

_____

Scoring the Motivation for Reading Questionnaire (MRQ)

Score the MRQ by computing the mean or average score for each of the seven scales listed below. For example, determine the students average score for items that assess curiosity (1, 12, 15, 22). A high score is a 3 or 4 and low score is a 2 or 1. You can also compute the average scores for all of the items that assess intrinsic motivation and the those that assess extrinsic motivation. Compare the means for intrinsic and extrinsic motivation and you will have some ideas of what motivates each student to read.

Intrinsic Factors and Items

Curiosity 1, 12, 15, 22
Involvement, 7, 10, 18
Relief from boredom, 6, 9. 17
Emotional regulation, 5, 8, 11

Extrinsic Factors and Items

Grades, 2. 16. 19
Competition, 4, 13, 14, 23
Social recognition, 3, 20, 21, 24

Lesson Plans and Materials

In this appendix, we have included some lesson plans and some for helping you prepare for a lesson. Each procedure or lesson plan is related to a chapter, and you can learn more about the types of instruction illustrated in each lesson plan by consulting the appropriate chapter in the book.

The first procedure that follows provides information about selecting and teaching individual words. We introduced the SWIT concept in Chapter 10 and here we present a more elaborated version of it. SWIT helps you decide what words to teach and how to teach them. Chapter 10 then provides the procedures for teaching these words. The lesson that follows the SWIT procedures in this appendix describes how to use semantic mapping to introduce new words. Semantic mapping is an alternative to the lessons for teaching new words we included in Chapter 10.

The first lesson plan is a detailed description of an in-depth procedure for teaching students to infer the meanings of unknown words they come across as they read. Teaching students to use context clues is both very important and something that takes a good deal of time and effort on your part and on the part of your students. More information on teaching context clues can be found in Chapter 10, Vocabulary Development.

The second lesson plan is a detailed description of an in-depth procedure for teaching students to unlock the meanings of unknown words using their knowledge of prefixes. Teaching students to use prefixes to unlock the meanings of words they do not know is another important word learning strategy, and it too requires in-depth instruction. A list of the most frequent prefixes, those that are most worthy of instruction, is included in Chapter 8, Word Recognition. More information on teaching students to use prefixes and information on teaching them to use other word parts is included in Chapter 10, Vocabulary Development.

The third lesson plan is a Scaffolded Reading Experience (SRE) for teaching Kate DiCamillo's award-winning novel *Because of Winn-Dixie.* In addition to helping students learn strategies such as using context and using prefixes, it is important to help students read, understand, learn from, and enjoy the books and other materials they read for your class. SREs are research based, powerful, and flexible ways to do that. More information on SREs can be found in Chapter 11, in the section Four Frameworks for Scaffolding Students Reading.

The fourth lesson plan is a description of the first three days of instruction on making inferences designed for third- through fifth-graders. Comprehension is, of course, the ultimate goal of reading, and one of the most vital things that readers do is infer knowledge and connections that the authors imply. More information on comprehension strategies and how to teach them can be found in Chapter 11, Teaching Reading Comprehension: Focusing on Narrative Text.

The fifth lesson plan is a fairly detailed description of Questioning the Author (QtA), a type of comprehension instruction developed by Isabel Beck and Margaret McKeown. QtA is a whole-group questioning and discussion strategy designed to help students clarify any misunderstandings they have and construct significant meaning for what they read. It is one of several procedures for assisting students in building rich and lasting understanding of important topics, which we discuss in Chapter 11 Teaching Reading Comprehension Focusing on Narrative Text. While we introduced QtA in the narrative chapter it can be used equally successfully with informational text.

At the end of the appendix we include several lessons where we apply the principles of the Scaffolded Reading Experience to English learners. These lessons extend what we presented in Chapter 14. In one of the lessons we share the details of teaching an informational text about earthquakes and the other lessons shares how to scaffold the reading of a narrative story.

Selecting Words for Instructional Text: The SWIT Procedure

Although there are some situations in which you may teach words from a specific list, particularly with younger children or ELs, for the most part you are likely to be selecting words to teach from the selections students are reading. Here, we discuss an approach several colleagues developed called Selecting Words from Instructional Text or SWIT (Graves, Baumann et al., 2014). Two beliefs underlie this approach. One is that the principal goal in teaching the vocabulary from a selection students are reading is to support their comprehension of the selection and, particularly with information text, to support their understanding of a particular subject matter. The other underlying belief is that, while the differences between selecting vocabulary from narrative texts and informational text are relatively small, they are important to keep in mind, particularly because, with the advent of the Common Core, the use of informational texts has become more common in many classrooms.

In describing the SWIT approach, we will first discuss some types of words to teach, next consider how many words to teach at one time, then briefly describe four levels or intensities of instruction, and finally give examples of the SWIT procedure with upper elementary students reading a narrative text, primary grade students reading an informational text, and high school students reading an informational text. Key processes of the SWIT approach are shown in Figure 1.

Figure 1   Key Processes of the SWIT Approach

	Identifying Words	Teaching Words
Narrative	Essential	Powerful
Text		Instruction
	Valuable	
Unfamiliar		Brief
Words	Accessible	Explanations
Informational	Imported	Infer
Test		Meanings

Types of Words To Teach

As shown in Figure 1 the approach deals with teaching four types of words, each of which are described here.

ESSENTIAL WORDS

Essential words are *crucial for comprehending the text students are reading*. In narrative texts, these words often relate to understanding the central story elements and the characters and their actions. Essential words in narratives often appear just once or a few times in a given text. In Andrew Clements *Frindle*, for example, typically read in the upper elementary grades, Essential words might include *troublemaker, dictionary,* and *launch*. Essential words in informational texts are necessary for understanding the content of the text and key concepts in the content area the text represents. These words are likely to be conceptually complex and are often repeated several times in the text because the concepts they represent are discussed repeatedly. In Jay Winik's *April 1865,* for example, which might be read in a history class, essential words might include *confederacy, abolistion,* and *reunification.* Without understanding the meanings of Essential words, students' comprehension and learning from text will be impaired significantly.

WIDELY USEFUL WORDS

These words have broad, general utility for students' reading and writing and thus have importance beyond the selection students are currently reading. Some of the words listed as Essential words, for example, *dictionary* and *totalitarianism,* would be considered Widely Useful words if they were not essential to understanding the selection students were reading. Widely Useful words are identified not only in relation to the text itself and their prevalence outside of the text but also in relation to the vocabulary sophistication of the students. For example, Widely Useful words from a text for tenth-grade students would be quite sophisticated, words like *inhospitable* and *perplexing.* Widely Useful words from a text for sixth-grade students would likely include some fairly complex words used by advanced language users, words like *discord* and *inevitable.* And Widely Useful words from a text for second-grade students would include words not likely to be known by many second graders, but they would be of higher frequency than the Widely Useful words identified for sixth graders, words like *accommodate* and *reconcile.*

MORE COMMON WORDS

These are higher frequency words that are not likely to be understood by students who have limited vocabulary knowledge. More Common words must be taught to students whose vocabularies lag significantly behind their age- or grade-level peers because of limited exposure to sophisticated language, fewer world experiences, limited prior knowledge, or the fact that they are learning English as a second language. These students need to acquire More Common words so that they can accelerate their vocabulary growth. These words are not the most common in our language—for example, they are less common that the 220 Dolch Sight Words—but developing language learners need to learn them in order to understand most written texts. Examples for ELs or other students who have mastered basic words but still have limited vocabularies might include words like *consider* and *recent.*

IMPORTED WORDS

These are words that enhance a reader's understanding, appreciation, or learning from a text but are not included in it. For narrative texts, imported words may capture key thematic elements (e.g., *prejudice*) or address important character traits (e.g., *gullible*); for informational texts, they may connect to or enhance key concepts presented in the text (e.g., *democracy, environmentalism*). Carefully selected Imported words will help students analyze and extend what they learn from the text.

How Many Words to Teach

Deciding how many words to teach is frequently a challenge because many selections contain more words that at least some students in your class don't know than you have time to teach. Moreover, there is a limit on how many words you can teach, or at least how many students are willing to learn. Generally, when teaching something the length of a short story or chapter, most teachers suggest teaching no more than ten words. And most formal instructional studies we are aware of taught about ten words in their units, which typically lasted about a week. Still, because students need to learn about 3,000 words per year, you would like to teach as many as is reasonable. Thus, while you may not want to teach more than ten words for a particular selection or segment of a selection, you can increase the number students learn by teaching words in all content areas, not just in reading and language arts, by suggesting words or sets of words students can learn on their own, by teaching word learning strategies thoroughly and repeatedly encouraging students to use them, by immersing students in rich and varied language experiences, and by fostering students' word consciousness.

Types or Intensities of Vocabulary Instruction

Because there are typically more words to teach than there is time to teach them, vocabulary instruction should be the least intensive, most efficient form necessary to provide students with the knowledge they need to understand word meanings and comprehend the texts containing the words. Here, are four types of vocabulary instruction: (a) Providing Rich Instruction on specific words whose meanings are complex and essential to comprehending the text, (b) Providing Introductory Instruction for words that have clear-cut definitions or are not essential to comprehending the text, (c) Giving students glossaries for words that you do not directly teach, and (d) Suggesting words for students to learn independently, perhaps using their context, word part, or dictionary skills.

In summary, the process of selecting the types and numbers of words to teach, as well the nature of instruction, involves considerable judgment and decision making on the part of teachers. We illustrate this decision-making process and further describe the SWIT approach in the following section, which gives an example of SWIT used with an elementary grade narrative text. Graves, Baumann et al. (2014) *The Reading Teacher* article, in which the SWIT procedure was first described, gives an example of SWIT used with a primary-grade informational text and with a secondary-school informational text.

Using SWIT with an Upper Elementary Grade Narrative Text

Jacquelyn, a fourth-grade teacher, has her students read a selection each week from their literature anthology and participate in small literature discussion groups in which they read related texts at their instructional levels. This week, the common selection is an excerpt from the classic Newbery Medal winning *Island of the Blue Dolphins* (O'Dell, 1960). This short novel tells the story of Karana, a young Indian girl who was left alone on a beautiful but isolated island off the coast of California for 18 years. Over that period, Karana survived, showed great courage and self-reliance, and found a measure of happiness in her solitary life. In the excerpt that the class will read, Karana attempts to paddle to the mainland but has to turn back when her canoe begins to leak. Jacquelyn uses the SWIT process to identify and teach words from this *Island* excerpt.

1. **Identify Unfamiliar Words:** Jacquelyn reads the selection carefully, underlining in pencil those words she believes are likely to be Unfamiliar to a number of her students. She identifies 15 words as potentially Unfamiliar: *advice, ancestors, befall, calm, faint, fortune, headland, kelp, lessened, omen, pause, pursued, sandspit, serpent, skirted.* She then creates a chart like that shown in Figure 2 that lists these words in column 1.

2. **Identify the Four Types of Words to Teach:** Jacquelyn returns to the chapter and determines which of the 15 words are Essential, Widely Useful, or More Common, and decides if she should add any Imported words. In doing so, she tries to think like the fourth graders in her classroom—who have varying levels of vocabulary, reading ability, linguistic facility, and prior knowledge—in order to identify the words that will best facilitate their comprehension of the reading selection and general vocabulary development.

Figure 2 Categorizing Types of Words and Determining Types of Instruction

	Type of Word			Type of Instruction				
	Essential	Widely Useful	More Common	Powerful	Introductory	Provide Glossary	Handout List	Ignore
1. advice	✔			✗				
2. ancestors	✔			✗				
3. befall		✔			✗			
4. calm			✔		✗			
5. faint		✔			✗			
6. fortune	✔				✗			
7. headland							✗	
8. kelp							✗	
9. lessened							✗	
10. omen	✔			✗				
11. pause			✔		✗			
12. pursued	✔				✗			
13. sandspit							✗	
14. serpent							✗	
15. skirted							✗	
Imported Word	determination							

ESSENTIAL WORDS

Jacquelyn focuses first on words whose meanings students need to know to understand the selection. She considers central narrative elements and O'Dell's portrayal of Karana. For example, she determines that the words *advice* and *ancestors,* which occur in the following passage, are necessary for students to understand Karana's cultural heritage and motivation to leave the island.

> I remembered how Kimki, before she had gone, had asked the *advice* of her *ancestors* who had lived many ages in the past, who had come to the island from that country, and likewise the *advice* of Zuma, the medicine man who held power over the wind and the seas [italics added]. (pp. 57–58).

In contrast, Jacquelyn decides that students' comprehension of the chapter would not be impaired if they did not know the word *serpent,* which O'Dell uses simply to name a constellation Karana saw. From going through the excerpt, Jacquelyn decides that the following five words are Essential: *advice, ancestors, fortune, omen, pursued.* Jacquelyn places checks (✓) in the Essential words column of her chart.

WIDELY USEFUL WORDS

Jacquelyn reviews the chart looking for Unfamiliar words that, although not Essential for comprehending the selection, are Widely Useful for students to know for general, long-term reading and writing development. Jacquelyn decides that two words are Widely Useful (*befall* and *faint*), and she places checks in the Widely Useful column of the chart.

MORE COMMON WORDS

Jacquelyn next determines which of the remaining words are More Common words that are not likely to be understood by her students who have limited vocabularies, particularly the English learners in her class. Jacquelyn determines that two words fall into this category (*pause* and *calm*) and places checks in the More Common column of the chart.

IMPORTED **WORDS:**

Jacquelyn recognizes that the theme of the *Island* excerpt revolves around Karana's determination to overcome the obstacles she faced while attempting to paddle from the island to the mainland. Therefore, she decides to teach *determination*, which she writes in the Imported row at the bottom of her SWIT chart.

3. **Determine the Optimal Type of Instruction:** Having chosen which words to teach, Jacqueline next determines which of the four forms of instruction described earlier is best suited for each word. She does this by considering (a) how abstract or concrete each word is, (b) which of the four types of words it is, making sure that Essential words are taught in a way that ensures that students learn them well; and (c) if her students can determine the words' meanings independently.

    Applying these criteria, Jacquelyn determines that four words—the Essential words *advice, ancestors,* and *omen* from the selection and the Imported word *determination*—will require Powerful Instruction, and that six words—*befall, calm, faint, fortune, pause,* and *pursued*—can be taught using Introductory Instruction. Jacquelyn places an ✗ in the appropriate Type of Instruction column in the table. In all, she will directly teach a total of ten words. This leaves six words she identified as unfamiliar—*headland, kelp, lessened, sandspit, serpent,* and *skirted.* Jacqueline decides that her fourth graders can learn these words independently and places an ✗ in the Handout List column on her chart. Her completed list is shown in Figure 2.

IMPLEMENT VOCABULARY INSTRUCTION:

At this point, Jacqueline provides Powerful Instruction for the four words she has identified as needing it and Introductory Instruction for the six words she has decided can be taught using a less time consuming approach. Several possibilities for each of these sorts of instruction are described in detail in Chapter 5. She also hands out the list of the remaining six unfamiliar words, telling students to use their context skills, word part skills, dictionary skills, or each other to be sure they know the words' meanings.

In addition to initially teaching these words, Jacqueline plans a variety of review activities. It is essential that students repeatedly see, use, and review all new words.

Semantic Mapping

Semantic mapping (Heimlich & Pittelman, 1986; Johnson & Pearson, 1984) is a widely used and effective method for teaching new concepts—if the concepts are not too difficult and if students already have at least some information related to them. It is also useful in preteaching unknown words to improve students' comprehension of a selection, one of the most important purposes of vocabulary instruction. It works particularly well because focus is not only on the word being taught but also on related words and on the part the word plays in the selection. Here are a description of the procedure and a completed semantic map for the word *tenement*.

Semantic mapping makes use of a graphic organizer that looks something like a spider web. Lines connect a central concept to a variety of related ideas and events. Figure 3 shows a semantic map for the word *tenement*. You and your students might create a map such as this before or after reading a social studies chapter on urban housing.

Purpose

-   To enrich and clarify students' existing knowledge of a concept by having them identify categories of ideas and events related to that concept.

Figure 3 Clue Web: An Example for the Word *Tenement*

Conditions	Owners
Run down	Hard to reach
Small	Make good money
Crowded	Don't live there
Drab	Often don't care

TENEMENT

Costs	Tenants
Not cheap	People without a lot of money
Lower than some places	New immigrants
Too high	City people
	Large families

Procedure

- Put a word representing a central concept, such as *tenement*, on the whiteboard.
- Have students form groups, brainstorming as many words as they can think of related to the central concept.
- Write students' words on the whiteboard, grouped in broad categories.
- Have students name the categories and perhaps suggest additional ones.
- Discuss with students the central concept, the other words, the categories, and their interrelationships.

Vocabulary Lesson: Using Context Clues to Infer the Meanings of Unknown Words

Using context clues to infer the meanings of unknown words is the first word-learning strategy to consider because it is the most important one. Most words are learned from context, and if we can increase students' proficiency in learning from context even a small amount, we will greatly increase the number of words they learn. It is, therefore, vital that we provide students with rich, robust, and effective instruction on using context clues. Providing such instruction takes a good deal of time and effort on the part of both teachers and students. The instruction outlined here takes place over ten 30–45 minute sessions. A sample schedule is shown in Figure 4. In what follows, we describe the first two days of instruction in some detail and then much more briefly describe the rest of the unit. The instruction is described as it would be presented to students in the upper elementary grades. With younger or older students, the language and examples would be adjusted accordingly.

Figure 4 Overview of a Unit on Context Clues

DAY 1	DAY 2	DAY 3	DAY 4	DAY 5
Introduction and motivation to using context to infer meaning using a videotape	Introduction to using context clues to infer word meanings and to the four-step strategy	Detailed instruction in the first two steps of the strategy: Play and Question and Slow Advance	Detailed instruction in the second two steps of the strategy: Stop and Rewind and Play and Question	Game in which students earn points for using the four-step strategy to infer word meanings
DAY 6	**DAY 7**	**DAY 8**	**DAY 9**	**DAY 10**
Review of using context clues and the four-step strategy Renaming of the four steps without the VCR terminology	Guided practice—and further instruction if necessary—in using the four-step process with teacher provided narrative texts	Guided practice—and further instruction if necessary—in using the four-step process with teacher provided expository texts	Guided practice—and further instruction if necessary—in using the four-step process with authentic texts currently being used in the class	Review of using context clues and the four-step strategy Student–teacher planning on strategically using and learning more about context clues

Day 1: Introduction and Motivation

Because learning to use context clues is a demanding and challenging task, the teacher introduces the unit with a substantial motivational activity designed to both gain students' interest and enable them to relate the task of using context clues to infer word meanings to an activity they are familiar with—using a VCR/DVD or the Internet.

She begins by telling students that over the next few weeks the class is going to be working on using context clues to figure out the meanings of unknown words they come across while reading. Using clues to figure out things they don't know, she tells them, is something they do all the time, something they're good at, and something that is fun. Then, she tells them that they'll begin their study of context clues by viewing a brief video showing a place they might know and that their job is to look for clues to what the place is.

Just before showing the video, the teacher passes out the Clue Web, a type of graphic organizer, shown in Figure 3, puts a copy of the Clue Web on the overhead or document camera, and tells students that they will use the Clue Web today as they watch the video and over the next few weeks as they learn to use context clues. She goes on to tell them that they probably won't be able to answer all of these questions and should jot down brief answers while trying to figure out as much as possible about the place described in the video.

Lesson adapted from Michael F. Graves, *The Vocabulary Book: Learning and Instruction*. New York: Teachers College Press. Reprinted by permission of the publisher. All rights reserved.

At this point, the teacher shows the video, gives students a few minutes to fill in clues on their Clue Webs, and then begins a dialogue with them.

> "Was everyone able to get all of the information they needed to answer the questions after watching the video once? Did you catch all that the tour guide said? What would help you figure out even more of the answers?"

Students will almost certainly say that they could learn more if they could watch the video again. If they don't, the teacher points this out and then replays the video.

After this, she asks for a volunteer to identify the place described in the video, which is Hawaii.

Next, the teacher asks students what clues suggested it was Hawaii. Likely responses include "Hawaiian music," "palm trees," "the beach," and "tropical fruits." The teacher writes these clues on the Clue Web and compliments students on their efforts. Then, she challenges them to identify more clues that this is Hawaii and replays the video as many times as students request.

The teacher concludes the introductory lesson by noting that finding all of the clues and figuring out that the place shown in the video was Hawaii required hard work and persistence, that each time they viewed the video again they found more clues, and that this same sort of sleuthing is what they need to do when they are trying to figure out unknown words they meet while reading. She goes on to say that beginning tomorrow they will learn a particular strategy for figuring out the meanings of unknown words they come across. And, she notes, they will find that the strategy is a lot like the approach they used to figure out that the place shown in the video was Hawaii.

Day 2: Introduction to Using Context Clues and the Four-Step Strategy

The teacher begins Day 2 with a brief review of what the class did on Day 1, and then moves quickly to the topic for the day, learning a strategy for figuring out the meanings of unknown words they meet while reading.

> "Today, we're going to learn a strategy for using clues to figure something out. But this strategy will not be for figuring out what place is shown in a video. Instead, it will be for figuring out the meanings of unknown words that we meet when we're reading."
>
> "Actually, we won't exactly be 'figuring out' meanings. Instead, we'll be 'inferring meanings.' The strategy is called 'inferring word meanings from context.' When we infer something, we make an educated guess about it. And when we infer word meanings from context, we are making educated guesses about the meanings of the words. The context in which we find a word doesn't usually tell us the exact meaning of a word, but it often gives us a good idea of the word's meaning, and that is often enough to understand what we are reading."

At this point, the teacher puts up a large and colorful poster with the name of the strategy and the four steps and begins discussing the strategy. A sample poster is shown in Figure 5.

Figure 5 Four-Step Strategy for Inferring Word Meanings from Context

and ?	**Play and Question**
	• Read carefully.
	• Frequently ask yourself, "Does this make sense?"
	Slow Advance
	• Notice when you don't know the meaning of a word and slow down.
	• Read that sentence at least once more, looking for clues.
	• Ask yourself, "What is this paragraph about?"
and	**Stop and Rewind or Fast Forward**
	• If necessary, go back and reread, looking for clues that help you figure out what the word might mean. Read ahead to look for clues.
and ?	**Play and Question**
	• When you figure out what the word might mean, substitute your guess for the difficult word and see if the sentence makes sense.
	• If it does, keep reading.
	• If it doesn't, stop, rewind, and try again.

"Do you recognize this strategy?"

A number of students note that they do recognize it, that it is the VCR/DVD strategy they worked with the day before.

"Right. This is the same strategy we used yesterday, but now we are applying it to figuring out unknown words we meet in reading rather than to figuring out an unknown place we see in a video. Here's how it works."

"As you can see, the first step in the strategy is Play and Question. That means you read carefully, always asking yourself if you are understanding what you are reading. Also ask yourself, 'What is this paragraph about?'"

"Then, when you come to a word you don't know, you move to the second step—Slow Advance. At this point, you slow down, read the sentence at least once more looking for clues to the meaning of the word, and see if you can infer its meaning."

"If you can infer the word's meaning from just rereading the sentence, that's great. You continue to read. But if you can't infer the word's meaning from rereading the sentence, it's time to move to the third step of the strategy— *Stop* and *Rewind* or *Fast Forward*. At this point you stop, go back, and read the sentence or two that comes before the one with the unknown word, again looking for clues to the meaning of the word. Then you might *Fast Forward* and read a sentence or two beyond the difficult word and see if the added information helps.

"If you can now infer its meaning, excellent! You can move on to the fourth step of the strategy, which is also called Play and Question. But this time, Play and Question means to try out the word you inferred. Substitute your educated guess for the word you didn't know and see if that works. If it does, keep on reading. If it doesn't, you'll need to Stop and Rewind again, ask someone about the word, look it up in the dictionary, or simply continue to read, understanding the passage as well as you can without knowing the meaning of the word."

"I know that all of this sounds pretty complicated. And using context clues to infer the meanings of unknown words is going to take some work. But the work is well worth it because learning to use context clues helps to make you an independent and powerful reader, a reader who can read anything because you know what to do when unknown words come up."

SAMPLE TEACHER–STUDENT DIALOGUE

Shown below is a sample dialogue in which the teacher and the class work together to infer the meaning of a difficult word.

Teacher: Much like we did with the video, we are going to take a small section of a book and make sure we understand it before moving on. I will read a paragraph aloud *(give students a copy)* and then stop and check to make sure everyone understood the words and ideas. The book is *The Phantom Tollbooth* by Norton Jester. As you will see, the story is set in a very strange place. Here is the paragraph we're going to work with.

"A-H-H-H-R-R-E-M-M," roared the gateman, clearing his throat and snapping smartly to attention. "This is Dictionopolis, a happy kingdom, advantageously located in the Foothills of Confusion. The breezes come right off the Sea of Knowledge and cool the foothills gently. In this kingdom we don't have the cold temperatures like at the top of the mountains, nor the rain that the other side of the mountain gets."

Teacher: This gateman is welcoming the main character, Milo, into his city of Dictionopolis. Notice that Foothills of Confusion and Sea of Knowledge are capitalized. What does that tell you?

Students: They're proper nouns. They're names of places.

Teacher: Exactly. Knowing what sorts of words are capitalized will help you understand this section.

Did everyone understand the paragraph completely? If we don't understand everything, what could we do?

Students: Reread it. Read it again. Read it slower. Ask ourselves questions as we are reading it.

Teacher: Good thinking. You came up with two of the steps to our strategy, Slow Advance and Stop and Rewind. Let's use those two steps now. As I reread the sentence, listen for words that you don't know.

The teacher again reads the paragraph aloud.

Teacher: Were there any difficult words in that sentence? If so, what were they?

Students: Advantageously.

Teacher: Let's highlight that one. Now, let's reread just the sentence that *advantageously* is in and the one after it. We don't need to reread the whole thing every time, just the section we're focusing on.

The teacher rereads just the one sentence.

Teacher: Does *advantageously* sound like a positive thing?

Students: It does to me. It says that it is a happy kingdom. I think that it has a positive meaning.

Teacher: What are some of the things the paragraph tells us about this kingdom?

Students: That it gets nice breezes off the sea. It's not as cold as the mountain peaks and it's not as rainy as the other side of the mountain.

Teacher: Would that make it a pleasant place to live?

Students. Yes. It's nice to have a breeze. It's also good that it's not too cold. And being not so rainy is a good thing, too.

Teacher: What is the word *advantageously* describing?

Students: Where this city is located.

Teacher: That's right. The city is located in an advantageous place. What do you think that *advantageous* could mean?

Students: Nice?

Teacher: Let's add an -ly to that because our unknown word had an -ly. Then, let's write *nicely* above the word *advantageously.* Now, we should reread the paragraph with our replacement word to see if it makes sense. This time, while I'm reading, ask yourself if you understand what sort of place the story takes place in.

The teacher crosses out *advantageously* on the overhead and replaces it with *nicely.*

Teacher: What do you think? Did *nicely* fit in the sentence OK? Does the sentence make sense now?

Students: Yes. It does make sense. Dictionopolis sounds like a good place to live.

Teacher: I agree. I think that we now have a better understanding of the whole paragraph because we understand the word *advantageously* better. That's what learning to use context to infer word meanings can do. It can help us learn words, and it can help us better understand what we read.

INDEPENDENT PRACTICE

In addition to the guided practice illustrated in the teacher–student dialogue, each session from the second day of instruction includes independent practice. This first independent practice activity is brief and does not require the students to do a lot on their own. The teacher gives them a brief paragraph with some difficult words, asks them to read it several times and mark any words they don't know or are uncertain of, and tells them they will discuss using the context clue strategy with this paragraph the next day. As the instruction continues, the guided practice portions of the lessons will become much shorter, and the independent practice sessions will become longer and more challenging.

REVIEW AND QUESTION SESSION

Each session ends with a review and question session. The teacher reviews what students have learned that day and throughout the unit, primarily by calling on students to recap what they have learned. Each ending session also gives students an opportunity to ask questions and get clarification on anything of which they are uncertain.

The Remaining Eight Days of Initial Instruction

As shown in Figure 4, over the next eight days, the class receives detailed instruction on the four-step strategy, interrupts the hard work with a game using the strategy, does guided practice with both narrative text and expository text, uses the strategy with authentic text, and makes plans for using the strategy in the future. There are also several important things that the figure cannot show: Increasingly, the students talk more and the teacher talks less. The students do more of the work. They take more responsibility for the strategy, and they increasingly self-monitor and self-regulate their use of the strategy. At the same time, the teacher is always there to support students' efforts, providing encouragement, scaffolding, and feedback as needed.

Transfer, Review, and Integration Activities

It is vital to realize that this initial unit of using context clues, substantial as it has been, is only the first step in assisting students in becoming competent and confident users of this important strategy. In the weeks, months, and years after the initial instruction, students need lots of independent practice, feedback, brief reviews and mini-lessons, opportunities to use the strategy, reminders to use it, and motivation to do so. It is only with such a long-term effort that students will fully learn the strategy, internalize it, and make it a part of their approach to building their vocabularies.

Vocabulary Lesson: Using Prefixes to Unlock the Meanings of Unknown Words

Teaching students to use context clues is the most important word-learning strategy to teach, but teaching them to use word parts is a close second. In fact, about half of the new words that students meet in their reading are related to familiar words. Once students can break words into parts, they can use their knowledge of word parts to attempt to deduce their meaning—if, of course, they understand word parts and how they function. Of the three types of word parts to consider teaching—prefixes, suffixes, and roots—prefixes are the most powerful elements to teach for the reasons shown below.

- There are relatively few prefixes to teach.
- They are used in a large number of words.

- They are consistently spelled.
- They appear at the beginnings of words, where they are easy for students to spot.

Here, we describe a procedure for teaching prefixes in detail.

Day 1: Introduction, Clarification, Motivation, and Overview

On Day 1, the teacher introduces the concept of prefixes and the strategy of using prefixes to unlock the meanings of unknown words, attempts to motivate students by stressing the value of prefixes, and gives students an overview of the unit. It is particularly important to be sure that students understand exactly what prefixes and prefixed words are.

The teacher might say something like this: "Over the next few days, we're going to be looking at how you can use prefixes to help you figure out the meanings of words you don't know. If you learn some common prefixes and how to use your knowledge of these prefixes to understand words that contain those prefixes, you're going to be able to figure out the meanings of a lot of new words. And, as you know, figuring out the meanings of words you don't know in a passage is an important step in understanding the passage."

Next, the teacher asks students what they already know about prefixes, reinforcing correct information students provide and gently suggesting that any incorrect information they give is not quite on target. It is critical that students have a clear understanding of prefixes, and for this reason, the teacher follows the discussion with a presentation supported by graphic image projected through a document camera. Figure 6 or 7 is the image that the teacher shares with the students.

This is a lot for students to remember—too much in fact. For this reason, the teacher constructs a shortened version of these points and writes them on a "Basic Facts about Prefixes" poster (see Figure 6) or a shorter version in Figure 7. As the unit progresses, the prefixes, their meanings, and example words can be added to the poster.

Figure 6 Prefix Transparency or Projection

BASIC FACTS ABOUT PREFIXES

- A prefix is a group of letters that goes in front of a word. *Un-* is one prefix you have probably seen. It often means "not."
- Although you can list prefixes by themselves, as with *un-*, in stories or other things that we read, prefixes are attached to words. They don't appear by themselves. In *unhappy*, for example, the prefix *un-* is attached to the word *happy*.
- When a prefix is attached to a word, it changes the meaning of the word. For example, when the prefix *un-* is attached to the word *happy*, it makes the word *unhappy*, which means "not happy."
- It's important to remember that, for a group of letters to really be a prefix, when you remove them from the word, you should still have a real word left. Removing the prefix *un-* from the word *unhappy* still leaves the word *happy*. That means it's a prefix. But if you remove the letters *un* from the word *uncle*, you are left with *cle*, which is not a word. This means that the *un* in *uncle* is not a prefix.

Figure 7 Prefix Poster

Basic Facts About Prefixes

1. A prefix is a group of letters that goes in the front of the word.
2. In *unhappy*, the prefix is *un-* and the root word is *happy*.
3. A prefix changes the meaning of a word. If you remove a prefix, you still have a real word.
4. Knowing about prefixes can help you determine the meaning of a new word.

Some Important Prefixes

Prefix	Meaning	Example
un-	not	unhappy
re-	again	review
in-	not	incomplete

At this point, the teacher asks students if they know any additional prefixes, prefixes beyond those they have already discussed. The teacher should be generally accepting of their answers, but (assuming that some responses are incorrect) noting afterwards that some of the word parts given are not actually prefixes and that the class will continue to work on what is and what is not a prefix as the unit progresses.

Finally, the teacher introduces the three prefixes for study the next day—*un-* (not), *re-* (again), and *in-* (not)—putting them on the poster, asking students to copy them down, and asking each student to bring in a word beginning with one of the prefixes the next day.

Day 2: Instruction to the First Three Prefixes

At the beginning of the session, the teacher refers to the "Basic Facts" poster, briefly reminding students what prefixes are, where they appear, and why it is important to know about them. Then, the teacher calls on some students to give the prefixed words they have located, jotting those that are indeed prefixed words on the board, and gently noting that the others are not actually prefixed words and that they will be discussed later.

Lesson adapted from "Teaching Prefixes: As Good as It Gets?" by Michael F. Graves. In J. F. Baumann and E. B. Kame'enui, *Vocabulary Instruction: Research to Practice* (pp. 81–99). New York: Guilford Press. Copyright © 2003 Guilford Press. Reprinted with permission of the Guilford Press.

After this, the teacher begins the standard instructional routine for teaching prefixes and prefix removal. We suggest this standardized routine for three reasons. First, there is experimental evidence that it works. Second, using the same routine for teaching all prefixes means that students can soon learn the procedure itself and then concentrate on learning the prefixes and how to work with them. Third, the routine suggested can serve as a model teachers can use in creating a complete set of materials for teaching prefixes and the strategy of prefix removal and replacement.

Next, the teacher tells students that today they will be working with the three prefixes introduced the day before and how to use them in unlocking the meanings of unknown words. The three prefixes are *un-*, meaning "not"; *re-*, meaning "again"; and *in-*, also meaning "not." In teaching these three prefixes, the teacher will use several types of materials—transparencies introducing each prefix, worksheets with brief exercises requiring use of the prefix just taught, transparencies of these worksheets, exercise sheets requiring additional use and manipulation of each prefix, and review sheets on which students manipulate the three prefixes and the words that were used in illustrating the prefixes for the day. On the back of the worksheets, exercise sheets, and review sheets are answer keys so that students can immediately check their efforts.

Each introductory transparency presents one prefix, illustrates its use with two familiar words and two unfamiliar words, and uses each of the four words in a context-rich sentence. Below each sentence, the word and its definition are shown. And below these sample sentences is a fifth sentence, which gives students a root word and requires them to generate the prefixed form of the word. The introductory transparency for the prefix *re-* is shown in Figure 8.

Instruction begins with the teacher displaying the first sentence on the introductory transparency and leading students from the meaning of the familiar prefixed word to the meaning of the prefix itself as illustrated in the following dialogue.

Teacher: If Tom were asked to rewrite a test, what must he do?

Students: He has to take it over. He has to take it again.

Figure 8 Introductory Transparency for the Prefix *re-*

THE PREFIX <u>RE-</u>

1. Tom was asked to <u>rewrite</u> his spelling test a second time.
   rewrite—to write again
2. Carmen had to <u>repeat</u> her joke because her grandfather did not hear it.
   repeat—to say again
3. After the heavy doors were battered by the enemy, the soldiers rushed to <u>refortify</u> their stronghold.
   refortify—to make strong again
4. The original movie had been a big hit, so they decided to <u>remake</u> it with some current stars.
   remake—to make again
5. If <u>commence</u> means "begin," then <u>recommence</u> means _____.

Teacher: That's correct. Using your understanding of the word *rewrite,* what is the meaning of the prefix *re-?*

Students: Again. A second time. Over again.

The process is repeated with the next three sentences on the transparency. With some prefixes, students are likely to be able to volunteer the response without difficulty. With others, they may need further prompting, in which case the teacher rephrases the sentence to add more clues. If students are still unable to respond after the prompting, the teacher gives the definition. After going through the first four sentences on the *re-* introductory transparency, the teacher presents the fifth sentence, which defines the unknown root word and asks students to define the prefixed word.

After completing introductory instruction on the first prefix, students individually complete their check sheets while a student volunteer completes the check sheet on a transparency. Part of a check sheet is shown in Figure 9. As soon as students complete their check sheets, the volunteer puts the transparency on the overhead so that all students receive immediate feedback on their work. If the volunteer has made an error, the teacher corrects it at this time.

Figure 9 Part of a Check Sheet for the Prefix *sub-*

CAN YOU FIND IT?

A word or prefix is hidden in each line of letters below. Read the definition of the word or prefix. Then circle the word or prefix when you find it.

1. Find the prefix meaning "under" or "below"
   antidissubplegohnobitto
2. Find the word in each line that means:

   a. "underground railroad"
      shelaunomessubwaywathoning
   b. "to put under water"
      lasubmergersinthergerows
   c. "a plot beneath the main plot"
      thisenroutelesubplotrudiw
   d. "underwater boat"
      mopeitaqksubmarinetshowl

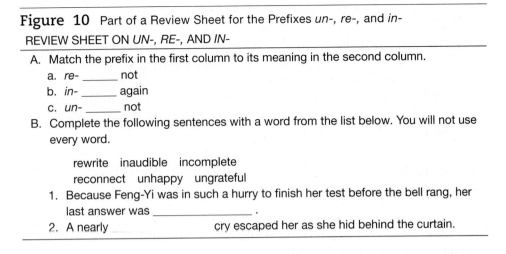

Figure 10 Part of a Review Sheet for the Prefixes *un-*, *re-*, and *in-*

REVIEW SHEET ON *UN-, RE-,* AND *IN-*

A. Match the prefix in the first column to its meaning in the second column.
   a. *re-* _____ not
   b. *in-* _____ again
   c. *un-* _____ not

B. Complete the following sentences with a word from the list below. You will not use every word.

   rewrite   inaudible   incomplete
   reconnect   unhappy   ungrateful

   1. Because Feng-Yi was in such a hurry to finish her test before the bell rang, her last answer was _____ .
   2. A nearly _____ cry escaped her as she hid behind the curtain.

These same procedures are then completed with the two remaining prefixes for the day—*un-* and *in-*. Following initial instruction on the three prefixes, the students complete a review sheet and immediately receive feedback by checking the answers on the back of the sheet. Part of a review sheet is shown in Figure 10. While students are completing the review sheet, the teacher monitors their work and provides assistance when requested. This concludes the second day of the unit.

Day 3: Review the Prefix Strategy and the Remaining Three Prefixes

Day 3 begins with the teacher reviewing the basic facts about prefixes on the poster. Then students complete a review sheet on the three prefixes taught the previous day and immediately correct their work.

Next comes another crucial part of the instruction—instruction in the prefix strategy. The teacher introduces the strategy by telling students that now that they have worked some with the strategy and understand how useful prefixes can be in figuring out the meanings of unknown words, the teacher is going to teach a specific strategy for working with unknown words. The teacher titles the procedure "Prefix Removal and Replacement," emphasizing that they are using a big name for an important idea.

The teacher then puts up the "Prefix Removal and Replacement" transparency, which is reproduced on a prominently displayed "Prefix Removal and Replacement Strategy" poster (shown in Figure 11), and talks students through the procedure with one or two sample prefixed words.

Figure 11 Prefix Removal and Replacement Poster

THE PREFIX REMOVAL AND REPLACEMENT STRATEGY

When you come to an unknown word that may contain a prefix:

- Remove the "prefix."
- Check that you have a real word remaining. If you do, you've found a prefix.
- Think about the meaning of the prefix and the meaning of the root word.
- Combine the meanings of the prefix and the root word, and infer the meaning of the unknown word.
- Try out the meaning of the "unknown" word in the sentence, and see if it makes sense. If it does, read on. If it doesn't, you'll need to use another strategy for discovering the unknown word's meaning.

Following this explicit description of the strategy and modeling of its use, the teacher tells students that they will continue to work on learning the meanings of prefixes and learning to use the strategy today, tomorrow, and in future review sessions. The teacher then points out to students that they now have two posters to refer to when they come to an unknown word that may contain a prefix—the "Basic Facts" poster and the "Prefix Strategy" poster. Finally, the teacher teaches and reviews the remaining three prefixes (dis-, en-, and non-) using procedures and materials that exactly parallel those used on Day 2. This concludes the third day of the unit.

Day 4: Review of the Information about Prefixes, the Prefix Strategy, and the Prefixes Taught

Day 4 begins with the teacher reviewing the four facts about prefixes, again using the "Basic Facts" poster in doing so. As part of the review, the teacher asks students a few questions about these facts to be sure they understand them and answers any questions students have.

Next, the teacher reviews the prefix removal and replacement strategy using the "Prefix Strategy" poster. After this, the teacher continues with the explicit instruction model, first modeling use of the strategy with two of the six prefixes taught and then collaboratively using the strategy in a whole-class session with two more of the six prefixes. After this, the teacher divides students into small groups and provides guided practice by having the groups use the strategy with the final pair of prefixes. The teacher also has some of the groups share their work and their findings, thus providing guided practice.

As the final activity of the initial instruction, small groups of students work together on a quiz. The quiz requires them to state the four facts about prefixes, state the steps of the prefix removal and replacement strategy, and give the meanings of the six prefixes taught. As soon as students complete the quiz, they correct the quiz in class so that they get immediate feedback on their performance and hand the corrected quizzes in so that the teacher has this information to plan reviews.

Reviewing, Prompting, and Guiding Students to Independence

At this point, the instruction is far from complete. If we really want students to remember what a prefix is, recognize and know the meanings of some prefixes, and use the prefix removal and replacement strategy when they come to unknown words in their reading, reviewing what has been taught and prompting students to use the strategy while reading is crucial.

By reviewing, we mean formal reviews. Have the first review about a month after the initial instruction, a second review two months after that, and a third review, if it seems necessary, several months after that. Each review might last 30–45 minutes. Two somewhat conflicting considerations are important in undertaking these reviews. The first is that it does no good and in all probability does some harm to spend time "teaching" students things they already know. Thus, if at the beginning of a review, it is apparent that students already know the material, the review should be very brief or should be conducted for that small group of students who still need additional instruction.

By prompting, we simply mean reminding students about prefixes and the prefix strategy at appropriate points when they are reading. Thus, when students are about to read a selection that contains some unknown prefixed words, the teacher might say something like, "In looking through today's reading, I noticed some pretty hard words that begin with prefixes. Be on the lookout for these, and if you don't know them, try using the prefix strategy to figure out their meanings." This sort of prompting should probably be fairly frequent, as it can do a lot to move students toward independent use of the strategy.

Comprehension Materials: Role Sheets for Literature Circles

We provide the following role sheets for implementing Literature Circles in your class. Each sheet describes a role and each must be introduced and practiced with the class. The role sheets outline the type of preparation required of the students. One student must create discussion questions, another must identify vocabulary words, and others reflect, critique, or summarize. Pick and choose the roles. A discussion director is essential, but you can vary the other roles depending on the needs of the students.

Vocabulary Monitor

Purpose: Find, teach, and discuss new and important words and/or phrases to the group.	Name: _____ Book title: _____ Discussion of pages _____ Date _____

Preparation

Your job is to look for words and phrases we need to know. Write down the page numbers and the context clues for each word. Note why you picked these words.

Words or Phrases we need to know	Page #	Context clues, meaning, or synonym

During the Discussion

1. Choose one or more words to discuss.
2. Show the words and pronounce them correctly.
3. Give your reasons for choosing the words. How does each word contribute to your understanding of the passage?
4. Ask others to discuss the words or suggest another definition.
5. Discuss how the context clues helped you determine the meaning of the words.

Visualizer

Purpose: To identify descriptive passages, visualize them, and use visual images to improve comprehension.	Name: _____ Book title: _____ Discussion of pages _____ Date _____

Preparation

Your job is to find passages with rich descriptions such as strong use of adjectives, adverbs, concrete nouns, and explicit verbs. Note these passages and think of ways to bring them to light. You might draw diagrams, charts, pictures, cartoons, or maps.

The Passage and Page #	Why Did You Pick This Passage?	What Image Does It Create in Your Mind?

After Reading – During the Discussion

1. Read a passage with rich description.
2. Discuss why you picked it.
3. Share the image you created or what you pictured in your mind.

The Connector

Purpose: To find important connections within the passage and connections to your experiences, to books, and to ideas.

Name: _____
Book title: _____
Discussion of pages _____ Date _____

Preparation
Your job is to look for and note important connections that can be made within the story or between the story and what you know. Write about the connections you made.

Connections You Can Make

Connect one idea in the story to another Connect the story to something in your life	Connect the story to another text Connect the story to something you know
Page #	Describe the Connections That You Made

During the Discussion

1. Discuss the connections that you made.
2. Ask others what other connections they made while reading.
3. Discuss why all of the connections are important to understanding the story.

Discussion Director - Questioner

Purpose: To ask important questions that promote inferential and critical thinking.

Name: _____
Book title: _____
Discussion of pages _____ Date _____

Preparation
Look for parts of the story that raise questions about plot, character development, theme, mood, point of view, and author's purpose. Write questions that will help others in your group develop their understanding of the story.

Page #	Question

During the Discussion

1. Ask your questions and call on people to answer the questions. They should label the questions literal and inferential as they answer them.
2. Ask group members to ask their own questions during the discussion.

The Critic

| Purpose: To highlight parts that are important or interesting enough to share with the group. | Name: _____
Book title: _____
Discussion of pages _____ Date _____ |

Preparation

Look for passages in the book that the group should share. Share passages that are:

- interesting
- confusing
- well written
- funny
- important
- thought provoking
- scary
- informational
- controversial

Page #	Passage You Are Sharing	Why You Picked this Passage

During the Discussion

1. Share with the group at least one of your passages.
2. Tell the group why you are sharing that passage.
3. Ask other group members what passage they would like to share.

The Predictor

| Purpose: To help the group think along with the author and use text clues to determine what will happen next | Name: _____
Book title: _____
Discussion of pages _____ Date _____ |

Preparation

1. Look for clues that help the reader anticipate what might happen next. Look for some clues and then write down your prediction.

Passage Clues	What are your predictions for the next chapters?

After Reading – During the Discussion

2. Ask the group if the first prediction came true.
3. Ask the group to make a prediction or share yours.
4. Ask people to justify their prediction.

The Summarizer

Purpose: To help the group integrate what they have read and develop a concise understanding of the story.

Name: _____

Book title: _____

Discussion of pages _____ Date _____

Preparation

Your job is to sum up what has been read. As you are reading, look for: 1. Changes in the setting; 2. Changes in the behavior of the main characters; 3. Resolution of problems and conflicts; 4. Development of new conflicts.

Your Summary

_____

_____

_____

_____

_____

_____

_____

_____

_____

_____

_____

After Reading – During the Discussion

1. Read or recite your summary.
2. Ask the group if there is anything we should add to the summary.
3. Ask people if there is anything we should leave out of the summary.

Character Cartographer

Purpose: To help the group track the characters, their relationship to other characters, and how characters influence each other.

Name: _____

Book title: _____

Discussion of pages _____ Date _____

Preparation

Your job is to keep a list of characters. After each character's name write down their relationship to other characters, and how they influence each other.

Characters	Relationships	Influences/Interactions

After Reading – During the Discussion

1. Help to explain who the characters are and how they are related.
2. Point out the most important conflicts.
3. Discuss how some characters support each other.

Comprehension Lesson: Teaching Students the Strategy of Making Inferences

Strategies are mental actions we use to understand and remember what we read. Teaching comprehension strategies—such as establishing a purpose for reading, using prior knowledge, asking and answering questions, making inferences, determining what is important, summarizing, dealing with graphic information, imagining and creating graphic representations, and monitoring comprehension—is important at all grade levels. Only when the reader has acquired some word recognition fluency is he able to turn his mental energy to comprehension strategies. Starting in second grade, students are able to use comprehension strategies to construct meaning and can begin to do so without continual teacher support. Described below are the first three days of a unit on making inferences as it might be presented to third-, fourth- or fifth-grade students.

Day 1: Making Inferences Introduction

MOTIVATION AND INTEREST BUILDING (ABOUT 5 MINUTES)

Make a small chart on the whiteboard (see Figure 12). Ask the students what toy or game they would very much like to have. Answers will vary, but Wii or Playstation 4 will most likely be included. Label these as goals. Then ask the students how they plan to acquire a Wii. They might say they will ask for it as a birthday present, do odd jobs, or beg. Explain that these are strategies, actions we can take to achieve a goal.

Now switch the discussion to reading and ask, "What are your goals when you read?" Some possible responses might include finish the assignment, remember new ideas, enjoy a good story, or learn information. If the students leave out any of these ideas, add them to the chart yourself. After you have established the goals, begin to discuss strategies. "What are some strategies that we use that help us achieve these goals?" The students' responses might include rereading a story, making notes, sounding out words, and so forth. You might add other strategies you have studied, such as making predictions and asking questions. Explain that today the class will learn a new strategy called making inferences.

EXPLANATION AND MODELING (ABOUT 20–30 MINUTES)

Write the following sentence on the board and begin the discussion leading the students to understand what inferences are and how we make them.

> Mary looked at her menu trying to find the cheapest entrée while John gazed lovingly in her eyes.

First ask, "Where are John and Mary?" Almost all students will infer that they are in a restaurant, but your goal is to discover how that inference is made. Ask the students what clues in the sentence tell them that John and Mary are in a restaurant. Most will focus on the word *menu* and a few on the word *entrée*. Now that they have discovered the text information necessary to draw an inference, lead the students to examine their

---

Figure 12   Just What Is a Strategy?

	Your Goals	Your Strategies
Toys & Games	To have a Wii or a Playstation 4	Ask for it as a birthday present Do odd jobs Save up my allowance
Reading		

Figure 13 Making Inferences Chart

Clues in the Text	Your Knowledge/Experiences	Inferences/ Conclusions
Menu, entrée	All restaurants I have been to have a menu, even McDonalds.	Mary and John must be in a restaurant.

own experiences or knowledge, the second component of an inference. Ask the students, "Have you been to a restaurant?" "Do all restaurants have menus?" "Does your mother hand you a menu before dinner at home?" As these questions are discussed, explain that we make an inference by considering text clues and our prior knowledge to add to a text what the author has left out. Enter the students' responses on the "Making Inferences" chart (Figure 13).

Briefly discuss why the author does not have to explain everything and why he can leave out the important fact that Mary and John are in a restaurant. He counts on the reader to add his or her knowledge and experiences to the text to complete what the author has omitted. We call this process *making inferences,* or *reading between the lines.* At times, we can infer how a character feels, what kind of person the character is or what causes a character to act or behave in a certain way.

Reveal more about how the strategy works by reading the next paragraph and discussing with the students what inferences they might make. Make sure that the students think about what the author did not explain, what was left out. Next, tell students to look for clues in the text and think about what they know or have experienced in their own lives.

> The team boarded the school bus and started out for the big game. If they won this game, they would be champions! Suddenly, fifteen miles from the site of the game, the bus broke down. There they sat, waiting. Nobody seemed to know what to do, and it was getting closer and closer to game time.

As the discussion about this paragraph develops, point out the salient text clues if the students do not. They should note that the bus has broken down, the students are going to an important game, and nobody knows what to do. If they don't point out these clues, you must. Next, ask the students how they might feel if they were trapped in a similar situation. Update the "Making Inferences" chart with text clues, the students' prior knowledge, and the inferences they have drawn.

Have the students read the next paragraph and then work with a partner to discover what the author left unsaid. The goal is to discover the feelings, goals, or motives of the characters. Use the chart in Figure 13 to record the text clues and the students' personal experiences.

> Mario was smiling. There were cute little puppies lined up in cages and lots of goldfish swimming around in a huge tank. He could hear birds chirping, kittens meowing, and gerbils running on their little wheels. He had a big decision to make. His dad looked at him, smiled, and said, "Well, here we are! Are you ready for your new responsibility?" Mario's heart started beating faster. He was so glad Dad said yes to what he had wanted for so long!

End the lesson by introducing the anchor chart (see Figure 14). At this time you will review what an inference is and the thinking process that most readers employ. Check to see if students were following you by asking a few students to explain the strategy and tell why it is important when they read.

Figure 14 Inference Anchor Chart

MAKING INFERENCES

- Think about what the author did not tell us—feelings, character traits, motives.
- Look for clues in the text.
- Think about what you know. Think about similar experiences you have had.
- Relate your experiences to the clues in the story. Make the inferences.
- Do the inferences make sense in the context of the story?

Day 2: Large-Group Student Guided Practice (20 minutes)

Begin the lesson by asking the students to explain the strategy they were studying yesterday. Ask students to name the strategy, explain how to make an inference, and explain the importance of making inferences. Expand on the question of importance by exploring with the students when we make inferences. The discussion should focus on the following ideas.

- We make inferences when we sense that the author has left something out. Often it is a clear statement about a character's feelings, traits, or motives.

- We make inferences when we add something to the text that helps the story make more sense.

Continue the discussion and have the students explain how we go about making inferences, using the inference anchor chart (Figure 13) as a guide. Remind them that the strategy of making inferences has several different names. At times it will be called "making inferences," others may call the strategy "drawing conclusions" and sometimes "making generalizations." The underlying thinking is the same. You need to read between the lines and think about what the author did not tell you. Next, you need to search for text clues and at the same time relate what you are reading to your own knowledge and experiences.

Then, using the following paragraphs, engage the students in a third round of making inferences. Have the students consider what the author might have left out. What can they infer about the characters, what they are doing, and what they are feeling?

> Billy was crying. His hands were scraped up and his knees were bloody. Grandpa said, "You have tried so hard today and you haven't given up! You know they say, 'Practice makes perfect.' I know you can do this." Billy stood up and let out a big sigh. "I know, Grandpa. But I'm getting tired." "How about two more tries and then we'll go get some ice cream?" "Okay, sounds good," Billy responded.
>
> He grabbed the handles, pulled on the button, and rang the bell. The tinkling sound always made him feel better. He slowly straddled the seat and put his left foot on the pedal. "Take your time," Grandpa warned. As he picked up a little speed, Billy put his right foot on the other pedal. He could sense Grandpa close behind him holding the seat. All of a sudden, he felt the wind blowing into his face. Grandpa let go and started clapping. Billy was doing it! He swallowed the lump in his throat and laughed out loud. Grandpa was right! The more you practice, the better you will get.

Add the students' comments to the "Making Inferences" chart in Figure 13. Be sure to discuss the clues in the text and the students' prior knowledge or experiences. Several more paragraphs for you to use with your students are included at the end of this lesson.

Day 3: Making Inferences with Real Text (20 minutes)

It is now time to apply the task of making inferences to the reading and comprehending of a real text, not just a few well-formed paragraphs. We can support students' inference generation by asking many inferential questions, but we should also help them discover these inferences on their own. For this next lesson, review all of the information on the inference poster. Students should have a decent understanding of an inference and the thinking process that underlies it. They should think about what the author has omitted, search for text clues, and relate their prior knowledge and experiences to the text.

PLANNING THE THIRD DAY LESSON

Planning is key to the success of helping students make inferences with lengthy texts such as short stories or novels. First, pick a text that demands that the reader make inferences—a text that demands that the reader think along with the writer. Next, read the selection twice, first to gain an overall understanding and second to determine what inferences will be necessary to fully comprehend the selection. Examine the text and determine whether you need to teach any vocabulary words to support the students' comprehension. Consider what prior knowledge you will need to develop before the students read and discuss the selection. Next, pick the points where students will stop reading to discuss portions of the selection. Finally, prepare the questions and prompts you will use to stimulate the inference generation process and encourage discussion.

INTRODUCE THE SELECTION AND DEVELOP PRIOR KNOWLEDGE

Begin the lesson by giving the students a brief preview of the reading selection and taking some time to develop their prior knowledge. Remember, if the students are to make inferences, they must draw upon their prior knowledge. So this portion of the lesson is critical to their success in making inferences. If, for example, the story is about a boy wishing his father would take him fishing and the father is avoiding the idea at all costs, begin with a few simple questions.

1. What do you like to do with your parents?
2. Do your parents always do what you want them to do? How do you feel when they say no?
3. How do you get your parents to do what you want?

This discussion will build the knowledge that the students need to make the necessary inferences. Before reading, it is also important to teach a few of the critical vocabulary words that the students do not know.

READING THE SELECTION AND MAKING INFERENCES

Have the students read a portion of the selection and then stop to discuss it. Begin the discussion by asking the students to summarize what they have read. Ask, "What is the story about? What did the author tell us?" Next, begin the inferential thinking by starting with broad questions. "What did we learn about the character?" "What kind of person is he or she?" "What did his words or actions tell us about his feelings or his character?" If these broad questions do not solicit the necessary inferences, then become more specific and focus on particular events and reactions in the story. Remember to ask students to search for important text clues.

When students have difficulty answering these inferential questions, it is important to take them into their own experiences. For example, if in the story the child repeatedly asks about going fishing, but the father has excuses and puts the son off, ask the following question: "How do you think that the son feels?" If the students struggle to construct an answer, remind them of their own experiences. "How do you feel when your parents don't do what you have asked?" Making the questions personal helps the students apply what they know and have experienced to answering the questions.

You will continue discussing the selection in this manner. When you have completed the discussion, review some of the important inferences that your students made.

What have you and the students learned about the characters, their feelings, and their motivations? Consider what clues in the text helped you make these inferences and what prior knowledge was necessary to make these inferences. As you and the students continue to read and discuss short stories, picture books, and novels during the year, making inferences will always be an important strategy. Return to the poster whenever students need a review of the strategy.

Sasha licked her bowl clean. She grabbed her bone, jumped up on the chair, and started chewing. When she heard keys jingle in the doorknob, she started wagging her tail. Jermaine was home!

PARAGRAPHS FOR PRACTICE IN MAKING INFERENCES

My forehead started sweating as I pumped my arms in the wind. My new sneakers felt great on my feet. I picked up my pace. I could see the finish line in the distance. The crowd was going wild for me!

Mom and Jeffrey raced around the house collecting Jeff's spikes, glove, water bottle, cap, and uniform. His stuff was hard to find because it was still dark outside and they didn't even think to turn the lights on. Jeff yawned as he searched every corner of the house. When they finally gathered everything in Jeff's bag, they ran out the door. This was going to be a long day, but Jeffrey was excited!

Jenny's arms were sore and her legs were tired. She let out a heavy sigh. She was sick of putting her belongings in all the boxes. As she took down pictures of her friends off the wall, she wiped her tears away. Who knew when she would see them again? Her room was almost empty. By tonight her family would be gone.

The boys snuck slowly up the front sidewalk. The sun was almost behind the trees so it was pretty dark. They tiptoed up the creaky stairs of the front porch. The door squealed as David slowly pushed it open. Spider webs hung in the dark corners of the tall ceiling. It looked like no one had lived there for years. There was dust covering everything. All of a sudden, there was a loud BANG upstairs. John screamed! David felt a chill run up his spine. It sounded like someone was slowly walking down the stairs! The stories they had heard were true! They ran out the door and never went back again.

Mario was smiling. There were cute little puppies lined up in cages and lots of goldfish swimming around in a huge tank. He could hear birds chirping, kittens meowing, and gerbils running on their little wheels. He had a big decision to make. His dad looked at him, smiled, and said, "Well, here we are! Are you ready for your new responsibility?" Mario's heart started beating faster. He was so glad Dad said yes to what he had wanted for so long!

Comprehension Lesson: A Description of Questioning the Author (QtA)

Questioning the Author is a large- and small-group questioning and discussion procedure developed and validated by Isabel Beck and Margaret McKeown (Beck, McKeown, Hamilton, & Kucan, 1997, 1998; Beck, McKeown, Worthy, Sandora, & Kucan, 1996; McKeown, Beck, & Sandora, 1996). It is, as Beck and McKeown explain, "an approach to text-based instruction that was designed to facilitate building understanding of text ideas" (Beck et al., 1997). Beck and McKeown developed the procedures after several years of research on textbooks (Beck, McKeown, & Gromoll, 1989). They found that textbooks were often difficult for students to understand because they often assumed that students had more prior knowledge of the topics being dealt with than they actually did. As a result, the explanations of ideas and events given in the text were often insufficient to allow students to construct much meaning. This shortcoming of the textbooks was further compounded by the fact that students assumed the texts to be absolute authorities and thus beyond question. When students read a text and did not understand what they had read, they repeatedly saw themselves as totally responsible for their lack of understanding and failed to even consider the possibility that the text itself might be less than perfect.

Prompted by these findings, Beck and McKeown developed QtA with two ideas in mind: (1) to encourage and assist young readers in getting under the surface of the material they were reading, dig into it, and engage with the ideas the texts presented and (2) to assist students in realizing that textbooks are simply someone's ideas written down and that readers frequently need to work hard to figure out what the author is trying to say.

Their procedure for doing this is simple and straightforward. First, the teacher explains to children that texts are, in fact, written by ordinary people who are not perfect and who create texts that are not perfect. Consequently, readers need to continually work hard to figure out what the authors are trying to say. QtA proceeds by having the class read a text together, with the teacher stopping at critical points to pose queries that invite students to explore and grapple with the meaning of the text. The queries include initiating prompts such as "What's the author trying to say?" to get students started in grappling with the text, follow-ups such as "What does the author mean by that?" to encourage them to dig for deeper meaning, and follow-ups such as "How does that connect with what the author told you?" to encourage them to put ideas together. However, queries are not scripted, and teachers are encouraged to modify those suggested and make up their own to fit the students and texts with which they are working.

The key purpose of QtA is building understanding from text. As Beck and McKeown note, understanding does not come from a casual reading of the text and the assumption that the author's meaning will somehow be absorbed by the reader. Instead, understanding comes when the reader considers, manipulates, grapples with, and integrates information gleaned from the text with his existing knowledge. QtA involves students as they read the text for the first time rather than after they have read or during a second reading. This is a very important characteristic of QtA and one that distinguishes it from many other questioning and discussion techniques. The goal of QtA is that students will actually have the experience of constructing meaning for text as they are reading, not that they will be told about what they might have experienced after the fact.

Another very important characteristic of QtA that distinguishes it from many other questioning and discussion techniques is that QtA discussions focus specifically on the text. QtA discussions are not wide-ranging conversations in which students are encouraged to engage in sharing a wide range of opinions and ideas. Instead, the discussion focuses on clarifying, collaboratively constructing meaning for, and ultimately understanding the ideas in the text they are reading. The QtA queries are strategically used by the teacher to direct the discussion to that end. They are general probes that have a very specific purpose—engaging students in grappling with and constructing meaning for the ideas in a text.

In the remainder of our discussion of QtA, we present a segment of a QtA session, consider queries in a bit more detail, explain the process of planning a QtA session, characterize the types of discussion you are trying to prompt with QtA, and suggest how you might introduce QtA to a class.

A Sample Questioning the Author Segment

The following classroom scenario, taken from Beck and colleagues (1996, 1997), shows a fifth-grade social studies class studying Pennsylvania history. The class has been working with QtA for some time and is quite skilled in grappling with text ideas. The class is discussing a text segment about the presidency of James Buchanan, a Pennsylvania native. The text indicates that many people believed that Buchanan liked the South better than the North because he believed that it was a person's choice whether or not to have slaves. Following is the class discussion (McKeown, Beck, & Sandora, 1996, pp. 112–113).

FIFTH GRADERS QUESTIONING THE AUTHOR

Teacher: All right. This paragraph that Tracy just read is really full of important information. What has the author told us in this important paragraph?

Laura: Um, they, um, think that Buchanan liked the South better because they, he said that it is a person's choice if they want to have slaves or not, so they thought, um, that he liked the South better than the North.

Teacher: Okay. And what kind of problem then did this cause President Buchanan when they thought that he liked the South better? What kind of problem did that cause?

Next, Janet gives her interpretation of how Buchanan's position on slavery might have affected the voters in Pennsylvania.

Janet: Well, maybe, um, like. less people would vote for him because. like. if he ran for President again, maybe less people would vote for him because, like, in Pennsylvania we were against slavery and we might have voted for him because he was in Pennsylvania, because he was from Pennsylvania. That may be why they voted for him, but now since we knew that he was for the South, we might not vote for him again.

At this point, the teacher summarizes Janet's remarks.

Teacher: Okay, a little bit of knowledge, then, might change people's minds.

Then, another student acknowledges Janet's explanation and offers some of his own thoughts.

Jamie: I have something to add on to Janet's 'cause I completely agree with her, but I just want to add something on. Um, we might have voted for him because he was from Pennsylvania so we might have thought that since he was from Pennsylvania and Pennsylvania was an antislavery state, that he was also against slavery. But it turns out he wasn't.

Finally, a third student acknowledges her classmates' thoughts and contributes her ideas to the developing interpretation.

Angelica: I agree with the rest of them, except for one that, um, like, all of a sudden, like, someone who would be in Pennsylvania you want to vote for them but then they wouldn't, they be going for the South and then you wouldn't want to vote for them after that.

The scenario illustrates several key attributes of a QtA discussion. The students are indeed grappling with text meaning; they are really trying to understand the author's meaning. The teacher adroitly directs the discussion, but she does not dominate it. She leaves plenty of room for student input because the purpose is for the students to understand the text; if they're the ones who are going to understand the text, they're the ones who must do most of the talking and thinking. The students respond at some length. Finally, they listen to each other and build on each other's responses as they jointly construct meaning for the text.

Queries

One way to begin to understand queries is to contrast them to traditional questions, with which we are more familiar. Beck and McKeown suggest three dimensions on which the two differ. First, traditional questions assess comprehension with the goal of finding out whether the students understand what they have read. Queries assist students in grappling with text ideas, with the goal of helping them put ideas together. Second, traditional questions serve to evaluate individual student responses and foster teacher-to-student exchanges. Queries "facilitate group discussion about an author's ideas and prompt student-to-student interactions." Finally, traditional questions are generally used either before reading or after reading. Queries "are used on-line during initial reading" of the text.

As we have already pointed out, queries are not scripted and teachers are encouraged to adjust their queries to fit their students, the text, and the purposes in reading the text. Nevertheless, Beck and McKeown have identified a set of queries that are quite useful and serve to illustrate the nature of successful queries. These are shown in Figure 15.

These, of course, are general queries. In posing queries for a specific text, they become more specific. We have already seen specific examples of initiating and follow-up queries in the QtA segment on President Buchanan. Here, the teacher's initiating query and its lead-in were "All right. This paragraph that Tracy just read is really full of important information. What has the author told us in this important paragraph?" In this same segment, one of the teacher's follow-up queries was "Okay. And what kind of problem then did this cause President Buchanan when they thought that he liked the South better? What kind of problem did that cause?"

Narrative queries, a type we haven't yet discussed, are uniquely suited to narratives. They are used with narratives in addition to initiating and follow-up queries. A representative example of a narrative query comes from a teacher whose class was using QtA as they read George Seldon's *The Cricket in Times Square* (1970). In the part of the story students have just read, Mario Bellini's pet cricket, Chester, ate half of a two-dollar bill. This is a problem because two dollars is a lot of money to the Bellinis. Here is the next paragraph of the story.

> Chester Cricket sat frozen on the spot. He was caught red handed, holding the chewed-up two dollars in his front legs. Muttering with rage, Mama Bellini picked him up by his antennae, tossed him into the cricket cage and clicked the gate behind him. He half expected that she would pick him up, cage and all, and throw him onto the shuttle tracks.

Figure 15 Some Questioning the Author Queries

INITIATING QUERIES

- What is the author trying to say here?
- What is the author's message?
- What is the author talking about?

FOLLOW-UP QUERIES

- So what does the author mean right here?
- Did the author explain that clearly?
- Does that make sense with what the author told us before?
- How does that connect with what the author has told us here?
- But does the author tell us why?
- Why do you think the author tells us that now?

NARRATIVE QUERIES

- How do things look for this character now?
- How does the author let you know that something has changed?
- How has the author settled that?
- Given what the author has already told us about this character, what do you think he (the character) is up to?

SOURCE: Beck, I. L., McKeown, M. G., Hamilton, R., & Kucan, L. (1997). *Questioning the Author*, p. 45. Newark, DE: International Reading Association.

After students have read the paragraph the teacher poses this narrative query: "How do things look for Chester?"

As you can see from the sample queries and these examples, the purposes of initiating queries are to make the text information public in the classroom and to get the discussion underway, and the purposes of follow-up queries are to keep the discussion focused and to assist students in elaborating and integrating ideas. The purposes of narrative queries are to focus students' attention on characters and the roles they are playing in the story and on the way the author is crafting the plot.

Planning

There are three steps in planning a QtA lesson. The first step is to read and study the text thoroughly in order to identify the major understandings that you want students to achieve and the potential problems that they may have in achieving those understandings. For example, in reading the text on President Buchanan mentioned above, the teacher might determine that one thing she wants students to understand is that President Buchanan was supported and influenced by people representing diverse views and had to somehow deal with these diverse views. She might further infer that students are unlikely to appreciate the very different views on slavery advanced by different states.

The second step is to segment the text, to divide it into short sections that are read and discussed before students go on to the next section. Sometimes a segment will be quite lengthy, perhaps a page or so. At other times, a segment will be relatively short; for example, the sample discussion we presented for the Buchanan text dealt with a single paragraph—"All right. This paragraph that Tracy just read is really full of important information. What has the author told us in this important paragraph?" At still other times, a segment might be even shorter, dealing with a single sentence, as fifth-grade teacher Rona Greene tells us.

> My fifth-graders are familiar with the Questioning the Author procedure, so when I come up with just a single sentence for them to analyze, they're not surprised. Recently, while reading R. Lawson's *Ben and Me* (1939), I ran across a sentence that was challenging enough and important enough to constitute a Questioning the Author segment. In the story, in which Benjamin Franklin has a mouse companion named Amos, who narrates the story, there comes a point at which Franklin is about to send Amos up in a kite to examine lightning. The text reads, "This question of the nature of lightning so preyed upon his mind that he was finally driven to an act of deceit that caused the first and only rift in our long friendship." I decided that this particular sentence, which indirectly reveals the depth of the friendship between Amos and Franklin but does not directly describe it, was worth serious consideration.

Finally, in addition to deciding what is important in a text, what the likely stumbling blocks are, and how the text will be segmented for the discussion, you need to write down the queries. Although many queries will be modified or even discarded as the discussion proceeds, queries such as "What has the author told us in this important paragraph?" and "How do things look for Chester?" are planned in advance.

Discussion

We have already given one fairly lengthy example of a QtA discussion and described the sort of discussions that QtA is designed to foster. Here, we give another example of a QtA discussion, also from Beck and colleagues (1997), and conclude with a quotation emphasizing that students need to be the principal participants in QtA discussions.

This discussion deals with the sentence from *Ben and Me* just given—"This question of the nature of lightning so preyed upon his mind that he was finally driven to an act of deceit that caused the first and only rift in our long friendship"—and begins with the initiating query shown in the following dialogue (McKeown, Beck, & Sandora, 1996, pp. 110–111).

Teacher: What's the author trying to tell us about Ben and Amos?

Temika: That their friendship was breaking up.

Teacher: Their friendship was breaking up? OK, let's hang on to that. What do you think, April?

April: I agree with the part that their friendship did break up, but, um, I think that they got back together because when you were reading, um, further, it said that he was enjoying the mouse.

Teacher: OK, so let me make sure. You say that he knows that they're friends, and something happened that made them almost not be friends? But they're still friends?

Alvis: I think that, um, Amos is just, I think Amos is just lying because in the story it said if they weren't good friends, why would, um, um, Ben build a, um, kite for, build a kite for him so he could have fun.

Teacher: OK, so Alvis is telling us that, why would Ben go to all that trouble and build that beautiful kite if they weren't friends? A lot of people agreed that their friendship was broken up. Alvis doesn't think their friendship is broken up. Can somebody help me out? What's the author want us to figure out here?

(The teacher sees that April and Alvis are making sense of this sentence by bringing in supporting information from other parts of the text, and she attempts to rephrase their statements to better clarify the nature of the friendship.)

The discussion continues, with two more students grappling with the meaning of the sentence.

Tammy: Um, um, deceit was an act of lying so that means, that means, um, sometimes a lie broke up a friendship and, because it made a rift and, um, so, and deceit was an act of lying, so their friendship must've broke up because of somebody told, um, some kind of lie.

Teacher: Oh, that's interesting. Tammy said that if there were some lying going on, something to break up their friendship, because that's what Amos said, "the first and only rift in our friendship," something must've happened. How many of you agree that something had to happen?

Jamal: I disagree, cause a break in their friendship don't mean they gotta break their friendship.

Teacher: OK, so Jamal thinks that they might still be friends, even though something happened. OK? We're gonna continue 'cause the only way we're gonna find out is if we read some more.

In addition to illustrating how a teacher rephrases and clarifies ideas and keeps the discussion focused as she guides students toward full understanding of this important sentence, this excerpt shows how QtA discussions are dominated by students rather than by teachers. "Students do the work. They construct the meaning, wrestle with the ideas, and consider the ways information connects to construct meaning." Thus, "the discussion becomes an opportunity for students to formulate complete thoughts, respond to the text, react to each other's ideas, and consider new notions" (Beck et al., 1997).

Introducing QtA

Introducing QtA is a straightforward matter, but it is important to include several points in your introduction. First, tell students that the way they are going to be reading and discussing text is probably different from they way they have typically dealt with it. Next, tell them that you and they are going to be reading and discussing short sections of text at some length. That is, they will read a segment of text and then stop and discuss what it means with their classmates. Explain that the reason they need to do this is that a text is simply somebody else's words written down and that sometimes, in fact in quite a few cases, understanding what the author is saying requires close attention to, and a good deal of discussion of, the text. Finally, note that the discussions you are going to have will deal with the text and the meaning the author is trying to convey rather than with more wide-ranging matters.

That's it. With this ground work laid, and after thoroughly familiarizing yourself with the QtA procedure, you are ready to begin QtA sessions.

The Impact of Using the Questioning the Author Procedure

Beck and McKeown and their colleagues have worked with QtA for several years and have gathered several sorts of data on its efficacy. First, they implemented QtA with two teachers who had had been using a very traditional pattern of teacher-initiated questions aimed mainly at retrieving information directly from the text and brief student responses that were quickly acknowledged before the next question was asked. A more recent study indicated that QtA helped students achieve greater comprehension than did a more strategy-focused discussion (McKeown, Beck, & Blake, 2009).

But with QtA, their lessons began to change. Typically, a QtA lesson showed collaborative construction of meaning. A student would offer an idea in response to a query, and the teacher and other students would build and elaborate on that idea. As an example, here is a brief excerpt from a QtA social studies lesson on "international cooperation." The class had just read a text segment about countries cooperating to share resources through world trade.

Teacher: What's the author reminding us of here? Reggy?

Reggy: That we, um, that we trade resources out of their countries and they trade us out of our resources and we cooperate, by helping each other.

In this excerpt that Reggy's response is in his own words, strongly suggesting that he is presenting his ideas rather than simply parroting text information. Now notice in the following excerpt how the teacher handles Reggy's response by summarizing part of it and then extending the discussion by forming a question from another piece of what Reggy said.

Teacher: OK, Reggy said we help each other, and that's how we cooperate. When you cooperate, you're working together to get something done. What does Reggy mean by, "we trade resources out of their countries?" What's he talking about? Darleen?

Darleen responds with an explanation about how trade works.

Darleen: He's talking about, when he says we're trading resources out of our country, he means that other countries, like Britain and Japan and China, we get our cotton and our resources that we have that are really popular, and we trade them for money sometimes.

Darleen's response is a fitting conclusion to our discussion of QtA because it indicates the amount of listening, thinking, and connecting that a QtA lesson can elicit. This is the sort of active engagement students need to demonstrate if they are to fully understand a text.

Comprehension Lessons: English Learners

The Scaffolded Reading Experience or SRE is an instructional framework that one of us (Mike Graves) has worked with for a number of years. The framework provides a number of options for providing prereading, during reading, and postreading activities to support students as they read a selection. Although SREs can be designed for English-only students as well as for English learners, they can be very useful for English learners. The SRE below is taken with permission from J. Fitzgerald & M. F. Graves (2004) *Scaffolding Reading Experiences for English-Language Learners.* Norwood, MA: Christopher-Gordon.

A Very Supportive SRE on Seymour Simon's *Earthquakes*

This SRE uses the K-W-L procedure recommended by Donna Ogle (1986). K-W-L includes pre-, during, and postreading activities in which students actively consider what they Know, what they Want to know, and what they Learn.

Students: Fourth-grade students with low to average English-reading ability in an ethnically diverse classroom in California, including several English-language learners.

Selection: *Earthquakes* by Seymour Simon. This informational book gives a dramatic photographic account of the causes and effects of earthquakes around the globe.

Reading Purpose: To learn about earthquakes, what causes them, what effects they have on people and property, and what might be done to prepare for them.

Overview		
Students	**Selection**	**Purpose**
Day 1		
Prereading	**During Reading**	**Postreading**
Motivating and Relating Reading to students' lives (10 mins.)	Reading to Students (5 mins.)	Discussion (10 min.)
Activating Background Knowledge (10 mins.)	Guided Reading (5 min)	Questioning (10 min.)
Prequestioning and Direction Setting (5 mins.)		
Day 2		
Prereading	**During Reading**	**Postreading**
Prequestioning and Direction Setting (5 min.)	Guided Reading and Silent Reading (30 mins.)	Discussion (10 min.)
		Application—jigsaw groups (10 min.)

PREREADING FOR DAY 1

MOTIVATING and RELATING READING TO STUDENTS' LIVES—*What's Your Story?*

In this activity, an event relating to the topic of the text is described and then students relate their own similar experiences.

Goal of the Activity: To pique students' interest in a topic and activate their background knowledge.

Rationale: Describing an event in a way that requires students to infer what is happening can be an effective way to stimulate interest and introduce a topic at the same time. Having students then discuss their own experiences requires that they access relevant knowledge, which will help them build meaning from the text.

Procedure: Begin by describing a scenario similar to the following. "Imagine yourself in this situation. You are asleep in bed. Suddenly, the bed begins to move back and forth. Half awake, you say to the sibling in the bed next to yours, 'Stop shaking the bed.'" Ask students to explain what is going on. Tell students this was an experience you had with earthquakes and encourage them to talk about their own experiences.

ACTIVATING BACKGROUND KNOWLEDGE—*WHAT I KNOW*

In this activity, students brainstorm to find out what they know about a topic and then generate categories of information that are likely to be found in the text they will read.

Goal of the Activity: To have students activate their prior knowledge about a topic and consider what information on that topic might be included in a specific text.

Rationale: Students who have been in California for some time are likely to have some knowledge of earthquakes. Activating this knowledge before reading can help establish a framework to aid them in understanding and remembering. If some of the English-language learners are new to California and unfamiliar with earthquakes, they can learn from their classmates.

Procedure: On the whiteboard, write the title *Earthquakes*. Underneath that title and to the left, write the heading *What I Know*. Ask students to give some of the facts they know about earthquakes. Jot their responses under the heading *What I Know*.

EARTHQUAKES

What I Know
Can cause damage
Are unpredictable
Are scary
Happen in California
Not all are the same

Shake the earth
Don't happen at night
Are getting worse

As you will notice, not all of the students' responses are accurate. During this brainstorming session, you might ask students various questions such as, "How did you learn that?" or "How could you prove that?" Later, during the postreading discussion, you can clear up any remaining misconceptions.

After students have given a variety of responses, show them the cover illustration on the book *Earthquakes*. Ask them to think about the kind of information that might be included in the book and write their suggestions on the board to the left of their initial responses. Some of their suggestions might include: How earthquakes happen, where they happen, what we can do about them, how much damage they do, why they happen, and descriptions of some of the worst quakes.

PREQUESTIONING AND DIRECTION-SETTING—*WHAT I WOULD LIKE TO KNOW*

In this activity, students consider what they would like to know about a topic that might be discussed in a specific text.

Goal of the Activity: To turn students' interest in earthquakes into a desire to read about them.

Rationale: Having learners think about what they would like to know about a topic sets up a purpose for reading. If students have questions in mind, they will be looking for answers to those questions as they read and comprehension will be facilitated.

Procedure: Explain that informational books such as *Earthquakes* are written to give us information that we might need or want. Ask students to think about what they would like to know about earthquakes—things they don't already know or aren't quite sure of. Write their responses on the board in a column to the right of the *What I Know* column.

EARTHQUAKES

What I Would Like to Know
What causes earthquakes
How earthquakes are measured
What places have earthquakes
What was the worst earthquake
Where most earthquakes are
What we can do about earthquakes

DURING READING FOR DAY 1
GUIDED READING—*WHAT I FIND OUT*

In this activity, students write down answers to the questions they posed prior to reading that are given in the text, and then they consider which of their questions still need answering.

Goal of the Activity: To have students transform questions into answers and thoughts into writing.
Rationale: Having students search for answers to their questions requires active reading on their part. Transforming what they learn into writing requires and promotes even deeper understanding. Having students go a step further and check what questions still need answering lets them know that the information an author chooses is selective and they may need to check other sources to get their answers.
Procedure: On the whiteboard to the right of the previous two headings, write *What I Found Out.* Explain to students that this will be the last part of the K-W-L procedure—a procedure they can use when they read informational books and articles. They have already completed the first two steps—thinking about and writing down what they know about earthquakes and what they would like to know. The last step is to record what information they do learn.

Direct students' attention to the information they wanted to know. Explain that as they read they will look for the answers to these questions.

READING TO STUDENTS—*THE APPETIZER*

In this activity, you read the first few pages of an informational book aloud to students.

Goal of the Activity: To interest students further in the topic of the book and motivate them to read it on their own.
Rationale: Reading aloud can help ease many students into the material. A good enthusiastic rendition can also be an enticement for students to read on their own. At the same time, some of your English-language learners may be stronger readers than listeners, so be sure to allow any students who want to to follow along in the text. In addition to getting students off to a good start, this shared experience allows you to complete the third step of the K-W-L procedure as a group and provide clarification of the task before students read and record answers on their own.

Ask students to listen carefully as you read the first five pages in the book aloud. They should be thinking about the questions they had listed on the board and decide whether or not they are answered in these pages.

POSTREADING FOR DAY 1
DISCUSSION—*QUESTIONS ANSWERED?*

In this activity, students decide which questions were answered in the text.

> **Goal of the Activity:** To have students realize that, although a specific text may answer some of their questions, it may not answer all of them and they will need to seek other sources for some questions.
>
> **Rationale:** To become critical thinkers and readers, students need to realize that, while our questions about a topic might be answered in a text, they also might not be. Authors have to be selective in what they include. What we may wish to know may not be in the scope of the text and, therefore, we need to consult others.
>
> Procedure: Draw students' attention to the questions asked in the prereading activity.

EARTHQUAKES

What I Would Like to Know
What causes earthquakes
How earthquakes are measured
What places have earthquakes
What was the worst earthquake
Where most earthquakes are
What we can do about earthquakes

Begin by asking students, "Was the first question, *'What causes earthquakes?'* answered in the first five pages of the book?" If students answer "yes," ask them to tell you, if they can, what the answer is and write that answer in the column *What I Found Out*. Proceed in a similar manner with each of the questions. If questions aren't answered, tell students that these questions still might be answered in the remainder of the text or that they may not be answered in this particular text at all and they will need to consult other sources for the answers.

PREREADING FOR DAY 2
PREQUESTIONING AND DIRECTION-SETTING—*K-W-L*

In this activity, students record what they know about a topic, what they would like to know, and what they learned from reading a text.

> **Goal of the Activity:** To have students access their knowledge on a topic, think about what more they would like to learn about that topic, and better understand and remember the information that interests them most.
>
> **Rationale:** Having students access appropriate knowledge before reading a text, posing their own questions, and writing down the answers to those questions can help them better understand and remember text material.
>
> **Procedure:** Hand out the *What I KNOW—What I WANT to Know —What I LEARNED* chart shown below.

WHAT I KNOW—WHAT I WANT TO KNOW—WHAT I LEARNED

When students have their charts, review the three types of information they will record. First they will think about and record what they **know** about earthquakes, then write down what they **want** to know in the second column. As they read the book, they will write the answers to their questions or what they **learned** in the third column. Remind students of what they had done as a group the day before and explain that today they will have the opportunity to focus on their individual knowledge and interest in earthquakes or perhaps work with one other student as they read. Quietly invite each of your English-language learners to team up with a native English speaker who is a good reader if they like.

Remind students that not all of their questions will be answered in the text. This might be a good opportunity to talk about other resources for finding answers if this particular text doesn't provide them.

Explain that when they finish they will get a chance to share what they learned about earthquakes.

MODIFYING THE TEXT—*TAPE IT*

In this activity, an audio tape recording is made available for students to listen to as they follow along in the text.

> **Goal of the Activity:** To make the concepts in the text accessible to readers who might have difficulty reading the text on their own.
>
> **Rationale***:* Although this text is richly illustrated and not particularly dense, some English-language learners may have difficulty with it. Having an audio tape available will help make the concepts accessible for those students whose oral skills are more developed than their reading skills.
>
> **Procedure:** Make a recording of the story on an audio tape or have an older or more competent student do it. Make as many copies as necessary or hook up one tape player to several receivers.

POSTREADING ACTIVITY FOR DAY 2

DISCUSSION I—*WHAT DID YOU LEARN?*

Students meet in small groups to discuss what they learned from the text.

> **Goal of the Activity:** To give students the opportunity to express their ideas to an audience and hear other students' ideas as well.
>
> **Rationale:** Expressing themselves in an informal small-group setting gives students the opportunity to clarify their thoughts and also receive new information and insights from their classmates.
>
> **Procedure:** After students have finished reading the text and have completed their K-W-L charts, have them meet in groups of 3–6, with no more than one or two English-language learners in any one group. Appoint a facilitator—perhaps an English-language learner—and a recorder for each group. In the groups, students take turns telling what their questions were, which ones were answered, and what the answers were. The facilitator's job is to make sure everyone gets a chance to speak and the recorder keeps an account of the questions that were *not* answered in the text.

DISCUSSION II—*RESEARCH IT*

The recorders from each small group discussion session report to the class what questions are still left to be answered and then each group takes a question to research.

> **Goal of the Activity:** To have students work in small groups to check multiple sources in order to find answers to a question.
>
> **Rationale:** As previously mentioned, students need to realize that finding the information they want sometimes requires searching in one or more additional sources. Working in heterogeneous groups to locate these sources and answers requires that group members support one another in their efforts. Learning to work cooperatively is a skill that is not only necessary in school, but in many aspects of life.
>
> **Procedure:** After the groups have met to discuss what they learned in *Earthquakes*, have the recorders report to the entire class what questions their group members still have. Write these questions on the whiteboard. Have each group choose one question to research. That group is then responsible for finding the answer and reporting their findings to the entire class.

This may also be a good time to compare the statements students listed in the *What I Know* activity with what they actually did learn from the text. For example, one student had said, "They are getting worse." Ask students if the idea that earthquakes are getting worse was validated by the text. If the consensus is "no," the student who offered this initial comment may concur or perhaps decide to pursue independent research to try to confirm his statement.

Because this class is familiar with library research techniques, students need only be reminded at this time on how to proceed. This may require only a brief discussion to activate students' prior knowledge and review guidelines they might follow.

APPLICATION AND OUTREACH—*LET'S JIGSAW*

Students form cooperative Jigsaw groups (Aronson & Patnoe, 1997) where each student completes a different part of the process, and take a topic that emerged from their readings to make posters that will be displayed in the school cafeteria, library, or other public places.

Goal of the Activity: To help reinforce the concepts students learned in their reading and to provide the opportunity for students to apply their knowledge in a practical, helpful way.

Rationale: Having groups of students—again with no more than one of two English-language learners—work together to create posters designed to communicate information they learned from reading about earthquakes can provide students with practice in working cooperatively, recalling, analyzing, and summarizing information, and thinking creatively about how to present information in a clear, concise, yet eye-catching way. It also demonstrates that information garnered from reading can be shared with others and can be important and useful.

Procedure: After students have met in their discussion groups, bring the entire class together again. Discuss some of the major points of interest in their reading about earthquakes and ask students to think about what information might be of interest to other students in the school. Have students offer their suggestions and write these on the board. Some of their suggestions might include:

How earthquakes are measured
What you should do to prepare for an earthquake
What you should do when an earthquake happens
How earthquakes happen
Where earthquakes happen

Assign (or let each group choose) one of the topics and have them make a poster about it. If sample posters are available, show these to students. Or you can clip appropriate advertisements from magazines and discuss what makes these informative and eye catching. Be aware that some of your English-language learners may be able to do a particularly good job with this nonverbal activity, and be prepared to fully support their efforts.

Each group will then meet to decide what information, graphics, and illustrations will go onto their poster. Next, they will use the resources available to them to produce a poster that will communicate information on their topic in the most interesting way possible. Finally, they will publicly display their poster.

Adapting the Activity: The K-W-L activity can be used any time students' purpose for reading is to learn information. Students might use this procedure while reading content-areas textbooks, magazine articles, or any number of informational trade books. For example, students might use a K-W-L chart to help them learn more about Benjamin Franklin while reading *The Many Lives of Benjamin Franklin* by Mary Pope Osborne, to learn more about space exploration in *Can You Hear a Shout in Space?* by Melvin and Gilda Berger, to discover what it means to be president when reading the Caldecott-winning picture book *So You Want to be President?* by Judith St. George and illustrated by David Small, or to learn more about the California condor and the efforts to save this very endangered species when reading *California Condor: Flying Free* by Bonnie Graves.

Reflection: This SRE is based primarily on the K-W-L teaching model. Although K-W-L is not the only procedure that might be used with Earthquakes, *it's a good one. The prereading and postreading activities, of course, will reflect the material students are reading and their purposes for reading it. The essence of the model, however, includes three phases— brainstorming, purpose-setting through asking questions, and finding answers to those questions. The procedure provides a scaffold which helps support students' own interests and inquiries. According to Ogle, K-L-W "helps students keep control of their own inquiry, extending the pursuit of knowledge beyond just the one article. The teacher is making clear that learning shouldn't be framed around just what an author chooses to include, but that it involves the identification of the learner's questions and the search for authors or articles dealing with those questions."*

SRE for *The Girl Who Struck Out Babe Ruth* for Students Who Need a Lot of Scaffolding

Students	Selection	Purpose
A class of fourth graders, about a third of whom are ELs who need a good deal of assistance in reading English	*The Girl Who Struck Out Babe Ruth* by Joan L. S. Patrick	To understand and enjoy an inspiring biography

Prereading	During Reading	Postreading
• Motivating • Preteaching Vocabulary • Building Background Knowledge • Suggesting a Strategy	• Guided Reading • Oral Reading by Teacher • Silent Reading	• Discussion • Drama • Artistic Activity • Reteaching (This became part of the SRE when it became apparent that students were having problems using the strategy suggested during prereading.)

SRE for *The Girl Who Struck Out Babe Ruth* for Students Who Do Not Need a Lot of Scaffolding

Students	Selection	Purpose
A class of largely above average third graders that includes native-English speakers and English-language learners who have been in dual-language immersion classes since kindergarten	*The Girl Who Struck Out Babe Ruth* by Joan L. S. Patrick	To understand and enjoy an inspiring biography

Prereading	During Reading	Postreadimg
• Building Background Knowledge (using an approach that also provides some motivation for reading the selection)	• Guided Reading • Silent Reading	• Discussion • Artistic Activity

References

Adams, M. J. (1990). *Beginning to Read: Thinking and Learning about Print*. Cambridge, MA: MIT Press.

Adams, M. J., Foorman, B. R., Lundberg, I., & Beeler, T. (1998). *Phonemic Awareness in Young Children*. Baltimore: Paul H. Brookes.

Adler, M. J., & Van Doren, C. (1972). *How to Read a Book*, rev. ed. New York: Touchstone.

Afflerbach, P. (2007). *Understanding and Using Reading Assessment, K–12*. Newark, DE: International Reading Association.

Afflerbach, P., & Cho, B. Y. (2009). Identifying and describing constructively responsive comprehension strategies in new and traditional forms of reading. In S. E. Israel and G. G. Duffy (Eds.), *Handbook of Research on Reading Comprehension* (pp. 69–90). New York: Routledge.

Afflerbach, P., & Johnston, P. H. (1986). What do expert readers do when the main idea is not explicit? In J. F. Baumann (Ed.), *Main Idea Comprehension*. Newark, DE: International Reading Association.

Afflerbach, P., Pearson, P. D., & Paris, S. G. (2008). Clarifying differences between reading skills and strategies. *The Reading Teacher, 61*(5), 364–373.

Afflerbach, P. P. (1990). The influence of prior knowledge on expert readers' main idea construction strategies. *Reading Research Quarterly*, 31–46.

Airasian, P. (1994). *Classroom Assessment*. New York: McGraw-Hill.

Alexander, P. A. (2003). The development of expertise: The journey from acclimation to proficiency. *Educational Researcher, 32*(8), 10–14.

Allington, R., Guice, S., Michelson, N., Baker, K., & Li, S. (1996). Literature-based curricula in high-poverty schools. In M. F. Graves, P. van den Broek, & B. M. Taylor (Eds.), *The First R: Every Child's Right to Read* (pp. 73–96). New York: Teachers College Press.

Allington, R. L. (1977). If they don't read much, how they ever gonna get good? *Journal of Reading, 21*, 57–61.

Allington, R. L. (1983). The reading instruction provided readers of different abilities. *Elementary School Journal, 83*, 548–559.

Allington, R. L. (1984). Oral reading. In P. D. Pearson, R. Barr, M. L. Kamil, & P. B. Mosenthal (Eds.), *Handbook of Reading Research* (Vol. 1, pp. 829–864). New York: Longman.

Allington, R. L. (2001). *What Really Matters for Struggling Readers: Designing Research-based Programs*. New York: Longman.

Allington, R. L. (2014). How reading volume affects both reading fluency and reading achievement. *International Journal of Elementary Education, 7*(1), 13–26.

Allington, R. L., & Johnston, P. H. (2002). *Reading to Learn: Lessons from Exemplary Fourth-grade Classrooms*. New York: Guilford Press.

American Educational Research Association. (2004). English language learners: Boosting academic achievement. *Research Points: Essential Information for Educational Policy, 2*(1), 1–4. Washington, DC: Author. Available at www.aera .net/publications/?id=314

American Federation of Teachers. (1999). *Teaching Reading Is Rocket Science: What Expert Teachers of Reading Should Know and Be Able to Do*. Washington, DC: Author.

Anderson, L. W., & Krathwohl, D. R. (2001). *A Taxonomy for Learning, Teaching, and Assessing: A Revision of Bloom's Taxonomy of Educational Objectives*. New York: Longman.

Anderson, R. C. (1996). Research foundations to support wide reading. In V. Greaney (Ed.), *Promoting Reading in Developing Countries* (pp. 55–77). Newark, DE: International Reading Association.

Anderson, R. C., Hiebert, E. F., Scott, J. A., & Wilkinson, I. A. G. (1985). *Becoming a Nation of Readers*. Washington, DC: National Institute of Education.

Anderson, R. C., & Pearson, P. D. (1984). A schema-theoretic view of basic processes in reading. In P. D. Pearson (Ed.), *Handbook of Reading Research* (pp. 255–291). White Plains, NY: Longman.

Anderson, R. C., Wilson, P., & Fielding, L. (1988). Growth in reading and how children spend their time outside of school. *Reading Research Quarterly, 23*, 285–303.

Anderson, T. H., & Armbruster, B. B. (1984). Content area textbooks. In R. C. Anderson, J. Osborn, & R. J. Tierney (Eds.), *Learning to Read in American Schools* (pp. 193–226). Mahwah, NJ: Erlbaum.

Anson, C. M., & Beach, R. (1995). *Journals in the Classroom: Writing to Learn*. Norwood, MA: Christopher-Gordon.

Applegate, A. J., Applegate, M., McGeehan, C. M., Pinto, C. M., & Kong, A. (2009, February). The assessment of thoughtful literacy in NAEP: Why the states aren't measuring up. *The Reading Teacher, 62*(5), 372–381.

Ardoin, S. P., Williams, J. C., Christ, T. J., Klubnik, C., & Wellborn, C. (2010). Examining readability estimates' predictions of students' oral reading rate: Spache, Lexile, and Forcast. *School Psychology Review, 39*(2).

Arias, M. B. (2018, February). *How Can the U.S. Overcome Its Linguistic Deficit? The Findings of Two National Reports on Language Learners*. Washington, DC: Center for Applied Linguistics.

Armbruster, B. B., McCarthey, S. J., & Cummins, S. (2005). Writing to learn in elementary classrooms. In R. Indrisano & J. R. Paratore (Eds.), *Learning to Write, Writing to Learn: Theory and Research in Practice* (pp. 71–96). Newark, DE: International Reading Association.

Aronson, E., & Patnoe, S. (1997). *The Jigsaw Classroom: Building Cooperation in the Classroom*. New York: Longman.

Atwell, N. (1998a). *In the Middle: New Understandings about Writing, Reading, and Learning* (2nd ed.). Portsmouth, NH: Boyton/Cook.

Atwell, N. (1998b). *In the Middle: Writing, Reading, and Learning with Adolescents* (2nd ed.). Portsmouth, NH: Heinemann.

Au, K. H. (1993). *Literacy Instruction in Multicultural Settings*. New York: Harcourt, Brace, Jovanovich.

Au, K. H. (1999). Foreword. In J. T. Guthrie & D. E. Alvermann (Eds.), *Engaged Reading: Processes, Practices, and Policy Implications* (pp. 17–45). New York: Teachers College Press.

August, D. (2005, October). *Building Vocabulary in English-language Learners.* Paper presented at the 3rd Guy Bond Memorial Conference on Reading, Minneapolis, MN.

August, D., Carlo, M., Dressler, C., & Snow, C. (2005). The critical role of vocabulary development for English language learners. *Learning Disabilities Research & Practice, 20*(1), 50–57.

August, D., & Shanahan, J. (Eds.). (2017). *Report of the National Literacy Panel on Language Minority Children and Youth: Acquiring Literacy in a Second Language.* Mahwah, NJ: Erlbaum.

Avalos, M.A., Plasencia, A., Chavez, C. & Rascon J. (2007/2008). Modified guided reading: Gateway to English as a second language and literacy learning. *The Reading Teacher, 61*(4) 296–307.

Avery, P. G., & Graves, M. F. (1997). Scaffolding young learners' reading of social studies texts. *Social Studies and the Young Learner, 9*(4), 10–14.

Baildon, R., & Baildon, M. (2008). Guiding independence: Developing a research tool to support student decision making in selecting online information sources. *The Reading Teacher, 61*(8), 637–647.

Baker, L., & Wigfield, A. (1999). Dimensions of children's motivation for reading and their relations to reading activity and reading achievement. *Reading Research Quarterly, 34*(4), 452–477.

Balu, R., Zhu, P., Doolittle, F., Schiller, E., Jenkins, J., & Gersten, R. (2015). *Evaluation of Response to Intervention Practices for Elementary School Reading* (NCEE 2016-4000). Washington, DC: National Center for Education Evaluation and Regional Assistance, Institute of Education Sciences, U.S. Department of Education.

Bamford, R. A., & Kristo, J. V. (1998). *Making Facts Come Alive: Choosing Quality Nonfiction Literature K–8.* Norwood, MA: Christopher-Gordon.

Barr, C. (Ed.). (1998). *From Biography to History.* New Providence, NJ: R. R. Bowker.

Baumann, J. F. (1988). *Reading Assessment: An Instructional Decision-making Perspective.* Columbus, OH: Merrill.

Baumann, J. F., Font, G., Edwards, E. C., & Boland, E. (2005). In E. H. Hiebert & M. Kamil (Eds.), *Teaching and Learning Vocabulary: Bringing Research to Practice* (pp. 179–205). Mahwah, NJ: Erlbaum.

Baumann, J. F., Kame'enui, E. J., & Ash, G. E. (2003). Research on vocabulary instruction: Voltaire redux. In J. Flood, D. Lapp, J. R. Squire, & J. M. Jensen (Eds.), *Handbook on Research on Teaching the English language Arts* (2nd ed., pp. 752–785). Mahwah, NJ: Erlbaum.

Bear, D. R., Invernizzi, M., Templeton, S., & Johnston, F. (2015). *Words Their Way: Word Study for Phonics, Vocabulary, and Spelling Instruction* (3rd ed.). Upper Saddle River, NJ: Merrill.

Bear, D. R., & Templeton, S. (2017). Word study, research to practice: Spelling, phonics, meaning. In *Handbook of Research on Teaching the English Language Arts* (pp. 218–243). Routledge.

Beaver, J. (1997). *Developmental Reading Assessment.* Parsippany, NJ: Pearson Learning Group.

Beaver, J., & Carter, M. A. (2013). *DRA: Developmental Reading Assessment. Grades 4–8.* New York: Celebration Press.

Beck, I. L., & Beck, M. E. (2013). *Making Sense of Phonics.* New York: Guilford Press.

Beck, I. L., & McKeown, M. G. (1981). Developing questions that promote comprehension: The story map. *Language Arts, 58,* 913–918.

Beck, I. L., & McKeown, M. G. (2001). Text talk: Capturing the benefits of read-aloud experiences for young children. *The Reading Teacher, 55,* 10–20.

Beck, I. L., & McKeown, M. G. (2004). *Increasing young children's oral vocabulary repertoires through rich and focused instruction.* Unpublished paper. University of Pittsburgh, Learning Research and Development Center.

Beck, I. L., McKeown, M. G., Hamilton, R., & Kucan, L. (1997). *Questioning the Author: An Approach for Enhancing Student Engagement with Text.* Newark, DE: International Reading Association.

Beck, I. L., McKeown, M. G., Hamilton, R., & Kucan, L. (1998). Getting at the meaning: How to help students unpack difficult text. *American Educator, 22*(1–2), 66–71, 85.

Beck, I. L., McKeown, M. G., & Kucan, L. (2013). *Bringing Words to Life: Robust Vocabulary Instruction.* New York: Guilford Press.

Beck, I. L., McKeown, M. G., Sandora, C., Kucan, L., & Worthy, J. (1996). Questioning the author: A yearlong classroom implementation to engage students with text. *The Elementary School Journal, 96*(4), 385–414.

Beck, I. L., McKeown, M. G., Sinatra, G. M., & Loxterman, J. A. (1991). Revising social studies text from a text-processing: Evidence of improved comprehensibility. *Reading Research Quarterly, 26*(3), 251–276.

Beck, I. L., McKeown, M. G., Worthy, J. (1995). Giving a text voice can improve students' understanding. *Reading Research Quarterly, 30*(2), 220–239.

Beck, I. L., McKeown, M. G., Worthy, J., Sandora, C. A., & Kucan, L. (1996). Questioning the author: A year-long classroom implementation to engage students with text. *Elementary School Journal, 96,* 385–414.

Begeny, J. C., & Greene, D. J. (2013). Can readability formulas be used to successfully gauge difficulty of reading materials? *Psychology in the Schools, 52*(2), 198–215.

Benedetto, S., Drai-Zerbib, V., Pedrotti, M., Tissier, G., & Baccino, T. (2013). E-readers and visual fatigue. *PLos ONE, 8*(12): e83676.

Berliner, D., & Biddle, B. (1995). *The Manufactured Crisis.* White Plains, NY: Longman.

Berliner, D. C. (1979). Tempus educare. In P. L. Peterson & H. J. Walberg (Eds.), *Research on Teaching: Concepts, Findings, and Implications* (pp. 120–135). Berkeley, CA: McCutchan.

Betts, E. A. (1946). *Foundations of Reading Instruction.* New York: American Book.

Biancarosa, G., & Griffiths, G. G. (2012). Technology tools to support reading in the digital age. *The Future of Children, 22*(2) 139–160.

Biemiller, A. (2001). Teaching vocabulary: Early, direct, and sequential. *American Educator, 25*(1), 24–28, 47.

Biemiller, A. (2003, April). *Teaching Vocabulary to Kindergarten to Grade Two Children.* Paper presented at the annual meeting of the American Educational Research Association, Chicago.

Bigot, L. L., & Rouet, J. F. (2007). The impact of presentation format, task assignment, and prior knowledge on students' comprehension of multiple online documents. *Journal of Literacy Research, 39*(4), 445–470.

Bissex, G. L. (1980). *Gnys at Wrk: A Child Learns to Read and Write.* Cambridge, MA: Harvard University Press.

Blachowicz, C. L. Z., & Fisher, P. (2000). Vocabulary instruction. In M. Kamil, P. Mosenthal, P. D. Pearson, & R. Barr (Eds.), *Handbook of Reading Research* (Vol. 3, pp. 503–523). New York: Longman.

Black, P., & Wiliam, D. (2009). Developing the theory of formative assessment. *Educational Assessment, Evaluation and Accountability.* 21(1): 5–31.

Block, C. C., & Pressley, M. (Eds.). (2002). *Comprehension Instruction: Research-based Best Practices.* New York: Guilford Press.

Bloodgood, J. R. (1999). What's in a name? The role of name writing in children's literacy acquisition. *Reading Research Quarterly, 34,* 342–367.

Bloom, B. S., Englehart, M. D., Furst, E. J., Hill, W. H., & Krathwohl, D. R. (1956). *The Taxonomy of Educational Objectives. Handbook I: Cognitive Domain.* New York: David McKay.

Boaler, J. (2002). *Experiencing School Mathematics.* Mahwah, NJ: Erlbaum.

Bogner, K., Raphael, L., & Pressley, M. (2002). How grade 1 teachers motivate literate activity by their students. *Scientific Studies in Reading, 6,* 135–165.

Bond, G. L., & Dykstra, R. (1967/1997). The cooperative research program in first-grade reading instruction. *Reading Research Quarterly, 2*(4), 1–142. (Reprinted in *Reading Research Quarterly, 32*(4)).

Boyles, N. (2012/2013). Closing in on close reading. *Educational Leadership.* 70(4), 36–41.

Bransford, J. D., Brown, A. L., & Cocking, R. R. (Eds.). (2000). *How People Learn: Brain, Mind, Experience, and School* (Expanded ed.). Washington, DC: National Academies Press.

Bransford, J. D., & Johnson, M. K. (1972). Contextual prerequisites for understanding: Some investigations of comprehension and recall. *Journal of Verbal Learning and Verbal Behavior, 11*(6), 717–726.

Bransford, J. D., & Schwartz, D. L. (1999). Rethinking transfer: A simple proposal with multiple implications. *Review of Research in Education, 3*(24), 61–100.

Brenner, D., & Hiebert, E. H. (2010). If I follow the teachers' editions, isn't that enough? Analyzing reading volume in six core reading programs. *The Elementary School Journal, 110*(3), 347–363.

Brooks, C., & Warren, R. P. (1938). *Understanding Poetry: An Anthology for College Students.* New York: Holt.

Brophy, J. (1986). Teacher influences on student achievement. *American Psychologist, 41,* 1069–1077.

Brophy, J. (1987). Socializing students' motivation to learn. In M. L. Maehr & D. A. Kleiber (Eds.), *Advances in Motivation and Achievement: Enhancing Motivation* (Vol. 5, pp. 181–210). Greenwich, CT: JAI Press.

Brophy, J. (2004). *Motivating Students to Learn* (2nd ed.). Mahwah, NJ: Erlbaum.

Brown, A. L., & Day, J. D. (1983). Macrorules for summarizing text: The development of expertise. *Journal of Verbal Learning and Verbal Behavior, 22,* 1–14.

Brown, J. S., Collins, A., & Duguid, P. (1989). Situated cognition and the culture of learning. *Educational Researcher, 18*(1), 32–42.

Brown, L. T., Mohr, K. A., Wilcox, B. R., & Barrett, T. S. (2018). The effects of dyad reading and text difficulty on third-graders' reading achievement. *The Journal of Educational Research, 111*(5), 541–553.

Brown, R., Pressley, M., Van Meter, P., & Schuder, T. (1996). A quasi-experimental validation of transactional strategies instruction with low-achieving second-grade readers. *Journal of Educational Psychology, 88,* 18–37.

Brozo, W. G. (2002). *To Be a Boy, To Be a Reader.* Newark, DE: International Reading Association.

Bruck, M., & Treiman, R. (1992). Learning to pronounce words: The limitations of analogies. *Reading Research Quarterly, 27,* 375–388.

Burns, M. S., Griffin, P., & Snow, C. E. (1999). *Starting Out Right: A Guide to Promoting Children's Reading Success.* Washington, DC: National Academies Press.

Calet, N., Gutiérrez-Palma, N., Defior, S. (2017). Effects of fluency training on reading competence in primary school children: The role of prosody. *Learning and Instruction,* Vol. 52, Issue undefined.

Calfee, R. C. (2000). Writing portfolios: Activity, assessment, authenticity. In R. Indrisano & J. R. Squire (Eds.), *Theoretical Models and Processes of Writing* (pp. 278–304). Newark, DE: International Reading Association.

Calfee, R. C., & Perfumo, P. (1993). Student portfolios: Opportunities for a revolution in assessment. *Journal of Reading, 36,* 532–537.

Calkins, L. M. (1983). *Lesson from a Child.* Portsmith, NH. Heinemann.

Calkins, L. M., Montgomery, K., Santman, D., & Falk, B. (1998). *A Teacher's Guide to Standardized Achievement Tests: Knowledge Is Power.* Portsmouth, NH: Heinemann.

Campbell, Donald T. (1979). Assessing the impact of planned social change. *Evaluation and Program Planning* 2, no. 1, 67–90.

Canney, G. F., Kennedy, T. R., Schroeder, M., & Miles, S. (1999). Instructional strategies for K–12 limited English proficiency (LEP) students in the regular classroom. *The Reading Teacher, 52*(5), 540–544.

Caplan, A. L., & Igel, L. H. (2015). The common core is taking away kids' recess—and that makes no sense. *Forbes.* www.forbes.com/sites/leeigel/2015/01/15/the-common-core-is-taking-away-kids-recess-and-that-makes-no-sense/#29881b4e128d

Cazden, C. (2001). *Classroom Discourse* (2nd ed.). Portsmouth, NH: Heinemann.

Center for Educational Policy. (2005). *From the Capital to the Classroom: Year 3 of the No Child Left Behind Act.* Washington, DC: Author. Available at www.cep-dc.org.

Cervetti, G. N. & Hiebert, E. H. The sixth pillar of reading instruction: Knowledge development. *The Reading Teacher, 68*(7), 548–551.

Cervetti, G. N., Pearson, P. D., Bravo, M. A., & Barber, J. (2006). Reading and writing in the service of inquiry-based science. http://citeseerx.ist.psu.edu/viewdoc/summary?doi=10.1.1.136.1449

Chall, J. S. (1996). *Stages of Reading Development* (2nd ed.). Fort Worth, TX: Harcourt-Brace.

Chall, J. S. (1967). *Learning to Read: The Great Debate.* New York: McGraw-Hill.

Chall, J. S., & Dale, E. (1995). *Readability Revisited: The New Dale-Chall Readability Formula.* Boston, MA: Brookline Books.

Chen, H-C., & Graves, M. F. (1996). Effects of previewing and providing background knowledge on Taiwanese college students' comprehension of American short stories. *TESOL Quarterly, 29,* 663–686.

Chomsky, C. (1978). When you still can't read in third grade: After decoding, what? In S. J. Samuels (Ed.), *What Research Has to Say about Reading Instruction* (pp. 13–30). Newark, DE: International Reading Association.

Clark, K. F., & Graves, M. F. (2005). Scaffolding students' comprehension of text. *The Reading Teacher, 56,* 570–580.

Clay, M. (1991). *Becoming Literate: The Construction of Inner Control.* Portsmouth, NH: Heinemann.

Clay, M. (1993). *An Observation Study of Early Literacy Achievement.* Portsmouth, NH: Heinemann.

Clay, M. M. (1979). *The Early Detection of Reading Difficulties.* Portsmouth, NH: Heinemann.

Clay, M. M. (1994). *Reading Recovery: A Guidebook for Teachers in Training.* Portsmouth, NH: Heinemann.

Cobb, L. (1835). *The North American Reader.* New York: B and S Collins.

Cohen, E. (1994). *Designing Group Work: Strategies for Heterogeneous Classrooms.* New York: Teachers College Press.

Coiro, J. (2011). Predicting reading comprehension on the Internet: Contributions of offline reading skills, online reading skills, and prior knowledge. *Journal of Literacy Research, 43*(4), 352–392.

Coiro, J., & Dobler, E. (2007). Exploring the online reading comprehension strategies used by sixth-grade skilled readers to search for and locate information on the Internet. *Reading Research Quarterly, 42*(2), 214–257.

Coleman, D., & Pimental, S. (2012). Revised publishers' criteria for the Common Core State Standards in English language arts and literacy, grades 3–12. Washington, DC: Council of Chief State School Officers.

Coleman, J. S. (1966). Equality of educational opportunity. https://files.eric.ed.gov/fulltext/ED012275.pdf

Coleman, R., & Goldenberg, C. (2012). The Common Core Challenge for ELLs. *Principal Leadership, 12*(5), 46–51.

Coleman, R., & Goldenberg, C. (2012). The Common Core challenge: English language learners. *Principal Leadership,* (February) 46–51.

Collinge, S. (2011). *Raising the Standards through Chapter Books: The C.I.A. Approach.* Seattle, Washington: Peanut Butter Publishing.

Collinge, S., & Robinson, B. (2015). *C.I.A. Unit of Study, 4th Grade, Vol. 4.1.* Seattle, WA: Peanut Butter Press.

Colon-Vila, L. (1997, February). Storytelling in an ESL classroom. *Teaching K–8,* 48.

Commission on Language Learning. (2017). American languages: Investing in language education for the 21st century. Cambridge, MA: American Academy of Arts and Sciences. Available at www.amacad.org/language

Connor, C. M., Jakobsons, L. J., Crowe, E., & Meadows, J. G. (2009). Instruction, student engagement, and reading skill growth in reading first classrooms. *The Elementary School Journal, 109,* 221–250.

Connor, C. M., Morrison, F., & Petrella, J. N. (2004). Effective reading comprehension instruction: Examining child instruction interactions. *Journal of Educational Psychology, 96*(4), 682–698.

Connor, C. M., Morrison, F. J., Schatschneider, C., & Underwood, P. (2007). Algorithm-guided individualized reading instruction. *Science, 315,* 464–465.

Connor, C. M., Morrison, F. J., & Underwood, P. S. (2007). A second chance in second grade: The independent and cumulative impact of first- and second-grade reading instruction and student's letter-word reading skill growth. *Scientific Studies of Reading, 11,* 199–234.

Cooke, C. L., & Graves, M. F. (1995). Writing for an audience—for fun. *Middle School Journal, 26*(3), 31–37.

Cordray, D., Pion, G., Brandt, C., Molefe, A., & Toby, M. (2012). *The Impact of the Measures of Academic Progress (MAP) Program on Student Reading Achievement. Final Report.* NCEE 2013-4000. National Center for Education Evaluation and Regional Assistance.

Costa, A. L., & Kallick, B. (2004). Launching self-directed learners. *Educational Leadership, 62*(1), 51–55.

Coyne, M. D., Kame'enui, E. J., & Simmons, D. C. (2001). Prevention and intervention in beginning reading: Two complex systems. *Learning Disabilities Research & Practice, 16*(2), 62–73.

Cremin, L. A. (1990). *Popular Education and Its Discontents.* New York: Harper & Row.

Cronbach, L. J. (1960). *Essentials of Psychological Testing* (3rd ed.). New York: Harper & Row.

Csikszentmihalyi, M. (1990). *Flow: The Psychology of Optimal Experience.* New York: Harper & Row.

Culham, R. (2010). *6+ 1 Traits of Writing: The Complete Guide.* New York, NY: Scholastic Inc.

Cullinan, B. (1993). *Pen in Hand: Children Become Writers.* Newark, DE: International Reading Association.

Cummins, C., Stewart, M. T., & Block, C. C. (2005). Teaching several metacognitive strategies together increases students' independent metacognition. In S. E. Israel, C. C. Block, K. L. Bauserman, & K. Kinnucan-Welsch (Eds.), *Metacognition in Literacy Learning* (pp. 277–298). Mahwah, NJ: Erlbaum.

Cummins, J. (2001). *Negotiating Identities: Education for Empowerment in a Diverse Society* (2nd ed.). Los Angeles: California Association for Bilingual Education.

Cummins, S. (2013). *Close Reading of Informational Texts: Assessment-driven Instruction in Grade 3–8.* New York: Guilford.

Cunningham, A., & Stanovich, K. (2003). Reading matters: How reading English influences cognition. In J. Flood, D. Lapp, J. R. Squire, & J. M. Jensen (Eds.), *Handbook of Research on Teaching the English Language Arts* (pp. 666–675). Mahwah, NJ: Erlbaum.

Cunningham, A. E,. & O'Donnel, C. R. (2012). Reading and vocabulary growth. In E. J. Kame'enui & J. F. Baunann (Eds.), *Vocabulary Instruction: Research to Practice* (2nd ed., pp. 256–279). New York: Guilford.

Cunningham, A. E. (2005). Vocabulary growth through independent reading and reading aloud to children. In E. H. Hiebert & M. L. Kamil (Eds.), *Teaching and Learning Vocabulary: Bringing Research to Practice* (pp. 45–68). Mahwah, NJ: Erlbaum.

Cunningham, J. W., Spadorcia, S. A., Erickson, K. A., Koppenhaver, D. A., Strum, J. M., & Yoder, D. E. (2005). Investigating the instructional supportiveness of leveled text. *Reading Research Quarterly, 40*(4). 410–428.

Cunningham, P. (2005, June). *What Good Is Phonics If They Don't Use It?* Paper presented at the 2005 Minnesota Reading First Summer Literacy Institute, Minneapolis.

Cunningham, P., Hall, D., & Heggie, T. (2001). *Making Big Words, Grades 3–6: Multilevel, Hands-on Spelling and Phonics Activities.* New York, NY: Good Apple.

Cunningham, P. M., & Allington, R. L. (1999). *Classrooms That Work: They Can All Learn to Read and Write* (2nd ed.). New York: Longman.

Cunningham, P. M., & Cunningham, J. W. (1992). Making words: Enhancing the invented spelling-decoding connection. *The Reading Teacher, 46,* 106–115.

Daniels, H. (2002). *Literature Circles: Voice and Choice in the Student-centered Classroom.* New York: Stenhouse.

Deeney, T. A. (2010). One-minute fluency measures mixed message in assessment and instruction. *The Reading Teacher, 63*(6), 440–451.

Delpit, L. D. (1988). The second dialogue: Power and pedagogy in educating other people's children. *Harvard Educational Review, 58*, 280–298.

Delpit, L. D. (2006). *Other People's Children: Cultural Conflict in the Classroom.* New York: The New Press.

Demarest, A. J., & Van Sickle, W. M. (1900). *New Education Readers: A Synthetic and Phonic Word Method: Book Four: Reading for the Third Year* (Vol. 1082). American Book Company.

Deno, S. (1991). Curriculum-based measurement: The emerging alternative. In J. Kramer (Ed.), *Curriculum-based Assessment: Examining Old Problems, Evaluating New Solutions.* Mahwah, NJ: Erlbaum.

Derewianka, B. (2000). *Exploring How Texts Work.* Sydney, NSW: Primary English Teaching Association.

De Temple, J., & Snow, C. E. (2003). Learning words from books. In A. van Kleeck, S. A. Stahl, & E. B. Bauer (Eds.), *On Reading Books to Children* (pp. 16–36). Mahwah, NJ: Erlbaum.

Dewitz, P., Carr, E., & Patberg, J. (1987). Effects of inference training on comprehension and comprehension monitoring. *Reading Research Quarterly, 22*(1), 99–121.

Dewitz, P., & Collinge, S. (2018). A new approach to comprehension instruction. Paper presented at the National Council of Teachers of English. Houston, TX.

Dewitz, P., & Dewitz, P. (2003). They can read the words, but they can't understand: Refining comprehension assessment. *The Reading Teacher, 56*(5). 422–445.

Dewitz, P., & Jones, J. (2013). Using basal readers: From dutiful fidelity to intelligent decision making. *The Reading Teacher, 66*(5), 391–400.

Dewitz, P., Jones, J., & Leahy, S. (2009). Comprehension strategy instruction in core reading programs. *Reading Research Quarterly, 44*(2), 102–126.

Dewitz, P., Leahy, S., Jones, J., & Sullivan, P. M. (2010). *The Essential Guide to Selecting and Using Core Reading Programs.* Newark, DE: International Reading Association.

Diamond, J. B. (2012). Accountability policy, school organization, and classroom practice: Partial recoupling and educational opportunity. *Education and Urban Society, 44*(2), 127–142.

Dillon, J. T. (1988). *Questioning and Teaching: A Manual of Practice.* New York: Teachers College Press.

Dole, J. A., Brown, K. J., & Trathen, W. (1996). The effects of strategy instruction on the comprehension performance of at-risk students. *Reading Research Quarterly, 31*, 62–88.

Dolezal, S. E., Welsh, L. M., Pressley, M., & Vincent, M. (2003). How do grade 3 teachers motivate their students? *Elementary School Journal, 103*, 239–267.

Donovan, C. A., & Smolkin, L. B. (2002). Children's genre knowledge: An examination of K–5 students' performance on multiple tasks providing differing levels of scaffolding. *Reading Research Quarterly, 37*(4), 428–465.

Donovan, M. S., Bransford, J. D., & Pellegrino, J. W. (Eds.). (1999). *How People Learn: Bridging Research and Practice.* Washington, DC: National Academies Press.

Downing, S. M., & Haladyna, T. M. (2009). Validity and its threats. *Assessment in Health Professions Education*, 21–55.

Dreher, M. J., & Singer, H. (1980). Story grammer instruction unnecessary for intermediate grade students. *The Reading Teacher, 34*(3), 261–268.

Duffy, G. G. (2002). The case for direct explanation of strategies. In C. C. Block & M. Pressley (Eds.), *Comprehension Instruction: Research-based Best Practices* (pp. 28–41). New York: Guilford Press.

Duffy, G. G. (2009). *Explaining Reading: A Resource for Teaching Concepts, Skills, and Strategies.* New York: Guilford Press.

Duffy, G. G., & Roehler, L. R. (1982). Commentary: The illusion of instruction. *Reading Research Quarterly, 17*(3), 438–445.

Duffy, G. G., Roehler, L. R., Meloth, M., Vavrus, L., Book, C., Putnam, J., & Wesselman, R. (1986). The relationship between explicit verbal explanation during reading skill instruction and student awareness and achievement: A story of reading teacher effects. *Reading Research Quarterly, 21*, 237–252.

Duffy, G. G., Roehler, L. R., Sivan, E., Rackliffe, G., Book, C., Meloth, M., Vavrus, L. G., Wesselman, R., Putnam, J., & Bassiri, D. (1987). Effects of explaining the reasoning associated with using reading strategies. *Reading Research Quarterly, 22*, 347–368.

Duin, A. H., & Graves, M. F. (1988). Teaching vocabulary as a writing prompt. *Journal of Reading, 22*, 204–212.

Duke, N. K. (2000). 3.6 minutes per day: The scarcity of informational texts in first grade. *Reading Research Quarterly, 35*(2), 202–224.

Duke, N. K. (2004). The case for informational text. *Educational Leadership, 61*(6), 40–44.

Duke, N. K., & Bennett-Armistead, V. S. (2003). *Reading and Writing Informational Text in the Primary Grades: Research-based Practices.* New York: Scholastic.

Duke, N. K., & Pearson, P. D. (2002). Effective practices for developing reading comprehension. In A. E. Farstrup & S. J. Samuels (Eds.), *What Research Has to Say about Reading Instruction* (3rd ed., pp. 205–242). Newark, DE: International Reading Association.

Duke, N. K., Pearson, P. D., Strachan, S. L., & Billman, A. K. (2011). Essential elements of fostering and teaching reading comprehension. In S. J. Samuels & A. Farstrup (Eds.). *What Research Has to Say about Reading Instruction* (4th ed., pp. 51–93). Newark, DE: International Reading Association.

Dyson, A. H., & Freedman, S. W. (1991). Writing. In J. Flood, J. M. Jensen, D. Lapp, & J. R. Squire (Eds.), *Handbook of Research on Teaching the English Language Arts* (pp. 754–774) New York: Guilford Press.

Echevarria, J., Vogt, M. E., & Short, D. (2016). *Making Content Comprehensible to English Learners: The SIOP Model* (5th ed) New York: Pearson.

Education Market Research (2007). *Elementary Reading Market Teaching Methods, Textbooks/Materials Used and Needed, and Market Size.* Rockway Park, NY: Author.

Ehri, L. C. (2005). Learning to read words: Theory, findings, and issues. *Scientific Studies of Reading, 9*(2), 167–188.

Ehri, L. C. (2015). How Children Learn to Read Words. *The Oxford Handbook of Reading*, Oxford, GB: Oxford University Press 293.

Ehri, L. C., & Robbins, C. (1992). Beginners need some decoding skill to read words by analogy. *Reading Research Quarterly, 27*, 13–26.

Emig, J. (1971). *The Composing Process of Twelfth Graders.* Urbana, IL: National Council of Teachers of English.

Englert, C. S., Zhao, Y., Dunsmore, K., Collings, N. Y., & Wolbers, K. (2007). Scaffolding the writing of students with disabilities through procedural facilitation: Using an Internet-based technology to improve performance. *Learning Disability Quarterly, 30*, 9–29.

Every Student Succeeds Act. (2015). *Current Events in Context.* ABC-CLIO, 2018. Web. 4 November 2018.

Farr, R. (1993). Writing in response to reading: A process approach to literary assessment. In B. E. Cullinan (Ed.), *Pen in Hand: Children Become Writers* (pp. 64–79). Newark, DE: International Reading Association.

Fernald, A., Marchman, V. A., & Weisleder, A. (2012). SES differences in language processing skill and vocabulary are evident at 18 months. *Developmental Science, 16,* 234–248.

Fetterman, D. M. (1998). *Ethnography Step by Step* (2nd ed.). Newbury Park, CA: Sage.

Fielding, L. G., Wilson, P. D., & Anderson, R. C. (1986). A new focus on free reading: The role of trade books in reading instruction. In T. E. Raphael (Ed.), *The Contexts of School-based Literacy* (pp. 149–160). New York: Random House.

Fillenworth, L. I. (1995). *Using Reciprocal Teaching to Help At-risk College Freshmen Study.* Unpublished doctoral dissertation, University of Minnesota, Minneapolis, MN.

Fisher, D., & Frey, N. (2012). Close reading in elementary schools. *The Reading Teacher, 66*(3), 179–188.

Fitzgerald, J., & Graves, M. F. (2004). *Scaffolding Reading Experiences for English Language Learners.* Norwood, MA: Christopher-Gordon Publishers.

Five, C. L., & Dionisio, M. (1999). Revisiting the teaching of writing. *School Talk, 4*(4), 5.

Flesch, R. (1955). *Why Johnny Can't Read—and What You Can Do about It.* New York: Harper.

Fletcher, J. M., & Vaughn, S. (2009). Response to intervention: Preventing and remediating academic difficulties. *Child Development Perspectives, 3*(1), 30–37.

Fletcher, R. & Portalupi, J. (1998). *Craft Lessons.* Portland, ME: Stenhouse.

Foorman, B. R., Schatschneider, C., Eakin, M. N., Fletcher, J. M., Moats, L. C., & Francis, D. J. (2006). The impact of instructional practices in Grades 1 and 2 on reading and spelling achievement in high poverty schools. *Contemporary Educational Psychology, 31*(1), 1–29.

Forsythe, S. J. (1995). It worked! Readers theatre in second grade. *The Reading Teacher, 49*(3), 264–265.

Forzani, E. (2018). How well can students evaluate online science information? Contributions of prior knowledge, gender, socioeconomic status, and offline reading ability. *Reading Research Quarterly, 53*(1), 3–13.

Fountas, I. C., & Pinnell, G. S. (1996). *Guided Reading: Good First Teaching for All Children.* Portsmouth, NH: Heinemann.

Fountas, I. C., & Pinnell, G. S. (1999). *Matching Books to Readers.* Portsmouth, NH: Heinemann.

Fountas, I. C., & Pinnell, G. S. (2001). *Guiding Readers and Writers: Grade 3–6.* Portsmouth, NH: Heinemann.

Fountas, I. C., & Pinnnell, G. S. (2006). *Leveled Books, K–8: Matching Texts to Readers for Effective Teaching.* Portsmouth, NH: Heinemann.

Fountas, I. C., & Pinnell, G. S. (2012). Guided reading: The romance and the reality. *The Reading Teacher, 66*(4), 268–284.

Frayer, D. A., Frederick, W. D., & Klausmeier, H. J. (1969). *A Schema for Testing the Level of Concept Mastery* (Working Paper No. 16). Madison: Wisconsin Research and Development Center for Cognitive Learning.

Friedland, E. S., & Truesdell, K. S. (2004). Kids reading together: Ensuring the success of a buddy reading program. *The Reading Teacher, 58*(1), 76–79.

Frith, U. (1985). Beneath the surface of developmental dyslexia. *Surface Dyslexia, 32,* 301–330.

Fry, E. (1977). Fry's readability graph: Clarifications, validity, and extension to level 17. *Journal of Reading, 21,* 242–252.

Fry, E. (2002). Readability versus leveling. *The Reading Teacher, 56,* 286–291.

Fry, E. B. (2004). *The Vocabulary Teacher's Book of Lists.* San Francisco: Jossey-Bass.

Fry, E. B., Polk, J. K., & Fountoukidis, D. (2000). *The Reading Teacher's Book of Lists.* Upper Saddle River, NJ: Prentice Hall.

Fry, E. F. (1998). *Phonics Patterns: Onset and Rhyme Word Lists* (4th ed.). Laguna Beach, CA: Laguna Beach Educational Books.

Fuchs, D., Fuchs, L. S., & Vaughn, S. (2008). *Response to Intervention.* Newark, DE: International Reading Association.

Fuchs, L. S., & Fuchs, D. (2000). Building students' capacity to work productively during peer-assisted reading activities. In B. M. Taylor, M. F. Graves, & P. van den Broek (Eds.), *Reading for Meaning: Fostering Comprehension in the Middle Grades* (pp. 95–114). New York: Teachers College Press.

Fukkink, R. G., & de Glopper, K. (1998). Effects of instruction in deriving word meanings from context: A meta-analysis. *Review of Educational Research, 68,* 450–469.

Fulwiler, T. (Ed.). (1987). *The Journal Book.* Portsmouth, NH: Boyton/Cook.

Galda, L., Ash, G. E., & Cullinan, B. E. (2000). Children's literature. In M. Kamil, P. Mosenthal, P. D. Pearson, & R. Barr (Eds.), *Handbook of Reading Research* (Vol. 3, pp. 361–379). Mahwah, NJ: Erlbaum.

Galda, L., & Cullinan, B. E. (2016). *Literature and the Child* (7th ed.). Belmont, CA: Wadsworth.

Galda, L., & Graves, M. F. (2010). *Reading and Responding in the Middle Grades: Approaches for All Classrooms.* Boston: Allyn & Bacon.

Gambrell, L. B., & Mazzoni, S. A. (1999). Principles of best practice: Finding the common ground. In L. B. Gambrell, L. M. Morrow, S. B. Neuman, & M. Pressley (Eds.), *Best Practices in Literacy Instruction* (pp. 11–21). New York: Guilford Press.

Gamse, B. C., Jacob, R. T., Horst, M., Boulay, B., & Unlu, F. (2008). *Reading First Impact Study. Final Report. NCEE 2009-4038.* National Center for Education Evaluation and Regional Assistance.

Gardner, H. (1985). *The Mind's New Science.* New York: Basic Books.

Gardner, H. (1999). *Intelligence Reframed: Multiple Intelligences for the 21st Century.* New York: Basic Books.

Gaskins, I. W. (2005). *Success with Struggling Readers: The Benchmark School Approach.* New York: Guilford Press.

Gaskins, I. W., Ehri, L. C., Cress, C., O'Hara, C., & Donnelly, K. (1997). Procedures for word learning: Making discoveries about words. *The Reading Teacher, 50,* 312–327.

Gavelek, J. R., & Raphael, T. E. (1996). Changing talk about text: New roles for teachers and students. *Language Arts, 73*(3), 182–192.

Gergen, K. J. (1985). The social constructionist movement in modern psychology. *American Psychologist, 40,* 266–275.

Gersten, R., & Baker, S. (2000). What we know about effective instructional practices for English-language learners. *Exceptional Children, 66,* 454–470.

Goatley, V. J., Brock, C. H., & Raphael, T. E. (1995). Diverse learners participating in regular education "Book Clubs." *Reading Research Quarterly, 30,* 352–380.

Goldenberg, C. (2013). Unlocking the research on English Learners: What we know—and don't yet know—about effective instruction. *American Educator, 37* (2), 4–11, 38. (Available at http://www.aft.org/periodical/american-educator/summer-2013/unlocking-research-english-learners)

Goldenberg, C. (2013). Unlocking the research on English learners. *American Educator, 37*(2), 4–12, 38.

Goldenberg, C. (2015, July 10). Congress: Bilingualism is not a handicap. *Education Week, commentary published only online.* Retrieved 5/15/18 from https://www.edweek.org/ew/articles/2015/congress-bilingualism-is-not-a-handicap.ht

Goldenberg, C., & Coleman, R. (2010). *Promoting Academic Achievement among English Learners.* Thousand Oaks, CA: Corwin.

Goldenberg, C., Tolar, T. D., Reese, L., Francis, D. J., Ray Bazán, A., & Mejía-Arauz, R. (2014). How important is teaching phonemic awareness to children learning to read in Spanish? *American Educational Research Journal, 51*(3), 604-633.0

Good, R. H., & Kaminski, R. A. (Eds.). (2002). *Dynamic Indicators of Basic Early Literacy Skills* (6th ed.). Eugene, OR: Institute for the Development of Educational Achievement. Available at http://dibels.uoregon.edu

Good, T., & Brophy, J. (2003). *Looking into Classrooms* (9th ed.). Boston: Allyn & Bacon.

Goodman, K. (1970). Behind the eye: What happens in reading. In K. S. Goodman & O. S. Niles (Eds.), *Reading: Process and Program* (pp. 1–38). Urbana, IL: National Council of Teachers of English.

Goodman, K. (1986). *What's Whole in Whole Language?* Portsmouth, NH: Heinemann.

Goodman, K. (2005). Making sense of written language: A lifelong journey. *Journal of Literacy Research, 37*, 1–24.

Goodman, K. S., Goodman, Y. M., & Hood, W. J. (1989). *The Whole Language Evaluation Book.* Portsmouth, NH: Heinemann.

Gordon, E. W. (2004). Closing the gap: High achievement for students of color. *Research Points, 2*(3), 1–4. Available at www.aera.net/publications/?id=314

Goswami, U., & Bryant, P. (1992). Rhyme, analogy, and children's reading. In P. B. Gough, L. C. Ehri, & R. Treiman (Eds.), *Reading Acquisition* (pp. 49–63). Mahwah, NJ: Erlbaum.

Goswami, U., & Mead, F. (1992). Onset and rime awareness and analogies in reading. *Reading Research Quarterly, 27*, 153–162.

Graesser, A., Singer, M., & Trabasso, T. (1994). Constructing inferences during narrative comprehension. *Psychological Review, 101*, 371–395.

Graham, S., & Hebert, M. (2010). *Writing to Read: Evidence for How Writing Can Improve Reading.* New York: Alliance for Excellent Education. Carnegie Corporation of New York.

Graves, D. H. (1975). An examination of the writing processes of seven-year-old children. *Research in the Teaching of English, 9*, 227–241.

Graves, D. H. (1983). *Writing: Teachers and Children at Work.* Exeter, NH: Heinemann Educational Books.

Graves, D. H. (1991). *Writing: Teachers and Children at Work.* Portsmouth, NH: Heinemann.

Graves, D. H. (1996, April). Spot the lifetime writers. *Instructor, 105*(7), 26–27.

Graves, M. F. (1998, October/November). Beyond balance. *Reading Today, 16* (1), 16.

Graves, M. F. (2000). A vocabulary program to complement and bolster a middle-grade comprehension program. In B. M. Taylor, M. F. Graves, & P. van den Broek (Eds.), *Reading for Meaning: Fostering Comprehension in the Middle Grades* (pp. 116–135). New York: Teachers College Press.

Graves, M. F. (2004a). Teaching prefixes: As good as it gets? In J. F. Baumann & E. B. Kame'enui (Eds.), *Vocabulary Instruction: Research to Practice* (pp. 81–99). New York: Guilford Press.

Graves, M. F. (2004b). Theories and constructs that have made a significant difference in adolescent literacy—but that have the potential to produce still more positive benefits. In T. Jetton & J. A. Dole (Eds.), *Adolescent Literacy Research and Practice* (pp. 433–452). New York: Guilford Press.

Graves, M. F. (Ed.). (2009a). *Essential Readings on Vocabulary Instruction.* Newark, DE: International Reading Association.

Graves, M. F. (2009b). *Teaching Individual Words: One Size Does Not Fit All.* New York: Teachers College Press and International Reading Association.

Graves, M. F. (2016). *The Vocabulary Book: Learning and Instruction* (2nd ed.). New York: Teachers College Press, International Literacy Association.

Graves, M. F., Baumann, J. F., Blachowicz, C. L. Z., Manyak, P., Bates, A., Cieply, C., Davis, J. R., & Von Gunten, H. (2013). Words, words everywhere; but which ones do we teach. *The Reading Teacher, 67*, 333–346.

Graves, M. F., & Dykstra, R. (1997). Contextualizing the first-grade studies: What is the best way to teach children to read? *Reading Research Quarterly, 32*, 342–344.

Graves, M. F., & Graves, B. B. (2003). *Scaffolding Reading Experiences: Designs for Student Success* (2nd ed.). Norwood, MA: Christopher-Gordon.

Graves, M. F., Graves, B. B., & Braaten, S. (1996). Scaffolded reading experiences: Bridges to reading success. *Educational Leadership, 53*, 14–16.

Graves, M. F., & Philippot, R. A. (2001). High interest-easy reading book series. In B. E. Cullinan & D. G. Person (Eds.), *The Encyclopedia of Children's Literature.* New York: Continuum.

Graves, M. F., Sales, G. C., & Ruda, M. (2008). *The First 4,000 Words.* Minneapolis, MN: Seward Inc.

Graves, M. F., & Slater, W. H. (in press). Vocabulary instruction in content areas. In D. Lapp, J. Flood, & N. Farnan (Eds.), *Content Area Reading and Learning: Instructional Strategies* (3rd ed.). Mahwah, NJ: Erlbaum.

Graves, M. F., & Watts, S. M. (2002). The place of word consciousness in a research-based vocabulary program. In S. J. Samuels & A. E. Farstrup (Eds.), *What Research Has to Say about Reading Instruction* (3rd ed., pp. 140–165). Newark, DE: International Reading Association.

Graves, M. F., & Watts-Taffe, S. W. (2008). For the love of words: Fostering word consciousness in young readers. *The Reading Teacher, 62*, 185–193.

Greene, F. (1979). Radio reading. In C. Pennock (Ed.), *Reading Comprehension at Four Linguistic Levels* (pp. 104–107). Newark, DE: International Reading Association.

Guthrie, J., & Wigfield, A. (2000). Engagement and motivation in reading. In M. Kamil, P. Mosenthal, P. D. Pearson, & R. Barr (Eds.), *Handbook of Reading Research* (Vol. 3, pp. 403–424). Mahwah, NJ: Erlbaum.

Guthrie, J. T. (2002). Preparing students for high-stakes test taking in reading. In N. Duke & P. D. Pearson (Eds.) *What Research Has to Say about Reading Instruction,* (pp. 370–390). Newark, DE: International Reading Association.

Guthrie, J. T., & Anderson, E. (1999). Engagement in reading: Processes of motivated, strategic, knowledgeable, social readers. In J. T. Guthrie & D. E. Alvermann (Eds.), *Engaged Reading: Processes, Practices, and Policy Implications* (pp. 17–45). New York: Teachers College Press.

Guthrie, J. T., Van Meter, P., Hancock, G. R., Alao, S., Anderson, E., & McCann, A. (1998). Does concept-oriented reading instruction increase strategy use and conceptual learning from text? *Journal of Educational Psychology, 90*(2), 261–278.

Gutierrez, K. D. (2005). The persistence of inequality: English-language learners and educational reform. In J. Flood & P. L. Anders (Eds.), *Literacy Development of Students in Urban Schools: Research and Policy* (pp. 288–304). Newark, DE: International Reading Association.

Hakim, J. (2003). *A History of US: The New Nation.* New York: Oxford University Press.

Hannon, J. (1999). Talking back: Kindergarten dialogue journals. *The Reading Teacher, 53*(3), 200–203.

Hansen, J., & Pearson, P. D. (1981). The effects of inference training and practice on young children's reading comprehension. *Reading Research Quarterly, 16*(3), 391–417.

Harlen, W. (Ed.). (1994). *Enhancing Quality in Assessment.* London: Paul Chapman.

Hart, B., & Risley, T. R. (1995). *Meaningful Differences in the Everyday Experiences of Young American Children.* Baltimore: Paul H. Brookes.

Hart, B., & Risley, T. R. (2003, Spring). The early catastrophe: The 30 million word gap. *American Educator, 27*(1), 4–9.

Hart, D. (1994). *Authentic Assessment: A Handbook for Educators.* Menlo Park, CA: Addison-Wesley.

Harvey, S., & Goudvis, A. (2017). *Strategies That Work.* York, ME: Stenhouse.

Harwayne, S. (1993). Chutzpah and the nonfiction writer. In B. E. Cullinan (Ed.), *Pen in Hand: Children Become Writers* (pp. 19–35). Newark, DE: International Reading Association.

Hasbrouck, J., & Tindal, G. (2005). *Oral Reading Fluency: 90 Years of Measurement* (Tech. Rep. No. 33). Eugene: University of Oregon, College of Education, Behavioral Research and Teaching. Available at http://brt.uoregon.edu/tech_reports.htm

Heath, S. B. (1983). *Ways with Words: Language, Life, and Work in Communities and Classrooms.* Cambridge, MA: Cambridge University Press.

Heckelman, R. G. (1969). A neurological-impress method of remedial-reading instruction. *Academic Therapy Quarterly, 4,* 277–282.

Heimlich, J. E., & Pittelman, S. D. (1986). *Semantic Mapping: Classroom Applications.* Newark, DE: International Reading Association.

Henderson, E. (1981). *Learning to Read and Spell: The Child's Knowledge of Words.* DeKalb: Northern Illinois University Press.

Henderson, E. H. (1990). *Teaching Spelling* (2nd ed.). Boston: Houghton Mifflin.

Hidi, S. (2001). Interest, reading, and learning: Theoretical and practical considerations. *Educational Psychology Review, 13*(3), 191–209.

Hidi, S., & Renninger, K. A. (2006). The four-phase model of interest development. *Educational Psychologist, 41*(2), 111–127.

Hiebert, E. H. (1994). Reading recovery in the United States: What difference does it make to an age cohort? *Educational Researcher, 23*(9), 15–25.

Hiebert, E.H. (1999). Texts matters in learning to read. *The Reading Teacher, 52*(6), 552–569.

Hiebert, E. H. (2002). Standards, assessment, and text difficulty. *What Research Has to Say about Reading Instruction, 3,* 337–369.

Hiebert, E. H. (2002). *QuickReads: A Research-based Fluency Program.* Parsippany, NJ: Modern Curriculum.

Hiebert, E. H. (2014). Knowing what's complex and what's not: Guidelines for teachers in establishing text complexity, Santa Cruz, CA: TextProject Article Series.

Hiebert, E. H. (2014). *Changing Readers, Changing Texts: Beginning Reading Texts from 1960 to 2010.* Santa Cruz, CA: TextProject & University of California, Santa Cruz.

Hiebert, E. H., & Calfee, R. C. (1992). Assessment of literacy: From standardized tests to performances and portfolios. In A. E. Farstrup & S. J. Samuels (Eds.), *What Research Says about Reading Instruction* (pp. 70–100). Newark, DE: International Reading Association.

Hiebert, E. H., & Martin, L. A. (2008). Repetition of word: The forgotten variable in text for beginning and struggling readers. In E. H. Hiebert & M. Sailors (Eds.) *Finding the Right Text for Beginning and Struggling Readers: Research-based Solutions* (pp 47–69). New York, NY: Guilford.

Hiebert, E. H., & Martin, L. A. (2015). Changes in the texts of reading instruction during the past 50 years. In P. D. Pearson and E. H. Hiebert (Eds.) *Research-Based Practices for Teaching Common Core Literacy.* (pp. 237–257). Newark: DE: International Literacy Association.

Hiebert, E. H., & Mesmer, H. A. (2013). Upping the ante of text complexity in the Common Core State Standards: Examining its potential impact on young readers. *Educational Researcher, 42*(1), 44–51.

Hiebert, E. H., Pearson, P. D., Taylor, B. M., Richardson, V., & Paris, S. G. (1998). *Every Child a Reader: Applying Reading Research in the Classroom.* Ann Arbor, MI: Center for the Improvement of Early Reading Achievement.

Higham, J. (1988). *Strangers in the Land: Patterns of American Nativism, 1860–1925.* New Brunswick, NJ: Rutgers University Press.

Hoffman, J. V. (2017). What if "just right" is just wrong? The unintended consequences of leveling readers. *The Reading Teacher, 71*(3). 265–274.

Hoffman, J. V., McCarthey, S. J., Abbott, J., Christian, C., Corman, L., & Curry, C. (1994). So what's new in the new basal? A focus on first grade. *Journal of Reading Behavior, 26,* 47–73.

Hoffman, J. V., McCarthey, S. J., Elliot, B., Bayles, D. L., Price, D. P., Ferree, A., & Abbott, J. A. (1998). The literature-based basal in first-grade classrooms: Savior, Satan or same-old, same-old. *Reading Research Quarterly, 33,* 168–197.

Hoffman, J. V., Sailors, M., Duffy, G. R., & Beretvas, S. N. (2004). Effective elementary classroom literacy environment: Examining the validity of the TEX-IN3 observation system. *Journal of Literacy Research, 36,* 303–334.

Hoover, W.A., & Gough, P. B. (1990). The simple view of reading. *Reading and Writing, 2*(2). 127–160.

Horn Book Guide to Children's and Young Adult Books. (2002). Boston, MA: Horn Book.

Ihnot, C. (2004). *Read Naturally* (Software ed., version 2.0). Saint Paul, MN: Read Naturally.

Individuals with Disabilities Education Improvement Act, H.R. 1350, 108th Congress (2004).

International Reading Association. (1997b). *The Role of Phonics in Reading Instruction.* Newark, DE: Author.

International Reading Association. (2005, April/May). Wordsmiths: Helping students develop as writers. *Reading Today, 23*(5), 14.

Invernizzi, M., Juel, C., & Rosemary, C. A. (1996/1997). A community volunteer tutorial that works. *The Reading Teacher, 50*, 304–311.

Invernizzi, M., Meier, J., Swank, L., & Juel, C. (2015). *PALS: Phonological Awareness Literacy Screening*. Charlottesville, VA: University of Virginia Printing Services.

Jacobi-Karna, K. (1996). Music and children's books. *The Reading Teacher, 49*(3), 265–269.

Jiménez, R. T. (2000). Literacy lessons derived from the instruction of six Latina/Latino teachers. In B. M. Taylor, M. F. Graves, & P. van den Broek (Eds.), *Reading for Meaning: Fostering Comprehension in the Middle Grades* (pp. 152–169). New York: Teachers College Press.

Johns, J. L. (2005). *Basic Reading Inventory: Pre-primer through Grade Twelve and Early Literacy Assessments* (Vol. 1) Dubuque IA: Kendall Hunt.

Johnson, D. D., & Pearson, P. D. (1975). Skills management systems: A critique. *The Reading Teacher 28*, no. 8, 757–764.

Johnson, D. D., & Pearson, P. D. (1984). *Teaching Reading Vocabulary* (2nd ed.). New York: Holt, Rinehart & Winston.

Johnson, D. W., & Johnson, R. T. (1989). *Cooperation and Competition: Theory and Research*. Edina, MN: Interaction Book Company.

Johnson, D. W., & Johnson, R. T. (2002). Teaching students to resolve their own and their schoolmates' conflicts. *Counseling and Human Development, 34*(6), 1–12.

Johnson, D. W., Johnson, R. T., & Holubec, E. J. (1987). *Structuring Cooperative Learning: Lesson Plans for Teachers*. Edina, MN: Interaction Book Company.

Johnson, D. W., Johnson, R. T., & Holubec, E. J. (1994). *The New Circles of Learning: Cooperation in the Classroom*. Alexandria, VA: Association for Supervision and Curriculum Development.

Johnson, F. R., Invernizzi, M., & Juel, C. (1998). *Book Buddies: Guidelines for Volunteer Tutors of Emergent and Early Readers*. New York: Guilford Press.

Johnston, P. H. (1990). Steps toward a more naturalistic approach to the assessment of the reading process. In J. Algina & S. Legg (Eds.), *Cognitive Assessment of Language and Mathematics Outcomes* (pp. 92–143). Norwood, NJ: Ablex.

Johnston, P. H. (1992). *Constructive Evaluation of Literate Activity*. New York: Longman.

Johnston, P. H., & Winograd, P. N. (1985). Passive failure in reading. *Journal of Reading Behavior, 17*, 279–301.

Juel, C. (1988). Learning to read and write: A longitudinal study of fifty-four children from first through fourth grade. *Journal of Educational Psychology, 80*, 437–447.

Juel, C. (1990). Effects of reading group assignment on reading development in first and second grade. *Journal of Reading Behavior, 22*, 223–254.

Juel, C. (1994). *Learning to Read and Write in One Elementary School*. New York: Springer-Verlag.

Juel, C. (2005). The impact of early school experiences on initial reading. In D. K. Dickinson & S. B. Neuman (Eds.), *Handbook of Early Literacy Research* (Vol. 2, pp. 410–426). New York: Guilford Press.

Juel, C., Griffith, P. L., & Gough, P. B. (1986). Acquisition of literacy: A longitudinal study of children in first and second grade. *Journal of Educational Psychology, 78*, 243–255.

Juel, C., & Minden-Cupp, C. (2000). Learning to read words: Linguistic units and instructional strategies. *Reading Research Quarterly, 35*(4), 458–492.

Juel, C., & Roper/Schneider, D. (1985). The influence of basal readers on first grade reading. *Reading Research Quarterly, 18*, 306–327.

Just, M. A., & Carpenter, P. H. (1980). A theory of reading: From eye fixations to comprehension. *Psychological Review, 87*, 329–354.

Kame'enui, E., Simmons, D., & Cornachione, C. (2001). *A Practical Guide to Reading Assessments*. Eugene: University of Oregon, National Center to Improve the Tools of Educators.

Kamil, M. L., & Lane, D. (1997). *Using Informational Text for First-grade Reading Instruction*. Paper presented at the annual meeting of the National Reading Conference.

Kaminski, R. A., & Good, R. H. (2006). *Dynamic Indicators of Basic Early Literacy Skills: DIBELS*. R. H. Good (Ed.). Dynamic Measurement Group.

Kaufman, G., & Flanagan, M. (2016, May). High-low split: Divergent cognitive construal levels triggered by digital and non-digital platforms. In *Proceedings of the 2016 CHI Conference on Human Factors in Computing Systems* (pp. 2773–2777). ACM.

Keenan, J., Betjeman, R., & Olson, R. (2008). Reading comprehension tests vary in the skills they assess: Differential dependence on decoding and oral comprehension. *Scientific Studies of Reading, 12*, 281–300.

Kim, J. S., & Quinn, D. M. (2013). The effects of summer reading on low-income children's literacy achievement from Kindergarten to Grade 8: A meta-analysis of classroom and home interventions, *Review of Educational Research, 83*(3), 386–431.

Kim, Y.-S. G., Boyle, H. N., Zuilkowski, S. S., & Nakamura, P. (2016). *Landscape Report on Early Grade Literacy*. Washington, D.C.: USAID.

Kingston, N., & Nash, B. (2011). Formative assessment: A meta-analysis and a call for research. *Educational Measurement: Issues and Practice, 30*(4), 28–37.

Kintsch, W. (1998). *Comprehension: A Paradigm for Cognition*. Cambridge, UK: Cambridge University Press.

Kintsch, W. (2004). The construction-integration model of text comprehension and its implications for instruction. In R. B. Ruddell & N. J. Unrau (Eds.) *Theoretical Models and Processes of Reading, 5*, 1270–1328. Newark, DE: International Reading Association.

Kirsch, I., & Jungeblut, A. (1986). *Literacy: Profiles of America's Young Adults*. Princeton, NJ: National Assessment of Educational Progress and Educational Testing Service.

Klingner, J. K., & Vaughn, S. (1996). Reciprocal teaching of reading comprehension strategies for students with learning disabilities who use English as a second language. *The Elementary School Journal, 96*(3), 275–293.

Klingner, J. K., Vaughn, S., & Schumm, J. S. (1998). Collaborative strategic reading during social studies in heterogeneous fourth-grade classrooms. *The Elementary School Journal, 99*(1), 3–22.

Knapp, M. S., et al. (1995). *Teaching for Meaning in High-poverty Classrooms*. New York: Teachers College Press.

Knipper, K. J., & Duggan, T. J. (2006). Writing to learn across the curriculum: Tools for comprehension in content area classes. *The Reading Teacher, 59*(5), 462–470.

Koch, K. (1970). *Wishes, Lies and Dreams*. New York: Vantage Books.

Koch, K. (1974). *Rose, where did you get that red?* New York: Vantage Books.

Kontovourki, S. (2012). Reading leveled books in assessment-saturated classrooms: A close examination of unmarked processes of assessment. *Reading Research Quarterly, 47*(2), 153–171.

Koretz, D. (2008). *Measuring Up*. Cambridge, MA: Harvard University Press.

Koretz, D. (2017). *The Testing Charade*. Chicago, IL: University of Chicago Press.

Koziol, S. M., Minnick, J. B., & Riddell, K. (1996). *Journals for Active Learning: A Two-day Workshop Module for Primary Teachers in Bosnia*. Pittsburgh, PA: University of Pittsburgh, International Institute for Studies in Education.

Krashen, S. (2004). False claims about literacy development. *Educational Leadership, 61*(6), 18–21.

Kucan, L., & Beck, I. L. (1997). Thinking aloud and reading comprehension research: Inquiry, instruction, and social interaction. *Review of Educational Research, 67*(3), 271–299.

Kuhn, M. (2004/2005). Helping students become accurate, expressive readers: Fluency instruction for small groups. *The Reading Teacher, 58,* 338–344.

Kuhn, M. R., & Morrow, L. M. (2003). Taking computers out of the corner: Making technology work for struggling intermediate grade readers. *After early intervention, then what,* 172–189.

Kuhn, M. R., & Stahl, S. A. (2003). Fluency: A review of developmental and remedial practices. *Journal of Educational Psychology, 95,* 3–21. An earlier version is available at www.ciera.org/library/reports/inquiry-2

Kurlansky, M. (1997). *Cod: A Biography of the Fish that Changed the World*. New York: Walker and Company.

Kurlansky, M. (2002). *Salt: A World History*. New York: Walker and Company.

LaBerge, D., & Samuels, S. J. (1974). Toward a theory of automatic information processing in reading. *Cognitive Psychology, 6,* 293–323.

Lane, B. (1993). After the END. *Teaching and Learning Creative Revision*. Portsmouth, NH: Heinemann.

Langer, J. (1995). *Envisioning Literature*. Newark, DE: International Reading Association.

Language and Reading Research Consortium. (2015). Learning to read: Should we keep things simple? *Reading Research Quarterly, 50*(2), 151–170.

Leavitt, J. (1832). *Easy Lessons in Reading*. Keene, NH. J. and J. W. Prentiss.

León, J. A., Escudero, I., & van den Broek, P. (2000). Genre of the text and the activation of elaborative inferences: A cross-cultural study based on thinking-aloud tasks. In *Annual Meeting of the Society for Text and Discourse, Lyon, France*.

Leslie, L., & Allen, L. (1999). Factors that predict success in an early literacy intervention project. *Reading Research Quarterly, 34*(4), 404–424.

Leslie, L., & Caldwell, J. (2017). *Qualitative Reading Inventory-6*. New York: Pearson.

Leu, D. J., Kinzer, C. K., Coiro, J., Castek, J., & Henry, L. A. (2017). New literacies: A dual-level theory of the changing nature of literacy, instruction, and assessment. *Journal of Education, 197*(2), 1–18.

Leu, D. J., O'byrne, W. I., Zawilinski, L., McVerry, J. G., & Everett-Cacopardo, H. (2009). Comments on Greenhow, Robelia, and Hughes: Expanding the new literacies conversation. *Educational Researcher, 38*(4), 264–269.

Leu, D. J., Zawilinski, L., Forzani, E., & Timbrell, N. (2014). Best practices in teaching the new literacies of online research and comprehension. *Best Practices in Literacy Instruction,* 343–264.

Liebfreund, M. D. (2015). Success with informational text comprehension: An examination of underlying factors. *Reading Research Quarterly, 50*(4). 387–392.

Lovett, M. W., De Palma, M., Frijters, J., Steinbach, K., Temple, M., Benson, N., & Lacerenza, L. (2008). Interventions for reading difficulties: A comparison of response to intervention by ELL and EFL struggling readers. *Journal of Learning Disabilities, 41*(4), 333–352.

Lovett, M. W., Lacerenza, L., Borden, S. L., Frijters, J. C., Steinbach, K. A., & De Palma, M. (2000). Components of effective remediation for developmental reading disabilities: Combining phonological and strategy-based instruction to improve outcomes. *Journal of Educational Psychology, 92*(2), 263–283.

Lundberg, I. (1984, August). Learning to read. *School Research Newsletter*. Sweden: National Board of Education.

Lysynchuk, L. M., Pressley, M., d'Ailly, H., Smith, M., & Cake, H. (1989). A methodological analysis of experimental studies of comprehension strategy instruction. *Reading Research Quarterly,* 458–470.

Maclean, M., Bryant, P., & Bradley, L. (1988). Rhymes, nursery rhymes, and reading in early childhood. In K. E. Stanovich (Ed.), *Children's Reading and the Development of Phonological Awareness* (pp. 11–37). Detroit, MI: Wayne State University Press.

Mandler, J., & Johnson, N. (1977). Remembrance of things parsed: Story structure and recall. *Cognitive Psychology, 9,* 111–151.

Mangen, A. (2006). New narrative pleasures? A cognitive-phenomenological study of the experience of reading digital narrative fictions. Doctoral thesis, Norwegian University of Science and Technology [NTNU], Trondheim, Norway. Retrieved from http://urn.kb.se/resolve?urn=urn:nbn:no:ntnu:diva-1833

Mangen, A., Walgermo, B. R., & Brønnick, K. (2013). Reading linear texts on paper versus computer screen: Effects on reading comprehension. *International Journal of Educational Research, 58,* 61–68.

Mann, H. (1965). Method of teaching young children on their first entering school. In N. B. Smith (Ed.), *American Reading Instruction* (2nd ed., p. 117). Newark, DE: International Reading Association. (Original work published in 1884.)

Mariedwari, M., & Prema, N. (2016). Effectiveness of peer tutoring in learning English among tutors and tutees of class VIII students in Kancjeepiram DT. *English Language Teaching, 9*(11), 1–5.

Marshall, J. (2000). Response to literature. In M. Kamil, P. Mosenthal, P. D. Pearson, & R. Barr (Eds.), *Handbook of Reading Research* (Vol. 3, pp. 381–402). Mahwah, NJ: Erlbaum.

Marzano, R. J. (2000). *Transforming Classroom Grading*. Alexandria, VA: Association for Supervision and Curriculum Development.

Mather, N., Sammons, J., & Schwartz, J. (2006). Adaptations of the Names Test: Easy-to-Use Phonics Assessments. *The Reading Teacher, 60*(2), 114–122.

Mathes, P. G., Denton, C. A., Fletcher, J. M., Anthony, J. L., Francis, D. J., & Schatschneider, C. (2005). The effects of theoretically different instruction and student characteristics on the skills of struggling readers. *Reading Research Quarterly, 40*(2), 148–182.

Mathes, P. G., Pollard-Durodola, S. D., Cárdenas-Hagan, E., Linan-Thompson, S., & Vaughn, S. (2007). Teaching struggling readers who are native Spanish speakers: What do we know? *Language, Speech, and Hearing Services in Schools, 38*, 260–271.

McClure, A. A., Harrison, P., & Reed, S. (1990). *Sunrises and Songs: Reading and Writing Poetry in an Elementary Classroom.* Portsmouth, NH: Heinemann.

McConkie, G. W., & Zola, D. (1981). Language constraints and the functional stimulus in reading. In A. M. Lesgold & C. A. Perfetti (Eds.), *Interactive Processes in Reading* (pp. 155–175). Mahwah, NJ: Erlbaum.

McFarland, J., Hussar, B., de Brey, C., Snyder, T., Wang, X., Wilkinson-Flicker, S., . . . Hinz, S. (2017). Condition of Education 2017 (NCES 2017-144). U.S. Department of Education. Washington, DC: National Center for Education Statistics. Retrieved 5-15-18 from https://nces.ed.gov/pubsearch/pubsinfo.asp?pubid=2017144

McGill-Franzen, A., Zmach, C., Solic, K., & Zeig, J. L. (2006). The confluence of two policy mandates: Core reading programs and third-grade retention in Florida. *The Elementary School Journal, 107*(1), 67–91.

McGuffey, W. H. (1857). ... *McGuffey's New First [-sixth] Eclectic Reader.* (Vol. 6). WB Smith & Company.

McKenna, M. C., Conradi, K., Lawrence, C., Jang, B. G., & Meyer, J. P. (2012). Reading attitudes of middle school students: Results of a U.S. Survey, *Reading Research Quarterly, 47*(3), 283–306.

McKenna, M. C., Kear, D. J., & Ellsworth, R. A. (1995). Children's attitudes toward reading: A national survey. *Reading Research Quarterly,* 934–956.

McKeown, M. G., & Beck, I. L. (2003). Taking advantage of read-alouds to help children make sense of decontextualized language. In A. van Kleeck, S. A. Stahl, & E. B. Bauer (Eds.), *On Reading Books to Young Children* (pp. 159–176). Mahwah, NJ: Erlbaum.

McKeown, M. G., Beck, I. L., & Blake, R. G. K. (2009). Rethinking reading comprehension instruction: A comparison of instruction for strategies and content approaches. *Reading Research Quarterly, 44*(3), 218–253.

McKeown, M. G., Beck, I. L., & Sandora, C. A. (1996). Questioning the author: An approach to developing meaningful classroom discourse. In M. F. Graves, P. van den Broek, & B. M. Taylor (Eds.), *The First R: Every Child's Right to Read* (pp. 97–119). New York: Teachers College Press.

McMahon, M. M., & McCormack, B. B. (1998). To think and act like a scientist: Learning disciplinary knowledge. In C. R. Hynd (Ed.), *Learning from Text across Conceptual Domains* (pp. 227–262). Mahwah, NJ: Erlbaum.

McMahon, S. I., Raphael, T. E., & Goatley, V. J. (1995). Changing the context for classroom reading instruction: The Book Club project. In J. Brophy (Ed.), *Advances in Research on Teaching* (Vol. 5, pp. 123–166). Greenwich, CT: JAI Press.

McNamara, D. S. (2001). Reading both high-coherence and low-coherence texts: Effects of text sequence and prior knowledge. *Canadian Journal of Experimental Psychology/Revue Canadienne de Psychologie Expérimentale, 55*(1), 51.

McNamara, D. S., Kintsch, E., Songer, N. B., & Kintsch, W. (1996). Are good texts always better? Interactions of text coherence, background knowledge, and levels of understanding in learning from text. *Cognition and Instruction, 14*(1) 1–43.

McTighe, J., Seif, E., & Wiggins, G. (2004). You can teach for meaning. *Educational Leadership, 62*(1), 26–30.

Menand, L. (2015). Out of Bethlehem. *The New Yorker*, August 24, 2015.

Mesmer, H. A., Cunningham, J. W., & Hiebert, E. H. (2012). Toward a theoretical model of text complexity for the early grades: Learning from the past, anticipating the future. *Reading Research Quarterly, 47*(3), 235–258.

Meyer, B. J. F., & Ray, M. N. (2011). Structure strategy interventions: Increasing reading comprehension of expository text. *International Electronic Journal of Elementary Education, 4*(1) 127–152.

Miciak, J., Roberts, G., Taylor, W. P., Solis, M., Ahmed, Y., Vaughn, S., & Fletcher, J. M. (2018). The effects of one versus two years of intensive reading intervention implemented with late elementary struggling readers. *Learning Disabilities Research & Practice, 33*(1), 24–36.

Mills, H., Stephens, D., O'Keefe, T., & Waugh, J. R. (2004). Theory in practice: The legacy of Louise Rosenblatt. *Language Arts, 82*, 47–55.

Mokhtari, K., & Reichard, C. A. (2002). Assessing students' metacognitive awareness of reading strategies. *Journal of Educational Psychology, 94*(2), 249–259.

Moll, L. C. (1992). Literacy research in community classrooms: A socio-cultural approach. In R. Beach, J. L. Green, M. S. Kamil, & T. Shanahan (Eds.), *Multidisciplinary Perspectives on Literacy Research* (pp. 211–244). Urbana, IL: National Council of Teachers of English.

Molnar, M. (2017). Market is booming for digital formative assessment. *Education Week*, May 24, 2017.

Moore, D. W., Moore, S. A., Cunningham, P. M., & Cunningham, J. W. (2003). *Developing Readers and Writers in the Content Areas K–12.* Boston: Allyn & Bacon.

Muijselaar, M. M., Kendeou, P., de Jong, P. F., & van den Broek, P. W. (2017). What does the CBM-Maze test measure? *Scientific Studies of Reading, 21*(2), 120–132.

Mullis, I. V. S., Martin, M. O., Foy, P., & Hooper, M. (2017a). *ePIRLS 2016 International Report Results in Online Informational Reading.* Boston: International Study Center, Boston College.

Mullis, I. V. S., Martin, M. O., Foy, P., & Hooper, M. (2017b). *PIRLS: International Results in Reading.* Boston: TIMSS and PIRLS International Study Center, Boston College.

Murray, B. A., Brabham, E. G., Villaume, S. K., & Veal, M. (2008). The Cluella study: Optimal segmentation and voicing for oral blending. *Journal of Literacy Research, 40*(4), 395–421.

Murray, J. D., Klin, C. M., & Myers, J. L. (1993). Forward inferences in narrative text. *Journal of Memory and Language, 32*(4), 464.

Nagy, W., & Townsend, D. (2012). Words as tools: Learning academic vocabulary as language acquisition. *Reading Research Quarterly, 47*(1), 91–108.

Nagy, W. E., & Anderson, R. C. (1984). How many words are there in printed school English? *Reading Research Quarterly, 19*, 304–330.

Nagy, W. E., & Scott, J. A. (2000). Vocabulary processes. In M. Kamil, P. Mosenthal, P. D. Pearson, & R. Barr (Eds.), *Handbook of Reading Research* (Vol. 3, pp. 269–284). Mahwah, NJ: Erlbaum.

National Assessment of Educational Progress. (2018). *2017 NAEP Mathematics and Reading Assessments: Highlighted Results at Grades 4 and 8 for the Nation, States, and Districts.* NCES Number: 2018037. Retrieved 5-15-18 from https://nces.ed.gov/pubsearch/pubsinfo.asp?pubid=2018037

National Center on Education and the Economy. (1997). *New Standards: Performance Standards. Volume 1: Elementary Schools.* Pittsburgh, PA: University of Pittsburgh.

National Council of Teachers of English (NCTE) Commission on Reading. (2004). *On Reading, Learning to Read, and Effective Reading Instruction.* Retrieved December 2005 from www.ncte.org/about/over/positions/category/read/118620.htm

National Governors Association Center for Best Practice & Council of Chief State School Officers. (2010). Common Core State Standards for English language arts and literacy in history, social studies, science and technical subjects. Washington, DC: Authors. Available at www.corestandards.org/assets/CCSSL_ELA%20standards.pdf

National Reading Panel. (2000). *Report of the National Reading Panel: Teaching Children to Read.* Bethesda, MD: National Institute of Child Health and Human Development.

National Research Council. (2004). *Engaging Schools: Fostering High School Students' Motivation to Learn.* Washington, DC: National Academies Press.

Nebraska Department of Education. (2014). English Language Arts Standards https://www.education.ne.gov/ela/

Nelley, E., & Smith, A. (2000). *PM Benchmark Kit Teacher's Notes.* Oxford, England: Nelson Thornes.

New Standards Primary Literacy Committee. (1999). *Reading and Writing Grade by Grade.* Pittsburgh, PA: National Center on Education and the University of Pittsburgh. Available at www.ncee.org

Newmann, F. N. (1996). *Authentic Achievement: Restructuring Schools for Intellectual Quality.* San Francisco: Jossey-Bass.

Newmann, F. N. (2000). Authentic intellectual work: What and why? *Research/Practice, 8*(1), 15–20.

Nichols, S. L., & Berliner, D. C. (2007). *Collateral Damage: How High-stakes Testing Corrupts America's Schools.* Harvard Education Press.

Nicholson, T. (1991). Do children read words better in context or in lists? A classic study revisited. *Journal of Educational Psychology, 83*(4), 444.

Nitko, A. J. (1996). *Educational Assessment of Students* (2nd ed.). Englewood Cliffs, NJ: Merrill.

No Child Left Behind Act of 2001. Public Law No. 107-110. 115 Stat. 1425 (2002).

Noddings, N. (2003). *Happiness and Education.* Cambridge, UK: Cambridge University Press.

O'Connor, R. E., Bell, K. M., Harty, K. R., Larkin, L. K., Sackor, S. M., & Zigmond, N. (2002). Teaching reading to poor readers in the intermediate grades: A comparison of text difficulty. *Journal of Educational Psychology, 94*(3), 474–485.

Oczkus, L. (2004). *Super 6 Comprehension Strategies.* Norwood, MA: Christopher-Gordon.

Ogle, D. (1986). K-W-L: A teaching model that develops active reading of expository text. *The Reading Teacher, 39,* 564–570.

Olness, R. (2005). *Using Literature to Enhance Writing Instruction: A Guide for K–5 Teachers.* Newark, DE: International Reading Association.

Olson, J. F., & Goldstein, A. A. (1997). *The Inclusion of Students with Disabilities and Limited English Proficient Students in Large-scale Assessments: A Summary of Recent Progress.* Washington, DC: National Center for Education Statistics.

Ophir, E., Nass, C., & Wagner, A. D. (2009). Cognitive control in media multitaskers. *Proceedings of the National Academy of Sciences, 106*(37), 15583–15587.

Otto, W., & Askov, E. N. (1971). *Wisconsin Design for Reading Skill Development: Rationale and Guidelines.* Madison, WI: National Computer Systems, Incorporated.

Owocki, G., & Goodman, Y. M. (2002). *Kidwatching: Documenting Children's Literacy Development.* Portsmouth, NH: Heinemann.

Palincsar, A. M., & Brown, A. L. (1984). Reciprocal teaching of comprehension and monitoring activities. *Cognition and Instruction, 1*(2), 117–175.

Palincsar, A. M., & Brown, A. L. (1986). Interactive teaching to promote independent learning from text. *The Reading Teacher, 39,* 771–777.

Palincsar, A. M., & David, Y. M. (1991). Promoting literacy through classroom dialogue. In E. Hiebert (Ed.), *Literacy for a Diverse Society: Perspectives, Programs, and Policies.* New York: Teachers College Press.

Paré, A., & Smart, G. (1994). Observing genres in action: Towards a research methodology. *Genre and the New Rhetoric,* 146–154.

Paris, S. G. (2005). Reinterpreting the development of reading skills. *Reading Research Quarterly, 40*(2), 184–202.

Paris, S. G., & Luo, S. W. (2010). Confounded statistical analyses hinder interpretation of the NELP report. *Educational Researcher, 39*(4), 316–322.

Paris, S. G., & Winograd, P. (1990). How metacognition can promote academic learning and instruction. *Dimensions of Thinking and Cognitive Instruction, 1,* 15–51.

Pearson, P. D. (1990). Foreword. In T. Shanahan (Ed.), *Reading and Writing Together: New Perspectives for the Classroom* (pp. v–vi). Norwood, MA: Christopher-Gordon.

Pearson, P. D. (2000). Reading in the twentieth century. In T. L. Good (Ed.), *American Education: Yesterday, Today, and Tomorrow* (pp. 152–208). Chicago: National Society for the Study of Education.

Pearson, P. D., & Cervetti, G. N. (2017). Fifty years of reading comprehension theory and practice. In P. D. Pearson & E. H. Hiebert (Eds). *Research-based Practices for Teaching Common Core Literacy* (pp.1–224). New York: Teachers College Press.

Pearson, P. D., & Duke, N. K. (2002). Comprehension instruction in the primary grades. In C. C. Block & M. Pressley (Eds.), *Comprehension Instruction: Research-based Practices* (pp. 247–258). New York: Guilford Press.

Pearson, P. D., & Gallagher, M. C. (1983). The instruction of reading comprehension. *Contemporary Educational Psychology, 8,* 317–344.

Pearson, P. D., Garavaglia, D., Lycke, K., Roberts, E., Danridge, J., & Hamm, D. (1999). The impact of item format on the depth of students' cognitive engagement. Unpublished manuscript. NAEP Validity Study Panel.

Pearson, P. D., & Hamm, D. N. (2005). The assessment of reading comprehension: A review of practices—past, present, and future. In S. G. Paris & S. A. Stahl (Eds.), *Children's Reading Comprehension and Assessment,* (pp. 5–38). New York: Routledge.

Pearson, P. D., Hiebert, E. H., & Kamil, M. L. (2012). Vocabulary assessment: Making do with what we have while we create the tools we need. In E. J. Kame'enui & J. F. Baunann (Eds,), *Vocabulary Instruction: Research to Practice* (2nd ed., pp. 231–255). New York: Guilford.

Pearson, P. D., Roehler, L. R., Dole, J. A., & Duffy, G. G. (1992). Developing expertise in reading comprehension. In S. J. Samuels & A. E. Farstrup (Eds.), *What Research Has to Say about Reading Instruction* (2nd ed., pp. 145–199). Newark, DE: International Reading Association.

Perfetti, C. (2007). Reading ability: Lexical quality to comprehension. *Scientific Studies of Reading, 11*(4), 357–383.

Perie, M., Moran, R., Lutkus, A. D., & Tirre, W. (2005). *NAEP 2004 Trends in Academic Progress: Three Decades of Student Performance in Reading and Mathematics*. Washington, DC: U.S. Department of Education.

Perkins, D. (1992). *Smart Schools: From Training Memories to Educating Minds*. New York: The Free Press.

Perkins, D. (1994). *Knowledge as Design: A Handbook for Critical and Creative Discussion across the Curriculum*. Pacific Grove, CA: Critical Thinking Press.

Perkins, D. (2004). Knowledge alive. *Educational Leadership, 62*(1), 14–18.

Perrin, A. (2016). Who doesn't read books in America? Pew Research Center. Retrieved from URL: http://www.pewresearch.org/fact-tank/2018/03/23/who-doesnt-read-books-in-america/

Persky, H. R., Daane, M. C., & Ying, J. (2003). *The Nation's Report Card: Writing 2002*. Washington, DC: U.S. Department of Education.

Phillips, D. C. (Ed.). (2000). *Constructivism in Education*. Chicago: National Society for the Study of Education.

Piasta, S. B., Connor, C. M., Fishman, B. J., & Morrison, F. J. (2009). Teachers' knowledge of literacy concepts, classroom practices, and student reading growth. *Scientific Studies of Reading, 13*(3), 224–248.

Picton, I. (2014). *The Impact of ebooks on the Reading Motivation and Reading Skills of Children and Young People: A Rapid Literature Review*. London: National Literacy Trust.

Pikulski, J. J., & Chard, D. J. (2005). Fluency: Bridge between decoding and reading comprehension. *The Reading Teacher, 58*, 510–519.

Pinnell, G. S., Fried, M. D., & Eustice, R. M. (1990). Reading Recovery: Learning how to make a difference. *The Reading Teacher, 43*, 282–295.

Pintrich, P. R., & Zusho, A. (2002). The development of academic self-regulation: The role of cognitive and motivational factors. In A. Wigfield & J. S. Eccles (Eds.), *A Vol. in the Educational Psychology Series. Development of Achievement Motivation* (pp. 249–284). San Diego, CA: Academic Press.

Poindexter, C., & Oliver, I. (1998/1999). Navigating the writing process: Strategies for young children. *The Reading Teacher, 52*(4), 420–423.

Popham, W. J. (1999). *Classroom Assessment: What Teachers Need to Know* (2nd ed.). Boston: Allyn & Bacon.

Pressley, M. (2000). What should comprehension instruction be the instruction of? In M. Kamil, P. Mosenthal, P. D. Pearson, & R. Barr (Eds.), *Handbook of Reading Research* (Vol. 3, pp. 545–561). Mahwah, NJ: Erlbaum.

Pressley, M. (2002). Comprehension strategies instruction: A turn-of-the-century status report. In C. C. Block & M. Pressley (Eds.), *Comprehension Instruction: Research-based Best Practices* (pp. 11–27). New York: Guilford Press.

Pressley, M. (2005). Final reflections—Metacognition in literacy learning: Then, now, and in the future. In S. E. Israel, C. C. Block, K. L. Bauserman, & K. Kinnucan-Welsch (Eds.), *Metacognition in Literacy Learning* (pp. 391–411). Mahwah, NJ: Erlbaum.

Pressley, M. (2006). *Reading Instruction That Works: The Case for Balanced Teaching* (3rd ed.). New York: Guilford.

Pressley, M., & Afflerbach, P. (1995). *Verbal Protocols of Reading: The Nature of Constructively Responsive Reading*. Mahwah, NJ: Erlbaum.

Pressley, M., Allington, R. L., Wharton-McDonald, R., Block, C. C., & Morrow, L. M. (2001). *Learning to Read: Lessons from Exemplary First-grade Classrooms*. New York: Guilford Press.

Pressley, M., Dolezal, S. E., Raphael, L., Mohan, L., Bogner, K., & Roehrig, A. (2003). *Motivating Primary Grade Students*. New York: Guilford Press.

Pressley, M., El-Dinary, P. B., Wharton-McDonald, R., & Brown, R. (1998). Transactional instruction of comprehension strategies in the elementary grades. In D. H. Schunk & B. J. Zimmerman (Eds.), *Self-regulated Learning: From Teaching to Self-reflective Practice* (pp. 42–56). New York: Guilford Press.

Pressley, M., Harris, K. R., & Marks, M. B. (1992). But good strategy instructors are constructivists! *Educational Psychology Review, 4*, 3–31.

Pritchard, A., & Cartwright, V. (2004). Transforming what they read: Helping eleven-year-olds engage with Internet information. *Literacy, 38*(1), 26.

Proctor, C. P., Dalton, B., & Grisham, D. L. (2007). Scaffolding English language learners and struggling readers in a universal literacy environment with embedded strategy instruction and vocabulary support. *Journal of Literacy Research, 39*(1), 71–93.

Purcell-Gates, V. (1989). What oral/written language differences can tell us about beginning instruction. *The Reading Teacher, 42*, 290–294.

RAND Reading Study Group. (2002). *Reading for Understanding: Toward an R&D Program in Reading Comprehension*. Santa Monica, CA: Rand Education. Also available at www.rand.org/multi/achievement-forall/reading

Ransom, J. C. (1979). *The New Criticism 1941*. Westport, CT: Greenwood Press.

Raphael, T. E. (1982). Question-answering strategies for children. *The Reading Teacher, 36*(2), 186–190.

Raphael, T. E. (2000). Balancing literature and instruction: Lessons from the Book Club project. In B. M. Taylor, M. F. Graves, & P. van den Broek (Eds.), *Reading for Meaning: Fostering Comprehension in the Middle Grades* (pp. 70–94). New York: Teachers College Press.

Raphael, T. E., & Au, K. H. (2005). QAR: Enhancing comprehension and test taking across grades and content areas. *The Reading Teacher, 59*(3), 206–221.

Raphael, T. E., Florio-Ruane, S., & George, M. (2001). Book Club Plus: A conceptual framework to organize literacy instruction. *Language Arts, 79*, 159–169.

Raphael, T. E., Florio-Ruane, S., George, M. A., Hasty, N. L., & Highfield, K. (2004). *Book Club Plus! A Literacy Framework for the Primary Grades*. Lawrence, MA: Small Planet Communications.

Raphael, T. E., & McMahon, S. I. (1994). Book Club: An alternative framework for reading instruction. *The Reading Teacher, 48*, 102–116.

Raphael, T. E., & Wonnacott, C. A. (1985). Heightening fourth-grade students' sensitivity to sources of information for answering comprehension questions. *Reading Research Quarterly, 20*(3) 282–296.

Rasinski, T., Blachowicz, C. L. Z., & Lems, K. (Eds.). (in press). *Teaching Reading Fluency: Meeting the Needs of All Readers*. New York: Guilford Press.

Rasinski, T. V. (2003). *The Fluent Reader: Oral Reading Strategies for Building Word Recognition, Fluency, and Comprehension.* New York: Scholastic.

Rauch, D. P., & Hartig, J. (2010). Multiple-choice versus open-ended response formats of reading test items: A two-dimensional IRT analysis. *Psychological Test and Assessment Modeling, 52*(4), 354.

Ray, M. N., & Meyer, B. J. F. (2011). Individual differences in children's knowledge of expository text structure. *International Electronic Journal of Elementary Education, 4*(1) 67–82.

Renaissance Learning. (2005). *Fluent Reader.* Wisconsin Rapids, WI: Author.

Resnick, L. B. (1987). *Education and Learning to Think.* Washington, DC: National Academies Press.

Reutzel, D. R., Jones, C. D., Fawson, P. C., & Smith, J. A. (2008). Scaffolded silent reading: A complement to guided repeated oral reading that works! *The Reading Teacher, 62,* 194–209.

Reynolds, R. E., & Anderson, R. C. (1982). Influence of questions on the allocation of attention during reading. *Journal of Educational Psychology, 74*(5), 623.

Richards, I. A. (1926). *Poetries and Sciences* (Vol. 2). London, England: Routledge & Kegan Paul, Limited.

Robertson, C., & Salter, W. (2007). Statistics manual. *Phonological Awareness Test-2,*Lutz, FL. Psychological Assessment Resource.

Robinson, H. M, Monroe, M., & Artley, A. S. (1962). *Fun Wherever We Are.* Chicago, IL: Scott, Foresman and Company.

Rodgers, E., D'Agostino, J. V., Harmey, S. J., Kelly, R. H., & Brownfield, K. (2016). Examining the nature of scaffolding in an early literacy intervention. *Reading Research Quarterly, 51*(3), 345–360.

Rosenblatt, L. (1978). *The Reader, the Text, the Poem: The Transactional Theory of the Literary Work.* Carbondale: Southern Illinois Press.

Rosenblatt, L. M. (1938/1995). *Literature as Exploration.* New York: Modern Language Association.

Rosenshine, B., & Meister, C. (1994). Reciprocal teaching: A review of the research. *Review of Educational Research, 64*(4), 479–530.

Routman, R. (1995). *Invitations: Changing as Teachers and Learners K–12.* Portsmouth, NH: Heinemann.

Routman, R. (2002). *Reading Essentials: The Specifics You Need to Teach Reading Well.* Portsmouth, NH: Heinemann.

Routman, R. (2005). *Writing Essentials: Raising Expectations and Results while Simplifying Teaching.* Portsmouth, NH: Heinemann.

Rumelhart, D. E. (1977). Toward an interactive model of reading. In S. Dornic (Ed.), *Attention and Performance* (Vol. 6, pp. 573–603). Mahwah, NJ: Erlbaum.

Rumelhart, D. E. (1980). Schemata: The building blocks of cognition. In R. J. Spiro, B. C. Bruce, & W. F. Brewer (Eds.), *Theoretical Issues in Reading Comprehension* (pp. 33–58). Mahwah, NJ: Erlbaum.

Rupp, A. A., Ferne, T., & Choi, H. (2006). How assessing reading comprehension with multiple-choice questions shapes the construct: A cognitive processing perspective. *Language Testing, 23,* 441–474.

Sales, G. H., & Graves, M. F. (2005). *Teaching Comprehension Strategies.* Minneapolis, MN: Seward Incorporated.

Samuels, S. J. (1979). The method of repeated reading. *The Reading Teacher, 32,* 403–408.

Samuels, S. J. (2002). Reading fluency: Its development and assessment. In S. J. Samuels & A. E. Farstrup (Eds.), *What Research Has to Say about Reading Instruction* (3rd ed., pp. 166–183). Newark, DE: International Reading Association.

Samuels, S. J., & Farstrup, A. E. (Eds.) (2006). *What Research Has to Say about Fluency Instruction.* Newark, DE: International Reading Association.

Santoro, L. E., Chard, D. J., Howard, L., & Baker, S. K. (2008). Making the very most of classroom read-alouds to promote comprehension and vocabulary. *The Reading Teacher, 61*(5), 396–408.

Scarcella, R. C. (1996). English learners and writing: Responding to linguistic diversity. In C. B. Olson (Ed.), *Practical Ideas for Teaching Writing as a Process at the Elementary School and Middle School Levels* (pp. 97–103). Sacramento: California State Department of Education.

Schiefele, U., & Schaffner, E. (2016). Factorial and construct validity of a new instrument for the assessment of reading motivation. *Reading Research Quarterly, 51*(2), 221–237.

Schiefele, U., Schaffner, E., Moller, J., & Wigfield, A. (2012). Dimensions of reading motivations and their relation to reading behavior and competence. *Reading Research Quarterly, 47,* 427–463.

Schlesinger, A. M., Jr. (1986). *The Cycles of American History.* Boston: Houghton Mifflin.

Schmitt, N. (2000). *Vocabulary in Language Teaching.* Cambridge, England: Cambridge University Press.

Schon, I., & Berkin, S. C. (1996). *Introducción a la Literatura Infantil y Juvenil.* Newark, DE: International Reading Association. (Available only in Spanish.)

Schraw, G., & Dennison, R. S. (1994). Assessing metacognitive awareness. *Contemporary Educational Psychology, 19*(4), 460–475.

Schumaker, J. B., & Deshler, D. D. (2003). Can students with LD become competent writers? *Learning Disability Quarterly, 26,* 129–141.

Schunk, D. H., & Zimmerman, B. J. (Eds.). (1998). *Self-regulated Learning: From Teaching to Self-reflective Practice.* New York: Guilford Press.

Searle, J. R. (1993). Rationality and realism: What is at stake? *Daedalus, 122*(4), 55–83.

Sellen, A. J., & Harper, R. (2002). The myth of the paperless office. Cambridge, MA: MIT Press.

Shahaeian, A., Wang, C., Drob, E.T., Geiger, V., Gus, A. G., & Harrison, L. J. (2018). Early shared reading, socioeconomic status, and children's cognitive and school competencies: Six years of longitudinal evidence. *Scientific Studies of Reading, 22*(6), 485–502.

Shanahan, C., & Shanahan, T. (2014). Does disciplinary literacy have a place in elementary school? *The Reading Teacher, 67*(8), 636–639.

Shanahan, T., & Barr, R. (1995). Reading Recovery: An independent evaluation of the effects of an early instructional intervention for at-risk learners. *Reading Research Quarterly,* 958–996.

Shanahan, T., Kamil, M. L., & Tobin, A. W. (1982). Cloze as a measure of intersentential comprehension. *Reading Research Quarterly, 17*(2), 229–255.

Shany, M. T., & Biemiller, A. (1995). Assisted reading practice: Effects on performance of poor readers in grades 3 and 4. *Reading Research Quarterly, 30,* 382–395.

Share, D. L. (1995). Phonological recoding and self-teaching: Sine qua non of reading acquisition. *Cognition, 55,* 151–218.

Share, D. L. (2004). Orthographic learning at a glance: On the time course and developmental onset of self-teaching. *Journal of Experimental Child Psychology, 72,* 94–129.

Share, D. L., Jorm, A. F., Maclean, R., & Matthews, R. (1984). Sources of individual differences in reading acquisition. *Journal of Educational Psychology, 76,* 1309–1324.

Shaywitz, S. (2003). *Overcoming Dyslexia: A New and Complete Science Based Program for Reading Problems at Any Level.* New York: Knopf.

Shea, M., Murray, R., & Harlin, R. (2005). *Drowning in Data: How to Collect, Organize, and Document Student Performance.* Portsmouth, NH: Heinemann.

Shepard, L. A. (2010). What the marketplace has brought us: Item-by-item teaching with little instructional insight. *Peabody Journal of Education, 85(2),* 246–257.

Shinn, M. R., & Shinn, M. M. (2002). *Aimsweb Training Workbook.* Eden Prairie, MN: Edformation.

Short, D., & Echevarria, J. (2004–2005). Teacher skills to support English language learners. *Educational Leadership, 62(4),* 8–13.

Short, K., Kaufman, G., Kaser, L. H., Kahn, L. H., & Crawford, K. M. (1999). "Teacher-watching": Examining teacher talk in literature circles. *Language Arts, 76,* 377–385.

Short, K. G., & Klassen, C. (1993). Literature circles: Hearing children's voices. In B. E. Cullinan (Ed.), *Children's Voices: Talk in the Classroom* (pp. 66–85). Newark, DE: International Reading Association.

Simmons, D. C., & Kame'enui, E. J. (2003). *Early Reading Intervention.* Glenview, IL: Pearson, Scott Foresman.

Singer, L. M., & Alexander, P. A. (2017). Reading across mediums: Effects of reading digital and print texts on comprehension and calibration. *The Journal of Experimental Education, 85(1),* 155–172.

Slater, W. H., Graves, M. F., & Piche, G. L. (1985). Effects of structural organizers on ninth-grade students' comprehension and recall of four patterns of expository text. *Reading Research Quarterly, 20,* 25–32.

Slatin, J. M. (1991, July). Composing hypertext: Discussion for writing teachers. In *Hypertext/Hypermedia Handbook* (pp. 55–64).New York: McGraw-Hill, Inc.

Slavin, R. E. (1987). *Cooperative Learning: Student Teams* (2nd ed.). Washington, DC: National Education Association.

Slavin, R. E., & Cheung, A. (2005). A synthesis of research on language of reading instruction for English language learners. *Review of Educational Research, 75,* 247–284.

Smith, F. (1971). *Understanding Reading: A Psycholinguistic Analysis of Reading and Learning to Read.* New York: Holt, Rinehart & Winston.

Smith, L. E., Borkowski, J. G., & Whitman, T. L. (2008). From reading readiness to reading competence: The role of self-regulation in at-risk children. *Scientific Studies of Reading, 12(2),* 131–152.

Smith, N. B. (2002). *American Reading Instruction* (Special ed.). Newark, DE: International Reading Association.

Snow, C., & O'Connor, C. (2013). Close reading and far-reaching classroom discussion: Fostering a vital connection (Policy brief). Retrieved from International Reading Association: http://www.reading.org/Libraries/lrp/ira-lrp-policy-brief—close reading--13sept2013. pdf

Snow, C. E. (Ed.). (2004, Winter). English language learners: Boosting academic achievement. *Research Points: Essential Information for Educational Policy, 2,* 1–4. Available at www.aera.net

Snow, C. E., Barnes, W. S., Chandler, J., Goodman, I. F., & Hemphill, L. (1991). *Unfulfilled Expectations: Home and School Influences on Literacy.* Cambridge, MA: Harvard University Press.

Snow, C. E., Burns, M. S., & Griffin, P. (1998). *Preventing Reading Difficulties in Young Children.* Washington, DC: National Academies Press.

Snow, C. E., & Kim, Y. (2007). Large problem spaces: The challenge of vocabulary for English language learners. In R. K. Wagner, A. E. Muse, & K. R. Tannenbaum (Eds.), *Vocabulary Acquisition: Implications for Reading Comprehension* (pp. 123–139). New York: Guilford Press.

Spandel, V. (2005). *The 9 Rights of Every Writer: A Guide for Teachers.* Portsmouth, NH: Heinemann.

Sparks, S. D. (2016). Teaching English-language learners: What does the research tell us? *Education Week 35(30),* 3–6. Retrieved 5-15-18 from www.edweek.org/ew/articles/2016/05/11/teaching-english-language-learners-what-does-the-research.html?r=2135472880

Spichtig, A. N., Hiebert, E. H., Vorstius, C., Pasco, J. P., Pearson, P. D., & Radach, R. (2016). The decline of comprehension-based silent reading efficiency in the United States: A comparison of current data with performance in 1960. *Reading Research Quarterly, 51(2),* 239–259.

Spiegel, D. L. (1998). Reader response approaches and the growth of readers. *Language Arts, 76,* 41–56.

Stahl, K.A.D. (2004). Proof, practice, and promise: Comprehension strategies in the primary grades, *The Reading Teacher, 57(7),* 598–609.

Stahl, S. A. (1998). Four questions about vocabulary knowledge and reading and some answers. In C. R. Hynd (Ed.), *Learning from Text across Conceptual Domains* (pp. 73–94). Mahwah, NJ: Erlbaum.

Stahl, S. A., & Nagy, W. (2006). *Teaching Word Meanings.* Mahway, NJ: Erlbaum.

Stanovich, K. E. (1986). Matthew effects in reading: Some consequences of individual differences in the acquisition of literacy. *Reading Research Quarterly, 21(4),* 360–383.

Stanovich, K. E. (1991a). Changing models of reading and reading acquisition. In L. Rieben & C. A. Perfetti (Eds.), *Learning to Read* (pp. 19–31). Mahwah, NJ: Erlbaum.

Stanovich, K. E. (1991b). Word recognition: Changing perspectives. In R. Barr, M. L. Kamil, P. B. Mosenthal, & P. D. Pearson (Eds.), *Handbook of Reading Research* (Vol. 2, pp. 418–452). New York: Longman.

Stanovich, K. E. (1992). Speculations on the causes and consequences of individual differences in early reading acquisition. In P. B. Gough, L. C. Ehri, & R. Treiman (Eds.), *Reading Acquisition* (pp. 307–342). Mahwah, NJ: Erlbaum.

Stanovich, K. E. (1994). Constructivism in reading education. *Journal of Special Education, 28,* 259–274.

Steiner, S. F. (2001). *Promoting a Global Community through Multicultural Children's Literature.* Portsmouth, NH: Teacher Ideas Press.

Sternberg, R. J., & Grigorenko, E. L. (2004). Intelligence in the classroom. *Theory Into Practice, 43,* 274–280.

Sternberg, R. J., & Spear-Sperling, L. S. (1996). *Teaching for Thinking.* Washington, DC: American Psychological Association.

Stiggins, R. J. (1994). *Student-centered Classroom Assessment.* New York: Merrill.

Strickland, K., & Strickland, J. (2000). *Making Assessment Elementary.* Portsmouth, NH: Heinemann.

Sulzby, E., & Teale, W. (1996). Emergent literacy. In R. Barr, M. Kamil, P. B. Mosenthal, & P. D. Pearson (Eds.), *Handbook of Reading Research* (Vol. 2, pp. 727–758). New York: Longman.

Sum, A., Kirsch, I., & Taggart, R. (2002). *The Twin Challenges of Mediocrity and Inequality: Literacy in the U.S. from an International Perspective*. Princeton, NJ: Educational Testing Service.

Taylor, B. M., & Beach, R. W. (1984). The effects of text structure instruction on middle-grade students' comprehension and production of expository text. *Reading Research Quarterly, 19*(3), 134–146.

Taylor, B. M., Hanson, B. E., Justice-Swanson, K., & Watts, S. M. (1997). Helping struggling readers: Linking small-group intervention with cross-age tutoring. *The Reading Teacher, 51*, 196–209.

Taylor, B. M., Pearson, P. D., Clark, K., & Walpole, S. (2000). Effective schools and accomplished teachers: Lessons about primary-grade reading instruction in low-income schools. *Elementary School Journal, 101*, 121–165.

Taylor, B. M., Pearson, P. D., Peterson, D. S., & Rodriguez, M. C. (2003). Reading growth in high-poverty classrooms. *Elementary School Journal, 104*, 3–28.

Taylor, B. M., Pressley, M., & Pearson, P. D. (2002). Research-supported characteristics of schools and teachers that promote reading achievement. In B. M. Taylor & P. D. Pearson (Eds.), *Teaching Reading: Effective Schools, Accomplished Teachers* (pp. 361–373). Mahwah, NJ: Erlbaum.

Taylor, B. M., Pressley, M., & Pearson, P. D. (2002). *Supported Characteristics of Teachers and Schools That Promote Reading Achievement* (pp. 361–374). Mahwah, NJ: Erlbaum.

Taylor, B. M., Short, R. A., Frye, B. J., & Shearer, B. A. (1992). Classroom teachers prevent reading failure among low-achieving first-grade children. *The Reading Teacher, 45*, 592–597.

Taylor, B. T., Pearson, P. D., Peterson, D. S., & Rodriguez, M. C. (2003). Reading growth in high-poverty classrooms. *Elementary School Journal, 104*, 3–28.

Taylor, B. T., Pearson, P. D., Peterson, D. S., & Rodriguez, M. C. (2005). The CIERA school change framework. *Reading Research Quarterly, 40*, 40–69.

Temple, C., Nathan, R., Temple, F., & Burris, N. A. (1993). *The Beginnings of Writing* (3rd ed.). Boston: Allyn & Bacon.

Texas Education Agency. (1996). Proclamation of the State Board of Education advertising for bids on textbooks. Austin, TX: Author.

Thorndike, R. M., & Thorndike-Christ, T. M. (2010). *Measurement and Evaluation in Psychology and Education*. Upper Saddle River, NJ: Pearson.

Thorndyke, P. (1977). Cognitive structures in comprehension and memory of narrative discourse. *Cognitive Psychology, 9*, 97–110.

Tierney, R. J., & Readence, J. E. (2005). *Reading Strategies and Practices: A Compendium* (6th ed.). Boston: Allyn & Bacon.

Tollefson, J. W. (1995). Introduction: Language policy, power, and inequality. In J. W. Tollefson (Ed.), *Power and Inequality in Language Education*. Cambridge, England: Cambridge University Press.

Tompkins, G. E. (1996). Becoming an effective teacher of reading. *WSRA Journal, 13*(2), 1–7.

Torgesen, J. K. (1998). Catch them before they fall. *American Educator, 22*(1–2), 32–39.

Toyama, Y., Hiebert, E. H., & Pearson, P. D. (2017). An analysis of the text complexity of leveled passages in four popular classroom reading assessments. *Educational Assessment, 22*(3), 139–170.

Treiman, R. (1992). The role of intrasyllabic units in learning to read and spell. In P. B. Gough, L. C. Ehri, & R. Treiman (Eds.), *Reading Acquisition* (pp. 65–106). Mahwah, NJ: Erlbaum.

Trelease, J. (1995). *The New Read-aloud Handbook* (4th ed.). New York: Penguin Books.

Tunmer, W. E., & Nicholson, T. (2011). The development and teaching of word recognition skill. In M. K. Kamil, P. D. Pearson, E. B. Moje, & P. P. Afflerbach: *Handbook of Reading Research* Vol 4. (pp. 405–431). New York: Routledge.

Turner, J., & Paris, S. G. (2010). How literacy tasks influence children's motivation for literacy. *Essential Readings on Motivation: International Reading Association*.

Ulanoff, S., Quiocho, A., & Riedell, K. (2009). The use of questioning in inquiry-based lessons with bilingual learners. *Curriculum & Teaching Dialogue, 17*, 35–56.

U.S. Department of Education. (1995). *Listening to Children Read Aloud*. Washington, DC: Author. Available at http://nces.ed.gov/pubs95/web/95762.asp

United State Department of Education (2009). *Race to the Top*. https://www2.ed.gov/programs/racetothetop/executive-summary.pdf

United States Department of Education (2013). *Long-Term Trends*. https://nces.ed.gov/nationsreportcard/ltt/

Vacca, R., & Linek, W. M. (1992). Writing to learn. In J. W. Irwin & M. A. Doyle (Eds.), *Reading/Writing Connections: Learning from Research* (pp. 145–159). Newark, DE: International Reading Association.

Valli, L., & Buese, D. (2009). The changing roles of teachers in an era of high-stakes accountability. *American Educational Researcher Journal, 44*(3), 519–558.

Valli, L., & Chambliss, M. (2007). Creating classroom cultures: One teacher, two lessons, and a high-stakes test. *Anthropology & Education Quarterly, 38*(1), 57–75.

Valli, L., Croninger, R. G., & Buese, D. (2012). Studying high-quality teaching in a highly charged policy environment. *Teachers College Record, 114*(4), n4.

van den Brock, P., & Kemer, K. E. (2000). The mind in action: What it means to comprehend during reading. In B. M. Taylor, P. van den Broek, & M. Graves (Eds.), *Reading for Meaning* (pp. 1–31). Newark, DE: International Reading Association.

Vandervelden, M. C., & Siegel, L. S. (1995). Phonological recoding and phoneme awareness in early literacy: A developmental approach. *Reading Research Quarterly, 30*, 854–875.

Vaughan, S. (2005, October). *A Three-tier Model for Preventing and Remediating Reading Difficulties: Response to Intervention*. Paper presented at the 3rd Guy Bond Memorial Conference on Reading, Minneapolis, MN.

Veenendaal, N. J., Groen, M. A., & Verhoeven, L. (2015). What oral text reading fluency can reveal about reading comprehension. *Journal of Research in Reading, 38*, 213–225.

Vellutino, F. R., Scanlon, D. M. Sipay, E. R., Small, S. G., Pratt, A., Chen, R., & Denckla, M. B. (1996). Cognitive profiles of difficult to remediate and readily remediated poor readers: Early intervention as a vehicle for distinguishing between cognitive and experiential deficits as basic causes of specific reading disability. *Journal of Educational Psychology, 88*(4), 601–638.

Venesky, R. (1999). *The American Way of Spelling*. New York: Guilford.

von Glaserfeld, E. (1984). An introduction to radical constructivism. In P. Watzlawick (Ed.), *The Ivented Reality* (pp. 17–40). New York: W. W. Norton.

Vygotsky, L. S. (1978). *Mind in Society: The Development of Higher Psychological Processes*. Cambridge, MA: Harvard University Press.

Walpole, S., & McKenna, M. C. (2007). *Differentiated Reading Instruction: Strategies for the Primary Grades*. New York: Guilford Press.

Wanzek, J., & Vaughn, S. (2007). Research-based implications from extensive early reading interventions. *School Psychology Review, 36*(4), 541–561.

Wanzek, J., Wexler, J., Vaughn, S., & Ciullo, S. (2010). Reading interventions for struggling readers in the upper elementary grades: A synthesis of 20 years of research. *Reading and Writing, 23*(8), 889–912.

Watts, S. M., & Graves, M. F. (1997). Fostering middle school students' understanding of challenging texts. *Middle School Journal, 29*(1), 45–51.

Watts-Taffe, S., Fisher, P., & Blachowiz, C. (2017). Vocabulary instruction: Research and Practice. In D. Lapp & D. Fisher (Eds.), *The Handbook of Research on Teaching the English Language Arts* (4th ed., pp. 130–161). New York: Routledge.

Webster, N. (1821). *The American Spelling Book: Containing the Rudiments of the English Language, for the Use of Schools in the United States*. Philadelphia, PA:Holbrook and Fessenden.

Wells, J., & Lewis, L. (2006). *Internet Access in US Public Schools and Classrooms: 1994–2005. Highlights. NCES 2007-020*. National Center for Education Statistics.

Werderich, D. E. (2002). Individualized responses: Using journal letters as a vehicle for differentiated reading instruction. *Journal of Adolescent and Adult Literacy, 45*(8), 746–754.

Wertsch, J. V. (1998). *Mind as Action*. New York: Oxford University Press.

Wharton-McDonald, R., Pressley, M., & Hampston, J. M. (1998). Literacy instruction in nine first-grade classrooms: Teacher characteristics and student achievement. *Elementary School Journal, 99*, 101–128.

White, T. G., Graves, M. F., & Slater, W. H. (1990). Growth of reading vocabulary in diverse elementary schools: Decoding and word meaning. *Journal of Educational Psychology, 82*(2), 281–290.

White, T. G., & Kim, J. S. (2008). Teacher and parent scaffolding of voluntary summer reading. *The Reading Teacher, 62*, 116–125.

White, T. G., Slater, W. H., & Graves, M. F. (1989). Yes/no method of vocabulary assessment: Valid for whom and useful for what? In S. McCormick & V. Zutel (Eds.), *Cognitive and Social Perspectives for Literacy Research and Instruction*. Chicago: National Reading Conference.

White, T. G., Sowell, J., & Yanagihara, A. (1989). Teaching elementary students to use word-part clues. *The Reading Teacher, 44*, 302–307.

Whitehead, A. N. (1929). *The Aims of Education and Other Essays*. New York: Macmillan.

Wigfield, A., & Eccles, J. S. (2002). *Development of Achievement Motivation*. San Diego, CA: Academic Press.

Wigfield, A., Gladstone, J., & Turci, L. (2016). Beyond cognition: Reading motivation and reading comprehension. *Child Development Perspectives, 10*(3), 190–195.

Wigfield, A., & Guthrie, J. T. (1997). Relations of children's motivation for reading to the amount and breadth of their reading. *Journal of Educational Psychology, 89*(3), 420.

Wiggins, G., & McTighe, J. (1998). *The Understanding by Design Handbook*. Alexandria, VA: Association for Supervision and Curriculum Development.

Wilkinson, G. S. (1995). *Wide-range Achievement Test 3*. Wilmington, DE: Jastak.

Williams, J. P., Hall, K. M., Lauer, K. D., Stafford, K. B., DeSisto, L. A., & deCani, J. S. (2005). Expository text comprehension in the primary grade classroom. *Journal of Educational Psychology, 97*(4), 538–551.

Williams, J. P., Pollini, S., Nubla-Kung, A. M., Snyder, A. E., Garcia, A., Ordynans, J. G., & Atkins, J. G. (2014). An intervention to improve comprehension of cause/effect through expository text structure instruction. *Journal of Educational Psychology, 106*(1) 1–15.

Willingham, D. T. (2006a). How knowledge helps: It speeds and strengthens reading comprehension, learning and thinking. *American Educator, 30*(1), 30–37.

Willingham, D. T. (2006b). The usefulness of brief instruction in reading comprehension strategies. *American Educator, 31*(Winter), 39–45.

Wise, B. W., Olson, R. K., & Trieman, R. (1990). Subsyllabic units in computerized reading instruction: Onset-rime-versus postvowel segmentation. *Journal of Experimental Child Psychology, 49*, 1–19.

Wiske, M. S. (Ed.). (1998). *Teaching for Understanding: Linking Research with Practice*. San Francisco: Jossey-Bass.

Wittrock, M. (1986). Students' thought processes. In M. C. Wittrock (Ed.), *Handbook of Research on Teaching* (3rd ed., pp. 297–314). New York: Macmillan.

Wollman-Bonilla, J. E. (2001). Can first-grade writers demonstrate audience awareness? *Reading Research Quarterly, 36*(2), 184–201.

Wollman-Bonilla, J. E., & Werchadlo, B. (1995). Literature response journals in a first-grade classroom. *Language Arts, 72*(8), 562–570.

Wonder-McDowell, C., Reutzel, D. R., & Smith, J. A. (2011). Does instructional alignment matter? Effects on struggling second graders' reading achievement. *The Elementary School Journal, 112*(2), 259–279.

Worcester, S. (1832). *First Book for Reading*. Boston, MA. Jenks, Palmer & Co.

Wood, D. J., Bruner, J. S., & Ross, G. (1976). The role of tutoring in problem-solving. *Journal of Child Psychology and Psychiatry, 17*(2), 89–100.

Woodcock, R. W., McGrew, K. S., & Mather, N. (2001). *Woodcock-Johnson III Tests of Achievement*. Itasca, IL: Riverside Publishing.

Wright, T. S., & Cervetti, G. N. (2016). A systematic review of the research on vocabulary instruction that impacts text comprehension. *Reading Research Quarterly, 52*, 203–226.

Wylie, R. E., & Durrell, D. D. (1970). Teaching vowels through phonograms. *Elementary English, 47*, 787–791.

Yogt, M. A. (2018). *Journeys*. Boston, MA. Houghton Mifflin Harcourt.

Yopp, H. (1995). A test for assessing phonemic awareness in young children. *The Reading Teacher, 49*(1), 20–29.

Yopp, R. H., & Yopp, H. K. (2006). Informational texts as read-alouds at school and home. *Journal of Literacy Research, 38*(1), 37–51.

Young, T. A., & Vardell, S. (1993). Weaving readers theatre and nonfiction into the curriculum. *The Reading Teacher, 46*, 396–406.

Zevenbergen, A. A., & Whitehurst, G. J. (2004). Dialogic reading: A shared picture book reading intervention for preschoolers. In A. V. Kleeck, S. A. Stahl, & E. B. Bauer (Eds.), *On Reading Books to Children: Parents and Teachers* (pp. 177–200). Mahwah, NJ: Erlbaum.

Zhang, S., Duke, N. K., & Jimenez, L. M. (2011). The WWWDOT approach to improving students' critical evaluation of websites. *The Reading Teacher, 65*(2), 150–168.

Name Index

Subject Index